Edmund Hogan

The Description of Ireland

And the State thereof as it is at this Present in Anno 1598

Edmund Hogan

The Description of Ireland
And the State thereof as it is at this Present in Anno 1598

ISBN/EAN: 9783337186678

Printed in Europe, USA, Canada, Australia, Japan

Cover: Foto ©ninafisch / pixelio.de

More available books at **www.hansebooks.com**

THE
DESCRIPTION OF IRELAND,

AND

The State thereof as it is at this present

IN ANNO 1598.

NOW FOR THE FIRST TIME PUBLISHED

From a Manuscript preserved in Clongowes-Wood College,

With Copious Notes and Illustrations

BY

EDMUND HOGAN,
Priest of the Society of Jesus.

Tuille feara ar Eirinn óiʒ:	Addition of knowledge on holy Erin :
Triallam timceall na Fotla,	Let us pass round Ireland,
Gluairio fir ar furrógra;	Let men go by order ;
Ar na fóirib a bfuileam	From the lands on which we are
Na coiʒeaba cuarcuiʒeam.	The provinces let us visit.
	Irish Topographical Poems.

Dublin :
M. H. GILL & SON, 50 UPPER SACKVILLE STREET.
London :
BERNARD QUARITCH, 15 PICCADILLY
1878.

Printed by
DUBLIN STEAM PRINTING COMPANY,
94, 95, 96, MIDDLE ABBEY STREET,
DUBLIN.

TABLE OF CONTENTS.

General Description of Ireland, 1.
Ulster, 2, 246, 295.
Louthe, 3, 260, 296.
Downe, 6, 260, 296.
Antrim, 13, 260, 296.
Armagh, 19, 250, 261, 296.
Monaghan, 23, 262, 296.
Fermanagh, 24, 247, 262, 297.
Tyrone, 25, 249, 262, 297.
Coleraine or Derry, 28, 249, 262, 297.
Dunigal, 29, 248, 262.
Leinster, 35.
Dublin, 35, 263, 298.
Wicklow, 39, 259, 264.
Kildare, 44, 252, 264.
Catherlagh, 50, 253, 265, 298.
Wexford, 55, 256, 265, 298.
Kilkenny, 65, 254, 266.
Queen's County, 73, 267, 325.
King's County, 81, 268.
Countie of Elye, 87.
Meath, 89, 268.
West Meath, 102, 270.
Longford, 113, 270.
Cavan, 117, 246, 271, 300.
Connaught, 122.
Clare, 124, 271.
Galway, 131, 272, 300.
Mayo, 140, 275, 300.
Sligo, 144, 275.
Leytrim, 147, 276, 300.
Roscommon, 150, 276.

Mounster, 156.
Waterford, 157, 277.
Cork, 167, 278.
Kerry, 187, 282.
Limerick, 196, 283, 300.
Tipperary, 207, 284.
Noblemen, 217, 349.
Bishops, 233.
Havens, 238.
Revenue, 240.
Names of the Council of Ireland, 244.
APPENDIX, 246.
  1. Chichester's Account of Ulster, 246.
  2. Present Known Representatives of the Families Extant in 1598, 260.
  3. Catholic Clergy, 285.
  4. Catalogue of Irish Jesuits in 1609, 290.
  5. Irish Writers; Irish Colleges Abroad, 294.
  6. Additional Notes from Camden, 296.
  7. Barnaby Riche's Description of Dublin, 299.
  8. Records of Events, Battle of Bellanaboy, &c., 301.
  9. Some Original Letters Written this Year, 339.
  10. Parliamentary Lists of 1560, 1585, and 1613, p. 349.
  11. Addenda et Corrigenda, p. 353.
  12. Round Towers and Index, p. 357.

PREFACE.

THE manuscript book, from which this description of Ireland has been printed, is a royal quarto, bound in vellum, containing ninety-two pages of "The Description of Ireland as it is in hoc anno 1598," and fifty-four pages of "Haynes' Observations on the State of Ireland in 1600"—both specimens of the same exquisite penmanship. It bears on the first page the autograph of the celebrated Father Betagh, S. J., after whose death, in 1811, it passed, with his other MSS., to his distinguished pupil, Father Kenny, S. J., by whom it was deposited in Clongowes Wood College in the year 1814. It is said by competent judges to be about one hundred years old, and it is proved by the Betagh autograph and the *Blauw*[a] watermark to have been written between the years 1756 and 1811.

It is therefore a transcript; and such it professes to be in the following marginal notes[b]:—'These lines from being a note in the margin hath crept into the text;' 'cancelled in the Original;' 'In the original the word seemeth to be Omelie, but in my opinion it should be O'Reillie.' 'The original' was compiled in the winter of 1598, as appears from the title and the following entries: 'O'Rourke hath bene a Rebell saving a little time *this last sommer*, but he revolted again;' 'Sir Thomas of Desmonde's Son latelie made Earle of Desmonde, Capten of the Rebellion in Mounster raised in *October last;*' 'Donell Spaniaughe of late sturred up by the Earle of Tyrone;'

---

[a] "The firm of Blauw was established in 1756"—Letter from that Dutch firm, received through the kindness of Heer Nyhoff.

[b] The marginal notes of the MS. have, for the sake of appearance, been inserted, within brackets, in the text.

'Sligo Castle was demolished four years ago and since not reëdified.'[c] These entries, and the references to O'More and Tyrrell in Queen's County, to O'Ferrall, to Westmeath and to the political state of each county, point to the winter of 1598,[d] while the silence about the death of Sir T. Norreys in June 1599, and of Sir E. Denny in February 1599, seems to indicate that our MS. was written before these dates.[e] However, the list of Noblemen appears to have been penned between the year 1603, and 1607 (the year of "The Flight of the Earls);" the list of Bishops between 1605 and 1610; and the list of the Members of the Council between December 1607 and December 1608, as 'Lord Davies' came to Ireland after October 1, 1608, and Winche came after November 11, 1607, and, on the 8th December, 1608, succeeded Ley as Chief Justice. Again, of the many marginal notes, which correct or supplement the text, and which are here inserted in brackets, two were added after Mountjoy's death in April, 1605, one after O'Dogherty's death in July, 1608, and one after 1617, when Rothe's 'Analecta' was published.[f]

The author was a man of English sympathies, and, no doubt, an Englishman, and an English official; his initials are, I strongly suspect, those given in the marginal note, at page 31, 'Belleke is now the possession of S. H.';[g] and his name was, I presume, S. H[aynes], as Haynes is the writer of the second treatise in the book. But since I cannot name the author with certainty, I may be told—

> To "pass the foundling by, a work of chance;
> Why into noble families advance
> A nameless issue?"[h]

[a] pp—:49, 181, 63, 147.
[d] See Record of Events of the Year, p. 305, etc., and pp. 78, 115, 112, 44, 39.
[e] pp. 184, 190.
[f] pp. 30, 160. pp.—22 & 23 were written soon after August, 1598.
[g] Quaere, is it S(ir) H(enry) Folliott?
[h] Dryden.

Why place this thing of obscure or questionable origin by the side of the authentic Descriptions by Stanihurst, Derricke, Dymmok, Camden, and Riche? The answer is, that 'the original,' spoken of above, whose existence cannot fairly be doubted, and which may be slumbering in some home or foreign archivium, is a respectable relative, if not the parent, of the best descriptions of Ireland hitherto published, and is superior to all of them. The 'Dobbs MS.' description of Antrim, written[i] *circ*, 1598; Lord Burghley's copy of Marshall Bagnall's description of Ulster, written[k] in 1586; the Carew MS. description of Ulster, written[l] in 1586; and Dymmok's 'Treatise of Ireland,'[m] written *circ.* 1600, are all, *as far as they go*, substantially, and, I may say, verbally the same as the Betagh MS.; while the 'Perambulation of Leinster in 1596,'[n] and the state papers given in the published Calendars, in the 'Life of MacCarthy Mor,' and in Hardiman's 'Iar-Connacht,' respectively corroborate its statements regarding Leinster, Munster and Connaught. These concurrent accounts are enough, I think, to give authority to our MS., which besides, as far as one can judge from an extract on Wexford, printed in the 'Annuary of the Kilkenny Archaeological Society for 1855,' resembles 'The Description of the Provinces of Ireland, Carew MSS. 635,' which Dymmok is said to have abridged.

Thus the critical and corrective tests of collation, to which it has been subjected, establish and illustrate its genuine character, and entitle it to the respect shewn to other published descriptions; moreover it challenges special attention on account

---

[i] Published by Dubourdieu in 1812.
[k] Published by Hore in 1854.
[l] Printed as "a very interesting and instructive survey" in the Calendars of State Papers by Dr. Russell and Mr. Prendergast.
[m] Edited by Rev. R. Butler, A.B. in 1843.
[n] Published in the calendar of Carew Mss. ad an. 1596. N.B. The Calendar of Carew Mss. (1589 to 1600) is often quoted and its title abridged to *Car. Cal*,

of many particulars, which it alone gives, relating to the chief towns and castles, the chieftains, noblemen, and gentlemen, and the political state of each county. Finding that it was much valued by antiquarians highly qualified to gauge its worth,[o] and that it occupied ground, which has been hitherto unappropriated or treated with but scant attention ; and hoping that it would reward, while it invited editorial care, 'I gave the venture' to edit, supplement, and illustrate it, and to try (though unsuccessfully) to raise it to the dignity of an old-world Topographical Dictionary and primitive *Directory* of the year 1598—a hard and humble task, 'a work suerly full of unsavoury toyle . . . which I write, not of vanity to commend my diligence, but of necessity to excuse mine imperfection.'[p] The records of the same time and character[q] were ransacked, 'which would minister furniture'[p] for my notes ; the archaic, or rather the perverse and profligate, spelling of the 16th century has been followed in all its freaks ; and the notes are put together according to the method of Hardiman, O'Donovan, and Dr. Reeves, except in the case of Ulster, where the peculiar social condition of that province, and the necessity of collating the 'Dobbs,' Bagnal, and Betagh MSS. made me sacrifice symmetry and reserve the notes for the Appendix. The reader will find mentioned over one hundred epitaphs, wayside crosses, and other *souvenirs* of those times ; but not much concerning the round towers and the manners and customs of the people, as these things are outside the object of the original work, and the editor is preparing a separate book on the manners and customs of the 16th century, and is too lightly equipped to deal with the towers and such antiquarian matters. On the other hand many may find an

[o] Among others, Mr. Gilbert, the author of "the Manuscript Materials of Irish History."

[p] Campion's Historie of Ireland.

[q] See list of Descriptions of Ireland p. xi.

interest in the Original Documents, the Parliamentary Lists, the List of the present known representatives of the old families,[r] and the full record of the events of 1598, which is given in the very words of the State Papers and other contemporary authorities.[s] From the inspection of this record (p. 315), and of the old map of the escheated county of Armagh, done in 1609, it is clear that O'Donovan, Tucker, and Larcom,[t] were mistaken with regard to the site of the battle-field of Belanahabuy, and that the trench was two-thirds, or 'two miles' of the distance from Armagh, and one-third or 'one mile' from Blackwater Fort. This trench is now a drain crossing the solid ground *Anaha*,[u] and carrying its water under *Bagnall's* Bridge; and beyond it is still the 'scons made on the top of the hill beyond the same,'[v] and near it there is 'a mayne bogg.'[v] Moreover, in the map of 1609—'ye long trenche of ye forde' is distinctly sketched, and also the Armagh road, which here branches off to Blackwater Fort and Charlemont.

Having written this much of the history, the author, authority, and merit of our MS., of the method of its editor, and of the site of the battle of Anaha or Bel-Anaha-buy, 'it remaineth that,' with Campion, 'I request my countrymen to bend their good liking to my good will, and to deliver me from all unjust suspicions,' as I have endeavoured to be sternly archaeological, and to handle my documents with an antiquarian temper, or, shall I say, 'with a benevolent neutrality.' I may add, with Camden, that 'if some there are who contemn this study of antiquitie as a back-looking curiosity . . . I am not destitute of reasons by

---

[r] Compiled from the works of Sir B. Burke, Lodge, Archdall, O'Donovan, and others.
[s] The memoirs of O'Neill, M'Carthy, and Tyrill, promised at p. 176, could not be inserted for sundry reasons.
[t] Annals of the Four Masters, note p. 2060; and the Ordnance Survey, Armagh, in the R. I. Academy.
[u] See Ordnance six-inch Map of Armagh.
[v] pp. 316, 317.

which I might approve this my purpose to well-bred, well-meaning men, who tender the glory of their native land . . . but if any there be, who are desirous to be strangers in their own soile, and forrainers in their own city, they may so continue—for such I have not taken these pains.' Finally, with the Four Masters, I think 'it is clear through the whole world, wherever there is nobility or honour, that nothing is more glorious than to give the knowledge of antiquity of old authors, and the knowledge of the chiefs who lived in the days of yore . . . . . and that it was a cause of pity (for the glory of God and the honour of Erin) that the race of the Gael have gone under a cloud:" and hence I publish this Description of Ireland—

To the glory of God and the honour of Erin.

Do cum Gloipe Dé agur Onopa na h-Epeann.

Milltown Park, Dublin,
May, the 1st, 1878.

LIST OF DESCRIPTIONS OF IRELAND.

1. Topographical Poems of O'Duggan and O'Heerin.
2. MS. Abbreviate of Ireland and Description of the Power of Irishmen, by Dean Nowell who died in 1576.
3. Campion's, in 1575.
4. Derricke's 'Image of Ireland,' 1581.
5. Carew MSS., No. 635.
6. Stanihurst's 'Plaine and Perfect Description,' 1586.
7. A brife Description by Payne, in 1589.
8. Dymmok's 'Treatice of Ireland,' circ. 1598.
9. Camden's in 1607; the best hitherto published.
10. Barnaby Riche's 'New Description of Ireland,' in 1610.'
11. Moryson's, in 1617.

DESCRIPTIONS OF PARTS OF IRELAND.

1. Bagnall's Slender Description of Ulster, in 1586; published in 1854.
2. Carew MSS., Description of Ulster, 11. p. 437.
3. Carew MSS., Description of Ulster, Vol. 621.
4. Sir A. Chichester's Description of Ulster, in Calendar of State Papers, an. 1609.
5. 'Dobbs MS. Description of Antrim,' circ. 1598; published by Dubourdieu in 1812.
6. Loughfoyle in 1601; published in Ulster Journal of Archaeology.
7. 'Perambulation of Leinster in 1596,' in Calendar of Carew MSS.
8. 'Counties of the Pale,' Ussher MSS. E. 4 33.
9. Barony of Forth, printed in the Kilkenny Journal of Archaeology.
10. Composition of Connaught in 1585 in Hardiman's Iar-Connacht and O'Donovan's Hy-Many and Hy-Fiachrach.
11. Description of Connaught in 1612, printed in Archaeologia Vol. 27.
12. Description of Clare, MSS. E. 2. 14., Trinity College, printed in this book.
13. O'Flaherty's Chorographical Description of Iar-Connacht in 1684, published by Hardiman.
14. O'Roddy's Description of Leitrim, MS. T.C.D.
15. Ordnance Survey MSS., in Royal Irish Academy.
16. Old Maps—the first in 1567; the second in 1571 for the Government; Nowel's; Jobson's Ulster in 1590; Janson's; Speed's; Maps of the Escheated Counties in 1609; Maps in the Pacata Hibernia.

THE notes have been taken from the foregoing Descriptions, from the publications of the Irish Archaeological Society's, the Kilkenny Journal of Archaeology, the Ulster Journal of Archaeology, the Life and Letters of McCarthy Mor, the Calendars of the Carew Manuscripts, and other Calendars. The Calendar of the Carew MSS. from year 1589 to 1600 is meant by the reference *Car. Cal.*, which is so frequently repeated. I have also ransacked the various County Histories and Statistical Surveys, the Topographical Dictionaries of Seward and Lewis, and the Parliamentary Gazetteer of Ireland, the Annals of the Four Masters., and the Historia Catholica of O'Sullevan Beare.

The gentlemen, who preside over the libraries of The Royal Irish Academy, of The Royal Dublin Society, and Trinity College, gave me every facility for examining the treasures which are under their care. To them and to the gentlemen of the Record Office I beg.to tender my best thanks.

THE DESCRIPTION OF IRELAND
AND THE STATE THEREOF, AS IT IS AT THIS PRESENT IN ANNO 1598.

IRELAND containeth in length from the old head of Kinsale in the South (which is West and to North from St. Michel's mount in Cornwall) unto Ramshead Hand in the North of Ulster, which is from Loghryan in Scotland, about 260 Miles; and in Breadth from Hoth, near Dublin, which is East, to Croghe Patrick in Maio Westward, 120 Miles.[a] There are in Ireland, according to the old number of their division of Lands, 6814 Town Lands; in Leinster, 1930; in Munster, 2200; in Connaught, 1600; in Meath, 84; in Ulster, 1000.

Every Town containeth Eight Plowlands arable, besides pasture for 300 Kyne; the Sume of the arable Plowlands is 54,512, besides Woods, Marshes, moores, pastures and Hills. Every Plowland containeth 120 Acres, every Acre is in Breadth 4 Roodes or Perches, in Length 40 Perches, and every Rood 21 Foot, so the Irish Acre exceedeth the English Acre by $5/8$. If Ireland were re-formed, it might yield every year of common

---

[a] 'Irelande lieth a-loofe in the West Ocean; in proportion it resembleth an egge, blunt and plaine on the sides, not reaching forth to sea, in nookes and elbowes of land, as Brittaine doth.'—*Campion.*

'Its shape is that of a rhomboid, the great diagonal of which is 302 miles, and the less 210 miles; its greatest and least breadths are 174 and 111 miles.'—*Thom's Directory.*

'From the South forelande to the northe pointe called Thorach, about 300 myles; and in breadthe from Dublin to St. Patrick's mounte and the sea beating alongst Connaught, 140 miles Irish, which are somewhat larger than our Englishe myles.'—*Dymmok.*

A

Subsidies upon every Plowland vj$^s.$ viij$^d.$, which would amount yearly to 18,170$^l.$ 13$^s.$ iiij$^d.$, besides Customs of Havens, Ports, and offices, which was in old time 20,000 marks yearly, besides the Inheritance of the Crowne; that was, in Ulster, 32,000 marks and an half; in Connaught, 28,000 marks x$^s.$ vj$^d.$; in Meath, 18,000 marks, besides Munster and Leinster, and besides all advowsons of Churches, Wards, Marriages, Reliefs and Escheats, first fruits, xx parts, imposts, and other Casualties.

Ireland is Divided into five parts or provinces: Ulster, Meath,^{b} Munster, Leinster, and Connaught.^{c} The province of ULSTER lyeth in the furthest part North of the Realm. It is divided from Meath with the River Boyne on the South-east part, and with the Breyine, which is called Omelies^d Country, on the South, and on the South-west it boundeth upon Connaught, namely, upon the County of Leytrim and the County of Sligo; the rest is altogether invironed with the Sea, and containeth in it Nine Counties^e, three of Antient and old making, and six new made, the names whereof are these:

Louth, }
Doune, } Old Counties.
Antrim, }

Armagh,   Tyrone,   Fermanagh, } New
Monaghan, Coleraine, Donegall,   } Counties.

^{b} 'Meathe, so called, as lying in the midst of the country, and composed of a part of every province; or else for that it conteyneth but 18 cantreds, whereas the others contain 34 or 35 a piece.'—*Dymmok.*

^{c} 'The insurgents of all Ireland in 1599 amounted to 18,368 foote and 2346 horse.'—*Moryson.*

^{d} 'O'Relye's countrey.'—*Bagnall.*

^{e} 'Some attribute the co. of Cavan for a tenth.'—*Dymmok.* 'The Irish forces of these counties were 1702 horse and 7220 foote.'—*Moryson.* 'The places of strengths and fastnesses in Ulster are the woodds and boggs of Clanbrasselogh, Clancane in the co. of Armagh, and the woodds and boggs of Killulto, Kilwarlin, Killoutry, and south Clandeboye, in ye co. of Downe.'—*Dymmok,* p. 26.

THE COUNTY OF LOUTHE.

The Countie of LOUTH containeth all the Land by the Sea coast, from the River of the Boyne by Drogheda to the Haven of Carlingford on the East, and it hath the Countie of Meath to the South, and South-west the barbarous Countries of the Fewes, part of the County of Armagh to the North, and the Countrie of Feony, part of the same County to the West, by means whereof it is exposed to the incursions of the rude people inhabiting these Countries,¹ who in times past kept a great part of this Countrie lying next them wast; but of late years Tyrone and his adherents hath made the whole Countie desolate, that it might not yield to the English Armie, whensoever it should invade him, any succour or relief, either of men, or Victuals for men or Horses, or any convenient place for soldiers to garrison in, now againe re-inhabitted.

It is part of the English paile, and beareth contribution with the rest of the English countries.

TOWNES INCORPORAT in the Countie of Louth are these, and walled:
- Drogheda, standing upon the Boyne, 2 Miles from the Sea, with a barred Haven very dangerous to enter in, governed by a Mair and 2 Sheriffes.
- Dundalk, Carlingford, Both Sea Townes, and walled, but barred; Ardee, a drie Towne within the Land westward, walled.

¹ 'It hath the most dangerous borderers and neighbors of any county; for it lyeth on the MacMahons of Monaghan, upon the O'Neiles of the Teenes, and the O'Hanlons of Armagh.' —*Dymmok.* Feony should be Ferny.

STATE OF IRELAND ANNO 1598.

THE LORDS SPIRITUAL.—The Primate Armagh, his chief Hous and Seat at Armagh; but he hath much Lande in this Countie, and at this time his whole Residence is in Drogheda or thereabout.

LORDS TEMPORALL.—The Lord of Louth, whose surname is Plunket, his chief Hous is Louth.

KNIGHTS.—Sir Gerrot Moore, his chief Hous is Millefont.
Sir Chyver [Christofer] Bedlow, his Hous is called of himself Bedlowstoune.
Sir Nico. Bagnell, the Father, and Sir Henrie, his Sone, both Knight Marshalls of Ireland, had much possessions in this Countie, and sometimes had their residence at Carlingford, where Sir Henry was borne [but for many years they have resided at the Newrie, the L. whereof is now called Arthure Bagnell, an idiot.]

GENTLEMEN^e of better and meaner sort are these:

Plunketts,	Dartoyes,
Brandons,	Bedlowes,
Taffes,	Garlands,
Cashells,	Warrens,
Barnwalls,	Clintons,
Verdons,	Moores,
	Dowdals.

^e We have here forty names. We find only twenty-five in the *Perambulation of the Pale*, which, however, gives fourteen additional names: 'Tath (*sic*, but it should be Taaffe), of Clintonstown; Tath of Cookstown; Tath of Stevinstown; Tath of Rathclare; Dowdal of Glassepestell; Clinton of Drumcashell; Plunket of Nuchowse; Gernon of Gernonstown; Gernon of Donmoghan; Babe of Derver; Stanley of Merlinstown; Warren of Warrenstown; Barnwall of Rathesker; Talbot of Castlering; Rice Ap Hugh, Provost Marshal of the Ardye.' It also informs us that Fleming lived at Crowmerton, and that Verdon of Clonmore was 'descended of Theobald Verdon, High Constable of Ireland.'

COUNTY OF LOUTH. 5

Of Plunketts in this Countie are—
    Plunket of Bewlie.
    Plunket of Correstone.

Other Gentlemen.

Dowdall of Newton.
Taffe of Ballibrayen.
Drake of Drakeston.
Peppard of Ardy.
Bath of Raferghe.
Clinton of Clintonstoune.
Dromgold of Dromgoldstoune.
Wotton of Rochestoune.
Garland of Bothnan.
Garlond of Garlondstonne.
Verdon of Clonmor[vel Clonnor]
Allen of Ardy.
Cusack of Richardstoune.
Hadsor of Keppock.

Cashells, } of Dundalk.
Brandons, }
Sagrave of the Grange.
Dowdon of Dowdonstonne.
Merriman, } of Carlingford.
Butler, }
Hurlestone of Killany.
Garlond of Killoncowle.
Brett.   Car.
Fleming.   Cooke.
Worrall.   Sherlock.
Birrell.   Nugent.
Chamberlayne. Barnwall.
White.[h]

[h] The Members of Parliament for Louth in 1560 were Taf de Ballebragane and Dowedal de Glassepistell; in 1582 the members were Gerlone and Moore. In this county there are of the Queen's troops, 350 foote at Dundalk, under Egerton, Bisset, and Bingley; 200 foote at Artherdee, under Sir Garret Moore and Captaine Roe.—*Moryson*, p. 43. The garrison of Drogheda in 1595 consisted of 120 footmen of Sir H. Norris, 60 f. of Captain Wingfield, and 60 f. of Captain Brett.—*Calendar of Carew MSS.* Captain Brett was probably of the Louth family mentioned in the text. 'Fleming' was Captain Garret Fleming, at whose castle the truce was concluded between the commissioners of Tyrone and Essex, on the 8th Sept. 1599.—Vide *Carew Calendar*. He was the grandson of Sir Garret Fleming, Marshal of Ireland, and was the father of the celebrated Franciscan, F. Fleming, who was born in 1599, at Belatha Lagain, in Louth.—Vide *Ulster Jour. of Arch.*, No. 8, p. 254. Only three of these names are now to be found among the magistrates or among the 'County Families' of Louth, viz., Lords Louth and Bellew, and Mr. Taaffe of Smarmore Castle.—See *Thom's Directory*, and *Walford's County Families*.

THE COUNTIE OF DOUNE.

This shyre contayneth all the Countries between the Haven of Carlingford and the Borry[a] of Knockfergus, viz. :—
    The Topp[b] of the Newrie.
    The Topp[b] of Mourney.
    Evaghe, otherwise called McGennes'[c] Country.
    Kilulto.   lecahell.
    Kiwarlen.   Duffrin.
    Kinalewarten.   little Ardes and great Ardes.
                           South Clandeboye.
Clonbrassell M^{c}yoolechan.[d]

THE TOPPS OF NEWRIE AND MOURNE are the Inheritance of the Heyres of Sr Nich. Bagnoll, who at his first coming hither found them altogether Wast, and Shane O'Neall dwelling within less than a Mile to the Newrie, at a place called feidem. Suffering no subject to Travel from Dundalk Northwards, but Sithence the Buildings and Fortifications made there by the said Sr Nicolas, all the Passages were made free, and much of the Countrie next adjacent reduced to reasonable tributs [civilitie], till this late Rebellion of Tyrone hath stopped againe all the said Passages, and layed the Countrie in a manner Wast, as it was in the said tyme of Shane O'Neall, [e]but since the King's tyme returned to the former State.[e]

---

[a] 'The Bay of Knockfergus.'—*Dobbs* and *Dymmok*.

[b] A curious mistake for Lopp, *i.e.*, 'Lordshipp,' as it is in *Dobbs* and *Bagnall*.

[c] '*All* Maginnes' country' is in *Dobbs*; but it is a mistake for *called*, which is in the *Betagh* and *Bagnall* MSS.

[d] Written McBoolechan further on; but McCoolechan in *Dobbs*, and McGoolechan in *Bagnall*. It is MacDuilechain in Irish; perhaps it is the present northern name of Dullagan?

[e] The words from [e] to [e] are not in *Dobbs*.

In this Countrie are few Gentlemen of name, the whole Inhabitants being Tenants to late ᶠ Sʳ Henrie Bagnoll.

EVEAGHE [Evaghe], otherwise called MᶜGennes Countrie, was lately governed by Sʳ Hugh MᶜGenne, ᵍand now by his Sone, Sʳ Arthure MᶜGennes,ᵍ the civilest of all the Irish in these parts. He was brought of by Sir Nicholas Bagnoll from the Bonnoght ʰ[paying of meal, butter, and some money for paying of O'Neall's soldiers]ʰ of the O'Neall's, to contribute to the Prince [Queene], to whome he did paie an Anual Rent for his Lands, which he took by Letters patents to hold after the Inglishe manner, for him and his Heyres males ;ⁱ So as in this place onlyᵏ of Ulster the rude custome of Thanistshipˡ was taken away. But this old Knight being dead, his Sone that succeeded being a young Man, hath ioyned himself with Tyrone, his Brother-in-law ᵐ[for Tyrone hath to his Wife the sister of this MᶜGennes],ᵐ and thereby hath cast away his Father's civilitie, and returned to the rudeness of the country. MᶜGennes is able to make four Score Horsemen and near 200 Footmen.ⁿ °Of late he hath carried himself well, and admitted Freeholders in his Country by advice of the State.°

KILULTO is a very fast Countrie, full of Wood and Boggs. It bordereth upon Lough Evaghe and Clonbrassell; the Capten thereof was one Cormack MᶜNeal, who likewise was brought by

---

ᶠ This word is not in *Dobbs.*

ᵍ ʰ The words from ᵍ to ᵍ, ʰ to ʰ, are not in *Dobbs.*

ⁱ 'He lyeth very cyvilly and Englishe like in his house, and every festival day weareth Englishe garmentes amongst his own followers.'—*Bagnall.*

ᵏ After 'only' in the *Bagnal* MS.

Lord Burghley inserted 'amongest the Irishry.'

ˡ This word is misspelled 'Thom ship' in *Dymmok.*

ᵐ From ᵐ to ᵐ is a marginal note in our MS.; in *Dobbs* it is in parenthesis.

ⁿ He had 610 f. and 120 h. in 1592. —*Carew Calendar.*

° From ° to ° is not in *Dobbs.*

Sr Nich. Bagnoll from the Bonnaghts^p of O'Neall's to yield to the Prence [Quene], but at this present the captaine thereof is Bryan McArt, Brother's Son to the Earl of Tyrone. He is able to make 30 Horsmen^q and 180 Shot and Kearne. ^r[The Kearnes' arms are swords, tergats, and darts.]^r This countrie, before the barons' Warrs in Ingland, was possessed and Inhabitted by Inglishmen, and there doeth yet remain an old defaced Castle, which still beareth the name of one Sr Miles Tracie.

KILWARTEN,^s Bounding upon Kilulto, is a verie fast Woodland; the Captain thereof was one McRorie,^t and sometymes did contribute and yield to Clandeboy, and after reduced to have dependance upon the Quene; But of late the Earl of Tyrone hath given this Countrie to one of his Coosons, named Owen McHughe: this Countrie is able to make xx Horsemen and aboute 100 Footmen.

KINALEWARTEN, otherwise called McCartie [forsan McCartan]^u Countrie, is likewise a Woodland and Boggie. It Lyeth between Kilwarton and Lechaell, the Capten thereof is called Acholie McCartan, and did yield to the Quene, but lately adherred to the Earl of Tyrone, as one of O'Neall's vassals. It is able to make 260 Footmen, but few or no Horsemen, by reason that the Country is so full of Woods and Boggs.^v

---

^p 'From the bondage of the O'Neils.' —*Bagnall;* but it should be bonnaght, as in our MS. and in *Dobbs.*

^q 'Twenty h. and 160 foote and Kerne.'—*Dobbs.* The *Carew Calendar* states that Bryan McArt was captain of 300 foot, 'trained after ye English manner, besides rascals and Kerne.'

^r From ^r to ^r is not in *Dobbs.*

^s *Recte* Kilwarlin, as in *Dobbs* and *Bagnall;* yet also written Kilwaren in *Bagnall,* and Kilwartin in the index to the *Carew Calendar.*

^t By sirname is McGenis called Ever McRorie.—*Bagnall.*

^u 'Kincleartie, or McCarthaney's Country'—*Dobbs;* but *Bagnall* has McCartan.

^v McArtan and the Sleaght McNeill hath 100 f. and 20 h. in 1599.—*Carew Calendar.*

COUNTY OF DOWN.

CLONEBRASSELL McBOOLECHAN (so called for difference between this and another Countrie of the same name in the Countie of Armagh), is a verie vast Countrie of Wood and Bogg, Inhabitted with a sept called the O'Rellies,ᵃ verie Savage and Barbarous people, given altogether to Spoiles and Robberies. They contribute, but of their own pleasure, to the capten of Glandeboy, ᵇbut were lately followers to Tyrone.ᵇ They can make few Horsemen and 160 Kearne and Shott.

LECHAELL is, ᶜfor most part,ᶜ the Inheritance of ᵈthe Earls of Kildare,ᵈ the abbey Lands whereof were given to Gerrot, Earle of Kildare, and his wife and the heyres Males of his Bodie, by Queen Marie at their Marriage, and the Earl's restitution to his Blood and Lands, in place of some of his livings given away to others by patent by King Henrie the 8ᵗʰ in the tyme of his attainder. ᵉ*But by reason the Heyres Males are now all extinct, the King gave these lands to the late Earl of Devonshire, and he disposed of them to the late L. Cromwell, whose heyres now enioy them.*ᵉ ᶠ[These lines (in italics) from being a note in the margin, hath crept into the text.]ᶠ It is almost an Iland, and no trees in it; in it is the Bishop's seat called Downe. First built and Inhabitted by one Sʳ John Coursey, who brought with him sundrie Inglish Gentlemen and planted them in this Countrie, where some of their posteritie yet remaine;ᵍ their names are—

    Savages.   Audlies.
    Russells.   Jordans.
    Fitzsimons.   Bensons.

ᵃ 'The Kellies greatly affected to the Scott, whom they often draw into their countries for the spoilinge of the subjects.'—*Bagnall.* 'The O'Rellies.'—*Dobbs.*

ᵇᶜᵈᵉᶠ From ᵇ to ᵇ, ᶜ–ᶜ, ᵈ–ᵈ, ᵉ–ᵉ, ᶠ–ᶠ, is not in *Dobbs*; from ᶠ to ᶠ is a marginal note.

ᵍ 'Where some of them yet remayne, though somewhate degenerate and in poore estate; yet they hold still their freeholdes.'—*Bagnall.* 'I assure your

[h]This Country of Lecahell, before it was spoyled by the Rebells, yielded yearly to the Earl of Kildare 800^{li} ster. in Rent, besides much Service and many other duties.[h]

DUFFRYN, sometimes the Inheritance of the Mandevills, and now appertayning unto one Whyte, Gent.,[i] who, by reason of his residence in the pale, cou'd not defend same in the late Rebellion. [j]It is now come to be held by Lease by Mr. James Hamilton.[j] This Countrie is for the most part Woodie, and lieth upon the Lough called *lough coyne*, which issues into the Sea at the Haven of Strangford; this lough is farr navigable within the Land, wherein are divers Isles, and in some of them Strong Castles. This Countrie is able to make 120 Footmen and 20 Horsemen.

LITLE ARDES lyeth on the North side of the River of Strangford [k]by the Sea,[k] a fertile Champion Countrie. [l]The Inhabitants are an old colonie of the English.[l] It is the Inheritance of the Lord Savage, who, being not able to withstand the violence of the O'Neals, was constreyned to take what they will give him. There are besides dwelling here certen ancient Freeholders of the Savages and Smithes, able to make amongst them all 30 Horsemen and 60 Footmen, but of late being spoiled by their Neighbours, some were compelled to remove,

Lordship I have been in many places and countries in my days, and yet did I never see for so much a pleasanter plott of grounde than the sayd Lecayll, for the commoditie of the land and divers islands in the same, environed with the sea.'—*Lord Grey the Deputy in* 1539, *quoted in note to Bagnall MS.*

[h] From [h] to [h] is not in *Dobbs.*

[i] 'A mean gentleman, who is not of power sufficient to defend the same; therefore it is usurped and inhabited by the neighbours.'—*Dobbs.* 'It is usurped by a bastard sorte of Scotts, who yield to White some small rent at their pleasure. There are of those bastard Scottes dwelling here some 60 bowmen and 20 shott, which live most upon the praie and spoil of their neighbours.' —*Bagnall.*

[j k l] From [j] to [j], [k] to [k], and [l] to [l], is not in *Dobbs* or *Bagnall.*

some others, that knew not whither to go, ᵐcontinued there to this daie.ᵐ

GREAT ARDES is almost an Iland, a Champion, and fertile Land, and now possessed by Sʳ Hugh Montgomery and Mr. James Hamilton. But the Ancient dwellers there are the ⁿ[. .], a rich and strong Sept of people, always followers of the O'Neall's of Clandeboy. The force of the Inhabitants now dwelling there is small, the ᵒsame being yet a Beginning of a Plantation fromᵒ [. . .].

SOUTH CLANDEBOYE is for the most part a Woodland, and reacheth from the Duffrin to the river of Knockfergus;ᵖ the Capten of this was Con O'Neal,ᑫ his chief Hous is called Castlereagh. This Countrie was able to make 40 Horsemen and 80 Footmen, ʳbut the late Rebellion hath consumed them all.ʳ

ᵐ 'They are often harrowed and spoiled by them of Clandeboy, with whom the borders of their lands do joine.'—*Bagnall.* *Dobbs* says, 'not knowing what to do, they have joined themselves to the enemy.' From ᵐ to ᵐ is not in *Dobbs* or *Bagnall.*

ⁿ 'The Ogilmers, a rich, &c. The land is now possessed by Sir Con Mac-Neil Oige, who hath planted there Neil MᶜBryan Ferto with sondrey of his owne sirname. The force of the inhabitants now dwellinge there is 60 horsemen and 300 footemen.'—*Bagnall.*

ᵒ From ᵒ to ᵒ is not in *Dobbs.*

ᵖ 'The river of Knockfergus, Kilulto, lyinge upon Lough Eaghe and Clanbraselo.'—*Dymmok.*

ᑫ 'Nial MᶜBryan Flain.'—*Dobbs.* 'Sir Con MᶜNeil Oige O'Nele, who in the time that th' Erle of Essex attempted this country was prisoner in the castle of Dublin, together with his nephewe, Hugh MᶜPhelim, Capten of North Clandeboye, by mean whereof Sir Brian MᶜPhelim, younger brother to Hugh, did then possess both countries. The Southe parte is able to make 40 horsemen and 80 footemen.'—*Bagnall.*

ʳ The *Dobbs* MS. has not these remarkable and significant words from ʳ to ʳ. In 1598 the Lords of Upper and Lower Clannaboy had 120 h. and 300 f.; and in 1599 Neil MᶜBryan Fertagh, Lord of Upper Clannaboy, had 80 f. and 50 horse in the service of Hugh O'Neil.—*Carew Calendar.*

TOUNES in the Countie of Doune are— { The Newrie,' Downe, and Arglas. } All unwalled, and without any priviledges of a Corporation.

CASTLES in the said Countie— { Green Castle, 'belonging to the Queene,' near the barr of Carlingford, upon the Sea.

Dundrum, "belonging to the Earl of Kildare," in the Bottom of the Bay, that divideth lecahell from Evaghe. The Castle of the narrow Water which kepeth the River that goeth to the Newire, passable.

Stranyford.

Ranechadie, Scatterig, } within the Iles of Lough Coyne.

Castlereaghe, in the Great Ardes.ᵛ

This Countrie hath the Sea to the East, the Countie of Armagh to the West, the Haven of Carlingford and that river to the South, the Countries of Brasilagh, Clancan, and Lough Eaghe to the North.

' At the Newrie in 1599 there were 50 h. under Sir S. Bagnoll, and 950 f. under Bagnoll, Blayney, Bodley, Freckleton, Tobias Caufield, Stafford, and Leigh.'—*Moryson.*

' From ' to ', and " to " is not in *Dobbs*, nor is there anything about the towns and castles in *Bagnall*.

" 'Doundrome, one of the strongest holts that ever I saw in Ireland, and most commodious for the defence of the whole country of Lecayll, both by sea and land.'—*Lord Grey, in* 1539.

ᵛ By mistake, the *Dobbs'* MS. has 'Castlereagh in Lough Coyne.' The Savages of Down are still represented by Col. Andrew Nugent, of Portaferry, of the Scots Greys, the old name of whose family was Savage. The Russels are represented by Mr. Russell, proprietor of Quoniamstown, near Down Patrick, in whose family the property has remained for six centuries, and by C. Russell, Esq., of Killough. The Whytes are represented by J. J. Whyte, Esq., of Loughbrickland, J.P. & D.L., of the Co. of Down.

THE COUNTY OF ANTRIM.

The Countie of ANTRIM stretcheth from the River of Craigfergus to the River[a] of the Bann, and containeth these Countries:—
North Clandeboy.
Iland magie, Bryan Carroghes Countrie.
The Glynnes.
the rout.

NORTH CLANDEBOY is for the most part a plain Country, being in length from the River of Belfast and Craigfergus to the Rout, and in bredth from the Glynnes to the great Lough called Eaghe, otherwise called Lough Sidney. This Land was given by the Quene by Letters Patents to S[r] Bryan McPhelim's Sones, notwithstanding by a division made by S[r] John Perrott the one moyetie thereof was allotted to Hugh McPhelim's Sones, whereby great dissention fell out between them, and several Slaughters on both parts hath been committed. [b][But Shane McBrian possesses some part thereof at this day; the rest for the most was given by the h. L. Sir Arthure Chicester to the L. Dep.][b] The principall of all was[c] in this Countrie were these:—the M^c . . . .

---

[a] 'To the goinge out of the Bann.'—*Bagnall*.

[b] From [b] to [b] is a marginal note, and is not in *Dobbs*.

[c] 'The principal followers in this countrey are these:—the McGies, McOnulles, Onulchalons, Durnam, and Tarturs.'—*Bagnall;* but, according to *Dobbs*, they were MacYnes, MacQuillens, Ownilechabees, Dawmans, and Bertiers.' The writer of our MS. could not make out the names in the copy which he had. The *variantes*, 'Tartur' and 'Bertier,' and 'the principal *followers*,' and 'the principal *of all was*,' are very remarkable; the latter seems to be due to a *lapsus linguæ*.

Dymmok says, 'North Clandeboy is divided into two partes, the river of Kellis being the mear bounde. The south parte thereof was geven for a rent to the sonnes of Brian McPhelim

The force which they were able to make was 80 Horsmen and 300 Footmen, ^dbut the most part in the last Rebellion killed.^d

ILAND MAGIE.

ILAND MAGIE is a portion of Land within five Miles of Craigfergus, almost environed with the Sea, the head Land thereof maketh the Haven of Olderfleet. It is five Miles long, but little more than a Mile broad, all plaine without any Wood, very fertile. It was given by the late Quene to the then Erle of Essex his Grandfather, and from him lately purchased by the L. Dep^r.

BRYAN CARROGHES COUNTRIE was a portion of North Clandeboy, but wonne from it by some of the Scottish Irysh^f of the Sept of the Clandonnels, who entered the same, and yet do hold it, being a verie strong piece of Land, lying upon the North side of the Bann. The name of the now Capten thereof is Bryan Carraghe, who possesseth also another piece of the Countrie upon Tyrone's side upon the Bann, for which he did contribute to the Quene^g and for the Lande on the north Side to the Lorde of that part of Clandeboy. This man, by reason of the Fastness and Strength of his Countrie, having succour on each side of the

O'Neill, who were all pencioners in Ireland to her Majestie; and the eldest, Shane McBrian, yet lyvinge, was cheeffe. The north parte beyond Kellis to the river of Bann by Lough Eaugh was assigned to the sonnes of Hugh McPhelim, elder brother to Sir Bryan, whose eldest son in that part is Hugh Oge McHugh.'—*Dymmok.*

^d From ^d to ^d is not in *Dobbs.*

^e 'Iland McGye, a portion of land within 3 miles of Knockfergus. It is almost all waste; such as be there be the McGyes, and contribute to the Lord of Clandeboy, but doth of right belong to the Quene's Castle of Carikfergus.'—*Bagnall.* 'It is the inheritance of the now Erle of Essex.'—*Dymmok.* 'It hath its name from the McGies, it is granted in lease to one Savage, one of the Erl of Essex his men.'—*Dobbs.*

^f A bastard kinde of Scotts.—*Bagnall* and *Dobbs.*

^g He doth contribute to O'Neil.—*Bagnall* and *Dobbs.*

COUNTY OF ANTRIM. 15

Bann, was so obstinate and careless as he never wou'd appear before any deputie, [h]untill this Deputie came to be Governor of Craigfergus,[h] but yielded what relief he could to the Scotch. His force in People is very small, he standeth only upon the Strength of his Country, which indeed is the fastest Ground of Ireland.[i]

THE GLYNNES is a Countrie so called, because its full of rockie and wooddic dales; it stretcheth[j] in length xxiv Miles on the one side, being backed with a very steepe and Boggie mountaine, and on the other part with the sea, on which side there are many Creekes between Rocks and Thicketts where the Scottish Gallies do commonly land; at either end are verie narrow Entries and passages into the Countrie, which lieth directlie opposite to Cantyre, from which it is xviii Miles distant. The Countrie of Glynnes containeth Seven Barrónies, whereof the Ile of Raghlins is compted half a Barronie. The Names of the Barronies are these:—

This Countrie of the GLYNNES was possessed by Agnes McConnell of Cantyre; but these three or four years past, they have been possessed by Sr Randoll McDonell, Brother to Sr James McConnell, who enjoys them at this present, and is able to make 120 Footmen and 16 Horsemen.[m]

Larne.
Parke.
Glanarme.
Radboy.[k]
Lade.[l]
Carie.
Mowberry.

---

[h] From [h] to [h] is not in *Dobbs*.

[i] 'The fasted and safest ground of Ireland—it is very hard to hurt him.'—*Dymmok* and *Bagnall*.

[j] 'It stretcheth from the haven of Olderfleete to the Route.'—*Dymmok*.

[k] Redbay where Randal, now Lord of the country, has his residence.—*Dobbs*.

[l] Lade is not in *Dobbs*, but it is in *Bagnall*.

[m] 100 f. and 100 h. *Carew Calendar;* but *Dymmok* says: 'James McSurly Buy and his two brothers, Neece and Randol, possessing the country of Towany (being the Route), and ye seven Glynnes, hath 400 f. and 100 h.'

These were sometymes the Inheritance of Baron Misset, from whom it is descended to a Daughter, who was married to one of the Clandonnells in Scotland, by whom the Scottish now make their claime to the whole, and did quietlie possess the same for many years, till not long agoe being spoiled of their Goods they were whollie banished into Scotland. But againe, the Countrie, by Instructions from the Quene, was let to Agnes M‘Connell and her[n] Uncle Surleboy, to be holden from her,[n] and Her Heyres and Successors for a certen Rent yearly payable. The force of this Countrie is uncertaine, for that they were Supplyed as need required, from Scotland with what Nombers they Listed to call for, by making of Fires upon many Steepe Rockes hanging over the Sea. The ancient followers of this Countrie are these—Some few of the Missetts yet remaining, but in poor State; the Magies,[o] . . . M‘Carnocks, and the Clanalasters, who are by Original Scottish, and all of them are most desirous to Live under the Scotch, because they

---

Angus M‘Connell, Lord of Cantyre. ‘His’ and ‘her’ are used in the *Dobbs* and *Betagh* MSS.; but *Dymmok* writes, Angus and *his*, and says, ‘by instructions from her Majesty it was divided by Sir John Perrott, between Angus M‘Connell, chief of his name, and Sourley Buy, his uncle bysides in the land of the Route.'

Margery Bissett married Ian Mór M‘Donnell, son of the Lord of the Isles. The Bissets were originally de Miset; they soon changed their name to Bissett, and adopted Irish customs. It was in Bissett's island of Rathlin, that the Bruce formed the resolve of reconquering Scotland, and it was at Sir Hugh Bissett's manor of Glenarm, that Edward Bruce landed with the victors of Bannockburn. Some of the family formed a Celtic clan, and took the name of M‘Eoin or M‘Keon. (*Four Mast. An.* 1383-7, and *O'Donovan Introd. to Topogr. Poem*).

[o] ‘The Magies, O'Nowlanes, MacNygells, MacAroulbyes, MacCarnocks, and the Clanacasters.'—*Dobbs*. ‘The MacKayes, the Omulrenies, the Mac y Gilles, the MacAwnleys, the MacCarnocks, and the Clanalsters.'—*Bagnall*.

do better defend them, and less spoile them then the Irysh doth.ᵖ

The Route is a pleasant and fertile Country, being between the Glynnes and the River of the Bann, and from Clandeboy to the Sea; it was sometime inhabitted with Inglishe, for there remayneth yet certain defaced Castles and Monasteries of their Buildinge. The Captain that made claime to it is called ᵠ [. . .] the posteritie as is thought of Walsheman; but S: James M⁽ᶜ⁾Surlie wholy expulsed him and drove him to live in Knockfergus, where he remayneth in a very poor Estate. The cheif Hous is called Dunluce, standing upon a rock in the Sea Shore, where the said Sir James had his residence,ʳ and since his decease his Brother Sir Randoll M⁽ᶜ⁾Donnell has enjoyed it, first under pretence of Succession, but now by virtue of the King's grant to him and his heyres for ever of both the Rent and Glynnes.ʳ The cheife followers and Inhabitants of this Country are the O . . .ˢ and O'Guinnes, who dwell upon their Lands and yield rent and Service to the foresaid S: Randoll. This Countrie was able latelie to make 140 horsemen and 300 Footemen.ᵗ

ᵖ 'Are lest spent upon, and better defended than by the Irish or English.' *Dymmok*.

ᵠ 'M⁽ᶜ⁾Guillim.'—*Bagn*. 'M⁽ᶜ⁾Guillin.'—*Dobbs*. 'M⁽ᶜ⁾Willi.'—*Dymmok*. It was, it appears, a corruption of M⁽ᶜ⁾Llewellyn. In 1541 the Chief of the M⁽ᶜ⁾Guillins declared that no captain of his race 'ever died in his bed sith the first conqueste of their said lande.'—(*Council Book An.* 1541). *Bagnall* says: 'The Scot hath well nere expulsed M⁽ᶜ⁾Guillin and driven him to a small corner near the Bann, which he defendeth rather by maintenance of Turloch O'Neil, than by his own forces.'

ʳ From ʳ to ʳ is not in *Dobbs*. It is strange that *Bagnall* does not mention Dunluce, which a State Paper of 1584 declared to be an impregnable fortress.

ˢ 'O'Furries and O'Quins.'—*Dobbs*. 'O'Harries and O'Guines.'—*Dymmok*. 'O'Haryes and O'Quins.'—*Bagnall*.

ᵗ *Moryson* says, the Glynnes and Route had 400 f. and 100 h.; but our MS. estimates at 450 h. and 156 f., the forces they *were able* to raise.

CRAIGFERGUS[u] is the onlie Towne in this Shyre upon the River, three Miles broad over against the Towne, walled partlie with stone, partlie with Soades. There were in it 2 Wardes, the one in the Castle in the South end of the Towne, the other in the Abbey in the North end thereof; [v]but the Abbey Warde is taken away.[v] This Towne is governed by a Maior and Two Sheriffes, and at this day there is not may freemen of this Towne.[w]

CASTLES WARDABLE at this day,
{ Bellfast, viii Miles by the River from Craigfergus, where the passage is over the River at low water.
O . . .[x] near Lough Eaghe.

Defaced.
{ Olderfleete.[y]
Glanarne.
Castle marten in the Route.

[u] "In 1599 the Queen had at Carrigfergus 30 h. under Neale M{c}Hugh, and 550 f. under Sir A. Chichester, Sir R. Percy, and Captains Lington and Norton.—*Moryson.*

[v] From [v] to [v] is not in *Dobbs.*

[w] At this day there are but 16 freemen of this towne.—*Dobbs.*

[x] 'Edenduffee Carrig, near Lough Eagh.'—*Dobbs.* 'The Castles Wardable in 1586 are Belfast, Edenduchar and Olderfleete; and the castles defaced are these—Portmuck in Iland Magy, Glanarne, and Redbaye in the Glynnes, and Castlemartyn in the Route.'—*Bagnall.*

In 1523 the Earl of Kildare took Hugh M{c}Neil's castle of Belfast, and 'burnt 24 myle of his country.' This Hugh M{c}Neil kept 1,500 Scots, besides his own soldiers. In 1591 Belfast castle was almost surrounded by woods, 'okes and other wood for many miles' (*See Notes of the Editor of Bagnall's Description of Ulster in Ulst. J. of Arch.*)

[y] On the narrow peninsula called the Corran, which projects into the bay of Larne, stands this castle, once a place of strength. After M{c}Donnell overthrew the English under Sir J. Chichester in the end of 1597, this castle was sold to him by its English commander. In announcing this treachery to Elizabeth, Ormond calls it 'Alderfleet standing upon the north seas.'

THE COUNTY OF ARMAGH.

This Countie hath to the South the Countie of Louth, the blackwater to the North, the River of the Newrie to the East, and the Countie of Monaghan to the West. It contayneth all the Land between the River of Dundalk and the black water, saving a small proportion called Cowley,[a] joining to Carlinford, belonging to Louth. In it are those several Countries comprehended.

   Ornaugh, otherwise O'Hanlon's Countrie.
   Clanbrassell,
   Clancane, Mucknoe, Oneylans,
   Clanant, Tirriaugh, Feues.

Most of these have Several Captens, to whom the Countries do appertain, but in time of Sr John Perrott were all made contributories to the Earle of Tyrone, to whom they were subject in the latter times.

O'HANLON'S COUNTRIE reacheth from the Newrie and from Dundalk to Ardmaghe; it is for the most part without Wood, but full of Hills and Boggs. It is able to make 50 Horsemen and 250 footemen.[b]

---

[a] 'Couray.'—*Dymmok*.

[b] 'Forty h. and 200 f.'—*Bagnall*. 'In 1598, in the army of Hugh O'Neil, there were 80 h. and 200 f. under O'Hanlon, McGyniesse, and Bryan McArt.'—*Carew Calendar*, p. 287. Sir H. Sydney informed the English government that a 'Mr. Chatterton undertooke to expulse and subdue the O'Hanlons . . . in troth, my Lords, the poor gentleman hath utterly undone himself in wrestling with them; and his brother, likewise, an honest, valiant gentleman, was wounded and maimed in the service, and lost and spent all that ever he had. . . The Countrie is large and long, yet is waste, altogether without a house, pile, or castle left standing in it, but a little sorry fort pitched of sods and turves.'—*Collins*, vol. i., 148.

CLONBRASSELL is a verie Woody and Boggie Countrie upon the great Lough side, called Oaghe or Sidney. It hath in it no Horsemen, but able to make 160 Kearnes.[c]

CLANCANCANE[d] is a verie strong Countrie, almost all Wood and deep Bogg; it is invironed on one side with the foresaid great Loughe, and on the other side with a great Bogg, and two deep Rivers, the one called the Black Water, the other the little Banne, which both within this Countrie do fall within this Lough. In this Countrie are no Horsemen, but about some 150 kearne,[e] who live for the most part in tyme of peace upon Stealth and Robberies.

CANTAULE[f] is a peece of a Countrie, which of right appertaineth to the Arch-Bishop of Ardmagh and his Freeholders, and Lieth between Ardmagh and the Blackwater. There is in it now[g] to the River much underwoode and Loughes,[h] but the rest lying towards Ardmagh is champion and Fertile.[i] The Capten of this Countrie was called Turleighe Brasilaghe, who held this peece of Land from the Earle of Tyrone, to whom he payed his Rents and Service. The said Turloghe and his Sonnes were Liable to make 40 Horsemen and 100 Footmen.

MUCTIONOE and TIRRIAUGHELIE,[j] between Ardmaghe and McMahon's Countries, not Long since appertayning to him, but of late possessed by the Earl of Tyrone, who hath placed certen of his waged followers, that paid their Rents and Services only unto him.

[c] McCane's country hath 100 f. and and 12 h.—*Carew Calendar*, p. 299. Clanbrassil was McCann's country.
[d] Called Clancan by *Bagnall*.
'McCan in Clancan hath 100 f. and 12 h.'—*Dymmok*.
[f] Written Clanant *supra*, but Clanawle by *Bagnall*, and Clanowlo by *Dymmok*.

[g] 'nere.'—*Bagnall*.
[h] 'boggs.'—*Bagnall*.
[i] 'Upon parte of this land is the bridge and fort of Blackwater built.'—*Bagnall*.
[j] 'Muckno and Tireawh.'—*Bagnall*. 'Muckro and Tragh.'—*Dymmok*.

FUES bordereth upon the Inglish Pale, within 3 Miles to Dundalke. It is a verie strong Countrie of Wood and Bogg, peopled with certen of the O'Neals, accustomed to live much upon the Spoiles of the Pale.[k] The Capten hereof is Sir Turloghe McHenrie O'Neall, Brother by the Mother to the now Earle of Tyrone, but no way affected to the Earle. For while the Earle of Tyrone was a good Subject, he overruled the said Sr Turloghe with his strength and Authoritie, and thereby kept him from annoying the Pale. But afterward, when Tyrone was a Rebell, the said Sr Turloghe rebelled from his Brother and came in to the L. Burrowes, Late L. Deputie, whom he served Fathfullie during the Life of the said Deputie, after which he was won by fair promises to returne from the Quene to Tyrone, with whom, when he had remained a certen tyme, he was committed to close Prison in a Castle within a Loughe upon a Suspicion of a Second revolt from the Earle to the Quene, where he remayneth in cheynes cruelly used for a long time, for whose deliverie divers attempts were made, but without success. At length he got his liberty by force, and ever since hath been a good Subject. He hath this Countrie by Letters Patents from his Majestie. This country is able to make about Fiftie Horsemen and 200 Footemen.[l]

ONEYLANE is likewise a Woodie land, lyeing between Ardmagh and Clanconcane. This Earle of Tyrone hath and claimeth it to his inheritance; he hath placed there some of the O'———[m] and ———, who fostered him, and for the most part

[k] All that follows, down to the end of the chapter on Armagh, is not in the *Bagnall* MS.

'In the Fewes Tirlo M^{c}O'Neale hath 300 f. and 50 h.'—*Carew Calendar*.

[m] 'Some of the Quins and Hagans who fostered him.'—*Bagnall*. The learned Editor of the *Bagnall* MS. says that 'Henry O'Hagan was the Earl's secretary, and *probably* his foster-brother.' But the *Cal. of Carew* MSS. removes all doubt regarding O'Neill's fosterers.

he dwelleth himself amongst them in a little Iland within a small Loughe called Lough Cotos." In this place lay his store of Munition, his money and jewels, and whatsoever precious things he had, namlie his Wife and Children.

There be no places of importance in this Countrie, but the church of Ardmagh, which was wont to Serve for a Garrison place, and a little Fort upon the Blackwater, which the old Earle of Essex first Builded on the South side of the River, together with a Bridge over the River; but Tyrone demolished the Bridge and raysed the Fort, and builded it on the North side of the River to Stopp the Passage of the Foord, which the L. Burrowes, late L. Deputie, surprised in July 1597, and placed in it a Garrison of 200 Men, who kept the same till August 1598, at which tyme, after the overthrowe given the

---

Under the year 1594, at p. 87, the Earl of Tyrone says:—'The Earl's *foster-brothers*, Captain Richard and Henry Hovendon, having the leading of 200 f. upon the Earl's charges, overthrew 500 or 600 Spaniards in Tir-Connell . . but neither they nor the Earl had any recompense of such service.' Again, in the negotiations with Elizabeth's commissioners, Jan. 15th, 1596, O'Neil says he cannot give them full satisfaction, because *his secretary*, Henry Hovendon, was absent, and he could not trust another to write for him on such matters.—*Carew Calendar*, an. 1596, pp. 133 and 136.

" 'In a little island called Lough Coe.'—*Bagnall*. Island fastnesses in inland lakes formed the universal system of defence in the north. Phetti-place, a famous pirate, informs the Council that John O'Neal the Proud 'dependeth for fortification on sartin freshwater loghes in this country. It is thought that there, in the said fortified islands, lyeth all his plate, which is much, and his money, prisoners, and gages. He hath razed the strongest castles of his country.' See what Mr. Evelyn Shirley says on this subject in his admirable work, called *Account of the Territory of Farney*. As Hugh trusted his foster-brothers, so, according to Phettiplace, 'Shane's strength and safety consists, not in the noblest of his men, nor in his kinsmen nor brothers, but on his foster-brothers, the O'Donnelly's, who are three hundred gentlemen.'

Inglyshe at Ardmaghe, it was yielded upon Composition to Tyrone, who possesseth the same at this instant.

The Principall men of this Country are :
- The Primate of Ardmaghe.
- The Earl of Tyrone.
- O'Hanlons.
- Turloghe Brasilagh.
- Sir Turloghe McHenrie of the Fewes.
- Art McBarons Sonnes.[o]
- The Clergie of Armagh.

THE COUNTIE OF MONAGHAN.

This Countie was in tymes past called Oriel, given at the time of the conquest to one Reinold FitzUrse, or Baresone, supposed to be one of the 4 Knights that slew Thomas Beckett.[a] His offspring are grown mere Irysh, and called McMahon, which signifyeth in Irish the Sone of a Beer.[b] He hath under him three Captains, all of his own surname, and possesseth the Countries of Loughty, Dartire, and Ferny,[c] which last bordereth

---

[o] Art MacBaron had 30 f. and 30 h.—*Dymmok.* Cormack McBaron had 300 f. and 40 h., and O'Neil had always about him 700 f. and 200 h.—*Carew Calendar,* p. 299.

[a] 'Sanct Thomas of Canterbury.'—*Dymmok.* From this extract of *Dymmok,* and from a blank before Thomas in our MS., it appears not unlikely that Sanct, or Saint, was in the original.

[b] Sir Henry Sydney, Spencer, Dymmok, Campion, and others, laboured under this delusion; but Mr. Evelyn Shirley gives the pedigree of the McMahons, and shows them to be pure Celts. Marshal Bagnall says nothing of the 'Bear's Son.'

[c] 'Iriell, Dartry, Loghtie, and Trow.'—*Bagnall.* 'Iriel, Bartrey, and Ferney.' *Dymmok.*

upon the Countie of Louth, and being a parcell of the Ancient Possessions of the Crowne, was given to the Grandfathers of this Earle of Essex, the title whereof remayneth in the now Earle, his Grandsonne. There is not in this Countie any Corporat Towne or place of importance, save 2 or 3 defaced Monasteries and the Lp. of Dunamore belonging to the Earle of Essex.

McMahon, now Capten hereof, is Sister's Sone to the Earle of Tyrone, and was able to make 120 Horsemen and 600 Footmen.[d] This Countie bordereth upon the Countie of Louth to East, to the Countie of Cavan or Omelies Countrie[e] to the South and South East, to the Lough, called Lougherne, north-west, and to the Countie of Ardmaghe to the North.

THE COUNTIE OF FERMANAGH.

This Countie, called commonlie McGwyres countrie,[a] lyeth upon both sides of the great Lough called Erne, and Stretcheth northward toward O'donnell's Countrie, called Tyrconnell; it hath the Countie of Tyrone to the East, Leytrim to the West, and to the South Monaghan and part of the Countie of Cavan.

[d] 'In 1599, McMaghone, Ferry Clancarvell, and Patrick McArte Moyle, in the co. of Monaghan, have 500 f. and 160 h.'—*Carew Calendar.* 'McMahon, with Ferney and Glancarvell, McArty Moyle (being a competitor for ye co. of Monahan').—*Dymmok.* 'McMahowne in Monaghan, Ever McCoolye in the Ferney, and others of that name in Clankarvil, 500 f. and 160 h.'—*Moryson.*

[e] *Recte*, O'Reilly's Countrie. There is in No. 9 of *Ulster Jour. of Arch.* a curious, coloured old map of Clones and Dartrie, showing the 'watch toure' (*i.e.*, round tower), the four or five churches, the Cross, ' the chapel,' and the Abbey; and the bogs, woods, and mountains all around.

[a] Conteineth all Farmanaghe, Termingraghe, and Tyrmin-Omungan. *Bag.*

This Countrie for the most part is verie Strong of Wood and Bogg, especiallie near the great Lake called Erne, wherein is diverse Ilands, full of Woods. Buildings in this Countrie are none of importance, the chief Hous is Inishkellen, demolished, which is Situat in one of the greatest Ilands in the Lough. The present Capten is named Sr Conner roe McGwyre, an old man . . . was able to make almost of his own Surname 120 Horsemen and 600 Footemen.[b]

THE COUNTIE OF TYRONE.

The Countie of Tyrone contayneth all the Land from the Black Water to the Laffer and fyne.[a] This was the portion assigned to Turloghe Lenoghe O'Nealle in the Treatie between him and the Earle of Essex, who before had comandemend of all Lands Southward to the Inglysh Pale.

This Countie hath the great Loughe called Eaghe to the East, and the Countie of Coleraine to the West, the Countie of Ardmagh to the South, and Tyrconnell to the North. The

---

[b] 'He hath 600 f. and 100 h.'—*Carew Calendar*. 'He is able to make (and most of his owne nation), 80 horsemen, 240 shot, and 300 kerne.'—*Bagnall*. 'He is left always to the rule and commandment of O'Neil, and yet be very desirous to depend on the Queen.'—*Bagnall*. However, this Maguire, six years afterwards, *i.e.*, in 1594, would not suffer any man to pass through his country, who wore an English hat or cloak (S. Paper, 10 Feb. 1594). 'He is one of O'Neil's Uraughts; he hath not any of name under him but his owne kindred; he is under the bishop of Clohn in the Co. of Tyrone.'—*Dymmok*.

The Uriaghs just mentioned were 'sub-kings' (*Oir-righ*) who paid tribute to their King, and joined his standard in time of war.

[a] 'from Blackwater to Liffer.'—*Bagnall*.

now *Earle of Tyrone* claiming this Countrie from his Grandfather, and growing Strong upon Turloghe Lenaghe, the last O'Neall, and wynning his followers from him, lest it should burst out into Warr, a composition was made between them by Sir John Perrot, L. Deputie, that for the life of the said O'Neale, the Earle should paie to him for a portion of Land being almost the halfe[b] of the Countie Southwards, 1000 marks Stir. yearlie, which Composition thoghe the Earle did not observe,[c] yet the Deputies succeeding wou'd not have the same broken during the Life of the said O'Neall, after which the Earle of Tyrone became M[r] of all, first under the name of Earle of Tyrone, but in the entire of his Rebellion perceiving the Iryshric more to affect the name of O'Neall, he caused himself to be chosen O'Neall after the ancient manner, thereby disannulling the Act of Parliament, which had altogether [abrogated] the name and Creation of O'Neall, made when his Grandfather Con O'Neall was made Earle of Tyrone.

The Inhabitants of this Countrie and the chief Gentlemen of the O'Nealls[d] amongst whome were the Sonnes of Shane O'Neall, Henrie, Hugh, Con, and Arthur. The Eldest and

---

[b] 'the half thereof and more.'—*Bagnall*.

[c] which (1000 marks a year) hath been detayned by the Erle: *where throughe it is like that some trouble will arise betweene them or it be longe*. Turlough desireth from her Ma[tie] to his sonne that portion of Tyrone, wherein he dwelleth, and is the remotest parte from th' English Paleward. The granting whereof were very expedient; the one for extinguishing their barborous custom of Tanestship, which is th' occasion of much mischiefe and disorder; th' other that by this division it will weeken the force and greatness of such as shall succeede, whereby they shall not be of power to do the hurt they were wont.'—*Bagnall*.

[d] 'first the Oneyles, who most are all horsemen; the Clandonnells, all galloglas; the Odoonelles, a very strong sept, and much affected to Shane Oneil's sonnes, the Hagans and Quyns.'—*Bagnall*.

the youngest were Prisoners in the Castle of Dublin, but escaped; in which escape Henry wounded himself negligentlie [accidently] with a knife as he was slipping down the Cord to Escape, and died of the wound; Con and Arthur are Prisoners with the Earle; Hughe was Hanged by the Earle upon a Suspicion that he had intended his death, which was the cause of the great hatred between Tyrone and McSleyne in Scotland, Hugh's Mother being McCleynes Father's Sister. In this Countie also is O'Neall's Turlogh's Grand Son to the last O'Neall.

This Countie hath not Townes, but divers ruined Castles, as Dungannon, the Earles principall Hous, which himself cast down to the middest after he had well . . . builded it and covered it with Lead, when Sir William Russell, late Lord Deputie, approached with the Armie thereto; Omaghe, Newcastle, Benburge,^e and Strabane, which was the place, where the last O'Neall had his Residence, whose Wife being a Scottish woman drew great repair of Scottishmen thither insomuch as at this present there are above 3 or four Score Scottish Familes inhabitting there. This Countie is able to make 450 Horsemen and 800^f Footemen.

The Odoonells were the O'Donnellies who were foster-brothers of Shane O'Neil, and who numbered ' 300 gentlemen of their name' according to the pirate Phettiplace.

^e called Benburb by Shane O'Neil.

^f '300 h. and 1,500 f., but alwaies the strength and greatness of the Oneyles stoode chiffest upon bandes of Scottes, whom they caused their Uriaughes to victual and paye.'—*Bagnall.*

In 1592 'the forces of Tyrone were 930 h. and 5,260 f., of which 20 horse and 1,000 foot were retained by the Earl of Tyrone.'—(*Carew Calendar*, p. 73). 'Where the Earle of Tyrone hath rule is the fairest and goodliest countrie in Ireland, and many gentlemen of the Neyles dwell therein.' (*Letter of Lord Chancellor Cusack of the 8th May 1552, quoted by the Editor of Bagnall's MS.*)

THE COUNTIE OF COLERAINE.

This Countie beareth this name of the Castle of COLERAINE upon the North side of the Banne, and not of the Abbey of Coleraine, which is on the other side of the River. It contayneth all the Land[a] between the Rivers of Banne and Loughfoile along the Sea coast. It hath the Sea to East, Tyrone and the Woods of Clanknockkeyne to the West, the Banne to the South, and Loughfoile to the North. There is no man of name in it, But Sir Donald Ocaen and his Freeholders; This OCAEN is the cheif of O'Neall's Vassalls,[b] and createth him O'Neall by casting a Shoe over his head upon a Hill in Tyrone.

He is able to make near 200 Horsemen, which are esteemed the best Horsemen that O'Neall hath, and 500 Footmen;[c] and because he Lyeth near Scotland, he was well affected to the Scotch and gave them yearlie great relief; he hath 2 strong Castles upon Loughfoyle—Armagh[d] and Limevady, and upon the Banne, near the Salmond Fishing, 2 Castles—the Castle of Coleraine somewhat defaced yet Wardable, and Castle Roe wherein O'Neall was wont to keep a Ward to receive his part of the Fishing.

[a] 'all o'Cahan's country.'—*Bagnall.*
[b] 'Uraughts.' *Dymmok.*

In 1590 the Earl of Tyrone renounced meddling with the 'Uriats;' but said o'Cane was none of the 'Uriatts,' being an inhabitant within the county of Tyrone.

[c] In 1592 'the forces of Colrane were 400 h. and 1,000 f. (*Carew Calendar,* p. 73). 'A garrison should be placed at Derry, bordering upon O'Cahan, the chief strength of horse that the Earl has.'—*Mr. Francis Shane, Discourse on the Rebellion in Ulster* 1596.—*Carew Calendar.*

[d] 'Anagh.'—*Bagnall.* In 1542 the Lord Dep. and Council wrote to Henry VIII. about a proude obstynate Irysheman called O'Cathan. (*Printed State Papers,* Vol. iii. p. 408). The O'Cahans were descended from O'Cathan, grandson of O'Niall of the Nine Hostages. They ruled Ciannacta from at least the year 1138, and were styled in Irish *Righ* (Kings), or *Tighearna* (Lord), or *Taoiseach* (Chief).

THE COUNTIE OF DUNNIGALL.

This Countie contayneth all Tyrconnell, and is the greatest of all the Shyres of Ulster, and contayneth all the Land to the River of Fynne northward to the Sea. From the East Sea to the *County* [River] of Earne near the Countie of Sligo, so hath it the Sea upon the East and North, the River Fynne to the South, and Earne to the West. This Countie contayneth all O'DONNELLS and ODOCHERTIES Countrie. [The first year that the K. came into England this Country was erected into an Earldom, etc.] O'Donnell is Captain and Governor of Tyrconnell, the chief strength of whom standeth upon 2 Septs of People called O'Gallochies[b] and McSwynes who are all Galloglasses [That is men armed with Coates of Mayl Steel Bonetts, Swords and pole axes]. He is able to make about 300 Horsemen and so many more Footmen.[c]

---

[b] ' O'Galchoule.'—*Carew Calendar.*

' O'Gallochelles.' — *Bagnall.* In *Dymmok* it is O'Chaloganes, and the learned Editor surmises, that perhaps it is O'Halagan; but the *Betagh* and *Bagnall* MSS. point to the O'Gallaghers, 'a sept which inhabit the middle of Tir-Connell,' says the 'Description of Lough Foyle in 1601.' (Published by Herbert F. Hore, in No. 18 of *Ulster J. of Arch.*) The O'Galchoule of the *Carew* MSS. is called *O'Gallchubhar* in the F. Mast. an. 1586 and 1587.

[c] ' 200 h. and 1,300 f.'—*Bagnall.* In 1592 there were in O'Donnell's country of Tir-connell 310 h. and 2,680 f., of whom 80 h. and 500 f. were retained by O'Donnell. In 1599 O'Donnell had 180 h. and 1,250 f., of whom he kept round him 60 h. and 200 f.—*Carew Calendar.* According to *Dymmok* he had 3,000 f. and 200 h. for his whole country. 'His country is large, profitable and good—a ship under sail may come to four of his houses.' (*L. Chancellor Cusack in* 1552).

According to *Carew* MSS. 614, O'Donnell was 'the best Lorde of fyshe in Ireland, and exchangeth fyshe alwaies with foreign merchants for wine; by which his call in other countries is *King of the Fishe.*' (No. 7 *Ulst. J. of Arch.* p. 148-9).

Between O'Donnell and O'Neall in tymes past hath been continual Warr for the Castle of Liffer and the Lands thereabouts, Lying between both their Countries and bordering upon Loughfoyle, by which means of their dissention it was kept altogether Wast and uninhabitted, until the late Quene took it into her hands, and made it a Garrison place, and so remayneth unto this day. This controversie was taken away by a double Marriage. Tyrone having married O'donnell's Sister, by whom he hath divers Sonnes, and O'Donnell having married his Daughter, whom many yeares he hath cast off for Barronness.

O'DOGHERTIES COUNTRIE is a promontory almost environed with the Sea, namlie, with Lough Swilly on the South, and Loughfoyle on the North. It is Governed by a Capten, called Sir Caher O'doghertie, who not being of power able to defend himself was forced to contribute both to O'Neall and O'Donnell, and by turne to Serve them both. His Country lying upon the Sea, and upon the Isles of Ila and Jura in Scotland, was wont almost yearlie to be invaded by the Scotch, who tooke the Spoyles at their pleasures, whereby O'Doghertie was forced always to be at their devotions [He was latelie Killed.]

He was able of his own Nation, and others his followers, to make 80 Horsemen and 300 Footemen.[d] Buildings in this Countrie are the Ordy [Orey][e] which is defaced, and Creen Castle,[f] which is also defaced.

---

[d] 60 h. and 300 f.—*Bagnall.*

[e] 'Dery, which is defaced, and Greencastle, and [. . .] which are wardable.'—*Bagnall.* All that follows about Tir-connell is not in the *Bagnall* MS.

The Derie stood three miles above Culmore; there the Bishop dwelt, who is one of the sept of the O'Gallocars. He dwelled in 1600 at the Castle and Church of Fanne. (*Lough Foyle in* 1601 *by H. J. Hore*).

[f] On the south syde of the country at the coming to the Loughe, an ould ruined Castle called Newcastle. Here dwells Hugh Boy mack Caire, one of

This Countie hath some principall Castles belonging to it—Dunigall,[g] O'Donnell's chief Hous, from whence the Countie hath the name; Ballyshannon,[h] standing upon the Earne, a Strong Hous, by the means whereof O'Donnell passeth the River of Earne at his pleasure, and entereth Conaught in a manner quietlie, Lyffer and Fynne,[i] he had also Beleeke and Bundroose beyond the River of Earne on Conaught side; besides the Abbeys of Dunigall, Asherowe, and Darrie, all ruined saving Dunigall, latelie re-edifyed by the Earl of Tyrconnell, and Sundrie other small Fryries.[j]

The Principal men in this Countie [It is now in the King's hands and kept with a Garrison. Defaced. Beleke is now the possession of S. H.] are Sir Roger O'donnell, Earle of Tyrconnell, The Bishops of Derrie and Rafoe, Hugh Duff O'Donnell,[k] who challengeth a title the whole Countrie. [Hugh Oge Roe, Sonne and heyre to the said S[r]. Hugh by the Daughter of James M[c]Connell. Defaced. S[r]. Hugh, Chief of his name, who hath resigned his place to his Sone and betaken

---

the O'Doghertie sept; It is called also Greencastle, but in Irish *Caislean nua, i.e.,* the new Castle.—*Hore.*

[g] Here is a good haven, and the river Esk falls into it, also an Abbey and a Castle. Three miles above it is Lough Eske, O'Donnell's chief keeping and chief store-house for the warr.—*Hore.*

[h] 'Where dwells M[c]O'Dongonrye.'—*Hore.*

O'Donnell dwelt at Liffer, and Cul MacTryne; and Neal Garve, at Castle Fenc; Shane M[c]Manus Oge, at the fort of Dunboye; O'Donnell's mother at the forts of M[c]Gwyvelin and Cargan.

[j] The Fryars dwell in the abbayes of Kil O'Donnell, of Ballaghan, of Asheroe, and of Donegall. Bishop O'Gallogher's houses were the Derry, the Castle and Church of Fanne; and at the Castle of Kilmerrish at the lower end of O'Boyle's country lived the Bishop of O'Boyle. At a Castle and Church called Clonmeny lives a priest called Amerson. (*Condensed from Mr. Hore's Lough Foyle in* 1601).

[k] Hugh M[c]Hugh Duffe, I presume, who lived in the Castle of 'Ramaltan,' which stands upon the Lanan.

himself to the Monasterie.] Hugh M*c*Connell,[1] adopted, who is also a Competitor for the Capitencie, and was many years accompted the Sonne of Dronisk O'Gallochie.

The 2 Sonnes of Con O'Donnell.
S*ir* Caher O'Doghertie,[m] Knight, Capten of his Countrie.
Sir Owen O'Gallochie.[n]
M*c*Swyne Baine.[o]
M*c*Swyne faine.[p]
M*c*Swyne a Doagh.[q]

⇒ Quaere, was he the 'Seneschal M*c*Gonell who dwelt at the haven of Calboy?'—(*See Hore*).

[m] Of this name, the Chief, Sir Cahir, lived at Don-yrish fort, at the Castle of Elloghe (*Oileach*), and at the Castle of Birt he had a ward of 40 men; Hugh Boy M*c*Caire at Greencastle, and his brother Shane M*c*Duffe at Moville; Phelimy Og, the chief's brother, at the fort of Culmore. In the island of Ench lives Doultach O'Dogherty; Conor M*c*Garret O'D. at Buncrana Castle; Phelim Brasleigh O'D. at Carrigbraghey Castle; Phelim Brasleigh's two sonnes at the Castle of Caslan-Stoke, and the fort of Don-Owen; M*c*Shane O'Doghertie at Caldanylie.

This country is called Inishowen; the midland country is mostly mountainous, and hath few inhabitants. Also in this country Hugh Carrogh M*c*Loughlin, chief of his sept, dwells in the Castle of Caire MacEwlyn, and Brien Og M*c*Loughlin at the Castle of Garnegall. (*Condensed and arranged from the Description of Lough Foyle, edited by Hore*).

[n] Donel Gallocar, one of O'Donnell's chief councillors, lives at the fort of Ballakit. The O'Galloghers lived in the Baronies of Raphoe and Tirhugh, had a Castle at Ballyshannon, were the Constables of the Castle of Lifford and commanders of O'Donnell's cavalry. Perhaps 'M*c*O'Dongonry who dwells in Ballashannon,' mentioned in *Mr. Hore's MS.*, is a mistake for O'Gallogher.

[o] dwells at M*c*Swyn O'Bane's Tower; Hugh Boy M*c*Swyne (O'Bane's brother) at the Castle of Bromoyle.

[p] At the castle and abbey of Ramellan is M*c*Swyn O'Fane's chief country House; Menrice (near Red Haven) is also a castle of M*c*Swyn O'Fanets. Red Haven (where dwells Alexander M*c*Donologe) separates the countries of M*c*Swyne O'Fane's and M*c*Swyn O'Doe's.

[q] of the castle of Conogarhen. 'O'Boyle's chief house is O'Boyle, where the ships used to ride.' (*The notes in this column are taken from Hore's Lough Foyle*).

Our MS. does not state the forces

COUNTY OF DUNNIGALL.

All Ulster' is now joined together in Rebellion against the Quene, saving the Countie of Louth, a little piece of land about the Newrie and the Towne of Craigfergus; all the Captens of Countries are bound to the Earle of Tyrone, either by Affinitie or Consanguinitie or duetie; for O'Donnell is his Brother-in-law, his first Wife being O'Donnell's Sister, McGwyre is his Coosen Germane, for the Earl's mother was this McGwyres Father's Sister; Ocaen is his Coosen Germane, for his Father's Sister was Ocaen's mother; further, Ocaen is his chief Vassell, and of late he hath married this Earle's Daughter, whom O'Donnell hath divorced from him; McMahon is his near Kinsman; McGynnes is his Brother-in-law, for his present Lady is McGynnes's Sister.

Tyrone is a man valiant, Temperate and wise, well brought up, partlie in the Court of Ingl., and a Speciall actor in all the Warrs of Ireland these xxx years, whereby he is become a man of great expereance, to which parts some ambition is joyned. He is now become impotent to contayne himself within his bounds; but Seeketh to Usurpe the whole province.

His forces, when the Countrie is as hath been said, 5,800 Footemen and 1,870 Horsemen, To whom many ill disposed persons from all parts of the Land hath conjoyned themselves,

of O'Donnell's sub-chiefs or *Oir-righ*, viz., 'The Donnelagh's country, betwixt the river Fynn and Lough Swilly, possessed by Con O'Donnell's sons and McHugh Duff, hath 150 f. and 30 h.; McSwyne's cuntry, McSwine de Band, McSwyne de Fand, and MacSwyne de Doe, hath 500 f. and 30 h. O'Boyle's country reached to Calebegge, hath 100 f. and 20 horse.'—*See Carew Calen.*

'' *Ulster.*—A country so strong and so wild, as never conquered nor quiet; wholly in rebellion except some scores(?), the climate unwholesome; the passages so difficult as that my Lord Burgh——. The General Norreys never could look over the water. Good soldiers well armed and in blood. The Scottish islands, which yield men and provisions. Clyfford betrayed; Bingham lightly condemned.'—*Memorial for Ireland*, *written in Cecil's hand, Nov.* 4, 1598.

besides a certen number of Scots whom he entertayneth upon the Bonnaghts of the Countrie, whereby his Forces will extend to the number of about *One* [Ten] thousand.[s]

[s] The *summa totalis* of such horse and foote as the Erle of Tyrone hath very lately plotted to be cessed and waged by the several Captaynes and Lords of Cuntries in ye Province of Ulster is foote 8430, horse 1130; in all 9560.—*Dymmok*, p. 30. 'In 1600 the main strength of the chieftains of Ulster was 9000 f. and 800 h.'—*Carew Calendar*, p. 405. In 1598 Capt. Francis Stafford gave 'The List of the Horse and Foot of Ulster under the Earl's command in 1598.'—Cormac McBaron of Carrick-Teague, 60 h. 200 f.; Art McBaron in O'Neale's land, 30 h. 80 f.; Henry McShane of the Tynan, 30 h. 80 f.; Phelimy O'N. of Dunavall, 10 h. 40 f.; Con McTerlagh of the Tynan, 10 h. 40 f.; Con McHenry, between Tynan and Clougharde, 12 h. 40 f.; Sir Art O'N. of the Onye, 30 h. 50 f.; Tirlogh McHenry, 50 h. 100 f.; Cormac O'N. of Lenough, 10 h. 30 f.; Con O'N., 5 h. 20 f.; John O'N. of Carrick-Teall, 20 h. 50 f.; Shane McBryan O'N. and Neal McHugh O'N. (Lords of the Lower Clonduboyes), Neal McBryan Erto O'N. and Owen MacHugh O'N. (Lords of Upper Clanduboy), and McSowrlie of the Rowte, 60 h. 200 f.; 'Tyrone 60 h. for himself and his men, 200 f. under Nugent and Tirrell, and 100 naked Scots with bows' = 60 h. 300 f.; Neal O'Guin of Curran, 10 h. 30 f.; Oge Guin, 20 h. 30 f; John McDonnell Grome of Bunburbe, 8 h. 40 f.; Edmund Gynclagh of Knock-la-Glynche, 6 h. 30 f.; Bryan Carrough McDonnell, 30 h. 60 f.; O'Mallow (Mallon ? Ed.) of Ellis Flynn, 6 h. 20 f.; O'Hagan, 16 h. 40 f.; Cormac O'Hagan, 10 h. 20 f.; O'Cane, 60 h. 60 f.; O'Hanlon, McGenyese, and Brian McArt, 80 h. 200 f.; Maguyre, 50 h. 200 f.; The McMahounds together, 100 h. 300 f.; O'Donnell, O'Doherty, and Tirconnell, 140 h. 1000 f. Total 1043 h. and 3540 foot.—*Carew Calendar*, p. 287.

In April 1599, the Ulster forces consisted of 1470 h. and 6180 f. The mustering of O'Donnell's forces in that year is thus quaintly chronicled in the Irish Annals: 'First of all assembled the Kinel-Connel, among whom were Hugh Oge (the son of Hugh Duv, son of Hugh Roe, son of Niall Garv O'Donnell); and Niall Garv (the son of Con, son of Calvach, son of Manus, son of Hugh Duv); O'Dogherty (John Oge, the son of Felim, son of Conor Carragh); O'Boyle (Teig Oge, the son of Teig, son of Torlogh, son of Niall); MacSuiny Fanad (Donnal, the son of Torlogh, son of Mulmurry); MacSuiny Banach (Donogh, the son of Mulmurry Meirgeach, son of Mulmurry, son of Niall) : all these with their forces. To the same rendezvous came Maguire (Hugh, the son of Cuconnacht, son of Cuconnacht, son of Cuconnacht, son of Brian, son of Philip, son of Thomas); the son of O'Rourk; and the MacWilliam.'

LEINSTER.

CONTAYNETH that portion of Land which was conquered by the Inglysh, including the Counties of Dublin, Kildare, Catherlaghe, Wexford, Kilkenny, King's and Quene's countie, and latelie one other Countie taken out of the Counties of Dublin and Wexford, called by the name of Wickloe.[a]

DUBLIN.

DUBLIN contayneth all the Land from Baleratherie, nere the Countie of Meath, to Bray, which is the Length of the Shyre, and includeth all the Land between the Naas and Dublin, which

[a] 'The Irish Septs planted in Leinster are, according to *Sir H. Sydney's Collections*, the Byrnes, Tooles, Cavanaghes (which is the nation of the Macmurrow), Omores, O'Connores, Odempsyes, Odun.' 'The Irish coursed the English into a narrow circuite of certaine shires in Leinster, which the English did choose as the fattest soyle, most defensible, their proper right, and most open to receive help from England. Hereupon it was termed their pale, as whereout they durst not peepe. But now both within this pale, uncivill Irish and some rebells doe dwell, and without it Countreyes and cities English are well governed.'—*Campion*, p. 2 & 4. Ed. 1633.

'Leinster includeth all that ground from Dublin southwarde to the river Suyre, and the Cytty of Waterforde, which parteth it from Munster. The river of Shenin in MacCouglian's country devideth the west parte from Connaght and Meath; northwarde yt endeth with the barony of Balrothry and the ryver Boyne, and on the east side it is bounded by the sea. They have gone about of late to add two other shires, the counties of Wicklo and Fernes; but because these two shires are unperfett, not having sufficient freeholders and gentlemen to choose Shriffes and other principal officers, or to make a jury for the Queen, they may be well omitted.'—*Dymmok*.

is the bredth thereof. In it is comprehended the Kings[b] and the mountains, some of the O'Burnes and O'Tooles, and the crosse of the Countie of Dublin, being the Libertie of the Archbishop, also his Ilands in the Sea, as Lambay, Ireland's Eye, and Dalkey. So hath it the Sea to the East part, the Counties of Meath and Kildare to the West, the Counties of Caterlaghe and Wicklow to the South, and the Countie of Meath to the North.

In it are Townes, viz.

The CITTY OF DUBLIN, the seat of the Government,[c] the See of the Archbishop Walled with a Barred Haven.

Dumboyne
Swords
Luske } market Townes unwalled and without priviledges.
Ratoth

'The whole number of the Rebels in this Province of Leinster was 3048 foot and 182 horse.'—*Moryson.*

'Strangers within Leinster. With Pheagh M'Hugh's sonnes are ye Clamoles with 80 f.; with Murrogh M'Edmunds' sons, 30 Scotts under Donogh Ganco; of Ulstermen under Con the bastard 800 foote.'—*Dymmok.*

'The Fastnesses of wood and bogge in Leinster are Glandilore, a fastness in Pheagh M'Hugh's cuntry. Shilogh in the co. of Dublin. The Duffrin in the co. of Wexford. The Dromes and Leverough in the co. of Catherloghe. The great bogge in the King's Co. called the Tougher. The Fewes in the co. of Kildare. The woodes and bogges of Monasterevan, Gallin, and Slymarge in the Queen's Co. The Roure near S[t] Mollines. Part of Consteragh, joining upon Kilkenny.'—*Dymmok,* 26.

[b] The King's lands and the mountains of the O'Byrnes, O'Tooles and Banilagh, called Pheagh MacHugh's cuntry, also Shilo and Ferderrogh and the crosse of the country.'—*Dymmok.*

[c] 'Dyvelin, the beauty and eye of Ireland, fast by a goodly river. The seat hereof is in many respects comfortable, but less frequented of marchant strangers because of the bard haven. Its Mayorality, both for state and charge of that office, and for the bountifull hospitality exceedeth any City in England, except London.'—*Campion,* p. 2 and 96.

DUBLIN.

The names of the best Villages in this County.

Balerotherie	Clondalkin	Kilshaughlin
Hoth	Brey	Finglass
Newcastle	Fieldstowne	Ballimore
Kingsland		

Principal Castles in this Countie are these

Swords \
Tallowghe } both belonging to the Archbishop of Dublin.

Rathfernen [Built by Sr Adam Loftus]

Dromconren	Castle Knock	
Monckton	Dunshughlin	Donibroke
Newcastle	Dromnaghe	Malahide
Merron	Balgriffen	Belgard
Turvey	Lucan	Hoth
Donamore	Luttrelstone	
Holme Patrick	The Ward	

Men of name in this Countie are

The Arch Bishop of Dublin his Deane and clergie	Sr Willm Sarsfield, Kn$^{t.}$ his hous is Lucan
L. of Hoth his name St. Lawrence [alias Tristram]	Allen of St Wolstans Allen of Palmerston
Sr Henrie Harrington	Talbott of Balgard
Preston of Balmadon	Talbot of Templeoge
Sir Garot Elmer[d]	Talbot of Fash[d]
Preston of Tassagard	Talbot of Kilmarocke

---

[d] Garret Aylmer at Munkton; Talbot of Faghsaghere; Couran of Wyartstone, Coran of Curragh. Only sixty names are given in the *Perambulation of the Pale in* 1596; there are ninety-eight in our manuscript, to which we will add the following from the *Perambulation of the Pale*:—Ashpoole of Kenleston, John Bath of Balgriffin, Richard Netterville of Corballies, Philip Couran of

Barnwall of Dromnaghe
Walshe of Shaunogherghe [Shanganagh]
Fitzwilliams of Merrion
Fitzwilliams of Jobston
S[r] William Usher of Donabroke
Phelim O'Toole of Powerstoune
Walshe of Kilbegan
Walshe of Carrickmayne
Harold of the Grange
Archbold of Kellister
Archbold of Bray
Bath of Dromconraghe
Burnell of Castle Knock
Hollywood of Tartayne
Nugent of Kilmore
Golding of the Grange
Hackett of Sutton
Talbot of Malahide
Russell of Seaton
Fitzsimons of Swords

Tailor of Swords
Caddell of Moreton
Caddell of Caddelston
Stokes of Knockyngen
Wycam of Drynan
Blackney of Riknhore
Sinothe of Sinot court
Foster of Killerghe
S[r] Chris[r] Plunket Knt of Dunshoghley
Bealing of Bealingston
Jordan of[d]
S[r] Patrick Barnewall of Turvey
Barnewall of Broymore
Stanihurst of Carduff
Cruis of the Naale
Conran of[d]
Beg of Borranston
Sedgrave of Killeglan
Barnwall of Dunbroe
Scurlock of Rathcredon
Hamlen of Smitheston
Field of Carduff

Wyartown, Coran of Curragh, Sedgrave of W. . . . , Golding of Tobbirsowle, Fagan of Feltrim, Bath of Balgriffin, Bellew of Weston, Belling of Kilcoskan, Brown of Kissak, Fagan of Feltrim, Cardiff of Dunsink, Dillon of Huntstown, FitzGerot of Damaston, Fitzwilliam of Holmpatrick, King of Clontarf, Pypho of Hollywood, Plunket of the Grange, Russell of Dryneham, Walshe of Killegarge, Walshe of Ballawlie, Walshe of Kilgobbon, Warren of Drumconrath, and Peter Travers of Ballykey. Doubtless Beg of Boranstown, Scurlock of Rathcredon, and Finglas of Tippersold are the same as Bigg of Borarstown, Scurlock of Rathcredant, and Finglas of Tobberton given in the *Carew Calendar*, p. 188.

DUBLIN. 39

Luttrell of Luttrelstone
Whyte of St Kathrens
Eustace of Confy
Dillon of Keppoch
Taylor of Feltrim
Finglas of Wespelston
Finglas of Tippersole
Goodman of Laughanston
Delahide of Loughfenny
Bath of Carrendeston
Bath of Beccanston
Sarkey of the Hintch
Barnwall of Laspelston
Bath of the new l.
Tallen of Weston^e
Bedlow of Reynoldston
Hewitt of Gareston
Young of Gareston
Plunket of Brownston
Sedgrave of Borranston
Chamberlon of Kilresk
Clinshe of Newcastle

Reynold of Newcastle
Russell of Newcastle
Linche of
Mason of
Taylor of Ballown
Den of Tassagard
Fount of Tassagard
Lock of Colmanston
Tappock of Colmanston
Fitzsimons of Balmadroght
Protford of Protfordeston
Tyrrell of Powerston
Byrne of Ballyeane
Mangen of Loughton
Dungan of Loughton
Pierce of Cromelin
Caddell of Harbardstone
Fitzsimons of the Grange
Newtervile of Kilsoghlie
Ulverston of Stalorgan
and many meane freeholders

Of this Countie of Dublin there is some in this action of Rebellion. The Countrie commonlie called by the late Capten thereof Fewghe McHugh his contrie is full of Woods and Hills that it administereth a mervalous Succour to the Rebells that lie therein, for there they lie safelie in a manner, and the Cattle having pasture in abondance can hardlie be driven away there being so few Entries and Outgates into the Countrie. In this

^e First written Callen, and then the C was changed to T.

the Rebells remaynes commonlie all day, and in the beginning of the Night they come abroad and wast the Countries farr and nere, and the Vicinitie of this Countrie to Dublin doth much annoy the Cittie,[f] for it being within four or Five Miles of the Cittie, the Cittie is constreyned to keep strong watch least on a sudden these Rebells that Lurke in these Mountains do set the Suburbs on Fire which hath heretofore been done by them in the Goverment of the late L. Grey. The now head Capten of this Countrie is called PHELIM M^cFEWGHE[g] who is able to make some 300 or 400 Footmen but no Horsemen. He is confederat

[f] 'Campion thus quaintly speaks of the Dublin mountaineers:—'While the Deputy staggered uncertain of continuance, the *Tooles* and the Cavanaghes waxed cockish in the Countie of Divelin, ranging in flocks of seven or eight score, on whom set forth the Marshal and the Sheriffes of Divelin, *Buckley* and *Gygen*, with the cities helpe, and overlaid them in sudden skirmishes, of which three score were executed for example.'—*Campion's Historie*, p. 124. Ed. of 1633.

[g] 'Those that dwell even within the sight of the smoke of Dublin are not subject to the laws. The very gall of Ireland, and the flame from which all others take their lights is our next neighbour Pheaghe McHugh, who, like one absolute within himself, with his den of thieves, ruleth all things in his own country at his own will, refusing in person to come to the Governor, and spoiling his neighbours, who for fear dare not complain. His force does not exceed one hundred persons. His neighbours would help to cut him off. The Cavanaghs, who rely upon him, are entered into the like kind of life.'— *Sir G. Carew to Mr. Vice-Chamberlain, Nov.* 1590, *Carew Calendar.*

Fewghe or Fiach, though not the chief of the O'Byrnes, was the most warlike and powerful man of his name since the death of Dunlang, who was the last inaugurated O'Byrne. He was chief of that sept of the O'Byrnes called Gaval-Rannall, and lived in Glenmalure. His battles and victories are recorded in several poems of the *Leabhar Branach, or Book of the O'Byrnes.* The jealousy of the senior branches of the O'Byrnes led to his betrayal and death. Fiach left three sons, viz: Felim who was M.P. for Wicklow in 1613; Raymund and Torlogh; also a daughter, who was m. to Walter Reagh FitzGerald. His eldest son, Felim, had eight sons and a daughter, of whom the eldest, Brian, had a son Shane McBrian McFelim of Ballinacor, who was a Colonel of the Confederate army in

with Tyrone and comonlie doth most mischief when the companies withdrawes from Dublin ether against Tyrone or the Omoores, then do they besturr themselves burning, Spoiling, and praying thereby Seeking either to draw back the Forces from any prosecution, or else to divide the Forces and so to weaken them that they may either be the more easilice overthrown or be com-

1641, in which also Hugh, a grandson of Fiach, was a lieutenant-colonel. After the year 1641 the family of Ballinacor disappears from history.— See *O'Donovan's Notes to Four Masters*, an. 1597.

'Fiach McHugh continually troubleth the State, though he lyeth under their nose; plays the *Rex*, gives heart and succour and refuge to all against her Majesty. Through his boldness and late good success the rebels Byrnes and Tooles threaten perill even to Dublin over whose necke they continually hang. He is a most dangerous enemy to deal withall. Through his own hardinesse lifted himself to such a height, that he dare now front Princes and make tearmes with great potentates. ... A thousand men should be laid in six garrisons in order to reduce him—200 f. and 50 h. at Ballinacor to shut him out of his great glynne; at Knockelough, 200 f. and 50 h. to answer the co. of Catherlagh; at Arclo or Wicklow 200 f. and 50 h. to defend all on the Sea side; in Shilelagh 100 f. to cut him off from the Kavanagh's and Wexford about the Three Castles 50 h. which should defend the co. of Dublin; at Talbotstown 100 f. to keep him from breaking out into Kildare and to be always on his necke on that side. These garrisons will so busie him that he shall never rest at home nor stir abroad but he shall be had; as for his Creete they cannot be above ground and must fall into our hands. By good espialls, *whereof there they cannot want store*, they shall be drawn continually upon him; so as one of them shall be still upon him, and sometimes all at once, bayting him—unto the eternall quietness of that Realme.'—Abridged from *Spencer's View*, p. 81. Ed. 1633.

The *Four Masters* thus record his death: 'Fiach, son of Hugh, son of John from Glenmalure was slain in the first month of Summer in this year, having been treacherously betrayed by his relation at the bidding of the Chief Justiciary of Ireland, Sir W. Russel.'

Carew called him 'the firebrand, the gall of Ireland, the ancient traitor of Leinster.' In 1596 Elizabeth made offers, 'honorable for herself and not over hard for Fiach:' 1st, 'Pardon for himself, his wife, sons and followers; and restoration to his house and livings by letters patent, yielding some service. If he insists on getting back Ballinacor and will not be reduced without

pelled more warlic to prosecute the Rebells. All the Gents betwixt Dublin and these mountains do daylie susteyn great losse in their Goods, and sometimes lose their Lives.[h] There is joyned with this Phelim some few of the *Walshes*, and some of the *O'Tooles*.[i]

it, let him have it, and hold it of the Queen, who is at great charges to keep it. 2nd, He must promise to banish all strangers,' etc.

[h] The joy of these gentlemen of Dublin at Fiach's death appears from the following entries in the Lord Deputy's Journal: 'May 8, Sunday.—Early in the morning our foot entered the Glynnes, and fell into that quarter, where Fiach lay; and coming several ways on him, it pleased God to deliver him into our hands, being so hardly followed, as that he was run out of breath, and forced to take a cave, where one Milborne, sergeant to Captain Lea, first lighted on him, and *the fury of our soldiers was so great* as he could not be brought away alive; thereupon the said sergeant cut off Fiach's head with his own sword, and presented his head to my Lord, which with his carcass was brought to Dublin to the great comfort and joy of all that province. Many of his followers were slain and 200 cows were taken with much pillage, which was divided among the soldiers. My Lord returned to Rathdrome, and there before the fort Knighted Sir Calistinas Brooke, Sir Thomas Maria Wingfield, and Sir Richard Trevers. 9th of May.—My Lord rode to Dublin. All the way the people of the country met him with great joy and gladness, and as their manner is, bestowed many blessings on him for performing so good a deed and delivering them from their long oppressions. The Council, divers noblemen, and the citizens of Dublin with many others met his lordship, and he was welcomed with universal joy.'

O'Sullivan Beare says that he was betrayed by some one in whom he had the greatest confidence, '*quodam, quem fidissimum habebat, prodente et hostes ducente.*' Dr. O'Donovan thought it was Cahir McHugh Duffe; perhaps it was Hugh Duffe himself who figures in Russell's Journal as 'being out on service,' and as 'certifying that he had taken certain of the traitors' heads.'

Russell's Journal tells us that Fiach's wife, Rosa O'Toole was found guilty of treason and 'sentenced to be burned.' A constant entry in this Journal is, 'Heads of so many of Fiach's followers brought in.' If followers meant husbandmen, or old men or women of his clan, the journal is black indeed. On the 9th of March 1597, 'my Lord pledges his word to Ormond that he will pardon Garret McMurtagh if he cut off 20 heads of rebel kernes.'

[i] However, on St. Patrick's Eve 1597, Phelim O'Toole brought in one

DUBLIN. 43

This Countie of Dublin is verie fruitfull, and yealdeth great plentie of all kind of cornes; but if the Rebells fear prosecution, they burn the Corn that the Subject may not have means to

head to the Deputy and made a prisoner of one of Fiach's followers. In 1595 Sir H. Harrington 'complained of Capt. Lea about the murdering of one of the O'Tooles, protected by Council.' Old Sir Owen O'Toole, Knight, though the Lord Deputy pledged his word he should not be molested, was imprisoned for six years, from the hardships of which he died.—(See *Carew Calendar*, pp. 89, 153). Felim O'Toole of Teara-Cualann lived at Powerscourt; he and Brian O'Toole forfeited their territory of 'Fercuolen,' which was five miles in length and four in breadth. O'Toole of Castlekevin, was Fiach O'Byrne's brother-in-law. His son Fiach, was deprived of his property by James I.; in 1641 he was a Colonel in the Confederate Army in which two of his sons held commissions as Lieut.-Colonel and Major.

The Wexford O'Tooles are the most respectable representatives of the name.

According to the *Carew Calendar* the O'Tohills, O'Bernes, the Galliglasses with other Irish septs had 500 men whereof 200 were horse. *Moryson* is more explicit, and perhaps more accurate. He says:—' The Mountainers of Dublin have 480 h. and 20 f. They are Felim McFeagh, and his brother Redmond with their sept of the O'Byrnes, and Phelim McFeagh with his sept of the O'Tooles, and Walter McEdward, chiefe of the gallowglasses, with his sept of the McDonnells. Only two castles, Newcastle and Wickloe, Sir H. Harrington held for the Queen, and all the rest of the countrie continued loyal.'—*Moryson*, p. 31.

Essex tells us that near this castle of Wickloe Harrington 'was overthrown in 1599, and our troops, having advantage of number and no disadvantage of ground were put in rout and many cut to pieces without striking a blow. I called a martial court upon the captains and officers. Walshe, lieutenant to Captain Loftus, was executed; the other captains and officers were all cashiered and imprisoned; the soldiers were all condemned to die; but were pardoned, and only every tenth man was executed. Sir H. Harrington, because he is a privy councillor in this Kingdom, I forbear to bring to trial till I know her Majesty's pleasure.'—*Essex to Privy Council*, July 11, 1599.

At Dublin Sir H. Foulkes commands the L. Lieutenant's guard of 200 f. In Fingall and the Navan 300 horse under Sir W. Evers, Sir H. Davers and J. Jephson; in the co. of Dublin 60 h. under Sir H. Harrington, Sir E. Herbert, Sir Gerald Aylemer, and Murrogh McTeig Oge; Sir Jn Talbot has 22 f. undisposed; Sir Wil. Warren has 50 horse and 100 f. at Newcastle.—*Moryson*, p. 43.

relieve the Soldiers in the tyme either of prosecution or cessation, whereupon ensueth extream miserie either to the Countrie man Souldier, or both; for the Souldiers being for the most Part disordered and verie Licentious, will violentlie draw from the poor Husbandman that which shou'd sustain himself and his Familie, and so doth dailie drive him to begg, or if the Souldier be restreyned which seldom falleth out, he perisheth for want of Food, of both which these last years hath given infinit Examples, and it is to be feared that if the Cornes be burnt up this Winter that there will be little Sowing of Summer Corn this year, and consequentlie a dearth and plague, which comonlie followeth dearth, the next year.

THE COUNTIE OF KILDARE.

This Countie hath Dublin to the East, Catherlogh to the South, the Kings and Quenes Counties to the West, and Meath to the North. It reacheth no where the Sea; in it are no Townes of importance, saving Castledermott and Athie, which hath been walled but now ruined, and the Townes of Kildare, Kilcullen, Naas, Leslip, and Maynooth, the principall fors of the Earles of Kildare with other Scattered Villages.[a] It hath many Fayre Castles and Houses.

The Castle of Kildare, } the Earles of Kildare,
Castle of Maynooth,

S[t.] Wolstans, a Hous belonging to M[r.] Allen,

The Castle of Leslip belonging to M[r.] Whyte,

---

[a] 'Divers proper villages lie scattered about the cuntrie,' says *Dymmok*, who dispatches the county of Kildare in four lines.

COUNTIE OF KILDARE.

S:· Kathrens a Hous belonging to him, also
Lecagh a Castle belonging to one of the Geraldines,
Kilkea a Hous of the Earles of Kildare,
Woodstock a Castle of the Earle of Kildares,
Castle martin belonging to M:r· Eustace,
Carberie belonging to one Coolie,
Domfert to one[b] .... Reban belonging to Henrie Lee,
Mottinsey,
Monasterevan or the pleasant Abbey, belonging to the L. Cromwells,
Baltinglass belonging to S:r· Henry Harrington, sometyme the chief Hous of the Viscount Baltinglass,[B]
Rathangan a Castle of the Earle of Kildares, latelie raysed by the Rebells,
Rathcoffy,[c]
Tipper a hous belonging to one Sutton,
Osberts Toune belonging to one FitzGerrald.

[b] To one Bremingham.—See *infra.* In the church of Dunfierth near Enfield, there is, or was not long ago, a sepulchral effigy carved in high relief, representing a knight in complete plate armour; round the neck was suspended by a chain a large crucifix—according to tradition it represents one of the Berminghams. Elizabeth wrote to the Council, Nov. 1599: 'What will be the answer of the traitor (O'Neil) for the last treason of the bridge where Esmond's company was defeated, and what reason will he yield for usurping so unjustly in the time of the Cessation to place Bremingham in the county of Kildare.'—*Car. Cal.,* Nov. 6, 1599.

[B] The monastery of Baltinglass, founded by Mc Morogh in 1148, was granted, with its manor and castle, to Sir Th. Eustace in 1541; his grandson, the third Viscount Baltinglass, confederated with the OByrnes, and with them slew 800 English at the battle of Glenmalure, in 1580; after the defeat of Desmond in 1583, he retired to Spain and his lands were confiscated. His brother William's descendant, C. S. Eustace, Esq., of Robertstown, claims the title.—See *O'Sullivan Bere's Hist. Cath., Lewis's Top. Dict., Burke's Peerage.*

[c] Belonging to Wogan.—See *infra* and the *Car. Cal.*

Principal men[d] *in this Countie are:*

Gerrot[e] Earle of Kildare,
David Sutton,
Fitz Gerrald of Allen,
Flatesburie of Johnston,
Fitzgerrald of Osbertston,
Edw[d.] Fitz James of Blackhill,
Long of the Dour,
Eustace of Castlemartin,
Barnet of Reban, called S[t.] Michell now belonging to Hen. Lee,
Wolf of Benford,

[d] The Clongowes MS. gives 58 names; the *Car. Cal.* contains only 35—from both we gather the names of 72 gentlemen, of whom 13 were FitzGeralds, 8 Eustaces, 4 Berminghams, and 4 Aylmers. The only remaining representatives of any of these seventy-two gentlemen are the Duke of Leinster, FitzGerald of Geraldine, Eustace of Ballymore-Eustace, the Aylmers (formerly) of Lyons, of Donadea, of Painstown, and of Courtown.—See *Walford's County Families.*

[e] This name would show that our 'Description' was written before 1585, or in or after 1599; since Gerot E. of Kildare died in 1585, and the next of the name of Gerot got the title in 1599. The former Garret was some time a prisoner in the Tower. His son Henry, who had married a d. of the Earl of Nottingham, enjoyed the title until 1597. 'The L. Deputy, having taken the fort of Blackwater, was with the whole army rendering thanks to God'; the Irish interrupted their prayers, and in the conflict killed 'Sir F. Vaughan, the L. Deputy's brother-in-law; R. Turner, the Serjant Major of the Army; and two foster-brothers of the E. of Kildare, who, with his troop of Horse served valiantly upon the Rebells, and tooke the death of his foster brothers so to heart (after the education of the Irish) as shortly after he died. Many also were wounded of whom T. Walker was of chiefe name.'—*Moryson.* O'Neil in his letter to the King of Spain writes: 'Kildare was hurt and died of his hurt;' but Carew wrote in the margin, 'a lie; he died of no hurt.' O'Sullivan-Bere says: 'Kildare was unhorsed by push of pike, and was wounded; but was put on horseback again by his two Irish foster-brothers, named O'Hickey, who were killed while saving him. Kildare died a few days afterwards.' The *Four Masters* say that 'in consequence of a wound or of a fever he went homewards, and died at Drogheda and his brother William was installed in his place. William with eighteen chiefs of Meath and Fingall was drowned coming from England,' in 1598; and 'his kinsman Garret, the son of Edward, son of Garret, son of Thomas, son of John Cam succeeded.' He was 14th Earl, and with a dispen-

Baronet[f] of the Noraghe,
Eustace of Blackrath,
Sutton of Tipper,
Eustace[g] of
Rochfort of Laraghes,
Fitzgerrald of Dunor,
Owgan of Newhall,
Eustace of Mulahasse,

Sherlock of the Naas,
Owgan of[h]
Fitzgerrald of Leccaghe,
Young of Newton,
Browne of Browneston,
Fount of Founteston,
Pipard of
Young of Youngstone,

sation from the Pope, married his second cousin Elizabeth who was a d. of the 14th Baron of Delvin and was born in the Tower of London. This Garret, according to O'Sullivan, was poisoned by the English in 1612.

[f] Wesley or Wellesly was Baronet of the Noragh. The *Car. Cal.* has 'Wesley at the Norragh' in Kildare; and again, 'Garrat Westie (Wesley?) of the Dengin' in Meath. The Wesleys of the Dangan came to Ireland in 1172, and are ancestors of the Duke of Wellington through Alison Wesley of Dangan, who was married to Sir Henry Colley and died in 1597. Among those pardoned by the English government in 1598 was R. Wesley; and in 1600 'Walter Wesley of the Narrowe,' co. of Kildare, and Richard Wesley.— See *Morrin's Cal. of Close Rolls*, ad an. 1598 and 1600.

[g] There are five Eustaces in our MS.; but this Eustace, mentioned without the name of his place, may be ' E. at Newlande, E. at Cradockstowne, E. at Coffy, or E. at Clangloswoodd.' This is clearly Clongoweswood near Clane, to which our MS. belongs.— See *Car. Cal., Peramb. of the Pale*, p. 191.

[h] Wogan of Rathcoffy.—*Car. Cal.* This family produced some remarkable men, of whom the Editor of this book published an account some years ago. John Wogan was twice ruler of Ireland in the 14th century; R. Wogan was High Chancellor in 1443; Colonel Wogan of Rathcofty saved the King's life at the battle of Nazeby; young Captain Wogan's enterprising character has been drawn by Clarendon, and by Walter Scott in *Waverley*. Sir Charles Wogan of Rathcoffy, a near kinsman of the aforesaid colonel and nephew of Talbot Duke of Tirconnell, a Roman Patrician and Senator, and Colonel in the Spanish Army, 'with but 1400 men held out for four hours against 20,000, losing half his soldiers, and thus secured a victory and conquest for the Prince he served.' He was one of the most dashing and daring men of his day, and, with the help of three Irish officers, he rescued Maria Sobieski from an Austrian fortress and brought her safe to

Creaff of Thomaston,
Wale of
Elmer[j] of Lions,
Allen of S[t.] Wolstanes,
Allen of Kilheele,
Weslie of Barringstone,
Fitzgerrald of Brecaston,
Fitzgerrald of Breton,
Whyte[k] of Sherlockstone,
Fitzgerrald of Kilune,
Fitzgerrald of the Grange,
Bremingham of Doinfert,
Bremingham of Corrikeris,
Bremingham of the Graunge,
Bremingham of Rosewood,
Misset of Dowdingleston,
Calf of Duriforth,
Fleming of the Naas,
Golding of Harberston,
Eustace of Ballecotlan,
Dongan of Fontistone,
Cowley[l] of Carberrie,
S[r.] Edward Fitzgerald,[m] Knt.,
Walshes of Morten,
Stanihurst of Ballincapoch,
Buggon of Rathmore,
Howlet of Rathmore,
Row of Branganston,

Rome to the Pretender, whose *fiancée* she was. All Europe wondered at this exploit, and the Duke of Wharton complimented him on it thus :

'Great in your verse as on the martial scene,
Whose essay was to free a captive Queen.'

[l] Also Aylmer at Clancurry, Aylmer at Downada, and Aylmer at Hardwell.—*Car. Cal.* The head of the Aylmer family and representative of the Aylmers of Lyons is Michael Valentine Aylmer, Esq., Derry, Rathcabbin, co. Tipperary. 'Aylmer of Downada,' the ancestor of Sir Gerald G. Aylmer of Donadea Castle, was son of A. of Cloncurrie, and grandson of A. of Lyons. His lady was the widow of Viscount Baltinglass

[k] 'and Whyte of Leixlip'—*Car. Cal.*

'at Carbry Castle.'—*Car. Cal.* He was the direct ancestor of Wellington. He was grandson of Walter Colley, Solicitor-General and then Surveyor-General for Ireland. In 1595, as appears from Sir W. Russell's Journal, 'the L. Deputy went to the Nasse (Mr. Coolie's) ; also in April, that year, Lieut. Greemes brought in one Hall, a priest, taken at the Lady Colie's house ; he was committed close prisoner to the Castle of Dublin.'

[m] Also, 'FitzGerald at Castle Iskin, F. at Ballysonan, and F. at Dunnocks.' To which may be added from the *Car. Cal.*, 'Allie at Rathbrede, Beling at Killussy, Cheevers at Rathmore, Sir W[m.] Sarsfield at Tully, Sarsfield at Turning, Herbert at Collanstowne, Sir H. Warren at Castletowne, and Sir Harry Harrington at Golmoorstowne.'

COUNTIE OF KILDARE. 49

Fitzphillips of Clain,   Tyrrell of Ardchille,
Branaghe of Leslip,   Delahide of Moyglare.
Fyan of Leslip,

Few of this Countie[n] are yet entered into action of Rebellion, saving some younger Brethren of the Geraldines that followed Thomas, base Brother of this Earle of Kildare's, into Rebellion, who was apprehended and Executed by the Earle of

[n] 'Touching the five shires of the English Pale, though many of them have showed more backwardness to answer the service and their own defence than were meet, which, we think, groweth more upon their poor estate and waste of their countries, than of any wilfulness or corrupt mind; yet in many of the meaner sort, upon the borders towards the North and the co. of Kildare some of the Bastard Garraldines, especially two base brothers of the now Earl of Kildare are in open rebellion with two of the Eustaces.'—*State of Ireland in* 1597. 'Kildare is for the most part spoiled, wasted and consumed by burning or otherwise, save some castles, where the owners do shroud themselves from the rebels. This waste has been caused by the incursions of the rebels, the daily outrages and disorders of the soldiers and the burthens imposed by the governors, the Council and the commanders.'—*Car. Cal.*, p. 260. 'Two base brethren of the Earl of Kildare, called the Bastard Geraldines, having drawn to them a number of loose people, do range up and down the Pale, extorting meat, drink and money at their own wills, and so terrify the subjects as many do forsake their dwellings. These Bastard Geraldines are now upon protection, and what will further come of them we know not, having often written to the Earl of Kildare to temper with them and to stay them, but we have not as yet heard anything from him.'—*Report of the Dublin Council*, 5th Nov. 1597. 'In Kildare James Fitz Piers a Geraldine, Sheriff of the shire, the two Bastard Geraldines, one (some) of the Delahydes, Glashane O'Dempsie, and Lisaghe O'Dempsie with the rest of the O'Dempsies, and certain of the Eustaces of kindred to (of the sept of) the late Viscount Baltinglasse attainted are in actual rebellion; their forces are 230 f. and 30 h. (220 f. and 30 h.).'—*Car. Cal., State of Ireland, April* 1599; but the words in parenthesis are from *Moryson.*

The Queen's troops in Kildare were: '*Horse,*—in and about the Nasse: Earl of Kildare, 50; Capt. R. Greame, 50; Capt. Gifford, 25; Capt. Lee, 12. *Foote,*—in and about the Nasse were: Earl of Kildare, 150; Earl of South-

G

Ormond. These, becaus they have no head of themselves and are but few, they abide out of their owne countrie amongst Strangers, and serve onlie for Guyders to Lead others through the Countrie.°

THE COUNTIE OF CATHELAGH.

This Countie is a long slip of Land lying for the most part between the 2 Rivers Slaine and Barrowe, and contayneth divers Baronies ancientle inhabited by the Inglyshe, but not long after the conquest a good part thereof was recovered by the Cavanaghs, which did inhabit both it and the Countie of Wexford.ᵃ

ampton, 200; Sir M. Morgan, 150; Sir T. Loftus, 100; Williams, 150; Esmond, 150; W. McEdmond, 100; E. Loftus, 100; Lea, 100; Eustace, 100; J. Masterson, 100; Flood, 100; Trevor, 100.'—*Moryson*, p. 43.

° The following Kildare worthies were *pardoned* in 1598 and 1600, so I presume they aided the 'Geraldines': 'Piers Walshe Fitz Piers of Moynally, and Howel Walshe; Wm. Fitz Oliver FitzGerald; R. Fitz Maurice Fitz G.; W. Fitz Maurice Fitz G.; W. Fitz Edward Fitz G., Wm. Bremingham of Dunfert; E. Bremingham of Derite; R. Bremingham Fitz James; Garret Bremingham Fitz Redmond; Richard Mac William Oge Bremingham of Muckland, Cecily Linch his wife, Wm. B. his son, and Piers Fitz James Bremingham, Gerald Wogan of the Downings; R. Wesley, Walter Wesley of the Narrowe; Wm. Eustace of Castlemartin; Christopher Eustace of Ballycallen and Ellinor his wife; Thomas Rochford of the Laragh; Donal Enos and Wm. Moony of the Laroghs; Sir Wm. Sarsfield of Lucan; Christopher Flattesburie of Johnstown; Carroll, Boylan, and Ashe of the Naas; Keatinge, Doyne, Gilliglas O'Scott, Brenan, Morogh O'Hanlon, O'Conlan, D. O'Byrne, H. O'Byrne, O'Kellie, Coffie, O'Halegan, O'Donnell, Tallen, O'Rhawley.'—See *Morrin's Cal. of Close Rolls.*

ᵃ The Cavanaghs held the strong mountain fastnesses lying between the Counties of Wexford and Carlow, and extending down the left bank of the Barrow to the neighbourhood of New Ross. In the description accompanying Speed's Maps we read: '*Cavenaghi hic* (*i.e.*, in Carlow) *circumquaque agunt, in numerosam familiam propagati—viri*

COUNTIE OF CATHLAGH. 51

It hath in it certan high mountains upon the East part and the rest of the Countrie is nere plain. The third part of the whole Shyre is accompted to belong to the Earle of Ormond and his brother Sr Edmond Butler. One baronie called Idrone was the ancient Inheritance of Sr Peter Carew.[b]

This Countie is bounded with the Countie of Kildare to the North, with the Quene's Countie to the West and Southwest, and Kilkenny to the East and Southeast. It hath onlie one Towne called Catherlaghe, from which the Shyre hath its name.

Principall Castles are:— Catherlaghe, Tully,
Leighlin, St Mollins,
Rathvilley, Cloughgrenan,
Fortovollon,[c] Rathmore.

bellicosi, sed qui per mutuas clades se quotidie conficiunt.' Circa 1568 five Cavanaghs owned Idrone East. In 1587 Murtagh C. chief of his name, dwelt at Garryhill, though his chief house was the Castle of Rathnegarry in Idrone. As he was wantonly murdered by Dudley Bagnall's men in 1587, his two sons made a raid on Bagnall's land, plundered it, and being pursued, killed Bagnall and thirteen of his men, inflicted on him sixteen wounds, drew his tongue out of his mouth and slit it.—*Kilk. Arch. Jour.*

Three years afterwards Hugh O'Donnell was helped to escape from the Castle by 'a certain renowned warrior of Leinster, Art Cavanagh by name, who was a champion in battle and a commander in conflict.'—*Four Masters.*

[b]. Belonging to Sir Dudley Bagnoll.—

Dymmok. In the *Kilk. Jour. of Arch.*, April 1870, the Rev. J. Hughes gives an account of this barony, from which we take the following details: The ninth Earl of Ormonde purchased the Dullogh and gave it to his son Sir Edward Butler. Carew claimed it in right of his ancestors and in 1568 got possession of Idrone from the Sheriff of Carlow. Sir Edward, who had done great service against the O'Mores, rebelled, and after holding out for some time was pardoned in 1573. He had four sons, one of whom succeeded to the father's estates in 1603, got the title of Viscount Tullophelim, and married the only daughter of his uncle Ormond, but died without issue.

[c] 'In the co. of Catherlagh, being little and all wasted, the castles of Carlogh and Laghline, and her Majesty's

52   STATE OF IRELAND ANNO 1598.

Principall   Sr Edmond Butler^d
Gentlemen :—   Dudley Bagnoll's^e sons

house of Fernes, held by the Queene's Warders, and six castles belonging to the Earl of Ormond held for the Queene, but the Cavanaghs and Keytons were in rebellion.'—*Moryson*, p. 31.

'The Earl of Ormonde's chief manor there is Ravelly, and his territories reach along Clonmore and Fortanolan to Arclow.'—*Car. Cal.* The Fothart O'Nolan, or country of O'Nolan is now the barony of Forth in the co. of Carlow. O'Flaherty in his *Ogygia*, p. iii., c. 64, says O'Nolan the last proprietor and chief of this territory died a short time before O'Flaherty wrote his book, so there must have been a chief of that name in 1598. O'Heerin thus sings of the chief in his time :

'O'Nuallain, hero without fault
    Chief prince, fine and bountiful of
        Fothart.'

O'N. was senior Vassal of McMurrogh ; 'O'N., the Lord of Fotharta was slain in 1133; his son was slain in 1154; Shan O'N. was chief of Fogharta in 1394 ; and in 1406 Laighsech O'N. the royal heir of Foghart died.'—See *Four Masters* and *Annals of Loch Ce.*

^{d} Sir Edmond Butler of Cloghgrennan, was brother of Ormond, and is called Edmond *an Caladh* (of the Port) by the *Four Masters.* In 1569 this Edmond and his brother Edward 'seized at the fair of Eniscor-

thy, on Great Lady Day, an immense quantity of property—horses, cattle, gold, silver and foreign goods ; but Ormond having returned made peace for his Kinsmen with the State.' In 1582, these brothers with their cavalry, galloglasses, and *giomanachs* were defeated by the Earl of Desmond. In 1596 this Edmond, son of James, son of Pierce Roe, son of James, son of Edmond, son of Richard Butler, was imprisoned for the crimes of his sons who turned out to plunder.'—See *Four Masters*. In 1596 the Lord Deputy wrote to him : 'Your son, Pierse Butler, hath received a commandment to come to us, and yet hath obstinately refused to do so : these are therefore to will and command you to apprehend him and deliver him to his uncle, the Earl of Ormonde.' In the month of December 1596, the heads of his son James and two others were sent to the Deputy ; and in 1597 his son Pierse was taken and executed by his own uncle Ormond, who sent his head to Dublin.—See *Car. Cal.*

^{e} Sir W. St Leger was governor of the fort of Leighlin, had 150 men, and was guardian of Dudley Bagnall's son, who owned Idrone Barony.—*Car. Cal.,* p. 191. Dudley's brother, Marshal B. owned the premises and castle of Leighlin Bridge until his defeat and death by O'Neil in 1598. Dudley's son, Sir Nicholas B. was constable of

Sr William Harpole^f
The Heirs of Henry Dowels
Edmond Gline
Turloghe McDonnell Galliglass
The Bishop of Laghlein, the Sonnes of Bryan McCawer
Cavanagh^g of St Molins

the Castle of Leighlin in 1602. Dudley's grandson, Colonel Walter B. had an Irish mother, who was d. of the 11th Earl of Ormond ; he was a Catholic, and though a Confederate officer, he allowed Ormond's army to pass Leighlin Bridge and thus enabled Ormond to escape from Owen Roe. He was tried for 'murder' by the Parliamentarians, was put to death in 1652; his property of 15,000 acres in Idrone was confiscated, as he was '*an Irish papist*,' and his brother Colonel Thomas Bagnall was 'transplanted' into Connaught as '*an Irish papist.*'—See the papers published by Mr. Prendergast in *Kilk. Arch. J.* of 1860.

^{f} Perhaps a son of Hartpole, constable of Catherlogh who died in 1594, aged 70, whose effigial tomb was found many years ago in the cemetery of St Mary, Castle Hill, Carlow. 'He was matched with a Coltyonean (*i.e.*, an O'Birne) and was a maintainer of rebels.'—*Survey of Ireland in* 1572 and 1602. The *Car. Cal.* mentions a William Wall ; who, I presume, was of the Carlow family of Wall that afterwards rose to some eminence in France. The *Survey of Ireland circa* 1575 *and circ.* 1602 says, 'there are in Carloe Keating's kerne ill-disposed and now rebels.'

^{g} 'Garret McMurtagh Cavanagh, Morgan McBrian Cavanagh at Poble Tymolin.'—*Car. Cal.*, p. 191.

According to the Cavanagh Pedigree in the *Kilk. Arch. Journal* of July 1856, Donnell Spaineach fl. 1600, attainted an. 1617, was father of Sir Murrough McMorrough ; Morgan, son of Brian of Borris (who died in 1572) d. 1636; his great grandson was governor of Prague in 1766 ; Murtogh attainted in 1605 ; Dowling Cavanagh of Ballyleigh lived in 1598 ; Art McMorrough Kavanagh of Borris is the 7th in descent from Morgan of Borris who died in 1636.

The 'Sects of the Cavanaghes in Carloe : (1) Morchage of Garlile [Garryhill—ED.] chief of that sect. (2) Gerard McCahair Carragh of Glennmulle [Clonolyn—ED.] chief of another. (3) Cahir Begge of Leinerocke chief of another sect. (4) Bryan McMurtagh of the country of the Melaghe, chief of another sect. (5) Bryan McCahir McArte, dwelling in the barony of St Malyne, between Sir Peter Carew and Rosse on the river of Barrouglie—all open rebels or doubtful ; and Bryan McCahir McArte, a notable rebel, who

Hugh
Owen O'Gormoghan
John Barrie.

killed Browne in 1572, with a number of other good gentlemen of Wexford. The Coltyoneans *alias* Byrnes notable rebels; all the rest faithful to her Majesty. Wm. M‹Hubberd, chief of these hanged in 1602. There are 10 septs of the Kavanaghes, *i.e.*: (1) Gerald M‹Moridaghe Oge of Slught Moritaughe; he is upon protection; his sept in rebellion; his house Rathengerge in O'Dorne. (2) Brian M‹Donoghe (both of these are of Slewght Morrogh Ballaghe), upon protection; his house Castle Balliboghare in O'Dorne. (3) Morietaghe M‹Donogh, dead; his sept in rebellion. (4) Morietagh M‹Morish in rebellion; both these septs are of Slewght Ayte More; both these men's lands in O'Dorne. (5) Dowghe M‹Cahir in rebellion; his house was the castle of Fenes. (6) Donell M‹Dowghe *alias* Donell Spanaghe in rebellion; his chief house was Huysceethy. (7) Dermond M‹Morish a pensioner in pay; his sept in rebellion; those three septs are of Slewght Donell Reaghe; his pension in Kilkennin in Wexford. (8) Morogh M‹Brian upon protection; his sept in rebellion; he is of Slewght Dermond Langrett; his land in S‹ Nolin in Wexford. (9) Moroghe Leighe M‹Cahir dead; his sept in rebellion; he is of Slewght Art More; his land in S‹ Nolin in Wexford.'—*Survey of Ireland*, written *circ.* 1574, with additions *circ.* 1597 and 1602. *Car. Cal.* in year 1603. p. 447.

'In 1597 there were some of the Butlers who range up and down the borders of Carlowe having of their adherancy some of the Connaughts (*sic*, perhaps bonnaughts—ED.) and sundry of the O"Tooles and OByrnes.' —*State of Ireland, Car. Cal.*

'In 1599 most of the Cos. of Carlow and Wexford were in rebellion; the chief in these two counties are the Kevanaghes, who with their followers are 750 men and whereof 50 are horse.' —*Moryson* and *Car. Cal.*

In a tract of the British Museum, written by Nowel, Dean of Lichfield, who died in 1576, the power of the Carlow Irish in his time is thus stated: 'M‹Murghowe is prince of Leinster. He and his Kinsmen will be 200 horse well harnessed, a bataile (*i.e.*, about 80) of Galoglas and 300 kerne—his; O'Moroghowe l. of Yphelim 16 h. and 40 k.; O'Nowlane L. of Tohyrly 12 h. and 20 k.; O'Brenan of Idough 40 kerne.' A later paper, *circ.* 1572, mentions as of estimation the Cavanaghs of 'S‹ Molyns, of Garryhill and Clonolyn; but none of them able to make 8 horsemen of his own byinge, and every one of them is enemy to the other.'

THE COUNTIE OF WEXFORD.

This Countie being the first conquered by the Inglysh men, hath so much written in several Books now extant, as it were superfluous to speak more of this Shyre, than of the present State thereof. Sr Henrie Sidney and Sr William Drury caused it to be Surveyed, and had a meaning to have it divided into Two Shyres, and to have called the North part the Countie of fearnes as the south part the Countie of Wexford, but for want of Sufficient Freeholders to be of Juries, or to be Sheriffe, or to bear any other Office, this purpose of Division took no Effecte.

This Shyre serveth to be an Inglyshe Pale, and an Irish Countie. The Pale or civill part is contayned within a River called the Pill,[a] in the which the most of the posteritie of the ancient Gentlemen, that were conquerors do inhabite.[b] The other without the Pill is yet Inhabited by the Originall people,

---

[a] Weisford with the territory baied and perclosed within the Pill was so quite estranged from Irishrie, as if a traveller of the Irish (which was rare in these days) had pitched his foot within the Pill and spoken Irish, the Weisfordians would command him forthwith to turn the other end of his toong, and speake English, or else bring his trouchman with him. But in our days (*circa* 1578) they have so acquainted themselves with the Irish as that they have made a mingle mangle or gallimanfreie of both the languages, as commonlie the inhabitants of the meaner sort speake neither good English nor good Irish.—*Stanihurst's Description of Ireland.*

[b] 'The mansion houses of most gentry were fortified with Castles, some neere 60 foot high, having walls at least 5 foot thicke to the number of Thirty, of which few as yet becom ruinous,' says one who wrote in 1680.

'The people of the B. of Forth spoke the same tongue and wore the same dress and professed the same Faith as the first settlers, their predecessors.

as the Cavenaghes and Kinshelaughes^c possessing the Woodie part thereof; into which, notwithstanding, some of the Inglysh have intruded, and planted Forts and Castles within them.

This Countie hath the Sea to the East, the County of Wicklo to the North, the Countie of Catherlagh to the West and the River of Barrowe and the County of Waterfoord to the South.

Both Wexford and Rosse hath walled and Haven Townes, the first upon the East Sea, the other upon the River Barow being amplyfied by the Rivers of Nuer and Suer, and the mouth of the Haven is the Haven of Waterfoord, yet hath it other ancient ruined Townes as Fearnes whereof the Bishop hath his name, Clomyne B . . . . and Federt.

[1] In that single barony there were no less than eighteen churches, thirty three chapels, one religious hospital and two convents, and very many crosses in public roads.'—Description of B. of Forth, ed. by H. F. Hore in *Kilk. Jour. of Arch.* The Gentlewomen of Wexford, in 1634, 'wore good handsome gownes, petticoates, and hatts,' and for mantles, had 'Irishe ruggs with handsome comely large fringes, which go about their necks; thick rugg fringe is joined to a garment, which comes round about them and recheth to the very ground; it is much more comely than the rugg short cloaks used by the women on festival days at Abbeville and Boulogne.'—*Sir W. Brereton.*

[c] 'That part of the county north of the river Slane is possessed chiefly by the Irish called Cavanaghs. It hath on that side also many English inhabitants; sc. Synot of Clelande, Roth of Roth, Synot of Ballinerah in the Murros (?), Masterson at Fernes Castle, where also the Bishop's see is, Peppard of Glascarrig.'

'The Irish on that side the Slane are —Donell Murtagh, Edmund O'Morowe of 'the O'Morowes' country, and others, ever bad neighbours and rebellious people, under the government of William Synot, by lease from her Majesty. Other Irish nations are by east them to the sea. The countries are called the Kinshelaghes, Kilconelin, Kilhobock, Farinhamon, inhabited by Art McDermot, McDaMore, McVadock, Darby McMorish, all under the government of Mr. Masterson. On the south-west of the Slane are four English baronies called Fort, Barge, Sherberre, and Shelmalen, and an Irish barony called the Duffree. In the Duffree dwell Sir H. Wallop, and Lord Mountgarret.'—*Car. Cal.*, p. 190.

COUNTIE OF WEXFORD.

The Principall Castles are:

Wexford[d] belonging to the Quene,
Fernes to the Bishop,
Tinterne to S[r] Tho. Cocle,
Donbrodie Abbey,
Doncannon,
The Towre of Hooke,
Ballihack,
Adamstone,
Inishcortie to Sir Henrie Wallop,
Bromestone,
Rosegarland,
Old Crosse,
Mountgarret, and
Kilclogher.

Principall Gentlemen :[e]

The Bishop of Fearnes,
Sir Henrie Wallop,
Sir Dudley Loftus,
Richard Mastersone,
Sir Tho. Colclough,
Roche[f] of Rochesland,

[d] 'Washfort was very populous in 1644, owing to its great commerce. The fortress a small square regularly enough fortified, at the foot of which were many ruins of churches; the people came chiefly from France.'— *Boulaye Le Gouz' Travels in Ireland in 1644.*

'In the co. of Wexford, being wasted, all the castles held for the Queene, and Sir T. Colclough, Sir R. Masterson, and Sir Dudley Loftus, the only English there inhabiting, held for the Queene. But Donnell Spaniagh, alias Cavanagh, with all that Sept, the Omorroghs, Macony More, all the Kinsellaghes, Dermot M[c]Morice, etc. were in rebellion and had 750 f. and 50 h. In 1599 there were 200 f. at Eniscorthy, under Sir Oliver Lambert, and 150 f. under Sir R. Masterson.'— *Moryson*, p. 43.

[e] An old barony of Forth alliterative rhyme conveys the supposed hereditary characteristics of several Wexford families :—' Stiff Staffort, Dugget [dogged] Lamport, Gay Rochford, Proud Deweros, Lacheny [laughing] Cheevers, Currachy [obstinate] Hore, Criss [cross] Calfer, Valse [false] Furlong, Shimereen [showy] Synnot, Gentleman [gentle] Brune.'

[f] Sir J. Fitz George Roche, Knt. was summoned to the war in Scotland in 1335. The Roches of Roche's land waxed very Irish in their ways; for the Wexford jury of 1537 'do present that Walter R. with his followers went to the suburbs of Wexford by night for the most part feloniously, burned a boat of

H

Synnots of Clayland,

R. Canton; and burned a towne of Wm. Meyler and T. Synnot in ye parish of Kilkevan; and so ye said Wm. and Thomas must give unto the said Walter 20s. to have license to build ye same towne; that the said Walter came with a banner displayed of Irishmen, and took with them ye prey, that is to say, of kine and cattle of the towne of Wexford; and also as yet holdeth an Irishwoman to his wife.'

'In 1552 Roche of Artramont, Lord of Rochesland, wrote to the L. Deputy that his father retained the yearly rents of money, sheep, butter, etc., of the tenants and dwellers of Rathalvey, and that *whenever any goods were taken* from the tenants *by the English Pale* of the co. of Wexford, *being in wars with the Morrowes*, Roche caused the same to be restored; and that the said lands had ever been freed from O'Morrowe's galloglasses and other charges.'

g 'The Sinnots exceed in number any ancient name; the house of Ballybrennan in Forth was the most eminent, from which sprang men remarkable for school learning, persons endowed with heroic spirits and martially disposed minds. Richard S. of Ballybrennan, for his noble services with his sons, relations and dependents, was rewarded with forfeited lands. His son Walter being slain in battle, his grandson Martin S. inherited Ballybrennan; his son James S. got the Manor and Barony of Rosegarland, John got Cooledyne with 1200 acres; Nicholas

FitzHenric of Maghemorne,[h]

got Park, Logh and other villages with several houses in Wexford; Sir Wm. S. got Ballyfarnocke with 24 plowlands intire in the Murrowes; Edmond S. got Lingstown and other villages.

'The following were gentlemen of the name enjoying good estates for many descents, from whom also several persons famous for learning and chivalry—in Germany, France, Spain and Muscovie, etc., were extracted.

'In the *Barony of Forth*—
'Sinnot of Balligery; S. of Rathdowney; S. of Stonehouse of Wexford; S. of Gratkerock. In *Ballaghene* Barony—S. of Owlert, S. of Ballymore, S. of Garrymusky, S. of Tinraheene. In *Shilmaleere*—S. of Garrymusky, S. of Owlortvicke, S. of Ballinhownemore, S. of Ballinvacky, S. of Belleareele, S. of Balliroe, S. of Ballinkilly, S. of Monyvilleog, S. of Mogangolie.

'These gentlemen, compleatly armed and mounted on horsebacke in Q. Elizabeth's warrs vigorously opposed such as appeared Rebellious.'—*Description of the Barony of Forth*, Edited by H. F. Hore.

h Maghmayne.—*Ussher M.S.* FitzHarris of Killkevan is given in the *Car. Cal.* in which are found only twelve names, whereas there are fifty or sixty in our MS. I fancy this is the 'Fecffarris, a malefactor matched with the Cavanaghs in Carlow, and holding with them;' he is thus described by the *Survey of Ireland*, written between 1575 and 1602.

In 1537 the jury of New Ross 'pre-

Deverox[i] of Balmagere,
Foorlong[k] of Hoorton,

Browne[l] of Malrancan,
Hay[m] of Tancomshanee,

sent that one FitzHarry, that now is, of Kilkevan, robbed ye towne of Rosse, and killed a man within ye liberties of the said towne, and that ye said Fitz Harry did take a pray to the some and valew of £100.'—*Annuary of Kilk. Arch. Society*, Vol. i.

[j] The Devereuxes were the wealthiest and most powerful of all of the Strongbonian race in Wexford. In 1566 Sir Nicholas D. makes 'bold to refresh his acquaintance' with his schoolfellow, Lord Burleigh; in 1574, 'he was spoiled of a great part of his inheritance by the Cavanaghs;' in 1599, Devereux, Earl of Essex, on his march from Waterford to Dublin, passed a day at Balmagir, and Knighted Sir J. Devereux.—p. 43, *Ann. Kilk. A. Soc.* and *Car. Cal.*, p. 308.

[k] 'Furlongs, malefactors matched with the Cavanaghs.'—*Survey of Ireland*, 1574-1602. In 1539 Philip Furlong of Carrigmenan gent. granted to Th. Rosseter of Rathmance gent. his town and manor of Carrigmanan; in 1638, Furlong of C. sold his large estate for £2500 to R. Devereux, Esq. Eleven gentlemen named Furlong were summoned to attend an expedition against O'Brien in 1345. Their chief house was Horetown near Taghmon. John F. was Knight of the Shire in 1613, and owned the manors of Camross, Bridgestown, etc.; another branch lived at Davidstown in the Glynn.

[l] The following letter of Q. Elizabeth, dated 1572, throws some light on this family and on Wexford: 'El. R. Where we are informed that R. Browne of Mulrancan (a yonge gentilman of great valour, wholy given to our sarvice against the disobedient Irish of that Countie, upon whom his father hath valiantly builded a fortress, and he after his father's death hath as valiantly kept and defended the same, to the amplifying of our obed^{ce}, being also near of bloud to the houses of our r^h t^n and well beloved Cosins Th' Erles of Kildare and Ormond) is traitorously murdered by Brene McCoder Kavanagh, and his brethren, Hugh McShan's sons . . . . [These Cavanaghs were kinsmen of Elizabeth through the Kildare alliance.—ED.] And whereas we are informed likewise that two gentlemen of our said co. of Wexford, the one, J. Furlong of Horeton, who hath of late procured the pitiful murder of the s^d Browne's sister, to bring home her jointure to his house, the other M. Fitzhenry of Magsmagh, being under Off^n to Thos. Stukeley, bearing the s^d Browne malice, and both of them cosins of blood to the said murderers of the Kavanaghs, have been procurers of the s^d Murd^r.—We think it good,' etc.—Forwarded by John P. Prendergast, Esq., to the *Kilk. Arch. Jour.*

[m] Henry the 6th, 'on account of the services Hay and his progenitors had

Tod of Carne,[n]
Lamport of Ballyhinch,[o]
Scurlock of Roseland,[p]
Keting of Kilcowan,[q]

Chevers of Ballyhaly,[r]
Rawceter of Rathmokue,[s]
Wadding of Ballicoiley,[t]

rendered to the King and his predecessors, in many times resisting the enemy, *accepit cum in intimum amicum.*' The Hays owned the Towers of Hill, Slade, Tacumshene, and Castlehaystown.—*Kilk. Annuary.*

[n] Nich. Codd of Carne d. in 1564 seised of the castle and lands of Rathaspig. In 1599, Nicholas Codde of Castleton, son of Martin Codde and Margaret da. of A. Roche, Lord of Rochesland, was marshal of Wexford Liberty; he was slain in 1600.—(See 'Description of the Barony of Forth,' written *circ.* 1680, edit. by Hore in *Kilk. Arch.*, Vol. iv., p. 62). 'These Coodes of Castletown expressed singular loyaltie and valour in Q. Eliza. warrs several of them being therein slain.'

[o] Of Ballyhire near Greenore. The Wexford jury of 1537 'present that Lamport of Ballyhire did take James Kent prisoner, and took from him feloniously £8.'

[p] 'Scurlocke of Roslare.—*Ussher M.S.* ' He owned two manors with a valuable estate in Ballymore and Roslare, unto whom the Copyholders by their tenures performed homage, divers customary duties and services not elsewhere used, many of which were servile; none could marry in his Lordships without his previous License nor build a house, nor suffer it to be demolished or to fall to decay. If a Copyholder married a maide, a certaine fine was payable to the Lord; if a widow, double as much; if a woman whose virginity had been violated, more; which fine or duty was termed *Lotherwite* (*i.e.*, Lother's law). All tenants deceasing were liable to *Heriots.* Transgressors of such and many other strange customs incurred forfeiture of their interest by Copyhold.' —*Descrip. of B. Forth.*

[q] W[m.] Keting was commander of Kilklogan, *circ.* 1537; Baldwin and R. Keting were witnesses of the Charter of the Earl of Pembroke to Tintern Abbey. The eldest house had the title of Barons K. of Kilcowan.

[r] Cheevers, a Flemish family named Chevre, long settled in Wexford; Patrick C. witnessed the charter given to Wexford in 1317; Edward C. was created Viscount Mount Leinster by James II.—*Hore.*

[s] The family came from Rocester in Lincolnshire; Rossieter of Rathmacnee was expulsed in 1653; Bargy castle was built by a Rosseter, whose initials are on an oak panel in the house. Slevoy belonged to Walter R. in 1608; another R. lived at Tacumshane and owned the manor of Tomhaggard. Colonel R. of Rathmacknee is said to have married a sister of the famous Sarsfield.—*Hore.*

[t] R. Wadding of Ballycogly m. a da. of Rowseter of Rathmacnee, Esq., and

Stafford of Balmakeryn,[u]
Barry of Bonecarry,
Rochford[v] of [   ],
French of Ballitorie,
Eliot of Rathshillan,
Sutton of Ballikerock,[w]
Prendergasse of the Gorchins,[x]

Bourcher of Balliconnick,[y]
Mayler[z] of
Redmond of the Hooke,
Laffan of the Slade,[aa]
Sygin of Syginston,[bb]
Cullen of Cullenston,
Osmond of Johnston,[cc]

had four sons and seven daughters; his eldest son, Thomas, was one of the Knights of the Shire in 1613, and was married to a d. of Eustace of Castlemartin; his daughter Elenor was m. to Th. Scurlock of Bolgan in the Glynn.

[u] Ballymacarne, the principal castle of the Staffords, who were a numerous and distinguished family. There was a branch at Balliconnor, where Denis Stafford of Balliconnor and his wife Katerina Synnot of Byllygeary built a tower in 1570, which still stands. Their son Hamond S. died in 1630.

[v] Of Taghunnan (Mountpleasant) under the mountain of Forth. The Rochfords were barons in the 13th century and owned the barony of Duffyr, but were driven northwards by the Irish.—*Kilk. Annuary*, p. 41.

[w] Ballykeroge, a castle of unusual dimensions in 'Sutton's parish' near Ross was the chief house; but branches lived at Oldcourt, Ballysop, and Priesthaggard.

[x] Gurteen—The Prendergasts owned the territories of Fernes and Kinsellagh; but were driven southward, and in 1598 lived in a tower called Gurteen near the mountain of Forth.

[y] Written also Bosher or Busher.

[z] 'Walter Meyler of Duncormack and his ancestors have been in possession of Mountgarret beside Ross with the appurtenances, as their inheritance of right until the Earl of Ossory entered and kept it by force in 1518.' In 1570 Walter M. of Doncormock, gent., addressed the Government, stating that he was possessed of the manor of Prystown, 'adjoining the salvage nacion of the Cavanaghes, and the Key of the country upon the very frontiers of the Irishry, and therefore wasted by their continual incursions, and they have oft times shed his blood.'

[aa] 'Mac Laffan of the Sladd' is included among the gentlemen of Shelburne in the grand panel of the co. of Wexford 1608. In 1638 Henry Laffan of Slade Castle died.

[bb] Siggins, perhaps S[t.] John; one S[t.] John had land at Tomhaggard and at Monsyu in 1472; and about 1537 W. Browne 'did take Stephen S[t.] John in ye highway and did lead him to his castle and did imprison him after his own use, contrary to the King's laws till he paid his fine.' There was also a Sigon on the Wexford Jury of 1537.

[cc] Esmond—'Lord Esmond served as a Martialist in the Low Countries,

Whyte of Tromer,
Eshingham of Dunbrody,
Isham of Bryanston,
Walshe of [dd]
Hore of S[dd]
Butler of[ee] Clonkyraghe,
FitzJohn of Ballicoppock,
Fitzneal[ff] of Ballyharth,
Nevell[ff] of Rosegarland,
Turnor of[ff]
St. John of Wexford,[bb]
Whitty of Baltitege,[gg]
Butler of Wexford, Brother to the L[d.] Mountgerat,

Lewes[ff] of Leweston,
Chyver of Killyan,
Hasson of Wexford,
Bryan of the[ff]

And of the *Irishe*—
Donell Cavanaghe, commonlie called Donell Spaniaughe, or Donell the Spaniard, being broght with Stuckly in Spaine, also
the Sept of Croan [Shean] McMurrow,
The 3 Lo. of Kinsheloghe,

and then against the Kavanaghes, Birnes and O'Tooles; his countenance terrible, with a formidable voice when exasperated ; of sanguine complexion, compact, solid corpulent body with robustious Limms, terrible to his Enemy, maintaining always a numerous Retinue of well accomplished young gentlemen, well accoutred and compleatelie armed with excellent serviceable horses, He was abstemious and continent.'—*Description of the B. of Forth*, edited by H. F. Hore.

[dd] 'Walshe of Polrankan ; Hore of Harpiston.'—*Ussher M.S.* In 1649 there were H. of Pole-Hore, H. of Harperstown, and H. of Kilvashlan. In Taghmon Church there is a very ancient monument to Hore of Harperstown. Wm. Hore of Harperstown was Knight of the Shire in 1559 ; and was in 1572 seised of the castle

and lands of Harperstown, held of Roche of Drinagh, and of the castle and lands of Taghmon, held of the Queen.—*H. F. Hore.*

[ee] Perhaps 'Piers Butler, who has a portion of the Fassasse of Bentry, who is reported to be a rash young man.'—*Survey of Ireland.*

[ff] 'Fitznicol ; Nevil baron of Rosegarland ; Turner of Ballyasshin ; Lowes of Lowston ; Brian of the Starr ; Graye.' —*Ussher M.S.* (E. 4. 33) T.C.D. There was also a 'Pippard of Glascarrig,' according to the *Car. Cal.*; and there was an influential family, named Gerot, as appears from a paper *penes me.*

[gg] R. Whitty of Ballyteige b. 1546, d. 1623, was J.P. for the co. of Wexford; held three manors, three carucates and 523 acres; married a d. of Sir N. Devereux of Ballymagir, 'the

McVadock,ʰʰ   Edmond Duff.
McDanore,

The whole Countie of Catherlaghe, and the one halfe of the Countie of Wexford was in tymes past inhabitted by the Cavanaghes, who being by Warr driven out have from time to time greatlie disturbed the Inhabitants of the foresaid Counties; there remayneth of them but few, and these of four Septs or Families, of which Griffyne McMorroghe and his Brethren were chief and dwelt nere Fearnes; the Elder Brother being Executed, the younger doth altogether depend upon Sr Henrie Wallop.

The Second Familie is Donell Spaniaughe and his Kinsmen, who also pretended to be much at the devotion of Sr Henrie Wallop, who procured to the said Donell a yearlie Pension from the quene, but of late being Sturred up by the Earle of Tyrone, he took Armes against the quene and challingeth the Hous of Enishcortie, possessed and sumptuouslie Builded by Sr Henrie Wallop, without which he purposeth not to live in quiet.ⁱⁱ The 3ʳᵈ was the Sept of Bryan McCare of   or

White Knight;' his son married a d. of Stafford of Ballyconnor, and his grandson married a d. of Oliver Eustace of Ballynunry. There is a fine monument to the Whittys in the ruined Church of Kilmore.—See *Kilk. A. Jour.* year 1872, p. 62.

ʰʰ McVadock and McDamore were descended from *Murchadh* a brother of Dermot McMurrough. McVadock's sept dwelt round Gorey. Hi Kinsellagh, *Ui Cennselach*, was in the north-east of the co. of Wexford.

ⁱⁱ In June 1599 Essex 'viewed the skirt of the Duffry, the chief fastness of D. Spaniaghe, who now pretends [to be chief?] of the Cavanaghs and McMurragh, which in the Irish account is no less than to be King of Leynister. His Lordship also viewed the ground between Eniscorthy and this fastness, where the garrison had not long before skirmished with D. Spaniaghe. Soon after, D. Spaniagh, Phelim McFeagh and McRowry fought against Essex. In Sept. 1599 he was in action with 300 or 400 of his followers in the co. of Wexford and greatly annoying these

64   STATE OF IRELAND ANNO 1598.

S^{t.} mollins and these depended upon Sr Antony Colclough in his Life tyme, and now I suppose they depend upon his Sone, Sir Thomas Colcloughe Sone-in-Law to the late Lord Chancellor. The 4th are of the Countie of Catherlagh in the Baronie of Idrone, whose chief dependance was upon the Earle of Ormond. The head of this last Sept was Mourtoghe oge latelie by one of the Omailies. The rest of them together with the Remainder of the third Familie, have joined themselves together with the foresaid Donell Spaniaughe who dailie vexeth the Counties of Wexford, Catherlaghe, Kildare and Dublin; he is not able to make above 200 Footmen, who, being prosecuted from Countie to Countie, hath continuall relief from Phelim McFeughe the Rebell of the Countie in Dublin, whose Brother-in-law he is.^{kk}

parts. Much of the lands of Donall Spaniaghe were possessed by Sir R. Masterson, Sir H. Wallop, Lord Mountgarrett, and Sir N. Walshe; his ancestor, Art Boy Kevanaghe possessed Enischortye, etc.'—*Car. Cal.*

A member of this clan, Morgan Kavanagh, was Governor of Prague in 1766, and was the largest man in Europe. Relatives of his were living in Austria in the year 1844, and were declared by Professor Niemann of Vienna to be the tallest men in all Germany. They were descendants of Bryan *na-Stroice* Kavanagh, who was the largest man in the army of James the Second.—See *O'Donovan on the Physical Characteristics of the Irish*, in *Ulster J. of Arch.*

^{kk} A souvenir of Wexford in 1598 has been recently discovered:—' Near the burial ground of Bannow have been found squared granite stones, forming the entrance to a house, and on one of the stones, a portion of which had been broken off, was the fragmentary inscription:—

. . . . mes . colli . fz
. . ence . builded . this
house . in . the . yeere . of
owre . lord . 1598 . and
marion . sinot . his . wife.

This may be read: "[Ja]mes Collin (Cullen) fitz [Lawr] ence builded this house in the yeere of our Lord 1598, and Marion Sinot, his wife."'—*Kilk. J. of Arch.*, October 1864.

THE COUNTIE OF KILKENNY.

This Countie hath the most shew of civilitie[a] of any other of the border Counties, in respect of the fayre Seats of Howses, the number of Castles and Inglysh manner of Inclosure of their Grounds. It is bounded with the River Barow to the East, with the River Suer to the South, with Ossorie to the North with Tipperairie to the West. These Counties being Ancientlie called Osseria seemeth to contayne the whole county of Kilkenny or rather Ossery, and the other part called upp. Osserie, and so to be all one Countie. But albeit many directions have been sent from the Queen and her progenitors for the deciding of this controversie, Yet McGillaPatrick, the ancient possessor of Upper Osserie and now baron[b] of it wou'd never consent to be of that Countie for the native malice between them, the one having been utter Enimie to the other; but pleadeth a Prerogative by custome to be out of all Shyreground and to be Sheriffe himselfe for the Execution of the civill cawses, and criminall cawses, he rather sorteth himself to be of the new

---

[a] A Kilkenny jury in 1537 declared that—'The gentylmen with all the comoners of the said counte, the Sovereine with all the heddes and comoners of the towne of Kilkenny, ben very desirous to be obedient to the Kinges lawe, and to lyve in good cevylitie; and albehit the Kinges laws in the said counte be not only clerly void and frustrate, but also all the exactions, suppressions and other enormities before presented, with many mo, be mentcyned only by the Erle of Ossory, my lady, his wyff, the Lord Jamys Butler, and other the said Erle's children and Kyne of his name; wherefor to provide that these persons may be reduced, the countie wyl be immediately prosperous and of gret strength to defend therselves against their enemyes.'—*Annuary*, p. 136.

[b] Florence, the 3rd Lord, lived in the time of Elizabeth, m. a daughter of O'More of Leix; his son, Thady the 4th lord, m. a daughter of Sir Edmund Butler of Tullow, and d. 1627.

Countie, and so in all criminall cawses to be tried by the late planted Inglyshe, then by their Ancient Enemies the Countie of Kilkenny.

The chief Tounes of this Countie are these:
{ Kilkenny[c]
Thomaston
Callan
I[d]
Gauran[d]
Balleragat
Burnchurche
and many other of meane reckoning.

[c] 'The best uplandish towne in Ireland .... famous for Peter White's school out of which have sprouted such proper Impes so as the whole weale publik of Ireland is thereby furthered.' —*Stanihurst.* 'Kilkenny the best dry towne in Ireland.'—*Campion.*

'The most pleasant and delightful town of y[e] Kingdom; the buildings are fair and people fashionable; its cituation is in the best Air of Ireland upon the river Nore of admirable cleer water upon a gravel—it is said that it hath—
"Water without mud, air without fog,
Fire without smoke and land without bog."'
—*Dynely's Tour, temp. Charles II.*

In 1644 it seemed to Le Gouz, a French traveller, as large as Orleans, which had 31,000 inhabitants.

The ten leading families or 'tribes of Kilkenny,' are thus given, in Galway fashion, by Mr. Prim:

'Archdekin, Archer, Cowley, Langton, Ley, Knaresborough, Lawless, Ragget, Rothe and Shee.'

The Shees, the only one of undoubted Milesian blood, was the most important, and next to them ranked Rothe and Archer.—*J. G. A. Prim, Esq.*

The Corporation of K. in 1537 :—Shee, Rothe, Lanton, Rothe, Hakket, Walshe, Rothe, Shee, Ragge, Archer, Raaour, Lawless, Savage.

'Commyners of the town of Kilkenny in 1537 :—Lye, Busser, Dormondus, Marshall, Clery, Brasell, Purcell, Thyvyn, Langton, Rothy, Machill, Gybbes, Ragge, Garrard, Archer, Cavin.'

[d] I is perhaps Inistioge; Gauran is Gowran. 'In 1608 Gowran got a charter, and N. Hackett was made Portreeve, and Everarde, Archer, J. Nashe, R. Nashe, J. Swayne, E. Staunton, Kealy, Raghtor, R. Swayne, M. Staunton, E. Walshe, and T. Staunton were Burgesses and of the Common Council

COUNTIE OF KILKENNY.

Castles:
{ Kilkenny
Gauran[d]
Kell
Ballingtoughe
Creey Toune
Whyte's Hall }

Men of Accompt.[e]

The Earle of Ormond,[f] his name Jam[s] Butler, his chief Hous Carrick; The L. Viscount Mountgarot[g]

his name Rich[d] Butler, The L. Bishop of Ossorie his Seat at Kilkenny,

of the Borough.'—*Kilk. J. of Arch.*, July 1871, p. 540. In 1608 David Archer was constable to the Earl of Ormond of the Castle of Gowran.

[e] The gentlemen of the jury of the Shire of Kilkenny in 1537 were:— Grace, Sweetman, Comerforth, Dobbin, Smith, Watonn, Cowik, Datowne, Howel, Forstall, Forstall, Purcell, Shortall, Shortall, Forstall, Croke and Blomfeld.

Jury of the Commyners of the Co. of Kilk. in 1537:—Troddye, Herford, Moteing, Fanneing, Mounsell, Howling, all of Callan; Forstall, Power, Walshe, Arland, and Karron, all of Inystioke; Power, Tywe, FitzJohn, Lacye, all of Knocktopher; Lorknan, Whyte of Knocktopher.—See *Annuary of Kilk. J. of A.*

[f] Thomas 10th Earl, called *The Black Earl;* his mother was daughter and heir of the 11th Earl of Desmond; his father's mother was a d. of the 8th Earl of Kildare; he enjoyed the title since the year 1546; in 1559 he was constituted lord treasurer of Ireland, and in the *Carew Calendar* he is styled 'Lord General, General of the Army, and Lord Lieutenant General.' He was a great favourite of Elizabeth; according to *Burke's Peerage* 'he was the first of his family to conform to the Church of England;' however, he became a Catholic a few years before his death, and was constantly visited by Fathers Walle and O'Kearney, S.J. He had six brothers.

[g] Edmund Butler 2nd Viscount Mountgarret, 1st cousin of the Earl of Ormonde; he married a d. of FitzPatrick 1st Lord of Upper Ossory; he died in 1602, and was succeeded by his son Richard, who had married the eldest d. of the Earl of Tyrone. His house is called Beallagarett and Ballinaggett in the *Car. Cal.* The 12th Viscount was made Earl of Kilkenny.

Garrot,[h] Baronet of Burnchurch,
Purcell[i] of Ballynfoyle,
Edw[d] Butler of Butlerswood,
Deane[k] of Thomastowne,
David Baron[l] of Brownsfoord,

[h] Rowland FitzGerald alias Baron de Burnchurch. In the churchyard of Burnchurch there is a tomb of 'FitzGerald alias Baron, dominus de Burnchurch, who d. in 1545. The castle of B. is in a good state of preservation. The representative of this family is Sir H. Winston Barron.'—*Kilk. Annuary of* 1858. The Baron of Burnchurche is the title given by the Kilkenny juries of 1537.—*Annuary.*

[i] To P. of Ballyfoyle was erected Purcell's Cross in St. Patrick's Cemetery: it bears the inscription, '*Orate pro anima Nobilimi D.D. Edmundi Purcelli, qui obiit* 16 *Aug.* 1625.' The Baron of Loughmoe in Tipperary was the head of the Purcells from whom N. Purcell O'Gorman is descended in the female line; but there were five respectable branches in Kilkenny, viz. :— of Ballyfoile, of Foulksrath, of Lismain, of Ballymartin and of Clone.—See *The Wayside Crosses*, by Mr. Prim, in Vol. I. of *Kilk. J. of Arch.*

The Purcells were hereditary captains of Ormonde's Kerne. The chief stock lived at Foulksrath, the offsets at Ballyfoyl, Lismain, Clone and Ballymartin. Edmund Purcell 'captain of Kerne' died in 1549, and is buried in S[t.] Canice, where his tombstone bears the inscription, '*Capitanus turbariorum Comitis Ormoniae*.'—Mr. Prim in *Kilk. J. of Archæology.*

There was a Patrick Porcell gent. of Lowyston in the year 1537; and Piers P. of Ballyen; also 'the Lorde Purcell.'—See *Annuary*, pp. 116, 117, 121, 123, 132.
The ruin of Ballyfoile Castle stands in the glen of that name at the foot of the Johnswell mountains.

[k] Also 'Mr. Den of Grenan.'—*Car. Cal.*

[l] David FitzGerald, alias Barron. This family, which had the title of Baron after it had ceased to be summoned to Parliament as such, was of the Geraldine stock. The title came at last to be a surname. A way-side Cross in the Square of Inistioge has the inscription, '*Orate pro animabus Domini David Geraldini, dicti Baron de Brownsfoord, obiit* 14, *Apr.* 1621; *et Joannae Morres.*'

The castle of Brownsford is situate over the Nore. In 1537 the Kilkenny 'Jurye present that the Baron of Brownesforde, and his officers doth use Blak men, that is to saye, the Baron will show the country that he hath VIII[xx] Gallawglasseis, and require wages of them therefor; where of truthe he hath not above the number of 100 Gallowglassheis, and doth take and levye of the country wages for VIII[xx] personnes, and so keepeth the residue of the money to himself, which amounteth to the some of 60 persons

COUNTIE OF KILKENNY. 69

Fostor[m] of Kilseraghe,
Sir Richard Shee[n] Knight,
Sir James Butler[o] Knight,

Sir Pierce Butler[p] Knight,
and divers more Families of

wages.'—See *Annuary*, pp. 117, 121, and Mr. Prim's *Wayside Crosses* in *Kilk. J. of Arch.*

[m] Gerald Forster. In 1537 R. Forstell of Kilferrouthe gent. From a pedigree it appears the name was originally Forrester, but the name was afterwards written Fforstall. The head of the family held the manors of Kilferagh and Ballyfrunck by Knight's service from the Crown in *capite*. Monsieur Forestall of Paris is believed to be the head of the Kilkenny Forstalls of Rochestown.

[n] Of Upper Court and Cloran; he was descended from O'Seagha, chief of Iveragh in Kerry. He was son of Robert Shee and Margaret Rothe; he was a member of Gray's Inn, seneschal of Irishtown in 1568, in 1576 deputy to the E. of Ormonde (lord high treasurer of Ireland), he was knighted in 1589; he died at his castle of Bonnettstown in 1603, and in his will left an injunction on his son, Lucas, to build an Alms' House, and left his curse on any of his descendants who should ever attempt to alienate the property provided for its maintenance, which consisted chiefly of impropriate tithes. A cross was erected to Sir Richard by his wife Dame Margaret Fagan. His son Lucas married a sister of Lord Mountgarret, and at Freshford there is or was a Wayside Cross erected in memory of Lucas and his wife, and the site is called in Irish *Bun na Croise*.

Colonel Count O'Shee, of the French service, is the representative of Sir Richard, whose old vellum Cartulary he possesses. From Sir Richard's second son, Marcus of Sheestown, is descended J. Power O'Shee, Esq., of Sheestown and Gardenmorres. Sir Richard's brother, Elias Shee of Cranmore was, says Hollingshed, 'a scholar of Oxford, of passing wit, a pleasant conceited companion, full of mirth without gall;' from him was descended Sir G. Shee of Dunmore, co. of Galway.

[o] Perhaps 'Sir James Oge Butler of Slewardaghe.'

[p] 'M[r.] Peers Butler of Old Abbey.' —*Car. Cal.*

Piers Fitz Thomas Butler of Duiske Abbey and Lowgrange, illegitimate son of the Earl of Ormonde, died in 1601, leaving (by his wife, a da. of Lord Slane) two sons, Edward, afterwards Viscount Galmoy, and Sir Richard Butler of Knocktopher. Piers was a zealous Catholic, and did his best to save Archbishop O'Hurly; he died in 1601. In 1697 the third Viscount Galmoy was attainted, but James the Second created him Earl of Newcastle— a poor recompense for the broad acres which he had lost.—See an account of Galmoy and his regiment in *O'Callaghan's Irish Brigades*.

Butlers,[q] Graces,[r] Shees, Cantwells,[s] Comberfords,[t] Deanes, Archdeacons,[u] Walshes,[v] Roothes,[w] Archers,[x] Dormers, Stronges, which are thought

[q] 'Richard B. now sheriff, of Pallistoun.'—*Car. Cal.* From the B. of Paulstown came Colonel B. the slayer of Wallenstein, and Sir W. Butler who defended Kilkenny against Cromwell.

[r] There is a 'Grace's Cross' near Bonnetstown, erected by Edward G. and his wife Catherine Archer; he was of the family of the Barons of Courtstown; he d. in 1619. Sir J. Grace, Baron of Courtstown, died after 1568; his tomb is in St. Canice's.

[s] 'Of Cantwellstown.'—*Car. Cal.* Cantwell's Court is four miles north-east of Kilkenny.

[t] 'Garret Comerford of Inchiolegan.' —*Car. Cal.* The head of the Comerfords was Baron of Danganmore; junior members were settled at Ballymack, Ballybur, Callan and Inchebologhan Castle; *circa* 1572 'Thomas C. late of Ballymacka, having been in his lifetime one of the chiefest conspirators and actual dooers in this last rebellion, was attainted.' At Danganmore there is a Wayside Cross with a Latin inscription, asking prayers for the souls of Richard C. and his wife, Domina Joanna S[t.] Leger.

[u] 'Archdeacon of Bawnmore.'—*Car. Cal.* Also A. of Dangan; they were descended from Odo le Ercedekne, and hence, when the family *waxed Irish* it took the name of Mac Odo, shortened to Cody. Of this family was Father Arsdekin, S.J., the celebrated Author of the *Theologia Tripartita*.

[v] 'Walsh of Castle Hely and Mr. Justice Walshe of Glomemore.'—*Car. Cal.* W. of Castlehowell was the head of the Kilkenny Walshes or the Brennachs of the Walsh Mountains. By the Kilkenny Jury of 1537 they are called Brennach, and Walter B. and his sons are presented as exacting coyne and livery. Walter W. the head of the family died in 1619. 'The Walshes are a great sect at the Earl of Ormond's commandment,' says a state paper of this time, to which I cannot now give a reference.

[w] 'The most distinguished man of this family in 1598 was Dr. D. Rothe afterwards Bishop of Ossory.

[x] In 1597 Thomas Archer was sheriff of Kilkenny City; in 1601, Patrick A. and in 1603 Martin A. were sheriffs. In 1602 John Archer FitzLaurence, burgess of the city of Kilkenny, in his will mentions his sons William and Matthew, and his daughters, to whom he leaves his land in fee. In 1605, Megge Archer FitzEdward mentions her son Jenkan Roth and desires her 'body to be buried with her husband Jenkan Rothe in the Choire of our Ladye Chapell Kilkenny.' In 1599 'the Sovraigne Burgesses and Commons demised to Walter Archer FitzArcher Esquire, S[t.] James' Castle, provided he

Thought to be Stranges,[y] their Armes agreeing with the Stranges of Ingl.; St. Legers,[z] Blanchviles,[aa] Staffordes, Sweatman,[bb] Geraldin, Tobyn,[cc] Dobyn, Forestall, Crooke, Hullen, Arnold White Dalton Smethes Dryling Shortall,[dd] Wales, Waton Row

cover the same with oken timber and maintain it stiff, strong, staunch and tenentable; but the Soveraigne, etc., should have the use of it in time of war or danger.'

[y] Peter Strong of Dunkit and Aylwardstown, where the present head of the family, Peter Strange, Esq., resides.

[z] The Jury of 1537 present that Lord Sleggar charged his tenauntes with coyne and livery. In 1549 he is called Baron Lyster. S[t.] Leger (or Slyggar) lived at Tullaghanbroge, also a branch resided at Ballyfennon; they were called Barons or 'Banrets' of Slewmargie, and by Stanihurst are described as 'mere Irish.' Hanmer states that Slieve Margie was granted to S[t.] Leger with the title of Baron, and that of late years (*circa* 1598) a gentleman of the name dwelling at Danganstown near Carlow laid claim to the same, as descendant of S[t.] Leger.

[aa] Gerald Blancheville of Blanchvillestown was Knight of the Shire in 1584; his son, Sir Edmond B. was living in 1616, and was maternally descended from the Earls of Ormond. The Blanchfield living in 1537 is called by the Kilkenny Jury 'lorde Blanchefeld.' Sir John Blanchfield Knt. was summoned to the war in Scotland in the year 1335.

[bb] 'Sweetman of Castlelyf.'—*Car. Cal.*

Sir R. Sweetman was summoned as a Baron to Parliament in 1374; Edward S. of Hoodgrove died in 1616 seised of a castle in Gowran, a castle in Thomastown, etc. The chief seats of the S. were Castlereife, and Newtown D'Erley.

William S. of Castlelyf in the co. of Kilkenny, Gent. tried to persuade Sir Edmund Butler to submit to the Government in 1569. By the jury of 1537 S. is called 'the lord Sweetman.'

[cc] Originally S[t.] Aubin. They were titular Barons of Comsey in the co. of Tipperary, a branch seems to have settled at Ballaghtobin in the co. of Kilkenny.—*Annuary*, p. 127.

[dd] 'Shortall of Ballylorcan, S. of Clagh.'—*Car. Cal.* J. Shortalls, 'Lord of Ballylorcan,' whose tomb was erected in 1507, is buried with his wife Catharine White in the Cathedral of S[t.] Canice. Sir Oliver S. of Ballylorcan, and Castle Idough, etc., married the widow of N. Shortal of Upper Claragh; he died in 1630. The jury of 1537 presented that 'the Lorde Shertell (written also here Sortall) useth the same exaccyons as the Earl of Ossory.' The war-cry of the Shortalls was *Pucansac-abo!*

Frayne^ee Dowley Knaresburghe
Conway, Baggad,
Davels Ledwyshe
Lancton^ff Troddy, Lawles
Brenan,^gg Swayne, Cormicke^hh
Of these the L. Mountgarrat accompanied with many Butlers,

^ee Frenge, French, Fulke de la Freigne was first of the gentlemen of the shire summoned to the war of Scotland in 1302. The head of the F. lived at Ballyreddy where Lord Freny died in 1611. Lord de Freyne is of this family, being descended from Oliver de Freyne who was seneschal of Kilkenny in 1336. We find a cross at Ballyneale near New Ross, and a tomb to Robert Frayne, '*viro vere pio, munifico et hospitali*,' erected by his wife Eleanor Geraldine, d. of the Baron of Brownsford; he died in 1643. The de F. was usually seneschal or chief officer to Ormond.—See *Mr. Prim's Wayside Crosses.*

^ff In 1598 the Rev. J. Langton was one of the vicars choral of St. Canice. In the same year Edward L. was sovereign of Kilkenny. Nich. L., Alderman, and P. Archer Esq. were members for Kilkenny in 1613. Mrs. Peter Grehan, of Rutland Square, Dublin, is of this family; her brother, F. Langton, Esq., of London, is its representative, and also heir and representative of the Comerfords, Palatine Barons of Danganmore. The Rev. E. Madden R. C.C. is also a representative of the Langtons and Comerfords, and owns the 'great stone house' of Langton in Kilkenny. Alderman Langton, M.P., who was born in 1562 and d. 1632,

had twelve sons and thirteen daughters. —See *Memoirs of the Langtons by Mr. Prim in the Kilk. J. of Arch.*

^gg The following were the septs of O'Brenans *circ.* 1603: 'The sept of Gilpatrick O'Brenan of Rathcally which are called Clanmoriertagh hath seven towns or hamlets; the sept of Edmund O'B. of Kildergan, alias Hokercty, and Edmund O'B. of Smithstown, which sept are called Clan McConill, they own four towns and hamlets; the sept of Ffarr McDonoghoe of Croghfenaly, which are called Clanvickelowe, they have three towns and hamlets; the sept of Moriertagh McDonoghoue Killy, which are called Clanowly, they own KyledonoghoueKilly, and three other places.'—*Rev. James Graves in 1st Vol. of Kilkenny J. of Arch.*

^hh Also 'Lovell of Ballymaka.'—*Car. Cal.* There were also Barnabe Bolgyr at Bishopscourt, the Cowleys ancestors of Wellington, the Grants of Curluddy and Ballynabooly, Le Poer of Powers Wood; the Rochfords, whose feudal residence was the Black Castle of Kildare. There was also a family of Gall or Gall-Burke of Gallstown, from which Dr. O'Donovan, the Irish scholar, was sprung. Walter Gall de Burgo of Gallstown was M.P. for Kilkenny county in 1560. Of his sons, Walter d. in 1642; William (Count Gall von

Graces, and all the younger Brethren of Gent of this Countie are now in Rebellion he is able to make about 150 *Horsemen and* 500 *Footemen, they Stop the Passage from Dublin to Mounster which lieth through this Countie and do much harm to all the Counties adjacent* [The lines in italics are Cancelled in the[ii] Original].

THE QUENES COUNTIE *alias* LEASE.[a]

This Countie contayneth all the Lands in effect between the Water of Barrow and Ormond, including all that did belong to Omore Odwine [ODunn] upper Ossyrie and Sleumaghe [als

---

Bourckh of the German Empire) d. 1655; James was slain at Torgau; David was slain at Leipsig in 1631; Patrick was in the Spanish service, and Thomas was living in 1636, in the Austrian army, and had a son William Walter Gall de Burgo, Count Gall von Bourckh of Gerstorf and Holstein.— See *Dr. O'Donovan's Memoir of the Gall-Burkes, in the Kilk. J. of Arch.*

[ii] In April 1599, Mountgarret with his brother's sons, Richard, James and Edward, and followers, are in rebellion with the O'Carrolls : their forces 150 ; whereof 20 are horse, besides continual assistance from Tyrone, to whose daughter Mountgarret married his son. —*Car. Cal.*, p. 298.

The English had in Kilkenny 230 horse under Ormond, Sir J. Lambert, Sir Walter Butler, Sir Chr. S[t.] Lawrence, and Captains Fleming and Taffe; also 800 foot under Ormond, Sir Carew Reynel, Sir H. Follyot, Croft, Sheffield and Pinner.—*Moryson*, p. 43.

N.B.—Most of these notes on Kilkenny have been put together from the *Annuary of the Kilk. Arch. Soc.*, an. 1868, and from various papers by the Rev. J. Graves and J. Prim, Esq., in the *Kilk. J. of Arch.*

[a] 'Let us approach *Laoighis*,
Brown-haired heroes for whom showers fall ;
The great territory of Laoighis of slender swords
Belongs to O'Mordha, bulwark of battle,
Of the golden shield of one colour.'
—*O'Huidhrin*.

Laoighis, pronounced Lee-ish, comprised, not the baronies of Upper Ossory, Portnahinch, and Tinnahinch,

Slewmargie]. The Soyle is Fruitfull[b] and Exceeding pleasant,

but only the northern and eastern baronies of Queen's Co.

'*Lease* est regiuncula sylvestris et uliginosa; primarium oppidum est Maryburgh, ubi cum suo Seneschallo præsidiarii agunt, qui sese ægre defendunt contra *O'Moores* (qui se ut antiquos hujus dominos gerunt), *Mac-Gilpatrick, O'Dempsios* et alios, malefica et tumultiosa hominum genera, qui ad Anglos deturbandos nihil non quotidie moliuntur.'—*Letterpress prefixed to Jansson's old Map of Leinster.*

[b] 'It seemed incredible, that by so barbarous inhabitants (as the people of Leix) the ground should be so manured, the fields so orderly fenced, the Townes so frequently inhabited, and the high waies and paths so well beaten as the Lord Deputy here found them—*the reason whereof was that the Queene's forces during these warres never till then came among them.* His Lordship staying in Leax till the twenty three of August did many waies weaken them—he fought with them every day and as often did beate them—our Captaines and, by their example (for it was otherwise painful) the common souldiers did cut down with their swords all the Rebels come to the value of ten thousand pound and upward, *the only means by which they were to live,* and to keepe their Bonaghts (or hired souldiers).'—*Morysón, Ireland anno* 1600, p. 77.

'The Lord Deputy's journey into the Queen's Co. in 1600.'—Vol. 601 of *Carew MSS.* 'Aug. 14. His Lordship left Sir J. FitzPiers and Sir H. Follyott with 400 men, "to fall into Leix another way that night for a prey; Aug. 15. Rory McRory with 100 Kerne skirmished with them and they got no prey. The L. Deputy burned and *spoiled Keating's country and the corn thereabouts.*" Aug. 16. He sent Sir O. Lambert with 600 foot who marched through the fastness of Slemarge, *spoiling* their plots of corn within the woods, burning their towns, with some skirmish in the passes. His Lordship coasted along the plain "burning and spoiling likewise. At the river there were some skirmishes. Aug. 17. Encamped at Ferney Abbey. The army marching along the valley, the rebels coasted along the mountains. Divers of them came from the hill waving us to them with their swords, and calling us, as their manner is, with railing speeches." Aug. 18 and 19. The army passed to Kilgighy in Ossory, "all the way we burned all their houses in their fastnesses and woods." Aug. 22. We spoiled the corn about Teig Fitz-Patrick's Castle.'—*Car. Cal.,* p. 432.

On the 5th of Sep. the Deputy wrote to Carew: 'With 800 foot and 100 horse I entered Leixe, burned and spoiled all their towns and cut down their corn; Owny McRory wrote to the Earl of Ormond desiring him "to stay this execrable and abominable

and hath on the one Side the River Barrow, and through a great part thereof the River Newer [Nore] well Sorted with plaines and Woods.ᶜ This Countie being throughlie conquered by the Earle of Sussex was planted with a mixed people of Inglysh and Irish, and in the tyme of King Phillip and Quene Marie this Countrie was called by the name of the Quenes Countie, and the

course (for so he termed it) of cutting down green corn." On our return the rebels charging our men hotly were beaten back.'—*Car. Cal.*

Owny declared himself 'outraged by the abominable new device of Mountjoy, to cut down green corn wherever he goes—an execrable course and a bad example to all the world. The English had taught him bad lessons before, and as they do not mean to give over schooling him in bad actions, which he protests he loathes, he declares he will give over tillage and take to living on the tilling of others.'—See his letter published in *Kilk. J. of Arch.*

ᶜ There is in the *Kilk. J. of Arch.* a fac-simile of an ancient map of Leix, Ofaly, etc., which was made *circ.* 1563. It excels all other Irish maps in archæological interest—it exhibits the huge and wide mountains of Slievebloom and Slievecomar, the primeval forests, as 'the great wood;' the vast heaths and morasses as Frugh-more (the great heath of Maryborough) and part of the bog of Allen; fort 'Protectour' (now Maryborough); the old feudal fortresses of Lea, Geashill, and Dunamase; smaller castellated houses of Celtic chiefs; the smaller dwellings of the bards, brehons, and physicians; clusters of cabins; considerable monasteries such as Abbey-Leix, Killeigh, and Monasterevan; a sprinkling of small churches; and some evidences of an armed settlement as 'Castle Cosby,' 'Castle Pigot.' The sylvan condition of the land is remarkable; the 'passes' or rude roads through the bogs and these 'backwoods' of the Pale are marked also. Finglas wrote in 1529 that among the most dangerous passes were 'two passes in Feemore (*Fiadh-mor* or *great wood*) in O'More's country.' In 1548 a pass in Leix was described as three miles long through a forest of great timber mingled with hazel; and in a state paper we are told the Irish 'repute the great woods of oak no fastness, but the thyke woods of hassel and sallies they take for great assurance.'—*Description of an Ancient Map of Leix by H. F. Hore, Esq.*

Leis was divided into seven parts, the boundaries of which met at a stone called *Leac-Riada*, on the plain of *Magh Riada*, now Morett; these regions were under seven petty kings, who were subject to an Arch-King, called *Righ-Riada*, who resided at Dunamase.

chief Towne called Marieborroughe, as the next Countie was called by the name of Kings Countie and the chief Towne thereof called Phillipstowne. The new planted Inhabitants Hath bene so molested continuallie with the multitudes of the first Natives thereof, and the Omoores, and especially at this present, as that they have in a manner recovered the Countrie againe and Expelled all the Inglysh Inhabitants saving 3 or 4 which contayne themselves within their Castles till they be relieved from Ingl. These Omoores was almost extinct, but they have increased againe chieflie for lack of good Government,[d] and due observation of such Orders as were appointed

[d] This is unjust to the government of Sir H. Sydney, who thus tells us in his 'Memoir' what he did to *extinguish* and extirpe the O'Mores : 'Rory Oge O'More was the sonne of another Rorye, chief of the O'M, and Captain of the country called Leish who married a daughter of the Earl of Ormond (and was first cousin of the tenth Earl). He called himself O'More. Against him in 1578 I advanced, being of horsemen and footmen a right good force; but he would not abide me, nor I overtake him; he carried away captive, to my heart's grief, my lieutenant, Sir Harrie Harrington, my most dear sister's son. I made on him as *actual and cunning a warre* as I could; I besett his cabanish dwelling with good soldiers and excellent good executioners; he had within it twenty-six of his best men, his wife and his marcial's wief, and Cormac O'Connor, an ancient and rank rebel of long mentyned in Scotland. All were killed, his wife and all his men; only there escaped himself and his marshall called Shane M'Rory Reagh, in trouth most miraculously, for they crept between the legs of the soldiers into the fastness of the plashes of trees. The soldiers saved the marshal's wife.'—*Sydney*.

As Shane O'Neill was subdued by the Scots, Desmond by Ormond, and the Kavanaghs by the Butlers, so were the O'Mores ruined by their neighbours and kinsmen, the M'Gillapatricks. 'M'Gillapatrick, Baron of Upper Ossory, my particular sworn brother,' says Sydney, ' was the faithfullest man for martial action that ever I found of that country. He followed O'More with great skill and cunning and with much or more courage assailed him and made the best fight with him that ever I heard of between Irishmen. Rory was killed by a household servant of the Baron's; his marshall escaped, and the rebel's bodye, though dead was so well attended and carried away as it

to the Livetennants thereof by the Earle of Sussex, (To wit) that the Freeholders of this Countie, and the King's Countie be compelled to keep for their own defence the Horsemen and Footmen, which they are bound to keep by their Tenures, which if it had been put to Execution without any charge to the Quene had bene able to have suppressed any power that the Rebells cou'd have raysed against them. The Capten of these Omoores at this present is one Orory McRoric—who is not able to make of himself above 160 or 180 Footemen;^e but when-

was the cause of the death of a good many men on both sides; yet carried away it was.'—*Sydney's Memoirs.*

^e When Owny captured Ormond on the 10th Apr. 1600, 'he had,' says Carew, ' 500 foot and 20 horse, the best furnished men for the war and the best apparelled that we have seen in this kingdom, whereof 300 were bonaghes.'—*Carew to Privy Council, April* 18, 1600. In April 1599, ' Owny with the rest of the Moores and their followers were 600, of whom 30 are horse.'—*Car. Cal.*

' The best service done at that time was the killing of Owny, *a bloody and bold yong* man, who had lately taken the Earl of Ormond prisoner and had made great stirres in Mounster. He was chief of the O'Mores and by his death they were so discouraged that they never after held up their heads. Also a *bold bloody* rebel Callogh Mac-Walter (O'More) was at the same time killed.'—*Moryson.*

' Callogh McWalter, the most bloody rebel in Leinster, was killed in helping of Owny; after the skirmish, we heard that Owny, being mortally wounded, and fearing his head should come into the L. Deputy's hands, had willed it to be cut off and buried after his death, and he appointed Owny McShane to be O'Moore.' 'L. Mountjoy's Journey.'—*Car. Cal.* 'Uaitne, son of Rury Oge, son of Rury Caoch O'Moore, an illustrious, renowned and celebrated gentleman, by right the sole heir to his territory, had wrested the government of his patrimony by the prowess of his hand and the resoluteness of his heart from the hands of foreigners, brought it under his own sway, and under the government of his stewards and bonnaghts according to Irish usage, so that there was not a village from one extremity of his patrimony to the other which he had not in his possession except Port-Leix alone.' —*Four Masters.* According to *Dymmok,* p. 32, 'Owny challenged Essex to fight 50 of his with 50 of ours with sworde and target which was consented to by the L. Lieutenant; but Owny

soever he intendeth any Robberie or Spoyle he is assisted partlie with his Neighbours of the King's Countie the Oconnors partlie by Phelim M⁄cFeughe whose coosen germaine he is, and partlie by Capten Tyrrell who is readie with his Companie to assist ether the Omoores or the Oconnors or the Omclaghlanes for in any Sudden and present exployt. This Countie is bounded with the Countie of Kilkenny to the South, with Tipperairie to the West, with the Kings Countie and the mountaynes of Slewblowe to the North, and the River Barrow to the East. It is governed by Sʳ Vaughan Sᵗ Leger who hath a commission of Lieutenancy for the Countie. The chief Towne whereof is Marieborrow ruled by a Portrise, and wherein is a Fort garded with 150 Footmen or Sometymes 200, as need requireth, and some few Horsemen.

*The chef Castles :*ᶠ

The Quene's Fort	Dunas
The Shyan	Blackfort
The Abbey of Lease	Baleclockan
Stradbellie	Disert
Pallace	Balliadams

*Principal Irysh Gentlemen :*ᵍ Sir Henrie Power Lieutenant and constable of the Fort

never came to perform it.'—See about his fight with Essex at the *Pass of the Plumes* in O'Sullivan Beare's *Historia Cath.*

ᶠ 'Master Hartpol, Mʳ· Bowen and Mʳ· Pygot were the only English inhabitants, by whom and some others certaine castles were kept for the Queen, besides the Fort of Mariaborough kept by the Queen's Garrison.'

'The English foote at Leax and the Barow side were Sir Warham Sᵗ Leger 150 f., Sir F. Rush 150, Captaine John Fitz-Piers 150, and Mʳ· Hartpoole 10.' —*Moryson.*

ᵍ Cosby (?) at Stradbally; Cosby at Castle Dirrhy; Harpoole of Coolbaneghar, he is constable of Catherlagh Castle; Bowen of BallyAdams; Edward Brierton of Laghtiog; Pigotts of

THE QUENES COUNTIE. 79

Alexander Cosbie
William Harpole
Robert Bowen
Bruerton
Rob' Piggot of the desert
Young Davels
Barrington[h]

Freeholders of the [   ] of Ireland
The Earle of Kildare
The Barron of upper Ossyrrie[i]
Pierce Butler Brother to the Earle of Ormond
O Dunne[k]
Bryan McCalloghe McDonell,[l] and many other inferior Freeholders.

Dysart; John Barrington of Cowlniagh. Earl of Kildare at Moyrit and Tymog; Hovendon at Taukardstowne, Hetherington at Tully, Sir Thos. Colclough of Ballyknockan, Loftus of Tymoghoe, Whytney of Shyan, Hugh Boy Clan Donnell of Tenne-Killeh; Edmund MacDonell of Rhahin, Tirence O'Dempsey of Ballybrittas.—*Car. Cal.*, p. 191.

[h] In fighting with the O'Mores there fell, 1° the son of Captain John Barrington, 2° Joseph Barrington, 3° Thomas Lighe, second husband of Mrs. Barrington.

[i] Florence FitzPatrick or Fineen MacGillapatrick, son of Brian, the first Baron. He and his father mainly contributed to ruin the O'Mores; but his son Teig was opposed to the English.

—See *Car. Cal.* year 1600. O'Dugan says, 'MacGillapatric of the fine seat, noble fairfaced is the tribe of the residence of the head chieftain.' Lord Castletown is descended of this family.

[k] 'Over Ui-Rigan of heavy routs,
A vigorous tribe who conquer in battle,
Is O'Duinn, chief of demolition,
Hero of the golden battle spears.'
—*O'Huidhrin.*

Iregan is co-extensive with the barony of Tinnahinch. General Francis Dunn, M.P., is the head of the O'Dunnes of Iregan.

[l] 'This county of Leax, lately all English is now usurped by O'More and all the sept of the O'Mores, and the chiefe of the galloglasses in that county of the sept of MacDonnell,

Ancient endwellers[m]

The whole race of the Omoores were excluded from having residence here by act of Parliament An° 2° Phill. & maria.

the sept of O'Dempsies (except Sir Terence O'Dempsey), the sept of O'Doyne, except Teig Oge O'Doyne.'—*Moryson.*

In Nos. 5 and 6 of the *Ulster J. of Arch.* there are interesting accounts of the M‘Donnells of Tennekille Castle by J. Huband Smith, Esq., and by Sir Erasmus Burrowes, Bart. From them we extract the following details: The Castle of Tennekille (*teach na coille* or house of the wood) was built *circ.* 1450; it is remarkable for its skilful design, groined ceiling, and finished execution; a few patriarchs of the forest still remain, venerable companions of the old keep. In 1578 an agreement was entered into between the L. Deputy and 'the three chiefe Captains of the three septs of Clandonnells of Leinster, her Majesty's Galloglas, viz.—Turlogh Oge M‘Alexander of Wicklow, M‘Edmund M‘Donnell of Rahin and Hugh Boy M‘Donnell of Tenekille.' It was agreed that—'In consideration of the auntient and continued fydelytie, loyaltye and true service of the Capitaynes, gent and septs of the said Clandonnills, the Bonaghts dead payes, and black-mail, heretofore levied, shall be commuted into a yearly pencon of £300 to be paid out of her Majesty's exchequer, unto th' ands of the said three chief captains—Provided that henceforth none of the said Capitaynes . . . shall use weapon or armor in serving of any other but her Majesty,' etc.—*Sir E. Burrowes in Ulster J. of Arch.*

About this time 1598 the castles and towns of Rahin and Derry, belonging to M‘Edmund M‘Donnell of Queen's Co., were forfeited and given to Sir R. Greame. In 1631 James M‘D. got a patent of his estates of Tennekille including 30 townlands; but was obliged to agree that 'his sons and servants shall use English dress and language, and he and they and all the males under their controul between the ages of 16 and 60 shall present themselves every year before the constable of Maryborough and get their names inscribed.' In 1641 James M‘D. of Tenekille was a Confederate colonel.'—*J. Huband Smith.* The M‘Donnells are still found about Strahard and Portarlington, but as peasants and blacksmiths on the lands of their galloglas ancestors.—J. M‘Grady in No. 7 *Ulst. J. of Arch.*

[m] The seven septs of Leix were the the O'Mores, O'Kellys, O'Lalors, O'Devoys, M‘Evoys, O'Dorans, and O'Dowlings.—See an account of them in *O'Byrne's History of Queen's County.* From Ruary O'More, Prince of Leix in 1555, is descended the Right Hon. R. More-O'Ferrall of Balyna.

The names Cosby, Bowen, Fitz-Patrick, Butler, Dunne, and Lalor are still among the 'County Families.'—See *Walford.*

THE KING'S COUNTIE.

The Countie being in tymes past called Offaly[a] was inhabited by the O'Connors, a wicked and Rebellious people, which for their sundrie Rebellions were by the Earle of Sussex in the tyme of Quene Marie banished and disinherited, their Countrie converted into Shyre ground and called the King's Countie,[b] and the chief Towne thereof called Phillipstowne appointed to be ruled by a portrise as Marieboroughe.

This Shyre contayneth all the Land between the Countie of Kildare and the River of Sheynen including all the Clonmillier or O'Dempsies Countrie on both sides of the Barrow also Galline

[a] 'King's County consisteth of Offaly lately possessed by the O'Connors; Fercal of the O'Meloyes; Moyntertagan or Foxe's cuntrie possessed by the Foxes; Delvin McCoghlan of the McCoghlans; and that parcel of Glenmaliry possessed by the O'Demsies.'— *Endorsement on Ancient Map of Idrone in the Rolls' House, London.*

There is as much of O'Faley in Queen's Co. as in the King's Co.; and the baronies of Garrycastle, Ballycowan, Fercal, Clonlish and Ballybritt were never included in O'Faley.

Ui-Failghe, i.e., the descendants of Failghe, eldest son of Cathaoir Mor, inhabited originally the baronies of East and West Offaly in Kildare, of Portnahinch and Tinnahinch in Queen's Co., and that part of King's Co. comprised in the diocese of Kildare and Leighlin.

The O'Conors were chiefs of this territory till the reign of Philip and Mary, when they were dispossessed, and then the O'Dempsies became the most powerful families till the Revolution in 1688. —*Note to Irish Topographical Poem.* The 'Lords of Offaly, the land of Cattle, are not unknown to the poets, they spend their lands on knowledge; O'Conor is the hero of the plain, on the green round hill of Cruachan.'—*Top. Poem.*

[b] 'O'Connor of Ofaly was the scourge of the Englishry,' from whose rich domains in Meath he levied a 'black' rent equivalent to £10,000 a year (i.e., £300 at that time). His territory was 'the gall of the Pale,' 'the doore whereby myche warre and myschyff entered emong the subjects.'—*Irish Archæol. Miscellany.*

and ferecall, or Omeloyes Countrie the Shenaughe or O'Foxes Countrie and Delvin McCoghlane commonlie called McCoghlanes Countrie to the brink of the Sheynen nere Myllick. So it is bounded East with the Countie of Kildare, West with the Sheynen and with Westmeath, South with the Quenes Countie and Slewblow and Elie or O'Carrells Countrie, and North with Meath there is no Towne in it but Phillipstowne.

Principall Castles The Fort called Dingan in Phillipstoune,
Croughan belonging to Sr Thomas Moore,
Balliburlie, belonging to Sr George Cowlie,
Baliburtane belonging to Sr Henrie Warren, *Munster-Oris*,
Castlejordan,
Eden Durick belonging to Sr Edw. Harbert.

Chief Gent.[c] The Earle of Kildare,
Sr George Bouchier, ⎫
Sr Edward Moore, Constable of the Fort, ⎪
Sr Henrie Warren, ⎬ Knights.
Sr Thomas Moore, ⎪
Sr George Cowley, ⎪
Sr Edward Herbert, ⎭
Capten Brabazon's Sonnes,
Sanchie,
Tyrrell,

[c] Sir Henry Warren at Ballybrittan; Sir Thomas Moore at Croghan; Sir George Colly at Edenderrie; Sir Edw. Herbert at Dorrown; Nicholas Sanky; Sir John Tirrell at Blacklowne; Francis Herbert at Monaster-Orys; Thomas Wakeley at Ballyburley.'—*Car. Cal.* an. 1596.

Of the Irysh Freeholders :[d]

Gerrot Fitzgerrald,
Thomas Fitzgerrald,
the Sonnes of Neall McGeogaghan,[e]
McCoyhlan[f] and his sept,
Omoloy[g] and his sept,

[d] Garret FitzGerald at Corbetstown; Redmond Og FitzG. at Clownebolche; Wm. FitzG. at Geishell; John Raynolds at Cloyduff; Barnaby Connor at Derrymollin.—*Car. Cal.*

[e] Mageoghegan's country of Kinalea (*Cinel-Fiachach*) originally extended from Birr in King's Co. to Uisnech in Westmeath; but subsequently the O'Molloys, a junior branch of the Cinal-Fiachach, asserted their sway over the southern portion. Mageoghan's territory was co-extensive with the barony of Moycashel. Of this race were R. Mageoghegan, the heroic defender of Dunboy in 1602, Connell M. of Lismoyny, who translated the *Annals of Clonmacnoise* in 1627, and the Abbé M. who wrote the *Histoire d'Irlande.* Sir R. Nagle inherited the property of the last chieftain, from whom he was maternally descended.—*O'D. Note to Top. Poem.*

'The manly sept, the illustrious Clan Geoghagan, host of the girdles, comely their complexion.'—*O'Dugan.*

[f] 'John MacCoghlan of Coghlan.'—*Car. Cal.*

'MacCochlan whose children are beauteous to behold, King of Dealbhna-Eathra.'—*O'Dugan.* His territory comprised the present barony of Garrycastle, except the parish of Lusmagh. The family retained their territory till this century when they were succeeded by the O'Dalys and Armstrongs, who are descended maternally from the MacCochlans. Mr. Coghlan of Castlebar is head of one of the most respectable families of this stock.—*O'Donovan's Notes to O'Daly's Tribes of Ireland.* About 1249 Conor McCoghlan of the Castles was 'a great destroyer of the English.'

[g] 'Connell O'Moloy of Ralyhen'—*Car. Cal.* O'Molloy's territory comprised the baronies of Fircal or Eglish, Ballycown and Ballyboy. 'O'Mulloy King of Feara-Ceall of ancient swords, noble the surname; every sword was tried by him.' The head of the sept in 1588 was Connell son of Caher, whose grandson was Chief in 1677. D. Molloy, Esq., of Clonbela, Birr, is supposed to be the present representative of the family.—*O'Donovan.*

'When Calais was taken, I during the Christmas holidays upon a sudden invaded Fyrcal, or O'Molloys country, burned and wasted the same; on my return was fought with by the O'Conors, O'Mores, and O'Molloy, and the people

Odempsie[h] and his sept,
OFoxe[i] and his sept,

of Mackgochigan, albeit he was with me in person in that skirmish; I received in a freize jerkin (though armed under it) four or five Irish arrows.'—*Lord Deputy Sydney's Memoir.*

'On the 10th of March 1596, my Lord Deputy (Russell) went from Durrough to Rathmagolduld (Tege O'Molloyes). The chief of the O'M. with other gentlemen and some kerne met my Lord and declared that the Scots were burning the country within view. His Lordship sent 100 shot with certaine kerne under the guiding of O'Moloy, and assisted by M[c]Goghlin they fell upon the Scots at break of day and slew 140 of them, others being drowned.'—Russell's Journal, *Car. Cal.*

O'Molloy—*O'Maolmuidh* (Conal son of Cahir) died in the spring of 1599, and his son Calvach took his place, being appointed by the Queen. Some of the gentlemen of his tribe contended with him for that name, according to the Irish law of tanistic succession.—*Four Masters.*

[h] 'Noble the degree of their race, a smooth plain this sept have defended, the land is hereditary to O'Diomosaigh.' —*O'Huidhrin.* Their land of *Clann Maoilughra,* or Clanmaliere, embraced the baronies Portnahinch in Queen's Co., and of Upper Philipstown in King's Co. Their chief was ennobled by Charles I. 'There was a Terence Dempsy of Clonegawny;' also a Sir Terence O'Dempsye lived at Ballybrittas; the Earl of Ormond was imprisoned in his castle by O'More in 1600. Glashane O'D. and Lisagh O'D. with the rest of the O'Dempsies were in actual rebellion in 1599.—*Car. Cal.*

[i] 'Hubart Fox of Lehinche.'—*Car. Cal.* The Foxes or Sinnachs were 'O'Caharny's, Kings of Teffia—the brown oaks of the valleys, the protection and bounty of Erin, of whom robbers were afraid.' *O'Dugan.* The Foxes owned *Muinter Tadhgain,* which became the barony of Kilcoursey. Darcy Fox of Foxville, in Co. Meath, is believed to be the head of this clan. Fox of Foxhall in Longford is of this family, and is descended from Sir Patrick Fox, Clerk of the Privy Council of Dublin from 1588 to 1610.

The following extract from a Patent Roll shows the extent and subdivision of Fox's country in 1598 :—
'Hubert Foxe of Lahinchie Barony Kilcoursie, *alias* the Foxe his countrie, Gent., commonly called The Foxe, chief of his name, by deed dated 1 May 1599 surrendered to the Queen all his estate temporal and spiritual within the whole barony and territory of Kilcourcie, with intent that her Maty should regrant the same to him in tail male. Wherefore from Richmond, Jan. 29, 1599, her Maty granted the same to him and his heirs male, remainder to his nephew Brissel F. son of his

The old Inhabitants, O'Connors," was by act of Parliament

brother Arte, to his uncle Owen F. of Lissinuskie, to Phelim F. of Tolghan ne Brenny, to Brissel F. of Kilmaledie, son of Neil F. who died lately in the Queen's service, with power to keep a Court Baron and a Court Leet, hereby appointing him Seneschal of that Barony.'—*Irish Arch. Misc.*, Vol I.

ª 'The O'Conors Faly, namely the descendants of Brian, the son of Cahir, son of Con, son of Calvagh, were for three or four years in the Irish Confederation up.to this time (1600). During this period they took and destroyed the most of the castles of Offaly, and indeed all except Dangan (Philipstown) and a few others. About Lammas this year 1600 the L. Deputy came into Offaly with scythes and sickles, and destroyed or reaped the ripe and unripe crops; the consequence of this was that the inhabitants fled to Ulster and other territories, where they remained to the end of the year.'—*Four Masters*, an. 1600.

'Henry Cooley, seneschal of the county with other English freeholders are sore pressed by the O'Conors, of whom Cormac O'Conor is chief, and by the Clandonnell Galliglasses, a naughty race and disposed to rebellion.' —*State Paper*.

'Nugent of Dysert, M.P. for Westmeath in 1585, m. a dau. of the Great O'Conor Offaley.'—*Lodge*.

'Shortly after the arrival of Essex the O'Connors slew 500 English horsemen and wounded their commander.'—*Lombard*, p. 417. About the same time Cahir Murtagh and John O'Conor of Offaly, with a hundred footmen took by assault the castle of Cruochan, which was defended by Sir Thomas More and Lifford—all the garrison was slain. The words of O'Sullivan are: 'Cathirius, Mauritius et Joannes O'Conchures Iphalii equites cum centum peditibus, improviso, scalis altissimis admotis Cruochanum castellum, quod in Iphalia principatu Thomas Morus eques Auratus et Liffirdus, Angli præsidio tenebant, ascendunt, et propugnatoribus occisis expugnant.'—*O'Sullivan*. Lib. v. cap. 8. *Hist. Cath.*

When Essex was in Offaly in 1599, Captain William Williams sallied forth from Philipstown with '300 men to recover a pray taken that morning by the rebels, lost 60 of his men, which fell improvidently between three enemies ambuscados.' 'A porcion of Offaly, called Fercal, is so strong as nature could devise to make it by wood and bogge, hence it was a storehouse for prays. Essex with 1200 foote and 200 horse went from Derrow to Ballycowen, where Sir Conyers Clifford, Governor of Connaught, arrived with 9 companies of foote. Sir Conyers Clifford was sore fought with at the entrance into Fercall, and had 10 men slayne and 40 hurte, which losse was doubled upon the rebel by the virtue of our men and specially of Sir Griffin

debarred from having Frehold here. There was a tyme of late when this Countie governed by a Lievetenant Sr George Bowchier grew wealthie and was verie quiet, both because it is by nature strong, and few passages, and those well garded; as also because the Inhabitants have better united in good Will one to another, and have better observed the Constitutions appointed unto them, than their Neighbors of Lease—besides they were in the beginning of her Majesties raigne verie well quieted with a prosecution which the old Earle of Kildare made upon the O'Connors who in manner did wholly extirpe them. But since the last Rebellion the O'Connors have from all quarters gathered themselves together againe to recover their ancient possessions, which in a Sort they have done, for they have ether banished the most of the Inglysh that dwelt in that Countrie, or else constreyned them to keep within their Castles, and albeit there are 40 knowen to be of the race of the O'Connors, yet at this present they lead of themselves their followers, and Strangers almost 400°. They are not yet agreed who shall be the chief; 4 men contending for it Moretoghe oge, Shane Glasse, Donoghe Pope, and

O'Foxe and O'Dempsie themselves kepe in but most of their friends and followers be in rebellion.

Markham. In the morning Essex sent into the woods 1000 choice men under Sir John MacCoughlin, Sir Theobald Dillon, and Sir C. St Lawrence, and his Lordship with the rest of the horse and foot took up the fittest places to second them; there was great slaughter of the rebels.'—*Dymmok.*

'The O'Conors, Princes of Ofaly and the O'Mores princes of Leix waged war on the English for more than sixty years continuously in this country; no counties were more dearly purchased by the English than the King's and Queen's Counties. Even the occasional notices of the battles of the O'Mores and O'Conors for these two counties would supply the poet or historian with one of the most thrilling episodes in Irish history.'—*Rev. M. Kelly's Note to O'Sullivan's Hist.*, p. 88.

° 'The O'Conors, O'Mollyes and

Nere unto this Countie is the Countie of Elie or O'carroll's[p] Countrie, which the Earles of Ormond have of long tyme challenged to have belonged to their Countie Palatine of Tipperarie; but by reason of the great dessention that have bene betwixt the Hous of Ormond and the OCarrell's, they wou'd never yeald to be of that Countie. This S[r] Charles O'Carrell's[q] Father did

O'donners had 468 f. and 12 h. The English foote in Offaly are Sir H. Cooly 20 f. Sir H. Warren 100 f. Sir Edward FitzGerald 100 f. Sir George Cooly 200; Sir G. Boucher 100 f. at Philipstown.'—*Moryson*, p. 43.

> 'Lords to whom the nut-trees bend
> Are the Munitir-Cearoll of Biorra's plain
> King of Ely to sweet Bladhma,
> The most hospitable mansion in Erin.
> Eight cantreds, eight chieftains east
> Under the King of Ely of the land of cattle,
> Brave the host gathering a prey,
> The host of yellow curling hair.'
> —*Top. Poem.*

In 1598 Ely comprised only the baronies of Clonlisk and Ballybritt. The freeholders of Sir W. O'Carroll in 1576 were O'Flanagan, M[c]Corcran, O'Hagan, O'Dooly, M[c]Gilfoyle, and O'Banan.—*O'Donovan's Notes to Top. Poem.*

[q] Sir Charles O'Carroll, was third son, considered illegitimate, of Sir William O'C. chief of Ely O'Carroll in the present King's County. In 1582 he succeeded his brother John, who was murdered by his kinsman Mulrony O'C.; in 1585 he attended the Dublin Parliament, and in 1588 was Knighted; in 1598 he committed an act of treachery towards some Ulster soldiers in his service. The *Four Masters* say: 'Some gentlemen of the MacMahons with one hundred soldiers were hired by O'Carroll (Calvach, son of William Owen, son of Ferganainm) in the spring of this year; and, at the time that their wages should be given them, O'C. with his people went to them by night and slew them on their beds and in their lodging houses. He hanged some of them from trees, but the party of one village made their escape. The evil fate deserved by that wicked deed befell Ely; for (in Hugh O'Neill's march southwards) nothing was left in it but ashes instead of corn, and embers in place of its mansions. Great numbers of their men, women, sons and daughters were left in a dying state, and some gentlemen of his own tribe were left in opposition to O'Carroll in the territory.' O'Carroll's territory comprised the baronies of Clonlisk and Ballybritt. The present chief of the family is unknown; the senior branch removed to America in Cromwell's time, and the head of that was grandfather of the late Marchioness of Wellesley. There is a letter of this 'Ch. O'Carroulle' from 'my chamber at London this present Monday, 1595.'

yeald himself to be under the Government of the Inglyshe, and namelie under the Government of the livetenant of the Kings Countie. But this O'Carrell having committed a Slaughter upon 3 of the Earle of Ormond's friends, and being summoned to abyde a Jurie in the Countie Palatyne of Tipperarie, obtayned by Letters from the Quene, that he should be tried by the Inhabitants of the Countie of Louth, which is a Countie farr distant from him. This Sr Charles O'Carrell hath continued his duetifull obedience to the Quene,' notwithstanding that his

It is 'A brief note of territories subtracted and concealed from her Majesty by the Erle of Ormond.' They were Dow Arra the contre of MacBrien Arra, O'Mulrian's is contre; Keelan a longforta or Shane Glasse is contre; Dow o Loyaghe or MacWalter is contre; Murkrybyry improperly and usurpedly called Heither Ormond,' *i.e.*, Upper and Lower Ormond.—*State Paper Office.*

'The Queen to the L. Deputy in 1595—'Whereas there is an indictment presented in the Co. Tipperary for a slaughter of some of the Cantwells by Sir C. O'Caroll the said Sir Charles has made complaint that the loss of his life is intended by means of that indictment laid in Tipperary, where he is mortally hated in regard of divers spoils between his country of Elye and the County Palatine; the trial is to be suspended until the difference of title betwixt the Earl of Ormond and Sir C. O'Caroll be determined whether Elye be in the co. Tipperary or not.'

On the 20th of July, 1600, Carew writes: 'No hour passeth within this Kingdom but some place or other produceth slaughters. This last week Sir Ch. O'Carroll (a good servant of her Majesty's) was murdered by one of his kinsmen. Four of the O'Carrolls are in competition for the lordship of that country. Before this case be decided it will cost much blood; but therein the State is nothing indemnified.'

The Four Masters thus speak of O'Carroll's death: 'O'Carroll, *i.e.*, Calvach, the son of William Odhar, son of Ferganainm, son of Maolruny was killed in July by some petty gentlemen of the O'Carrolls and O'Meaghers. This Calvach was a fierce and protecting man, a strong arm against his English and Irish neighbours, and a knight in title and honour by authority of the Sovereign.'

There was a Cian O'C. living at this time, who is savagely satirized by O'Daly in verses which begin thus: 'Cian O'Caroll and his spouse are a pair that never forgot inhospitality.' As O'Daly seems to have been em-

Countrie hath bene often Spoyled by the Enimie, and himself much Solicited and partlie threatned to enter into Rebellion. This Countie of Elie or O'Carrells Countrie is bounded with Ossory and a part of the Quens Countie to the South, with Ormond to the West with Delvyn M^ccoghlan to the North, and with the Mountayne of Shewblowne and a part of Fercall to the East, It hath Castles of some importance divers but the chief is Limevadie.ᵃ

MEATH.

This Countie hath his name of Medium the Middle partᵃ and contayneth properly but one Shyre under the name of Meath, being in the beginning a portion appointed for the Kings Demeasnes but long since divided into many barronies and Counties, and now latelie in the tyme of King Henrie the 8th made Two Townes [Counties] East Meath and West meath. And because 2 Iryshe Countries adjoining to these Shyres the one belonging to the O'Reillies and the other to the O'Ferralls be nowe converted to Shyre Grounde by the names of the Countie of Cavan and Longforde, it is not amissᵇ to lay these

---

ployed by the English to put calumnies in verse, his word could not injure Cian's character.

ᵃ Limwaddon.—*Dymmok.* 'At Ballymore and O'Carroll's countrie the Queen hath under Captaine Shane 100 f., Capt. Lister 100 f., Sir Charles O'Carroll 100 foote.'—*Moryson,* p. 43.

ᵃ 'A fifth plot defalked from every fourth part, lying together in the heart of the Realme, called thereof Media.' —*Campion.*

The Irish name is *Midhe.* The great plain of Meath was called *Magh Breagh,* or the Magnificent Plain; it included most of the present counties of Meath and Dublin.

ᵇ Keating says that the ancient Kingdom of Meath comprised the present counties of Meath and Westmeath,

Two to East meath and West meath and so to contayne them all four in this middle province, albeit by some these 2 last Countries hath bene esteemed part of Ulster.

EAST MEATH.[c]

This Countie contayneth all the Land betweene Balerotherie in the Countie of Dublin and the river of Boyne near Drogheda, and then not farr from Drogheda extendeth itself over the River and contayneth all the Land to the Border of Cavan and to the half Barone of Foore and from thence in breadth to the King's Countie and the Countie of Kildare. So hath it the Sea to the East, the Countie of Cavan to the West, Westmeath and the King's Countie to the South and South west, and the Countie of Louth to the North. It is in all Cesses and impositions double rated to any other Countie.[d]

and parts of Dublin, Kildare, King's County, Longford, Brefney and Orgial.

[c] 'The ancient manuscripts are very rich in topographical descriptions of this district, and one of our oldest coins is that of Aedh King of Meath. In it were four palaces of note in ancient times—Tara on the Boyne, Tailten on the Blackwater, Tlachta on the Hill of Ward, and Uisneach in Westmeath. In its bogs are remains of oxen, which for beauty of head and horn might vie with the finest modern improved breeds of England. The peasantry are handsome, well made, stout and healthy. The Meathmen were very Irish in the last century, used to boast that they spoke better Irish, had more poets, minstrels and men of genius, and had more energy than the boors of Leinster, whom they always defeated at hurling, boxing, wrestling and other athletic exercises.'—*Sir W. Wilde's 'Boyne,'* pp. 13, 15, 16.

[d] In 1515 it was 'ordered that every village and town in the barony of Kells, that lay within six miles of the Wylde Iryshe, be dycheyed, and hegeyed strongly about the gates, of tymbre, after the manner of the Co. of Kildare for dredde of fyre of their enymyes.'

In 1478, the Parliament of Drogheda, decreed at the prayer of A. Tuite gentleman — That, 'Whereas there is an open road for the Irish

It hath Townes

Drogheda
Aboy [Athboy] } Walled.
Kelles
Trim[e]

Navan
Dowlick } market Townes.[f]

enemies of the King between Rathconnyll and Queylan to enter Meath for the destruction thereof, a trench be made a mile in length.' Again in 1480 at Naas a Parliament decreed—'That it is very necessary for the safeguard of the King's subjects of his County of Meath, that a tower or pile of the new fashion should be built on the extreme frontier of the old march, not only in resistance of O'Conchie [O'Connor] but also for the chastisement of the Berminghams.'

'In 1584 Draper, Parson of Trim, writes to Burghley to urge the erection of a University or at least a grammar school in Trim. He says—'It is in a most fresh and wholesome ayre, full of very fayre Castles and stone houses, and hath in it five fair streets and the fairest and most stately Castle in Ireland. The Abbey and friary will be easily bought of the owner Edw. Cusack of Lesmollen; your suppliant will freely give a Friary having stanche walls with a pleasant backside.

The country round aboute is very fruitful of corn and cattle yeldinge besides plentifull store of firewood and turfe—a very good and sweet fewel.

Lastly the town is in the myddest of the English Pale and well and strongly walled about; a thing that will draw learned men and be great safety to the whole company of studentes; for your Honor knoweth wheresoever the University be founded, the town must of necessitie have a good wall, else will no learned men go from hence, or any other place thither, neither they of the country send their sons to any place that is not defensible and safe from the invasion of the Irishe.'—*Dean Butler's* '*Trim*,' p. 290.

'The Members for Meath in 1585 were R. Barnwall of Crickstown and J. Netterville of Dowth; in 1613 Hussey, Baron of Galtrim and Barnwall of Robertstown. The Members for Trim in 1585 were Hamon and Guyre, in 1613 Sir T. Ashe, and Sir Roger Jones; the Members for Athboy in 1585 were Browne and Ferrell of Athboy; and in 1613 Moore and Browne, gents, of Athboy.

The Members for Kells in 1585—Fleming of Stevenston, N. Daxe, and P. Plunket of Kells; in 1613 O. Plunket and G. Balfe gents., of Kells.

Members for Navan in 1585—Wakely

STATE OF IRELAND ANNO 1598.

It hath many Statelie Castles

Trim, the Quenes,
Killynee [Kyllyne] the Lords of it,
Dunsany the Lords of it,
Trivleston [Trimleston] the Lords of it,
Rathmore,
Meylaughe,
Moygare,
Newcastle,
Castle-towne of Athboy,
Jesucellin,
Ardmollan to [   ]
Bedlowston to S[r] To. Bedlow,
Stackallan,
Slane the Lords of it,
Moymet to Ja. Dillon,
Balldungan to the L. of Hoth,
Galtrim to the Baron of it,
Castle jordan to M[r.] Gifford[g]
Arbracan to the Bishop of Meath,
Cutmollen,
Dullerston,
Gillranston,
Gormanston to the Viscount thereof,
Colpe,
Murmudeye,
Platten to M[r.] Darsey [Darcey],
Dunmore,
Beste,
Castle lamerby,
Crinton,
Moyvally,
Bective,
Celcarne,

The Noblemen[h] of East-meath } The Lord Viscount Gormanstone his name Preston his chief Hous Gormanston,

of Ballyburly King's Co., and Waring of Navan; in 1613 P. Begg of Burranstown and J. Warren gent., of Navan.

[g] There are still many old, ruined castles in Meath; of which we find a description in Sir W. Wilde's *Boyne and Blackwater*, viz.—The castles of Carbury, Kinnafad, Clonmore, Grange, Carrig-Oris, Ticroghan, Trimblestown, Trim, Nangle's and Talbot's castles, Scurlogstown, Trubly, Assey, Riverstown, Athlumney, Liscarton, Dexter, Dowth, Proudfootstown, Naul and Termonfecken.

[h] In the *Barony of Dunboyne* are—Sir G. Fenton of Dunboyne, Pat. Phippes of Roan, Jn. Delahoyde of Bellander, Rich. Bremingham of Pace,

EAST MEATH. 93

The Bishop of Meath his name Jones,
his chief Seat Arbraccan,
The Lord Baron of Killyen his name
Plunket his chief Hous Killyen,
The Lord Baron of Dunsany his name
Plunket his chief hous Dunsany,

Simon Rowe of Waringstone, Rich. Sale of Salestowne, Alex. Barnwall of Luston, Christ. Hollywoode of Herbertstown.

Rising out of the general Hosting of Barony of Dunboyne—Phepo of Rowen, if he have freedom 1 armed horseman; Francis de la Hide 1 armed horseman.

Ratoathe. — Sir Pat. Barnwall of Crickston, Baron Sedgrave of Killeglan, Barnwall of Kilbrue, Th. Plunket of Loughgoure, FitzWilliams of Dunamore, Rich. Ball of Feydorffe, Jn. Birford of Kilrowe, Js. Lee of Clonresse, Pat. Lee of Licianstown, Jn. Sparke of Ratowthe, Gellouse of Gelloustown, Rich. Fowleing of Parsonstown, Delahoyde of Dunshaghlin, 'and many freeholders.' Rich. Reade of Rowestown, Th. Russel of Cookestown.

Rising out of Ratoath—Barnwall of Kilbrye in person 1 armed horseman, Berford of Kilrowe 1 ditto; Ichers of Dunshaughlin; Talbot of Robertston 2; Weafy of the Blackehil 2 armed horsemen.

Scrine—Baron of Killeen, Sir Rob. Dillon, Wil. Nugent, Baron of Scrine; Pat. Tankard of Castletown, Pat. Brimigham of Corballies; R. Caddell of Dowstown; R. Dillon of Scrine; Ed. Penteny of the Cabbragh; Nich. Cusake of Ballimolchan, Rob. Cusake of Geradstown, Rich. Cusake of Lesmollen, Walter Porter of Kingstown, Jn. Barnwall of Mouncktown, Jn. Barnwall of Cookstown, Mich. Barnwall of Branstown, Nich. Dracot of Oder, Jn. Dracot of , G. Harvy of Scrine, Wal. Evers of Tarraghe, Rob. Pentenie of Jordanstown, Jn. Plunket of Clonardran, Ellen Plunket of Kilcarne.

Rising out of Skreen—The Lord of Killeen, the L. of Dunsany, and the rest of the Plunketts 24; Nicholas Nugent in person 3; M. Draycott 1; Sir T. Cusack of Lismullen in consideration of his absence but 3; Sir C. Cheevers of Measton 4; Bath of Raphesk in person 3; Kent of Daneston 2; Cusack of Gerardston 2; T. Dillon of Riverston 3; P. Dillon 1; Tancred of Castleton 1; The Portriff of Skryne 1.

Duleeke—L. of Gormanstown, L. of Trimletstown, Justice Bath of Athcarne, Rich. Caddell of the Naul, Rob. Caddell of Herbertstown, Jn. Dracott of Normanton, Geo. Darcy of Platten, Rob. Preston of Rogerstown, Talbot of Dardistowne, Rich. Bellame of Donakernie, Rich. Stanley of , Ed. Tallon 'of the same,' R^d Aylmer of Dollardstown, Lawr. Tafe of Ardmolchan,

The Lord Baron of Slane his name
Fleming his chief Hous Slane,
The Lord Baron of Tribleston his name
Barnwall his chief Hous Tribleston.

Jn. Chivers of Mastoston, Chr. Bath of Rathfeigh, Js. Dillon of Ballgath, Jn. Cusake of Cusingstone, Wal. Gowlding of Pierstone, Pat. Moore of Duleek, R$^{d.}$ Plunkett of the Boles, Th. Kent of Dainstown, Th. Hamling of Smithstone, Pat. Whyte of Flemington, the Corporation of Dowleeke, Sir Jn. Bellew of Bellewstown, Sir Ed. Moore ; Birt of Tullock.

Rising out—L. Viscount Gormanston 8 ; Darcy of Platten 3 ; Talbot of Dardiston 3 ; J. Aylmer 2 ; Caddell of the Nall 2; Birt of Tullocke 2; Oliver Darcy 1 ; Holde of Paynestown 1 ; Hambige of Smithstown 1 ; Bath of Colpe 1.

Slane—Baron of Slane, Pat. Fleming of Gernenstown, Garret F. of Loghbracan, Piers F. of Killarie, Rich. F. of Rath-Reynolds, Edw. F. of Lobenstone, Pat. Barnwall of Gernonstown, Barnwall of Rowthstown, Walt. B. of Calcestown, Rob. B. of Starallan, Newterville of Dowth, Jn. Bath of Cashiel, Ivers of Bingerstown, Stookes of Mitchellstown, Lord Lowth of the Carrick, Rob. Mey of Slane, Geo. FitzJones of Slane, Jn. Botford of Protfortstone.

Rising out—Baron of Slane 6 ; Barnwall of Stackallen 4 archer horsemen ; Barnwall of Roweston 2 armed horsemen ; Netterville of Dowth 2.

Margallen—Wil. Fleming of Stephenstone, Jn. Newterville of Castleton, W. Veldon of Raffin, P$^{k.}$ White of Clongell, Pat. Beg of Fleshillstone, Wil. Garvey of Knightstone, Tallon of Wilkenstone, R. Plunket of the same, Th. Darcy of Donmore, Th. Plunket of Possickstone, Jn. Darcy of Rathoode, Jn. Waffer of Kilboy, Hen. Rooe of the same, Js. Veldon of Rathcon, Edmund —— of the Corballies, Jn. FitzJohn of Plainstone, Js. FitzGarret of Drakestone.

Rising out—T. Fleming of Stephenstone 3 ; White of Clongell 2 ; Veldon of Clongell 2.

Navan—Bishop of Meath, Baron of the Novan, Js. Dillon of Moymet, Rob. Rochfort of Kilbrid, Alex. Evers of Rathtain, R$^{d.}$ Bellew of Bellewestown, Jn. Waffer of Gainstown, Js. Warren of Philpottstown, Js. Hill of Allenstown, Jn. Eustace of Lescartan, R^{d} Misset of the same, Geo. Cusake of Rathallrone, Chr. Netterville of Black Castle, Steph. Blackine for Cowlneallven, Warren of Churchtown, W. FitzGarret of Ongestown, Pat. Manning of Hatton, Rob. Fleming of Rathkenny, Th. Teling of Mullagha, Th. Bath of Ladin-Rath, Th. Ashe of Trim, Rob. Hamon of the same, Js. Cusake of Tullegharde, Jasper Staples of Hollanstone, Chr. Birt of Curghton, Darcie

EAST MEATH.

Barnets   The Barnet of Navan his name Nangle his hous at the Navan,
The Barnet of Galtrim his name Hussy His Hous Galtrim,
The Barnet of Scryne his name Nugent his house Scryne.

of Balreske, Sir. Jn. Dillon of Doramestown, Melcher Moore of Escherowean, Th. Luttrell of Tankardstown.

Rising out—Bishop of Meathe 8; the Lord of Trimberton 6; the Baron of Navan 3; the Baron of Dillon 2; Rochford of Kilbride 4; Michael Cusack 2; Ivers of Racaghee 1; The Prortriffe of Trim 3; the Portriffe of Navan 4; Teeling of Mullagha 1; Hill of Allenstown 1; Misset of Laskerton 1; Eustace of Laskerton 1.

Kelles — Barnwall of Robertstown, Betaghe of Moynealty, Hen. Mape of Mape-Rath, Wil. Betaghe of Walterstown, Drake of Drakerath, W^m· Balf of Ardloman, Plunket of Ardmath, Plunket of Tath-Rath, Prountford of Morentstown, Th. FitzJones of Franstone, Hen. Garvey of Rossmine, Sir Pat. Barnwall of Killineighnam and Mitchmore, Alex. Plunket of Gibston, Js. Erwarde of Randallston, Garret Plunket of Preston, Garret Plunket of Irishton, Edw. P. of Ball-Rath, Th. P. of Thistle Keran, Plunket of Balnegin, P. of Robinstone, P. of Bolton, Forde of Fordston, Nic. Gillagh of Gillston, Balf of Ballnegin, Ledwitch of Cookstone.

Rising out of Kells (or Kenlis)— Alexander Barnwall 3; Everard of Randalstown 2; Mape of Mape-Rath 1; Drake of Rathode 2; Betagh of Moynaltie for his County 6; Ledwiche of Cookstown 6; FitzJohn of Fyanstown 1; The Soffreign of Kenlis 2 archers.

Dece—Js. Hussey of Galtrim, Wal. H. of Moylehussey, Rob. H. of Ballrodan, Martin H. of Curmollen, H. of Muchardroms, H. of Cullendragh, Boys of Gallgath, Geo. Garland of Agher, Pat. Barnwall of Arolstone, Rob. B. of Athshe, Barnwall of Killinessan and Athronan '*cum multis aliis*,' Js. Fleming of Derpatrick, Allen and Wiel of Knockmarke, Hen. Waring of Waringston, Rich. Delahoyde of Moyglare, Baron Eliot of Balreske, Th. Widder of Leemaraghstone, Jn. Cusake of Troneblie, R^d· Crumpe of Marshalstown, Jn. Gilsten of Collmollen, R^d, Talbot of Achar, Hen. Usher Ld Primate of Armagh of Balstown, Wal. Golding of Ballendel.

Moyfenragh — R^d· Barnwall of Newcastle, Garret Weslie of the Dengan, Pat. Lince of the Knocke, Hen. Dillon of Little Frefan, Th. Lynam of Adamstown, Rich. Misset of Bedlowstown, Edw. Kindellane of Ballnekill, Peter

The chief Gentlemen

Plunket of Rathmore
Plunket of Ballioth
Plunket of Irishtoune
Plunket of Longcrey
Plunket of Roses
Plunket of Drombar
Plunket of Gybston

Plunket of Fathrath
Plunket of Felten
Plunket of Castlekeren
Plunket of Armaghbeet
Plunket of Clonbrene
Plunket of Dromsaurie
Barnewall of Crickston[i]

Lynam of Frefans, Wm MacEvoy of Balleneskeagh, Edm. Keeting of Possickstown, Christ. Leins of Crobey, Edm. Darcy of Clondaly, R^d Gifford of Castle Jordan, Sir Ed. FitzGerald of Teighcroghan, Gerald FitzGerald of Moylagh, Ed. Aylmer of the same, Pat. Cusake of Clonmaghan, Hen. Burnell of Castle Richard, Edm. Darcy of Jordanstown, Hen. Kinge of Ardnemollen, Gregory Cole of Clonard.

Rising out of Deece and Moyfenragh—The Baron of Galtrim in person 4; Barnwall of Antislon 2; De la Hide of Moyglare 2; Westley of the Dengen 3; Goodall 2; B. Cusacke 1; Fleming of Dirpatrick 1; Mercler Hussey 2; De la Hide of Assye 1.

Lune—Rich. Plunket of Rathmore, Pat. Begge of Moyagher, Martin Blake, Js. Dowdall, Melchior Moore and Robert Misset, all of Athboy; Walter Scurlocke of the Frame, Roger Dillon of Ballenedramey, Jn. Rochfort of Keranston, Rob. R. of Clonekevan, Wal. Lince of Donowre, Wal. Nangle of Kildalkey.

Rising out of Lune—Lynch of Dunmore 1; Rochford of Keranston 1; The Portriff of Athboy 4; Bernaby Sherlock 2.

Fowere—Plunket of Oldcastle, P. of Newcaster, P. of Loughcrew, Chr. P. of Clonebreny, P. of Ballinacaldde, P of Thomastowne, P. of Drumsaurie, Balf of Collmoolestone, Rob. Barnwall of Moylaghoo, Tint (or Tuit?) of Baltraseney, Js. Dowdal of Athboy 'for Oliver Plunkett's lands in Ballegray;' Dardisse of Glevecktoan.

Rising out of Fower—The Plunkets, 24 horsemen; Balfe of Galmoweston 2; Barnwall of Morlow 1; Tuite of Beltrastin 1.

The names according to baronies are taken from *Car. Cal.* 'Perambulation of the Pale' in 1596; the 'Rising out of Meath' *circ.* 1586 is taken from 'the Statistical Survey of Meath.'

[i] There were 30 families named Barnwall who enjoyed considerable estates in Meath and Dublin. Sir Patrick B. of Crickstown brought 4 mounted archers to the general hosting of Tara;

EAST MEATH. 97

Barnewall of Kilbrew
Barnewall of Moylaghe
Barnewall of Roeston
Barnewall of Gerlonstone
Barnewall of Caufelston
Barnewall of Aronston
Barnewall of Flemingston[i]
Barnewall of Crackanston
Barnewall of Robertston
Barnewall of Staffordstone
Cusack of Lismollin[j]
Cusack of Cufyngston
Cusack of Gerardston
Cusack of Rahalion [Rathlion][k]
Cusack of Ballunalheu
Cusack of Trubloy[l]
Cusack of Cloneard
Cusack of Clomochain
Proteford of Protfordston
Tynt of Blayne
Loynes of Cuake
Caddell of the Nall
Caddell of Harberdston
Caddle of Doweston
Ivers of Ratoryn[m]
Luttrell of Tancardston
Bedge of Frencheston
Beedge of Harriston
Whyte of Clongell
Rochforde of Kilbride[n]

he m. a dau. of Sir P. Barnwall of Turvey, and had 5 sons and 3 daughters; his son Richard was m. to a dau. of Sir Oliver Plunket of Rathmore, ancestor of Chief Baron Palles.

John B. of Flemington was m. to Lord Howth's widow; he was a brother of Sir P. Barnwall of Turvey; he made his will in this year 1598.—*Lodge.*

[j] In 1598 Edward C. of Lismullen sold the lands of the Augustinian and Dominican Friars to Roger Jones. These lands are still in the possession of the Lords Essex and De Ros, representatives of Archbishop Jones.

Catherine Cusack of Cushinstown m. Sir H. Colley of Castle Carbery.

[k] On the wayside cross of Nevinstown there is an inscription in beautiful black-letter character. What remains of it runs thus: .... *Armigeri, et Margaretae Dexter uxoris ejus ac heredum eorum qui hanc crucem fecerunt anno Domini* 1588, *quorum animabus propitietur Deus. Amen.*

The *armiger* was found by Mr. J. Huband Smith to be Michael de Cusack, Lord of Portrane and Rathaldron, who got with his wife Margaret Dexter, the castle, town and lands of Rathaldron.

[l] On the southern bank of the Boyne we still find a remnant of the castle of Trubly or Turberville, the ancient seat of the Cusacks. It consisted of a square keep with circular corner towers.

[m] Walter Evers of Bingerstown in Meath was the cousin and executor of Sir W[m]. Taaffe who distinguished himself fighting against O'Neill.—*Lodge.*

[n] Rob. R. of Kilbryde, ancestor of

Veldon of Raffinall
Veldon of Raffen
Newtervile°
Drake of Drakerath
Porter of Kingstone

Wesley of Dingen
Wal of Blackhall
Bath of Rafeig
Justice Bath[p]
Bath of Dewleeke

Lord Belfield, brought 4 archers on horseback to the general Hosting at Tara in 1593 for the barony of Navan and one for that of Ratoath; he m. a dau. of Chief Baron Sir Lucas Dillon, and had 6 sons and 4 daughters. His son and heir, John, was 23 years old in 1598; his sons-in-law were Sir W. Dongan of Castleton Kildrought, and Luttrell of Tancardstown in Meath.—*Lodge.*

° John Netterville of Douth was M.P. for Meath in 1585; he died in 1601; his brother Richard N. of Corballies was a distinguished lawyer, and was M.P. for Dublin in 1585; his wife was a dau. of Sir J. Gernon of Kilmacoole in Louth; his son Nicholas, who was 18 years old in 1598, was made a Viscount in 1622, joined the Confederation of Kilkenny, was outlawed in 1642, and died in 1654, leaving 8 sons, two of whom were Jesuits, and four were Confederate officers. The present Lord is the 8th Viscount. Richard N. was reported by Sydney to Elizabeth to be 'as seditious a varlet and as great an impugner of English government as any this Lande beareth.' He married a dau. of Plunket of Dunsoghly; he died in 1607. — *Lodge and Burke's Peerages.*

[p] The inscription on the Wayside Cross of Athcarne runs thus—*On the front of the pillar*—

'This Cross was builded by Jennet Dowdall, late wife unto William Bathe of Athcarne, justice, for him and for herself, in the year of our Lorde God 1600, which justice deceased the xxv of October 1599, and buried in the church of Duleek, whose souls I praye God take to his Mercie. Amen. I.H.S.'

On the back—'Haile Marie full of Grace, oure Lord is with the. Haile sweet virgin the blessed mother of God, the excellent Queen of Heaven praye for us poore soules. Amen.'—See *Paper of J.H.S. in Proceedings of R.I. Academy.*

In the village of Duleek stands a remarkable Wayside Cross. The inscription on one side is—'This Cross was builded by Genet Dowdall, wife to William Bathe of Athcarne, justice of his Majesty's Court of Common Plees, for him and her, anno 1601. He deceased the 15th of Oct. 1599, buried in the church of Duleek; whose souls I pray God take to his mercie.' On the other side of the Cross are sculptured in relief figures of S[ts.] Andrew, Catherine, Stephen, Patrick,

EAST MEATH. 99

Bath beside Slane
Balf of Colmoleston
Balf of Fidorth
Balf of the Cleggs
Betaghe of Monaltie
Betaghe of Dunowie [Dunamore]
Justice Dillon of Newton
James Dillon of Moynet[q]
Bartholemew Dillon of[r] Riverston
Dillon of Prowdeston
Dillon of Harbeston
Warren of the Navan
Warren of Warrenston

Penteney of Cabragh
Tancard of Castletoune
Tylen of Molashe [Molahac]
Hussey of Adrain
Hussey of Moylaghe
Delahide of Balankey
Delahide of Dunsoghley
Delahide of knockconor
Nugent of Kilcarne
Elmer of Dullerston
Field of Payneston
Kent of Daneston
Chivers of Moreton
Talbot of Robertston
Talbot of Daideston

Kieran, Magdalene, Jacobus, and Thomas.

The bridge of Duleek was erected in 1587 by W[m.] Bathe and Genet Dowdall, as appears from an inscribed tablet inserted in the battlement.—See *Sir W. Wilde's 'Boyne,'* p. 277.

[q] This Sir James D. of Moymet became Earl of Roscommon in 1622; by his wife, Miss Barnwall of Turvey, he had 7 sons and 6 daughters; his son George was a Jesuit of great learning; his great grandson was the poet Earl of Roscommon.—See *Lodge.*

The father of James was Sir Lucas Dillon; he was a distinguished lawyer, and had great experience in military and civil matters; he was called by Sydney *meus fidelis Lucas.* Elizabeth conferred on him and his heirs the office of Seneschal of the Barony of Kilkenny West over the surname of Dillon and other inhabitants thereof. He m. a dau. of Chief Baron Bathe of Athcarne and Drunconragh, and had 7 sons and 5 daughters. He lies buried under a noble monument in Newtown; it is an altar tomb, on which are the recumbent figures of Sir Lucas and his lady, and it is adorned with the arms of Dillon, Bathe, and Barnwall.—*Lodge, and Sir W. Wilde's ' Boyne.'*

[r] Ancestor of Sir J. Dillon, Bart. of Lismullen, Baron of the Holy Roman Empire. Bartholomew was son of Chief Justice Sir R. Dillon and m. a dau. of Sir W. Sarsfield of Lucan; he was 25 years old in 1598 and distinguished himself against Tyrone—See *Lodge.*

Talbot of Agher
Tirrell of Johnston
Beerford of Kylbrowe
Bedlow of Bedlowston [5]
Sale of Saleston
Hill of Allenston
Phepoe of the Rovan
Scurlock of Kilmarton [1]
Lee of Clomesse
Fleming of Derpatrick
Flc. of Sedon

Flc. of Baligatlan
Flc. of Kilrory
Flc. of Stevinston
Fitz John of Franston
Dorran [Derran] of Derranston
Wafer of Grunston
Misset of Lascarten
Eustace of the same
Clinch of the Scryne
Arward of Randolfeston
Darcy of Dounmow

[5] Sir J. Bellew owned the manors of Bellewstown and Duleek, etc. He was in 1563 a Commissioner for the Preservation of the Peace in Drogheda and all Louth during the L. Deputy's Expedition against Shan O'Neill. In 1584 he and his wife Ismay Nugent built the bridge of Ballycorry in Westmeath where an Inscription still remains stating them to be the founders, and asking the Prayers of all who pass by. He and Dame Ismay erected the East window in the Church of Duleek; and also a 'Monument for their burial' in Duleek churchyard. In 1598 he made his Will, in which he says: 'To the intent that my heirs may be and shall continue dutiful subjects to her Majesty and her successors, Kings and Queens of England and Ireland, my will is that I demise... said Manors... to my sons Christopher, John, and Richard with these conditions that whensoever and as often as the said Christopher etc. shall, or do imagine, practice, compass, assent, go about, conclude, determine, commit, deal or execute any treason whatsoever, the Interest of such person and his heirs shall cease...'

Sir John's brother, Richard of Stamen, was M.P. for Dundalk in 1585; he died in 1616. Sir Christopher B. of Bellewstown m. a dau. of Sarsfield of Lucan, and died in 1610. He had 4 sons and 2 daughters. His heir was 27 years old in 1598. His son Robert owned Donemore. James B. was Mayor of Dublin in 1598.—*Lodge.*

[1] Barnaby Scurlock of Frayne in Meath m. a dau. of Sir T. Nugent of Moyrath, and died in 1633, leaving 4 sons and 6 daughters. Of this family was Barnaby Scurlock, who was reported to Elizabeth by Sydney as having 'purchased more and builded more than ever his father did; his chief mean to get this was by being attorney to your sister and yourself. From which office he was displaced; since which time he never ceased to impugn Inglishe

Darcy of Plattin
Moore of Uskerower
Moore of Mooreston
Black of Athboy
Tallon of Wilkinston
Gerald of the Rath"
Map of Mapston
Map of Maprath
Hamlen of Smythston
Cromp of Muchalton
Foord of Foordston

Lynch of the knock
Eliot of Baliesko
Russell of Cookeston
Telincs of Telinston
Dillon of Balinderomny
Cardiff of Flemingston
Ledwich of Cookeston
Bremingham of Corbally
Whyte of Flemingston
Foster of ^v
Usher of Balsound

government, and in especial your Majesty's Prerogatives.' Wherefore, when Scurlock went to England, he was imprisoned in the Fleet.—*Lodge.*

The castle of Scurlogstown was one of the strongest built watch-towers of the Pale—its massive and gloomy walls, its tall towers and unbroken battlements give it such a stern appearance that in passing it one still expects to hear the warders challenge from its gate.—*Sir W. Wilde's ' Boyne.'*

" Sir Edw. FitzGerald of Tecroghan in Meath m. Miss Barnwall of Turvey; his son, Sir Luke, m. a dau. of Viscount Netterville. Sir Edward was a distinguished man. The Jesuit Father, Christopher Holywood, under the *nom de plume* of John Geraldine, dedicated to his cousin (cognatus), Sir Edw. FitzGerald, his work *De Meteoris*, published in 1613—' Ornatissimo Viro D. Edwardo Geraldine de Teacrochane, Equiti aurato, bonorum ac literatorum patrono optimo . . . Cui, quaeso potiore jure quam tibi debetur, qui multis magnisque rebus, non sine multorum admiratione, domi forisque praeclare gestis, amplissima virtutis tuae testimonia exhibuisti, ita ut Familiae Nostrae Geraldinorum, post Illustrissimum Heroem, Kildariae comitem, fatali quodam nostro malo ereptum, lumen et columen habearis.'

^v Gerald Foster of Kilgrage—*Usher MSS.* (E. 4, 33). Prountford of Mounstowne.—*Car. Cal.* From the Carew and Clongowes MSS. we have the names of about 250 gentlemen of Meath. 'In Meath the son and heir of Sir William Nugent was in Rebellion, and the county, lying in the heart of the Pale, was greatly wasted by the Ulster Rebels, and many Castles lay waste without inhabitants; but no Rebels possessed either town or castle therein. At Kells and Navan Lord Dunsany has 50 horse and Sir G. Moore 25. There are 1700 f. under Lords Audley and Dunsany, Sir F. Conway and Sir

102   STATE OF IRELAND ANNO 1598.

Harvey of Odder Dracot of Marranston
Prenderfoote of ˅ Bysse of

THE COUNTIE OF WESTMEATH.

This Countie[a] contayneth all land from the red moore beyond Aboy to the river of the Sheynen by delven McCoghlan and in bredth from the King's Countie to the Countie of Longford comprehending all McGeoghaghans, McCawles, and Omelaughlines Countries. So hath it the King's Countie East and South, the Sheynen and part of the Countie of Longford West, and the Countie of Cavan and part of the Countie of Meath north.[b]

Townes   Mollingare governed by a Portrise, lately often burned.

Market Townes   Fower   Castletoune Delvin
Kilkenny West   Rawyre
Athloane   ~~Delvin~~ (*sic*)
Ballimore

[a] C. St Lawrence, Sir H. Dockora, Sir J. Chamberlaine, Syney, Sydley, Atkinson, Heath, Nelson, and Hugh Reilly. At Trim there are 50 h. under Sir Griffin Markham, and 400 f. under Sir C. Piercy, Orme, and Alford. At Athboy 260 f. under Sir R. Moryson. —*Moryson*, p. 43.

[a] *Hall* dismisses this county in half a page, and then says—'The limits of our work will not permit us to describe at length the counties which have no very peculiar feature; and we avail ourselves of the opportunity presented to us for supplying some information concerning Irish music'!

[b] In 1543 an Act of Parliament was passed, in the preamble of which we read, 'For the division of Methe into two shires, (because) the shire of Methe is great in circuit, and the west parte thereof laid about and beset with divers of the Kings rebells, and in several partes thereof the King's writs for lacke of ministration of justice, have not of late been obeyed, ne his Grace's lawes put in due exercise.'—See p. 270 of *Grand Juries of Westmeath*.

Castles and good Houses { Killean the Lord of Delvins chief Hous, Castle tounc delvin belonging to him also, Rawyre, belonging to the Earle of Kildare, Tristinaughe, a faire Abbey belonging to Henrie Pierce,[c] Waterston to one of the Dillons, Tuiteston to William Tuit, and many others belonging to the Several Surnames of

Nugents[d] Tyrrells[f]
Darcies[e] Daltons[g]

[c] Ancestor of Sir E. F. Piers, Bart., of Tristernagh Abbey. This Henry P. married a dau. of Dr. Jones, Protestant Archbishop of Dublin, and had 4 sons and 6 daughters; he was a distinguished traveller, and left behind him an account of his travels, which was placed among 'the Ware MSS.' He became a Catholic, and prevailed on some of his children to embrace the same faith; one of his sons became a Franciscan, and a grandson became a secular priest. H. Piers d. in 1623. His father, W[m] P., got 1000 marks for bringing in the head of Shan O'Neil, who was murdered by the Scots.—*Burke's Peerage.*

[d] *Barony of Delvin.* — Delvin the chief town is possessed by the L. of Delvin. His chief house is called Clonin. Other towns are Dromcree, Teghmon, and Ballenemonoe; a great sept of the Nugents inhabit this barony.

The half barony of Fowre.—The chief town, Fowre; it is inhabited by the Nugents, and the chief gentleman is the owner or heir of Corolanstown.

Barony of Corkry. — Multifernan, the chief town, is inhabited by the Nugents, of whom the best is Richard Nugent of Denewear.

The barony of Moyhassel.—Possessed by the Nugents and Tutes, 'of whom the principal is Chr. Nugent of Dardeston, and Edw. Tute, late slain in Connaught, of Killenan.'—*Car. Cal.* p. 192.

[e] *Barony of Ferbilly.*—Rathwire, the chief towne, the Earl of Kildare's. 'The Darcies be possessioners there.'

[f] *Barony of Fertullagh.*—Inhabited by the Tirrells, of whom Sir John Tirrell is chief. His house is called the Pace. Newcastle is held partly by Rich. Nugent, and partly by Will. Tirrell FitzMorice.

[g] *Bar. of Rathconred*, called the Dalton's country.—Chief town, Ballymore Lough Swedy, Francis Shane's; at Dondonnell, Hen. Dalton; at Milton, the heirs of Rich. Dalton; Edm. Dalton of Mollinmighan; Peter Nangle of

STATE OF IRELAND ANNO 1598.

Dillons,[h]
Delamaies,
Petits,[i]
Hop's,
Geraldins,
Tuites,[j]

Omelaghlins,[k]
McGeoghaghans,[l]
Coffies,
McGawlies,[k]
O birnes.

It hath many goodlie Loughes and marshes of freshe Water of great quantities, whereof the greatest part fall into the Sheynan, above Athloane and the rest into the River of Brosenaghe which also falleth into the Sheynan beneath Athloane not farr from Melick.

It hath no noble-men in it, but onlie the Baron of Delvin, whose name is Nugent, and is under the Bishop of Meath as Ordinarie thereof, whereunto is latelie united by Parliament the little Bushoprick of Cloine McKnoshe in Omeloughlines Countrie.

Bishopstown; Francis Shane of Killare.—*Car. Cal.*

[h] *Bar. of Kilkenny*, called Maghery-Cork or Dillon's country.—Kilkenny-the-West, possessed by James Dillon, son and heir to the late Sir Lucas Dillon, Chief Baron. The inhabitants for the most part are Dillons. Captain Tibbot Dillon dwelleth at Killenfaghney.

[i] *Barony of Maghery Dernan.*—Inhabited by the Petits, Tutes, and some of the Nugents. The chief of the Petits, called Thomas, at Irishetowne. 'Tutestown, the best Tutes; and Welchetown, Edward Nugent's.'

[j] *Bar. of Moyoise.*—Chief inhabitants, Tute of the Sunnagh, Piers of Triscornagh; R^d Nangle of Ballycorky, and Js. FitzGerald of the Laragh.—See also notes (¹) and (ᵈ).

[k] *Bar. of Clonlonan*, called O'Molaghlin's country.—Chief towns, Clonlonnan, Newcastle, and Kilgarvan possessed by the O'Molaghlins. Calry held by Magawle; 'the chief is Balliloghlow.' The Karne held by William MacGawle, Brawne-O'Burney is annexed to Athlaon—*Car. Cal.*, p. 192.

[l] *Bar. of Moycassell.*—Inhabited by the Magoghegans: Bryan at Donewer; Hugh, now sheriff, at Castletown; Art at Ballyconin; Con at Syonan; the heir of Thomas at Larath; and the heirs of Rosse Magoghegan, who hold Killuber, Moycassell, Lismoyne, Knockcosger, and the Abbey of Kilbeggan.—*Perambulation of the Pale* in 1596.—*Car. Cal.*

Chief Gent. in Nugent of Moyrath[m]   Nug. of Dromcree[p]
Westmeath   Nug. of Carlandston[n]   Nug. of the Disart[q]
                Nug. of Dunnore[o]   Nug. of Colambre[r]

[m] Sir Christopher N. of Moyrath in Meath and Farrow in Westmeath, was son of Sir Thomas N. M.P. for Westmeath in 1561 and of a daughter of Lord Delvin; in 1601 he married Miss Luttrell of Luttrellstown, he died in 1619 and was buried in Taghmon Church. His son, Sir Francis, became a Capuchine Friar; his son Sir Thomas, born in 1598, became a Baronet; his great grandson, Colonel Sir Thomas N. followed James II. to France.—*Lodge,* and *The Grand Juries of Westmeath.*

[n] Edmond N. of Carlanstown in Westmeath, grandson of Sir Thomas N. married first a d. of Lord Killeen and secondly a Miss Cusack. His son Robert became Confederate governor of Westmeath in 1642.

[o] Richard N. of Donour married in 1580 a dau. of Sir C. Barnwall of Crickstown and died 1616. On the large stone in the wall of the Church of Multifernan is the inscription—
"Sumptibus Jaco. Nugent
    Filii Rich. Nug. de Don-
    ower, qui ob. 18 Feb. Ao
    Dni 1615. W. N. B. N."
Richard's brother, Christopher N. of Clonlost d. 1613; his eldest son James was 25 years old in 1598. The present M[r] Nugent of Clonlost was High Sheriff of Westmeath in 1855.
Sir Walter G. Nugent, Bart., of Donore is maternally descended from this family, his ancestor Piers Fitzgerald, Esq., having m. a sister of Sir P. Nugent, second Baronet of Donore. —*Grand Juries of Westmeath,* and *Burke's Peerage.*

[p] Lavalin N. of Drumcree d. in 1610, leaving six sons, the eldest of whom, Nicholas, was forty years old and married to a Miss Birmingham; and four daughters, one of whom was m. to James Ledwyche of the Grange in Westmeath. From this family are descended the Nugents of Streamstown. —*Grand Juries of Westmeath.*

[q] Edward N. of Dysert and Tullaghan was Knight of the Shire for Westmeath with Edw. N. of Morton in 1585. He married a dau. of the Great O'Connor Offaley, and had two sons, Sir Robert and Andrew, the latter of whom was 18 years old in 1598. From this family are descended maternally the O'Reillys of Ballinlough.

Sir Robert was seated at Ballybranagh; he had a pardon granted to him in 1608, and dying in 1620 was succeeded by his brother Andrew, who was then 44 years old, and m. to a dau. of O'Ferrall of Mornin. On the death of John Nugent, Governor of Tortola, the Nugent property passed to his nephews Sir Hugh O'Reilly of Ballinlough, and A. Savage of Portaferry, both of whom assumed the name of Nugent. The family is now

Nugent of Doneames
Nug. of the Carne[s]
Nug. of moreton[t]
Nug. of Balrath
Nug. of Killaughe
Nug. of Ballneaghe
Nug. of Balliconiell
Nug. of Castlemollen

Nug. of Newcastle
Nug. of Bracklan[u]
Fitzsimons of Tallinall
Golding of Archertone
Frances Shaen of Ballimore
Whyte of Belletston
Dardrefe of Gibbonston
Darcy of Ratlen[v]

represented in the female line by Lord Talbot of Malahide, Sir C. Nugent of Ballinlough, and Colonel Nugent of the Scots Greys, owner of Portaferry.

[r] James N. of Coolamber, brother of the 8th Lord Delvin, d. in 1603; his heir, Edmund, then of full age, died that year also. A member of this family became Count de Valdesoto and Major-General in the Imperial service, another was murdered while Commandant of Prague in 1720; another was 26 years in the service of Venice, General of its Troops in Dalmatia, Governor of Verona, etc.— *Lodge.*

[s] A branch of the family of Drumcree. —*Lodge.*

[t] Edward N. of Morton was Knight of the shire for Westmeath in 1585.

[u] Edward N. of Bracklyn d. in 1599; his wife was Ismay Barnwall. From this N. was maternally descended Field Marshal N. of Austria. N. of Carlanstown was ancestor of Earl Nugent. See in the Appendix an account of some religious of that name.

[v] Descended from Lord D'Arcy, Viceroy of Ireland in 1324, whose grandson, Sir Wm. D. of Platten, carried Simnel on his shoulders through Dublin, after the coronation in Christ Church. Another descendant of Lord D. wrote *The Decay of Ireland.*

The attainders of 1642 present the names of Nich. D. of Platten, who attended the great meeting at the hill of Crofty; D. of Ballymount co. Kildare, and D. of Athlumney in Meath. Among the attainted in 1691 were the Darcies of Platten, of Porterstown, and Corbetstown co. Westmeath. The D. of Platten in 1598 was George D. son of Christopher and a dau. of Sir H. Draycot. George's grand-uncle settled at Dunmow, and on the attainder and forfeiture of the D. of Platten in 1696, and on the extinction of that line, George D. of Dunmow became the head of the race; in 1693 he was declared an 'innocent papist;' he entertained as guests on two successive days Kings James and William; and is said to have pronounced his policy in the lines—

'Who will be King I do not know ;
But I'll be D'Arcy of Dunmow.'

THE COUNTIE OF WESTMEATH.

Darcy of Clonecollain
Tuit of Killenan
Tuit of Mollenlyeth[w]
Tuit of Sonnaghe[x]
Petit of Mollingare[y]
S[r] John Tirrell of the Pace
Tirrell of Baloebrack
Water moyle Tirrell of Fertullaghe

Water Tirrell of Kilbride[z]
M[c]Geoghaghan of Larra
M[c]Geog. of Robinstown
M[c]Geog. of Moyhassell
M[c]Geog. of S. *(sic)*
M[c]Geog. of Kiltober
M[c]Geog. of Parres
Bryan M[c]Geoghaghan

Mr. D'Arcy of Hyde Park, Westmeath, is the present representative of the D. of Platten, and Dunmow.—*Westmeath Grand Juries.*

[w] Theobald T. of Monilea, m. a dau. of Aylmer of Lyons; he died in 1632.

[x] Oliver T. of Sonagh was b. about 1588, m. a dau. of Aylmer of Donadea; he was made a Baronet in 1622. Sir Mark A. H. Tuite is the 10th Baronet. Walter T. of Tuitestown, grandson (by his mother) of Sir Oliver, and grandson (by his father) of T. of Monilea, m. a dau. of O'More of Port Allen, and had thirteen sons, eleven of whom fell in the campaign of 1691.—*Lodge*, Vol. iii., p. 37. From this Walter was descended the famous French preacher Father Nicholas Tuite McCarthy, of the Society of Jesus.

[y] William P. styled Baron of Mullingar; his dau. was married to a son of the Lord of Drumraney, and had a son Edmund alive in 1611.—*Lodge*, Vol. iv., p. 170.

[z] There was also Edward T. of Caverstown, and John T. of Clonmoyle. Eight Tyrrels were attainted in Westmeath in 1691.

'I could not obtain much information respecting this family. The Tyrrell property has long since passed to other hands, and the name is here extinct,' says the author of *Grand Juries of Westmeath*, p. 317.

Sir John T. was 'the chief of the Tyrrells;' there was also William Tyrrell FitzMorrice of Newcastle.—*Car. Cal.*, p. 192. Perhaps he was the 'Captain Wiliam T. of the Irish,' who was wounded at the battle of the pass of Cashel, where part of Captain Richard T.'s men were engaged. O'Sullevan mentions a Water T., who, with Thomas Plunket commanded 580 men at the battle of Rower, which Desmond and M[c]Carthy fought with Essex. One of the Tyrrells was suspected of having been bribed to let Essex pass unmolested through a defile. The most distinguished of the T.'s was 'Captain Tyrrell;' Mountjoy wrote to Cecil that, 'next to Tyrone he was the most dangerous, being the most

McGeoghaghan of Castletowne[aa]

efficient soldier, and of the greatest reputation through all Ireland, and better able to perform anything in this country than any Captain they have ;' O'Sullevan calls him a veteran soldier, well skilled in war ; the *Four Masters* style him ' Captain Tirial (*Risderd mac Tomais mic Risdeird*).' See some details about him in the *Introduction* to this book.

[aa] ' Mag Eochagain, Lord of Kinalea, namely, Connla, son of Conor, son of Laighne, son of Connla, son of Hugh, died in 1588; his son Brian, and (his grandson) Niall, the son of Ross, were in contention with each other for the Lordship of the territory.' Niall's brother was Captain Risderd (son of Ross, son of Conla), the gallant defender of Dunboy, who was mortally wounded, and was slain while staggering to blow up the beseigers and the beseiged. O'Sullevan says of him ' Dux Ricardus M. vir nobilis, cujus animi magnitudo cum generis claritate de principatu contendebat.' 'So obstinate and resolved a defence hath not been seene within this Kingdome,' says the *Pacata. Hib.* p. 318, Ed. 1633.

At one time the M.'s were chiefs of Kinel Fiacha (the Barony of Moycashel with parts of Moyashell, Rathconrath and Fertullagh); they had various castles, the chief of which was Castletown Geoghegan. In 1328 the M.'s beat the English army, putting 3500 of them *hors de combat*.

Elizabeth directed a letter to her Deputy, of which the following extracts are of interest :—' Whereas Conley Mac Geoghegan...humbly submitted himself ...offering to surrender his estate for him and his sequele...we...are pleased to accept him as our liege man and faithful subject... 1° he is to deliver a full and pleyne particular note and extent of all the manors, castells, lordshipps, lands, tenements, seigniories, rules, rents duties, customs, and commodities whereof he is seized at present,' etc. —See *Hardiman's Iar Connacht*.

Conly M. had by his third wife (dau. of Lord Delvin), Hugh *buidhe*, ' the yellow,' who died in 1622, leaving a son, Art of Castletown, from whom is descended Mr. O'Neill of Bunowen Castle, whose father changed the name of Geoghegan to that of O'Neill.

In the ''41 wars,' three M.'s lost their lands in Kildare; Art M. lost 1500 acres and Castletown in Kinalea. In the Council of the Confederates, Doctor M. sat among the spiritual peers; in the Commons were Conly and Charles of Donore, Edward of Tyroterim, and Richard of Moycashel. Conly was one of seven sons of Hugh Buy M. by a dau. of W. Tyrrell of Clonmoyle ; by the Act of Settlement he was restored to his principal seat, and to 2000 acres of land. The Inquisitions of 1691 contain the Outlawries of the Mageoghegans of Newtown, Carrymare, Lougharlaghnought,

Bremingham of Milton
Bremingham of Balleuirton
Fitzgerrald[bb] of Am

Fitzgerrald of
Dillon of A.[cc]

Laragh, Donore, and Syonan. On the *magna panella* in 1703 we find in the Barony of Moycashel—Edrus and Hugh Geoghegan de Castletown, Gent. Bryan G. de Donore, Arm. Carolus G. de Syonan, Gent. Rich. G. de Ballybrechey,Gent. Jac. G. de Killour, Gent. Jac. G. de Ballyduffe, Gent.—*Grand Juries of Westmeath.*

Sir R. Nagle, Bart. of Westmeath inherited the property of the last chief of the Mageoghagans, from whom he was maternally descended; and had in his possession a compact written in Irish on parchment, and made by M. chief of Kinalea, and The Fox chief of Muinterhagan; it is dated 20th Aug. 1526, and by it M. was to be Lord over The Fox. It is is printed in Vol. i. of *Ir. Arch. Miscel.*

[bb] There were sixty FitzGeralds attainted in 1642; in Meath there were six, including F. of Tecroghan and F. of Rathrone. James C. Fitzgerald Kenny, Esq., of Kilclogher, co. of Galway, is the representative and heir general of the F. of Tecroghan and Rathrone. In 1691 seventeen F. were attainted in Westmeath. F. of Larah fought at the Boyne; after that he went to France. A dau. of F. of Pierstown (by his wife *née* Miss F. of Laragh) m. Dillon of Streamstown and Killinynen, in the territories of Dalton and Mageoghegan—Dillon d. in 1640.—*Westmeath Grand Juries*, and *Lodge*, Vol. iv., 159.

[cc] Edmund D. of the castle of Ardnegragh m. a dau. of O'Farrell, Lord of Callow, and had several sons, who were distinguished in the Army, Church, and State; his brother, Garret D. of Portlick Castle, was Captain of an independent company; his third brother was Sir Tibbot, who became First Viscount Dillon, of Castello Gallen. Tibbot commanded an independent troop; he was knighted on the field in 1559, he mar. a dau. of Sir E. Tuite of Tuitestown, and had 8 sons and 11 daughters, ; his 4th son, Thomas, was born in the Tower of London; the 5th and 6th became Franciscans; his 8th and 9th daughters became nuns of St. Clare and established a convent in Galway. Sir Tibbot died in 1624 at so advanced an age that at one time he saw assembled in his house of Killenfaghey above a hundred of his descendants. From him were descended the famous D.'s, of the Irish Brigade, '*nom célèbre dans les troupes Irelandaises*,' says Voltaire; and Dillon, Archbishop of Narbonne and 'Primate of the Gaules.'—See *Lodge*, Vol. iv. Colonel H. Dillon was M.P. for Westmeath in 1689, and had 15 officers named Dillon in his regiment.

Gerald D. Lord of Drumrany, by his wife, a dau. O'Conor Faly, had a

Dillon of Waterston
Dillon of Canerston
Dalton of Milton
Dalton of Dundanell[dd]
Dalt. of Mull[ee]
Dalton of
Hubert Dalton
Edmond Dalton

Delamaire[ff] of the Street
Ledwich of Ballinelock[gg]
Nangle of Ballinecorby[hh]
Nangle of Bishopstowne
Water Nangle
Walshe of Collanhroe
Evrell [Uriell] of Ballvomen
McGawlie[ii]

son James, a priest; a dau. Bridget a nun; and a second son Thomas, who married the sister of the 1st Viscount Dillon, and whose eldest son became a friar, and whose second son, Gerald, succeeded as Lord of Drumrany.

John D. of Low Baskin, grandson of Dillon of Drumrany, married a dau. of Sir John Hugan of co. of Kilkenny, Knt. and had two dau. and nine sons; his dau. Jane m. Dalton of Dalystown who died in 1636; three of his sons became priests.—*Lodge*, p. 152-168.

[dd] In 1636 died John Dalton of Dundonell, son and heir of Hubert D. He was the great great grandfather of D'Alton, who published *King James' Army List*, and other works, and who had some of the ancestral property. The attainders of 1691 include 17 Daltons of Westmeath. This family has given some distinguished officers to the continental armies.—See *King James' Army List*, p. 376.

[ee] Of Mollinmighan.—See note ([e]).

[ff] The Delamares had very extensive property before 1641. Peter D. served as Sheriff of Westmeath in 1773; he died without issue in 1805. He possessed the estates of Killeen, Knightswood, and Rathlavanagh.—*Westmeath Grand Juries*.

Theobald and William D. were among the Catholic gentlemen of Westmeath who signed a petition to the King in 1605. About 1407 Baron D. of Delamare's country married a dau. of the Lord of Drumrany.

[gg] Ledwich of Ballinalack was attained in 1691, and so was L. of Knockmory; the L. were benefactors to the Abbey of Tristernagh.

[hh] Ballycorky—*Car. Cal.* The Attainders of 1691 comprise the Nangles of Kildalky, Harberston, Navan, Mayne, and Kilmihill.

[ii] Of Balliloghlow—*Car. Cal.* Ballyloughloe was for centuries the chief seat of Magawley, Chief of Calry. One vault of his castle still remains. The late Count Magawley of Frankford, King's Co. was the last of this family that lived in Ireland.—*Notes to Irish Topogr. Poems*, p. xi.

The Emperor Charles VI. conferred upon Field Marshal Magawly, who married Margaret d'Este of Austria

W^m· more McGawlie
Obirne^kk
Edmond O'Brenan^ll
Edmond O'Byrne
Dionise O'Byrne
Moore of Rosemeane
Phypo of Huskinston
Adams of Fower

Casies of Fower
Dungan of Fower
Freines
Hamons of Mollingare
Hacklee of Killallon
Porter of Porterston
Russell of Russellston^mm

the dignity of Count of the Holy Roman Empire, and the rank and privileges of a grandee of Spain. The direct male representative of this family is Count Magawly-Cerati, whose grandfather was regent of the Duchies of Parma, Placentia, and Guastalla *circ.* 1812.—*Burke's Peerage.*

^kk O'Breen (*o'Braoin*) was chief of the territory of Brawney, which is now a barony; he lived at the castle of Creeve, in the barony of Clonlonan.— See *Ir. Arch. Miscel.* Vol. i., p. 195.

^l The names of the Westmeath Catholic Gentlemen annexed to the Petition of 1605 were: Edw. Brenaent; Wil. and Rob. Moore; Richard, Larkin, Edward, Nich., Walter, Christ. and Rob. Nugent; Theobald Dillon; J. Terrell; W. Browne; J. FitzGerald; Garret Fay; Edw. and Piers Ledwich; Th. Petit; D. Kyrane; Thomas and J. Dalton; Wil. and Theobald Delamare; Piers Nangle and R. Golding.—*Car. Cal.*

It is surprising that we do not find the names of Dease and Malone. In 'Cusack's Book' written in 1511, there is in the 'Baronia de Fower' Richard Dees of Turbitstown; in the *magna panella* of 1703 is found Jacobs Dease de Turbottstowne, Gent. Malone of Ballynahown married a dau. of Dalton of Milltown; his son Edmund m. a daughter of Coghlan, Esq. in 1599; they were ancestors of Anthony Malone, a distinguished lawyer, and of Lord Sunderlin.—*Lodge*, Vol. vii., p. 282.

The Malones were located in the barony of Brawney and Clonlonan, and eight of them are mentioned by the *Four Masters* as Abbots or Bishops of Clonmacnoise.

^mm There was a Patrick Fox of Moyvore in Westmeath, who had three sons, Nathaniel, Teig, and Garrett; he d. in 1618. Nathaniel was Knighted, and got the lands and Castle of Rathreagh, in Longford. A monument erected to him in the church near his Castle, bears the inscription: 'Hic Jacet Nathaniel Fox de Rathreogh, Armiger, Hujus templi fundator; imago, filius et haeres Patricii Fox de Moyuor in comitatu Westmediae, Militis, qui uxorem habuit Elizabetham filiam Walteri Hussy de Moyhussy Armigeri; ex ea genuit 8 filios et 5 filias, e quibus 8 filii et tres filiae super-

Of this Countie all the Omelaughlines,[nn] all the M⸱cGeoghaghans saving Two or three many of the Tirrells and M⸱cGawlies and some of the Nugents are entered into Rebellion, they will not all make above 400 Men, their chief head in any enterprise is Capten Tyrrell, otherwise everie Companie is lead by the chief of their own Nation. They wast all the Counties of Westmeath, King's Countie and Kildare, and Stop up the way betwixt Dublin and Conaught, which in tyme will prove the Loss of the province of Conaught.

stites sunt; Patricius praedicti Nath. filius et haeres, uxorem habet Barbaram, filiam Nobilissimi Domini Patricii Plunket, Baron de Dunsany; Idem Nath. et Elizabetha in sancto conjugii statu 25 an. vixerunt, et obiit apud Rathreogh 2 Februarii, an. 1634 aet. suae 46.'

His descendant is R. Fox, Esq., of Foxhall in Longford.—See *Westmeath G. Juries.*

[nn] The O'Molaughlines.—See note ([k]) p. 104. In Westmeath, lying for the most part waste, the O'Molaughlines and the Magoghegines, many of the Nugents, and some Geraldines, make 140 f. and 20 h; Capten Tyrrell 200 men, of whom 20 are horse. It is inhabited by many great Septs, as the O'Maddens, the Magoghegans, O'Molaghlens and MacCoghlans, which seeme such barbarous names.—*Car. Cal.;* and *Moryson.* Part III. p. 158, Part II. p. 31.

O'Melaghlin was King of Ireland, but was deposed by Brien Boroimhe; the O'Melaghlins were one of the five septs who had the privilege of using the English lawes. In the time of James I. the lands of O'M. were given to Clanricarde and Blundell. In Dillon's Infantry, in the time of James II. there was a Lieutenant O'M. The *Four Masters* record the names and deeds of one hundred of this royal family. The last entries are—'Nial, son of Phelim O'M.' tanist of Clan Colman, a prosperous and warlike man, and the best man of his age belonging to his tribe, was (in 1553) slain by O'M.' In 1557 'the castle of Rachra was demolished by O'M.; after which war broke out between M⸱cCoghlan and O'M.'

There were 750 f. at Mullingar under L. Delvin, Dillon, Mynne, Stafford, Lionel Ghest, Winsor and Cooche.

THE COUNTIE OF LONGFORD.

This Countie is a large quantitie of Land possessed by a people called the O'Ferralls,[a] and was in former tymes devided into 2, the Strongest of that Surname, the one which possessed the South part thereof, call Offerrall Bwy, or yallew O'Ferrall, the other Offerrall bane or Whyte Offerrall; which Two Surnames and Capitencies conjoined do make up this Countie. It hath the River of Sheynen and part of the Countie of Leitrim to the West, the Countie of Westmeath to the East and South, and the Countie of Dublin to the North. There is no Freeholders in it but the race of the O'Ferralls, saving of late one of the Nugents and one of the Nangles, and of the Dillons and Frances Shaen have *free* [Fee] farms and Leases of religious lands.

They yeald to the Quene for all ceasses £200 by year which was given to Sr Nic. malbee and his heyres males.

---

[a] 'Longford, seu Anale, a numerosa gente o'Pharoll colitur, e qua sunt duo dynastae; alter ad austrum dictus o'Pharoll Boy, i.e., Flavus; alter ad septentriones, o'Pharoll Ban, i.e., Candidus. Angli autem inter illos admodum pauci, et illi jampridem ingressi.'— Letterpress prefixed to *Janson's Map of Connaught*, published in 1610.

When William O'F. died in 1445, one chief, Rosse, was supported by the Clan Murtogh, and Donal was put forward by the Clan Hugh, and Clan Shane; after much bloodshed Annaly was divided between the two rivals. About the middle of the 16th century there were five branches—The O'F. Buidhe was Lord of Upper Annaly; the O'F. Bane was Lord of Lower Annaly; the Clan Muircheartaigh O'F. of Annaly; Clan Alave O'F. of Moydow near Sliev Goudry, the place of Inauguration of the O'F.; the Clan Hugh O'F. chiefs of Killoe.—*Cronelly's Irish Families.*

In 1615—17,904 acres were allotted to strangers, 13,000 to members of the O'F. families, and the rest, in parcels, to old inhabitants. In 1641 the whole county, with the exception of the Castle of Longford, and Castle Forbes, was seized by the O'F.; but at the close of that war it was nearly confiscated and distributed among new proprietors.— *Parliamentary Gazetteer* of Ireland, in the Article on Longford.

STATE OF IRELAND ANNO 1598.

Castles in this Countie.[b]
Longford belonging to the Quene.
Granard belonging to S[r] Frances Shaen.[c]

Chief Gentlemen. { Offarrell Bwy.[d]
Offarrell bane.[e]
Fergus Offarell.[f]

The B. of Ardagh, Uriall Offarrell, } Sonnes to O'Farrell
Roric Offarrell, } Bwy.
Terg Offerrall.

[b] The principal old castles which remain, either in whole or in part, are Granard, Tenalick, Castle-Cor, Rathcline, and Ballymahon.—*Imperial Gaz. of Ireland.* O'*Donovan*, in his Letters on the Antiquities of Longford, mentions the castles of Mornin, Ardandra, Cammagh, Castlereagh, Moat Farrell, Bawn, and Ballinclare.—*MSS. R. I. Academy.*

[c] He was Knighted in 1602; he was a member of the sept of Clan-Shane O'Farrell; he obtained considerable grants of land from the Crown, and successfully exposed great corruption in the Surveyors', Escheators', and Patent Offices in Dublin. He was M.P. for Galway in 1605.—*O'Donovan's* Preface to *Tribes of Ireland*, p. 25.

[d] The representatives for Longford in 1585 were William O'F. Bane, and Fachtna O'F. Boy.

[e] O'F. of Ballintober, son of O'F. Bane, was married to a dau. of the 2[d] Viscount Mountgarrett.—*Lodge.*

[f] In 1599 Fergus O'F. died, and his death was the cause of lamentations in his own territory.—*Four Masters.*

The 3rd L. of Upper Ossory, who succeeded to the title in 1581, had a son, Geffry of Ballyrahin, who married a dau. of Fergus O'F. of Tenelick.—*Lodge.*

A letter of Gerald Byrne to Sir J. Perrott in 1590, gives us a vivid picture of these old times, and of the son of Fergus O'F. He says—' Whereas you asked me whether Fergus O'Ferral's son hath been with that traitor Feagh M[c]Hughe, it may please you to understand that, I being from home, the said Fergus his son came to my house in harvest last, and not finding me there went away and staid baiting his horses in my way as I should return homewards. When I saw the company of horsemen I made toward them to see what they were, and I found him and another horseman well furnished with horse and armour, and a harper riding upon a hacney with them; and asking whence they came and whither they wolde, they said they came from my howse, and wolde that night lie at Morgh M[c]Edmond's howse, a neighbour of mine, whose daughter

Rosse Offerrall,[g] Sone and heyre to Offerrall bane, now in rebellion, and Usurpeth the Captenship of the whole Countrie by Tirons help.
Henrie Malbie's Sone.
Sir Frances Shaen.

Of this Countie some have followed Rosse Offerrall into Rebellion, his nomber is about 200.

was married to Feagh M{{c}}Hugh's son. From thence they would go to Feagh M{{c}}Hugh's howse. There they tarried certain days, and, at their departure, Feagh gave Fergus his son a horse which was taken by Feagh a littill before from Hugh Duffe M{{c}}Donnell, one of the L. of Ormonde's tenants in a prey.'

From Russell's Diary in the *Car. Cal.* we find that on the 5th of Feb. 1596, 'Phergus O'Farrell sent in the heads of Farrell O'Banne's son and another rebel.' 'June 20 the Lord of Delvine sent in one of the O'F. a notable rebel, who was taken and wounded by the Nugents—he died of his wounds.'

'Sept. 6th the L. of Delvin sent in three of the O'Farrells' heads.'

[g] Ross O'F. of Mornin, Chief of his name, married a dau. of the 1st Earl of Roscommon.—*Lodge.*

In 1599 all the O'Ferrals were in rebellion, except two chief men of that Family, and the Castle of Longford was held by an English Warde, and the Rebels were in number 120 foot.—*Moryson.*

'In 1595 O'Donnell marched into Longford or the two Annalys (the countries of the two O'F.) though the English had some time before obtained sway over them, and one of the English, Browne by name, was then dwelling in the chief house of O'F. The troops of O'Donnell set every place in a blaze, and wrapped it in a black heavy cloud of smoke. They took the Castle of Longford, saved Brown and his brother-in-law and their wives by a rope; but fifteen men of that country, hostages whom Brown held, could not be saved. Three other castles were also taken by O'Donnell, and on these occasions many were slain, of whom one of the freeborn, Hubert O'F., who was accidentally slain by Maguire.

'In 1597 an army was led by Maguire at the instance of the O'Farrells to Mullingar, and they preyed the country around them, pillaged Mullingar, and set the town in a dark red blaze. In 1598 O'Ruairc at the instance of Ross O'F. Bane, proceeded with his forces into Meath, and plundered Mullingar, and the country from Mullingar to Ballymore Lough Sewdy.' —*Four Masters.*

This Countie hath never a Towne but Longford, which is onlie a market Towne.[h]

[h] O'F., a Dominican, was made Bp. of Clonfert by Pope Sixtus V. in 1587, he died in 1602. O'F., a Franciscan, was put to death in 1588.

In 1689 Roger and Robert O'F. were Members for Longford, and Roger O'F. was M.P. for Lanesborough. Richard O'F. was a distinguished Commander under Owen Roe, and Col. Sir Connell F. of Tirlicken, and Charles and Francis F. of Mornin were in the Army of James II. Eight of the Sept were attainted in Longford in 1691. In the year 1703 Marlborough wrote to the Duke of Ormond: 'I give your Grace this trouble at the request of my old acquaintance Brigadier Offarel.' A daughter of this General O'F. married the first Earl of Effingham.

When O'Donovan, wrote his Letters on the Antiquities of Longford, Connell O'Farrell of Camlisk was the recognised senior of the O'Farrells, and retained fifty acres (free of rent) of the original territory. The chief representative of the name, at present, is the Right Hon. R. More O'Ferrall of Balyna in the Co. of Kildare, who has been a Lord of the Treasury, Secretary to the Admiralty, and Governor of Malta. He was in 1851 Member for Longford County, which is now represented by his nephew, George Errington, Esq., and by Major O'Reilly, who is a descendant of Edmond, Chief of Breifny O'Reilly in 1598. His brother, John L. More O'Ferrall, Esq., is D.L. for Longford, and proprietor of Lissard, concerning which historic spot consult O'Donovan's Letters on the Antiquities of Longford, in the Royal Irish Academy.

THE COUNTIE OF CAVAN.

This Countie of Cavan[a] contayned all the Lands called heretofore O'Reillies Countie [in the original the word seemeth to be Omelie, but in my opinion[b] should be read O'Reilie, as also in the names of the Chieftains], which was ever till Sir John Perot's tyme under one Capten, was then divided into fowre *Lps.*[c] and each subdivided into manie portions and Freeholders, and no one of the 4 principall depending upon ether, but all immediatelie upon the Quene.[d] The L. were Sir John Clankoe). To Moylmore mac an Prior, and his brother, the barony of Rathnarome.'—Note in O'D.'s *Four Masters,* p. 1899.

[a] In 1579 it was stated that 'never writ was current in O'Reilly's countrie, and it was almost a *sacrilege* for any Governor of Ireland to look into that territory.'—S. P., quoted by *H. F. Hore.*

[b] The transcriber is right in this marginal note. Dymmok calls it 'OReilie's country,' and says it 'conteyneth 30 miles in length and 30 in breadth.'

[c] i.e. 'Lordships.' Marginal note.

[d] In a Lambeth Manuscript we read that—'The Breny, now called the countie of Cavan, hath been tyme out of minde whollie in the jurisdiction of him that for the tyme was O'Reillye, that is to say Lord of the Countrie; but when the partition was made by Sir H. Sidney, the baronies were then divided among the principal gentlemen of the O'Reillies—viz., to Sir John O'R. and his heirs the baronies of Cavan, Tollaghgarvy, Tolloconho, and Tolloha. To Edmond O'R. and his heirs the barony of Castlerahin. To Philip O'R. and his heirs the bar. of Iniskine (now

Sir W. Drury wrote to Walsingham about the O'Reillies—'In June 1579, when I was staying at Sir Lucas Dillon's howse seven miles from Kelles, four German Barons came, who were visiting Ireland, and said that after having seen Galway, Limerick, and some other post towns, they would go to Scotland. I lodged them at Trim in Laurence Hammond's house, sending Patrick Barnwall, gent., with them as a companion. While they and I were at service the day after Whitson Sunday, Orelie with his brother Philip and his uncle Edmond and 30 horsemen well furnished cam (unlooked for) to present to me a submission in behalf of himself and his whole countrie—to have his people framed to English mannors, his countrie made shere ground, and subject to law under her Majesty's writ. I thought it good to honor with the title of Knighthoode.

Amelie,ᶜ Edmond Amelie, Phillip amelie, and Hugh reaghe

But how straunge the view of these savadges parsonadges (most of them wearing glibbes and armed in mail with pesantses and skulls and riding upon pillions), seemed to o' straungers I leave it to yo' wisdom to thinke of. And so myself and the traine together with these strangers and Oreighlie with his company, being entertained with the said Sir Lucas, we parted.'

ᶜ Sir John Ruadh O'R. was son of the chieftain Hugh, who died in 1583; he had two brothers Philip and Owen, and four sisters who were mar. to Hugh MacGuiness, Conor Maguire, Mac Ferroll O'Reilly, and Plunket of Clonbrene. This Sir John, 'by order out of England, anno 1587, was made Captain of Breny O'Reilly, and his uncle Edmond was confirmed Tanist.'— Note to *Four Masters*, p. 1811.

Shan was Knighted at the English Court in 1585; and then he described the extent and the rents of the five baronies of the Breny; he complained that 'his uncle Mulmore Mac Prior O'R. of Clonmahon hath threatened Sir John's tenants of Dowold-Donall, and their said lands are waste, etc. O'R., by ancient custom, had always out of the five baronies xlv libr. each, as often as he had any cause to cesse the said baronies, either for the Queen's rents, or for any charge towards O'Neil, or other matter, which sometimes was twice or thrice a yeare, and every time xlv lib. to his own use besides the charge of the cesse. Likewise all manner of charges, that his son or his men were put into by reason of their beinge in pledge or attending in Dublin or elsewhere for matter of the said O'R. Item, all manner of fees, etc., given to any learned counsell, solicitor, or agent for the causes of the contry; out of every 8 pooles of lande throughout the five baronies one fatt beeffe for the spendinge of his house, one horse for himselfe, one horse for his wife, one horse for his son and heir with one boy attending upon every horse, kept through the whole five baronies yearly. Item, to cesse upon the Mac Bradies, the MᶜEnroes, the Gones, and the Jordans, by the space of iii quarters of a yeare yearly, one foteman upon every poole, which the said surnames had, to keep his cattle, to reap and bynd his corne, to thrashe, hedge and ditch, etc., for the said O'R. Item, the said O'R. had upon the Bradies, the Gones, the McEnroes and the Jordans out of every poole of land yearly, thre quarters of a fatt beeffe, and out of every two pooles one fatt porke, and also the cessing of strangers, their men and horses, as often as any did come in friendship to the country. Item, all charges for workmen, stofe, and labourers, and victualls for the building and maintaining of his Castell of the Cavan; the duties of the town of Cavan as rent, drink, etc., now taken and not denied. —*Sir John O'R.'s Answers* to queries of the English Commissioners in 1585. —*Carew MSS.*

COUNTIE OF CAVAN.

Amilie; but so soon as Sr John died, Phillip Amelie,^f being the third (and Edmond being for Age impotent), Usurped the Countie and reversed all this division being chieflie sturred up thereunto by the Earle of Tyrone, whom he thought Especiallie good to draw into his Faction, because he was a Man of great courage and of many followers, and who might have much annoyed the Earle of Tyrone, if he had continued his Loyaltie. This Phillip being slaine by one of Tyrone's Souldiers negligentlie, Sr Edmond^g the old man enjoyeth the Government of the Countrie,

^f In 1596 Philip O'R. was nominated by O'Neill as O'R. over all Breifné, but he was soon after accidentally slain by O'Neill's people, and then Emann son of Maelmora, who was senior to the other two Lords, was styled O'R.—*Four Masters.*

'In 1601 Emann, the son of Maelmora, son of Sean, son of Cathal, died in the month of April. He was an aged, grey-headed, long-memoried man, and had been quick and vivacious in his mind and intellect in his youth. He was buried in the Monastery of St Francis at Cavan, and his brother's son, namely, Eoghan, son of Hugh Conallagh, was elected in his place.—*Four Masters,* p. 2243.

This Emann was chief of East Breifny; he was a member of the parliament of 1585. The *Four Masters* record that in 1583 'Emann's brother Hugh died; he was a man who had passed his time without contests, and who had preserved Breifne from the invasions of his English and Irish enemies; he was buried in the monastery of Cavan. The son of this O'R., namely John Roe, then exerted himself to acquire the chieftainship of the territory, through the power of the English, in opposition to Emann (his uncle) who was senior according to Irish usage. In consequence of this the country and lordship were divided between the descendants of Maoilmordha.'

Emann was elected chief in 1598. So early as the year 1558 Emann and his brother Hugh made a covenant with the English Government; and again in 1567, when they promised among other things that they would pursue their brother Cahier O'R., Owen O'R., and Thomas O'R., 'nunc rebelles, et eos ferro et flamma punire.'—Note to *Four Masters,* p. 1804 to 1808, see also p. 1997.

From Emann descend the O'R. formerly of Heath House, Queen's Co.; of Thomastown Castle in Louth; of Scarva in Antrim; and the Count O'R. of Spain; Miles W. O'R. of Knock Abbey, is descended from him by father and mother. Seventh in descent from Emann was Count O'R., Generalis-

who is assisted by the Sone of Sʳ John Amelie who having slaine one Mortaghe oge Cavanaghe that was upon protection, durst not abide Trial, but fled to Tyrone with whom he hath remained ever since.ʰ These Amilies is a strong and valiant clan, they are able to make 400 good Horsemen and some Footmen.ⁱ The chief Freeholder under them is one Mᶜbrady. This Countie is bounded with the Countie of Leytrim to the West, the Counties of Fermanagh and Monaghan to the North, the Countie of Eastmeath to the East, and Westmeath to the South. There

simo of His Catholic Majesty's forces, Inspector General of infantry, Grand Commander of the Order of Calatrava, Captain General of Andalusia, Civil and Military Governor of Cadiz, etc.

Emann married a dau. of the Baron of Dunsaney, and had Cahir, John, and Terence Neirinn (from whom O'R. of Scarva); he married 2ˡʸ a dau. of Baron Delvin, and had Myles, Farrell, and Charles. His son John married a dau. of Sir James Butler, and had a son Brian, who d. in 1631, and was the father of Maelmora, known as 'Myles the Slasher,' a distinguished cavalry officer of the war of 1641.

Emann had also two sons, Turlogh Gallda (or the Anglicised) and Turlogh-an-iarainn (or of the Iron).

Owen, who succeeded Emann as chief, d. in 1601, and was succeeded by Maelmora, the fourth son of Hugh Conallagh, and last chief of East Breifne, who enjoyed that dignity till the Plantation of 1609; he died in 1635.— Note to O'D.'s *Four Masters*, p. 2240.

ʰ Maolmora, another son of Sir John, 'a young man of fine person great valour and ambition,' mar. a niece of the Earl of Ormond, joined the English, was received with favour by Elizabeth, got a grant of lands in Cavan under letters patent with the promise of an Earldom. He was commander of horse in the English service, and was killed at the battle of the Yellow Ford in 1598 while covering the retreat of the English.—*D'Alton's Army List*, p. 925.

ⁱ Moryson says this county was in Ulster, and that 'the Orelyes in the Brenny had 800 f. and 100 horse.'

Dymmok writes, 'They are a stronge nation, able to make of their own sirname 400 horse; they are sayd to be aunciently descended from the Ridleys of England.'—*Dimmok*, p. 16.

This is an honour to which the O'Reillies cannot pretend, as they are 'meere Irishe.' Their Celtic pedigree is well known. Before the Normans came to Ireland, warriors of that name were slain in the years 1128, 1157, and 1161.

is no Towne in it but the Cavan[k] a market Towne wherein are 2 Strong Castles, Several small Castles, and the Several dwellings of the Amelies, whereof there is none of name.[l] The Bishop of Kilmore is Ordinarie both to Countie of Cavan and Leytrim.

[k] In 1595 an army was led by Maguire and MacMahon into Breifny O'R., and they quickly plundered that country, and left not a cabin in which two or three might be sheltered in all Cavan which they did not burn, except the Monastery of Cavan, in which English soldiers were at that time.—*Four Masters*, p. 1959.

[l] According to *Pynnar's Survey*, dated 1618—'The Precinct of Clanchie was allotted to Scotch undertakers; it contained 6000 acres; in the Precinct of Castlerahin 3900 to English, and 900 left to Shane M'Philip O'Reilly, on this he had an Irish House surrounded by a bawn of Sodds. In the Precinct of Tullaghgarry 2250 acres to English; 1000 acres called Itterry-outra to Mulmorie M'Philip O'R., he had a strong bawn of Sodds with four flankers, and a deep Moate, a good Irish house within it—he hath made no estates. Captain Reley hath 1000 acres called Lisconnor—all his tenants do Plough by the Tail. Mulmorie Oge O'R. hath 3000 acres, and in it an old Castle now built up. He hath made no estates to any of his tenants, and they do all plough by the Tail. Captain Richard Tirrell and his brother William have 2000 acres called Itterrery. Upon this is built a strong bawn of lime and stone 80 feet square, 12 feet high, with four flankers. He hath made no estates. Maurice M'Telligh hath 3000 acres called Liscurcron. Here is a bawn of sodds and in it a good Irish House. In the Precinct of Loghtee 12,004 acres allotted to English undertakers.

'In the Precint of Clonmahown 4500 acres to English; and Mulmory M'Hugh O'R. hath 2000 acres called Commot, and a strong house of lime and stones 40 f. long, 20 f. broad, three stories high, and a bawn about it of Sodds. He hath no estates. Philip M'Tirlagh hath 300 acres and an Irish House and bawn. In Tullaconchie 6000 acres to English. In Tullagha 4500 acres to English; and Magauran, a Native, hath 1000 acres.'

Dr. M'Dermot, in a note to the *Four Masters*, says that 'It is estimated that there are over 20,000 people named O'Reilly in the Co. of Cavan.' I may add that there are more priests of that name than of any other Irish name; they number about eighty.

CONNAUGHT.

CONNAUGHT[a] contayneth all the Lands Circuited with the great Ocean between the River of Earne near Asherow in Odonells Countrie and the River of Sheynen, where it falleth into the Sea beneath Limerick. It is in manner ane Iland, because to the North and West it hath the Sea, To the South and West the Sheynen, to the North-east the Lough and River[b] of Earne, onlie a small piece between the Earne and the Sheynen leaveth in that part not Circuited.[c]

---

[a] 'A Description of the Province of Connaught,' dated 'January, 1612,' preserved in British Museum, and published in Vol. 27 of the *Archaeologia*, says—'Connaght, by the antient division amonge the Irish was accompted the the fifte parte or Cocge of the Iland of Ireland, and was then and is still called by the name of Cocge Connaght, and contynewed the name and stile of a Kingdome in the posterity of Con Kedcagh, one of the three races discended of Mylle Spaynagh whome all the Cronicles of Ireland agree to be the absolute conqueror of the whole island.'

'Off this Cocge Conaght, a porcon now called Thomond, lyinge towards the Sowth, to the river of Shenan, whether by gift or conquest hath beene a long time possest by the O'Brians, beinge discended of another race of Mylle Spaynagh, whoe at this day enioye yt. The earle of Thomond beinge the Cheeffe of that name; yett it was helde within the government of Connaght till the beginninge of his Ma[ties] raigne to gratefie the Earle of Thomond. The Earle of Clanriccard was contented it shold be divided from the government of Connaght.

'Until the beginning of the reigne of Queen Elizabeth the ordinary Justice of the Kingdome hadd little passage in Conaght the English races remayninge under the rule of the Bowrks, and the Irishry under the Cheeffes of every particular septe, the whole province bearinge the name of the County of Conaght—whereof there was one Sherriffe whom the people little respected, at what time the said Queene erected a presideall seat, and establyshed a President and Councell for the administration of justice within the province, and devided yt into five shyers which ordinance continues unto this time.

[b] 'The river of Ballashennagh and the Loghe Ecarne.'—*Description of Connaght* in 1612.

[c] 'Leaveth that parte uninclosed.—*Dymmok*.

'It is a fruitful province but hath

In Connaught are Six Counties,

| Clare | Maio | Leytrim |
| Galway | Slego | Roscoman. |

many Boggs, and thick woods.'—*Moryson*, Part iii., p. 158.

'The insurgent forces there in April 1599, were 3090 f. and 260 horse.'—*Car. Cal.*, year 1599, p. 300.

'Her Majesty has to keep a force of 2300 f. and 75 horse; and such is the waste and ruin, specially in grain, as we are driven to victual most of these companies out of her Majesty's store.'—Nov. 5, 1597, *Car. Cal.*

The Queen's forces in 1599 were: *Horse*—Earl of Clanrickard, 50; Provost Marshal, 10; Sir Theobald Dillon, 15; Captain Blunt, 12. *Foote*—E. of Clanrickard, 100; E. of Dunkellin, 150; Sir A. Savage, 200; Sir Thomas Burke, 100; Sir H. O'Connor, 100; Sir T. Dillon, 100; Badbye, 150; Plunket, 100; Mostian, 100; Tibot ne Long, 100; Floyd, 150; Roper, 150; Oliver Burke, 100; T. Burke, 100; David Bourke, 100. Total, horse, 87; foot, 1800.—*Moryson*.

In 1602 there were 151 h. and 2100 f.—*Car. Cal.*

Connaught was of all provinces 'the most troublesome in 1588,' the most out of order in 1601; 'being ever a rebellious province of itself, the less counties the governor hath to govern the better, and hence Clare should not be added to it.'—*Car. Cal.* year 1588, p. 3; year 1601, pp. 49 and 174.

Sir Conyers Clifford reported in September 1597, that the total number of men now in action is 2600 at least. In April 1597, we are told that 'not one of the six shires is free from revolt; Clifford with 21 companies of foot and a half, besides horse, is not strong enough to reduce them, for his companies are weak, and O'Donnell tyranizeth over most of these people at his pleasure.'

Sir Conyers Clifford, a brave and good man, with 1900 foot under 25 ensigns and with about 200 horse, was defeated by 400 Irish under O'Rurke. He was wounded, and was so indignant at the flight of his men that 'he brake in a fury away from Sir J. Mac Swine and Capt. Oliver Burke's lieutenant, who wanted to save him by taking him off the field; and alone he rushed on the pursuers, in the midst of whom after he was stroake through the body with a pike; he died fighting.'—*Dymmok*.

'The Irish of Connaught were not pleased at his death, for he had been a bestower of jewels and riches upon them, and he had never told them a faslehood.'—*Four Masters*.

'In 1600 O'Donnell made an incursion into Clanrickard and Clare, in which he was joined by O'Rourke, O'Connor Sligo, O'Connor Roe, McDermot, and McWilliam.'—*Four Masters*.

THE COUNTIE OF CLARE.[a]

This Countie beareth the name of the Castle of Clare belonging to the Earle of Thomond. It contayneth Nine baronies[b]

[a] Carew writes to Cecil in June 1602, 'The Earle of Thomond hath no other suit in England but to annex Thomond to Munster, which if he may not obtain his heart is broken.'

'In the county of Clare when I beheld the appearance and fashion of the people, I would I had been in Ulster again; for these are as mere Irish as they, and in their outward form not much unlike them; but we found that many of them spake good English, and understood the course of our proceedings well. The best freeholders next to the O'Briens are the McNemaraes and the O'Laneyes, the chief of which appeared in civil habit and fashion, the rest are not so reformed as the people of Munster.'—Sir J. Davis, *Car. Cal.* May 1606.

[b] A Trinity Coll. MS., marked E. 2. 14, and the Carew MSS., vol. 611, give the following account of Clare:—

It conteyneth whole Thomond being in length from Leyme Concollen to Killalowe 45 myles, and in bredth from Lymericke to Beallaleynee 25 myles, which of auncient tyme was devided into 9 Troghkyeds or hundreds, and is nowe appoynted to be conteyned in 8 Baronies.

The Barony of Tullaghnenaspule conteyneth Macnemaries als Mortimers country by East; the Baron of Inshyquyn and Donel Reogh mac ne mare chief in the Same. The castles are 38 in number.

Gentlemen, and their Castles.
Donell Reogh, of Tullaghe
Edmunde O'Grady, of Toymegreene
Edmunde O'Grady, of Muyno
Donogh and   } of ffertan
Rory Macnemare } Garongharagh
Donell Reogh Macnemare, ffycklenearly
Rorye Mac ne Mares Sons, Iland Cahir
Donogh Mac ne Mare, of Kilallowe
Muriertagh, Custos of Obriens bridge
The Baron of Inshiquin, of Castell Loghe
S^ohane ne Geyllagh, of Dunasse
Donel Roe, of Cullistecke
Teige oge McConmea, Neadennury,
Tirilogh McDonel roo, Glanomra
Donel Reoghe, Sohort Castel in
Tirlagh Obrien, of Glanoradone
S^ohida McRory, Moynengeanagh
S^ohane McNamares, Son of Moyintallone
Donell Reogh, Tyrowanyn
S^ohane McMahoun, Euaghhowleyne
S^ohane McDonell, of Beallakullen
Brian McDonell Roo, Ballgarilly
Comea McMahown, Ballmitlayne
Therle of Thomond, of Castell Callogh
Donogh McConoghor, Ahereynagh
ffymyn McLaghlin, of Roscoe

COUNTY OF CLARE.

and 2 small Byshopricks, Killallo, and Kilfeneraghe, the former subject to the Archbishop of Cashell in Mounster the Latter to the Archbishop of Tooam. This Countie is situated between two Bayes of Limerick and Galloway, the one to the East and the other to the West the Countie of Galloway to the North and the Sheynan to the South-east. It hath 2 market Townes Inish and [   ] and in each ane Abbey,

Tege Oultagh, Ballymogashill
Coverey M⁰S⁰hanerey, Quaronenvyre Cullan
Rory M⁰Mahown, of Kelkissin Lysofine Lysmieghan
Tirilogh Obrien, of ffomara and of Tyriedagha
S⁰hane M⁰Nemara, Caeppagh
Edmund O'Grady, Sheriffe Trugh
Rory Moell M⁰ffynnyn, Beallagha

The Barony of Dangen conteyninge West Mac ne Mares Countrey. S⁰hane Mac ne mare Chief in the Same. Castles, 43.

Gentlemen, and their Castles.

S⁰hane Mac ne mare, of Dangen and of Croppoke
Tirilagh Obrien, of Croppoke
Sohane Mac ne mare, of Dangan breake
Donogh M⁰Murrogh Obrien, Qyynhi
Domea Mac Mahown, Dromollyn
William Nellan, Beallahanyn
Brene Obrien, of Castleton Nenenanogh
James Nellan, of Ballycaston Ballyally
Conoghor Maglanthy, Ballycharelle Mughane

Donogh Obrien, Ballychara
Donel M⁰S⁰hida Matagh, Granaghane
S⁰hane Omulhonery, Ballynegeyne
Donel M⁰Sohida, Ralahyn
Therle of Thomond, Rosmonagher
ffynnin M⁰laghlin, Legwaro
Donel M⁰Tege, Crathallaghmore
S⁰hane M⁰Nemare, Crathallaghmoello
Therle of Thomond, Bunratty and of Cloynmoneagh
Donel M⁰ne mare, Crathallaghkell
Muriertagh Obrien, Dromloyne
Donogh Maglanchy, of Claynloghane
Tege Maglanchy, of Balleneclogh
Muriertagh Maglanchy, Nerlyn
Brien na fforiry, of ffynis
Macenery heny, of Ballenecraige
Donogh Obrien, of Raehavellayne
Tege M⁰Murrogh, Ballyconill
Donogh O'Gradey, Cloyne
S⁰han Mac mahown, Corballe
Donogh Maglanchy, Bodovoher

The Baronie of Cloynetherala conteyninge East Corkewasten. Tege Mac Mahoone Chiefe in the Same, Castles, 7.

Gentlemen, and their Castles.

Tege Mac Mahown, of Dangen Myburke and of Cloynetheralla

STATE OF IRELAND ANNO 1598.

Principall Castles

Bonrattie the Earle of Thomond's chief Hous
Clare belonging to him also
Cowland
Inchequin belonging to the Baron thereof
Towne
Dunnas M^r· Waterhous
Ballivaghan belonging to Sir Turloghe O'Bryen

and of Cahiracon
and of Ballamacollman
Derecrossan
Tege McConer Obrien, of Corubirighane
Tege McMuriertagh Cam, Dunegroek

The Baronie of Moyartha which conteyneth West Corke-Wasken. Tirlagh McMahoun Cheife in ye Same. Castles, 8.

Gentlemen, and their Castles.
Charles Cahane, of Inyshkathyn. This man by inheritance is called a Courboe.
James Cahane, of Ballykette
Tirlagh McMahown, of Carrighowly
and of Moyartha
and of Dunlykill
Dunsumayn
So^r Donell Obrien, Knight, Dunmore
and of Dunbeg

The Baronie of Tuogh Morey Conor conteyninge Corkemroe. So^r Donell Obrien, Knight, Cheife in ye Same. Castles, 23.

Gentlemen, and their Castles.
O'Conor, of Inysdyman
So^r Donell, of Glan
and of Ballighanyre

Tullowmore
Tege McMurrogh, of ffante
Ballyngowne
Inshcovee
Ballighany
Ravine
Sir Donell O'Brien, of Beancoroe
Tege McMurrogh, of Cahirmenayn
So^r Donel Obrien, of Tullagh
Tege McMurrogh, Leymenegh
So^r Donell Obrien, of Dunegoir
Tege McMurrogh, of Dumnycphellen
Knockefyne
Conogher Maghanchy, Tuomolyn
Tege McMurrogh, of Ballenelakyn
and of Beallaghe
Loghbuligin
Kylmua
So^r Donell, of Dughe
and of Lyscanuire

The Baronie of Gragans conteyning the countrey of Buren. O'Loghlen, Cheife in the Same. Castles, 20.

Gentlemen, and their Castles.
Ologhen, of Cahirclogan
Lysiglysin
Cahiricnacty
Ballemoroghee
Moghenees
Glensteed

COUNTY OF CLARE.

Men of Name in this Countie The Earle of Thomond his name Obryan.
The L. Baron of Inchiquin, his name in like sort O'Bryen.

Ologhlen, of Gragan
    Glanoeynagh
    Ballyveaghane
    S°hanemokenes
    Novknesno
    Kynveare
    Turlagh
    Glancollayn
    Killy
    Nacapaghee
    Castleton
    Ballyheaghayne
    Kreaghwill
    Rugham

The Baronie of Tullagh Idea. So' Donell Obrien, Knight, Cheife in the Same. Castles, 24.

Gentlemen, and their Castles.
The Baron of Inshiquin, Inshiquin
S⁽ʳ⁾ Donell, of Killinbury
Mahown M꜀brene O'brien, Ballycrottry
    Quarowduffe
    Tirm꜀ brayne
Tege M꜀Murrogh, of Bohneill
Muriertagh Garagh, Cahir Corkrayne
    Rahe
Tege m꜀Murrogh, of Dromenglasse
Mahown Odea, of Beallnelykee
    Mowghowny
Ogriffee, of Ballygriffee
Donogh Duffee M꜀Cosedin, of Ballyharaghan
Therle of Thomonde, Mocthrie

The Baron of Inshiquin, Dereowen
    Manygriffane
Mahown Obrien, of Cloynenouayne
Dermot Obrien, of Cloyneseleherne
    Owarow negulc
Owen M꜀S°wyne, Dunymulvihill
    Carigentogher
Owen M꜀S°yne, Bealnefirvearnayn
Donell Moel Odea, Desert
Mahown the B. Sonne, Kilkidry

The Baronie Cloynerawde, conteyninge yᵉ troghkied of Cloynrawde and yᵉ Ilands. Therle of Thomonde, Cheife in the Same. Castles, 19.

Gentlemen, and their Castles.
Therle of Thomond, Clonrawde
    and of Clare
    and of Inish
The Baron of Inshiquyn, Killoyne
    and of Ballevecoode
Conogher Maglanchy, Enenshy
Brene Duffe, of S°hally
Tege M꜀Murroghe, Moghoony
Tege M꜀Conor O'brien, Inishvacwochny
    and of Inishdaghrome
    and of Inishnivar
M꜀Gylerervgh, of Craigurien
    Tirviglay
M꜀Graigh, of Ilandvecraigh
Tege M꜀Conor, of Beallchoricke
The Baron of Ibrikan the ⎫
  Earle of Towmond's ⎬ Moyobrakan
  eldest Sonne ⎭

The Two Byshops
Sʳ Turlogh O'Bryanᶜ
Mᶜne marre Reagheᵈ   Mᶜne marre feuᵈ
McMahonᵉ   George Blunt of Dunas

Therle of Thomond, Cahir Rivish
Tege Mac Conogher, Tromra
Tege Mac Murrogh, Dunogane

There are 8 Baronies, 79 parish churches, and 172 castles, and 8 Abbayes.

The Abbayes and Religious Houses are
Th abbay of Clare possessed by Sᵒʳ Donell and Tege McConoᶜ his brother.
    Inish by James Nellan.
    St. John's a nunrye by yᵉ Baron of Inshiquyn.
    Corkomoree.
    Iland Chanens by Therle of Thomonde.
    Kiltena.
    Quynhye, occupied by ffreers.
Th abbey of Insh Cronan.

From *Car. Cal.*, year 1601-1603, p. 472, it appears that this Description was written by Sir T. Cusack in 1574.

ᶜ In 601 Sir Torlogh's son and heir, Teig, was mortally wounded fighting against the English; he was taken care of by his enemy and kinsman, Lord Dunkellin; but soon died and 'was buried successively at Loughrea and Athenry.' 'He was expert at every warlike weapon, of remarkable energy, agility, mildness, comeliness and hospitality.' In 1602 Torlogh and Conor O'B. were driven out of the castles of Derryowen and Ballyanchaislen by the Earl of Thomond. Torlogh escaped, but the chieftains Conor and Brian O'B., with their followers, were hanged on trees in pairs face to face. In 1602 Torlogh, grandson of Bishop O'B. was slain by Burke of Derrymaclachtny.— *Four Masters.* Morogh O'B. of Duagh lived at this time, and had a son mar. to a dau. of Edward O'Hogan.—*Lodge.*

ᵈ ' The two Mac Namaras, if the countrie were quiet, might live like principal Knights in England.'—*Sydney's Letters*, fol. vol. i., p. 102. ' Mac Conmara Fionn (John son of Teig) d. in 1602; his son Donnall took his place.'—*Four Masters.*

ᵉ 'Teig *Caoch* McM., Lord of West Corcabhascin, captured an English ship in 1598, which put in near his Castle of Carriganchobhlaigh (Carrigaholt); he also took back Dunbeg, one of his own castles, from a Limerick merchant who 'held it in lieu of debt;' in 1599 he was driven out of his territory by Lord Thomond; he then joined the Earl of Desmond, assaulted by night Thomond's son, Donnall, wounded him, slew many of his people and imprisoned him. In 1602, being asked by O'Sullevan for a loan of

COUNTY OF CLARE.

Ogardie
Oneyland[g]
O'Laughlin
O'clanchey[h]

George Cusack[f]
Edward Mostyne
Edward Whyte
M[r.] Waterhous.

his ship to send to Spain for assistance, he refused, sent his son and other guards to defend it, and when O'Sullevan approached in a boat to seize it, Teig, who was with him, called to his men to fire on O'Sullevan, and was accidentally shot by his own son. 'There was no triocha-chead (barony) of which Teig was not worthy to be Lord, for dexterity of hand and bounty, for purchase of wines, horses and literary works. Mortagh M[c]M. of Cnocanlacha d. in 1598.'—*Four Masters.*

[f] Slain in 1599 by Turlogh O'Brien, whose lands he held.

[g] James O'N., who kept open house, d. in 1599.

[h] Baolach M[c]Clancy of Cnoc-Finn d. in 1598; he was fluent in Latin, Irish and English; was M.P. for Clare in 1585. Also Maolin Oge M[c]Brody, who in 1563 succeeded his brother as Ollav of Hy-Bracan and Hy-Fearmaac, d. at Ballybrody in 1602. There was no one in Eire who was, together, a better historian, poet, and rhymer than he.—*Four Masters.*

O'Daly had a white house at Finnyvara, 'great its wealth, bestowing without folly; it were a sufficiently loud organ to hear his pupils reciting the melodies of the ancient schools.'—*Tribes of Ireland.*

Dermot O'Dea of Tully O'Dea was killed in 1598; Hugh O'Hogan was slain in 1597, in a battle between the O'Briens and the Clanwilliam Burkes; 'he was by no means the least distinguished son of a chieftain for goodness and wealth.'—*Four Masters.*

In 1585 the 'Lords spirituall and temporall, chieftains, gents, &c., of Thomond were—Donogh Earle of Thomond; Murrough lord baron of Inchiequin; the Reverend fathers in God, Mauricius Bishopp of Kyllalowe; Daniell elect bishop of Kyllffinoraghe; Donogh O'Horane dean of Kyllalow; Daniell Shinnaghe, deane of Kyllfinoraghe; Denis, arch-deacon of the same; Sir Edward Waterhouse of Downassee, knt.; Sir Tyrrelagh O'Brien of Ennèstyvey, knt.; John M[c]nemara of Knappock, otherwise called M[c]Nemarra of Westcloncullun; Donell Reagh M[c]Nemarragh, of Garrowelagh, otherwise called M[c]Nemarraghe of East Cloncullin; Teige M[c]Mahoune of Clonderralae, otherwise called M[c]Mahoune of Castle-Corkowaskin; Tyrrelaghe M[c]Mahoune of Moyurtye, chief of his name in West Corkowaskin; Moriertagh O'Brien of Dromeleyne, gen.; Mahowne O'Brien of Clondewan gen.; Owny O'Laughleine of the Gragans, otherwise called

R

In this Countie the Earle of Thomond's Brother, called Teag O'Bryan,[1] and some few with him are in rebellion.

O'Laughlene; Rosse O'Laughlin of Glancollum-Kyllie, tanest to the same O'Llaghlen; Mahone and Dermott O'Dae of Tullaghadae, chieffe of their names; Connor Mac Gilreoghe of Cragbreane, chieffe of his name; Tyrrelaghe Mac Teig O'Brien of Beallacorege, gen.; Luke Bradey sonne and heire of the late bishopp of Meath; Edward White of the Crattclagh, gen.; George Cusacke of Dromoylen, gen.; Boetius Clanchie of Knockfynney, gen.; John McNemara of the Moetullen, gen.; Henry O'Grady of the iland of Inchecronan, gen.; Donnogh McClanchie of the Urlion, chieffe of his name; Donnoghe Garraghe O'Brien of Ballecessye, gen.; Connor O'Brien of Curharcorcae, gen.; and George Fanning Limerick merchant.'—See *Iar-Connacht*, p. 358.

[1] 'He had 600 f. and 50 horse in 1599, and not one castle there kept for the Queen.'—*Moryson*.

Teig had mar. Slaine, dau. of Teig O'Brien, of Smithstown, son of the 1st Earl of Thomond, and by her was father of Tirlogh of Ballyslattery, Colonel Morogh, and Dermot 'the Good.'—*Hist. Memoir of the O'Briens*, p. 496.

In 1598 Teig took the Bridge of Portcroisi, the castles of Cluain, and Sgairbh. In 1599 eight companies of English and Irish soldiers were marching from Kilkeedy, through Bealach an Fhiodhfail (Rockforest), Teig's people attacked them; more of the Queen's people were slain, but the Irish lost a gentleman named Dermot Roe O'Brien. Teig then made peace with the Queen, and dismissed his hirelings; and the English and Irish besieged and took the castle of Cahirminane belonging to Tirlogh O'Brien, whose brother Dermot was slain at Rockforest.—*Four Masters*.

THE COUNTIE OF GALLOWAY.

This Countie contayneth a great quantity of Land lying in a manner Square between thomond and maio, South and North between the Sheynen and the Sea East and West. It hath the River suck and the Countie of Roscoman to the Northeast thereof.

This Countie hath three Byshopricks
Tooam one Byshoprick
Clonfert a Byshoprick upon the Sheynen
Kilmacoughe a Byshoprick in Oshaghnes Countrie

Corporat Townes

Galloway[a] exceeding fayre and well built
Athenrie[b] all ruined saving the Wall

[a] 'A proper neat city.—*Campion.* The townsmen and wemmen present a more civil show of life than other towns of Ireland do.—*Lord Justice Pelham.* Noe towne in the three nations (London excepted) is more considerable for commerce.—*H. Cromwell* and Privy Council quoted by Hardiman. The *Description of Connaught* of the British Museum, dated 1612, which seems identical with that of the Lambeth MSS. written by Sir Oliver St. John in 1614, says—'Galway is small but all of fayer and stately buildings; the fronts of their howses towards the streets, being all of hewed stone, upp to the topp, and garnyshed with fayer battlements in an uniform cowrse, as if the whole towne hadd beene builte upon one modell. The merchants are riche and great adventurers at sea. They keepe goode hospitality and are kind to strangers, and in their manner of entertaynement and in fashioning and appearllinge themselves and their wives doe most preserve the ancyent manner and state of any town that ever I sawe. The towne is built upon a rocke envyroned almost with the sea and the ryver, compassed with a strong wall, and good defences, after the auncient manner, and such as with a fewe men it may defend itself against any army.'

[b] 'Eight miles from Galway, elder than yt, built by the English, whiles they hadd their swords in their hands, and kept themselves close in garryson.

STATE OF IRELAND ANNO 1598.

The principall Merchants[c] and Citizens in both are Linches[d]

Now it hath a very small and poore habitacion and people. Yet the walls stand still large in compass and very strong and fayer.'—*Descript. of Con.* 1612.

[c] 'The chief families or 'tribes' were 'Athy, Blake, Bodkin, Browne, Dean, Darcy, Lynch, Joyes, Kirwan, Martin, Morris, Skerret, French.'

From 1590 to 1609 there were 7 mayors and 16 bailiffs named Lynch; 4 mayors and 5 bailiffs named French; 3 mayors and 4 bailiffs named Martin. The Mayor of 1598 was Nicholas Kirwan Fitz-Denis; the Bailiffs were Marcus and Nat. Blake. The Members for Galway in 1585 were P. Lynch, Yonoke Lynch, and Robuck French. In 1518 the Corporation enacted that —'If any man should bring an Irishman to brage or boste upon the toune to forfeit 12d. That no man shall oste or receive into their houses any of the Burks, M[c]Williams, the Kellies, nor no cepte elles on pain of £5, that nether O ne Mac shall strutte ne swaggere thro' the streets of Galway.'—*Hardiman's Galway*, p. 201.

Names of Galway Jurymen in 1609: Lynch FitzEdmund, alderman; Browne, alderman; 2 Kirwans, 3 Lynches, 2 Bodkins, 1 Blake, Athie, Martin and Bige, merchants; Teig Ballaghe, shoumaker; M[c]Follane, brogmaker; M[c]Coghlane, weaver; O'Many, cottner; Shoy, taylour; Nolan, goldsmith; M[c]Inylley, glower; O'Mollhane, cooper; Duff, O'Fodaghe and Loghlin, fishermen.

[d] Ninety Lynches were Mayors from 1274 to 1654, and not one since. John L. made Bishop of Elphin by Elizabeth in 1584, surrendered the see in 1611, 'lived a concealed and died a public papist,' is buried in St. Nicholas' Church.—*Hardiman's Galway*, p. 235.

The Royal Visitation of 1615 says: Wee found in Galway a publique schoolmaster named Lynch, placed there by the citizens, who had a great number of schollers not only out of that Province but also out of the Pale and other parts resorting unto him. We had daily proof during our continuance in that city how well his schollers profitted under him, by verses and orations which they presented to us. We sent for that schoolemaster before us, and seriously advised him to conform to the Religion established, and not prevailing with our advices, we enjoyned him to forbear teaching: and I, the Chancellor, did take a recognizance of him and some others of his Kinsmen in that city, in the sum of £400 sterling, that from thenceforth he would forbear to teach any more.—*Iar-Connaught*, p. 215.

Nich. L., Mayor, had 12 sons; the

Blakes[e]
Martins[f]
Frenches[g]

Darcies[h]
Skerrets[i]

eldest, Henry became Mayor, M.P. and a Baronet and was ancestor of Sir H. Lynch Blosse. Sir Henry d. in 1633 leaving £500 for the marriage portions of 'poor maydens of the birth of Galway, for ever,' the Linches and then the Martines to be preferred.—See Will in *Iar-Connacht*, p. 36.

Lynch of Shruel lived with much splendor . . . was grandfather Fr. Dominick L. the learned Regent of the College of St. Thomas Seville. Dr. J. Lynch, Archbishop of Tuam in 1674, said that, 'Since the time of St. Patrick, the L. always preserved the Catholic faith.' Dominick L. in 1580 built the west side of the Town Hall at his own expense and founded a free school.— See *Irish Arch. Miscel.*, Vol. i., p. 48, 55.

[e] Blake of Ardfry was father of Sir R. B., Speaker of the Supreme Council, and ancestor of Lord Wallscourt. Blake FitzWalter, Mayor in 1611 and 1630, became a Baronet in 1622, is ancestor of Sir V. Blake of Menlough. Nicholas B., merchant, d. in 1620, owning Kilturroge etc. and lands around Athenry.

[f] Francis M., merchant, d. 1615 seized of Ballyglasse, etc. in Mayo. Robert M. d. 1622 seized of several lands in Iar-Connaught.

[g] R. French d. 1628 possessed of the castles of Dongendrick, Menlagh, etc. in Iar-Connaught. Patrick F. of the Castle of Monivea, d. 1630. Oliver Oge F. was Mayor in 1597; his wife, née Joyce, was called *Margaret na Drehid*, Margaret of the Bridges, as she built stone bridges all through Connaught.—*Iar-Con.* p. 41, and *Hardiman's Galway*.

[h] Dorseys were Mayors in 1602 and 1614, and Bailiffs in 1602 and 1608. On Darcy's vault in the Franciscan Abbey we read—'Epitaphium D. Jacobi Darcy Majoris, Connaciæ Praesidis, Galviæ Praetoris etc. Qui ob. an. 1603

Hic Amor Heroum, Decus urbis, Norma Senatus,
Mensa peregrini, pauperis arca jacet.

This tomb was repaired by the descendants of James Darcy in the year 1728. Pray for the dead.' This was Darcy *Riveach* (the swarthy); his 7th son, Patrick, born in 1598, was a famous lawyer and a member of the Confederate Council.

[i] Edmund S., head of the race, owned the castle of *Ath-cin* or Headford in 1641: Skerrets were Mayors in 1594 and 1605. Brownes were Mayors in 1574, 1575 and 1609. Bodkin in 1610; Kirwans in 1598 and 1608; Mareis (Morris?) in 1588. In the Church of St. Nicholas there are tombs with the

STATE OF IRELAND ANNO 1598.

Principall Castles Meleeke belonging to the Quene
Portumno to the Earle of Clanrickard
Balliloughreaghe, the Earle of Clanrickard's chief Hous
Ouran belonging to him also
Letrim to the Earle's eldest Sone
Goorte
Dunlaghlen, to one of the Odallies[k]
Longfoord
Clonfert to the Bishop thereof.
Ballineslo to Capten Brabazon's Sone
The Castle of Teaquin belonging to one of the O'Kellies[l]
The Castle of Athenrie belonging to the Lord Bremingham

inscription, 'Pray for the Soule of Alderman Dominick Browne and his Posterity, who dyed in 1576.' 'Here lieth the Bodys of Richard Browne, his son Matthew Browne and their children—God rest their souls. Amen. 1635.' 'Moriertha O'Fiernagh, and his wife Kate Kernanigonohiv, and his brother Teig Og. An. 1580.'—*Hardiman's Galway*, p. 268.

[k] 'Donnall O'Daly, a gentleman, who had command of a party of soldiers on the English side, in 1589 fell fighting against the Burkes of Tirawly.'— *Four Masters*. In 1641 Lieutenant Dermot O'D. with 3 companies of foot and 30 musketeers defended the Castle of Tirellan against the insurgents—a brave officer, grandson of Dermot O'D.

of Lerra Co. Galway, gent. who in 1578 obtained from Elizabeth the lordship, castles and lands of Lerra.—*Hardiman's Galway*, p. 112.

[l] Hy-Many or O'Kelly's country comprises the baronies of Athlone and Athcarnan in Roscommon, and of Tiaquin, Kilconnell and Killian in Galway. In 1585, Hugh O'K. of Lisdallon in Roscommon, who was chief, renounced the title of O'KELLY. His Tanist, Teig McWilliam O'K. of Mullaghmore, was chief in the baronies of Tiaquin and Kilconnell; and Teig's rival for the Tanistship was Conor Og O'K., of Killian barony. Under Teig was O'Mannin of Mynloch (whose castle, says O'Donovan, was lately destroyed by lightning); under Conor was

COUNTIE OF GALLOWAY.

The Castle of Donemone and Turlevaghan belonging to him also[m]
The Cabboyhe belonging to Frances Shayn
The Abbey of Kilconnell belonging to the Quene

Men of Name The Earle of Clanrickard[n] his name is Burke
The L. Brymingham his name is Bremingham
Sir Hubert McDavie[o] his name is Burke Mackoogh

O'Concannen of Kiltullagh.—*Hy-Many* p. 18; *Iar-Con.*, p. 320.

[m] '*Brymegham's Country, or Barony of Donemore;*' Ullick, earle of Clanrickard; Edmond Brymidgham, lord barron of Athenrie; Tibbot boy McJonen, of Tobberkeoghe; Donyll O'Higgin, of Killelona; J. duffe Brymidgham, of Feartemore; R. Fowlle, of Feartemore; W. Brymidgham, of Miltoun.

[n] *The Baronie of Clare.*

▸ John Burke FitzThomas, and McCreamon, chiefe in the same.

Gents and Castles.

Therle of Clanricard, Clare; Ullig Keogh, Dromghriffin; J. Lynch fitz-William, Yowhule; Tybbot Lyogh, Loscananon; M^acWalter, called Thomas McHenry, Ballenduffe; Moyler Mc Shean, Cloynebow; Walter Fitz-Ab, fitz-Ed., Masse; N. Lynch, Anaghcoyne; H. fitz-Edmond, Leagkagh; McReamon, Cloghenwoyr; Ullig Mc Reamon, Castle Hackett; Walter Burke, Kilnemanegh; McWalter's sept, Cahermorise; Moyler McReamon, Anaghkyne; Wil. Grana McRic, Cloghran; Redmund McMoyler McRoe, Bealclarhome; Redmund McWalter, Aghkyne; Ullig McRichard, Comor; W. Gaynard, Carigin; Meyler McRickard, Tawmagh; R. Burke, Coroffyny; J. fitz-Ambrose, Anbale; Thomas Balue, Qworanonyn; Th. Ballagh, Beallabeanchere; J. Burke fitz-Thomas, of Ballindere, and of Deremaclaghlyn; Murrogh McSwyne, Kyleskiegh; Edmund Owhny, Achrym; Walter Boy, Grange; J. oge fitz-John fitz-Ed., Carnan; R. Burke fitz-Tho., Beallena; Tirlagh Caragh McSwyne, Cahirnefieke; Ffoxe's castle. Cas, 33.'—*Division of Connaught in 1586. Brit. Mus.* See *Iar-Con.*, p. 148.

[o] '*M^acDavye's Countreye.*'

'Sir Hubert Bourke McDavie, of Glenske, Knight; Davie McEdmond, of Kilcroan; Thomas McHenrie, of Ballyme; R. Betaghe, of the Cregg; Hobert buy McEdmond, of the Moate; Shane McUllick Bourke, of Rahenile,

The several Houses of the Burches[p] of Leytrim Of Clonrickard.
A great Sept of the O'Kellies[l] whereof are manie Houses.
The Omaddens[q]

otherwise called M{c}Walter, chiefe of his name Shane M{c}Ullicke, of Kilmogher, all having lands or holdings within the barony of Bellamoe and M{ac}Davie's Country by the east the river of Succke in the countie of Roscommon.'—*Iar-Con.*

[p] 'There are more able men of the surname of the Burkes than of any name in Europe.'—*Sir J. Davies, Car. Cal.* an. 1606, p. 465.

Country of Clanrickard.

Ulick, Earl of Clanrickard, the Lord Baron of Leitrim ; R. Bourke, of Derry M{c}Laghny, esquire ; Sherone M{c} Knowge, of Killenedyaine, otherwise M{c}Kowge ; Ullick Carraghe M{c}Hubbert, of the Dissharte, called M{c}Hubberte ; Hubbert M{c}Edmund, of Gortnemackin ; Johnesone, of Binmore ; William Mostonne, of the Downe ; Shannock M{c}William Roe, of the Naile, called MacWilliam Roe; Walter Wall, of Droghtye, chiefe of his name ; Redmond Dolphine, of Rarroddy, chiefe of his name ; H. M{c}Swine, of Cloghervanae ; O. M{c}Swine, Kiltullage ; Oene Mantagh O'Heine, of Downgorye, called O'Heine ; Connor Crone O'Heine, taneste to the said O'Hiene ; Hubbert boy Bourk M{c}

Redmond, otherwise M{ac}Edmond ; D. O'Shaghnes, of Gortynchgory ; J. O'Shaghnes, of Ardmollyvan, compettytors for the name O'Shaghnes ; N. Follane, of the Newtone ; E. M{c}Ullick Bourke, of Ballily ; R. M{c}William, of Rahale; Shane Oge Bourke, of Mannyne ; Brian Reogh M{c}Kilkelly, of Cloghballymore.—*Iar-Con.*, p. 323.

[q] *O' Madden's Country.*

'Donyll O'Madde, of Longford, otherwise called O'Madden ; Owen Balluff O'M., of Lusmagh ; Cogh O'M. of Killyan ; Edmond M{c}Downy, of Rathmore ; Donyll M{c}Brasill, of Dryowen ; Cathall Carragh O'Madden . . . having lands and holdings within the barony of Longford, otherwise called Syllanmuighie.'—*Iar-Con.* p. 321.

In 1596, when the Deputy summoned O'Madden's Castle, Cloghan, to surrender, the ward answered that if all his soldiers were Deputies they would not yield, and about 186 persons were killed in the Castle, or around it. Among them were these chiefe men — O'Madden, of Corglogher ; O'M., of Kineghan; two O'M., of Tomaligh ; two O'M., of Clare Madden ; O'M., of Clare. In 1602 O'M. attacked O'Sullevan

COUNTIE OF GALLOWAY.   137

O'Shaghnes' Oflagherties'
Frances Shaen.
Thomas Dillon, Justice of Conaught.

Beare, who was marching through O'Madden's country to the north. In 1611 Donnell O'M., of Longford, Co. of Galway, 'captain of his nation,' left his manor and castle of Longford, etc., to his son.—*Hy-Many*, p. 150.

'Sir Roger O'Shaughnessy of Gort-Inchigory; 'he used to have 280 reapers in harvest;' his fourth son, Sir Dermot, d. in 1606, seized of the territory of Kinalea, or O'Shaughnessy's country, which he left to his heir Gilliduffe O'S.—*Hy-Fiacrach*, p. 379.

'A rich and noble family.'—*Description of Connaught* in 1612.

'' The barony of Ballenehence, containing the ii Conymares, viii myles long and vi broad; Murrogh ne doo O'Flarty, chief in the same.

Gentlemen, and their Castles, viz.:—

Donnell Ecowga, Ballenehense; Edmund Oflartie, Kyllindowne; Edmund McHugh, A new Castle; Ochaghy, of Lettermellan; Donell Ecowga, Bonowyn; Tege ne Buly, of Arddearee; Miles McTibbot, Reynivylie; Castles, 7—*Division of Connaught in* 1586; *Iar-Con.*, p. 93.

'The Country of the O'Fflahertyes called Eyre-Conaght in 1585, Sr Morogh ne doe of Aghnenure, otherwise called O'Fflahertie; Donell Crone O'F., of the Cnocke, competitor for the name of O'Fflahertie; Teig ne Boolye (na buile), of the Arde, otherwise called O'Fflahertie of both Con o Marrice; Owine fitz-Donyell Coghie O'F., of Bonowen; Moroghe O'F., of the sam; Roger O'F., of Moycullen; Danyell McRory O'F. of the Owre; Rory O'F. and Danyell, his brother, sonnes to Moroghe ne Mooe; McThomas; Mc Connor; O'Halloran; McCahill Boy McDonoghe; and McEnry; Lynche, of the Ballaghe; Browne, of Bearny; Martyne, of Gortetleva; Martyne, of Ballyerter; Linche, of the Dengine; Marcus Linch fitz-Nichollas, of Furboghe; and Patrick ffrence, of Curcholline.

'The barony of Muckullen, in 1586, Murrogh ne doe, chief.

Gentlemen and Castles (20) viz.:—

Rory O'Flahairte, of Muykullen; Murrogh ne doe, of Nowghe, and of Achneuir (Aghnenure); T. Colman, of Mynlagh (Menlo); Jonick O'Halorane, O'hery; O. O'Halorane, Bearne (Barna); D. Lynche, Tyrellan; R. Skeret, Short Castle (Castlegar); Donell oge O'Hologhan, Qwarown Brown (Carrobrown); W^m. and Redmond M^cW^m. Ffiegh, Kellyn; Redmond McThomas, Ballymuritty; Redmond Reogh, Ballindully; Richard Beg, Cloynecanyn; Darby Augny, Lysacowly; J. Blake fitz-Ricard, Kiltullagh; J. Blake fitz-

The 3 Ilands of Arien' are in this Countie within a Kenninge of the Towne of Galloway.

This Countie is in a manner unpeopled by reason of the Spoyles committed in the last Rebellion, partlie by the rebell and partlie by the Souldier, and the great famine that followed thereupon, which hath so wasted this countie that scarce the

Ricard, Kiltorogh; Thomas Blake, Ballemicro; Thomas and John Blake, Turlagh ne sheamon; Muriertagh O'Conor, Tullekyhan; M. Lynch, New Castle.'—*Iar-Con.* pp. 252 & 311.

O'Flaherty, of the Castle of Moycullen, d. in 1599, and was succeeded by his son Hugh, who was the last chief of his name, and d. in 1631, leaving a son, aged two years, who became the famous Irish Antiquary. A considerable part of the Castle of Aghnenure still remains.

'The barony of Ross or Joyce's country contains the Joyes, Walshes, Partrish (Partry) lands; McThomas and McTybod chief in the same.

Gents, and their Castles, viz.:—

MacThomas, Castlekirke; Murrogh ne dow, Ballynonagh; McEnvile, Ballenesleo; Albè McEnvile, Cloynlaghell; R. McMoyler Joy, Castlenew.' Titus B. xiii. fo. 399.—*Division of Connaught* in 1586.

'In 1588 the Mayor and citizens of Galway petitioned Elizabeth in favour of Morogh McTurlogh O'Brien, and said that 'he and his ancestors under the name of McTeig O'Brien, of Arran, were captains or lords of the Islands of Arran, until of late he was expulsed by the usurping power of the O'Flaherties.'

In 1575 Morchow McTirrelagh Mc Donill, chiefe of his nacion, called Clanteige, of Arran, claimed the ancient custom of connow and meales due to him and his ancestors, *i.e.*, for two days and nights in Galway. The 'Gentlemen of the isles in 1575 were, besides this captain, Eturgh, Morowe, McMorchowe, Meeagh, McTirrelagh, McMorchowe, McTirrelagh Oge, and McBrene.' This clan descended from Brian Boromhe.—See *Hardiman's Galway,* pp. 207 and 52.

Teig *an t-sleive* (of the mountain) O'Fahy and 8 gentlemen of the name had fee-simple property in the barony of Loughrea in 1617. There were the O'Lynes, of Ballinvoggan, Lisnagree, and Lehergen, in the bar. of Kilconnell, they were proprietors of handsome estates, and looked on themselves as Firbolgs. E. O'Horan, of Carrowanmeanagh; R. O'Horan, of Carrowanclogha, on which stood a castle; and others of the name in the bar. of Leitrim. In the bar. of Dunmore, the Lallys, of Tullaghnadaly, Ballynabanaby, and Lisbally, paid chief rent to Lord Bermingham; from the Lallys of

hundereth men or Hous is to be found now that was Several years ago. There is in Rebellion some of the Kellies and Burkes" and Omaddens, and in a sort all the Countie saving the Towne of Galloway and the Earle of Clanrickard and some of his Friends.

Tullaghnadaly descend the Counts Lally, of France.

In the bar. of Leitrim, M{c}Cnavin, of Cranog MacCnaivin; the head of the Clan, Hugo M{c}Nevin, *alias* M{c}Kelly, having joined the insurgents, was hanged in 1602; there were 8 other gentlemen of the name; the last supposed head of the clan was D{r.} M{c}Nevin, of 1798 celebrity.—*Hy-Many* pp. 36, 28, 88, 182, 68.

John Donelan, son of the Protestant Archbishop of Tuam, lived at Ballydonelan. John's brother became Lord Chief Justice of the Common Pleas; and his grandson, John, erected the stone cross of Kilconnell, which is said by the country people to bow when a Donelan is taken by it to the grave; it bears the inscription—' Orate pro D. Johanne Donelano, ejusque familia, qui hanc crucem erigi fecit A.D. 1682.'—*Hy-Many*, p. 172.

In 1594 Dermoid Duff O'Halloran, gent, of Bearna, for a certain sum of money, 'dedit, concessit, barganizavit to Edmund Halloran, Merchant, of Galway, all his maneria, dominia, castra, etc., of Rinemoyly,' etc. In the same year John O'Halloran, of Galway, 'piscator,' gave to A. Martin, merchant, omnia manerium, castrum,

etc. . . . boscos, suboscos . . . montium . . . in villis, campis, et hamletis de Rynvile.—*Iar-Con.* p. 255.

In the bar. of Kilconnell were Brian M{c}Cooleghan, of BallyM{c}Couleghan, and seven other proprietors of that name. In the bar. of Clanmacnowen O'Coffey owned 4 cartrons of land.— *Hy-Many*, p. 184, 84.

In the bar. of Kiltartan, and chiefly in the parish of Dawros Kinvara, there were 13 persons of the name O'Heyne in 1641. The *Four Masters* record the death of O'Heyne, of Lydegan, in 1594; he left a son, Hugh Buy O'H. There was a Knougher Crone O'Heyne, of Ledygan, gent., 100 years old and upwards in 1615, and O'Heyne, of Killaveragh, aged 80.—*Hy-Fiachrach*, p. 378 and 405.

" In 1599 the sons of Redmond Na Skoab, uncle to the Earl of Clanrickard, 300 f.; in Sillanchie, four sons of Owen O'Madden, who was lately killed in action, 50 f.; in Iar-Connaught the Joyes, M{c}Donoghe, and the Flaherties, 140 f. In 1598 John Burke, 'Baron of Leitrim,' led some hundreds of O'Neil's soldiers, fighting through Connaught, Leinster and Munster.—*Car. Cal.*, p. 300; and *Four Masters*.

THE COUNTIE OF MAYO.

This Countie[a] contayneth all the Land of McWilliam Euter,[b] and the Lands of the Omaylies,[c] Clandonels,[d] McMorice, McJordan, McCustologhe and the [   ]; this Countie hath in the Sea certain Ilands both Fertile and most comodious

[a] In 1574 the chiefs of the baronies were McMoris in Crossbwyhin, McMoris' Country; in Kilvean Wm. Burk Fitz-John, E. Burke Vaghery, and the Clan Jonyns; O'Maley in Murisk; Richard en-Iren in Burres; McVadin in Kunermore (Envyremore); John McOliverus or McWilliam, and McVadin called Baron Barret, in Many (Moyne); McWilliam Burk, and McPhilipin in Burrisker; McJordan or Baron D'Exeter in Beallalahane; McCostello otherwise Baron Nangle in Beallahaunes.—*Car. Cal.* 1601-1603, p. 474 and 450.

In 1587 'McCostello his country' was inhabited by Sir Theobald Dillon and his tenants.—*Iar-Con.* p. 340.

Sir Theobald m. a daughter of Tuite of Tuitestown; he saw assembled at one time in his house of Killenfaghny above one hundred of his descendants.—*Lodge.*

[b] 'I found McWilliam verie sencible, though wantinge the English tongue, yet understanding the Latin. . . . Surely, my Lords, MacWilliam is well wonne, for he is a great man; his Land lyeth along the West North West Coast wherein he hath manie goodlie Havens, and is Lord of a Territorie of three times as moche Land as the Earl of Clanricarde is.

'O'Maylle came likewise with him, who is strong in galleys and seamen.

'Also MacPhaten or Barrett, MacIvyle Staunton, MacJordan or Dexter, Mac Custelo or Nangle, MacMorris or Prendergast . . . all five have been Englishe, which everye man confesseth, but also Lords and Barons in Parliament, as they theim selves affirme, and surely they have lands sufficient for Barons, if they might weeld their owne quietlye. But so base and Barbarous Barons are they now, that they have not three hackneyes to carry them and their train home. There were with me many more of lower degree and no deeper of wealth, as the Chiefe of Clanandros and Mac Thomyn; both they, and many more Barretts, Cusacks, Lynches (Lynottes), and of sundrie English surnames now degenerate.'—*Sir H. Sydney,* in 1576.

[c] By inquisition taken A.D. 1607, it appeared, that Owen O'Maly, chief of his name and nation, and his ancestors, had chief rents, of barley, butter, and money, out of several lands within the barony of Murrisk; that he was seised of the Castle of Cahir-na-mart (now

COUNTIE OF MAYO.   141

for Shipping, for which purpose both Inglyshe and Strangers had Intercourse there. It hath the Ocean to the West and North, the Counties of Sligo and Roscommon to the East and the Countie of Galloway to the South.

The most part of this Countie is possessed by the Burkes,* whose Capten they commonlie call M<William. They are many of the name and Stoute men able to make in tymes past before the Warr consumed many of them 1500, the rest of the Countrie is inhabitted by the McJordans, McCustulaghes, and the rest above Specified, who be dependers upon McWilliam, and in a manner

Westport), the castle and island of Carrowmore, etc., in right of tanistry; and that he, as chief, ought to have, as his ancestors had 'all fines for bloodshed, all skins of animals killed, or to be killed, within that barony.'—*Iar-Con.* p. 58.

'The O'Mallies and O'Flaherties purposed with 600 men, whom they had gathered, to invade Kerry.'—Carew to Privy Council, May 2, 1601.—*Car. Cal.* The O'Mallies are celebrated in several Irish poems as expert seamen, as the sea-gods of the West. Graine O'M., mother of Tibbot ne long, first Viscount Mayo, was renowned for her bravery at sea. The O'M. were chiefs of the two Ualls, *i.e.* baronies of Murrisk and Borrishoole. O'Dugan says, 'A good man there never was of the O'Malleys, but he was a seaman.'

ᵈ The Lord Deputy wrote to the Council in 1576—' Out of the Countye of Maio came to me to Galway first seven principall men of the Clandonnells, for everye of their seven Linagies one, of that surname, inhabiting that Countye, all by profession mercenarie soldiers by the name of Galloglas; they are very stronge, and moche of the wealth of the countrie is under them; they are able to go where they will, and with the countenaunce of any meane Lorde of Force, to make Warre with the Greatest. I won MacWilliam Ewghter's chief force from him in getting these Clandonnells.'

* The Burkes of Mayo were 'noble of mind and of good courage,' and with the O'Flaherties were considered 'the greatest nation, and possessing the strongest country of any people in Ireland;' and were joined with the O'Rorkes and O'Connors—forming a league of the 'proudest, wildest, and fiercest clans.'—*L. Deputy to Walshingham* in 1589.

In 1586 the Bourks, very badd and loose people, very hardlye continued themselves two years together within compass of obdyence. The sons of Edmund Bourk of Castlebar were seven in number; he was an oulde man, a

his Vassals. They are whollie out in Rebellion saving one principall man called Tibbotnelong.'

There are no Townes in this Countie of any importance, but competitor for the MacWilliamshippe, a most badd member to the state, and his wife as bad as himself.—*Docwra's Narrative*, p. 214.

'There are more able men of the surname of Bourke than of any name wheresoever in Europe.'—Sir J. Davis in 1606.—*Car. Cal.*, p. 465.

In 1589 the Lower Burkes of Tirawly went on their defence, beat the English and Irish under Brown at Bealach and Diothruibh, slaying Brown, Donnell O'Daly an officer, and Redmond oge Burke of Benmore Castle, Galway; then they were joined by the sliocht of Oliverus FitzJohn Burke of Tirawly, by the Clan Donnell Galloglach, etc. ; they ravaged Connaught by day and night during the spring.

In 1595 Tiboid Burk (son of Walter Kittagh son of John, son of Oliver, son of John) laidseige to Belleek Castle near Ballina, took it, beat and pursued Captains Bingham, Foal, Mensi and Tuite (son of Wᵐ Boy Tuite) slaying Foal, Mensi and Tuite. Then, as Clan William Burk were at variance concerning the Lordship of the territory, O'Donnell nominated Tiboid chief in presence of the forces of O'Donnell and Clanwilliam.

In 1601 Walter (son of the late Mᶜ William Burke) was shot in a battle near Ennis. Up to the spring of this year Lord McWilliam and Tibot-na-Long were at peace, but then the descendants of Ulick and Tibot-na-Long chose as McWilliam, Rickard Burke, the son of *Deamhan an Chorrain* ('Daemonis Falcati filius' says O'Sullivan, or, as Docwra puts it, 'the Devil's Hook son'). But O'Donnell's McWilliam at Michaelmas got help from him, came back, beat his rival, and the sliocht Ulick Burke and Tibbot-na-Long, in a fierce battle, in which they were mindful of their ancient grudges and recent enmities, and in which Rickard was slain.—*Four Masters*.

This Tiboid, the last McWilliam, retired to Spain, where his son Tiboid was made Marquess of Mayo; he had seven brothers—Oliver of Iniscoe ; Ulick Ruadh of Crossmolina; John *an t-sleibhe* (of the Mountain); William *Fada* (the Tall) of Castlelacken ... *Lodge*.—' Viscount Mayo.'

' McWilliam was in action with 600 foot and 60 horse. Tibbot *na Long*, ' of the ship,' so called because he was born at sea, was son of Sir Richard *an Iarain* (of the iron) and the famous Graine ni Maille, dau. of Owen O'Malley of the Owles. His brothers Walter and Edmond were slain by the English. He defeated and hanged his brother-in-law, O'Connor, who was going to join the English interest ; in 1599 he with his followers maintained 600 f. and 60 horse against Elizabeth ; at the

many good Havens and fayre Castles belonging to the Gentlemen before named, whereof the chief is Castlebury Ardenery Belike, and the Castle of [   ] belonging to the Earle of Ormond

battle of Kinsale he fought on the English side; got, with his step-brothers Morogh and Donall Ikeggie O'Flaherty, a re-grant of his lands, was member for Mayo in 1613, became Viscount Mayo in 1626. He married a dau. of O'Connor Sligo. He had 4 sons—Miles, David, Tibot *Riveagh* (the strong) of Cloghans, and Rickard (called *Iron Dick*). His daughters were mar. to O'Conor Dun, O'Flaherty of Aghnamurra, Burke of Castlehacket, and Burke of Turlogh.—*Lodge.*—'Viscount Mayo.'

In 1597 he undertook with the aid of her Majesty's forces to banish Tibbot McWalter, the now McWilliam; for reward to have McWilliam's lands, and in lieu of the name of McWilliam to have a title, etc.

In 1597, the people of Mayo (except Wm. Boork of Shroul, his son Oliverus McShane, and his brother Edmond, Wm. Boork FitzRichard who fled into Munster, and McMorrice) in number 1500 men in action. Tibbot ne Long with the Devil's Hook and others had put in pledges. MacWilliam is in action, in July last lost 200 of his men; at his late coming his brother Thomas, equal in mischief to himself, was slain, and one of the chief commanders of the Clandonnels, with 30 or 40 of his men—their heads sent to me by Tibbot ne Long. McWilliam's forces, with 400 out of O'Donnel's country amount to 700.—*Car. Cal.*, year 1597, p 265, 270.

The chief men in 1585 were—Sir Richard Bourke of the Newton, knight, otherwise called McWilliam Eughter—Walter Kettagh Bourke of Bealycke and Crossmalyene—Bourke of Ardnery—E. Bourk McOliver of Ropa—Barret of Ross, otherwise called McPadin, chief of his name—Barret of Ballasseekery—Myly McEvily of Kenturk, otherwise called McEvily, chiefe of his name—Bourke of Castlebar, tanest to the said McWilliam Eyghter—Bourke of Ballenecarrae, otherwyse called the blinde abbote—Moyler B. of Castle McKerra—Tybbott Reoghe Bourke of Boherfayne—Evagher McJordan of Bellalahen, otherwise called McJordan, chief lord of the barony of Bellalahan or Gallen—Moyller McJurdan of the Newcastell—Walter Leaghe McStevane of Corran McStephane—Jordan Mc Thomas of Ballahaghe—R. McMoryse of the Bryse, otherwise called McMoryshe, chiefe of his name—McMoryshe of Castell McGeralte—Walter McErydry of Castell-Reoghe—William Bourke of Shrowell—Bourke of Conge—R. oge Bourke of Cloynecashell—Molaghlyne

STATE OF IRELAND ANNO 1598.

THE COUNTIE OF SLIGO.

Sligo[a] contayneth all the Lands betwcene the River of Earne and the plaine of Conaught by the Skirts of the Mountains of Ballibyan and Curleges to the river of the Boyle in M<sup>c</sup>Dermots Countrie and from thence North west by the River of Moyne which divideth the Countie of Maio from the Countie of Sligo. So hath it the River of Earne to the East, Maio to the West, the Sea to the North, and the Countie of Roscomon to the South.

O'Mayle of Belclare, otherwise called O'Mayle, chiefe of his name—Teige roe O'Mayle of Cahairenemart—Ouan O'Mayle of the same—Dermot M<sup>c</sup>Arte of Clare—Gilleduffe M<sup>c</sup>Gibbon of Ballynekellye—R. oge M<sup>c</sup>Gibbon of Glankyne—Sherrone M<sup>c</sup>Gibbon of Lackane—fitz Symons of Dunmacknynye—Walter M<sup>c</sup>Phillipyne of Brehe, otherwise called M<sup>c</sup>Phillypyne, chiefe of his name—Ferraghe M<sup>c</sup>Tirrlage roe of Carrickmadye—E. oge M<sup>c</sup>Gibbon of Derrymacgornan—W. Bourke of Torrane—R. oge M<sup>c</sup>Tomyne of Ballicroen—Barret of Dowlaghe—J. Browne of the Neyle—Barret of Kyrenan—Caree of Downmacknyny. — *Iar-Connaught*, p. 331 to 338.

. "'It hath of auncyent or new English none; off Irishie—O'ConnorSligoe, the M<sup>c</sup>Donoghes, the O'Dowdes, the O'Haraes, the O'Hartes, some of the M<sup>c</sup>Swynes and others.'—Description of Connaught in *Archæol*, vol. 27. The Lord Deputy reported in 1576 that O'Connor 'hath under his Tyranny O'Dowd, two M<sup>c</sup>Donoghes, two O'Hares and Agare, and yet he himself trybutarie to O'Donnell. They be all men of great lands, the countye is well inhabited, and ritche and more haunted with strangers than I wish it were.'—See *Iar-Con.* p. 300.

'The lords and chieftains in the year 1586 were—Sir Donyll O'Connor of Sligo, knight; Pheolyme O'Harte of Ardtarmon, otherwise called O'Hart, chief of his name; O'Connor of the Grawndge; Edmond O'Dowey (O'Dowda) of Killglasse, otherwise called O'Dowey, chief of his name; Hubert Albenaghe of Rathly; Breene M<sup>c</sup>Swyne of Ardneglas; Dowdy of Castle-Connor; Cormocke O'Harry (O'Hara) of Cowlany, otherwise called O'Harey buy, chief of his name; Ferral O'Harry of Ballinefennock, otherwise called O'Harry reoghe, chief of his name; O'Harry of Tulwy; O'Harey of Cowlany; Ferrdorraghe M<sup>c</sup>Donoghe of Cowlea, otherwise called M<sup>c</sup>Donoughe Tyrreryll, chief of

It hath in it no Towne but Sligo, a Sea towne with a Haven, which the Castle Shot.

Principall } Sligo belonging to the Quene.
Castles } Baller[b] belonging also to the quene.

Bondrois } belonging to O'Donnell who claimeth a
Belike } chief rent of £240 per Annum out of
O'Connor Sligoes Country.

The chief L. of this Countie is O'Connor Sligoe.[c] It is his name; M‹Donogh of Ballyndowne; M‹Donogh of Cowlwonye; M‹Donoghe of Clonemahyne; Cene M‹Hughe of Bryckleawe; Croftone of Ballymote; Goodman of Taghtample; Manus Reoghe of Rathmollyne; Manus M‹Teig buy of Lysconnowe; Mac Swyne of Loughtnevynaghe; Uryel Garrey of Moye, otherwise called O'garry, chief of his name; Rory O'Garry of Kearrowercogh; Manus M‹Bryene Reoghe of Levally. . . . Sir Donill O'Connor shall have the castles of Sligo in the barony of Carbry, and Meynlagh in the bar. of Magherylenye, etc. In the bar. of Corran Carmac O'Harry Buy shall have his castle of Cowlany, Ferragh Carragh O'Harry reogh his castle of Ballinefenock or Ballyharry; Hugh M‹Donoghe shall have land in the bar. of Corran removing from Ballymote; in the bar. of Tirrerel Ferdoragh M‹Donogh of Cowlea, and M‹Donogh of Cowlwony Castle; in the bar. of Tirrereagh Edmond O'Dowd his castle of Kylglasse, his cousin and heir apparent Davy O'Dowd of Castle Connor; Urrel O'Garry his castle of Moygarry,

John O'Crean his house or town of Ballynegare.—*Iar-Connaught*, p. 340 to 345.

[b] Ballymote had belonged to the Queen for the space of thirteen years, but in the summer of 1598 it was taken by its rightful inheritors the Clan Donogh of Corran, namely, Tomaltach and Cathal Dubh M‹Donough. In autumn they sold the castle to O'Donnell for £400 and 300 cows.—*Four Masters*, p. 2076.

Maurice M‹Donogh of Tirerill was slain in Breifney-O'Rorke in 1598 as he was carrying off a prey, and then Conor M‹Donogh of Ballindoon was appointed MacDonogh.—*Four Masters*.

[c] 'Donogh O'Conor Sligo, after his return from England in 1596, proceeded on behalf of the English to reduce Connaught; was joined by the Clan Donough of Collooney, and had Ballymote in his power. The O'Harts also adhered to him, for they had always been faithful to the man who held his place; and they began to threaten the Kinel-Connell. But O'Donnell plundered their territory; and in February 1597, he defeated O'Conor Sligo who had mustered an army of English and

most inhabitted by men of his name, and few Vassals the chief whereof is called Odood.[d] This Countrie is in a manner Subject to the Quene, yet are Rebells but against their Will, for their chief L. O'Connor being in Suite for the Lordship of Sligo in England 7 years and the Rebellion beginning long before he

Irish and was marching on Sligo.' However in that year O'C. Sligo with the help of his brother-in-law, Tibbot na-Long, twice beat McWilliam out of Mayo, and soon after, having joined Tibbot and Sir Conyers Clifford, he was severely wounded in a smart skirmish with O'Donnell's cavalry. Towards the end of the year he went to England and remained there to the end of 1598. He went with Essex on his hosting through Munster, then joined Clifford in Connaught, reached Collooney Castle (belonging to McDonogh of Tirerrill) the only castle which held out for O'Conor Sligo. It was deemed impregnable; O'Donnell besieged him; Clifford going to his relief with 1900 foot and 200 horse was beaten by O'Donnell, and lost his life in August 1599. O'Conor Sligo submitted and was reinstated in his territory by O'Donnell, and got from him 'a countless deal of cows, horses, etc., of corn and other necessaries to replant and inhabit his territory, after it had been a wilderness.' In 1600 he joined O'Donnell in his invasion of Galway and Clare; in 1601 for dealings with the enemy O'Donnell imprisoned him in Lough Esk. Donogh's brother, Dermot O'Conor was a distinguished captain of Connaught buonaghes serving in Munster in 1600 with 1400 men, and 'knoweth not better how to spend his time than to be resident where he gaineth so much; is grown to such reputation that he could bring 2000 more, were the Munster chiefs able to give them content.' Dermod took O'Sullevan More prisoner out of Munster; he himself was soon after, while going to join the English, attacked near Gort and hanged by Tibbot na-Long.—*Four Masters* and *Car. Cal.*, p. 401, 491.

Dermot had married the sister of Elizabeth's Earl of Desmond.

[d] 'O'Dowda of Tireragh (Dathi son of Teig) was slain by one of the queen's soldiers in one of his own castles in Tireragh of the Moy; his brother Teig Buy was made O'Dowda by O'Donnell in 1595—they were 7 brothers. Dathi had mar. Miss Lyons, who became successively wife of O'Dowda, of Sir L. Ghest, of Wm. May and of FitzMorrice FitzGerald. Her son Dathi O'Dowda was ordered to be brought up in the English religion and habits by Lionel Ghest. Sir R. Musgrave, in his narrative of the Irish rebellions, states, that this family counted 25 castles on their lands, "and they have a burying place appropriated to them in the Abbey of

cou'd end his Suite, O'Donnell tooke the best of the Countrie Prisoners and to this day detaineth them, and thereby constreyneth their followers to obey him at his pleasure, all the foresaid Castles be in O'Donnell's hand saving Sligo which was demolished by O'Donell 4 years ago, and since not re-edified.

THE COUNTIE OF LEYTRIM.

This Countie was erected by Sir John Perrott,[a] being before a parcell of the Countie of Sligo; it contayneth all O'Rorkes Countrie[b] called Breany Ororke also part of

Moyne, where may be seen the gigantic bones of some of them, who have been very remarkable for their great stature, as one of them exceeded seven feet in height." Mac Firbis was hereditary historian to O'Dowd, held the rod over O'Dowd at his inauguration, and drank at the banquet even before the acknowledged senior of the race. Ciothruadh and James McFirbis and their cousin John Oge built the Castle of Lecan in Tireragh in 1560. Ciothruadh had a son Ferfeasa. In 1672 Duald McFirbis, the last of these hereditary antiquaries of Lecan, was murdered.'—*Hy-Fiachrach*, p. 407.

[a] 'An Indenture was made in 1585 betwixte Perrotte, Lord Deputy Generall of Ireland, for and on the behaulfe of the Queene's most excellent Majesty of the one partye, and John, bishop of Kilmore—Lysaghe, bishop of Ardaghe

—Sir Briane O'Royrke of Dromahire, knt. —Cahall McConnor—Carragh Magrannyll of Inishmurryne, otherwise called Magrannell of Moynishe, chiefe of his name—Tirlaghe McMolaghline oge Magrannyll of Dromarde, otherwise called Magrannyle of Clonmologhlyne, chief of his name—Tyrelaghe Magawryne of the Largine, chief of his name—Teige oge Maglanchie of Rossclogher, chief of his name—Owyne McPhelline O'Royrke of the Garre—Rory McEnawe of Inyshimylerye, chiefe of his name—Melaghlyne McOwyne McMurrye of Loghmoyltagher—Farrell McTernan of Cloyloghe—Bryan McLoghlyne of the Fayhee—Phelyne Glasse of Cloncorycke—Wonye MacSheane O'Royrke of Lloghnecouhye, and Tyernane O'Royrke of Dromahyre of the other parte.

[b] 'Wytnesseth, that wheare the whole

McGwyres, and lying[c] upon the West part of Lough Earne and the Countie of Moynterrolis bordering upon the Countie of Longford and McSlenayes[d] Country near Bundras So as Leytrim hath the Countie of Sligo to the North the Sheynen to the West and South-West, the Countie of Longford South and part of the Countie of Cavan to the East. It hath neither Townes nor Castles of importance but such as be raised saving the Castle of Leytrim.

This O'Rorke[e] is the base Sone of the last Ororke apprehended in Scotland and Executed in Ingland who ever since his

territory called O'Royrk's country, comprehendeth Breny O'Royrke, both the Moynterolyes, the Largan, Cowleovlyne, Kinaloghane and the Dartry.'—*Iar-Connacht*, p. 346.

[c] 'McGuynies landes lyinge.'—*Dym.*

[d] 'MacGlanes Cuntrie lyinge on Bondroies.'—*Dymmock*, p. 20.

[e] This O' Rourke was Brian-na-Samhthach, or Brian Oge. In 1590 he spoiled everything belonging to the English, in Leitrim, when his father was driven out of his territory. In 1591 his father, Brian-na-Murtha O'R. was hanged in London, refusing to be tried by a jury, and refusing the ministrations of the Protestant Archbishop of Cashel, who was a pervert priest. Sydney had pronounced this Brian-na-Murtha the 'proudest man that ever he dealt with in Ireland.' 'No one of his tribe for a long time excelled him in bounty, hospitality, in giving rewards for panegyrical poems, and in sumptuousness, in numerous troops, in comeliness, in firmness, in maintaining the field of battle.' His son Brian in 1593 attacked Sir G. Bingham of Ballymote, burned Ballymote, and thirteen villages around it. In 1597 he joined O'Donnell and helped him to drive back the English army. In 1598, being annoyed with O'Donnell for having plundered O'Connor Roe, and being at variance with his own brother Teig about the partition of their territory, O'Rourke formed a friendship with Clifford and the English. But soon, on account of O'Donnell's persuasion and threats he joined O'Donnell, then plundered Mullingar and all around it; and made a second raid on that country.—*Four Masters*. On the 15th August 1599, he defeated at the Curlieus 1900 foot and 200 horse who were led by the gallant Sir C. Clifford.—*Tracts relating to Ireland*, Vol. II., p. 47.

He went to Kinsale with O'Donnell in 1601. He died at Galway in 1604, and was buried in Rosserilly. He was 'the battle prop of the race of Aedh Finn, the star of valour and chivalry, the brave protecting man who had never suffered Brefney to be molested in his

his Father's Execution hath bene a Rebell, saving a little time this last Sommer when upon a discord betwixt him and O'Donnel fearing Least O'Donnell should reject ͬthe Lawful Sone of the last Ororke to be Capten of the Countrie whom he hath in Custody and so displace him, he submitted himself to the State, but so soon as that controversie was composed he revolted againe, and since hath returned a great Enemie to the State, Spoyling and Wasting Especially the Counties of Longford and Westmeath; he is able to make of his owne men about 100 Horsemen and about 300 Footmen.ᵍ

time, a sedate and heroic man, kind to friends, fierce to foes.'—*Four Masters*.

ᶠ Elect, *recte*. In 1604, Teig O'Rourke only legitimate son of Sir Bryan O'R., got a grant of various lordships and manors in Leitrim. This Teige was 'Lord of Breifny, a man who had experienced many hardships while defending his patrimony against his brother, Brian Oge; a man who was not expected to die on his bed, but by the spear or sword; a man who had fought many difficult battles, and encountered many dangers while struggling for the dignity of his father, until God permitted him to obtain the Lordship, died in 1605, and was interred in the Franciscan Monastery of Carrigpatrick, *i.e.* Dromahare.'—*Four Masters*.

In 1601 Teig was sent by O'Neill with 800 men into Munster, and Redmond Burke with 600 men.

ᵍ According to the *Carew MSS.* O'Rourke's forces consisted of 600 f. and 60 horse.

The territory of the Magranails or Reynolds comprised *Mag-Rein* or the southern and level portion of the Co. of Leitrim. The late Squire Reynolds who was murdered at Sheemore was the last head of this family; his dau. is Mrs. Mᶜ Namara, of Lough-Scur House.

The last entry in the Annals of *Loch Cé* tells us that in the year 1590 'a Saxon army entered Dartry, or Maglancy's country; O'Rourke and Maglancy were in a fortified camp in the district before them; when Maglancy was leaving O'Rourke's camp, his enemies encountered him, viz., Maelsechlain Maglancy and another part of the army under Maglancy; and they killed him and eight persons with him, and his head was sent to Athlone.'-- *Annals of Loch Cé*.

O'Rodachans or O'Rodys were Comharbas of St. Caillin in the Church of Fenagh; they had several remarkable relics in their possession before Cromwell's time, viz., bells, sacred standards,

THE COUNTIE OF ROSCOMAN.

Roscoman[a] contayneth all the plaines of Conaught, beginning at the Abbey of Boyle nere the mountaines of the Cirlewes and Stretching along by the Sheynen to the River of the Suck. And so it hath the Sheynen to the East and South, the Countie of Sligo to the North, and the Counties of Galloway and Maio to the West.

This Countie is under the Diocese of the Bishop of Elfin, and the Townes are Roscomon, re-edified by Sir Nich. Malbie and the ruined Towne of Elfin.[b]

the shrine of St. Caillin. A very remarkable bell, called *Clog-na-righ* or Bell of the Kings, and an ancient vellum MS. are still preserved. The Coarbs or Herenach families looked on themselves as of the rank of gentleman, and not mere 'Antiquaryes.'

O'Roddy of Crossfield, hereditary *comharb* of Fenagh Monastery, was grandfather of Teig O'Roddy, who was an eminent Irish scholar and a great patron of Irish literature.—See *Irish Arch. Miscellany*, p. 115.

In 1696 were attainted the O'Rourkes of Galovrea, of Carnegreve, of Lallagh and of Dungebb, all in Leitrim. Several members of this family have held high command in the armies of France, Austria and Russia. In Russia there is a Prince O'Rourke.—*D'Alton's Army List.*

[a] A Jury finds at Roscommon in the year 1607 that—'Roscommon extendeth from Athlone to Lahaghnelahareebane, near and on this side of Beallanafadd, 33 miles, and from Beallaleige at the river of Sheanon to Owenmore, near Coystullath, 16 miles. . . . Item that it consisteth of fower barronyes and a halfe, viz. Athlone, Rosscommon, Boyle alias Moylagh (Moylurg) and the half barony of . . .'—*Iar-Con.* pp. 353, 355.

[b] Terra in planiciem plerumque porrecta, fertilis, et quae numerosa pascit armenta, adhibitaque mediocri cultura fruges benigne producit . . . Sub Curlew montibus ad Sineum flumen est Baronia *Boile* ubi *MacDermot* rerum potitur; ad Succum Baronia *Balin-Tober*, ubi *O'Conor Dun* plurimum potest, cui adjacet *Elphin*, sedes Episcopalis. Inferius est *Roscoman, O'Conori Roo* Baronia, in qua est oppidum primarium, castro olim munitum, sed aedificiis culmeis tectis; et magis ad

COUNTIE OF ROSCOMAN. 151

*The Principall
Castles are:*—Roscomon ⎱ belonging to the Quene.
 Athloane   ⎰
St. John's, belonging to Mr. Goodman.
Balinesloe, belonging to Capt. Brabazon's Sones.

austrum *O'Kelliorum* Baronia, *Athlone*, a praecipuo oppido nominata, quod suum habet castrum, et praesidia, et pontem e vivo saxo pulcherrimum quem Elizabetha Regina construendum curavit.'—Letter-press affixed to *Jansonius'* Ancient Map of Connaught.

'The country is of excellent soyle; under O'Chonnor Donne's rule are O'Byrne and Offlun; under O'Chonnor Roe is O'Flanigan; under MacDermot is MacManus.'—*Sydney's Letters*, Vol. I., p. 104.

It was divided into six baronies in 1574, viz., Muikarnayn—Shane ne Moy Brene, O'Kelly and O'Naghten, chief in the same; Athloyne—O'Kelly, O'Fallon, M⁽ᶜ⁾Cogh, O'Murye and M⁽ᶜ⁾ Edmund, chief; Ballintubber—O'Connor Dun, O'Flyn, and O'Flanigan, chief; Manaster Buille—M⁽ᶜ⁾Dermot, and the sept of Owen M⁽ᶜ⁾Dermot, chief; Tireone—O'Birne and O'Hanly, chief; Roscommon — O'Connor Roe and O'Hanly, chief.—*Car. Cal.* 1601-1603, p. 475.

'The Lords, Chieftains, etc., of Moylurge, alias M⁽ᶜ⁾Dermott's countrye, O'Connor Roe's countrye, and O'Connor Dune's countrye,' who in 1585 came to an agreement with Perrott, were—Hugh O'Connor of Ballintobber, otherwise called O'Connor Dune, chiefe of his name; Fergonanym O'Hanley of Knockensheigh, chiefe of his name; Teig M⁽ᶜ⁾Towmultagh of Croghan; Towmultagh Oge of Ballinkillen; Towmultagh M⁽ᶜ⁾Hugh of Dromeharlagh; Oene Ernney of . . . Ferrall M⁽ᶜ⁾Dermonde Roe, chiefe of his name; Connor Oge M⁽ᶜ⁾Dermod of the . . . Taneste; Cahall Oge M⁽ᶜ⁾Mulmory of the Eaden; Mulmory M⁽ᶜ⁾Dermod, gald, chief of his name; Duwaltagh M⁽ᶜ⁾Toolie O'Connor of Bracklone; Cahall M⁽ᶜ⁾Toolie of Castlereagh; Feagh O'Ffloyne of Sleavline, chiefe of his name; Calloe O'Floyn of the Cladaghe; Turrelagh Keaghe M⁽ᶜ⁾Swiny Knocknetaghty; Teig O'Connor Roe, chiefe of his name; Hugh M⁽ᶜ⁾Tirrelagh Roe of Clonybyrne; Breene O'Flanegan of Ballaoghter, chiefe of his name; John Crofton of Canvoe; . . . of Ballingilly; Edward White of Ballinderry.'—*Iar-Con.* p. 352.

O'Connor Dune had under him O'Byrne, O'Hanlie, O'Fflynne, etc., in the barony of Ballintobber. Teig Oge O'Connor Roe had under him O'Flanegan, M⁽ᶜ⁾Brenan, etc., in the baroney of Roscommon; he lived in the castle of Bealnemully; his Tanest was Hugh M⁽ᶜ⁾Tirrelagh Roe, who lived in the castle of Clonybirne. Connor

Ballintabler,[c] Athleag, belonging to the Heyres of S[r] Nicholas Lestrange in Suffolk in Ingland.

Men of name :—
The Bishop of Elfin   Oconnor dun[d]

Oge M[c]Dermod, mentioned above as Tanest, lived at Incheaghochar. Theobald Dillon had Carrowe-Riogh in the barony of Ballintobber and Bally M[c]Moroghe and Bally-ne-shie in the barony of Boyle. There were also Clifford of Calae ; Cavanaghe of Newtown castle, and Morgan of Artagh.—See *Iar-Con.* pp. 356, 357.

[c] Belonging to Sir Hugh O'Connor Donn. Baile-an-tobair or Baile-tobair-Brighde, in the barony of Castlereagh, was taken by Sir Edward Fitton in 1571. In 1581 O'Coinnegan, an eminent cleric and keeper of a general house of guests, wished to be buried at the mound of Baile-an-Tobair. ' Diarmaid O'Connor Donn, the man who subdued his enemies the most, and who plundered and destroyed his adversaries the most, of the race of Turlogh Mor O'Connor, died in 1587, was buried in Baile-an-tobair, under the protection of God and Brigid, after he had been thirty-five years in sovereignty.'—See *Annals of Loch Cé.*

[d] Hugh, 9th O'Connor Donn, mar. a dau. of Bryan na Murta O'Ruarc. His eldest son, Charles, mar. a dau. of Viscount Bourke of Mayo. His son Hugh of Castlereagh mar. a dau. of Lord Dillon and died in 1635. His son, Captain Bryan Ruadh of Corrasduna, mar. Mary, dau. of O'Connor Ruadh of Castleruby. There is nothing remarkable concerning O'Connor Donn in the *Carew Calendar.* He d. in his Castle of Ballintubber in 1627.—See *Memoir of the O'Connors* by *Roderic O'Connor, Esq.,* p. 62 and 80 ; also, *Lineal Descent of the O'Connors,* by *R. O'Connor, Esq.*

The *Four Masters,* p. 2145, say that the famous leader of Connaught buonaghes, Dermot O'Connor (son of Dualtach son of Tuathal), was 'a gentleman of the house of O'Connor Donn.' But Archdall's *Lodge* says he was a brother of O'Connor Sligo, and brother-in-law of Tibot-na-long.—*Lodge,* vol. iv., p. 237. We have given an account of him at p. 146. 'O'Connor Donn, who had been for a long time imprisoned by O'Donnell, was set at liberty by him on the 4th Dec. 1597, after having given him his full demand ; and he solemnly bound himself to be for ever obedient to O'Donnell, by guarantees and oaths of God and the Church ; and he also delivered up to him as hostages for the fulfilment of this, his own two sons, the heir of O'Beirn, the eldest son of O'Hanly, the heir of O'Flynn, etc.' However, O'Connor Donn was on the English side in 1598.—See *Four Masters,* pp. 2047 and 2125.

Oconnor Roe[e]
M[c]Dermott[f]
O'Birne[g]

O'Flanegane
O'Hanlie[h]
O'Kellie[i]

[e] In 1597 Dubhaltach O'C. died. His two sons Con and the son of Dermot made an irruption into Glinske, the castle of MacDavid, and took preys; but on their return the son of MacDavid defeated them, slew Con O'C. and Mulrony M[c]Dermott and many other gentlemen.—*Four Masters.*

[e] Hugh Mirgagh O'Connor of Castleruby was 11th O'Connor Ruadh in 1596. He is ancestor of the O'Connors of Tomona and Ballagh in Roscommon. His uncle Teig was 10th O'Connor Roe, was M.P. in 1585, was hanged in 1592, and his sons were hanged in 1588 and 1595. In 1616 a jury finds that Hugh Mirgagh O'Connor was seised of Castlerone, Corneboy, etc. Hugh's brother was John O'Connor of Clonfree.—*Memoir of the O'Connors,* Appendix, p. ix.; also p. 79.

Hugh O'Connor Roe with his muster, and M[c]Dermot with his people joined O'Donnell in his raid into Clanrickard and Thomond in 1600; and in 1596 they joined him in his march against General Sir J. Norris. However, these chiefs formed 'a league of friendship' with Sir Conyers Clifford in that year 1596;
[f] O'Donnell in consequence plundered O'Connor Roe's territory in 1597, 'although O'C. Roe's position was secure and intricate, and he had near him a fastness, into which he could send his cattle,' etc. O'Donnell took all the cattle and plundered and burned all his country.—*Four Masters,* pp. 2195, 2003, 2037.

[f] Teig M[c]Dermot, chief in 1585, being too old to attend Parliament, sent his relative, Bryan of Carrig MacDermot, to represent the sept. This Bryan was chief in 1602; his wife was dau. of O'Connor Sligo. Bryan M[c]Dermot of Moylurg d. in 1592, 'and there was no one like him of the M[c]Dermots to succeed him in the chieftainship.' Conor M[c]Dermot is given by the *Four Masters* as chief of Moylurg in 1596, 1597, and 1600. In 1600 and 1601 M[c]Dermott joined O'Donnell in his march against General Norris, and against the English at Kinsale.—*Four Masters,* pp. 2041, 2195, 2275.

[g] O'Beirne, chief of O'Briuin-na-Sinna, a beautiful district between Jamestown and Elphin. Carbry O'Beirne was chief in 1585, and is said by the *Four Masters* to have attended Perrot's Parliament. Mr. O'Beirne, of Dangan-i-Beirne, possesses some of the old property, and is head of the race.—*O'Donovan.*

[h] His territory comprised the parishes of Kilglass, Termonbarry, Cloontuskert etc.—*O'Donovan's Notes to Topog. Poem,* p. xli.

[i] In 1585, among the chieftains in the Roscommon part of Imany were Hugh

M‹Garrot*
M‹Edmond¹
and divers freeholders
of ech surname
Henrie Malbie

Divers of the Nugents, and Tuits, and Dillons
The Heyres of Sir Nicholas Strange and Capten Barbazon.

This Countie is also all wasted[m] that Scarce in XX Miles shall a House be seen all are in a sort Rebells saving Hugh

O'Kelly (otherwise O Kelly) of Liscalhone; and Shane ne Moy O'K. of Criagh (now Creagh); Shane O'Naghten of Moynure; Donogh O'Murry of Ballymurry, and Covaghe O'Fallon of Milltowne. The ruins of O'Fallon's castle are still to be seen.—*Hy-Many*, p. 19.

* In 1585 lived Connor MacGeraghte, otherwise called MacGerraghte.

In 1585 lived Teig M‹Owen of Gallee, otherwise called M‹Edmond. He was of the sept of O'Kelly; his ancestor William O'Kelly built the castle of Gallee or Gaille on the margin of Lough Ree, where it still stands.—See *Iar-Con.*, p. 318, and *Hy-Many*, pp. 103, 104. There were also of Gallee—Teig Colle M‹Connor, and Ferdoragh M‹William Carragh.

In 1587, obiit Shane O'Naghten, seisitus, in jure Capitaneatus, de duobus quarteriis, in Les Ffaes de Athlone, alias O'Naghten's cuntry. Duo quarteria sunt in occupatione Connori O'Naghten filii antedicti Joannis. O'Naghten was the senior of all the Hy-Many. In 1604 a grant was made to Jane O'N. (widow of Robert O'N. of Mynure in the Faes, Co. of Roscommon, killed in the wars) of the wardship of John O'N., son and heir of said Robert. The present head of the family is E. Naughton, Esq., of Thomastown Park in the Faes. Of this stock were Baron O'Naghten, who attended the Prince of Hesse Homburg when he married Princess Elizabeth.—*Hy-Many*, p. 176.

* In 1566 Sydney wrote Elizabeth—'We passed M‹Dermott's country, Occonnor Roe's country, O'Connor Dune's country, and encamped near your Majesty's Castle and Monastery of Roscommon, leaving for twenty miles of length as fruitful and pleasant a country as is in England or Ireland, all utterly waste through the wars of Occonnor Dune and Occonnor Roe, and we suppose the breadth to be equal in manner with the length; which Castle of Roscommon, as we perfectly perceived and were surely advertised, was guarded with a ward put into it by Occonnor Dune; nevertheless they offered us no injury lying by them, neither were we able to do them any.'—*Journal of the R. Hist. and Arch. Assoc. of Ireland*, Jan. 1870, p. 23.

O'Connor Roe[a] but there is neither Inglysh nor Irysh left for the rebell or Souldier to Spoyle or prey upon.

[a] 'Roscomen in 1597.—All the Kellys in Imany between the Sock and the Shannon were in rebellion. When O'Donnell came into the country, Feriogh M'Hugh O'Kelly of Moycarnan, and the Kellys of Twoaleagh revolted; some fled to the North, some to O'Ruark's country. Donnell O'K. of Lysdallon, Edmund O'K., and Donogh Baccho O'K. of Culnegire, Kedogh O'K. of Cloghin, and Redmond O'Fallon of Myltown were never in action. O'Connor Roe, O'Birne, O'Hanly, O'Flanigan were in action. MacDermot with 150 followers revolted at the coming of O'Donnell. The M'Dermot Roes live about the Abbey of Boyle; but their followers are in action with O'Ruark. Con M'Dwaltogh O'Conor, cousin-german to O'Connor Don, pretending to be chief of that name, revolted; he was slain in action by Feagh Boork, son of Sir Hubert MacDavy Boork, with 16 others, including Mulrony MacDermott.'—*Car. Cal.* 1597, p. 269.—*Sir Conyers Clifford's Declaration.*

In Roscommon O'Connor Don, MacDermon, O'Brien, O'Hanlye, O'Flamergan, the MacSwynes, MacHugh, Duff Dalie, O'Kellye had in 1599, 500 foot and 30 horse. The rebells' forces in all Connaught are 3090 foot and 230 horse.—*Dymmok*, p. 28.

The Connaught Fastnesses were 'The woods and boggs of Kilbigher; Kilcallon, in MacWilliam's contry; Killalon, in the county of Leitrim; the woods and boggs near the Corleas.'—*Sir G. Carew.*

MOUNSTER.

MOUNSTER[a] being of all the provinces most commodious for the Soyle, Havens, Rivers, and Townes is devided into the counties of

    Waterford   Limerick
    Cork   Tipperarie
    Kerrie and Desmond

[a] In the *Pacata Hibernia*, published in 1633, there are maps of Munster, Cahir, Askeaton, Glynn, Carrigafoyle, Castle Mang, Limerick, Limerick Castle, Kinsale, Hallibolyn, Beare, Dunboy, Castle-ni-Park, Muskrey, Cork, and Youghal.

Spencer says of Ireland and specially of Munster, with which he was acquainted—' And sure it is a most beautiful and sweete countrie.' Sir H. Sydney wrote in 1566—' I have known Munster as well inhabited as many counties are in England, yet a man may now ride 40 miles and fynde no house standing nor any manurance of the earth.'

In 1584 the towns and villages were ruined and but one in thirty persons was left alive. Desmond's lands were 'replenished with wood, rivers, and fishings.'—*Sir V. Browne.* ' If y' honor did vewe the commodious havens and harbours, the bewtie and commoditie of ye river Shenan, you w^d say that you have not in any region observed places of more pleasure nor a river of more commoditie . . . the people of Munster be the most docile and reformable of all others.'—*Pelham's Letter in* 1580.

' The Irish did account Mounster to be the Key of the Kingdome, both by reason of the Cities and walled Townes (which are more than in all the Island besides), the fruitfulnesse of the Country being reputed the Garden of Ireland, and the commodious harbours lying open to France and Spain.'—*Pac. Hib.* p. 1, Ed. 1633.

On 23rd Apr. 1600, Mounster is compared by Sir H. Power, in his report to Carew, to ' a man diseased of a languishing and incurable sicknesse, the Head so sore, and the Heart so sicke, that every member refuseth his naturall office ; it was never more distempered. All the inhabitants of the countrey are in actual and open rebellion, except some few of the better sort, yet even all their tenants, Friends, and Followers, yea, for the most part, either their Sonnes or Brothers, pub-

THE COUNTIE OF WATERFORD.

Waterford contayneth all the Land between the River of the Suer which falleth into the Sea beneath Waterford and the River

lickly professed in this develish action—as, for example, the Lord of Cahir, Cormock M⁥Dermond Lord of Muskry, Gerald FitzJames Lord of the Decies, M⁥Carthy Keugh. The Rebells are absolutely Masters of the field, and her Majesty's Forces here garrisoned in Cities and walled Townes were in condition little better than besieged. Furthermore the Cities and walled Townes are so besotted and bewitched with Priests, Jesuits and Seminaries, that they are ready upon every small occasion to rise in arms against our soldiers, and minister all underhand ayde and succour unto the Rebells.'—*Pac. Hib.* pp. 31, 32.

'Nations of Munster chiefly noted as procurers of mischief :—The MacSyhis, MacSwynes, and the Leries. In Kerry and Desmond—the Clantey M⁥Gagh, and the Stacks, saving Morrice Stack and his brothers. They are closely allied one with another. Teig M⁥Owen's sons of Drissane are notorious malefactors, the elder Owen M⁥Teig excepted. They are supported by Cormac M⁥Dermody Lord of Muskrie ; their mother, one of the Swynes. O'Sulevan More and O'Sulevan Bere

continue faithful subjects. The Knight of Kerry, Thomas FitzMorris, and John O'Connor Kerry, " sworn to one another and intended to become subjects when they find an opportunity."

'Certain men sworn to continue in rebellion—The Lord FitzMorris, Thomas Oge of Ardnagreagh, E. Hussey of Balynahowe, Owen M⁥Moriartie of Skart, Cahir M⁥Brien of Traly, Thomas FitzJohn of Ballykely, heir of Ballykely.

'Cormock Oge faithful ; Cahir O'Kallahane alias Cahir Modurhte, dwelling by Moaloe to be maintained in his possessions, at least till these rebellions be assuaged—an instrument meet to be employed.

'Trusted instruments in Kerry—Moris Stack and his brothers, John Rice, Donel Faries, Richard Rice.

'To be trusted in Cork—Cormock Oge and his brother Teig, Miles Roch, James Nagle and his kinsmen, W. Malafont, Patrick Miagh of Kinsale, T. Fleming of Belguolan, Cormock Daly, Moris Roch, Cahir M⁥Donoghe.'—*Car. Cal.* year 1596.

'The provincial rebels are no less than 7000 able weaponed 'men. Florence M⁥Carthy, by his friends and followers,

STATE OF IRELAND ANNO 1598.

of Youghall called the great Water and includeth the Mountain Countrie called the Decies[a] the Bishoprick of Lismoore adjoining to the whit Knights Countrie Called Clongibbon. So hath it the Sea to the East Suer to the North part of the Counties of Tipperarie and Limerick to the West, the great Water and part of the Countie of Cork to the South.

will be the strongest and of greatest force of any Traitor in Munster; in so much that 1500 of her Majesty's forces must of necessity be employed against him!

'The entire province was disaffected; with sufficient worldy wisdom the great Lords continued subjects in show, but their followers were in action with Fitz-Thomas; the walled towns were corrupted; and the open country was wholly in the possession of the Geraldines and shut against the Queen's loyal subjects.

'Wee can neither looke, nor hope for any assistaunce from the Lords of the countreys, who are onely in personal shewes subjects, as the Lo. Power, the Lo: of Dunboyne, Lo: Roche the Lo of Cahir, Cormac McDermott chief of Muskerry. McCharty Reough chief of Carrebry, Garrald Fitz James chief of the Deasyes, Patrick Condon, O'Calloughan, and all others (except the Lo Barry who of late hath don good service) being assured from the rest to receive no ayde for her Matie with their forces, the most of them having either their brothers or next kinsmen in actuall rebellion. Florence McCartie (if he continue in this disloyall course, wch he hath begonn, (whereof as yet we have no other hope) by his friends namely, both the O'Sulyvans, McFynnen, the Carties of Desmond, O'Donnevan, O'Crowly, O'Mahon Carbrey, O'Mahon Fin, sundry of the Septes of the Carthies of Carbery, the McSwynes, most of the Carties of Muskerry, all the Carties of Dowallo, O'Keefe, McAwlye, and many of the O'Callaghans with his and their followers and kinsmen who before were better disposed by their outward affections, will be the strongest, and of greatest force of any traytor in Mounster; in so much that 1500 of her Mats forces must of necessitie be employed against him.'—*Life of Florence McCarthy Mór*, pp. 249, 259, 260.

'The Munster people are Spanish in heart, Popish in religion, and infinitely discontented. If the gentlemen could agree upon a leader, they would declare themselves in action.'—*Car. Cal.*

[a] 'Called the Denes, the Bishoprick of Rismore united to the sea of Waterford, Prendergast's lande, who was one of the first conquest and a most famous capten. The White Knightes cuntry called Clangibbon.'—*Dym.* O'Brics, O'Felans, and Fitzgeralds, were successively lords of the Deisi.

COUNTIE OF WATERFORD.   159

It hath Castles   Waterford[b]
and Townes   Lismore
                      Dungarvan[b]
                      Clonmell[c]
The Bishop of Waterford and Lismore[d]

[b] 'Waterford and Dungarvan full of trafique with England, France and Spain, by means of their excellent good haven.' —*Campion.*

'Waterford is properly builded, and very well compact, somewhat close by reason of their thick buildings and narrow streets. The citizens through the intercourse of foreign trafic in short space attaine to abundance of wealth. The soil about it is not all of the best, by reason of which the aire is not very subtile; yea nathelesse the sharpnesse of their wittes seemeth to be nothing dulled by reason of the grossenesse of the air. They are, as students, pregnant in conceiving, quick in taking, and sure in keeping; very heedie and warie, loving to looke before they leape, cheerful in their entertainment of strangers, hearty one to another, nothing given to factions. They love no idle benchwhistlers nor luskish faitors. The men are addicted to trafick, the women to spinning and carding. As they distil the best Aqua vitæ, so they spin the choicest rug in Ireland. The citie was never dusked with the least freckle of treason, and therefore the city's arms are decked with the words '*Urbs Intacta.*'—*Stanihurst*, p. 24, Ed. 1586.

In 1583 the militia of Waterford consisted of 300 shot and 300 billmen, that of Clonmel 40 shot and 200 billmen, that of the barony of Decies 20 shot and 200 billmen.—*Cox, Hib. Anglicana.*

[c] In 1600 Whyte, a lawyer, was elected sovereign and was as much Romish as any of the other magistrates of Munster towns. Father Thomas Whyte, S.J., a native of Clonmel, was founder of the Irish College of Salamanca, and was its Rector in 1602.—*Car. Cal.*
'Clonmel a well built and well-kept town upon the river of Sure, is more haunted of Jesuits and priests than any other towne or city within this province, which is the cause we found the burgesses here more obstinate than elsewhere. For when the Lord President did gently offer to the principal inhabitants that he would spare to proceed against them then, if they would yield to conference for a time, and become bound in the meantime not to receive any Jesuit or priest into their houses, they peremptorily refused.'—Sir J. Davys in *Car. Cal.* an. 1606, p. 475.

[d] *Vide infra* The Bishops; this was Mulmury, or Myler M'Grath, who was Archbishop of Cashel.

STATE OF IRELAND ANNO 1598.

Vid Analect Catholic. in Hiber. 2nd edit. 1617 P. 68 For an Account of the penitent death of this chief Justice.[f]

Chief men The L. Power[e] baron of Carroughmore Sir Nicholas Walshe[f] chief Justice of the common Pleas.
The Heyres of Fitzgerrald Late Viscount of Derie[g] and Baron of Droman.

[e] *Vide infra* The Peers. 'Only in personal shows a subject.'

[f] 'Tunc mortuus est Nicholaus Valois, insignis haereticorum in Ibernia judex, qui quod se haereticum, et in Ibernos saevum ostenderit, apud Anglos magnum dignitatis locum obtinuit. Senescens, appropinquantemque mortem timens, Catholicae ecclesiae misericordiam implorando impetrat.—*O'Sulevan Beare*, Hist. p. 333, Ed. Kelly.

[g] *Recte* Decies. 'The Lord of Desies, James, son of Gerald, son of John, son of Gerot Mór of Desies, son of James, son of Gerot Earl of Desmond, died in 1581.'—*Four Masters*. 'Gerald FitzJames, Chief of the Deasyes only in personal shows a subject.'—*Car. Cal.* an. 1600. 'Mrs. Alyson Dalton petitions the Queen in 1600, says she is a poor widow with eight orphans, driven out of Ireland, had defended her castle of Knockmoan for two years at her own charge, prays to be allowed 20 warders and 4 horsemen in the Queen's pay. Garret Fitz James, her spiteful neighbour, was bound in £500 for the loyalty of his base brother, Thomas FitzJames, to whom was committed her castle of Cappoquin, but he treacherously razed the castle, whereby said bond is forfeited.' The Privy Council decide that the demand about the forfeiture of the bond may be granted when the country is reduced to obedience.—*Car. Cal.* year 1600. p. 396. In 1600, Elizabeth's Earl of Desmond writes to Cecil that 'the Lord of the Decis' came to him. Sir Gerald FitzGerald Lord of Decies died in 1553, seized in fee of the baronies of Curraghmore, Rosmire and Athmeane, the manor of Dromanagh, the mountain and castle of Slygan, and the Grange in Old Parish, in all over 4000 acres. His grandson, Gerald FitzJames, mentioned above, was son of Sir James Lord of Decies and Elena, dau. of McCarthy Reagh. He mar. 1st a dau. of Lord Poer, 2^{ly} a dau. of Lord Barry. Dying without issue he was succeeded by his cousin, John FitzGerod Gerald, whose mother was dau. of Butler of Derryloskan. Sir John by a dau. of the

Divers other Howses of   Powers[h]   Walshes[l]
　　　　　　　　　　　　　Wises[i]   Maddons[m]
　　　　　　　　　　　　　Aylewards[k]   Waddings[n]

White Knight was father of John Oge who was aged 18 in 1598. John Oge's son was 'brought up in piety' by the famous Colonel Sankey, mar. a dau. of Lord Power, and then a dau. of the Earl of Clancartie. He had no son; his daughter's son, Earl Grandison, put an inscription on his tomb in the church at Youghal.

[h] 'The prisoners in Waterford jail for the most part were natives of that shire, of which there were very few that were not bastard imps of the Poores and Geraldines of the Decies, which two septs do overspread all that county.' —Sir J. Davys in 1606, *Car. Cal.*

There were Power of Culcfin, P. of Culroe, P. of Balinecurry.—*Archdall's Lodge*, Ed. 1789, vol. ii., p. 305.

'Powers Country may be well compared with the best ordered country in the English Pale.'—*Sir H. Sydney's Letter*, 27th Feb. 1575.

James Wyse, of the Manor of St. John, died in 1596. His son, John, was 26 years old in 1598; his son Thomas was Mayor, and Nicholas, Sheriff of Waterford in 1605. Of this family was M. Wise, S.J. In the Franciscan Monastery is the tomb of Thomas Wise and Mabelle Walshe, ' Religione ac pietate, necnon in pauperes charitate conspicuorum.' Thomas Wise died in 1604.

[k] Aylward's castle of Fatlock was beautifully situated near Passage. John Aylward had known Cromwell in London, and was informed by him that his castle would be spared if he would pretend conformity in religion; Aylward held his faith, and lost his castle by siege.—*Ryland*, p. 72. In John's Street is an ancient spacious house belonging to Sir Peter Aylward's family, over the chimney-piece of which, in the great room, the family arms are curiously cut in stone; they are also cut on each side of the street gate.

[l] The Walshes were Mayors in 1407, 1578, 1601, 1602, and at other times. Pilltown was the estate of the W.; there Judge W. lived, the supposed author of the forged commission in favour of the Irish in Charles the First's time. The Holy Ghost Hospital was founded in 1545 by Patrick Walsh, ' in order that the master, brethren, and the poor may pray for our prosperity while we live, and for our souls when we shall depart this life, and for the souls of all our progenitors, and for the prosperity of said hospital, and for the soul of Patrick Walsh, and for the prosperity of Catherine Sherlock his wife, and for her soul and for the souls of all the faithful.'—*Ryland*, p. 190.

[m] Richard Madan was Mayor in 1599; James M. in 1583; William M. in 1380.

[n] Thomas Wadding was Mayor in 1596. ' He holds a chief office under

Sherlocks[o]
Prendergrasses[p]
Geraldines[q]

Nugents[r]
Whytes[s]
Mandevils[t]

the Crown in the Co. of Waterford, and dwells in that city, a busy fellow inclined to breed dissension, allied in these parts.'—*Carew MSS.* 608. 'The Mayor of Waterford, which is a great lawyer, one Wadding, carrieth the sword and rod, as I think he should do, for her Majesty; but he nor his sheriffs never came to church sithence he was mayor nor sithence this reign, nor none of the citizens men nor women nor in any town or city throughout this province.'—*Letter written by Dr. Lyon in* 1596.

Thomas W. mar. Mary Walsh, and had three most distinguished sons, Jesuits—Peter, Professor of Divinity at Louvain, Antwerp, Prague, and Gratz, and Chancellor of the Universities of Prague and Gratz, and author of several books; Michael, a distinguished Professor of Theology, Rector of the Seminary of St. Jerome, Puebla, of the College of St. Ildefonso, Mexico, of the College of Guatemala, of the College of St. Ildefonse, Puebla, renowned for learning and sanctity; he wrote a remarkable work on ascetic Theology; Luke, a Professor of great fame in Spain, consulting Theologian of the Inquisition, Lecturer on Jurisprudence in Madrid, etc., '*quem summis aequiparare possis*,' as a Spanish writer says of him.

Thomas' brother, Walter Wadding, had two celebrated sons—Ambrose, a Jesuit Professor in the University of Dilingen, and Luke, the great Franciscan. Their kinsman Richard W., an Augustinian, was a famous professor in Coimbra, and their cousins, Paul Sherlock, S.J., and Dr. French of Ferns, were men of great name.—See *Harold's Life of Luke Wadding, and De La Requera's Memoir of Michael Wadding, S.J.*

[o] The Sherlocks filled the office of Mayor in 1462, and often afterwards. Paul S. was Mayor in 1594; John S. in 1606; and Walter in 1614.

[p] The Prendergasts, I believe, were of Tipperary; they are given in *Smith's List* as of Waterford.

[q] FitzGerald of Fernane.

[r] Nugent of Cloncoskeran Castle.

[s] John White was Mayor in 1414; Thomas W. was Mayor in 1598. In the cathedral, on a flat stone, are the words 'Hic jacent Patricius White filius Johannis, quondam civis Civitatis Waterfordiae, qui obiit, et Anastacia Grant, ejus uxor, quae obiit x. die Octobris A.D. 1592.' Thomas W. of Clonmel, a Jesuit, was Rector of Salamanca at this time; he was the first to found an Irish College on the Continent. Stephen W. of Clonmel, who afterwards became one of the most learned men in Europe, was a Jesuit novice in 1598. See a memoir of him by Dr. Reeves, and another by the Bollandist, Père de Buck.

[t] In the time of Edw. IV. there was

Condonns[u]
Craghes[v]

Brownes[w]
Dobins[x]
Leas[y] and Lees[z]

a grant from T. Mandeville and Anastace his wife to Earl Maurice of Desmond.—*Car. Cal.* 1589-1600 p. 104.

I find no mention of this name in *Smith* or *Ryland*, except in this passage of *Smith* :—' The principal inhabitants of the county in the reign of Elizabeth were the Aylwards, Browns, O'Briens, Bracks, Bourks, Condons, Creaghs, O'Connerys, Daltons, Dobbins, Everards, FitzGarrets or FitzGeralds, O'Feolains, FitzTheobalds, Leas or Leaths, Maddens, *Mandevils*, Merrifields, Morgans, O'Maghers, M[c]Henricks, Nugents, Osbornes, Poers, Prendergasts, Rochfords, Sherlocks, Tobins, Walls, Walshes, Waddings, Wyses, Whites, etc.' There were a captain, a lieutenant, and an ensign named Mandeville in Butler's Regiment.—See *King James' Army List.*

[u] *Ryland* states that 'a family of the Co. of Waterford assumed, with unaccountable reluctance, the name of Condon in place of MacMajoke.'

[v] In the parish of Modeligo are the remains of some ancient castles of the Magraths. The castle of Sledy was built in 1628 by Philip M[c]Grath, as appears from a date on a chimney-piece with the words 'Philippus M[c]Grath.' In the Abbey of Dungarvan is a tombstone with the inscription, ' Donald M[c]Grath 1400.' The castle near Dungarvan belonged to this family; the Abbey was founded by them also. The only old monument of the church of Lismore which has escaped the ravages of time, is their highly ornamented tomb, with an inscription that can be only partially deciphered—'Johes M[c]Grath ... uxor ... Katherina Thorne. 1548.' There was a Daniel M[c]Grath, Esq., of Mountain Castle, whose dau. married one of the Powers of Curraghmore.—See *Lodge*, vol. ii. p. 306.

[w] M. Browne was Mayor in 1612. In the Franciscan Monastery is a tomb with the inscription ' *Hic jacet Robertus Lincol filius Gulielmi civis civitatis Waterfordiae, qui obiit A.D.* 1630, *et uxor ejus Margarita Browne quae obiit* ... ' The inscription on the Rice monument shows that Rice's wife was Catherine Browne. Rice was six times Mayor from 1471 to 1488. Ignatius Browne, a distinguished Jesuit, who founded the Irish College of Poictiers, was born in Waterford in 1630.

[x] Laurence Dobbyn was Mayor in 1460, and Patrick D. in 1589. Whitfieldstown Castle was the seat of W. Dobbin at the time of Petty's survey.

[y] Laurence Lea of Waterford became a Jesuit in 1604. N. Lee was Sheriff in 1575 and 1580.

[z] Perhaps this should be Tews. Under the tower in the Franciscan Friary is a highly laboured monument with the inscription, '*Hic jacent Johannes Tew, filius . . quondam civis civitatis Waterford,*

Chief Castles } Dongarvan,[aa] the quenes
The hooke[bb]

qui obiit 1597 ... ejus uxor ... 1599.' The following inscriptions in the Friary give names omitted in our MS.—'*Hic jacet Johannes Skydye, civis quondam et Major hujus civitatis Waterfordiae qui obiit* 1641, *et Johanna White ejus uxor* ... *Hic jacet Franciscus Lumbard filius Nicolai* ... *obiit A.D.* 1590, *et Katerina Walshe, uxor ejus, quorum Animabus propitietur Deus. Amen.*' There is also a tombstone highly decorated of Agnes Lumbard, wife of Edward Walshe; of Thomas Meyler and his wife Isabella Walsh '*religione pe* ... *ac pietate non pauperes.*' J. Tew and Patrick Meyler were Sheriffs about this time. The first Mayor of Waterford was W. Lumbard, in 1377; J. Lumbard was Mayor in 1603. Dr. Peter Lombard was a theologian of European reputation, and was made Primate of Armagh in 1601. He was born in Waterford in 1554; his family, closely allied to the Whites and Waddings, gave many bright ornaments to both Church and State. He was educated by the famous Rev. Peter White of Waterford, called 'the happy schoolmaster,' on account of his marvellous success in teaching.—See *Lombard's De Regno Hiberniae Commentarius*, edited by Dr. Moran, p. v.

In the churchyard of Newcastle, near Tramore, is the tomb of Ronan of Hacketstown, a celebrated doctor who d. in 1626, and of his wife Anastatia Devereux, who d. in 1614. In Carrickbeg is a monument to *Giraldus Wale de Cuilmuck—nobilis, Caterina Comeford;* these Wales lived in the castle of Coolnamuck, which is still possessed by the family. A Jesuit named Walter Wale lived in 1598. At Churchtown is the inscription, '*Here lieth. IHS. one Boutlr. Fis. Gerott. of Bolendisert. And His Wif. Johan. Fis. Richads. Ano.* 1587.'

Add Hore of Shandon, whose descendant Colonel Hore was M.P. for Waterford in 1689, when two others of the family were members for Dungarvan. In the 'French Church' is the old monument of Michael Hore, merchant of Waterford; also a monument to M. Grant, who d. in 1626. T. Grant was Sheriff in 1546; Matthew Grant was Mayor in 1640.

There was a respectable family named Gough of Kilmanahan; N. Gough was Mayor in 1435 and 1441, and Sir Edward Gough in 1600. Members of the family of Strong were Mayors in 1431, 1434, 1485, 1560, 1581, 1588. Paul Strong was Mayor in 1597; in 1607 Tho. Strong was Mayor and Rob. Strong Sheriff. Among the Waterford gentlemen in 1592 was 'Eu. Roche.'—*Car. Cal.* A. Briver was Mayor in 1587; and a namesake of his was a Jesuit. Patrick Morgan was Mayor in 1593, and there was a Waterford Jesuit of that name, about that time.

[aa] A very strong castle.—*Camden.*
[bb] Perhaps Crook, near Passage, which

Moncollop[cc]
Kilmanahim[dd]
Kilm'Thomas[ee]
Ardmore[ff]
The passage a foot at the mouth of the River
Pilton[gg]

Clovey[hh]
Dermebeer[ii]
Domano[kk]
Carraghmore[ll]

Cappahun[mm]

had belonged to the Knights of St. John, and in 1565 belonged to A. Power.

[cc] Macollop consists of a large round tower, and several square towers flanking its intermediate base ; it was made a ruin by Cromwell in 1640.—*Parliam. Gazetteer of Ireland*.

[dd] Opposite Knocklofty.

[ee] Belonging to Power, in whose descendants the surrounding property is still vested.

[ff] "Urbem Lissimor pertransit flumen Avenmor, Ardmor cernit ubi concitus aequor adit."—*Necham, quoted by Camden*.

Smith in 1774 wrote that there was 'the stump of a castle, and not long since was a much larger one there, which was taken down.' A family named Mirnen had property here from the year 1197 to 1745, when they sold it.—*Smith*, p. 49. 'The Mirnynes were remarkable for their longevity, enjoyed an estate of ten pounds a year conveyed to them by 4 lives above these 400 years, notwithstanding the Insurrections, etc. They never changed their name ; once only wanted one heir in a direct line, which was supplied by a collateral branch. It is said the present possessor, being 80 years old, never saw Youghal nor any other town, nor will be courted to it.'—*Dynely's Tour in* 1687.

[gg] Belonging to the Walsh family.

[hh] Clonea or Clough. Clonea, a castle of the FitzGeralds of Decies, is one of the most perfect specimens of the fortified residence. Clough was built before the invention of firearms ; it is called in *Gough's Camden* an ancient square castle.

[ii] Perhaps Darinlar Castle, which stands on the land of the Earl of Glengall, 'a tower protected by four circular castles, that projected beyond the curtain.'—*Parl. Gaz. of Ireland*.

[kk] The Lord of Decies owned Dromana ; he was descended from the 7th Earl of Desmond. In 1561 FitzGerald of Dromana became Baron of Dromany and Viscount Desses. When he died without issue, his brother, Sir James FitzGerald of Cappagh, came to live at Dromana ; Lord Stuart de Decies owns the property, and is descended (maternally) from the FitzGeralds. The greatest portion of the old castle was destroyed by fire. See note [g].

[ll] Curraghmore, Lord Power's.

[mm] The FitzGeralds built the castle of Cappoquin.

STATE OF IRELAND ANNO 1598.

Kilmadin[nn]   Strangally[pp]
Balleconchin[oo]   Shyan[qq]

This Countie in the late Rebellion of Desmond was least infected with treasons, yet much Spoyled by the Souldiers that lay in Garrisone there, and at this day some few are rebellion without any man of name to be their head. There belongeth more Ships[rr] to the Cittie of Waterford and Wexford than to all Ireland besides.

[nn] Power's, 'boldly erected on the banks of the Suir,' now gone to decay.

[oo] There was a castle in the parish of Ballycashen.

[pp] In the neighbourhood of Tallow were several castles, the chief of which was Strancally, belonging to the Desmond family. In the 28th Eliz. James FitzJohn Gerrot of Strancally was attainted, also his son Gerrot FitzJames.

[qq] In 28 Eliz., Maurice McGerrot McenEarla of Shean was attainted. There were also the castles of Templemichael, Ballyheney, Lismore, Knockmoan, Cloghlack, Conagh, Cullen, Castlereagh, Ballyclough, Feddens, and Cloncoskeran (belonging to the Nugent family), Ballycavoge (of the Walshes). —See *Smith, Ryland, and Parliam. Gazetteer of Ireland.*

[rr] 'Between the rivers Broadwater and Suire extends the very pleasant and fruitful county of Waterford ... Waterford for wealth and resort may be ranked the second city in Ireland.'—*Camden.*

'The gentle Swire, that making way
  By sweet Clonmel adorns rich Waterford.'
                          —*Spencer.*

'A rich and well inhabited city, esteemed second to Dublin.'—*Moryson's Itinerary,* p. iii. ch. 5.

Waterford was famous also for its intellectual wealth at the close of the 16th century—the six Waddings (four of whom were Jesuits), the Lombards, Sherlocks, and Comerfords, Whites, and Walshes, shed lustre on their native city. The *Annuae Literæ* of the Society of Jesus (1641-1651) says:—'Waterfordia, magnorum ingeniorum fecunda parens, prioribus annis suppeditavit Societati doctissimos viros, quibus illustravit non cæteras modo Residentias Missionis, sed et alias quoque Provincias Societatis in Hispania, Germania, Belgio, atque ipsis Indiis.'—*Literæ Annuae Provinciae Hiberniae,* published in Rome, *circa* 1654.

N.B.—The information, contained in the notes without a reference, is taken from *Ryland's* and *Smith's* Histories of Waterford.

THE COUNTIE OF CORK.

Cork contayneth all the lande adjoining to the Sea from the River of Youghall, to the Bay of the Dingle and the River Margne[a] ioining to the Countie of Kerrie, comprehending the Counties of Kerrie Wherrie,[b] Kinnalo,[c] *Garvy* Roe's Countrie,[d] the Bishoprick of Rosse, the Country of Carbere on both sides

[a] 'Maigne, the cuntry of Kerrywherry, Kilaloa, Barry-Roe's cuntry, the Bishopricke of Ross, the cuntry of Carbrye on both sydes the leape, O'Mahons and Ordriscalls cuntry. The Bantry, O'Silvian bent, O'Silvian more, and all Desmond; all which lie along y[e] coaste. In the middle of the shire lyeth Muskry, devided betweene Sir Cormoc and Sir Dermot mac teig Clancark, allso O'Challagon, O'Heift, Mac Auly, Mac Donoho, followers of the erle of Clancar, and includeth the landes of the two viscounts Barry and Armoy.'— *Dymmok*. The *variantes* here would show that our MS. was written later than Dymmok's account, as it speaks of the sons of Sir Cormac and Sir Dermot M[c]Teg.

[b] Kerricurihy (*Ciarraighe-Cuirche*) 12 miles long by six broad, contains Passage, Monkstown, and Crosshaven; it belonged to Maurice, brother of the 15th Earl of Desmond.—*Parl. Gaz. of Ireland*. Monkstown Castle or Castlemahon belonged to the Archdekens or Mac Odos. John Archdeken of Dromdony and Monkstown had a son John, who restored the castle; the date 1636 is on the mantlepiece of the principal chamber. The tomb (with inscription) of this John A. is in the old ruin of *Teampul Oen Bryn*.—*Windele's South of Ireland*, p. 180.

[c] Kinnalea, 13 miles long by 7 wide, is south of Kerricurrihy; it belonged to the Desmonds; in it are Inishannon and Tracton, etc. The gentlemen of Kinnalea in 1592 were Long, Bostock, Barries *alias* Barricok (*sic*, perhaps Barry Oge), Golde, Robinson, Graunte, Leoffin Meade, Awlie O'Flinne, Sarsfield, Fleming, Roche, Roold, Cogan, Mac Shane, FitzMoris Roche, White, Risserd, Fitzwilliam Roche, Piers Golde.—*Car. Cal.*, an. 1591, p. 64.

[d] 'Barry Roe,' in the margin; at one time the O'Cowigs had seven castles in this district, viz., Dundeedy, Dunowen, Duneen, Dunore, Duncowig, Dungorley, and Dunworley.—*Smith's Cork*, Book ii. ch. 3.

the Leap,[e] Omahoun,[f] and O'Driscals Countries.[g] The Bantrie[h] of beer, O'Sullivant, More, and all Desmond, and which lie along the Coast. Also in the middle of this Shyre Liyeth Muskerie[i] now in some Sort devided between the Heyres of S[r] Dermot and S[r] Cormack Clancarties, also Ocallogan,[k]

[e] A romantic ravine at the head of Glandore Harbour. Carberie belonged to M[c]Carthy Reagh.

[f] O'Mahony's country, the present barony of Kinnalmeaky.

[g] *Corca Laidhe.* Their territory was co-extensive with the diocese of Ross; but in 1615 they owned only the seven parishes, which constitute the rural deanery of Colleymore and Colleybeg. They had the castles of Gleann, Bearchain or Castlehaven, Lough-Hyne, Ardagh, Baltimore, Dunnangall, Dunan-oir, Rincaliskey, and Sherkin.—See p. 143 of *Miscell. of Celtic Society.*

[h] Bantry and Bearra form the southwest portion of the Co. of Cork. The lord of Bantry was Sir Owen O'Sullevan; the lord of Bearra was his nephew, the famous Donnell O'Sullevan.

[i] 'O'Sullivan Beare's countrey conteyneth 160 ploughlandes; M[c]Carthy More claymeth there Risinge out, the findinge of 50 Galleyglas, the geavinge of the Rodd, and to the value of £40 a yeare in spendings and refeccons. The countrie of Clanlawras [in O'Sullevan Beare's country] conteyneth 32 ploughlands.'—*MacCarthy Mor,* p. 31.

O'Sullevan's forces, as given by Carew, are stated in *Miss Cusack's History of Cork*—O'Sullivan Bere, 30 companies; Owen O'Sullevan's sons in Bantry, 80; M[c]Fineen Duff, 30 in Bere and Glanarought; Clanlaura, 30 in Bere and Bantry; the Coubrey, 40 in Bere; O'Sullevan Mor, 60 in Dunkerron; M[c]Gillicuddy, 100 in Dunkerron; M[c]Crohan, 40 in Iveragh. The Egerton MSS. give the various branches as O'Sullevan Mor, O'Sullevan Bere, M[c]Fineen Duff, M[c]Gillicuddy, and the O'Sughrues.—*Hist. of Cork, by the Nun of Kenmare,* p. 332.

[i] 'Muskcray, a woody tract, in which the name of Cormac Mac-Teg is famous.'—*Camden.*

[k] Conor O'Ceallachain, called 'Conor of the Rock,' was lord of Poble Hy Ceallachain, (*i.e.*, the parishes of Clonmeen and Kilshanig,) owned Drumneen Castle, 'the ruins of which still present an august appearance.' His Tanist or heir elect was Shan M[c]Teig. In 1690 the Earl of Barrymore wrote to the Duke of Wirtemberg—'I have received a humble petition on behalf of Colonel M[c]Donogh, chief of the country called Dunhallow, and of another chieftain of a country called O'Callaghan. They will bring with them a thousand men, and at least seven or eight thousand cows.' This was Colonel Donogh O'Callaghan.—*D'Alton's Army List,* p. 867.

COUNTIE OF CORK.

O'Kief,[1] McAuley,[m] and McDonoghe,[n] followers to the late Earle of Cloncare and including also the Lands of the Two Viscounts Barrhy[o] and Armoy.[p] So this Countie is bounded with the Sea East, South and South east, with the Mountains of Slewlogher to the West, and partlie with the great Water and partlie with the Countie of Limerick to the North. This Countie being the greatest in the Realm have bene tollerated to have Two Sheriffs,

[1] Art Oge O'Keeffe, b. in 1547, inaugurated in 1583, d. 1610; mar. a dau. of McCarthie of Iniskeen. His sons were Daniel of Ballymacquirk, Donogh of Cuilbeggan, and his successor Manus of Dromagh, who was 'chief of his nacion,' and was b. in 1567. Art Oge owned the castles of Dromagh, Du-Ardgil, Drumtariff, and Drumsicane. Dixon Cornelius O'Keeffe of Dublin, Barrister-at-law, is of this family.—See *Tribes of Ireland*, and *D'Alton's Army List*.

[m] Of Castle Mac Auliffe, near Newmarket. The territory of Mac Auliffe, or *Eas-Ealla*, was the land between Newmarket and the boundaries of the counties of Limerick and Kerry. The head of this family, who had been born to a handsome estate, was weigh-master in the market-house at Kenmare in 1840.—*Tribes of Ireland*, p. 66.

Among the gentlemen pensioners in the Spanish army in 1606 were John McAwly, McAwly's son, Conogher McAwly his brother, Dermod McAwly of Clan Awlye, and W^m. McAuliffe, all from Cork.—*Car. Cal.*, an. 1606, p. 397.

[n] Lord of Duhallow, of the McCarthy race, built such a strong and large fortress at Kanturk, that Elizabeth's council ordered the work to be stopped. See a description of it in *Smith's Cork*. In 1598 Elizabeth wrote to the President of Munster—'If McDonnaght will serve us against Derby McOwen, who takes the title of McCarthy More, we will bestow upon him the country of Dually.'—*Car. Cal.*, p. 286.

[o] Lord Barry's lands are Barries-Court, Inchinibakye, Castell-Lions, Botevant and Liscarrall in Orrery, Timologe, Rathebarry and Lislie in Ybaune; total, 392 plowlands; also he has the use of three-parts of every freeholders' lands within these manors, which amount to 1000 plowlands.—*Car. Cal.*

The gentlemen of Orrery in 1592 were—Barry *alias* McShian, Lumbard, Eily Barry of Bregoge; P. H. Rirragus (?), Chillister, Miz of Lessfricken, Byrn, Nangle, Dalie, Rallaghan McOwen.—*Car. Cal.*, p. 64.

[p] *Recte* Fermoy, the Barony of Fermoy, Roche's country, a beautiful territory. It is called the 'country of fine roads' by the Bard Ruadh O'Daly.

Y

170   STATE OF IRELAND ANNO 1598.

the one particular in Desmond, the other in the rest of the Countrie, and this without any Ground in Law, but by discretion of the L. Deputies, the inconvenience thereof being espied it hath been of late thought good that one Sherriff should for Kerrie and Desmond, and so Two Sherriffs in one Countie against Law taken away.

Cities and Townes   Corke^q a walled Cittie with a good Haven.
Clone ⎫
Rosse^r ⎬ Bishopricks ruined.
Youghall^s a Haven toune walled.

^q 'Cork is of an oval figure, surrounded by walls, environed and intersected by the river, which is passable only by bridges; and consisting of one straight street, continued by a bridge. A little trading town of great resort and eminence, but so beset by rebellious neighbours as to require as constant a watch as if constantly besieged, and the inhabitants not daring to trust their daughters to marry in the country, are all somehow related.'—*Camden.*

'At this day (1575) the city of Cork is so encumbered with unquiet neighbours of great power, that they are forced to watch their gates continually, to keep them shut at service time, at meales, from sunneset to sunne rising; nor suffer any stranger to enter with his weapon, but to leave the same at a lodge appointed. They walk out for recreation at seasons, with strength of men furnished; they match in wedlock among themselves.'—*Campion,* p. 96.

Some Cork families are mentioned in the following monuments, etc., mentioned by *Windele:*—

In Shandon Churchyard is the tomb of Stephen Coppinger of Ballyvolane, 'chief of the name,' erected by his wife, née Goold; he was born in 1610.

Inscription on a chalice—'Dna Margareta Sarsfield me fieri fecit pro fribus minoribus de Shandon, Anno Domini 1627, orate pro ea, et pro marito ejus Waltro Coppinger.'

J. White the elder by his will in 1582 directs his body to be buried in St James' Chapell, Christ Church, 'where mine ancestors lye.'

Tomb (date 1584) of J. Coleman and his wife Anstace McDonnell—*Windele,* p. 56.

Tomb of Walshe and his wife An Goaghe, with Templars' ensigns, 1592. —*Windele's South of Ireland.*

^r 'Ross, formerly of great resort, but, since a bar of sand has been thrown up, it is deserted.'—*Camden.*

^s 'Youghall—no large town indeed,

COUNTIE OF CORK. 171

  Kinsale[t] in like sort.
  Buttevant[u] ane inland Towne belonging to the Viscount
   Barrhy.
  Moyallo,[v] a fayre market Towne unwalled belonging
   to the L. President, where he maketh his Residence.
Tallow. Tallowyhe, a market Towne upon the great Water.
Principal Viscount Buttevant[w] or Barrhy, his name is Barrhy,
Men.   his chief hous Buttevant.
  Viscount Armoy[w] or Roche, his name Roche, his
   chief Hous Armoy.
  L. Courcy,[w] his name so.

but encompassed with walls of an oblong form, with a commodious harbour, with a key fortified. The fertility of the neighbouring country so invites merchants, that it is much resorted to, and has for its chief magistrate a mayor.' —*Camden.*

'A seaport town scituate at the ffoot of high rocky mountains, upon the mouth of the Blackwater.'

In the church there is an 'altar tomb' of Piers Miagh, who died in 1633, aged 43. On it is a Latin Inscription with a Latin Distich, and there were also the following words in English (which are now effaced) :—' Pray for the Founders hereof, Piers Miagh FitzJames of Yoghal, Alderman, and Phillis Miagh *alias* Nagle, his onely wife, who made this monument for their last lodging in this world.'

In the Portingal Chapel are the tombs of the Youghal merchants, Edw. Coppinger, who d. in 1624, and R. Nagle, who died in 1605.—*Dynely's Tour.*

Adams, whose tombstone is in the Churchyard of St. Mary's, was born in 1588, when Raleigh was Mayor, and he d. in 1715, aged 126 years.—Note to *Dynely's Tour*, by *Rev. S. Hayman*.

The image of the Blessed Virgin, which formerly belonged to the Dominican Convent of Youghal, has the inscription—' *Orate pro anima Onoriae filiae Jacobi de Geraldine, quae me fieri fecit*, an. 1617.'—*Windele*, p. 81.

'See the Map of Kinsale, and the account of its siege in *Pacata Hibernia.*

"Wadding wrote, *circ.* 1640, ' The town had been large and frequented, is now reduced. Two illustrious families, the Barrys and Lombards, had their residence here.'—*Miss Cusack's Cork*, p. 490.

[v] Had belonged to the Earls of Desmond. It was defended by two castles.

[w] *Vide infra* among the Peers and Bishops.

The B.ᵂ of Cork, Clone and Roscarbery.
Sʳ Owen MᶜCarte reaghe.ˣ
Sʳ Thomas Barrhy oge.ʸ
Sʳ Owen O'Sullivan.ᶻ

ˣ 'In 1593, *Mag Carthaigh Riabhach* (Owen MᶜCarthy Reagh) Tighearna or Lord of Carbery, died. He was a sensible, pious, and truly hospitable and noble-minded man. Donal, son of Cormac na h-Aoine, took his place.' Owen had been inaugurated in 1575. —*Annals*, years 1576, and 1593. Owen, who was described by St. Leger as 'a notorious papist who would be in rebellion if he dared,' wrote to Elizabeth in 1583 that he had contributed £7497 out of his territory to crush the Desmonds. On the 23rd Dec. 1587, he wrote from his 'Lodgings at Westmystre' to the Lord Treasurer that he had spent all the money he had deemed enough to bring with him, asked a loan of £200 or £300, which he 'will pay in Ireland to the Lord Deputy.' In the postscript he asks 'a Loan of one fortie ponds to refreshe me theis holydays.' —*MᶜCarthy Mor*, pp. 19 and 99. Owen had three sons, but his nephew Donal, 'the eldest relative of the blood,' succeeded by Tanistry. Owen's sons, Donogh Mael, and Finin, commanded 400 of the insurgents in 1602.—*Car. Cal.*, 268 and 404, an. 1602.

Sir Owen's dau. Evline was the wife of Sir Finin O'Driscoll (*infra*, note ᵃᵃ).

ʸ The country of Barry Og (or 'young Barry') was Kinalea, in which was his castle of Rincorran near Kinsale.—See *Annals*, pp. 2269, 2271, and 2161. 'Barry Oge, and the barron's brother John in the Muskry command 120 foot, and 30 horse.'— *Dymmok*.

ᶻ Sir Owen O'Sullevan Beare; O'Sullevan Mor is mentioned, *infra*. Owen, in 1598, was negotiating a marriage between his dau. and Donal, base son of the Earl of Clencar, whom he tried to get elected MᶜCarthy Mor; in 1594 he died, and his nephew Donall became Lord of Beare, though Owen's son had 'the best part of Beare and Bantry.'— *MᶜCarthy Mor*, pp. 27, 37, 134. Owen's son Owen, and his other sons were on the English side at the siege of Dunboy, as they laid claim to the Lordship of Beare. Young Owen was Lord of Bantrie in 1615; he d. in 1617; he was nephew of Lord Barry, and brother-in-law of Sir Cormac MᶜCarthy of Muscry, of Sir Nich. Browne and O'Sullevan Mor. His cousin Donal Lord of Beare, after the defeat of Kinsale, held out against overwhelming odds; and his castle of Dunboy was so heroically defended by MᶜGeoghagan, that Carew in the *Pacata* says that 'so obstinate and resolved a defence had not been seen in this kingdom.' When Donal was deserted by his allies,

Sr Fyn O'Driscall.^aa
The Sones of Sr Dermott and Sr Cormack^bb McTeig.

he set out with 400 men and 600 women and children from Glengariff on Dec. 31, 1602; and fought his way through the Barries, the Butlers, the Burkes of Clanricard, and on the 16th of Jan. reached O'Rourk's Castle of Leitrim, with his numbers reduced to *thirty-five* people. He was assassinated in Madrid in 1618.—*Miscel. Celt. Soc.* p. 403, and Preface to the *Historia Catholica*, ed. by Dr. Kelly. His cousin, the Historian, Philip O'Sullevan Beare, says of him— 'Obiens annum 57 agebat. Erat vir plane pius et largus maxime in pauperes et egenos. Duobus vel tribus Missarum sacris quotidie interesse solebat, longas ad Deum et Superos quotidianas preces effundens . . . Erat procerus et elegans statura, vultu pulcher'—p. 338. The *Annals*, p. 2291, say he was 'the best commander in Munster, for wisdom and valour;' and the *Pacata Hibernia* (book iii. chap. 17) tells of 'his brave charge (at Aughrim) on our men, who were more in numbers than the rebels, in the which Captaine Malby was slaine, upon whose fall Sir T. Burke and his Troopes, fainting with the losse of many men, studied their safeties by flight, and the rebels, with little harm, marched into O'Rourk's Country.'

^aa *O'h-Eidirsceoil.* Sir Fineen O'Driscoll, chief of Collymore in 1585, was living in 1614. There is an Irish poem on his death by Teig O'Daly. From it we learn that his 'eye was rapid;' 'his hand early in seeking the heavy weapons;' 'his tongue powerful.' His son Conor was a Captain, and his grandson Conor was an ensign in Spain. Fineen mar. a dau. of Sir Owen McCarthy Reagh; his son mar. a dau. of Donal Mac Owen Mac Swyne of Muskrie. His grandson Conor Og was killed in a naval fight between the Spaniards and Turks in 1619. In 1601, 'Donogh O'Driscoll delivered to the Spaniards his castle of Castlehaven; Sir Fineen O'D. (who never had been tainted with the least spot of disloyaltie) rendered to them his castle of Donneshed at Baltimore and his castle at Donnelong.'— See *Miscell. Celt. Soc.* and *Pac. Hib.*

In 1602 Carew took and burnt Littertenlis, a castle belonging to the Traitor Sir Finyn O'Driscoll's son. 'Fynin's three sons abroad are ready to skip to Ireland and do mischief.'

Collymore contains 63 ploughlands, the Lord whereof is O'Driscoll More; Collybeg is O'Driscoll Oge's land, and contains 34 ploughlands.—*Car. Cal.*, year 1599, p. 353.

^bb Sir Dermot and Sir Cormac were brothers—their sons were enemies.

'Cormac Mac Taige, Lord of Muskery, a comely-shaped, bright-countenanced man, who possessed most whitewashed edifices, fine built castles and hereditary seats of any of the

McDonaghe.cc

descendants of Eoghan Mor, d. in 1583. The people were at strife after his death; some supported Callaghan, son of Teig, on account of his seniority; others joined Cormac, son of Dermot, who sought the chieftaincy on account of his father's patent; others supported the young sons of the deceased Cormac McTaig.—*Annals*, an. 1583. In 1597 Brown writes to Burleigh—'There has been much murdering among themselves (the McCarthies of Muskery) about their lands.' The sons of Sir Dermot were Cormac and Teig McDermot; the sons of Sir Cormac were 'Charles' or Cormac Oge, and Teig McCormac.

Cronelly, and Windele in his *South of Ireland* (p. 228) mistake Cormac McDermot or McDermond for Cormac McTeig.

'The Captain or Lo. of Muskery hath two sonnes, and a brother called Teigh Mac Dermonde, and Charles, sonne of Sir Cormac Teigh, last Lo. of Muskerry.' 'The countrey of Muskerie is very large, wherein five other countreis are conteyned; he claymeth of them risinge out; McCarthy Mor claimeth here the keapinge of thirtie galleglass, and findinge of him for a certen tyme.'—*McCarthy Mor*.

'The septs of the Carties themselves (with their Followers and Dependants) were known to bee no lesse than 3000 able men. The rest were no less than 4500 strong. Cormacke McDermond was Lord of Muskerry, a populous, a rich, and a fast Countrey,'—*Pac. Hib.*, p. 131.

During the siege of Kinsale there was a young gentleman of the Carties, Teg Mac Cormock, son to that well-deserving gentleman, Sir Cormack Mac Teg, who, being of the President's Troope of Horse, combined with the Enemie, stealing away his Horse and Hackney.' He writes from Carrigisuky, June 1602, to ask remission of his offences which he committed 'not to hurt her Majestie, but to recover against my Cosen Cormock Mac Dermody some means to maintain my decayed estate, and still likely *to be suppressed by his greatnesse*, who will by no means give me a portion of land to live upon.' 'This young man bearing no good will to Cormock Mac Dermody, his Cosen, Lord of Muskery,' makes some communications true or false. Whereupon Carew resolved to seize Cormock's castles of Blarney, Kilcrea, and Macrumpe. Sir C. Wilmot and Captaine Harvie, with a sergeant and 24 foote, make shew of going to hunt the Bucke neare the castle of Blarney. This castle 'is four piles joined in one, seated on a maine rock, and so free from mining, the wall 18 foote thicke, and well flancked at each corner to the best advantage. Sir C. Wilmot asked for wine and usquebagh (whereof Irish gentlemen are seldom disfurnished). But the Warders, whether out of the jealous custom of the Nation in general (which is, not to admit any strangers in their master's absence to

O'Kief.[dd]

come into their castles), neither Sir Charles (though he much importuned to see the roomey within) nor any of his company were permitted to go into the gate of the castle, nor hardly to looke within the gate of the Bawne.' Cormac himself was invited to Cork and imprisoned.

Cormack consented to hand over his castle of Blarney 'to Captain Taaffe, in whom he reposed much trust, so that no others might have the custody thereof. His castle of Kilcrey surrendered to Cap. Slingsbie; but Mocrumpe, seated in the heart of Muscrey, surrounded with woods and bogs, could not be gotten without the countenance of an Armie.' Cormock escapes from his prison in Cork, and Wilmot is ordered to raise the siege of Macrumpe; the castle took fire while a pig was singed, and the warders trying to cut their way to the woods, were killed to the number of 50. As Cormack's children and wife were prisoners, he did not wish to fight, and begged to be pardoned, and he was pardoned for good reasons—as he was the strongest man of followers in Munster, his Countrey reached even to the walls of Cork; he had been only a Jugling Traytor; not to forgive him 'might have bred new broyles, and protracted the warres of Mounster *ad infinitum*.' 'Her Majesty might have got his land,' which, 'in the opinion of all wise men, would have proved too dear a purchase.'

O'Gallogan.[dd]

'Owen Mac Teig of the Drisshan, a Carty of Muskerry, and his Cosen, Owen Ologh McSwiney, led Bagnall and his forces to Tirrell's quarters at night, which were surprised, 80 men killed. Tirrell, who with his wife had to run away half-naked, lost 50 horse and hacknies, 1000 cowes, sheep and garrans, great store of arms and baggage; only 17 of our men hurt. 'Tirrell rageth in fury against the inhabitants of Muskerry, burning their corn and cabbines and putting them to the sword, as he thought that Cormock had contrived this plot.'—*Pac. Hib.*, 599, 634, 641.

"Two of the McCarthies claimed to be McDonogh: Dermod McOwen, who seems to be meant here, and Donogh McCormac of note ([ee]) *infra*. I regret that I could not find any pedigree of the McDonogh Carthies. These 'two Chiefs,' as the *Annals* call them (p. 1837), were at strife for the Lordship of Duhallow, namely, Dermot (son of Owen, son of Donogh an-Bhothair, son of Owen, son of Donogh), and Donogh (son of Cormac Oge, son of Cormac, son of Donogh).' They could not be nearer than third cousins. O'Sullevan Beare says of them (pp. 196 and 199), 'Dermysius et Donatus Mac Carrhae de Allae principatu lite contendentes judiciis regiorum judicum stomachabantur. Allae principatus competitores conspirarunt.' See note [a].

'The 1st is the countrey of McDonoc-

M{c}Awlie.{dd}

hoe (called Duallo) w{ch} hath w{t}hin it thre other countreis, O'Chalachan's countrey. He claymeth in these countreis the gevinge of the Rod to the chieffe Lords at their first entrie, who by receivinge a whit wand at his hands, for which they pay him a certen dutie, are thereby declared from thenceforthe to be Lords of those countries. He claymeth allso that they are to rise out wth him when he makes warre; to maintaine for him seaven and 20 Galleglasses.—*State Paper given in the Life of Mac Carthy Mór.*

{dd} See *supra* notes {k, l, m}. M{c}Awly was 'very inward with O'Neill.' About 1602, Sir F. Barkley, 'finding good cause and fitt opportunity to plague Mac Awley (and his Tenants who, under protection, relieved the broken-hearted rebels) harassed all the countrey of Clanowlie, and took from thence 1000 Cows, 200 Garrans, besides Sheepe and other spoyle, and had the killing of many traitors.'—*Pac. Hib.*, p. 193.

{ee} Finghin Mac Carthaigh, 'M{c}Carthy More,' and Chief of Carbery. See his *Life and Letters*, by Mr. M{c}Carthy Glas, and a short sketch of his extrordinary career in the Appendix. He was the most powerful of Irish chiefs, after O'Neill and O'Donnell. This Finghin or 'Florens Mac Carthy myt be both M{c}Carthy More and M{c}Carthy Rewe, and thereby become farre greater in

Fynen{ee} M{c}Cartie.

Munster than ever was Desmond, and greater then any man in all Ireland, that hath ben in this age, for O'Sulivan More and O'Sulivan Bere they do depend on Mac Carthy More; The O'Driscoes do depend on Mac Carthy Rewe. The Lords of Muskry and Duallow, being both great territories, are of the Mac Cartyes, and depend upon that chieff house, and so do divers other pettie Lords of smaller territories, all w{ch} do lye, the one upon the other from Cork, above sixty miles together westward, upon the very uttermost p{ts} of Spayne.' —Report on Florence in 1595, supposed to be by *Popham*.—See *M{c}Carthy Mor*, p. 135.

'These that follow are allyd, and have matched with the House of Clan Kartie:—A Syster of the late Earle of Desmonde married to the Earle of Clan Kartie. A Syster of James Fitz Maurice was married to Sir Donoghe M{c}Carty, by whom he had issue, Florence and his brother. Corm{t} M{c}Dermode, now Lo. of Muskerys Mother was another Syster of the saide James Fitz Morrice the Traytor. The Lo. Roche married a third Syster of the said James, by whom she hath a sonne and a daughter; which daughter is married to Mac Donoghe, now Lord of Dowalla.

'The Seneschall is married to a daughter of the said James Fitz Morrice.' —*Notes for Her Majesty in 1588.*— *M{c}Carthy Mor*, p. 42.

Donell pipeⁿ McCartie.

Fineen wrote to Burghley in 1595— 'Where Yor Loᵖ hath enquired who was heir of the said contrey of Carbery —as for my parte I know not a more lawfull heir than myself, seeing Law doth allow custome as well in Englande as in Ireland, and that custome hath bene ever inviolablie kept there; and yoʳ Loᵖ shall fynd me more comformable than Donell Pypy himselfe, or Dearmed MᶜCarthy, or Donogh Oge MᶜCarthy, or Donogh MᶜOwen MᶜCarthy, or Florence MᶜOwen or any other of the Cept.'

'A not of such as are Lordes of Cuntries being Finnin Mac Carti's kinsmen and followers of the Earls of Clancarte within Desmond and the Co. of Cork adioining upon Desmond:—

Cormok Mac Dermonde   } Finnin's
Teg ᵃᶜ D'Dermond   } Aunt's
                      } Sonns.

O'Sullevan Mooar, married unto Finnin's Sister.
O'Sullevant Bear.   O'Donnaogh-Glan.
Mac Gillo Cuddie.   Mac Crehon.
Mac Gillo Newlan.   MᶜDonnell.
Hugh Cormok of Dungwill.
Clan Dermond.   Clan Lawras.
Hugh Donill Brik.   MᶜFinnin.
MᶜFinnin Duff.   Clan Teige Kettas.
MᶜDonogh Barret.   MᶜCawlef.
O'Kiffe.   O'Kelahan.   O'Dale.

With many others, and alied by himselfe and his wife unto most of the noblemen in Ireland.'—*MᶜCarthy Mor*, p. 152.

Of the 160 castles built in Cork, 26 were erected by the MᶜCarthies.— *Windele's South of Ireland.*

Irish Forces in Desmond.

	Horse.	Gallo-glas.	Kerne.
Mac Carthy More, Prince of that portion	40	160	2000
Mac Carthy Reagh, Lord of Carbry	60	80	2000
Donogh MacCarthy of Dowallie	24	80	200
Teig Mac Cormac of Muskry	40	80	200
O'Keefe	12	0	100
MᶜAwliffe	80	0	60
O'Donovan	6	0	60
O'Driscolls of Collimore and Baltimore	6	0	200
O'Mahon of Ivaghe	26	0	120
O'Sullevan Beare and Bantry	10	0	200
O'Donough More of Lough Lene	12	0	200
O'Mahoni of Brin	46	0	100
O'Dwyre of Kil-na-Managhe	12	0	100
MᶜTeig MᶜPlilip of Kilna-loghengarty	6	0	40

The last two were not followers of MacCarthy.—*Carew*, quoted in *MᶜCarthy Mor*, p. 9.

'These are of Carbery, of Florence his countrie, his followers, cosens, and kinsmen. Donell MᶜCarty, alˢ MᶜCarty Reogh; Donogh Oge O'Cullen, Reynold Oge O'Hurley th elder; Teighen-orsie MᶜCarty; Kyrone MᶜMoragho MᶜSweynie; Teig Oreigan; Moroghe MᶜDermod Oreigan, Dermod, John, and Donell, sonnes to the said Morgho. Teigh MᶜDonnell Icrooly alˢ Branagh; Owen MᶜDermodie MᶜDonnell Cartie.' —*MᶜCarthy Mor*, p. 103.

ⁿ Donal-na-Pipe MᶜCarthy Reagh,

Donaghe MᶜCormack.[gg]
Patrick Condorn.[hh]

Lord of Carbery, first cousin and great enemy of Florence, who was, as Tanist, to succeed him. He pledged himself in securities of £10,000 to Florence, not to interfere with the Irish custom of Tanistry. He was son of Cormac na-h-Aoine; he was elected MᶜCarthy Reagh in 1593; he mar. a sister of the 'Sugaun,' Earl of Desmond; he d. in 1612. In 1606 he succeeded in getting his castles of Kilbrittain, etc., and his lands settled on his children, thus robbing his Tanist and his sept. His mother was a dau. of the Lord of Muskery; his sisters were mar. to Butler of Kilcash, Butler of Shian, MᶜDonogh Lord of Duhallow, Fitz-Gerald Lord of Decies, and MᶜCarthy of Inniskeen, Chief of Slught Donogh. His son mar. a dau. of the White Knight; his dau. were wives of Lord Barry, MᶜCarthy of Dunmanway, and MᶜCarthy of Ballykay. In 1600 MᶜCarthy Reagh betrays Florence. 'The said Florence asked MᶜCarthie Reaugh (they twaine standinge in the windowe in Kilbrittaine Castell next to the sea) what course he would take? MᶜCarthie made answer that he proposed to houlde, as he had done, on her Majesty's side. Florence made answeare and said, take heede what you do! the Queene is not able to overcome us; trust not in the English, for they are not sound among themselves, and the Councill is divided, and no man knoweth it better than I do; and be suere that the Irish will prevaile,' etc.—*MᶜCarthy Mor*, p. 239, and *Cronelly*.

[gg] See note ([cc]). He was killed in a skirmish in Connaught in 1601, say the *Annals*, which call him MᶜDonough, i.e., Donough Mac Cormac Oge, MᶜCormac.—p. 2231.

There were also the Mac Carthies of Ballea, of Cloghroe, of Mourne or na Mona; Teig-an-Fhorsa MᶜCarthy Duna of Gleanacroim, who 1° mar. a dau. of MᶜSwiney, Constable of Thomond, and 2° a dau. of Rory MᶜSheehy.—See *MᶜCarthy Mor*, and *Cronelly's Family History*.

[hh] In 1582 the Seneschal of Imokilly and Gilla-Patrick Condun made a raid into Roche's country, slew his sons Redmond and Theobald, and a great number of the chiefs of their people and of their chief constables. Theobald's wife seeing her husband mangled, shrieked dreadfully, 'so that she died that night alongside the body of her husband.' In a second raid, at Allhallowtide, the Seneschal and Patriccin Condun slew two other sons of Roche, and only fourteen weaponed men of the territory outlived the engagement!—*Annals*, p. 1777.

In 1600, Mac Hawghe Condon, chiefe of a small country, submitted to the Queen. In 1601, O'Donnell de-

John Fitz Edmond.[ii]
Seneshall of Imokellie.[kk]

sires Fineen McCarthy to commend him to Patrick Condon.—*Pac. Hib.*, pp. 62 and 302. In 1591, the gentlemen of Condon's countrey were, Edmond Gangahe; Edmond Og Condon; Patrick C.; Walter C.; Wm. Edmond C.; and Edmond McJohn C.; Richard Condon *alias* McMaoge, Piers Gold, and Fynne Monsloe.—*Car. Cal.*, p. 64.

In 1598, Cecil writes—'Certain undertakers are clamouring for the lands of Condon; let this chief be told that his land shall be safe from them.'—*M'Carthy Mor*, p. 168.

'Condon was brother-in-law of Lord Barry, who in 1605 informed Lord Salisbury that Condon was descended of the ancient English, his ancestors maintaining their lands since the conquest, and was near allied to ancient English in general in the Province of Munster.' Strange to say, Condon's son, David, was a friend of Florence McCarthy, the enemy of his uncle Barry, and with the Earl of Thomond and others was surety for him 'in £250 a-piece.'—*Car. Cal.*, 1605; *Mc Carthy Mor*, p. 399. The second Earl of Desmond mar. a dau. of Lord Condon. Patrick Condon of Ballymac-Patrick mar. Honora, sister of David Lord Barry, who lived in 1598.—*Lodge*, vol. i., pp. 63 and 293.

In 1591, William, son of Gerald C. of Cork-beg sold his property to John FitzEdmond de Gerald of Cloyne; near Corkbeg House are the remains of Condon's castle.—*Windele's South of Ireland*, p. 197.

In 1605, David C. describes himself to the Secretary of State as 'Chief of his sept, of as noble a house of English race as most in Ireland, and by birth Baron of Ballyderrowen; the Lords C. had frequently been summoned as Barons to Parliament—his ancestors had never matched but with Earls or Barons.'

[ii] I cannot make out who he is, from the *Geraldine Documents*, or *Calendar of Carew Papers*. Perhaps he is the Geraldine under note ([kk]).

[kk] See *supra* note ([hh]). Gentlemen of the barony of Imokillie in 1592—John FitzEdmond Gerrald; R. Condon; J. Ca ✗ rew (his mark); Edmund ✗ Supell (his mark); Redmond Maguier; Mastine ✗ McPieris (his mark); Edmond Power; Gerott ✗ Condon (his mark).—*Car. Cal.* In 1602, 'William McShane, the Seneschal's son of Imokilly,' emigrated to Spain, after the battle of Kinsale. The daughter of James FitzMorris mar. John FitzGerald, Seneschal of Imokilly, and 2^{ly} Sir Edmond, son and heir of Sir J. FitzGerald of Cloyne and Ballymaloe. In 1565, 'Gerald FitzJames McSleyney, Captain of his nacion in Imokilly and true Lord

John Fitz Edmond[u] of Clone.

of Rostellan, sold unto John Fitz-Edmond James de Geraldinis his manor of Rosteilan.'—*Windele*, p. 199.

The 8th and last Seneschal of Imokilly was John FitzEdmund FitzGerald; he married the dau. of James Fitz-Maurice of Desmond, 'the Arch Traytor.' His son Edmund was twelve years old in 1598. His sisters were married to Condon of Corkbeg, Sir John Fitz-Edmond, and R. McBrien McShee; his illegitimate son was in Spain in 1602.—*Geraldine Documents in Kilk. Jour. of Arch.*

[u] 'A man very famous for his learning and liberall hospitality in entertaining of strangers.'—*Pac. Hib.*, p. 63.

A 'Bastard Geraldine, a man of great authority, commissioner of the peace and quorum, and trusted and employed in causes of State; he has £1000 revenue; has made show of religion and loyalty and affection to the English; but of late has been discovered a hippocrite and a traitor . . . as rebellious and hateful towards the English as any Desmond or Tyrone.'—*Justice Saxey in 1597, Car. Cal.* In 1600, O'Neile wrote to Edmond FitzJohn and Thomas FitzJohn, ' to come to himself and fight for your conscience and the right. And if you do not, be well assured by the will of God that O'Neylle will come and sojourn with you for a time;' and O'Neille 'utterly spoiled him.'—*Car. Cal.*, 1600, pp. 363 and 364.

FitzEdmund was Fyneen McCarthy's godfather.—*Carew, in McCarthy Mor*, p. 268. After the victory of Kinsale the Lord Deputy, the night that he left Cork, lodged at Clone, a towne and manor house sometime belonging to the bishop of that See, but now passed in Fee-farme to Master John Fitz-Edmond, who gave cheereful and plentiful entertainment to his Lordship and all such of the Nobility, Captaines, and gentlemen, and others as attended upon him—the Deputy did honour him with the Order of Knighthood to requite his perpetual loyalty, etc.—*Pac. Hib.*, p. 503.

FitzEdmond mar. a dau. of Lord Barry; died in 1612, aged 82. His monument, with effigies, is in Cloyne cathedral. He had four brothers; his sisters were married to Lord Inchiquin and Owen McDonal O'Sullevan. His family vanished with his great-grandson.

His epitaph runs thus—
Epitaphium Johannis de Geraldinis Militis.
Anno Domini 1611.
Hic situs est miles magni de stirpe Giraldi,
Aeterna cujus Patria laude sonat,
Hospitio celebris, doctrina clarus et armis;
Digna fuit virtus nobilitate viri.
Omnipotens animam rapiat miseratus in altum

COUNTIE OF CORK. 181

The White knight^(mm) called Fitzgibbon.
Sr Thomas of Desmonds Sone,^(nn) latelie made Earle of Desmonde, Capten of the Rebellion in Mounster raysed in October last.

Dura haec exanimum marmora corpus habet;
Illius et gesta in pace, et quam plurima bello
Te doceant vivi, lector amice vale.

Obiit prædictus Eques anno ætatis 85, die vero mensis Januarii 15, anno Dni 1612. Sub hoc etiam marmore requiescit filius cum patre qui immatura morte patri praeivit iter anno ætatis 43, die vero mensis Martii 10, anno Dni 1612.—See *Geraldine Documents in Kil. Jour. of Arch.*

^(mm) Edmond FitzGibbon *alias* the White Knight, had 400 foot and 30 horse in 1599 against the English.—*Car. Cal.* He is marked 'very dangerous' in 1588.

In 1600, Carew writes—'The White Knight hath sent sundry messages to me promising to submit and to be an honest man. A more faythlesse man never lived upon the earthe . . . if anything do move him to keep his promise, it is the internal malice between James McThomas and him, which is irreconciliable.' He was a Geraldine, a born follower of Fitz-Thomas Earl of Desmond, and brother of his wife; and yet he betrayed him, and took him prisoner in Slewgrott. And Carew says—'I protest I do not know any man in Munster but himself by whom I might have gotten him.' The White Knight got £1000 for his service.

'The name of the White Knight shall cease, and his race;
His castle down fall, roof and rafter!'
Aubrey de Vere.

In 1604, the King orders Edmund FitzJohn Oge Gibbon, *alias* Gerald, called the White Knight, to be restored to his ancient blood, and to hold in feefarm for ever of the King, Ould Castle Town, and Michell's Town in Cork; and, as he hath good scope of land, . . . to be countenanced with the style of Baron of Clangibbon.—*Car. Cal.*

There was also FitzGibbon of the half barony of Kilmore, near Charleville—'David an-Chomhraic (of the combat) FitzGibbon, Lord of Coill-mor, died in 1582.'—*Annals.*

See more about those FitzGibbons in the *Geraldine Documents, Kilk. Arch. Journal,* 4th series, p. 609.

^(nn) 'That Archtraitor and usurping Earle' of Desmond, writes Carew, was the most mightie and potent Geraldine that had been of any of the Earles of Desmond his predecessors; for he had 8000 men well armed under his command at one time.'—*Pac. Hib.,* pp. 250, 251. See notes (^(mm)) and *infra* under 'the Earls.' He had a brother John;

182   STATE OF IRELAND ANNO 1598.

Justice Gold,[oo] second Justice of Mounster.
O'Sullivan more.[pp]
Also sundrie other of meaner sort, as—
Barrhies.[qq]   Waters.
Condorns.   Flemings.

and a cousin in the Tower who was set up as Elizabeth's Earl of Desmond.

There was also a Geraldine seated at Prughus, between Charleville and Tullylease.—*Tribes of Ireland*, p. 69. Also FitzGerald of Broghill—'Redmund FitzGerald, Lord of Tuath-Brothaill, was executed in 1596 at Cork for . . . insurrection.'—*Annals*, p. 1997.

[oo] James Gold, according to Chief Justice Saxey, 'is Second Justice of Munster and Recorder of Limerick; he stands indicted seven times of several high-treasons which for several years have been smothered, but lately revealed to me by Hugh Cuffe, Esquire.'—*Car. Cal.*, 1597, p. 211.

There was Philip Gold in Kinalea, and Piers Gold in Condon's country.

[pp] See under Kerry and *supra* note ([z]).

[qq] In 1585 the members for Cork were Norries, Cogan, and T. FitzEdmond; for the city, Miagh and Sarsfield; for Youghal, Coppinger and J. Collen; for Kinsale, Galway and Roche. In 1652, there were in the city of Cork 38 Goolds, 30 Roches, 22 Tyrries, 19 Galways, 18 Meads, 18 Coppingers, 11 Sarsfields, 11 Martels, 8 Morroghs, 5 Skiddies, 5 Ronaynes; the others were, Walters, Creaghs, Meskills, Fagans,

Lombards, Verdons, Lavallyns, Whytes, Hores, etc.

Thirty-nine Gallways, 34 Skiddies, 30 Golds, 29 Roches, and 25 Tyrrys were Mayors of Cork.—See List of Mayors in *Hist. of Cork, by the Nun of Kenmare.*

Temp. Henry VI., the Wynchedons (or Nugents) were the chief family, their head, 'Chief of his nacion,' lived at Aughavarten Castle (which is now a fine ruin 52 feet high), near Carrigaline. The Goolds and Sarsfields had also 'Captains of their nacion.'—*Windele's South of Ireland*, pp. 6 and 196.

The County Jury of 1576 were—'Martell of Martellston; Tch[t.] Barry of Donboige; Mallefunte of Courteston; Hoare of Money; O'Mahowny of O'Mahowne's castle; Skiddie of Frissell castle; M‘Owen of Drishane; O'Herlihie of Ballycorny; James Oge Rooch of Knyvre; Cogan of Ballenecourtey; Fynen M‘Cormac of Bellem‘lashy, gentlemen.'—*M‘Carthy Mor*, p. 11.

The Jurors who acquitted W[m.] Mead, Recorder of Cork in 1603, when the Government wanted to find him guilty of High Treason:—1. Richard FitzDavid Oge Barrie of Robertstown, Ar. 2. Thomas FitzJohn Gerald of Res-

Meaghes.
Skiddies.[rr]
Barrots.[ss]
Nugents.[tt]

Goldes.[uu]
Russells.
Galloways.

tellan, gent. 3. W{m.} Power of Shangarry, gent. 4. Gregorie Lombart of Bottevant, gent. 5. David Nogle (Nagle) of Mondaumny, gent. 6. Myles Roche of Killeahie, gent. 7. Donell O'Donvaie *alias* O'Donvan of Castle Donovane, gent. 8. J. Ronane of Youghill, gent. 9. Nich. Galwane of Youghill, gent. 10. Mohenus M{c}Shehie of Killinetworragh (Kilnatoora), gent. 11. W{m.} Hadnett of Ballyvoady. 12. Donogh Moel (Moyle) M{c}Carthy of Fiall, gent. Meade was accused of refusing to recognise James I., and 'of levying war.' The Jurors who were present at the indictment of Meade previously were—O'Solivan of Carrig, gentleman; Teig M{c}Cormac Carty of Ballea; Tailor of Mallow; T. Gaukaghe of Ishinegreagh; Garret Boy Barry of Ballyncourty; John Barry *alias* M{c}Adam of Rathcormac; T. Barry *alias* M{c}Adam of Ballycloghie; Edmund M{c}Shane M{c}Edmund of Ballynecorry; Hyde of Carrigyneady; Cahir O'Callaghan of Dromynive; W{m.} Mallesant of Killeaghie (Malefont?); Bryan M{c}Owen of Cloghdoe; Redmund Magner of Aghaddy; Teig M{c}Dermod M{c}Donnell of Knockilly; Garret Barrie of Ballyregan, gentlemen.'—*Car. Cal.*, 1603, p. 68.

[rr] In 1596, d. Andrew Skiddie, possessed of the 'North Abbey of the Friars of Shandon.' Skiddy's Castle, on west of North Main Street, built by John Skiddy in 1445, was demolished in 1785. On a bell in Trinity Church is inscribed —'Andrew Skiddie, Mayor—R. Pennington made me in the yeare of our Lorde 1621.' See *infra* Elinor Roche, *née* Skiddy. In 1594, R. Skyddye was 'Chaplain of our Ladye Chapel;' in 1536, Reen ny Skiddy was held by R. Skyddy, 'chief of his nacion.'— *Windele*, p. 181.

[ss] Barret, the 'chief of his nacion,' owned the strong castle of Ballincollig and the castles of Carrigrohan and Castlemore (which are now ruins). Wm. B. of Ballincollig, 'chief of a small countrye,' submitted in 1599.'— *Windele*, pp. 252-6. In 1612, Andrew Barret was M.P. for co. Cork. In 1588, John FitzJames Barrett, Prior of St. Stephen's by Cork, to Wm. Kyent of Corck, Sheareman, and Honory ny Learie his wife, two beds of the garden situate in the *Nard*, to hold for 50 years, at the rate of two pence yearly. The prior puts 'his mark.'—*Windele*.

[tt] Of Ahamartha, castle still standing, see note ([qq]).

[uu] See note ([oo]).

Ronayn of Ronayne's Court. A chimney-piece bears the inscription—

Roches.ᵛᵛ

*Chief Undertakers*ʷʷ *in this Countie:—*
Sir Thomas Norriesˣˣ L. President.

'Morris Ronayn, and Margaret Gould builded this house in the yeare of our Lorde 1627, and in the 3 yeare of Kinge Charles, Love God and Neighbors, M.R. (I.H.S.) M.G.'

T. Ronayne of Ronayne's Court was Mayor of Cork in 1630. This family became extinct in 1798, and the representative in the female line is Sarsfield of Ducloyne.

In 1536, Cogan was 'Lord of the Manor of Bernyheylyc in the counties of Kerrycurihy.'

ᵛᵛ *Vide* Lord Roche. The Roches had in 1652 two castles, 'the Golden Castle' inside, and 'Short Castle' outside the walls of Cork. There is in Christ Church the old Roche tomb with the words still visible—'Jacobus Roche. Also a tomb of 'Morris Roche Fitz-James, Alderman, and his only wife, Elenor Roche, *alias* Skiddy, this being their last dwelling;' date 1634.

There is an anonymous inscription on another tomb in Christ Church—

'God's peace bee with yow my tow good shisters, Ellinor and Margarite. A.D. 1624.'—*Windele*, p. 56.

A stone, which belonged probably to St. Peter's Church, has the initials I.H.S. 'circled with a glory,' and the inscription—'Made at Cork i anno dni. 1586 xxiii. June.

'𝕿𝖍𝖞 sugred name, ☩ 𝕷ord,
𝕰ngrabe within my brest,
𝕾ith therein doth consist
𝕸y weal and only rest.'

ʷʷ Character of certain English settlers. 'They are freed from three of the greatest dangers: first, they cannot meet in all that land (Ireland) any worsse than themselves; secondly, they neednot feare robbing, for, that they have not any thing to lose; lastly, they are not likely to rune in debte, for that there is none will trust them.'—*Description of Ireland in* 1589 *by R. Payne, a Settler.*

'I have just caus to be agreavd that Her Majesty is abused with such undertakers, I associated with sutch companions, and an honourable accion disgraced with such *lewd, indiscreet, and insufficient* men. . . . My dislike of the proceedings hear hath drawn upon me the enmitea of Sir V. Brown, Sir E. Denny, and others of that sorte, *that measure conscience by commodite, and law by lust.*'—*Sir W. Herbert to Burghley in* 1588, *given in M'Carthy Mor*, pp. 51, 52.

ˣˣ In June 1599, General Norreys, while, charging at the head of his cavalry, the troops of Burke of Castleconnell, at Kilteely, was pierced through helmet and brain by John Burke, a Connaught gentleman. On the 5th March 1600, Maguire, in a cavalry

COUNTIE OF CORK. 185

    Hugh Cuff.
S{r} Walter Raleigh.
S{r} Christofor Hatton's heyre.
S{r} Warrham S{t.} Leger's[xx] heyre.
S{r} Ric. Greenfield's Heyres.

    The most of the Iryshe Gentlemen of this Countie are latelie entered in Rebellion, having the Noblemen and chief Captens of everie nation. The nomber of their Forces I know not.[yy]

    Castles[zz] and Howses of name are many belonging to the

---

skirmish, 'strake Sir Warham St. Leger through the brain.'

    In 1598, Spencer was burned out of Kilcolman Castle, and one of his children perished in the flames. In the following year he died in London 'for lack of bread.' This 'gentle,' poet had written a work to urge the wholesale starvation of the Irish, and the burning of their homesteads and crops.

    Undertakers in Cork in 1589.
    @ 1d. the acre.

	Acres.
Hugh Cuffe	12000
Arthur Hyde . . .	6000
Phaare Beacher . . .	12000
Hugh Worthe . . .	12000
Sir W. St. Leger and Sir R. Grynfield	12000
Arthur Robyns . . .	4000
George Robynson . .	4000
Mr. Read	3000

    [yy] See *supra*. The 'Sugaun' Earl had 8000 men well armed under his command.—*Pac. Hib.*, p. 251.

In 1599, according to *Moryson*, Edmond FitzGibbon, the White Knight, had . 400 f. 30 h.
James FitzThomas, 'Earl of Desmond' . . 250 f. 30 h.
The Lord of Dowallough . 200 f. 8 h.
Barry Oge, and Lord Barry's brother in the Muskerye 120 f. 3 h.
Davy Burke in the Carbrye 500 f.
O'Sulevan Beare, O'Sulevan More's country, and Dermot M{c}Owen usurping the name of M{c}Carthy More 500 f. 6 h.

    The Lord President reported that 'between March and November 1600, he had slain 1200 weaponed men, *besides husbandmen, women, and children.'*
—*Life of M{c} Carthy Mor*, p. 315.

    [zz] 'There were 160 castles in Cork.
Castles in Muskry in 1600.—Blarney, Kilcrea, Mocrompy, Carrignavar. Castle ny Hinshy with Cormack's mother, Castlemore and Carrignamuk with Callaghan M{c}Teg, Carrigdrohid

Noblemen and Gentlemen of the Countrie and to the undertakers, the chief whereof is Moyallo, latelie Builded by Sr Thomas Norries, L. President of Mounster.

with Sir Cormac McTeg's widow; Donogh McCormoc of Cloghphilip; Owen Loghie McSwyne of McShaneglasse; Brian McOwen Loghie of Cloghda; O'Lery of Carrinecorragh and Carrigneyleghe; Owen McTeg Cartie of Carrigfalcaghe, Drissan, and Carrigepookie; Finin McDonal Oge Cartie of Downdererige. *Septs of the Carties in Muskry*—Clan Cormac Oge, Slucht Decan, Slught Tuonedrum, Slucht Cloghroe, the Sept of Clanfaddaghe, Sept of Shane Killie. *Septs of Freeholders*—O'Lery and O'Mahons. The 'followers' were—Riordens, Morohoes, Clancallogans, McSwynes. 'The countries' were—O'Healies, O'Herlies, O'Long, O'Cronin; Hegans (brehons), Aulyves or O'Levies (surgeons), O'Dallies (rimers), O'Donins (chroniclers).—*Car. Cal.*, an. 1600, p. 152.

In Carbrie in 1599 were—McCarthy Reogh of Kilbrittain, etc.; O'Mahon Fun (Fionn) of Evaugh; O'Driscoll Mor of Collymore, and O'Driscoll Oge of Collybeg; O'Donovan of Clancahell; O'Dally of Munster-Vary; O'Crowly of Killshallow; O'Murrihie of Ballywiddan; O'Mahon Carbery of Kinalmeaky (escheated).—*Car. Cal.*, year 1599, p. 351.

O'Learys owned the castles of Dundarierk, Carrigafooky, Carrignancela, Drumcarra, and Carrignacurra (possessed by Dermod Oge O'Leary in 1588, and said by Smith to be 100 f. high). The pass of Keim-an-eigh separated the territory of O'Leary (Ibh-Leary) from O'Sullevan's lands.

In 1600, the O'Learies, to the number of 100, attacked the Carties of Carbery, and after a sharp skirmish, O'Lery, Head of that Sept, was slain, and 10 other the chiefe of his family, with some more of lesse note.'—*Pac. Hib.*, p. 171. O'Mahony's castle and his lands of Kinalmeaky for several miles on both sides of the Bandon river were granted to Beecher and Grenville.

The McSwineys built Castlemore *circa* 1598. They lived at the Castle of Cloghda, a solid keep 40 feet high with projecting battlement. They owned also Mushanaglass, and Castle McDermod Oge.—*Windele*.

Castle Donovan or Sowagh, a tall square keep with crenellated battlements, and projecting defences at the angles. Donal O'Donovan of this place got a regrant from James I. by English tenure of this castle, and a large extent of territory. Copious and curious details about this O'Donovan, Chief of Clancahill, are given in the *Annals* and *Hy-Fiachra*.

THE COUNTIE OF KERRIE.

This Countie[a] properlie contayneth onlie that Land which Lyeth between the River of Mayne and the Sheynen, and

[a] Desmond is a parcel of the countrie of Kerry, and is divided into three baronies and a half, viz., Magonny, Iuragha, Dunkerran, and the half barony of Glanaroghto. In the north side it is bounded by the river Mang, which doeth divide Desmond from the rest of Kerry. The south part doeth bound with certain mountains of Bear and Bantry, beginning from Kilmallockoshista, and continuing to O'Leary and O'Donovan's lands in the Co. of Corke in the mountain of Sleughlogher, and are divided by the head of the rive of Blackwater; the rest of Desmond is bounded by the main ocean sea.

The chief castles were the Palace, Bally Carbry and Castle Logh.—*Carew MSS.*, quoted in *McCarthy Mor*, p. 221.

There are in the Lambeth Library some maps of the baronies of Kerry which were made *circ.* 1598. In them the following places are marked:—

I. 'Island of Dariry (Valentia) and haven of Bealinche and Beginnis—1. Slucht Cormack's land. 2. Part of Sluch Donnell Brick's land. 3. Part of Earl of Clancar's land.

II. 'Half barony of Glaneroght— 1. McFyneen's lande. 2. Part of McGillicuddies' land. 3. Lands of Niddin Clan Tiege Kittagh. 4. Clandermot's land. 5. A quarter of the Bishop of Cork's land. 6. A Sept of the O'Sulevan Beare. 7. Another Sept of the O'Sullivan's. 8. O'Griffin's lande and part of the Prior of Inisfallen's land. 9. Philip O'Sullivan's land. 10. McFineen Duff's land.

III. 'Barony of Iveragh—1. O'Sullivan Mor's lande. 2. Slught Donell Brick's land. 3. Slught nyne Rudderie's lande. 4. Part of McCarthy's lande in Donell McCarthy's possession, ✠ Priory of Ballinskelligs. 5. Lands of Ballycarbery, in Brown's possession. 6. Clan Crohan's lande. 7. Slught Cormac of Dunguile's lande. 8. Slught Owen Mor of Coshmang's land. 9. Clandonell Fin's land, and part of Earl of Clancarthy's land, in Donnell McCarthy's possession. 10. Lands of Ballycarbery, in Denny's possession.

IV. 'Barony of Magonihy—1. Glanfleske or O'Donoghoe Glan's lande. 2. Onaght or O'Donoghoe Mór's, and Slught Owen Mor's lande, now Browne's

includeth the most part of the mountaine of Shewroyher, which mountaine being the most Easterlie part of this Countie, boundeth it upon the Counties of Limerick and Corke to the East, upon the Sheynen to the North, upon the Sea to the West, and the River of Mayne to the South.

seignory lande. 3. Kilegy, part of the Earl's lande, now in Donal McCarthy's possession. 4. Castle Lough, part of the Earl's lande. 5. Part of McFincen's land. 6. Slught Fineen Duffe's lande. 7. Slught Murry's (Moriarty's) land. 8. Slught Cormock of Dunguile's land. 9. Clandonnell Fin's lande. 10. Part of McCrohan's lande. 11. Killorgan and other landes of Conways. 12. The Knight of Kerry's lands. 13. Lands of the Abbey of Killaha.

V. 'Barony of Dunkerron—1. McGillicuddy's land. 2. McFineen's land. 3. The Priory of Ahamon's land. 4. O'Sullivan Mor's lande. 5. Slught Cormock of Dunguile's land (McCarthy's). 6. Part of the Earl of Clancor's land, in his wife's possession.'—*Miss Hickson's Kerry Records*, p. 254, 2nd series.

O'Donochoe More's countrey of 45 ploughlands is now in McCarthy More's hands. The Lord of Cosmaigne's countrey of 84 ploughlands in his hands also. The Lord of Kerslawny's countrey, otherwise called Slight Cormak, conteyneth 35 ploughlands, whereof some are in the Ile of Valentia. McCarthy Mor claymeth there the geaving of the Rodd, Risinge out, the findinge of 40 Galleyglas, and to the value of £40 stg. a yeare in spendinge.

The countrey of [Mac] Gelecuddé contayneth 46 ploughlands. He claymeth there Risinge out, the gevinge of the Rodde, the findinge of 30 Galleyglas, Risinge out and to the value £20 a yeare in spendinge.

Mac Fynin's countrey in Glenaraught contayneth 28 ploughlands. McCarthy Mor claymeth the givinge of the Rodd, the findinge of 15 Galleyglas, Risinge out, and to the value of £24 yearly in spendinge.

The countrey of Clandonoroe contayneth 24 ploughlands. McCarthy More claymeth theare risinge out, and it is in the Erle's hands by Her Mª Gyfte.

The eleventh is the countrey of O'Donocho Glân (O'Donoghue of Glenflesk in Kerry). He hath there no other dutie but onlly six and fortic shillings fourpence of yearlie Rent. The countrey conteyneth 20 ploughlands.

The twelfth is the countrey of Clan Dermonde. It conteyneth 28 ploughlands. He claymeth Risinge out, the keepinge of 16 Galleyglas, and in yearly spendinge to the value of £40.

'The countrey of Loughlegh or

COUNTIE OF KERRIE. 189

Principall Ardfert.
Townes   Dingley,[b] a walled Towne.
       Traley.
Castles[c] Iland belonging to S[r] Will[m.] Harbert.
       Castle mayne to the Quene.
       Carrigfoyle[c] to John O'Connor.

Teignitowin contains 32 ploughlands. M'Carthy Mor claymeth it to be excheated to him for want of heirs right and legitimate.—*M'Carthy Mor*, p. 32.

[b] 'The chief towne in all that part of Ireland. It consisteth of one main street, hath gates, as it seemeth at ether end to open and shut as a town of war, and a castle also. The houses are very strong built, with strong thick walls and narrow windows, and like unto castles; and all the houses in the town were burned and ruined by the Earl of Desmond . . . There remaineth yet a thick stone wall, that passeth overthwart the middle of the street, which was a part of their fortification . . . we had good muttons, though less than ours in England, for 2 shillings or 5 groats a piece; good pigs and hens for 3 pence a piece. We were entertained at the Sovereign's house, one of the four that withstood the Earl of Desmond.'—*English Narrative written circ.* 1598, *given at* p. 235 *of Hist. of Kerry, by the Nun of Kenmare.*

Concerning Dingle, Hakluyt's *Chronicle*, edited in 1599, says—'That part is full of great mountaines and hills from whence came running down the pleasant streams. The natural hardness of that nacion appeareth in this, that their small children runne usually in the winter up and down barefootte and barelegged with many a times only a mantle to cover them. The chiefe officer of the town they call their Souvereyne. In 1585 it got the same privileges as Drogheda. In 1592 R. Traunt was Sovereign of Dingle, the other gentle men in or near it were Stephen Rice, Conway N. Browne, Pattinson (agent to Denny), Gerot Duff Stack, N. Traunt, and O'Sulevan Beare.

Dingle belonged to Knight of Kerry. He was beaten by Wilmot at Ballinahowe (a place belonging to Edmund Hussey), and he lost Dingle and the Castles of Gregorie and Rahinane.

Trant and Hussey were members for Dingle in 1613, and the Trants, Rices, and Husseys monopolised the representation till 1641.—*Miss Hickson*, p. 158.

There were 12 or 13 castles in the one small barony of Carcaguiny, and there must have been much more than 30 in all Kerry; perhaps there were 90.—*A writer in the Kilk. Jour. of Arch.*

[c] 'Carrigafoyle, chief seat of John

Lixnaw[d] to the L: thereof.
Tarbert to the Quene.
Ardfert[d] to the L: of Lixnaw.
Traley to S[r] Edward Denny[e] in the court of Ingland.

O'Connor Kerry, who owned also the Castle of Ardee.'—*Smith's Kerry*.

This was John *na-Cathac* (or of the conflicts), son of Conor O'Connor and Honoria, a dau. of the 2[d] Earl of Thomond. He d. in 1640, leaving no surviving male issue by his wife, a dau. of O'Sullevan Mor; his sister Ellen mar. FitzMaurice of Ballykiely; his daughters mar. the Knight of Glynn, Oliver Delahoyde, and Ulick Roche.—*Hist. of Kerry, by Nun of Kenmare*, p. vii.

However, Fineen M[c]Carthy Mor repeatedly calls O'Connor his nephew. Carrigafoyle was the 'strongest castle in all Kerry.'—*Car. Cal.*, p. 412, year 1600.

[d] 'Also Listowel. Ballykeely belonged to James FitzMaurice, Castle Drum to Moriarty, Dunkerron to O'Sullivan Mor, Dunloe to Daniel O'Sullevan, Dingle to Hussey, Gallerus to the Knight of Kerry, Cahir Trant to Trant.' —*Smith's Kerry*.

'The O'Connells were Constables of the Castle of Ballycarbrey, near Cahirciveen, for M[c]Carthy Mor. Richard O'Connell, ancestor of "the Liberator," fought against the Earl of Desmond, surrendered his estates, and obtained a regrant of his lands. He mar. a dau. of M[c]Carthy of Carrignamult, in Co. of Cork; his son Maurice was High Sheriff of Kerry.'—*The Nun of Kenmare*, p. x.

[e] Ned Denny, as Lord Grey calls him in his despatch, distinguished himself at the head of his company at Fort del-Ore, in Nov. 1580. In the Sep[r.] of that year he wrote, 'The service here in boggs, glumes, and woods might better fit *mastives* than brave gentlemen that desire to win honour.' Yet he got the honour of Knighthood at Fort del-Ore, and a claim on the Desmond estates. His epitaph is in Waltham Abbey—'He took his deadly sicknesse in the service of his countrie, and died the 13th of Feb. 1599.'—p. 141 of *Kerry Records*.

[f] See *infra*, the 'Peers' and 'Bishops.'

A map of Munster in 1608, dedicated to Cecil, has appended to it—'Lists of men of note :—M[c]Fineen at Ardtully, M[c]Eligot at Ballymac Eligot, John M[c]Ulick at Castle of O'Brenan, M[c]Shane at Mornigane, Donel M[c]Fun at Tybrid, MacGellecudde at Boddesmeen, Donell M[c]Moriertagh at Castle Drym, M[c]Tirlogh at Balingown, M[c]Gray at Tarmin M[c]Gray, FitzJohn de Lickfournea, FitzMoris at Lixnaw, Brown at Brownogh, Herbert at Clonnmillane, Hussaye at Castle Gregorie, Trant at Caer Trant, Thomas Oge at Ardnagragh, Gray of

Principall Men   The Baron of Lixnaw[f] commonlie called the L: Fitzmorrice, his name is PatrickFitzgerrald, his chief Hous Lixnaw.
The Bishop of Ardfert.[f]
Fitzgerrald[g] Knight of Kerrie.

Liscahane, Raymond Oge.'—*Kerry Records*, p. 281, 1st series.

The English descent in Kerry, given by Carew:—'Lixnaw, Knight of Kerry, Bishop of Ardfert; Hussey, Chief of his name; Hores, Rices, Browne, John Oge of the Island and his sept; McHenrys. Mere Irish:—Moriertaghs, O'Conor Kerrie, MacHeligots.'

In 1592, in the 'barony and half barony of Clanmorris lived Pa. Lyksnaw, and John ✗ Piers (his mark); in the three baronies of Trughnacmye, Brownlonclone, and Offerbuye, and the barony of Corcaguinny, were—Rich. Trantte ("suffrain" of Dinglecouishe), John FitzEdward Gerald, M. Brown, Stephen Ryce, Gerald FitzMorish, R. Pattinson (agent for Denny), J. Traunt, Jenkyn Conway, Gerott Duff Stack, T. ✗ McEdmond (mark), J. McThomas Mc ✗ Shane (mark), Moris Mc ✗ Ulick (mark), John ✗ McUlick (mark), R. Trauntt, M. Traunt, John Morish, Nich. Brown, Owen O'Suilevan ✗ *alias* O'Suilevan Beery (his mark), Dermod ✗ O'Swilevan (his mark).'—*Car. Cal.*, year 1592.

[g] William FitzGerald, 9th Knight of Kerry, living in 1599, was of Rathannan and Inismore; had married a lady, of the family of Tobyn, who was widow of Morogh McShee. He was son of John the 8th Knight, and of Shela, dau. of O'Sullevan More. His brothers were Maurice, Patrick, Gerald, of whom Maurice was in the service of Spain in 1605. His sisters' husbands were—FitzGerald Oge of Kilmacow, and Teig O'Driscoll. From him is descended the Knight of Kerry, *qui nunc est.*'—*Geraldine Documents in the Kil. Jour. of Arch.;* and *Pedigree in the Records of Kerry.*

'The Lord FitzMaurice hath some 200 foot. The Knight of Kerry hath 300, and a dozen horsemen on a sudden, and 100 foot more on 3 or 4 days' warninge. He is my cousene, . . . but the hard usage of my nephew, O'Conor of Kerry, doth make a great number loathe to be persuaded by me.'—*Flor. McCarthy Mor;* see his *Life*, p. 291.

In 1600, Wilmot, Governor of Kerry, being conducted to the Quarter of the Knight of Kerry in the night, killed 40 of his men, took 500 cowes, 200 garrans, two moneths' provisions of meale and butter for his soldiers. Thereby being disfurnished of all his provision for his followers, he submitted; Thomas Oge, of the Island, and Donal, son of O'Sullevan Mor, followed his example.—*Pac. Hib.*, 652.

Traunts[h] of the Dingle.
Nic: Browne.[i]
James oge Perce.[k]
The Stackes,[l] a great name.

[h] The members for the borough of Dingle in 1613 were Thomas Trant and Michael Hussey. See *supra* about the Trants. 'One Traunt of the Dingle went to Spain with O'Sullivan Beare's son after the battle of Kinsale.' —*Pac. Hib.*

The Rices were a distinguished Dingle family. About 20 of them forfeited in 1641, in the barony of Corcaguiny. Piers Rice of Dingle owned 'a perty castle' in 1580; Dominick R. of Dingle d. in 1592, and his son had livery of his estates in 1603. Stephen R. of Ballinruddel was with Daniel O'Sullevan of Dunlogh, M.P. for Kerry in 1613. His broken grave is in Dingle churchyard, with the inscription (now fast becoming illegible)—

'Stephen Rice, Esquire, lies here,
Late Knight of Parliamente;
A happie life for fourscore yeare
Full virtuously he spente.
His loyal wife, Helena Trante,
Who died five years before,
Lies here also—Lord Jesus grante
Them life for evermore.
MDCXXII.'

—*The Nun of Kenmare's Kerry*, p. xxiii.

Also, there were men of note, named 'The Ferritor and Hubbers.'—*Car. Cal.*, 1603, p. 452.

In Ballyoughtra churchyard there is a tombstone with the inscription—'I.H.S. Nagle. P[n] L[at] Terry 1551. A[tt] L[li] Ferriter 1642.... Pray for us.' —*Kerry Records*, 1st ser., p. 259.

In 1641 Lady Kerry wrote—'To my very loveing friend, Mr. Piers Ferriter, at Ferriter's towne,' asking him to leave 'Florence M[c]Fineen and the rest of that rebellious crue.'—*Nun of Kenmare*, p. 246. This Piers wrote an Irish *Coaine* on the Knight of Kerry, which has been translated by Crofton Croker.

[i] Sir Nicholas Browne, 'of Molahaff,' ancestor of the Earl of Kenmare, son of Sir V. Browne, and Thomasine, dau. of Sir N. Bacon, Keeper of the Great Seal. He mar. a dau. of O'Sullevan Beare; he d. in 1616.—See a great deal about him in *Life of M'Carthy Mor.* Sir Nicholas' daughters mar. two sons of O'Sullevan Mor.—*Nun of Kenmare.*

[k] In the articles between the Government Commissioners and the Lord Fitz Morish, and the gentlemen of the country of Clanmorris in 1592, the only names are 'Pa. Lyksnawe' (Lord of Kerry) and 'John X Oge Piers' (his mark). I presume James was his brother, and that they were Fitz Maurices.—*Car. Cal.*, p. 67.

[l] 'Nations chiefly noted as procurers of mischief in Kerry and Desmond:

Mr. Conway.[m]

The Clantey McGagh and the Stacks, saving Morrice Stack and his brothers. Meet instruments to be employed in Kerry—Morrice Stack and his brothers, John Rice, Donal Faries, R. Rice.—*Car. Cal.*, 1596, p. 203.

In 1603, 'McMorris himself, Gerrott Roe Stacke, Donal O'Swillivan More, Hussey the Scholar,' were blockaded in the castle of Ballingarry in Clanmorris.

'Maurice Stack, a man of small stature but invincible courage, with 50 men, surprised by scale the castle of Liscaghan, put the ward to the sword, burnt Ardare and other towns. Before this none of her Majesty's forces had been seen in Kerrie. The country was strong in men, and full of victuals, yet this undaunted spirit of Stack (a native of that countrey), with a handful of men attempted the enterprize.'

Maurice was invited to dine by Lady Lixnaw in her husband's castle of Beauliew, at which time her brother, Donal O'Brien, brother of the Earle of Thomond, was with her. The young lady cried out unto Dermond Keugh McCorman, W^m. O'donichan, and Edmund O'heher—'Doe you not heare him misuse me in words?' Whereupon they with their skenes murdered him. —*Pac. Hib.*, pp. 121, 122, 143, 144.

[m] See in the *Kerry Records* some details about the Conways. Browne and Denny and Herbert, and these six gentlemen were adventurers or undertakers. Sir W^m. Herbert speaks of his fellow-undertakers in no complimentary terms—as 'men who measure conscience by commoditie and law by lust.'

Undertakers in 1589 *in Kerry and Desmond,* @ 8*d. per acre.*

	Acres.	People.	Rent.
Sir Valentine Brown	6000	20	£100
Sir Edwd. Denny	6000	,,	100
Sir William Herbert and Sir Charles Herbert	18,000	,,	300

McKelgot.[n]

[n] McEligott or McGillicuddy. In the parish of Ballymac Elligot there were three castles of the McElligotts—Carrignafeela, Arabella, and Bernagrillagh. In 1613 the lands of Ulick McEligott attainted were given to Sir T. Roper. A Colonel Roger McElligott commanded a Kerry regiment in England under James II.—*Nun of Kenmare* and *D'Alton's Army List.*

There was also a 'McGillicuddy, Lord of the Reeks.' Donogh McDermot O'Sulevan, *alias* McGillycuddy of Bodevysmine was slain in the Desmond wars; his territory was granted to Edmund Barret in 1595, who conveyed them to Edward Hussey; and in 1598 Hussey conveyed them to 'Donogh McDermody, *alias* McGillycuddy of Bodenesmeen. Donogh had a son Conor of Castlecurrig, who mar. a dau. of John Crosby (*alias* McCrossan), Protestant Bishop of Ardfert. Conor had for his second wife a dau. of Daniel

Mr. Grey.
Mr. Spring.
John Burtall.
John Middelton.

Oconnor Kerrie.°
and many other meane Freeholders.

Oge Carty of Dunguile; in 1630 he d. by shipwreck.—*Mac Gillicuddy Papers*, p. xviii.

There were also Thomas Oge of Ardnagreagh, Hussey of Ballynahowe, Owen McMoriarty of Skeart, McBrien of Tralee, FitzJohn of Ballykely.—See *supra*, p. 157.

Over a niche in Muckross Abbey is inscribed on a slab—'Orate pro Donaldo MacFinin, et Elizabetha Stephens, O. An° 1631. Q.S.H.F.F.'—*Windele*, p. 434.

° See in the *Historia Catholica* of O'Sullevan Beare an account of the sufferings and heroism of O'Connor Kerry in his march from Munster into O'Rorke's country. *The Annals*, p. 2095, say that 'in August 1599 was slain the son of Conor *Ciarraighe* (Donagh-Maol, son of Conor, son of Conor, son of John) by a party of the soldiers of the Earl of Desmond, namely, by the sons of Manus Oge McSheehy. This was a great loss, for O'Conor himself (*i.e.* John) was his ally in war, as was his brother, this Donogh, and all who were in their territory.'

There was also Hore of Castlegregory, in the 'barony of Corcaguiny; he was lampooned by Aenghus O'Daly.

In 1612 the collectors in the baronies for the building of Tralee were V. Browne for Magonihies, Hardinge for Iveragh, John O'Conor of Eraght, Croneen for Clanmaurice, Bowdler for Trughenackmie, McFinnan for Glenerought, Daniel O'Sullivan for Dunkernan, Wm. FitzGerald for Corcaguiny or Letterogh.

Jurors at Tralee in 1622—McDonnell of Castle Dunn, Coursey of Ballyronan, Roche of Lachabane, Offaly of Lisnagoun, O'Callaghan of Ballyvidane, Morris of Urly, Garret Oge Brennagh of Ardfert, Owen Oge Carthy of Dromkeare, Moore of Cauncaum, Trante of Dingly Coist, McCormac of Litter, McCrohan, FitzJames of Litters, McOwen of Ballingamboon, Mac Andrew of Ardfert, McDonogh Cullen of Ballybristine.—*Nun of Kenmare*, pp. 239, 243.

Though mentioned only under Cork in our MS., the chief men in Kerry were McCarthy Mór and O'Sullevan Mór.

An inscription carved on a chimneypiece preserved in a house attached to Dunkerron Castle in Kerry runs thus—'IHS. Maria Deo Gratias. This work was made the 11th of April 1596, by Owen O'Sulivan More, Sily Ny Donogh Mac Carthy Rieogh.'

This Countie is in a manner all out in Rebellion, the Inglyshe almost being expelled; their nomber is about 300 men.

This Countie was a Countie Palatyne to the Earle of Desmond, and in that tyme no small hinderance to the Government of Mounster, by reason the Liberties and Royalties thereof falling to a man of small discretion caused him to be insolent above measure, forbidding the L: President and Councill of the province to have any dealings within this Jurisdiction, and this was the verie ground and caus of his rebellion and utter overthrow—which evidentlie teacheth what may ensue when Princes do bestow places of Justice (as Justiceships or Sherrifships) or great priviledges upon any man for himself and his posteritie, Seeing no man can assure that his Posteritie shall be capable thereof.

There also are graceful figures supposed to be likenesses of O'S. and his lady in 'mere Irish' costume. The lady is dressed in a long close-fitting gown, which covers the feet, and her headdress is something 'stunning.'— *Mr. Dunoyer* in *Kilk. Jour. of Arch.*, March 1859, p. 291.

O'S. Mór lived at Dunkerron Castle, acknowledged the suzerainty of Mac Carthy Mór, was his hereditary Marshal, and ruled over 960 square miles of territory. The lesser septs, who owed fealty to O'S. Mór, were the O'S. of Beara, Bantry, Cappanacuss, Ardea, Tomies, and the Mac Gillicuddy of the Reeks. Their castles of Carriganass, Dunboy, Reendeshart, Ardea, Dunkerron, Cappanacuss, and Dunloe, are in more or less preservation, and attest the power of a race whose boast is conveyed in these lines—

'Nulla manus tam liberalis
Et generalis atque universalis
Quam Sullevanus.'
—*Kilk. J. of Arch.*, March 1859.

Owen of Dunkerron had four brothers—Dermod, m. to a dau. of Owen McCarthy Reagh; Boghe, m. to a d^r. of O'Donovan; Conor, m. to a d. of the Knight of Glynn; Donal, m. to a d. of O'Leary (widow of Mac Gillicuddy). He had two sisters m. to O'Sullevan Beare and the Knight of Kerry. Owen's son, Donal, mar. 1st a d. of the White Knight, and 2^d a d. of Lord Kerry.

THE COUNTIE OF LIMERICK.

This Countie contayneth all the Lands from the mountaine nere to the red Shard[a] joining to the Countie of Corke, to the Sheynen as well above Limerick as beneath in manner as far as Carrigfoyle, and from Slewlogher,[a] the mountaine that devideth it from Kerry, to the farthest part of McBryan O'Gonogher's Countrie : So hath it Tipperarie to the East, Slewlogher to the West, the Countie of Corke to the South, and the Sheynen to the North.

Limerick[b] a fayre Walled Cittie upon Sheynen.

---

[a] Redsherd ... the farthest part of Mac Bryan Ogannogh's cuntry, and comprehendeth in yt Glanwillim, Canolokerry *alias* the Knight of the Vallyes cuntry, and Cosmoy.—*Dymmok.*

Limericke hath in it the Knight of the Valley, *William Burcke,* Mac-Ibrine Ara, part of the White Knight's lands, *Cosmay, O'Brenes,* and upon the edge of Kerry the greene Knight, *alias* the Knight of Kerry. It hathe Kilmallocke, lately sacked by James FitzMaurice, and Limericum coasting on the sea, hard upon the river Shannon, whereby are most notably severed Mounster and Connaght.—*Campion,* pp. 3, 4.

There is two very rich countries called Kennory and Conclogh, both within the Co. of Lemericke, and they are called the Gardenes of the lande, for the variety and great plenty of all graine and fruites; and also there is more plenty of venison, fish, and foule than elsewhere in Ireland, altho in everie place there is great store. This land belonged some time to the Knight of the Valley, who for high treason was executed in Lemerick.'—*Payne's Description of Ireland in* 1589.

Ireland beares good corne of all sortes, in particular the county of Limerick.—*Dynely's Tour.*

[b] See a map of it in the *Pacata Hibernia.* 'We passed by Kilmalocke, a good corporate town, over a sweet and fertile cuntry, unto the city of Limerick, which is indeed a town of castles, compassed with the fairest wall that ever I saw, under which runs the goodly river of the Shannon, which makes it a haven for ships of good burden. Though it stands above three score miles from the sea, yet such is the sloth of the inhabi-

COUNTIE OF LIMERICK.

Principall Townes. Killmallock,[c] a Walled inland Towne.
Adare,[d]
Rakeall, } markett Townes.

tants, that all these fair structures have nothing but sluttishness and poverty within.'—*Sir J. Davis*, see p. 469 *Cal. S. P.*, 1606.

'The building of Limericke is sumptuous and substantial.'—*Stanihurst*, p. 25.

The Privy Council wrote to Carew in 1600—'We perceive by the Lord Deputy's writing, and your own opinion, how necessary it is to bridle the insolence of the town of Limerick.'—*Car. Cal.*, pp. 384 and 403. 'It was kept in check by the Castle in 1603; its people rescued, in 1604, a priest who had been arrested by warrant of the Lord President of Munster; 200 and more of the burgesses were indicted in 1606 for not coming to church.'—*Car. Cal.*

The Mayor in 1598 was James Cronwell. David Cronwell was Bailiff in 1561, and George Cromwell in 1574, and James Cromwell in 1586. The Bailiffs in 1598 were Roche and Bourke. In 1597 FitzJordan Roche was Mayor, and men of that name were Mayors in 1499, and often after. Stephen Roche was Mayor in 1601, and Philip R. in 1602. Among the mayors and bailiffs from 1588 to 1608 were—Galway, Roche, Creagh, W. Rice, Woulf, Bourke, Stackpol, Stretch, Fox, Arthur, White, Comyn of Parke, Fanning, Waters,

Sexten, Myeagh, and Hally. The Members for the city were, in 1585, Arthur and White; in 1613, White and Counsellor James Galway. In 1594, 'a hundred tall men were sent to ye north, under the leading of David Woulfe, capte.'—*Lenihan*, pp. 700 and 741.

'I saw in a Grammer schoole in Limerick one hundred and threescore schollers, most of them speaking good and perfit English, for that they have used to conster the Latin into English.'—*Payne's Description*, p. 3.

[c] Formerly the seat of the Earls of Desmond. The Members for this borough were, in 1585, T. Verdon and Hurley; in 1613, H. Verdon and P. Kearney. The churches contain sculptured monuments of the Geraldines, Verdons, and Halys; and tombstones of the White Knights and the Burgatts.

The houses, built of hewn stone, were three stories high, and ornamented with embattlements, and tasteful stone mouldings.—*Parl. Gazetteer*.

[d] In 1599 it was a town of the Earl of Kildare's, 'in the midst of bogs and woods.' Essex had to rebuke his soldiers for 'going so coldly on' against Desmond's men at Adare.—*Car. Cal.*, 304. For six days Desmond skirmished with Essex's army, and 'cut off great numbers of his men.'

Arny.[e] Carrigmlyhe.[i]
Crome.[f] Loughyn.[k]
Askton,[g] belonging to Capt. Barcley.
Carrigigonell,[h] to Bryan Duff.[h]

[e] Perhaps Owney, now Abington. There are here monuments to Sir E. Walshe, who d. in 1618; to O'Ryan, who d. in 1632; and to Barry, who d. in 1633.

[f] Belonged to Earl of Kildare. It was held in 1600 by Piers Lacy, and 'gave great annoyance to the subject being seated at the entry into Connelogh.' It was taken by Carew in 1600. *Car. Cal.*

[g] Anciently chief house of the Earls of Desmond. Its castle was pressed by the Irish in 1599, but was, with the loss of many men, revictualled by Essex.—*Car. Cal.*, pp. 304, 305.
See a map or sketch of this castle in the *Pacata Hibernia*.

[h] Carrigogunnell, now one of the largest and most romantic ruins of its class. The *Harleian MSS.* contain a pedigree of 'Brian Duff O'Brien, of Carrigconnell,' who was living in 1615. His cousin, Morough O'Brien, 'the most renowned and noble of the heirs of Carrig OgConnell and Aherlagh,' was slain by the English in 1577.—See *Annals*, 1577.

[i] Perhaps Cahirconlish, which belonged to the Burkes of Brittas.

[k] It may be Loughgur, or Glyn, which is in Irish *Clochgleanna*. The *Annals* tell how, 'In July, 1600, the President and the Earl of Thomond set out from Limerick. The castle at which this great host gathered was one of the castles of the Knight of Glyn; it is situated in Glean-Corbraighe, from which it received the name of Cloch-Gleanna, and the Knight the appellation of '*Ridire-an-Ghleanna.*' . . . They reduced it in two days, and slew a score or two of the Knight's people, together with some women and children. Some of the President's and Earl's men were also slain by the warders. In 1601 the Knight of Glin (Edmond, son of Thomas) was with O'Donnell in his famous march to Kinsale.—*Annals*, pp. 2175, 2275.

See a map of the castle of Glyn in the *Pacata Hibernia*. Of Loughgur Carew says, 'I marched to Bruff, a castle held since the war by the traitor, Piers Lacy, to annoy the passage between Kilmallock and Lymerick. Finding it of good strength, and accommodated to annoy the traitors in the castle of Logherr, I placed a ward in it. Owen Groom, a stranger of the north, to whose charge Desmond had referred the castle of Loughgerr, at the approach of our army, delivered it to Ulick Browne, a freeholder of the country. The castles of Loughgerr and Bruff, thus possessed, give better liberty to the cattle of Kil-

COUNTIE OF LIMERICK.   199

Principall Shenet.[1]
Castles. Castle connell[m] to the L: Burke.
Newcastle[n] to Jordan Roche.
Ballynitie.[o]
Robertstoune[p] to S[r] Edward Fitton.
and divers others belonging to the undertakers, which were Howses belonging to the Earle of Desmond and his followers.

Chief Men. The Bishop[q] of Limerick.
The L: Burk[q] of Castle connell.
Richard Burke[r] of Castletowne.
Burk of Carrig.[r]

mallock (which is the greatest prey pertaining to any town in Ireland) to graze abroad.'

[1] As the Earls of Kildare took their war-cry from the castle of Crom, viz., *Crom-abu*, so the Desmonds took theirs from Shanid Castle, viz., *Shanid-abu*. The hill of Shanid is still crowned with a Cyclopean fort, and with the ruins of Shanid Castle.—*Parl. Gazetteer.*

[m] Hibernice, *Caislean-ui-Conaing.*

[n] It had belonged to the Desmonds. Jordan FitzGerald Roche was Mayor of Limerick in 1580 and 1588.

[o] It belonged to the O'Briens.

[p] Ballyrobert Castle belonged to the McClanchys. From 1593 to 1600, the castle and lands of Rathmore were held from Maurice Shighane by James Oge Leo, who joined the rebels.—*Car. Cal.*, p. 449.

The castle of Ballycalhane was the chief residence of the Pursells of Kenry.

Ballyalinan Castle belonged to McSheehy, Chief Constable of the Geraldines, who d. in 1601; the castle of Lisnacullen belonged also to his sept.

[q] *Vide infra* 'Peers and Bishops.'

[r] The following Limerick Burkes flourished about this time :—Richard Burke FitzRichard of Cahirconlish Castle; John B. FitzRichard of Brittas Castle; his mother was Onore ni Mulrian; his wife a dau. of Sir G. Thornton; his brothers, Theobald and William, lived at Cahirconlish. Oliver Burke of Kilpeacon Castle d. in 1592, leaving a son, David FitzOliver B. Richard B. lived in Lismolane.—*Limerick Inquisitions* in Royal Irish Academy. There was also a Richard Oge B. of Drumkeen, who d. in 1596, and is ancestor to Lord Downes and Hussey Burgh.

The *Lambeth Carew MSS.*, No. 635, give in 1570 Sir William and Sir Richard

Lacie of B.[s]
Lacie[s] of Ballingorie.
Lacie[s] of the

Burghe, Lo. of Clanwilliam; Burke of Limerick; Lord Burgh of Castleconnell. John Burke of Brittas was 'pietate, et aliarum virtutum ornamento non obscurus, sacerdotum patronus clarissimus.' —*O'Sullevan.* 'He was of good strength, both in castles and followers.'—*Car. Cal.*, 1600, p. 400.

He was hanged in 1607 for 'rebellion,' *i.e.*, for hearing Mass and wishing to keep a priest in his house. While in Dublin he had given the greatest edification to his keepers by his spirit of prayer and mortification. 'Vir pientissimus.'—*Fr. Holiwood*, in a letter dated Nov. 27, 1606.

[s] Bruffe and Bruree, Ballinagarde and Ballingarry. The De Lacies were a race of warriors. I find in the *Inquisitions*—Piers L. of the castles of Bruffe and Derryclogh, half-brother of Burke of Brittas, at Adare entered into rebellion in 1578, and was slain in 1601, July the 23rd. His mother was Honore Ni Mulrian; Eddie Lacie of Bruree claimed to be his heir. Also there were Eddie FitzWalter L. of Ballinagarde, and David L. of Goreston.

The Gentry and Freeholders of Owney in 1570 were—Wm. Leashe of the Browfe, and his young son, William; David Leashe, Alleshaighe; James Fitzmaurice Leashe of the Clewhir.

The Gentry and Freeholders of Con-
nellogh—Edye Lacye of the Browery, Piers Purcell of the Croagh, John Lacy of Ballingarry, Wm. Lacy of Ballinderyhly, the Walls and others.—*Lambeth MSS.*

At this time (1597) Davie Lacie, with his brotheren, Pierce, Ulick, and William, played the rebels, being once pardoned. Davie was after killed in service; Pierce was hanged at Limerick; Ulick and William were hanged at Kilkenny.—*M'Carthy Mór*, p. 148.

In 1601 was slain in battle near Armagh, Piers Lacy (*Hibernice* Piers Oge Dolés), Lord of Bruff, 'equally illustrious,' says Mageoghegan, 'for his virtue as for his birth, and one of the most zealous defenders of Catholicity.' The ruins of his castle are still visible. Of his family were the famous Lacys of the Russian and Austrian armies.

In 1598 Piers L., 'Vir animi plenus nec eloquentiae inanis,' persuaded O'More to march into Munster; he commanded at Adare, and slew Plunket for not attacking Essex in a defile. He was one of the officers who rescued the Earl of Desmond from Castle Ishin. After Desmond's capture he went to O'Neill.—*O'Sullevan.*

Moryson mentions the death of this 'Arch-rebell from Munster.' He was exempted from all pardon by Elizabeth. —*Car. Cal.*

Roch\[t\] of Lickdowne.
Hurley of Knocklig.[u]
M\[c\]Bryan[v] of Connaghe.
M\[c\]Kennedie M\[c\]Bryan.[v]
M\[c\]Bryan rath. O'Bryan.[w]

[t] This castle belonged about this time to the family of Archbishop O'Hurley.

[u] In Irish, *Cnocluinga*. Knocklong Castle is now a ruin. T. O'Hurley of Knocklong was M.P. in the Parliament of 1585. His son Randal built Ballinacarrig Castle, Cork, and mar. the dau. of O'Collins, a Chief in Carbery. His son Maurice d. *circ.* 1632. His monument in Emly bears a long Latin inscription—'Perillustris Dominus D. Mauritius Hurlaeus, Armiger, Monument. Hoc sibi, suisque charissimis conjugibus Graniae Hoganae et Graciae Thorntonae, ... posuit elaborarique fecit. A.N.D.L. 1632.' Then follow eight distichs in his praise—

'Hic jacet hospitii columen, pietatis asylum
Ingenio clarus, clarus et eloquio,' etc.

In 1583 Archbishop O'Hurley was tortured and put to death in Dublin; in 1609 Edmund and Randal Hurly, notwithstanding their minority and defect of clerical orders, got from James I. the Chancellorship and Chantorship of Emly Cathedral.—*Patent Rolls*.

In 1606 Morice Hurly drew Redmond Purcell into a castle of his, and then brought the English on him, and they executed him by martial law. Redmund was a cousin-german of the Baron of Loughmoe.—*Car. Cal.*, p. 471.

[v] There was Donnell M\[c\]Brien of Crosse, whose dau. was wife of Teig O'Hogan; Tirlagh M\[c\]Kennedie M\[c\]B. of Callough; Donal M\[c\]B. of Pallice Greyney, whose son Moroughue Oge was born in 1600; Moriertagh M\[c\]B. of Trian Mona, and his brothers Tirlagh, Conogher M\[c\]Conogher, and Kennedie M\[c\]B.—*Inquisitions*. The *Annals* say that *Mac-Briain Occuanach*, *i.e.* Moriertagh, son of Torlagh, son of Moriertagh, went to the Parliament of 1585. This M\[c\]Brian Cuanagh was seated in the barony of Coonagh, where the ruins of his splendid mansion are still to be seen at Castletown. In 1598 the sons of this Moriertagh joined O'More.—*Annals*, p. 2079.

However, Carew informs us that in 1600 he 'took a castle of one of the Bryans, called Ballytarsny, 8 miles from Limerick, a place of no less strength and worth than Loghgerr, and upon good pledge delivered it to the safe keeping of M\[c\]Bryan O'Gonough.' —*Car. Cal.*, p. 400.

[w] Brian M\[c\]Brian O'Brian of Garraneny Manna slain in 1600. Brian O'B. of Ballyclogh Castle joined the Desmonds; but in 1598, being at peace with the

The Knight of the Valley,[x] Fitzgerrald.

English, he was slain by Redmund Purcell, an insurgent. There was O'B. of Ballygean; O'B. of Atherlae; O'B. of Palliebeg.—*Inquisitions*. The chief of the O'B. lived at the castle of Carrigunnell.—See *note* [h]. The *Annals* say that in 1580, James of Desmond was slain by the Lord of Pobble-Brien and Carrigogunnell, *i.e.*, by Brian Dubh, son of Mahon; and that in 1585 the Lord of Carrigogunnell and Fasach-Luimnighe, *i.e.*, Brian Dubh, son of Donogh O'Brien, attended Parliament.

The pedigree of Brian Duff O'B. of Carrigogunnell, who lived in 1615, is among the *Harleian MSS*. In 1584 'A grant was made to Brien Duffe O'B. Mac Donagh of Carrigogynnell, chief of his nacion in Pobelbrien and Lord of Pobelbrien (upon his surrender) of all and singular Manors, Lordships, Castles, etc. . . . to hold to the heirs male of his body, remainder to his brothers, Teig, Mathew, *alias* Mahowne, Dermond, Donalde, and Cnogher O'B. . . . to find 3 sufficient horsemen, well furnished with horse and armour, with three hackneys for the said horsemen, with their apparel, and 6 footmen, *alias* shott or kerne, either galloglas.'—*Rolls Office, Dublin*. See *Lenihan*, pp. 76 and 114.

[x] See *note* [k]. O'Sullevan calls him Edmundus Geraldinus, Eques Auratus Vallis, and says he joined O'More in 1598, and joined O'Sullevan and Tirrell after the defeat of Kinsale. He was lampooned by the 'Red Bard,' who says of him and his brothers that 'after being killed, they survive; you will find their track to Rathkeale; do not seek them except in time of fairs.' He means that they are marauders. The *Annals* call him *Ridire-an-Gleanda* (*Emany Mac Thomais*), and say that he was with O'Donnell in his famous march from O'Maher's countrey to Owncy, 'the greatest march with carriage that hath been heard of; an unreasonable infinite long march, incredible, but upon my reputation it is true,' says Carew.

In 1600 he was exempted by Elizabeth from the general pardon, by the name of 'Edmond FitzThomas FitzGerald, commonly called The Knight of the Valley.'—*Car. Cal.*, p. 502. His son and heir, Thomas, emigrated to Spain after the battle of Kinsale. The Knight, 'though he saw the canon ready to place on his castle, and his son in my hands threatened to be presently executed, would not yield. In winning his castle of Glann, in 1600, we lost 11 soldiers, whereof one ensign and 21 hurt. Captain Flower had four wounds, and the lieutenants of the Earl of Thomond and Sir H. Power were hurt. Of the enemy of all sorts, 80 slain. His son being an infant (for humanity's sake), I did commiserate.' —*Carew in Car. Cal.*

COUNTIE OF LIMERICK. 203

Purcell[y] of the crook.
Several Freeholders of the Purcells,[y] Supples,[z] Walshes,[aa] Obirnes,[bb] Ryans,[cc] Fyants,[dd] Verdons,[ee] Roches,[ff]

[y] Among the 'Freeholders of Connelogh' in 1570, was Piers Purcell of the Croagh. In the vicinity of Croagh are the remains of Amigan Castle, and the castle of Cappa. The 'Red Bard' lampoons the Purcells thus—'The Kenry men, hard, hissing griffins. Hungry, lean-bodied—a begrudging horde. All their infants are ill-favoured; before baptism they speak, ordering scanty food for the labourer.' Their chief residence was the castle of Ballycalhane in the barony of Kenry. In 1595 there was Purcell of Ballincarrigy. Among the open friends to the Earl of Desmonde were 'the Purcells of the Crowghe, the Supples, Chacies, Lacyes, Hurleyes, Brownes, Rory McShane, all the Shees.'—*Car. Cal.*, 1601-1603.
In 1581 David Oge P., son of David of the Lake, son of Thomas, son of John, son of Thomas, son of Philip, son of the Knight, defeated a body of Englishmen near his castle of Ballycalhane; to avenge which the English commander of Adare slew 150 women and children in and around that castle. David was afterwards taken by McMahon, and 'the heroic soldier' was put to death in Limerick.—*Annals.*
Supple of Kilmocua joined Desmond.—*Inquisitions.* Also S. of Ballenetubbred.—*Car. Cal.*, 1592.

[aa] The chief of them was Sir Edmond Walshe, whose tomb is in Owney; but he will be given under Tipperary. Perhaps this name is meant for Nashes. There were John FitzDavid Nash and his brother of Ballycullen killed in rebellion in 1581 and 1583. James and Philip N. of Ballycolla Castle lived *circ.* 1598; also Redmond Oge N. of Sesherra, and James Oge N. of Ballonekaherrogh.—*Inquisitions.*

[bb] Perhaps O'Briens. Anniver O'Brien of Skehannagh was slain in 1601.—*Inquisitions.* See also *note* [w]. Another O'Brien lived at Gortboy.

[cc] O'Mulrian of Clonkine.—*Inquisitions.* One of the gentlemen of the Co. of Limerick in 1592 was Connour O'Mulrian. There is in Abington a monument to W^{m.}, chief of the O'Ryans, who d. in 1632. See under Tipperary.

[dd] Called 'Plants' in the list of 1570. James Ffante of Ffantestowne, 'interfecit et *murderavit* Patricium Ffante,' *circ.* 1598.

[ee] A Verdune was Mayor in 1553; there is a monument of this family in Kilmallock.

[ff] Jordan, Dominick, Stephen, and Philip R. were Mayors in 1588, 1597, 1601, and 1602.

Whytes,[gg] Sheerhes,[hh] Arthures,[ii]

[g] James and Robert W. were Mayors in 1595 and 1569.

The 'Mayor's Stone,' near the cross of Killeely, outside Thomond Gate, has the inscription—

> 'This Paving was wh
> Oly ended at the
> Charges of the Corpo
> Ration, James Whit
> E FitzJames Esquir
> Being Maior Anni Di
> MDCXXXVIII.'

[hh] McSheehy of Ballenerogie; McS. of the castle of Ballynoe; McS. of BallymcKery, and Curraghmore.—*Inquisitions*. The McS. were hereditary galloglasses to the Desmonds, and had their chief residence at the strong castle of Lisnacullia, in the parish of Cloonagh. —See *O'Donovan in Ulst. Jour. of Arch.*, No. 22, and *Annals*, p. 28.

'Murtagh Oge Mac S. and his brothers Rorie and Edmund, from the cradle inclined to mischief, as all that sept hath been, being oft apprehended and imprisoned, and having broken prisons (Murtagh at Limerick, Rory at Kilkenny), after many favors went into oppen accion. Murtagh was marked by nature; he had a strong arm, a desperate villanie, and a skilful targeteer. He was taken in a wood killing of porkes, and making provision to entertain the rebels of Leinster. Being brought to Cork and arraigned, evidence was given against him that he had prayed, spoiled and murdered about fourscore English families. Sentence was given that he should have his arms and his thies broken with a sledge, and hang in chains. So he was executed without the north gate of Cork anº 1597. Rory was killed by an Irish kerne; and Edmund was killed by an Englishman at the spoil of Kilkolman.'—*Mc Carthy Môr*, p. 148.

[ii] Dr. Arthurs' father, William, d. in 1622, aged 60. His person was handsome, symmetrical and upright his form; a long beard graced his cheeks; courteous, polite, mild of eyes, of voice, of aspect, munificent, clement and kind, the prayers of all bless him. Far from him was wrath, treachery, malice, and the crime of odious avarice; a worshipper of faith and of God, estimable for guileless simplicity. His generous house was open in hospitality to foreign exiles. He married in 1587 Anastatia Rice, who was mother of a numerous offspring, long abstained from meat and wine, and d. in 1640, aged 70.—*Dr. Arthur*, quoted by *Lenihan*, p. 368.

James Stackpole had a son Bartholomew, who mar. in 1636 a dau. of the famous Dr. Arthur of Limerick. He gave his *fiancée* 25 wedding presents, amongst which were a small goulde cross, a goulde ring weighing 22 carats, 2 small gould rings, 5 carats each ... 1 payer of Spanish leather shoes.— *Arthur MSS.*

COUNTIE OF LIMERICK. 205

Sir George Bowcher, Sir Edwd. Fitton, Sir W[illm.] Courtney, with divers others of the Burkes,[r] Lacies,[s] Geraldines,[jj] Shees,[hh] Foxes,[kk] Jordans, Fannings.[ll] Of the undertakers,

---

[jj] Thomas M[c]Shane FitzGerald, *alias* Thomas Cam, of Clenglish, mar. a dau. of M[c]Carthy of Muskerry; he is ancestor of FitzGerald of Castle Ishin, Co. Cork. He had the castle of Gortnitybured.—*Inquisitions.*

[kk] Fox of Ballyheward.—*Inquisitions.* Edmund Fox was Mayor in 1605.

[ll] Often Mayors and Bailiffs.

In St. John's Church there was, anno 1763, a monument with figures of the Twelve Apostles sculptured in stone, and the inscription—

'Thomas Power, quondam Civis Limericensis, et ejus uxor Joanna Rice hoc monumentum haeredibus suis construxerunt, in quo ambo sepeliuntur. Ora pro eis pius lector.

    Quisquis eris qui transis,
    Sta, perlege plora,
    Sum quod eris, fueramque quod es.
    Pro me, precor, ora.
        Hoc finito, A.D. 1622.'

In Broadstreet there is an inscription on a chimneypiece—

    Petrus Creagh Filius Andrae et
    Elionora Rice uxor ejus
    Curarunt extrui has Aedes
    A suis Haeredibus in timore
    Amore et favore Numinis diu Possidendas viventibus
    I.H.S.
    1640.   —*Lenihan.*

Geoffry Galway, Mayor of Limerick, a man who had spent many years in England in studying of the common law, and returning to Ireland about three years since, did so pervert that citie by counsell and example, that he withdrew the mayor, aldermen, and generally the whole citie from coming to the church, which before they sometimes frequented. About a year ago he prevailed on the maior to disarm the soldiers, whereby a gapp was open to him to induce a massacre of his Majestie's forces. Galway was fined £400 for this by Carew.—See *Pac. Hib.*

Twelve of the name of Harold were Mayors, and 8 either Bailiffs or Sheriffs. Daniel Harold, Esq., of Limerick is of this family.

Edmond Sexten owned the Convents of St. Mary and St. Francis, given to his grandfather, Edmond Sexten, by Henry VIII. In 1636 he was buried in the ancestral tomb in St. Mary's, with 'all the solemnitie that the countie made and could afforde.'—*Lenihan,* p. 657.

Also O'Madden of Knocktorine, slain in 1598. M[c]Keough of the castle of Cloneleiffe; M[c]Canny of the castle of Drombanny; O'Riardon of the castle of Tholowie, and O'Riardon of Rostemple; Dondon of the castle of Ballystine; Teig M[c]Clancy of Robertstown, killed at Glynn in 1600; Strich

206   STATE OF IRELAND ANNO 1598.

Sir John Outrich.ᵐᵐ   Capt. Barcley.
Capt. Collam.   Mr. Billinglesloy.ᵐᵐ
George Thornton, provost Marshall of Mounster.

The most part of the Irish are joined together in this Rebellion, especiallie such who either themselves or whose Parents lost their Lands by the Earle of Desmond's rebellion.ⁿᵃ

of the castle of Rathward, and Stritch of Gort Veaghan; England of the castle of Englandstown, whose father was hanged for rebellion, his mother was Unie Ni Donell Clancie; Mahowne Mᶜडa of Kilmede and Atheveghan; Browne of Camus, in rebellion, ancestor of Marshal Ulick Browne, the opponent of Frederick the Great; Liston of Skehanagh; Bugget of Buggedstown; Donal Barry of Ballygeybeg d. in 1612; his son Dowle Barry's monument is in Owney; O'Hynowrane of Muskry; O'Hynowrane; O'Riodiallighe of Ballennodiallighe; Wale of Listordan; M. FitzEdmund Hubert of Rathkielly, and Hubert of Ballycooghane; Hubert of Camoye; Mᶜthomas of Pallice; FitzWilliam of Dromeard; Donogh Mᶜwilliam Oge of Glenstille, who murderavit Rochford, a Limerick merchant; MᶜGrath of Galbally; R. Oge Cusshine of Liscorroge; E. MᶜAllister Gavin of Ballynerine, who rebelled in 1584; Leo of Thollovine; John Crom FitzNicholas Sarsfield of Amogane; Woulfe of Williamstowne.—*Inquisitions.* Rawley of Ballingowley, O'Heyne of Cahirelly, MᶜMahown of Cragan, Wall of Cloghtreade, FitzJohn of Ballinemong, FitzEdmund of Gilliterstown,

MᶜTighe of Tuogh.—*Lenihan*, p. 138.

Gentlemen of Connyloughe in 1592: —Suppell of Ballenetubbred, Thomas MᶜEae, Doole MᶜMulmurry, David Lacie, R. Wale, J. Lacie FitzDavid, P. Lalor, Morys Cooswill, MᶜHenry, Cartrill MᶜGerrott, J. FitzThomas MᶜPhillipp, Gerrott Liston, J. Nashe, Wm. Oge England, David Barrie, Moriertagh MᶜMorghe, J. Russell. Among the gentlemen of Limerick county there were besides—E. Miaghe, Oliver Bourke, Conor O'Mulryan, J. Verdon (Sheriff), J. Golde, Stephen Sexten, MᶜBrene X O'Gonaghes (his mark), T. Yong, Jordan Roche, J. Monsloy, T. FitzEdmond, Wm. MᶜRickard, T. Brown, T. FitzWilliam, E. Whytte, Moroghe X MᶜBrene (his mark), Redmond FitzWilliam.—*Car. Cal.*, p. 67.

ᵐᵐ Sir H. Outred of Maghawnagh d. in 1599.

In 1589 Billingely, Oughtread, Barkley, Courtney, and Trencher got 12,000 acres each in Conclogh at 4d. an acre.—*Mᶜ Carthy Mór*, p. 17.

ⁿᵃ 'In Limbricke Piers Lacy, with the MᶜShees, Clanwilliam (Burkes), and other septs, 300 f. and 15 horse in 1599.' —*Car. Cal.*, p. 300.

THE COUNTIE OF TIPPERARIE.

This Countie is devided into Two Counties, the one called the crosse of Tipperarie, the other the Countie of the Libertie of Tipperarie, which is a Countie Palatyne belonging to the Earle of Ormond. In the Countie of the Crosse the Quene[a] appointeth yearlie a Sherriff as her onlie officer. The Countie Palatyne is ruled by a Constable [Seneschal], a Justice, and a Sherriffe, all three appointed by the Earle of Ormond.

These two Counties of the Crosse and of the Libertie of Tipperarie are so mingled together, as no plat or card can be made to shew any apparent division, but by observation and Custome whereby the Inhabitants do know the one from the other. The whole countie ioyntlie comprehendeth all the Land from Callan, in the Countie of Kilkenny, to[b] the [   ] of [   ] Westward, and from Emelie, which was the

---

[a] 'The Queene maketh the Shriff her head officer. The Palatyne is gouerned by sceneschall Justice, a shriffe, and divers other meaner officers, which two counties lye onelie by observation and custome.'—*Dymmok*.

[b] 'To Mac O'Brien O'Gannogh's cuntry in the county of Lymrike, O'Mulrean's cuntry, Mac Brian Ara, O'Downie's cuntry, upper and nether Ormond, Constinagh, Cosehi, Muskry whirke, a great part of Harlow, and by ancient division O'Carroll's cuntry, Elye, though he disclaim from yt.'—*Dymmok*.

A document of the 16th century in Kilkenny Castle states that, 'Kilkenny and Tipperary counties being joined together under one capteyn, have rated themselves to bear for their defense each "three score beds (every bed a horseman and 2 kerne), 8 score sparys of galoglas (*i.e.*, 6 score sherts of mayle, the rest is allowed to the capteynes and their men to carry their armor)." The total monteth to 60 horse, 120 kerne, and 120 galoglas for Kilkenny, and the lyke nombre in Typperary.'—*Kilk. Jour. of Arch.*, year 1855, p. 234.

'Tipperarie, which is now the only

Seat of a Bishop, to Conshilaghe, the West part whereof belongeth to this Countie, the rest to the Countie of Kilkenny, and so contayneth the Countries of Omulryans, Odwyers, upper and nether Ormond, a part of Conshelaghe, Cosheshany, Muskry Wherke a great part of Arklo, and all onaught. It extendeth from Tobragney (a Well) in the South, to the Field of Breynd in the North 40 Miles, and from east to West some 32 or 33 Miles. The Quene hath reserved only the Tryall of Treasons

Countie Palatine, is made a receptacle to rob the Countries about it, by meanes of whose privileges none will follow their stealthes, so as it being situate in the very lap of all the land is now made a border, which how inconvenient it is let every man judge.'—*Spenser*, p. 46.

The Baronies in the Co. of Tipperary, and what Septs inhabit them in 1600.

Lower Ormond—The three O'Kenedies. *Upper Ormond*—McTeg of the Kenedies, whose chief house is Badinedoghie; in it is also the castle and abbey of Nenaghe, the Earl of Ormonde's lands; the O'Mares, the Hegans, the Hogans.

Owney O'Mulrian (part of this barony is in the Co. Limerick)—O'Mulrians. In this barony is the abbey of Owney, Sir Edmond Welshe's house, which was built by the White Earl of Ormond.

Kilnemanaghe—O'Duire, descended from the O'Briens.

Ikerine—O'Magher and the Earl of Ormond's castle of Roskrey.

Eliogortie—Parcel, Baron of Loughmay; Cantwell of Mocanke. It hath in it the abbey of the Crosse, Thurles Castle, and Templemore, the Earl of Ormond's lands.

Slewardie—Sir James Oge Butler, Fanning, Cantwell, Leffar, Mariner.

Dow Arra—McBrien Arra, descended from O'Brien of Tomond.

Eliaghe and Killinaghlohart—McWalter Burke in Eliagh, Donogh Mac Shaneglasse O'Mulrian.

East Clanwilliam—The Burkes of Muskrie, the Burkes of Onaught, the Burkes of Coshnaie, part of the O'Briens of Arloghe.

Comshey (part in Co. Kilkenny)—The Tobins.

Middlethird—Butler, Baron of Dunboyne, the Hackets, Stapletons, and Mocleere.

Cantred of Clonmel—Butler, Baron of Cahir, the Prendergarsts, the Powers, and McCraghes.—*Car. Cal.*, p. 513.

Freeholders of Crosse Tipperary in 1600.

Cantred of Middlethird—Everard of Kilmocley, Butler of Morestowne-

to herself in the Countie of the Libertie, all other crymes^c and actions which are tried and decided before the Earle of Ormond's officers.

Chief Townes in this Countie. } Cashell,^d well walled.

Kirke, Butler of Garriarde, Mockler of Ballynattine, Stapleton of Thurles-beg, Hackett of Marshalstown, Hacket of Ballycomuske, Malladg Carran of Burdensgrange, Meagher of the same, T. FitzRichard Stapleton of Leynaghstown, E. Stapleton of Garranpheccard.

Slevardaghe—Piers Butler FitzJames of Ballinonetie, J. Laffane of Greystowne.

Eliogertie—Purcell of Kilcaske, Purcell of Burres-Lieghe, Stapleton of Kilcloine, Hugh O'Meagher of Kiloskehane, Conogher O'Meagher, D. O'Meagher, and P. O'Meagher of the same.

Cantred of Clonmel—T. Butler of Ballehymicknie, Lord Baron of Cahir, Butler of Clogheculie, P. Butler of Knockenamine, E. Butler FitzJohn of Mullaghenonie, T. Butler of Tample-Ehennie, Prindergaste of Ballyvorish, Prindergast of Grandg, P. of the same, P. of the Freghanes, P. of Kilvynnine, P. of Carrigetearhie, P. of Rath O'Kellie, Keating of Ardfinnane, E. White of the same, McDonoghe of the same, Eustace Englishe of Cloghemenecode, Eustace English of Rahine, Mansfield of Loghtogherie, Keating of Morestowne, Donoghowe of Blackcastle, E. Mocler of Ballycurrine, Sherlock of

Clearichanstowne, Geoffrey Mockler of the same, T. Butler FitzEdmond of Rathnelowre, T. Butler FitzJohn of Rathenuskie.

Clanwilliam—Wm. Ryane of Selchod, J. Hiffernane of Lattine, M. Hiffernane of the same, O'Hiffernane of the same, Pilline of Duncomyne, Burke of Kilbeckane, (O'Dwyer) of Kilnemannaghe, J. O'Dowyre of Ballingarrane.—*Car. Cal.*, p. 480.

^c *Vide* the last note on this county.

^d 'It is said 100 castles are visible from the Rock of Cashel.'—*Kilk. Jour. of Arch.*, an. 1851, p. 465.

'We passed from Limerick to Cashell over the most rich and delightful valley in Ireland for the space of 20 miles. In Cashel we found only one inhabitant that came to church, for even the Archbishop's own sons, and sons-in-law, dwelling there are obstinate recusants. We indicted more than 100 in this poor town. The cathedral is a fair ancient structure, on a high hill.'— *Sir J. Davys* in 1606—*Car. Cal.*, 475.

The Will of Cantwell of Moycarkey, Esq., dated 1618—'I recommend my soul to Almighty God, to be placed in ye bosome of Abraham; and do will my body, after my decease, to be buried in St. Patrick's Church at Cashel, in

Clonmell,[c]
Fedart,[f] } well walled.

mine ancestor's tombe there.'—*Jour. of Kilk. Arch. Soc.*, May 1859, p. 320.

In the old cathedral of Cashel there is a small shield, upon which are the arms of Boyton—'three spur rowels'—with the name of *Boyton* in old English letters inscribed upon it. Also the tomb of O'Kearney, the lord of many manors in the neighbourhood, who d. in 1460; his direct descendant, David O'K., was Archbishop of Cashel in 1602. The O'K. lived at the castles of Killusty, and Barretstown, at Cappaghmore, and Knockinglass.

[c] 'A well built and well kept town. Being in the liberty, is more haunted with Jesuits and priests than any other town or city in this province, which is the cause we found the burgesses more obstinate here than elsewhere. The Lord President did gently offer to the principal inhabitants not to proceed against them if they would yield to conference for a time, and become bound in the meantime not to receive any Jesuit or priest into their houses; they peremptorily refused.'—*Davys.* See *Car. Cal.*, year 1606, p. 475.

[f] 'Tombs in the Abbey of Fethard: 'Hic jacent Thaddeus O'Meagher de Ballidin, et Anastatia Purtia ejus uxor, qui me fieri fecerunt, 20 Maii anno Salutis 1600.' The present representative of that family is Mr. O'Meagher of Fethard.

In the market house, which had in former days been a monastery, there is the inscription—'Dama Everardus, *alias* Roche, relicta Joannis Everardi Junioris hæc insignia erexit . . . quæ obiit xii Aug. 1646.' She was the d. of Roche of Ballinard Castle, near Fethard. The noble mansion of the Everards is converted into a barrack. A few years ago the only representative of this once illustrious house was a little servant girl living in Mullinahone. The Roches of Ballynard Castle have also disappeared.

'Hic jacet R. Heñes qui obiit xxix Dec. 1615; cujus perdillectus fater, Thomas Heñes, etiam uxor ejus Anastasia Archer me fieri fecerunt.'

'Orate pro animabus Edmondi Tobin de la Briscelagh, gen. Margarae Tobin uxoris ejusdem, Thomae Tobin, filii et haeredis ipsius, et Joanae Tobin *alias* Marrenel, uxoris ipsius Thomae, qui hic jacent, et me fieri fecerunt

Anno Doni 1634.'

Briscelagh was the residence of the Tobins at Kylenagranagh; its foundation is still visible and is called *Seancloch*, 'the old stone.'

'Hic jacet Bernardus Kearney Burgi de Fiderdiae, Filius Mauritii Kearney Burgi ibidem, qui Bernardus obiit an. 1682 aet. 38, Cujus uxor Katherina Kearney *alias* Dwyer me fieri fecit an. Dni 1687.'—*Kilk. Jour. of Arch.*

Bryan O'Kearney, S.J., was probably of the Kearney family that preserved St. Patrick's Crozier. From their pos-

COUNTIE OF TIPPERARIE. 211

    Carrig,[g] well walled.
    Emelie,
    Tipperarie, } Wast.
    Holicrosse,

Men of   The Earle of Ormond[i] Butler.
Name.[h]   The L. of Caer[i]   Butler.
    The L. of Dunboyne[i] Butler.
    The Arch Bishop[i] of Cashell.

session of this valuable relic they were called *O'Kearney Bacula*, or *Kearney Crux*. This relic was in the possession of Bryan O'Kearney of Fethard, who d. in 1765. He was the last of the male line of the O'Kearney Crux family, and he sold the remnant of their estates to the ancestor of the present Lord Lismore.
'Hic jacent Ricardus Wale de Rath kynny,
Generosus, et Catherina Wale *alias* Carran filia Mathiae Carran de Mobarnane ejus uxor ... .
Quorum animabus orate ad Dominum. Datum ultimo Februarii, Salutis 1635.'
    —*Kilk. Jour. of Arch.*

[g] In the Church of Carrick is a flat stone with the inscription—' Here lieth entombed the bodie of Thomas Butler, Esq., sonne to the R. Hon. th' Erle of Ormond and Ossory, who died being Sheriffe of the Co. of Typerary the 12 Jan. 1605.'
On an altar-tomb at Ballyneale, near Carrig-on-Suir, is the inscription—'Hic jacet Philippus Quemerford, quondam collactaneus Comitis Ormoniae cum uxore sua Margarita Shea A. Dni 1630. Qui obiit 10 Juni.' It bears the arms of Comerford and Shea.—*Kilk. Jour. of Arch.*, year 1862, p. 10.

At Ballintemple, near Carrick-on-Suir, is a monument on which a handsome floriated cross with the legend in raised letters—' Here lyeth Jhone Boutlr FitzGeroit of Bolendesert, and his wyf Johana FitzRicardi Ano 1587 [ ] to be made.' Up to 1654 the Butlers owned Bolendesert, and the (now ruined) castle of Ballinclohy.

The other tombstone has the legend —' Hic jacet Doñs Carolus Everardus filius Gabrielis Everardi filii Joannis Everardi de Fethard, Equitis aurati et quondam Justitiarius Regis Banco, hic quoque jacet uxor ei' Catherina Wale filia de Gulielmo Wale de Cuilnemuc. Orate pro animabus suis [ ] Maii 1643.'

The Everards owned large possessions near Fethard, and also Burntcourt, near Clogheen; they may now be considered extinct.

[h] See at note [b], two very full lists.
[i] See *infra* 'Peers and Bishops.'

The Barronet of Loghmie[k] Purcell, and many Gentlemen depending upon these Noblemen, as the

Butlers.[l]   Cantwells.[m]
Purcells.[k]   Kennadies.[n]

[k] In 1598 'the Lord of Clonmel-Third and Cahir, and the Baron of Luachmhagh (Loughmoe), with many others of the young Butlers, joined in this war of the Irish.'—*Annals*. The magnificent ruins of Loghmoe Castle and mansion are still visible. A Baron Purcell of Loughmoe and his son were killed at Aughrim.—*Rawdon Papers*, p. 351. Thomas P., Baron of Loghmoe, had a dau. mar. to Butler of Ballynodagh and Moyaliffe, and a dau. mar. to John, brother of the 2^d Lord Dunboyne. Theobald, son of Richard, 'Baron of Loughmoe,' mar. a dau. of the 2^d Lord Dunboyne.—*Lodge*, under Lords Carrick, Mountgarret, and Caer.

There was a Piers Pursell of Kilnesier.—*Inquisitions*.

[l] Butlers of Ardmayle Castle, of Ballykyrin.—*Inquisitions*. B. of Ballyboe, B. of Rouskagh, B. of Shanballyduffe, B. of Cabragh. Sir James B. of Lismallen and Clonamelchon, mar. a dau. of the Earl of Ormond, and had a son who, in 1628, became Viscount Ikerrin; B. of Kilmoyler and Bellacarren.—*Lodge*.

Sir Walter B. of Kilcash, nephew of 10th E. of Ormond, with some gentlemen of Tipperary, defeated Redmond Bourk, and forced him to fly to Spain; in this action Sir Walter was wounded. He mar. a dau. of L. Mountgarret; he became 11th Earl, and d. at Carrrick in 1632. On account of his devotion to the Blessed Virgin, he was called 'Earl Walter of the Rosaries.' He had three sons and nine daughters. His sons-in-law were Power of Monaghalargy in Tipperary, son of Lord Power; Butler, Viscount Ikerrine; Butler of Grellagh, son of Lord Dunboyne; Bagnal of Dunleckney; Sir E. Blanchville of Blanchvillestown, and Richard 6th Earl of Clanrickard.—*Lodge*.

Piers B. of Ballynenodagh or Moyaliffe, son of W. Butler, and a dau. of McBrien Ogonagh, d. in 1627, and was buried in the Abbey of Holy Cross. His wife was a dau. of the Baron of Loghmoe; his sisters were m. to O'Dwyer of Dundroney in Tipperary, to Sherlock of Mothe in Waterford, to Esmond Baron of Limbrick in Wexford.—*Lodge*.

The Lord of Slewardagh, *i.e.*, James Butler, d. in 1600.—*Annals*, p. 2185.

[m] C. of Athassell.—*Inquisitions*.

[n] O'Kennedy of Ballyloghyappull.

Teig McRorie McManeny O'K. of Ballyrushane, O'K. of Annagh Castle, Belafinvoy Castle, Kyriagh Kearowe,

Odwyrs.º
Burkes.ᵖ
Englyshes.ᑫ

Loughshearnes.
Whytes.ʳ

Brackagh, Lackin, Curraghmoririn, Ballygibbon, Caragharnine, Ballycolytan, Ballyhinikyne, Delysinclonty, Knockmelura.—*Inquisitions.* All these were 'in accion.'

'McTeig of Ormond, *i.e.*, Conor of the Harbour, son of Teig, grandson of Mahon Don O'Kennedy, d. in 1583, a ready tranquil, domestic man without reproach. Philip, son of Dermot O'K. of Ropalach, was then styled McTeig. The son of McCoghlan, an intellectual youth, on his first assumption of chivalry, was slain by the son of Kennedy Finn in 1583.' In 1588 (Bryan) O'Kennedy Finn d., upon which Owny, son of Donogh Oge, and Gilladuffe, son of Dermod, were at strife about the Lordship; at length the territory was divided equally between them, and the name was conferred on Owny. In 1599 Sean, son of Giolla Dubh, son of James O'Kennedy from Ballingarry-Knocshiena in Ormond, was slain by Hugh, son of Morogh O'Kennedy from Ballyquirk. O'Kennedy Finn (Owny) of Ballyhough in Lower Ormond d. in 1599, and Gilla Dubh O'K. was then styled the O'Kennedy Finn.'—*Annals.*

º O'Dwyers of Torrehie, Kilnecree, Cwillo-Cotta.—*Inquisitions.*

O'Duibhidhir of Coill-na-manach d. in 1594, and his son Diarmaid took his place. O'D. joined O'More in 1598.

—*Annals.* 'In 1600 Redmond Burke with 600 men entered Odwire's countrie to burn and prey the same. Odwire, having assembled as many men as that short warning would permit, fell upon one of his Divisions which consisted of 200 foot; of them he slew 120 and many hurt. In revenge whereof Burke entered a second time into the said countrie where he slew Man, Woman and Child, burnt all the houses (castles excepted), and drove away all the Cattle of the countrie.'—*Pacata Hib.*, p. 59.

ᵖ Burkes of Banshagh Castle; R. Liagh B. and J. Moel B. brothers, of Shanganagh and Pollaghbeg; B. of Drominagh, B. of Drangan, J. Oge B. of Fehertagh, David B. FitzWilliam of Ballinesillagh, B. of Bellankoaly, Thos. B. FitzWilliam of Swyfine, B. of Ballydare, B. of Lassinagh.—*Inquisitions.* In 1583 'John Carragh B., heir to Cois-Suir (in Clanwilliam), who had been in rebellion, went and seized all the cattle of the Adare; the warders pursued him, and while with his small body of horse he was charging them, he was shot through the helmet. His people carried off the prey, but John was taken and hanged in Limerick.'—*Annals.*

ᑫ E. of Cloghemenecode, E. of Rahime in 1600.—*Car. Cal.*, p. 480.

ʳ Of Clonmel.—See Co. of Waterford.

Ryans,[3] Bryans,[4]
and divers Religious Houses.

[3] D. Mac Shaneglasse O'Mulrian of Graigeneskie, Loughlin McTeig McThomas Finn O'M. of Bollibane, O'M. of Craig.—*Inquisitions.* In 1598 the O'Ryans joined O'More.—*Annals.*

In the Abbey of Owney there was a monument of the Head of this race who died in 1632. The inscription was—

Nobilissimus Dns Gulielmus Rian Patriæ suae
De Ownii, necnon antiquae Rianorum familiae Caput
Et Princeps, sibi, uxori et liberis suis hanc sepulchri
Molem erigi curavit.'

—See the rest in *Dynely's Tour.*

[4] Mac-I-Brien Ara d. in 1601; his sons were Donogh, Mortogh, Bishop of Killaloe, Torlogh Carrach, Teig na buile, Morogh na Tuath.—*Memoirs of the O'Brians*, p. 546. The castles of Ballina, Casteltown and Cnoc-an-Ein-Finn belonged to them.—*Annals*, p. 1835, note.

'In 1592 More O'Carroll, wife of Mac-I-Brien Ara, died—she had spent a good life, without reproach.

'Mac-I-Brien Ara, *i.e.*, Torlogh, d. in 1601. There was no other lord of a territory so old as he on the night he died. He was an active, warlike man, who had led his followers in safety from every territory into which he had gone, and seldom had any troops who had entered his territory escaped from him scathless: a man who had defended the rugged and hilly district, which he possessed, till his death. He was interred in his own fortified residence of Baile-an-Chaislen.'—*Annals.*

There were also McBrien Roe of Tornonyne, O'Brien of Lahesheragh, O'B. of Killmostully, whose wife was Slany Ni Vrick.—*Inquisitions.*

In the Abbey of Owney the monument to Sir E. Walsh (spoken of under note [b]) bears the figures of Saints Peter and Bernard, of the Blessed Virgin, and St. Mary Magdalene. He d. in 1617, as appears by the *Hexasticon Chronologicon* in raised letters on it—

'Jam sexcenti mille annis septemque decemque
Virgo ex quo enixa est immaculata Deum . . .
Edmundus Torquatus eques, vir maximus armis,
Major at hospitio, nec pietate minor.'
—*Dynely.*

A tomb at Dangan has—'Hic jacet Thadeus Geankagh O'Meagher, generosus, qui obiit 19 Dec. 1627 cujus animae propitietur Deus.' O'Meagher lived at Drumsaileach, near Roscrea.

In 1602 the most distinguished branch of the Mac Egans lived in the castle of *Coillte Ruadha* or Red-Wood, in the parish of Lorrha, in the neighbourhood of which the head of that branch still retains a small patrimonial estate.'—*Hy-Many*, p. 168.

Chief Castles are— Carrig, Thurles, Templemore, Kilshelshane, Roscree, Kilfekle, Caer^u } All the Erles of Ormond.

belonging to the L. thereof.

I find in the *Annals* the following entries about the O'Meaghers and McEgans and O'Hogans of this period:— 'The son of O'Meachair (John of the Glen) d. in 1592. In 1601 the Connaught Burks were surprised in O'Meachair's country by the Butlers, and many of them were slain "throughout their tents and booths." In 1601 Cairpre Oge McEgan, ensign to the son of the Earl of Ormond, was slain in the attack on Rincorran. In 1602 Donogh McEgan of Killte-roe was killed while attacking O'Sullevan on his passage across the Shannon. Ogan O'Hogan of Ard-Croine d. in 1598; he had four brothers—Conor of Ardcrony, John Prior of Lorha, Gillapatrick, Erenach of Lorha, and William. His pedigree is given in McFirbis. Ogan's brother, "John, Prior of Lorha, was slain by a party of the O'Kennedies in 1599."'—*Annals.*

Also the O'Hogans of Knockmelora, Ballyhynkyne, and Gortneskehy; O'Maghers of Killballyhin, Ballyfoline, Gurtyn McPhilip, Towmenagh, Dangensallagh; O'Carroll of Cowleowenleane Castle, in Eli O'Carroll; O'Clery of Fydden; Cosmeagh McEgan of Agheway; M. McGerald Prendergast of Ballybeg, P. of Leackymack, P. of Newcastle; the McGillfoyles of Ballystyanch and Gortnebeist; Keating of Gormanstown Castle, killed fighting against Essex; the Conways, Youngs, and Salls of Cashel; the McCraighs of Downans and Ballynecourty; O'Fogertie of Monroe Lististie; Roche of Cranagh; the Stapletons of Rathlegty and Drom; O'Carran of Burretstown Castle; Moncell of Moglasse; Moclear of Moclearstown; O'Hiffernan of Killmorie; Tobin of Poulecapple.—*Inquisitions.* Tobin of Cumshinagh mar. to dau. of Lord Mountgarret; Prendergast of Newcastle.—*Lodge.*

Gerald Grace, called *Marcach* or the Horseman, of Carney, Co. Tipperary, and of Ballylinch and Legan Castles, Co. Kilkenny, d. in 1618, and was interred in Jerpoint Abbey; his mother was a dau. of Lord de Decies; his son, Oliver, called *Skevach* or the Handsome, d. in 1625.—*Memoirs of Family of Grace.*

^u See a map of it in *Pacata Hibernia.* 'It is a place of greater strength than

Loghmo to the Barronet thereof.

So this Countie hath Waterford on the South, Limerick directlie on the West, Cork South West, Thomond or Shenan Northwest, and Lough Degert upon the Sheynan, being in length 30 Miles to the North.

Of this Countie[v] the most are in Rebellion, especiallie the younger Brethern, and all the Dependers, althoughe the eldest keep in shew of obedience.

any other in this kingdom, and of great consequence.' It was besieged and taken by Essex in 1599.—See description of the place and siege in *Car. Cal.*, p. 302.

[v] Carew writes to Mountjoy in 1601—'I thought good to discover to you the distempered state of Tipperary and Kilkenny. Keddagh O'Magher hath gathered 300 rogues together, and doth many outrages. In Osserie the Baron of Upper Osserie's nephews are entered into rebellion. In Kilkenny the 3rd son of Viscount Mountgarret and some of the Graces ransacked that country, and do join with Keddaghe O'Magher; and lastly 200 men under the leading of T. Butler, a bastard son to Sir Edmond Butler, are drawing into Tipperary to assist Kidagh O'Magher. As this upstart rebel is in my Lord of Ormond's liberty (who by his good will did never like to have her Majesty's forces to intermeddle within his liberty), I have written to his Lordship to undertake the service, or to leave it to me. The poison of rebellion rests nowhere in Munster but in my Lord of Ormond's country. As long as he liveth I look for no good establishment in those borders ... his council about him will evermore abuse him, and under his authority will give impediments to all good proceedings.'—*Car. Cal.*, 102.

Forces in Tipperary in 1599—The Baron of Cahir and James Butler his brother, with their followers and dependencies, 300 f. and 12 horse; the White Knight, 400 f. and 30 h.; Raph Purcell, Baron of Loughmey, with his followers, 200 f. 6 h.; Cahir M[c]Shane Glasse O'Mulrian, and the rest of the O'Mulrians, 300 f. 60 h.; Keadaghe O'Magher, 60 f. 30 h.; Brian Oge O'Kennedie, Hugh O'Kennedie, with the rest of the O'Kennedies in Ormond, 500 f. 30 h.; Redmund Burke, pretending himself Baron of Letrym, and his bonoghs, 300 f. 20 h.; William Burke FitzJohn, with the rest of the Burkes of Clanwilliam, 200 f. 4 h.—*Car. Cal.*, p. 299.

THE NOBLEMEN[a] OF IRELAND.

Gerrot Fitzgerrald Earle of Kildare, Baron of Offallie, his eldest Sone is L. Baron of Offallie. The first creation of this Earldome was an° 1315—9 Edwd. 2^d.[b] The first Erle of Ireland by creation. Sir Thomas Butler[c] knight, L. Butler Viscount of Carrick and Gaurane Earle of Ormond and Osserie,

[a] 'By conference with certaine gentlemen attendants on Sir H. Sidney, Lord Deputie (who excelleth in that knowledge), I tooke notice of the most noble English families in Ireland, which here ensue with their surnames as they stand at this present.'—*Campion*, 1571.

[b] One record, that I have seene, nameth a *Geraldine* the first Earle of Kildare in anno 1289; but another saith there dyed a *Geraldine* the fourth Earl of Kildare in anno 1316. The family is touched on in the Sonnet of Surrey, made upon Kildare's sister, now Lady Clinton—

'From Tuscane came my Ladye's worthy race,
Fair Florence was sometimes her ancient seate;
The western Isle, whose pleasant shore doth face
Wilde Cambre's cliffes, did give her lively heate.'—*Campion*.

William 13th Earl of Kildare was drowned in 1599.—See *supra*, p. 46. His two base brothers, called 'Bastard Geraldines,' were 'in accion' in 1599. —*Car. Cal.*

[c] Called by the *Annals* (an. 1560), 'Thomas, son of James, son of Piers Roe, son of James, son of Edmund.' O'Sullevan styles him, 'Thomas Butler, cognomine Niger.' He was 10th Earl of Ormond and 3^d Earl of Ossery; was son of the 9th Earl and of Joan, dau. of the 11th Earl of Desmond; born in 1532, and d. in 1614; was brought up as 'playmate and bedfellow' of Edward VI., distinguished him at the battle of Musselburgh, against Wyat as 'Lieutenant of the horsemen,' against the Scots of Ulster, the O'Briens of Thomond, the O'Mores; took the Earle of Desmond prisoner and killed 46 of his captains, 800 'notorious rebels,' and 4000 of his private soldiers, and was Lord High Marshal of England, and Captain and Lieutenant General of the Army in Ireland. He was 'a man of great parts, admirable judgment, vast experience and prodigious memory, very comely, and of black complexion; he was called by the Irish, *Dubh* or the Black Earl, and by Elizabeth, her *black husband*. The

L. of the Libertie and regalitie of Tipperarie, L. High Treasurer of Ireland, and one of the Right Honorable Order of the Garter, his Eldest Sone is Viscount Thurles. The Second Earle by flower of his country, he kept the greatest house, and used the most hospitality of any in the kingdom, and for his valour, wisdom, liberality, and virtue was greatly honoured not only in England and France, but . . . and was commonly taken by them to be a pattern of true honour.'—*Archdall* in note to 'Lord Mountgarret,' v. 4.

To him Spenser wrote—

'But where thyself hast thy mansion,
  There indeed dwell faire Graces many one,
And gentler nimphs, delights of learned wits,
  And in thy person without Paragon
All goodly bounty and true honour sits.'

This 'true honour' shines in his letter to Burghley, who proposed to him a way of capturing Desmond by treachery. '*My Lord, I wol never use trechery to any*, for it wol both toche her highness' honor to moch, and myne owne credit, and who so ever gave the Queene advise this to write is fitter to execute such base sarvice than I am. *Saving my dutye to her Majestie, I wold I weare to have revenge by my sword of any man that thus persuadeth the Queene to wryte to me.*'—See *Life of Mac Carthy Mór*, p. 329.

When Elizabeth asked him to use his intimacy with Hugh O'Neill to entrap him, he wrote to Burghley—'I have been employed by her Matie in manie services . . . all which (I thank God) I have performed without using unhonest or filthy practices; if my thanks shall be to be put to execute trechery, my fortune is bad, and the service much better for such as devised the same, than for me, that never had, thank God, a thought of any such matter. I protest before God, etc.'—See 'The Taking of the Earl of Ormond' in *Kilk. Jour. of Arch.*

Davis writes in 1606—'My Lord of Ormond hath lain at Carrick ever since his last weakness, because the feast of St. George fell out on the Easter holidays. I was not suffered in any wise to depart until I had seen him do honor to that day. He was not able to sit up, but had his robes laid upon his bed, as the manner is.'—*Car. Cal.*, 477.

Sir Bernard Burke says, this *Black Earl* 'was the first of his family who conformed to the Church of England;' however, he was a Catholic for the last nine years of his life. About the 29th of Nov. 1604, two Jesuits of his county palatine were with him (cum languente Comite); they were Fathers Walter Wale and Bryan O'Kearney, of 'the devilish clergy of Tipperary'; in April 1605 Fr. Wale alone was with him, as all obstacles had been broken down—'*non sine totius Hiberniae gaudio.*' In October it was announced that Fr. Wale had gained the sick Earl to God some months previously; and in June 1606, he could not be used for general

creation but first by his place of Tresurership his first Creation was 1327 an⁰ 1ˢᵗ Edwᵈ. 3ᵈ.

The Earle of Desmondᵈ created the same year, his name

missionary work—'quod principi cuidam viro sit necessarius.' Fr. Wale's companion and uncle, O'Kearney, wrote thirty discourses ('Triginta Discursus) on the death of this Earl, which were preserved in MS. in the Archives of the Gesù, Rome.—*Letters* (penes me) of Fathers Hollywood, O'Kearney, and Wise, written in 1605 and 1606 to their Father-General Acquaviva. O'Sullevan's *Historia*, Dr. Lynch's *Alithinologia*, and *Hibernia Dominicana*, mention his conforming to the Catholic Church.

ᵈ The following were the children of Gerald the 15ᵗʰ Earl of Desmond, who was slain in 1583, and whose lands of 800,000 acres were divided among English adventurers—1° James the 16ᵗʰ Earl (the Queen's Earl) who died in 1601; 2° Thomas; 3° Margaret m. to Dermod O'Connor of Connaught; 4° Joane m. to Dermod O'Sullevan Bere; 5° Catherine m. 1ˢᵗ to Viscount Fermoy, 2ᵈˡʸ to Sir Donel O'Brien; 6° Ellen m. 1ˢᵗ to Sir Donogh O'Connor Sligo, 2ᵈ to Sir R. Cressy, 3ʳᵈ to Edmond Lord Dunboyne, she died in 1660. Their mother, the Countess, was a daughter of Lord Dunboyne; she re-married with Sir Donogh O'Connor Sligo, and died in 1636.

Their uncle, Sir Thomas Roe, had been recognized as 15ᵗʰ Earl by the Government, but was ousted by his stepbrother, Gerald. Sir Thomas had 1° a son James, who was elected and by right 16ᵗʰ Earl in 1598; he was the *Sugdn* Earl. He mar. first a d. of Lord Cahir, secondly a d. of Lord Power; 2° a son of Gerald, a Count in Spain; 3° John, living in Spain in 1615 as Conde de Desmond; his wife was a daughter of Comerford of Danganmore; his son Gerald was Conde de Desmond, and was killed in Germany in 1632. 4° Ada m. to Donogh, second son of the 7ᵗʰ Mac Carthy Reagh; 5° Margaret m. to the 8ᵗʰ MᶜCarthy Reagh.

James Paderagh, illegitimate son of the 15ᵗʰ Earl of Desmond, mar. a d. of Wall of Culnamuc, and had four sons, Maurice, James, John, and Maurice FitzJohn, who were all living in the year 1598.—'Unpublished Geraldine Documents,' *Kilk. Jour. of Arch.*

James FitzThomas was rightful Earl of Desmond in 1598. In 1598 he wrote—'To my very good Lo. and Cosen the Erle of Ormond—I have be'n in England from my Father claiming his inheritance of the House of Desmond, which is manifestlie known to be his righte; Her Matye promised to do me justice upon the decease of my uncle, who was then in accion. Ever since my uncle's decease I could gett no hearinge concerning my inheritance

Fitzgerrald, his hous extinct, his Sone is Viscount Desmond. Richard Burk Erle of Clonrickard and Baron of Dunkellyn,

of the Earldome of Desmond, but have bestowed the same upon divers undertakers to disinherite me for ever . . . seeing no other remedie, I will follow by all means I may to maintain my right, trusting in the Almightie to further the same.'—*Life of McCarthy Mór*, p. 177.

He writes to the King of Spain in 1599—'I have drawen the sword for the recovery, first of Christ's Catholike religion, and next for the maintenance of my owne right, wrongfully detained from me and my father who was lawfull heir to the Earldome of Desmond; for he was the eldest sonne to James my grandfather, who was Earle of Desmond; and for that Uncle Gerald (being the younger brother) usurped the name of the Earle of Desmond in my father's true title,' and being 'annoyed by the wicked English-prosecuted wars, was slaine and his country planted with Englishmen.'—*Pac. Hib.*, p. 253.

This James McThomas and his father sided with the English against 'uncle Gerald,' were the rightful owners according to English (though not by Brehon) law of 800,000 acres of land which the English undertakers had seized on, and consequently they must have been 'usurping and titulary Earls,' and they were 'extinct,' to use the word of our MS.

Carew writes to Elizabeth, June 3, 1601—'I thank God for it, I now have at length, by means of the White Knight, gotten into my hands the bodie of James FitzThomas, that Archtraytour and usurping Earle, whom for a present I will send to your Majestie with the best conveniencie and safetie I may find.' He was (says Carew, or his Secretary) within one year before his apprehension the most mightie and potent Geraldine that had been of any of the Earles of Desmond his predecessors . . . he had 8000 men well armed at one time.—*Pac. Hib.*, p. 250.

The son of 'uncle Gerald' wrote to Cecil from the Tower—'I am yong, yet olde in miserye; I have never, since my infancy, breathed out of prison.' He was physicked frightfully at the expense of the Government—perhaps to carry off the Geraldine poison out of his system.—See the bill for 'boluses, juleps, glisters,' etc., in *Life of McCarthy Mór*, p. 488. He was sent from the Tower to Ireland as Earl, set up against James McThomas. However, some about Elizabeth said—'Yea, but he maie proove a rebell hearafter;' and Cecil says to Carew—'Whensoever you fynd any cause toe doubt him, never feare to laie holde of him . . . he will never much lyke an Irish lyfe, for he is tender and sicklye, but time will shewe.'

He reached Kilmallock on a Satur-

his Eldest Sone is Baron of Dunkellyn[e] created by K. H. 8th.

Donogh O'Bryan[f] Erle of Thomond and Baron of Ibrackan, his Eldest Sone is Baron of Ibrackan, created 1550 an° 1° Edw. 6th.

day; the people crowded round him. 'Although he had a guard of soldiers which made a lane for him, the confluence was so great as he could hardly make his passage. The next day he went to church, and all the way his countrey people used loud and rude dehortations to keep him from church . . . he was railed at and spet upon, and thenceforward would walke as little regarded as any private gentleman . . . his Religion bred this coynesse in them all, if he had been a Romish Catholike, the hearts and knees of all degrees in the Province would have bowed to him.'—*Pac. Hib.*, p. 163.

[e] Ulick, 3rd Earl of Clanrickard, m. a dau. of Burke of Tullyra. He d. in 1601. His son John was made Viscount Burke of Clanmories; his son Edmund of Kilcornan was ancestor of the Redingtons of Kilcornan, and of the Burkes of Greenfield, Co. Galway.

This Ulick, son of Richard, son of Ulick of the Heads, was sedate and just judging, of a mild, august and chief-becoming countenance, affable in conversation, gentle towards the people of his territory, fierce to his neighbours, and impartial in all his decisions; he had never been known to act a feeble part on the field of danger from the day he had first taken up arms.—*Annals*, 1601. His son and heir, 'Richard of Kinsale,' so called for having contributed more than any one to the English victory at Kinsale, m. the widow of Essex; he became Earl of St. Albans. He killed an English nobleman in a duel for speaking disparagingly of Ireland, and he would have been killed himself had he not a reliquary on his breast, given him by the Jesuit, Fr. Gerard.—See *Fr. Gerard's Narrative.* See 'Earl Ulick's Tailor's Bill of the year 1578,' in *Kilk. Jour. of Arch.*

[f] Donogh O'Brien, 4th Earl of Thomond, called the *Great Earl*, a person of distinguished courage, conduct, loyalty, and worth, highly-esteemed by Elizabeth and James I. He was brought up at Court, and was of the Privy Council to both these Princes; had a principal share in the victory of Kinsale, and in 1605 was made President and Commander-in-Chief of Munster. He d. in 1624; by his first wife, a dau. of Lord Fermoy, he had a dau. who was married to Cormac M[c]Carthy, heir of Lord Muskerry; by his 2[d] wife, a dau. of the 11th Earl of Kildare, he had Henry and Bryan, successive Earls of Thomond.

Erle of Cloncare baron of valentia, created by this Quene 1565; his Erldome extinct for want of Issue male, his name was McCartie.[g]

Teig, a brother of Donogh, was long imprisoned in Limerick, but escaped. In 1599 he was committed to prison by his brother, but escaped again, and, with the O'Briens, McNamaras, etc., had 600 f. and 50 h. serving against Elizabeth. He had three sons, of whom Turlogh lived at Ballyslattery. His sons-in-law were the 18th Lord Kerry, 2d Lord Dunboyne, and Turlogh Roe McMahon.

The Earl's brother, Daniel of Moyartie and Carrighychoulta, received many wounds in the wars of Ireland, for which he was knighted and received considerable grants of lands in Clare, and particularly those of Teig Reagh McMahon of Thomond. He lived to see the Restoration of Charles II.; and for his own services and those of his children at home and abroad, was created Viscount Clare in 1662. He mar. a dau. of the 16th Earl of Desmond. His descendant, Lord Clare, received nine wounds at the head of his famous dragoons, fighting for the French at Ramillies in 1706.—See *Lodge*.

Florence McCarthy says of Lord Thomond in a letter to Carew—'Commend me to the Great Boar of Thomond.' Lord Hunsden praises him for his 'true nobleness of character.' However, he kept his brother Teig in prison in Limerick, though the following went security for him, and Mountjoy thought them sufficient, viz., the Lord Bishop of Killalowe, the Lord Burke of Castleconnell, Turlogh Roe McMahound of Clonderralagh, Lord Thomond's brother-in-law. That my Lord of Thomond refuseth to join with you in setting him at liberty argueth, in my conceipt, a desire in his Lordship to carry a more hard hand towards his brother than the State may in course of justice suffer . . . his son shall remain a pledge, for which purpose I have written to the Council at Dublin. —*Mountjoy* in *Car. Cal.*

[g] 'Onora, Countess of Cloncar, was wife, sister and daughter of an Earl, ever of verye modest and good demeanure, though matched with one most disorderlye and dissolute.'—*Sir W. Herbert's Letter*, an. 1588. *McCarthy Mór*, p. 45. The Earl of Clancar d. in 1596. 'Donal, son of Donal, son of Cormac, son of Teig, usually styled Mac Carthy Mór. His only child Ellen mar. Fineen, son of McCarthy Reagh, and all thought he was the heir of Donal McCarthy Mór.'—*Annals*. This Earl was an Irish poet, and wrote some pious things; but his life was not edifying, it seems. His base son Donal claimed to be McCarthy Mór, and was so recognized until Tyrone got Florence McCarthy elected.—See under *Kerry*

Rorie Erle of Tyrconnell,[h] created an[e] 1°.

Hugh O'Neall Erle of Tyrone baron of Dunganon, created Erle An° 1586; his eldest Sone is baron of Dunganon. He chalenged the Earldome from his Grandfather, Con O'Neall, whom K. H. 8 created Earle of Tiron, restrayning his authority within the Countie of Tyrone, which was afore spread throughout the most part of Ulster. This Con had divers Sones Legittimat, and one Illegitimate named Mathew, who was for many years reputed to be the Sone of one Kelly of Dundalk a Smyth; But the Woman, which was Wife to this Smyth, and mother to the foresaid Mathew, at her departure confessed to a Priest (as then the manner was), and Swore the Same before

and Cork. 'A dower was given to the Countess, in 1598, of a third of the late Earl's castles,' etc. In 1598 Norreys wrote—'The base son of the Earl opposeth himself to Darby M‘Owen M‘Carthy for the Earldom; but they agree both to be Traitors to her Matye.'

The Bastard was a dashing soldier, 'the Munster Robin Hood,' the terror of the undertakers; was secretly encouraged by his father. He and the Earl of Desmond with 2500 men attacked Essex near Adare, and made Munster too hot for him.—See *O'Sullevan's Historia*, and the *Life of M‘Carthy Mór* for an account of this Donal.

[h] 'The King to the Lieutenant of Ireland, Sep. 4 1603—To grant to Rorie O'Donnell and heirs male of his body the Co. of Tirconnell, with remainders to his brother Cafferie O'Donnell, and his cousin Donel Oge M‘Donel O'Donell . . . Rorie O'D. to renounce all claims upon Sir Cahir O'Doherty's and O'Conor Sligo's country, and to be raised to the dignity of Earl of Tirconnell in tail male, with remainders of like estate to his brother, Caffery O'D.'—*Car. Cal.*, p. 80.

He left Ireland with Tyrone, and d. in Rome, where his tomb is to be seen in the Church of St. Peter in Montorio. 'He was a brave, protecting, warlike man, and had often been in the gap of danger with his brother Red Hugh. He was a generous and truly hospitable lord, to whom the patrimony of his ancestors did not seem anything for his spending and feasting parties; he did not place his affections on wealth and jewels, but distributed them among those who needed them, whether mighty or feeble.' He died in Rome on the 28th of July 1608, 'after exemplary penance,' etc.—*Annals.* After the battle of Kinsale he commanded his

Witnesses, that her Sone Mathew, reputed to be the Smythes Sone, was the Sone of Con Oneall, whereupon Con O'Neall accepted of him as of his Sone, and adopted him into the Familie and name of O'Nealls, to whom his pretended Father procured from H. 8 Legittimation, and being elder than the Ligittimat Children, was preferred to them in Succession to the Earldome, and made baron of Dunganon. But the Legittimat disdayning that a bastard should be preferred to them, conspired against him and Slue him, The eldest of whom, named Shane O'Neall, usurped the Authoritie and Title of O'Neall, and kept it during his Life, whom Quene Eliz. continuallie did prosecute to have placed this man as Successor to his Grand Father, which at Length she performed, and was for her princelie favor verie unworthily by him requited.

VISCOUNTS.

S[r] James Barrhy,[k] L. Barrhy, baron of Ibaun, Viscount Buttevant.

brother's followers. He was a bold and dexterous swordsman, as his brave cousin and enemy, Nial Garve (himself 'vir animo magno et audaci,') had reason to know. *O'Sullevan*, p. 220, describes an extraordinary fight between him and two horsemen on one side, and 8 English foot on the other. He slew all the English, and for a long time he fought with their brave leader, and, not being able to pierce his corselet, he held him under water till he drowned him.

[i] See under the Co. of Tyrone, and in the Introduction, some account of this 'Archrebel,' Hugh of Tyrone.

[k] 'The Barry Mór, who was in captivity in Dublin, d. in 1581; he was of the true stock of the Barry Roes, yet had in the beginning no hope of obtaining even the title of Barry Roe. But God bestowed upon him the chieftainship both of Barry Maol and Barry Roe, and he was elected chief over the sept of Barry Mór when the true heirs of that chieftainship became extinct.

Sir David de la Rup, L. Roch, Baron of Poulescastle, Viscount
   of Armoy.¹
Christofer Preston, L: Baron and Viscount of Gormanstone.ᵐ

His son David was afterwards called 'The Barry' by the Earl of Desmond, and his second son was lord over the Barry Roes."—*Annals*, p. 1753.

He was first on the side of the Desmonds; but he flung himself on the English side afterwards. He was a deadly enemy of Florence McCarthy, in whose 'Life' will be found many letters of Barry's.

This David FitzJames Barry Viscount Buttevant and Barrymore, succeeded his father in 1581; his eldest brother was deaf and dumb, and died in 1622; his brother William lived at Lislee; his three sisters were m. to Viscount Fermoy, O'Sullevan Beare, and Condon of Ballymac-Patrick. In 1599 Lord Buttevant, that his brother John might be subject to the Crown of England, gave him and his heirs male the manors, castles, etc., of Liscarroll, Ballymacow, etc. He d. at Barry's Court in 1617. His son David mar. a d. of Lord Poer; his sons-in-law were Gerald FitzGerald of the Decies, Browne of Mulranken in Wexford, John son of Lord Poer, Thomas Earl of Ormond, Tobin of Cumshinagh, Co. Tipperary, and Sir J. FitzGerald of Ballymaloe, Co. of Cork.—*Lodge*.

¹ *Recte* Fermoy. 'As for the Lord Roche, if I have any judgment in me, I do not think any nobleman within the province of Munster to be more assured to the Crown of England, which all his actions do manifest; for I have not the company of any one of his rank so much as of himself; and therefore the Viscount is much wronged.'— *Carew* in 1602; *Car. Cal.*, p. 409.

Carew wrote in 1600, that 'he was only in personal show a subject.'

However, his base sons became 'Robin Hoods' in 1597. 'L. Roche that now is (1583) hath mar. the syster of Finyan McCarthy's mother, by which kindred Finyan is strongly allied. By her, who was a syster of James Fitz-Morris, he had a son, and a dau. mar. to McDonoghe Lord of Dowalla.'—*St. Leger's Letter in Life of MacCarthy Mór*.

'The Roche, *i.e.*, Maurice son of David, d. in 1600, a mild and comely man, learned in the Latin, Irish, and English languages. His son David took his place.'—*Annals*, p. 2187.

The castle at Castletown Roche was the chief seat of Roche. There is (or was) a stone near the parish church with the inscription—'Orate pro bono statu Domini Maurici Roche Vicecomes de Fermoy et Dominae Elionoriae Mauricii et pro anima ejus Anno Domini 1585.'—*Parl. Gaz. of Ireland*, under *Castletown Roche*.

ᵐ 'Whereunto is lately annexed the Barony of Loundres, their ancestor,

Sʳ Richard Butler,ⁿ Viscount of Mountgerat.
Sʳ Morrice Fitzgerrald, Viscount Dessie and baron of Dromane,° extinct without Issue male.
Eustace, Viscount of Baltinglas and L: of Kilcullen, extinct by attainder.ᵖ

LORDS.

Lord Bremingham,ᑫ Baron of Athenrie.

then Chief Baron of the Exchequer, was made Knight in the field by Lionel Duke of Clarence, Lieutenant of Ireland.'—*Campion.* Christopher was the 4ᵗʰ Viscount, and succeeded in 1559, and was succeeded by Jenico, whose brother Thomas was created Viscount Tara. 'Young Viscount Gormanston was committed to the Castle in 1605 for contriving with Sir P. Barnwall and others a Petition of the Pale in favour of freedom of religion. His brother was an officer in Tyrone's Regiment in the Netherlands.'—*Car. Cal.*

ⁿ See *supra*, p. 67.

Edmund 2ᵈ Viscount Mountgarrett m. a dau. of the 1ˢᵗ Baron of Upper Ossory; in the Parliament of 1559 he represented Carlow; in 1602 he was buried in Kilkenny Cathedral; he had 8 sons and 8 daughters.

Richard, his son and successor, was 20 years old in 1598, when he sided with O'Neil, his father-in-law; he joined the Confederates in 1642, and died in 1652, and though dead was exempted by Cromwell's Act of Parliament from pardon for *life* or estate. He lies buried under a handsome monument in the Chancel of St. Canice. He had 3 sons and 5 daughters.

His brother Theobald of Tynehinch m. a dau. of FitzGerald of Queen's Co.; his sisters were m. to Walter Earl of Ormond; Shee of Upper Court; Morgan Mᶜالبryan Cavanagh, Chief of the Sept, called *Sleight Dermot*, of Polomonty in Carlow; to O'Connor; to Daton of Kilmodalin in Kilkenny; to O. Grace of Carney in Tipperary, son and heir to Gerald Grace of Liegan; to Viscount Galway; to O'Farrell of Ballintobber, son of O'Farrell Bane of the Annaly.—*Archdall.*

The Keep of Mountgarrett's castle, in Wexford, near New Ross, is still in a tolerable state of preservation.

° See *supra* 'Waterford,' p. 160.

ᵖ See *supra*, p. 45.

ᑫ Now degenerate and become meere

Fleming^r baron of Slaine.
Plunket^s baron of Killeyne.
Sr Christofer Nugent,^t Baron of Delvin.
Sr Christofer St. Laurence,^u L: of Hoth.

Irishe, against whom his ancestors served valiantly in An. 1300.—*Campion*.

Edmund, 15th Baron, sat as the *auncientest* Baron of Ireland in the Parliament of 1585. He mar. a sister to Sir Roger O'Shaghnessie, and had three sons, Richard, Meyler *Buy*, and Thomas *Duffe*.

Richard the 16th Baron, born in 1570, died in 1635, and was buried in the Abbey of Athenry. The 22^d Baron lived at Turlovaughan, near Tuam, in the year 1754.

Meyler *Buy* Bermingham of Connagher got from his brother, the 16th Baron, in 1595, Dalgan and other lands in the Barony of Dunmore. He m. a dau. of Mac Jordan of Tobrachan, in Mayo, and had 7 sons. Thomas Duffe B. mar. a dau. of Burke of Clochrooke. —*Archdall's Lodge*.

^r A Lord Slane betrayed Archbishop O'Hurley *circ.* 1584; in 1597 a Lord Slane sent to the Lord Deputy the heads of two rebels; in 1605 a L. Slane signed the 'Petition of the Papists of the Pale.'—See *Car. Cal.*, an. 1597 and *Cal. of S. Papers*, 1605.

^s 'This family came of the Danes, whereof they have as yet special monuments.'—*Campion*. Christopher, 9th Lord of Killeen, mar. a sister of Dillon, 1st Earl of Roscommon; in 1598 he was made 'Knight Marshall of the Camp;' he d. in 1613, leaving Lucas Mór, 1st Earl of Fingal; Patrick, Catholic Bishop of Meath, who d. in 1679; and Nicholas, a lawyer.—*Lodge, under Lord Dunsany*.

Christopher, 9th Baron, was made Captain of Slewght William in Annaly in 1565; was ordered in 1567 to help to extirpate the O'Mores, sons of Ferrass McRosse, and to lead in person 150 kerne, 10 horsemen, and 50 boys of his own choice; in 1580 was sent a prisoner to the Tower on suspicion of correspondence with the Leinster Insurgents; in 1593 brought 20 horsemen to the hosting at Tara, with the Nugents, his kinsmen. For his 'valorous services' he got, in 1597, forfeited lands in Longford and Cavan. He had m. Mary, dau. of the 11th Earl of Kildare, by whom he had six sons and six daughters. He died in Aug. 1602.— *Lodge*. He d. a prisoner in Dublin Castle, to which he was committed on a charge of having assisted Tyrone. His son was first Earl of Westmeath, about whom consult *Fr. Meehan's Flight of the Earls*.

^u *Recte* Sir Nicholas, the father of Christopher. He was the 21st Lord, who d. in 1606; he brought 6 archers on horseback for Howth, and 1 for

O'Bryan,[v] baron of Inchequyn.
Barnwall,[w] Baron of Tribleston.
Butler,[x] Baron of Caer.

Killester, to the hosting at Tara. His son Christopher, 22[d] Baron, served as a colonel of foot under Essex and Mountjoy. Camden tells us that this Christopher was one of the friends who accompanied Essex on his visit to Nonsuch, and that he offered to kill Lord Grey, an enemy of Essex, and then to kill Cecil at the Queen's Court. —See *The Flight of the Earls* for a sketch of this nobleman's career.

[v] Dermot, 5th Baron, was 4 years old in 1598. His son Morogh became famous as Earl of Inchiquin; his father, Morogh, was slain in 1597 by O'Donnell's soldiers, while trying with the English army to cross the Erne. He was, by order of O'Donnell and the Catholic Bishops of Derry and Raphoe, buried with reverence and honour in the Franciscan Monastery of Donegal, having been previously buried by the Cistercians in their Monastery of Asseroe—the reason was that the Baron's ancestors had been buried in the Franciscan Monastery in his country.— *Annals*, pp. 2027, 2047.

Dermot mar. a dau. of Sir Edmund FitzEdmond of Cloyne. In the *Life of Lady Falkland*, whose husband was Lord Deputy in 1622, I find that, 'In Ireland she grew acquainted with my Lord of Inchiquin, an exceeding good Catholic, and the first (at least knowing one) she had yet met. She highly esteemed him for his wit, learning, and judgment, though he were but about nine-and-twenty years old when he died. Her Lord did the same, admiring him much as a man of so sincere and upright a conscience, that he seemed to look on whatever was not lawful as not possible; he did somewhat shake her supposed security in esteeming it lawful to continue as she was.'—*Life of Lady Falkland*, p. 23.

[w] Peter, 6th Baron of Trimlestown, d. on Good Friday 1598; his mother was a dau. of Taylor of Swords; by his wife, a sister of Lord Delvin's, he had a son Robert, the 7th Lord, who was 24 years old in 1598, and mar. to Miss Talbot of Dardistown. Peter, in his will, left £10 to be divided among poor priests and friars, and 40s. to Bishop Brady. Sir P. Barnwall of Turvey, Dublin, was one of a family of 18 children; his wife was a sister of Marshal Bagnal; his son became 1st Viscount Kingsland; his sisters were wives of Lords Dunsany, Roscommon, and Howth; of the Knights Fitzgerald of Tecroghan, Draicot of Mornington, and Masterson of Ferns, of Thomas and John Finglas of Westpalston, Stanihurst of Corduff, Delahyde of Moyglare, and R. Beling. —See *Lodge*, vol. 5, p. 46. See the curious Barnewall monument in Lusk.

[x] 'Theobald Butler, Lord of Cahair-Duna-Iascaigh and Trian-chluana-meala

Courcy,[y] L: Courcy.
L. Burke[z] of Castle-conell.

(Cahir and Clonmel-third), d. in 1596; a bounteous man, he had the largest collection of poetical compositions of almost all the old English of Ireland; his son Thomas took his place.'—*Annals*, p. 1997. The sisters of Thomas, 4th Baron, were mar. to Butler of Ballyboe and Sir Cormac M'Carthy of Blarney; his brother James Galdie was engaged in the risings of 1598 and 1641; his castle of Cahir was besieged and taken by Essex. He mar. a sister of Lord Mountgarrett.—*Lodge*, vol. 6, p. 219. His brother Edmund lived at Cloghcully.

'Mr. Piers Butler of Knock-in-anama, w[ch] is his chefe house. He is son to the Lo: of Caher, and brother to the Lo. of Caher that now is; his liveing stands in the com[e] of Tipperary, nere the towne of Clounmell.'—*Florence M'Carthy*; see his *Life*. He was deeply concerned in the rising of 1598, and Carew was anxious to seize his person and his castle.

[y] 'Curcy, Baron of Ringrone, now reduced by the fluctuation of human affairs.'—*Camden*.

Gerald de Courcy, 17th Baron of Kinsale, son of the 16th Lord, and Seive, dau. of MacCarthy of Dowallagh, succeeded in 1535; at the siege of Boulogne he commanded an Irish Regiment under Henry 8, and for his bravery was knighted by the King on the field, under the Royal Standard displayed, the most distinguished manner of receiving Knighthood; but by his great expenses in serving the Crown he considerably lessened his estate. He died at a very advanced age in 1599; his wife was dau. of Cormac M'Donogh M'Carthy of Carbery; Mary, his only child, m. Donogh O'Driscol.

John, 18th Baron of Kinsale (was son of Edmond Oge of Kilnaclone, and his wife, dau. of Dermod M'Teig O'Hurley, Chief of his Sept), succeeded in 1599; fought on the English side at Kinsale; m. a dau. of O'Cruley of Carbery, Chief of his Sept; and he died in 1628, and was buried in the Abbey of Timoleague.—*Lodge*.

[z] In 1591 Lord Castleconnell was slain.

John Bourke, Lord Castleconnell, was basely slain
By Captain Arnold Crosby, for they twain
Resolved to fight; but Crosby stops, demurs—
Prays Castleconnell to take off his spurs,
And as he stooped, yielding to his request,
Crosby most basely stabbed him in the breast;
Gave twenty-one, all dreadful wounds—base act!
And Crosby's only hanged for the horrid fact.
—*Davis's Annals of Limerick*, quoted by *Mr. Lenihan*, p. 121.

'In the days that Essex was storming Cahir-Duine-Iasaigh (1599), Sir T. Norris came to Kilmallock, and was in the practice of scouring the hills of Limerick every other day to see whether he could kill or capture any enemies. He fell in, near Kilteely, with Thomas

Eustace[aa] Viscount of Baltinglas and L. of Kilcollen, extinct by attainder.
Patrick Fitzgerrald[bb] baron of Lixsnaw.
M[c]Kilpatrick[cc] baron of upper Ossyry.

Burke, son of Theobald, son of William, son of Edmond of Castleconnell, neither being in search of the other. Thomas was on horseback at the head of 100 Irish foot; he was attacked by Norris, who slew 20 of his people, but Norris was mortally wounded.

'Dermot O'Connor led some of O'Neill's soldiers into Munster in 1600. When the Baron of Castleconnell (Richard, son of Theobald, etc.), heard of Dermot's arrival in Owney and Clanwilliam, he and his brother Thomas mustered horse and foot of his own and the Queen's people, and fought Dermot from the Monastery of Owney to the bridge of Bun-briste. As the Baron and his brother advanced with pride across the bridge of Bunbriste in front of their own forces, they were put to the sword. A cause of lamentation; for though they were young they were manly in renown and noble deeds.'—*Annals*, pp. 2115, 2145.

[aa] Vide *supra* note [p].

[bb] 'Mac Maurice of Kerry, *i.e.*, Patrickin, son of Thomas, d. in 1600, in the prime of life, after having joined the Earl of Desmond in the war. It was a cause of lamentation that a man of his personal form, blood, and hospitality should thus die in his youth; his son Thomas took his place. Patrickin in 1590 succeeded his father, who was the best purchaser of wine, horses, and literary works of any of his wealth at that time.'—*Annals*, pp. 1893, 2177.

This Patrickin, 17th Lord Kerry, was b. in 1541; was sent as a hostage to Queen Mary; bred at the English Court, was favoured by Elizabeth, but getting leave to see his father in 1561, he took up arms against the English; in 1599 he was at the head of 500 foot and 30 h. He died of grief at seeing the English take one of his castles, and he was buried with his uncle, Donal Earl of Clancarre, in the Franciscan Friery of Irrinlagh. By his wife, dau. of Lord Fermoy, he had 3 sons and 2 dau.; the daughters were m. to O'Sullevan Mór and the son of M[c]Carthy Mór. His son Thomas, born in 1574, mar. a sister of the Earl of Thomond; at his father's death was promised pardon on condition that he would perform such service as would deserve them, but he absolutely refused, because 'it stood not with his conscience;' after that he retired to the North, and came to Kinsale as a commander in O'Donnell's army. After the defeat of Kinsale, he was beaten out of his castle of Lixnaw. He was pardoned by King James, and in 1630 d. and was buried in the Chapel and Tomb of St. Cormac

Plunket L: Baron[dd] of Dunsany.
Butler[cc] Baron of Dunboyne.
L. Power Baron[ff] of Corraghmore.
Plunket L. Baron of Louth.[gg]

M<sup>c</sup>Cullenan. He was married, first to a dau. of the Earl of Thomond, 2<sup>ly</sup> to a dau. of Lord Poer of Curraghmore; and he had 7 sons and 4 daughters.—*Lodge.*

[cc] See p. 79. He succeeded as 3<sup>rd</sup> Baron in 1581; he m. a dau. of Patrick O'More of Leix, head of that Sept, or, as some say, a dau. of Ruary O'More, and had issue 5 sons and 2 daughters. His sons were, 1° Teig, who m. a dau. of Sir E. Butler of Tullow; 2° John of Castletown; 3° Geoffry of Ballyraghin, m. to a dau. of Fergus Farrell of Tenelick, in the Co. of Longford, who was widow of Sir J. O'Reilly; 4° Bryan of Water Castle; 5° Edmund of Castle Fleming. His dau. Catherine m. (in 1592) Eustace of Newland, in Kildare; and his dau. Joan m. the heir of Lord Dunboyne.

[dd] Patrick, 7<sup>th</sup> Lord, 'a person of learning, and a patron of learning and learned men.'—*Stanyhurst.* In 1601 he commanded a company of Irish in English pay; took away 1600 cows from M<sup>c</sup>Mahon, but being attacked by 140 men, he lost the prey and 50 men, 'but not one good subject.' His wife was 11<sup>th</sup> dau. of Sir C. Barnwall.—*Lodge.*

[ee] James, 2<sup>nd</sup> Lord; by his first wife, a dau. of Lord Upper Ossory, he had 5 sons and 3 daughters; by his 2<sup>d</sup> wife (a dau. of Lord Thomond), he had 6 sons and 3 daughters.

[ff] Richard, Lord Poer, mar. to a dau. of Lord Buttevant, d. in 1607; his son and heir was killed by the White Knight. His father, whose wife was a dau. of the 15<sup>th</sup> Lord Desmond, was thus spoken of by Sir H. Sydney in 1575:—

'I lodged at Corraghmore, the house that the Lord Power is Baron of, where I was so used with such plenty and good order entertained (as adding to the quiet of all the country adjoining, by the same people called the *Power Country*), it may well be compared with the best ordered country in the *English Pale.* And the lord of the country, though he be of scope of ground a far less territory than his neighbour is, yet he lives in shew far more honourably and plentifully than he or any other whatsoever he be of his calling that lives in this province.'

[gg] 'On the western face of the Baronstown Cross, beneath a figure of St. Patrick, we read—"I pray you, St. Patrick, pray for the soules of Oliver Plunket Lord Baron of Louth, and Dame Jenet Dowdall, his wife. This cross was builded by Dame Janet Dowdall, late wife unto Oliver Plunket,

L: Savage Baron of [hh]

Lord Baron of Louth, for him and herselfe, in the yere of Our Lord God" . . .'

Underneath a rude image of St. Peter on the east side—'I pray you, St. Peter, pray for the soules of Oliver Plunket,' etc. On the back is the 'Hail Mary.'

This Oliver was the 4th Lord; he died in 1607; his 2nd wife was a daughter of Dowdall of Termonfeighan; by his first wife, a dau. of Marshal Bagenal, he had 5 children.'—See *Lodge* and *Sir W. Wilde's Boyne and Blackwater.*

[hh] Lord of Ardes. See p. 10.

Campion adds—'Mac Suretan, Lord of Deseret, whom Sir H. Sydney called Jordan de Exeter. This was Lord in the time of Lionel, Duke of Clarence, An. 1361—now very wilde Irish.' Mac Costilaghe, L. Nangle, whom Sir H. Sidney called the Angulo, now very Irish. Mac William Burke, Lord of Eichter, Connaught, now very Irish.— *Campion.*

Baronets.

Saintleger, of Slemarge, meere Irish. Den of Pormanston, waxing Irish. FitzGerald of Burnchurch. Welleslye of Narraghe. Hussee of Galtrim. St. Michell of Reban. Marwarde of Scryne. Nangle of the Navan.—*Campion.*

THE NAMES OF B.— AND ARCH-B.—

The Archb. of Armagh, Primat of all Ireland, his name is Henrie Usher.[a]

The Archb. of Dublin, Primate of Ireland, his name is Thomas Jones,[b] now L. Chancellor.

The Archb. of Cashel.[c]

[a] Born in Dublin; Abp. (1595-1613). He had sons, Richard and Luke; to Luke 'he had disposed of his Archdeaconry of Dublin.' He was in great Honour and Repute among all Protestants.—*Ware.*

[b] *Recte* Adam Loftus, b. in Yorkshire; Abp. (1567-1605), and Jones succeeded. Nominated Abp. of Armagh 1561, at the age of 28; Abp. of Dublin in 1567; Lord Chancellor (1578-1605). By his wife, Miss Purdon of Lurgan-Race, Louth, he had 20 children—1. Dudley, of Rathfarnham Castle, which was built by the Abp. 2. Edward, Sergeant-at-Law and Knight, who d. at siege of Kinsale. 3. Adam, a captain of horse, killed in Byrne's country in 1599. 4 and 5—Henry and Thomas, twins. Thomas was of Killyan, Co. Meath; was Constable of Wicklow Castle in 1596; he m. a sister of Piers Hartpole of Carlow. His daughters were—1. Isabella, m. to Wm. Ussher, Clerk of the Council. 2. Anne, m. to Sir H. Colley of Castle Carbery, Blount of Kidderminster, and Lord Blayney. 3. Catherine, m. to Sir F. Berkeley of Askeaton, and H. Berkeley, Esq. 4. Martha, m. to Sir T. Colclough of Tinterne Abbey. 5. Dorothy, m. to Sir J. Moore of Croghan. 6. Alicia, to Sir H. Warren of Warrenston or Ballybrett. 7. Margaret, to Sir G. Colley of Edenderry.—*Archdall's Lodge*, vol. 7, p. 246.

His 'great qualities were something tarnished by his excessive Ambition and Avarice. For, besides his promotions in the Church and his publick employments in the State, he grasped at everything that became void, either for himself or Family.'—*Ware.*

[c] Miler Magragh, born in Fermanagh, ex-Franciscan, Abp. of Cashel, and Bp. of Emly (1570 to 1622); he had also Waterford and Lismore in commendam (1582-1589, and 1592-1607). In 1611 he got a coadjutor, Wm. Knight, who soon after 'appeared Drunk in publick, and thereby exposed himself to the scorn and derision of the People;' 'and returned to England.' Magrath

The Archb. of Toam.[d]

THE BISHOPS.

The B. of Meath and Clonem'knois, his name is[e]
The Bishop of Derry, his name is Montgomerie.[f]
The B. of Ardagh,   Draper.[g]

made the most scandalous wastes and alienations of the Revenues and Manors belonging to his See. He erected a Monument for himself in his Cathedral, with the strange inscription written by himself—
'Venerat in Dunum primo sanctissimus olim,
Patricius, nostri gloria magna soli,
Huic ego succedens, utinam tam sanctus ut ille,
Sic Duni primo tempore Praesul eram.
Anglia! lustra decem sed post tua sceptra Colebam,
Principibus placui, Marte tonante, tuis.
Hic, ubi sum positus, non sum, sum non ubi non sum;
Sum nec in ambobus, sum sed utroque loco.
1621.
     Dominus est qui me judicat. 1 Cor. 4.
     Qui stat, caveat ne cadat.'—*Ware.*

Called 'Meillmorre M'Cragh,' by Tyrone; 'an ex-Friar, an avaricious and unprincipled man, and a most unscrupulous waster of the patrimony of the Sees under his administration; held 4 bishopricks and a great number of benefices in various dioceses. He m. Amy, dau. of O'Meara of Lisany, Co. Tipperary, and had issue—Turlogh, Redmond, Bryan, Mark, Mary, Cicely, Anne, and Eliza. His sons, or at least some of them, relapsed to Popery.'—*Cotton's Fasti.*

[d] Nehemiah Donellan, born in Galway, bred at Cambridge, Abp. from 1595 to 1609, when he voluntarily resigned.—*Ware.*

[e] Thomas Jones, b. in Lancashire; Bp. (1584-1605). His monument in St. Patrick's Cathedral has the inscription—'Thomas Jones, Archiepiscopus Dublin, Primas et Metropolitanus Hiberniae, Ejusdem Cancellarius . . .'

Margareta, ejusdem Thomae Uxor Charissima obiit decimo quinto Decembris, Anno a partu Virginis 1618. Jones had 6 children; his son, Sir Roger of Durhamstown, Westmeath, was made Viscount Ranelagh in 1628; his daughters were mar. to Domville, Clerk of the Hanaper, and Piers of Tristernagh, Westmeath.—*Archdall's Lodge,* v., p. 301.

'He laid the Foundation of a fair estate.'—*Harris's Addition to Ware.*

[f] Vacant in 1598; Dr. Montgomerie, b. in Scotland, was Bp. from 1605 to 1610, as well as of Raphoe and Clogher.

[g] Vacant in 1598. Robert Draper, Rector of Trim in 1598, Bp. of Ardagh and Kilmore (1603-1612).—*Ware.*

The B. of Kilmore,^g the same man hath both.
The B. of Clogher,^f united with Derrie.
The B. of Doune, his name is D. Tod.^h
The B. of Connor,^h the same man.
The B. of Raboo,^f united to Derrie.
The B. of Dromore,^h united to Downe.
All these are under the Archbishop of Armagh.
The B. of Glandelagh, annexed to the Archb. of Dublin.
The B. of Kildare, his name is Pilsworth.ⁱ
The B. of Fernes, his name is Mr Ram.^k
The B. of Ossorie, his name is^l

^h *Recte* John Charden of Devonshire, Bp. (1596-1601), had been a noted preacher. John Todd, 'Doctor of Divinity, Dean of Cashel, who had been a Jesuit, was Bp. (1606-1611); but being called to Account for some Crimes he had committed, he resigned, and a little after died in prison in *London* of Poyson, which he had prepared for himself.'—*Ware.*

ⁱ *Recte* Daniel Neylan, Rector of Iniscorthy in Killaloe Diocese; Bp. (1583-1603). Pilsworth, b. in London, was Bp. from 1604 to 1635. In 1591, out of 50 benefices in Kildare, 4 were vacant and in the bishop's possession, 22 were usurped by laymen; 24 were enjoyed by 22 incumbents, of whom one 'commorat in Anglia,' and 12 were pluralists who held livings in other dioceses.—See MS., T.C.D., E. 3, 14, quoted by *W. Maziere Brady.*

Pilsworth 'was determined to have a share in the spoil by leaving his Bishoprick poorer than he found it.'—*Harris's Addition to Ware.*

^k *Recte* Hugh Allen, b. in England, Bp. (1582-1599).

'He made long Leases of the Manor of Fethard, and of many other Farms, reserving very small Rents to his See. But Thomas Ram, who was afterwards Bishop, recovered the Manor,' after a long suit, and by giving a lease of Whitechurch to Allen's son for 21 years. Bp. Allen also leased in Fee 1500 acres to Sir H. Wallop, Vice-Treasurer, and the Parsonage of Carne for 61 years to N. Kenny, Clerk of the First-Fruits, who suffered him to detain money for which he was bound to account to the Exchequer, and which Ram was forced to pay.—*Harris's Ware.*

Thomas Ram, born in Windsor, was Bp. (1605-1634).

^l John Horsfall, b. in Yorkshire, Bp. (1586-1609).

The B. of Leighlin, united to Fernes.ᵏ
All these be under the Archbishop of Dublin.
The Bishop of Waterfordᵐ and Lismore.
The B. of Corke,ⁿ and Clone and Ross Carbery.
The B. of Ardfert,ᵒ his name is Crosbie.
The B. of Limerick, his name is Adams.ᵖ
The B. of Emelie,ᵐ annexed to the Archb. of Cashel.
The B. of Killallow,ᵠ his name is O'Bryan.
All these be under the Archbishop of Cashel.

ᵐ *Vide* note ᶜ.

ⁿ Wm. Lyon of Chester, Bp. (1583-1617), Vicar of Naas in 1573. A prelate of an active and liberal spirit. In the palace grounds in Cork was found a flagstone with the inscription—'This house was builded in anno 1589 by — Welleam lion, an Englis man born beshop of Cork, Clon-an-Ross, and this tomb was erected in anno dni. 1597,' etc. His portrait is in the see-house of Cork. He d. at Cork at a very advanced age.—*Cotton's Fasti*.

ᵒ Nich. Keenan, Bp. (1588-1599).— *Ware*. John Crosby, Bp. (1600-1621) m. the dau. of O'Lalor of Queen's Co.; he had two sons; his daughters were mar. to McElligott, McGillicuddy, Stephenson of Dunmoylin in Limerick, and Collum. Crosby was ancestor of the Earls of Glandore.—*Lodge*, vol. iii., p. 327.

ᵖ *Recte* John Thornburgh, of Salisbury, Bp. (1593-1603), performed many eminent services to the Crown after his advancement to the See of Limerick, which were the cause of his subsequent promotions; he was 'well furnished with Learning, Wisdom, Courage, and other as well Episcopal as temporal Accomplishments, beseeming a gentleman, a Dean, and a Bishop. He had great skill in Chimistry, by which it was thought he attained to so great an Age, arriving at his 89ᵗʰ year.' He was translated to Bristol, and then to Worcester, where there is a monument to him with a curious inscription, beginning thus—' Denarius Philoso-phorum. Dum spiro, spero.'

Adams of Middlesex was Bp. (1604-1625.) On his tomb is inscribed—

'Bernardus jacet hic en Adamus, Episcopus olim,
Omnia non vidit Solomonis, et omnia vana.
A Bishop once here *Bernard's* Bones remain;
He saw not all, but saw that all was vain.
Sufficient God did give me, which I spent;
I little borrowed, and as little lent.
I left them whom I loved enough in store.—
Increased this Bishoprick, relieved the Poor.'

ᵠ Maurice O'Brien, b. in Arra, Bp. (1570-1612), received the profits of the See six years before his consecration; he voluntarily resigned a year before

The B. of Kilmacow.'
The B. of Elfin,' his name is Linch.
The B. of Athcourie,' Vacant.
The B. of Clonfert,' his name Linch.
The B. of Maio, annexed to Toam.
The B. of Killallo,' Vacat.
These be under the Archb. of Toam.

So the BB. of Ulster and Meath be under the Primat of Armagh, the BB. of Leinster under the Archb. of Dublin. The BB. of Mounster under the Archb. of Cashell. The BB. of Conaught under the Archb. of Toam.

his death.—*Ware.* This Mortogh had two sons, Torlogh and John.—*Memoirs of the O'Briens*, p. 547.

' Kilmacduagh and Clonfert. Stephen Kerovan, b. in Galway, Bp. (1582-1602). Roland Linch, b. in Galway, Bp. (1602-1625.) The Members of the Royal Visitation say, '(Linch), Bp. of Clonfert and Kilmacduach and Clonfert hath dealt so fraudulently and perversely with us, that we cannot give the least Credit to his relation. We have undeniable Evidence that upon his first Promotion, Clonfert was esteemed worth £160 per Ann., and Kilmacduach £100. But now the Bp. hath returned us a Roll in Writing, in which he makes the value of Clonfert only £40, and Kilmacduach only £24, but gives us no account how this happened.'—*Harris's Ware.*

' John FitzJames Linch, b. in Galway, LL.B. of Oxford, Bp. (1584-1611), educated at Oxford; 'by Alienations, etc., so wasted and destroyed it (his See), that he left it not worth 200 Marks a year. It is said he lived a concealed and died a "Publick Papist."'—*Harris's Ware.*

' Achonry and Killala. Owen O'Connor, b. in Ireland; Bp. of Killala (1591-1607.)—*Ware.*

THE HAVENS OF IRELAND.

Loughfoyle.[a]
Oulderflecte.[b]
Carrickfergus, a wild road.[c]
Strangford.[d]
Arglas, barred.
Carlingford,[e] barred.
Dundalke,[f] barred.
Skerries,[g] dangerous for many rockes covered at ful Sea.
Rushe, a Creeke.
Malahide.
Hah,[g] a road.
The Sheynen,[h] and many places therein.
Galloway.[i]
The Iles of Arran the outer.
broad Haven.[j]
Inisbafin.[j]
Moyne.
Sligo.
Calbeg.

Havens.—3rd vol. *S.P.*, Henry 8, year 1543, p. 446.

[a] In O'Donnell's countrey.

[b] A good haven in the Irishe Scottes countrey. The Banne in Maccryllie's country.

[c] Knockfergus, a good haven and yours.

[d] A good haven.

[e] A good haven.

[f] A creek.

[g] Skyrries, a good rode. Howthe, Dalkey, Wicklow.—*Dean Nowel, MS.*

[h] Limerick, very good, but much hindered by certen Yrishmen bordering on either syde.

[i] Galway, very good.

[j] 'Inver, commonly called the broad haven; so it is broad within three hundred sayle may roade here without annoying one another. The fyshing is good and plentyfull for Codd, Lynge, Hearinge, etc. But the entry is such that a Poortie with artillery on the south side may sinke any vessell.'—*Descript. of Connaught in* 1612.

'Ince Bofin, the land of Saints, Tirke Mayne, and Clere, are under the rule of O'Malley; they are very pleasant and fertile, plenty of woode, a rabell grounde, pasture and fishe, and a very temperate ayer.'—*Apothecarie Smith*, anno 1561. See his MS. published in *Ulster Jour. of Arch.* Inish Bofin is called Inish Potin in *Nowel*, and Arran is called Arinnenewe

THE HAVENS OF IRELAND.

Lough Sulley.^k
Dalgoy,^l a wild road.
Wicklo,^m for small Vessels.
Arcklo,^m for the same.
Passage.ⁿ
Dungarvan.^o
Rosse.ⁿ

Youghall,^p good at half Tide.
Cork.^q
Kinsale, good at all tymes.
Rosse Carbery.
Baltimore.^r
Valentia.
Dingle.^s

The best of these Havens have no toune nere them as Calbeg, Loughsully, O-Lderfleet, etc.

^k Lough Swilly. Also Assero, Shepehaven, Northerborne, in O'Donnell's country.

^l Dalkey?

^m But a creek.

ⁿ Waterford and Rosse, very good.

^o A barred haven.

^p A good haven.

^q a good haven.

^r Wallentimore, good in Ohetheriscalle's country. Beare Haven in O'Sulyivan's country, very good.

^s Crook Haven and Dyngell Creek, in Machartie's country. *Nowel* calls Dingle, 'Dangyr Ighois.'

Also 'Wexford badde, Drogheda badde, Lambay Ylonde a good rode for all manner of windes.'—*St. Leger* to *Henry* 8, 6th April 1543—*State Papers*.

In addition to these, *Nowel's MS.* has—'Ardglasse Loghuen, Kilkele, Kilcloghir, Holmpatrick, Dublin, Tomalag, Kierie, Derrie, Downemore, Downeshead, Downelong, Artlanan, Croghan, Dunburie, Ballineskelligy, Tralee, Cassane, Inniskae, Belalem, Glanemagh, Ballywhyghan, Kinwarre, Dowrig, Woran, Roskain, Killenkillie, Rathsilben, Burske, Belaclare, Balala, Ardroute, Ardenoch, Ardremakow, Rosbare, Kilgholm, Kalbaly, Rabran, Bierweis our, Burwis Qare, Burweis nowe, Fattra Kattra'!!—*Nowel's MS.*, written before 1576. See a long description of the Connaught Havens in vol. 27 of the *Archaeologia*.

A NOTE OF THE REVENUES AND CASUALTIES OF IRELAND.

The old Rents and Revenues of the several counties here mencioned each half Year.

	£	s.	d.
Of the Countie of the Cittie of Dublin	218	15	2
Of the Countie of Dublin	174	9	6
Kildare	10	0	0
Meath	164	17	8
Longford	37	6	8
Westmeath	17	15	4
Drogheda	137	8	9
Roscommon	79	9	2
Galloway	5	10	0
Louth	5	0	0
Antrym	21	12	1
Cittie of Limerick	20	2	2
Corke	10	0	0
Dublin	939	18	8
Kilkenny	394	16	6
Westmeath	447	12	2
Clare	12	5	0
Louth	814	16	6
Kings	150	7	3
Roscomon	102	17	7
Galloway	209	13	8
Longford	111	11	0
Sligo	16	16	1
Reg	35	2	5
Drogheda	10	12	4
Downe	58	3	9
Maio	76	3	1
Kerry	91	17	0

THE REVENUES OF IRELAND.

Rents and Revenues of the Q. Lands and poss. in Ireland both Spirituall and Temporall in the Severall Counties thereof.	Cavan - - - -	£16 16	0
	O'Carrel's Countrie - -	6 10	4
	Kildare - - -	972 12	11
	Catherlagh - - -	107 12	5
	Limerick - - -	311 10	1
	Wexford - - -	430 1	0
	Tipperary - - -	252 16	4
	Waterford - - -	305 19	6
	Meath - - - -	1729 9	0
	Corke - - - -	310 4	8
	Summa totalis - - -	£8236 14	7
Rents reserved to the Quene, for territories and Lands resigned to her and taken back from her again.	O'Carrel's Countrie - -	200 0	0
	Corke - - - -	12 10	8
	Galloway - - -	21 11	2
	Roscomon - - -	6 0	0
	King's Countie - -	0 10	0
	Limerick - - -	6 16	0
	Province of Ulster - -	187 13	4
	Fercale in the King's Countie -	53 6	8
A Composition made by Sr Henrie Sidney for Bonnaught money.	King's Countie - -	40 0	0
	Wexford Countie - -	194 13	4
	For certen Personages let to the B. of Meath - -	84 1	0
Severall Compositions made by Severall Dep. with the Country for easing them of the Cesse of Soldiers and provision for the Dep hous.	Composition for Monaghan -	761 6	0
	Composition of the Pale -	2008 0	0
	Composition of Conaught -	3864 8	10
	Composition of Mounster -	1007 2	8
	Chief Rents in Mounster -	876 8	0
	Undertakers' Lands per Annum	5615 0	0

2 H

THE QUENE'S CASUALTIES WHICH IS YEARLIE UNCERTAINE.

Subsidies of Temporall Lands the *xx* of the clergie
The Office of the
Fines for Homages
Fines for Liverie
Fines for alienation
Fines for relief
Fines for Leases for term of Years
Fines for Ecclesiasticall causes
Fines for Pardones
The Sherriffs Accompts
Forfeitures of Recognizances
Office of the First Fruits
Office of the Clerke of the Crowne
Office of the Clerke of the Starr Chamber
Office of the Clerke of Faculties
Office of the Prerogative Court
Customs of all kinds of Merchandize brought or carried out
Imposts of Wines let to Sr Henrie Broncard for £2000 yearlie

Note that the Irish Pound or Shilling is lesse by the 4th part than the Inglysh, as the Irysh pound is but 18s. Ster., the Irish Shilling 9d. Ster.

The Summe of the Ordinarie receats by the half year, out of the Revenues and Impost is £24,952 4s. Irish.

A NOTE OF THE YEARLIE PAYMENTS ISSUED OUT OF THE REVENNUES.

To the Officers of the Exchequer	-	- £1188 13 0
To the Officers of the King's bench	-	- 543 6 8
To the Officers of the common Pleas	-	- 206 7 9
To the Officers of the Chauncerie	-	- 628 14 5

To the Officers attending the L. Dep. and counsail Sitting in the Starr chamber within the Castle of Dublin	£133	6	8
To the Collectors and Controllers of the Customs of Dublin and Drogheda	40	0	0
To the Clerk of Works, his Fee	34	vj	viij
The Fees of divers Constables of Castles within Ireland	286	vj	viij
Annuities and pensions granted either for Service or upon favour, some during Life, some during the parties' good behaviour, or during the prince's pleasure, paiable out of the Revenues and not out of the treasure	2835	vj	ij
To the Officers of the Countie of Wexford	67	0	0
To divers Officers attending the State	76	0	3
Expens	283	9	8
The Sume of all Issues and Disbursments	6322	5	0

The particulars of these reckonings, and of the disbursment of the rest of the Revenues may appear in a Book by itself, and also the issuing of the Treasure that cometh out of Ingl. extending everie of these late years to £120,000 in the Entertayment of the L. Dep. or Justices.

> The L: Lieutenant.
> The L: President of Mounster.
> The Knight Marshall.
> The Threasurer at Warrs.
> All the Officers of the Field and the Sergeant Maior.
> M^r of the Ordinance and his Officers.
> Minister Mr Controller and commissaries.

Campe, M^{r.}
Corporalls of the Field.
86 Capitens with their Lieutenante, Ensignes, Sergeants, Dromes and Fifes, and Trompeters, with Eight Thousand Souldiers, Horse and Foote.
Besides for Severall Wards in the Castles of

Dublin,	Knockfergus,
Catherlaghe,	Athloane,
Marreborrow,	Duncanon,
Phillipstowne,	Carlinford,
Laughlin,	Fearnes,
Trim,	Dondrome,
Dungarvan,	Castle and Abbey, besides
Castle mayne,	many Pensioners and 12
Limericke,	Alme.

Names of the Councill of Ireland.

Sr Arthure Chicester, L. Dep.
Thomas Jones, L. Chancellor.
Sr James Ley, chief Justice.
Sr Thomas Butler Knight Earle of Ormond Vi.
Earle of Clanrickard, President of Conaught.
Dod Bishop of Meath.
Sr Henrie Davies, L. Davies, L. president of Mounster.
Rich: Wingfield Knight Marshall of Ireland.
Thomas Ridgwae Knight at Warrs.
Sr Nicholas Walshe, Justice of the common pleas.
Sir Humphry Winch, chief Baron of the Exchequer.
Sr Anthony St Leger, Master of the Rolles.
Sir Oliver St John Knight, M^r of the Ordinance.

Sʳ Henrie Harrington.
Sʳ Edward Brabazon.
Sʳ Oliv. Lambert.
Sʳ Henrie Dowcra.
Sʳ William Godolphin.
Sʳ Francis Stafford.
The Bishop of Downe.

Sʳ James Fullerton.
Sʳ Rich. Morrison.
Sʳ Henrie Power.
Sʳ Gerrot Moore.
Sʳ Adam Loftus.
Sʳ Geffrey Fenton.
Sʳ Richard Cooke.

APPENDIX.

Sir Arthur Chichester's Instructions to Sir James Ley and Sir John Davys, touching the Settlement in Ulster. Sept. 1608.—See *Cal. of Irish S. P.*, an. 1608, p. 55.

CAVAN.—See p. 117, *supra*.

The Cavan is a spacious and large county, very populous, and the people hardy and warlike. The Chief of them are the O'Realyes (O'Reillys), of which Surname there are sundry Septs, most of them cross and opposite one unto another. By the division and Separation among themselves, the whole county, which heretofore made their dependancy upon the chief of the Sept by the name of O'Realye, may with the more facility and assurance be divided into parcels, and disposed to several freeholders, who, depending immediately upon the King, will not fear or obey their neighbours, unless some one or two be made so powerful as to overtop and sway down the rest; and therefore care must be in the Settlement of this country, that the greatest part of the people have their dependancy immediately from the King, and as little upon the Irish lords as may be without apparent hindrance to the plantation.

The natives of that County are not able in worth nor people to inhabit and manure the half thereof.

The books of Survey and other collections will disclose the chief pretenders to the lands in each barony, and in smaller circuits, who may be provided for as shall be directed, or as they (the commissioners) shall think fit, if it be left to their discretion.

The principal place to be cared for is the town of Cavan, which wishes to be made a corporation, and a ballibeto of land (if it may be) to be laid unto it out of the barony of Cavan. The Castle there is to be likewise reserved, and the like allotment of land to be made for the maintenance thereof.

Belturbet is likewise by situation a fit place to be strengthened by a ward or other residence of civil people.

The barony of Cavan (except Cloughouter) may be disposed in demesne and chiefry to young Mulmorie O'Relye, the grandchild of Sir John O'Relye. There are many freeholders in the barony, as the Bradies, and McCabies, and others, who will expect a good portion; but Mulmory, the head of the house, must get land out of other baronies or chief rents, as his father was slain in the Queen's service, and he is descended by the mother from the house of Ormonde.

FERMANAGH.—See p. 24, *supra*.

Fermanagh cannot be divided as the Cavan, by reason of Connor Roe Maguyre, who has a patent of the whole country passed unto him in the late Queen's time, but upon conference and advice had with him by the Deputy and Council for the settlement of his kinsman Cow Connaught (Couconaght) Maguyre, and of that country, he was content to submit himself to their order for a new division, upon which three baronies of the seven were allotted to him, the said Connor Roe, with a promise of letters for the same, which in his (Chichester's) opinion were meet to be passed to him with a clause to make a competent number of freeholders of the natives of that county, and with reservation of rent to His Majesty.

The other four baronies were intended to Cow Connaught Maguyre, and are now in the hands of his brother Bryen, but divers gentlemen inhabit thereupon, who claim a freehold in the lands they possess. It is to be considered and resolved by the Lords whether any part thereof shall be bestowed upon the pretenders to the freehold, or on the brethren and Sept of Cow Connaught, and, namely, on Tyrone's grandchild, son to Hugh Maguyre, slain in Munster. Bryen is a proper and active young man, and has a younger brother. These will be stirring and keep out if they be not cared for or restrained, and so will the freeholders with them, and the child when he comes to be a man. Therefore, either they must be provided for and settled, or the new plantation must be made strong and powerful to keep them in awe and subjection, which will require great charge and foresight; and to remove them with their followers and tenants to other countries will be found somewhat difficult.

Henry and Con O'Neale, sons to Shane O'Neale, are now seated in this county upon lands which they took from Cow Connaught Maguyre, to which certain freeholders pretend title. If the King think them worth the cherishing, they must be seated in something in this county or Armagh, or else removed clear out of Ulster; and if his Majesty could assume or purchase a Signory in Munster, it were good sending them thither; they are civil and discreet men, especially Harry, and have each of them 4s. a-day pension from His Majesty.

In this county there is neither town nor civil habitation. Iniskellin is the fittest place, in his opinion, for the Shire town, and to be made a corporation.

DONEGAL.—See p. 29, *supra*.

This has been so bangled by the Earl of Tyrconnell by sales, mortgages, and underhand conveyances, that he (Chichester) can make no certain demonstration thereof, only this is certain, Enishowen is come unto the King by O'Dogherty's attainders. Glanfyne and the greatest part of Monganagh was promised to Sir Neale O'Donnell, whereof he might have had letters patent, but he neglected to take them out, expecting greater quantities and pretending title to the whole country, which he (Chichester) thinks will hardly satisfy his ambition; but his case is such at this time that he will seem satisfied with a small portion, so he be assured of his life and liberty. Can say nothing of him until the pleasure of the King or the Lords of the Council be signified touching his arraignment or enlargement. His son is a dangerous youth, of whom, and of Caffer Oge O'Donnell, he (Chichester) has declared his opinion to them, together with the briefs and sundry examinations and voluntary confessions made against them.

Divers gentlemen claim freeholds in that county, as namely, the three Septs of the McSwynes, Bane (Banagh), Fanaght, and Doe, O'Boyle, and O'Galchare (O'Gallagher); but these men passed over their rights (if any they had) to the Earl (as it is said) which he got from them cautiously and by unworthy duties; in whose behalf his Majesty is to signify his gracious pleasure, and he (Chichester) is sure every of them has more land than they and their Septs will be able to manure and plant in any civil and good fashion these 40 years, albeit peace did continue among them; and they are for the most part unworthy of what they possess, being a people inclined to blood and trouble, but to displant them is very difficult. If His Majesty dispose the land to strangers, they must be very powerful to suppress them. Suggests that if his pleasure be to continue them in what they claim, the lands may be divided into many parts and disposed to several men of the septs, and some to strangers or some others of this nation, leaving none greater than another, unless it be in a small difference to the now chiefs of the name. If this cours displease the said chiefs, it will content many others, who will be good ties upon them if by Justice they be supported accordingly.

There are divers other places within this county fit to be reserved for the King's Service and to bestow upon civil and well chosen men, some of which are already possessed by Wards and garrisons, as namely, the Derry, Lyffor, Ballishanon, Dunegall, Castle Doe, and Culmore. . . .

COLERAINE.—See p. 28, *supra*.

This county is of small circuit, containing only three baronies, two of which are not so large as the barony of Dungannon. It has been of long time attempted for parcel of Tyrone. The chief septs that inhabit it are the O'Cahanes, and under them the O'Mullanes, Magilliganes, and M'Closkies. The Earl of Tyrone made challenge unto this country, as passed unto him by letters patents, and required Sir Donell O'Cahane, the now chief of that name, to give him £200 a year, in consideration of his challenge, but being unable to make him payment of so much, in respect of the waste and riotous expenses otherwise, he yielded one of the baronies up to the Earl in lieu of the £200, which the Earl possessed at the time of his flight; and albeit it is thought that neither Tyrone nor O'Cahane had any good and lawful estate in that country (the right being in the King by the Statute 11 Elizabeth), yet it is his duty to declare that the whole country (the castle of Annogh with a good quantity of lands thereunto annexed, and the Bishop's and Church's rights excepted) was promised to the said Sir Donell O'Cahane upon his submission in the year 1601, by the Lord Mountjoy, then Lord Deputy; and in confirmation hereof a custodiam was passed to him under the Great Seal. He is now prisoner in the Castle of Dublin.

In this county they neither hold ward nor keep men upon the King's charges. If Sir Donell O'Cahane be found unworthy of the King's favour by reason of his treasonable practices and misdemeanours, then is that country in the King's hands. The principal places to be cared for within this county are the Castles of Annogh, Lemavadie, Colerayne, and Downgeuyne (Dungiven), albeit most of them are ruinous and out of repair. If Sir Donnell O'Cahane be enlarged, or if, upon his trial, he escape the danger of the law, two parts of that country will not content him, nor, he thinks, the whole; but whatsoever becomes of him, good consideration must be had of his brother, Manus O'Cahane, Manus ut Quyvally O'Cahane, and some few others whom he (Chichester) has found honest in those last troubles, and before. . . .

TYRONE.—See p. 25, *supra*.

The great sept of this county is come to the King by the attainders of the Earl of Tyrone and his Sept. In this county they hold the forts of Mountjoy,

Omey, and the ruinous castle of Dungannon by the King's garrisons and wards; upon the division and settlement of the county, other places must be found out and strengthened for a time, as, namely, about the Clogher, where lies the country of Sir Cormac O'Neale, another in the Glynnes of Glancomkeyne, the Slute Artes (Slught Airta) country, and two or three other places. . . .

The chief Septs of this country are the O'Neales, and under them the O'Donnoles, O'Hagganes, O'Quynes, O'Delvynes (O'Devlins), O'Corres, the Clondonells, the Melans, and other septs, which are warlike people and many in number, and must be provided for or overmastered, without which they will not be ruled nor removed.

Has delivered the possession of the Newtown, with some three ballibetoes of land, to Tyrlowe and Neale M'Arte, the children of Sir Arte O'Neal, in respect of the good service they did against the traitor O'Doghertie and the relief they gave the Lyffer upon the burning of the Derry. . . . Thinks this sufficient for them, but they do not. If the King will be pleased to reserve the town of Straban, which stands within the lands now assigned to them, and give them a greater scope on the other side, he thinks it best for his Service, for divers Scottishmen will plant there and make it a pretty town, albeit it was all burnt to the ground by O'Doghertie. . . .

Downeganon (Dungannon) to be made a corporation.

ARMAGH.—See p. 19, *supra*.

The state of this county is much like that of Tyrone, and possessed by the same Septs, especially for as much of it as appertained to the Earl of Tyrone, which is the greatest part of the country. The rest belongs to the Lord Primate, and either is passed to Sir Tyrlogh and Henry O'Neale, and Sir Henry Oge O'Neale, lately slain in the service against O'Dohertie, or is Sir Oghy O'Hanlon's, who lately surrendered his interest to the King upon promise to have it repassed to him; which would have been performed before this time, if he had sought it, and would have permitted certain freeholders to take letters patent, and to hold immediately of the King as he promised. He is an old, lame man, of weake judgement, married to a sister of Tyrone's, who is as malicious and ill-affected to the King's government and country's reformation as her brother. She rules the old man. His only legitimate son was in rebellion with O'Doghertie, and is now hid and relieved by his friends in that country. The old man must be provided for as long as he lives. Hopes that after his death there may be no more O'Hanlons—he means as lord over the rest, but that that country may be disposed to the best affected of the sept and to other civil men.

The chief of this country under the Earl of Tyrone was his base brother, known by the name of Arte M'Barron, who is yet living, and claims the greatest part of the country of O'Neale, of which he is possessed. He has three sons with the Archduke, of whom two are captains. These youths, the sons of the Earl, and the children of Sir Cormock M'Barron, Sir Tyrlowe M'Henry, and Sir Henry Oge O'Neale, will kindle a new fire in those parts at some time or other, if they be not well looked to or provided for in some reasonable measure.

They are to declare to the Lords that there is a son of the Earl of Tyrone, of some seven or eight years old, and another to Caffer O'Donnell, brother to the Earl of Tyrconnell. Has committed them to the charge of two of the captains in Ulster. Should gladly receive directions to dispose of them, and in his opinion, the best course will be to send them to some remote parts of England or Scotland, to be kept from the knowledge of friends or acquaintance.

The countries known by the name of M'Cann Country and Braslowe (Bresilagh) are within this county, which are possessed principally by gentlemen, who claim the freehold thereof. They would gladly be tenants or freeholders to the King, and would pay a good rent to His Majesty.

Sir Tirlagh M'Henry wants to enlarge his possession of land of the Fues; it would be well to give him part of Toghrighie, if that will make him and his sons honest. Care to be had of Henry Oge O'Neile's children, of Con M'Tyrlowe and his brethren, who without such care are like to break out; and of Owine More O'Neale, more for his honest simplicity than for any harm he is like to do. The O'Hagans, O'Quinns, and Clandonnells were never better than tenants and followers of the Earl of Tyrone.

Many of the natives in each county claim freehold in the land they possess; and albeit their demands are not justifiable by law, yet it is hard and almost impossible to displant them.

The people must be drawn from 'creatinge,' and settle in towns and villages, and build houses like those of the Pale, and not cabins after their wonted manner.—*The L. Deputy Chichester, Cal. I. S. Papers*, 1608, p. 55.

Sir R. Jacob (Sol. Gen.) to Salisbury, April 1609 :—' The only thing that keeps them (the Ulster men) in subjection is the want of arms, for all their weapons are brought into the King's store. But they want no men, notwithstanding the late wars, the famine and the great plague that was amongst them ; for there are 5000 booked in Tyrone and Coleraine ; 4000 in Armagh ; 6000 in Tirconnell; and in other counties 3000 ; in others, 4000—so that in all that province there are at the least 20,000 men of the sword.'—*Cal. of I. S. P.*, p. 197.

KILDARE.—See *supra*, p. 46.

THE NAMES OF THE LORDS, KNIGHTS, COMMONS, AND OTHER OFFICERS IN THE COUNTY OF KILDARE ON THE 28TH OF JUNE 1608.

Names of the Lords Spiritual and Temporal.—Gerald Earl of Kildare; William Bishop of Derry.

Names of the Knights and Justices of the Peace.—R. Wingfield, G. Cowly, W. Sarsfield, G. Aylmer, R. Greame, G. Greame, J. FitzPiers FitzGerald, E. Blany, R. Digby, Knights; Allen of St. Wolstons, Sutton of Tipperary, Sarsfield of Surnings, Sarsfield of Tully, Nangle of Ballysax, Dallway of Castleton Kildrought, Lye of Rathbryde, Bartholomew Long of Dyrr, Meyres of Tullaghgrory, Rider (Archdeacon of Meath), Allen of Kilheele, Eustace of Castle Martin, Bellinge, Aylmer, FitzGerald of Laccagh, FitzGerald of Allen, Wogan of Rathcoffy, Downton, and Stokes, Esquires.

Names of the Coroners.—FitzGerrald of Osberstown, FitzGerrald of Blackhall.

Names of the Sovereigns and Provosts of the Towns.—Sheale, Sovereign of the town of Kildare; Aysh, Provost of the town of Naas; Smith, Provost of the town of Athye; Atwell Batwell, Provost of the town of Kildrought; Turlagh Doyne, Provost of the town of Rathmore; Peppard, Provost of the town of Leixlip; Dowlin, Provost of the town of Kill; Browne, Provost of the town of Woghterard.

Names of Constables.—Gilbert Sutton of Ardre, Allen of Bishoppscourt, Higgs of Cottlandstown, Sherlocke of Sherlockstowne, Eustace of Blackwood, Bath of Clane, Bellowe of Clougeswood, Eustace of Kylmorry, Dod of Connall, Myssett of Harberston, Gerrald FitzBryan of Ballysymon, Jacob of Srowlane, Segerson of Halveston, Danyell of Castle Dermott, Dowdall of Killen, Piers Brymingham of Garisker.

Names of the Jurors for the Lord King.—Barony of Sault.—Fyan of Leixlip, Gerrald Wellesley of Kildrought, Patrick Tipp of Tippston, Walsh of Moretown, Ayshe of Furnaghts.

Barony of Naas.—Eustace of Mullaghrash, Patrick Sanders of Newton o'More, Hasquin of Little Rath, Browne of Newton o'More, Sherlock of Naas, Kenna of the same, Latten of the same, Kelly of the same, and Walter Archbold of the same.

Barony of Clane.—FitzGerrald of Grages, Rochford of Newton o'Clane, FitzGerald of Ballandsox, FitzGerrald of Tymoghe, Wogan of Downings, Rochford of Clane.

Barony of Ikethy and Woghtereay.—Eustace of Clongoswood, Aylmer of Little Cappoth, Walsh of Cloncurry, Roe of Brangastowne.

APPENDIX. 253

Barony of Connally.—Wogan of Newhall, Goulding of Haubertston, FitzGerrald of Pinchers Grange, Eustace of Siggenston.

Barony of Ophaly.—FitzGerrald of Brownestowne.

Barony of Norragh and Rebon.—Walter Wellesley of Norragh, Wellesley of Blackehall, Eustace of Blackrath, Eustace of Crookestowne, Eustace of Collbinstowne.

Barony of Kilkullin.—Dougan of Tuberngan.

Barony of Killta and Moone.—FitzEdmond of Birton, Gerald FitzBrian of the same, Eustace of Moone, FitzGerrald of Bealan.

Barony of Carbry.—Brymingham of Donfort, Brymingham of Mucklane, Brymingham of Garisker, Brymingham of Grange, Brymingham of Longwood, Brymingham of Russellswood.

CARLOW.—See *supra*, p. 52.

THE COUNTY OF CATHERLOGH, THE 4TH JUNE 1608.

Lords.—Theobald Lord Viscount Butler of Tullagh; Thomas Lord Bishop of Laughlyn and Fearnes.

Knights.—Colclough, Maisterson, and Hartpoole.

Esquires.—Morgan M‹Brian, Davells, Wale, Bagnall, Eustace, Gerald M‹Mortagh, Donell Kavanagh, Harman, Hartpoole, Bryan M‹Donnogh.

Coroners.—Broune of Cloughchricke, Tomyne of Clonygagh.

Constables of the Barony of Catherlogh.—William Gorst of Carrickstowne.

Barony of Idron.—Donell O'Rian of Tomgarrough, Owen Byrne of Ballyrian.

Barony of St. Molyn.—Morris Kavanagh of Ballybracke, Donnough O'Neyle of Kiltarry.

Barony of Fort.—Rowry O'Nolan of Kilbracan, O'Nolan of Ballymoge.

Bailiffs Arrant.—Hugh Leaugh for the Barony of Catherlogh, D. Barron for the Barony of Idrone, W. Moyhill for the Barony of Fort, James M‹Teig Sergeant of Raville; Edmond Ower Sergeant, Sergeant of St. Moylyne.

Freeholders.—*Barony of Idrone.*—George Etherunton of Rahellin, Birne of Aha, Cahir M‹Teig of Knockscurr, Birne of Oldtowne, Walshe of Tomand, Dermonde Kavanaugh of Rahedin, M‹Gerrald of the Rath, Turlough Birne of Kilm‹·lapock (sic), Edmond M‹Tirlough of Kilree, Cahir M‹Donell Reough of Ballycromgan, Donell Roe M‹Dermott of Baldinge, Teig O'Rian of Balliellen, Donough Kavanaugh of Kilconyney, Dermott Kavanaugh of Ballifenyne, David M‹Mortagh of Clowater, Phoores (sic) M‹Cavell of Kilgreany, Donough M‹Garrott of Bordduffe, Garrat M‹Morris of Kilgreaney, James M‹Richard

Ballough of the Bunes, Donough MᶜMorrough of Bally William Roe, Fagon of Dunlockney, Birne of Seskinrem, MᶜGarratt of Balliteige, Geere of Kilamonine, Carron of Rathduffe, MᶜDonnough of Knockroe, Mortagh Kavanaugh of Kilkallatin, Thomyne of Ballydarmyne, Donell Fyn of Boreduffe, Walter Butler of Balliteigbeaugh, Patrick Morphue of Bollintollin.

Barony of Catherlogh.—Wale of Pollardstowne, Cooke of Staplestowne, Ferdonough Gormagan of Gruangfort, Birne of Ballilowe, Dermott MᶜShane of Balliterney, Birne of Ratroge, Birne of Moyhill, Birne of Teurelan, Arspoll of Freerstowne, Everson of Clough.

Barony of Fort.—Barry of Rarush, Morrough Birne of Straugh, Teige Nolan of Ballicallie, Donogh Nolan of Ballihemoge, Mortagh MᶜGarrott of Myssell, Donell MᶜHugh of Shangarry, Donell Nolan of Kilayne, Donnough Morrough of Carricknestayne, Patrick MᶜShane of Ballitample, Donnough Roe of Kilbreede, Cooke of Kilcoole.

Barony of Ravill.—Butler of Clomore, Leyn of Shroughbooe, Leyn of Lesenevae, Grace of Browalstowne, Mortagh Birne of Bennecerry, Birne of Balliduffe, Dermott Owen of Killelongart, Teige O'Gormagan of Ardriston, David MᶜSimon of Culliebege.

Barony of St. Moylyne.—Shane MᶜDermott of Ballihemoge, MᶜSheron of Ballybege, MᶜDermod of Lefallygan, Edmond Collatan of Ballicranigambege, Piers Collatan of Tennecarricke, Dermond MᶜDonell of Ballycramgain castlayn.

KILKENNY.—See *supra*, p. 67.

THE COUNTY OF KILKENNY, 9TH JULY 1608.

Names of the Lords as well Spiritual as Temporal.—Thomas Earl of Ormond and Ossory, Richard Lord Viscount Mount Garrett, Theobald Lord Viscount Tullagh; John Bishop of Ossory.

Names of Knights and Justices of the Peace.—Sovereigns for the Town of Kilkenny.—Richard Shee, Knt.; Jacob Butler, Esq.; Richard Butler, Knt.; Robert Roth, Esq.; Mannering, Esq.; Richard Deane, Deacon of Kilkenny; Helias Shee, Esq.; Gerald Grace, Patrick Archer, Walter Walsh, Nicholas Cleere, Thomas Denn, Robert Grace, David Serment, Piers Butler, Walter Archer, Henry Shee, John Butler Rector of Callan, Thomas Stronge, Esquires.

Names of the Coroners.—FitzGerrald of Gurtin, Waton of Growe, Shortall of Ratharding, Walsh of Kilkregan.

Names of the Constables of the Barony of Gawran.—Redmond Bleachfield of Rathgarvan, Purcell of Cloghla.

APPENDIX. 255

Constables of the Baronies of Igroin, Ida, and Iberton.—FitzGerrald of Gurtin, Aylward of Aylwardstown.

Constables of the Barony of Iverke.—Walsh of Kilkregan, Daton of Kilmodally.

Constables of the Barony of Kells.—Walsh of Doumogan, Howlinge of Kilry.

Constables of the Barony of Claragh.—John de Rochford of Kilary, George St. Leger of Woncestowne.

Constables of the Barony of Knocktofer.—Power of Knocktofer, Faing of Croambeg.

Constables of the Barony of Shillekyr.—St. Leger of Tulleghabroeg, FitzGerrold of Barntchurch; Archdecon, constable of Galmoy.

Constables of Fasagh de Myn and Odoghe.—Robnett Purcell of Foulksrath, William O'Brena of Ballyhomyn.

Barony of Gawran.—Blanchfield of Blanchveldstoune, Purcell of Ballyfoell, Butler of Old Aboy, Butler of Nogha, Tobyn of Lyrath, St. Leger of Clogha, Blanchveld of Milton, O'Ryan of Ullard, Power of Powerswood, Fanninge of Bally McCloghny, Tirlagh O'Rian of Barne Vedan, Piers McHenry Roe O'Rian of Thomnebaghy, O'Rian of Ballymorough, Milerus Payen of Ballynebally, Shortall of Leghrath, Shortall of Brownesborne.

Igroin, Ida, and Ibercon.—Gall of Gallstowne, Butler of Anaghes, Freny of Ballyraddy, Forstall of Forstalltowne, Daton of the same, Fortstall of Killred, Walsh of Ballycre, Forstall of Carrignegany, Walsh of Carrignory, Grace of Kilrmdony.

Barony of Overke.—Grant of Corlod, Grant of Portneholl, Daton of Grangowin, Daton of Bally McCrony, Walsh of Listroley.

Barony of Kerlis.—Butler of Rossnarowe, Butler of Rogerstowne, Howling of Damynbeg, Tobyn of Killollegha, Tobyn of Rosscommon.

Barony of Shillecher.—FitzGerrald of Barntchurch, Comerford of Ballybir, Forstall of Kilferagh, Comerford of Earlstowne, Mothell of the same, Raged of Waleslogh.

Barony of Knocktofer.—Walsh of Corbally, Purcell of Kilkerell, Walsh of Ballaghbregan, Walshe of Knockmoella, Walshe of Ballyncrowly, Grace of Aghviller.

Barony of Cranagh.—Shortall of Ballylorka, Drylin of Kilberagha, O'Roerk of Boresheis, Shortall of Purcellstiers, Grace of Cowle Ishell, Smith of Clastnoe, Butler of Woucestowne.

Barony of Fasagh, Denny, and Idogh.—O'Brena of Rathcally, Purcell of

256   STATE OF IRELAND ANNO 1598.

Esker, Purcell of Lysmayne, O'Brena of Uskertye, Farr McDonnogh of Croghtoncle, Duffe of Crint.

WEXFORD.—See *supra*, p. 57.

THE GRAND PANELL OF THE COUNTY OF WEXFORD, 25TH JULY 1608.

Justices of the Peace.—Thomas Lord Bishop of Fearnes and Leighline, Sir T. Colcloigh, Sir Dudly Loftus, Sir R. Mastersonne, Sir L. Esmond, Sir W. Sinot, Knights; Butler of Bellabow, Esq.; Devroux of Ballinagir, Morgan Kavanagh, Nicholas Kennay, Escheator; Donull Kavannagh, Brown of Malranckan, Esq.; Arthur Kavannaigh, Esq.; Murcus FitzHarvie, FitzHarvie, Dermott Kavannaigh, John Broune, Sovereign of Wex; Duffe of Cosse, Dode, Furlonge, Witty of Balleteg, Itchinghane, Dormer, Dale, Mastersonne, Furlonge, Alene, Devroux of Dipper, W. Talbot, R. Talbot, Esquires.

His Majesty's Coroners.—Hammond Stafford of Balleconnor, Rowsetor of Brigbargye, Hugh Ballaigh McDonaigh Oge of Killconky, Roche of Brianstoun, Sinot of the Rahen.

The Constables of the Barony of Forte.—Wadinge of Balleroghy, Elyot of Rathshillane.

Constables of Baigre.—Witty of Nimestoune, Devroux of Newcastle.

Barony of Shilbirne.—Redmond of the Hall, FitzHarvie of Witchurch.

Barony of Bantry.—Hoar of Bellaborow, Sutone and Scurlok.

The Portreves of Towns.—Furlonge, Portrief of Banno; Morgan McRory, Portreve of Taman; Ketinge, Portreve of Federt; Hea, Portreve of Clomem.

The Gentlemen of Fotherde.—Chevers of Killiane, gent.; R. Esmond of Johnstone, Rochford of Tugomane, Manton Synot of Ballebrennan, Robert Synot of Balehorron, Cod of Castletowne, Codd of Baleenfane, Codd of Cloess, John Stafford of Fursetime, Walshe of Polranctan, Hane of the Hill, Hane of Sladde, Walshe of the Buss, Turner of Belleushen, Synott of Ballegerce, Synot of Rathdownny, Devroux of Maglas, Witty of Balmacussen, Butler of Butlerstowne, Ketinge of Balemakeyan, Sigen of Sigenstoune, Hare of Redestoune, Frinss of Balletorie, Symotte of the Growgane, Hare of Harestoune, Esmond of Rathlonnane, FitzNicholl of Balecowanne, Rochford of Petettestoune, Hoar of Ionoclestoune, Ketinge of Balebeg, Wadinge of Asoalye, Synot of Gracekyrock, Derraigh O'Drycane of Remotestoune, White of Crommer, Synot of Ballohell, Synot of the Berlagh, Codd of Balmakeyrie, Stafford of the Gragene, Gentlemen.

The Gentlemen of the Barony of Bargie.—FitzHarvie of Kilkevan, FitzNicholl of Balehartie, Ketinge of Baldenestoune, Hammond Chevers of Balesestene,

Rowsetor of Tomger, Ketinge of Rosselletoune, Nevell of Tallokenaye, Barrie of Barriestoune, Devroux of the Woodgrage, Devrox of Caregeschurche, Broune of Holdhall, Broune of Rathronarie, Broune of Gragrobben, Tibald Roche of Killmannane, Wittie of Gentestounc, Prendergast of Sanshill, Hare of the Blackhall, Devroux of Coskayll.

The Gentlemen of the Barony of Shilmalyee.—Synnot of Fawlestoune, Synnot of Rosgarlande, Hoar of Ballesweillan, Rowsetor of Slevey, Hare of Cronwall, Hoar of the Poill, Meyler of the Dirr, Hoar of Muchwodd, Furlonge of Cargmannan, Furlonge of the Blackhall.

Barony of Bantrye.—Butler of Clonkeraigh, Furlonge of Daviestoun, Scurloh of the Balgan, Severaigh O'Doyrane of the Chaple, Dowloun M{c}Moigh of Ballegobbane, Dermot Ower M{c}Moigh of the same, Edmond M{c}Arte of Bolebann, Arte M{c}Bren of Tample Wodekann, Teg M{c}Morrishe Ley of Killovany, Caier M{c}Edmond of Rathepodenboy.

The Barony of Shilbirne.—Ketinge of Dungavestown, Luffane of the Sladd, Witye of Dongalpe, Sutone of the Prisugard, Prendergast of Balleforanch, Sutone of the Old Courte, Sutone of Balesope, Gent.; Ketinge of Galleystone.

The High Constables of the Barony of Ballaighene.—Synot FitzJames of Ballevelle, Connell M{c}Donnell Evallo of . . .

The Gentlemen of the same Barony.—Synot of the Owlorte, Donnill M{c}Arte of Tobberlomunaugh, Phelan M{c}Mahon of Balleshemes, Teg M{c}Mawen of Balerowane, Owen M{c}Arte of Tintubber, Synott of Babberdargh, Morishe Lacy of Tomlaine, Teg M{c}Miertargh of Lougherbege, James M{c}Brann of Balevek, Synott of Ballensar, Synot of Cowledoynge, Donull Dayrane of Killensu, Lisurgh M{c}Teg of Cloane, Cair M{c}Moriertaigh of the same, Cormack M{c}Donnell of Olortleighe, Edmond M{c}Arte of Balemute, O'Doyrane of the Dirr, Fardairaigh M{c}Dermott of Ballena, Sawle O'Doyrane of Tentober, Mortaigh O'Doiran of Clondae, Shane O'Doyrane of the same, Caier O'Doyrane of Blemony, Synot of Garrevadden, Dermott O'Doyran of the Davanargh, Donull O'Doyran of the same, Donull M{c}Donnaigh Tusker of Dondrom, Oyn M{c}Enn of Rahendarg, Gerald M{c}Innes of the same, Edmond Reaigh of Claranclariss, Dermott Reaigh of Ballemony Terrelaigh M{c}Oyn of the Courte, Synot of Balemoigh, Eff M{c}Phelim Art of Kilmannaigh, Oron M{c}Bran of Ballegresaigh, Shane O'Doyrane of Rainduf, Moraigh M{c}Adin of Baletrasine, Eff M{c}Urt Bry of Monclough, Teg Reagh of the same, Moraigh Reagh of Cloanatty, William M{c}Teg of Ballegowan, Phelim M{c}Donull of Garreden, Donnaigh M{c}Moriertargh of Balegore, Gerald M{c}Moraigh of Balevolo, Terrelaigh M{c}Moriertagh of the same, Synot of Balemore, Moriertaigh Duf McMoraigh of Balera, Cair McDonaigh of Banickard, Caier McRosse of Ballenellok, Phelim McYnnes of Ballevodick, Brenn McYnnes of the same, Synot of Balenosky, Geer of Garrenusky, Griffin McMoriertaigh of Teighm, Coiloigh McMoriertaigh of Ballevalle, Ef McDurlaigh of Ballegrand, Peppard of Glaskarge, Patrick McPhelin of Monalstrum, Waffer of Balemony, Caier McEf of Corranvredy, William McEdmond of Remremond, Caier Row of the Rahine, Edmond McCarr of Tomduff, Thomas Boy of Ballegerall, James McOyn of Rathnetesky, Dermot Boy of Moumecloigh, David Mor Phelin of Ascongeray, Redmond McPhelin of Balemees, Thomas McShane of Moymmer, Mortie Nur of Ballencurre, Thomas Finne of Ballewallken, Terrelaigh McPhelin of Balclosk, Broy of Killtynnen, Morraigh Mor of Kilbride, Shane Banne of Clowrann, Teg McDary of the Slaune, Brassell O'Bolger of Ballevalter, Dermot O'Bolger of the same, Donagh McGerott of Ballerah, Edmond McMoraighe of Balleheyne, Dermot McYllrem of Baleguffindowe.

The High Constables of the Barony of Gwery.—John Brassell of Balecargin, Teg McGerote Gill Patrick McThoms of Balchedin.

The Gentlemen of the Barony of Gwery.—Hugh Bellaigh McDermot of Balle, Edmond Duf McDermot of Lunnaigh, Donnaigh Oge McDermot of Balleolouagh, Terrelaigh McCreen of Balebane, Colloigh McKeen of Callonok, Teg Bellaigh McDonnaigh of the Cloane, Art McDonnell Ban of the Balekestan, Gillpatrick McDonill of Killpatrick, McDonill of Cowbrodd, Oyn McDonill Bane of Killpatrick, Gillpatrick Oge McLisaigh of Mongaroe, Walsh of Clonranye, Donill Reaigh, McPhelim of Killmehell, Donnaigh McGerrot of the same, Moraigh McBrene of Rathperise, Gerot McDonill Owr of Ballegolen, Art McDonnaigh Oge of Ballenrana, Donill McDonnaigh of . . . Fairdarraigh McBrane of Ballekargy, Moraigh Duff of Balleege, Braune McYnnes of Corratobbann, Gerot McDonull of Kildowdy, Gerot McOyn of the same, Edmond McCaier of the Cullentraigh, Gerot McCaier of Balle Arte, Lisaigh Duff McYnnes of Bellegarie, Phelin McMoriertaigh Bwy of Killnehell, Terrelaigh Buie McKenee of Ballemont, Teg McMiertagh of Rosmaynock, Dyn McMousseoge of Ballerayne, Edmond McBrene Bwy of Ballecarall, Morishe McDonull of Illanstrassock, Art Owr McMoroighe Oge of the Creagh Baleraen, Gerot McMoroighe Oge of the Creegh, Terrelaigh McMoroighe Oge of the same, Eff McThomas Oge of Ballentee, Gerald McEdmond of Coaleshill, Dermot Owr McShemmone of the Gesr, Edmund McMoriertaigh of Ballenrath, Moraigh McCormicke of Tomcoyle.

The High Constables of the Barony of Starrowalshe.—Synot of Ballevall, Moriertaigh McDonull of Ballenrayse.

APPENDIX. 259

The Gentlemen of the Barony of Starrowalshe.—Dowlen McBrenn of Tiscorre, Owen Donull of Tomm Dire, Richard McDonull of Garesinotte, Arte McCaier of Babbarne, Arte McDonull Owr of Killcowlen, Bren McDonill Owr of Marshallston, Gillpatrick McMalaghlyn of Ballebockran, Moraigh McArtmore of Straghmor, William McDonill Owr of Kowllungiste, Morishe McDonill Owr of Marshalstown, Farganman McMoriertaigh of Asconghin, Donnaigh Ballaigh of Monganestone, Donnell McEf of Davestoune, Edmond McGerot of Baledigane, Shane Duff McShemes of Ballelosch, Shane Reaigh of Balledegane, Dorlough McKowllse of Cromok, Teg McOyn Mor of the same, Art McMoriertaigh of Clonyardom, Gerotte McYnnes of Manglisse, Donull McBrenne of Balleouddane, Dermot Reaigh of Ballecullaigh, Dermot McPhersone of Mayne, Phersone, Robert McBreene of Rosseharde, Nicholas McEdmond of the same.

Copia Vera.

Per Walter Talbot, Clerke of the Crown and Peace in the County of Wexford.

Endorsed by Carew—Justices of the Peace, Coroners, Constables, Jurymen, &c., within the Counties of Kildare, Catherlough, Kilkenny, and Wexford, in anno 1608.—Abridged from *Car. Cal.*, an. 1608, pp. 23-35.

WICKLOW.—See *supra*, p. 40.

'Thence (from Wexford) we came to Wicklow, where there appeared such a multitude of the natives of that country, that it seemed strange that so many souls should be nourished in these wild and barren mountains.'—*Sir J. Davis, in Car. Cal.*, an. 1606, p. 16.

PRESENT REPRESENTATIVES OF THE FAMILIES OF 1598.

Families of 16th century.   *Representatives in the 19th century.*

LOUTH.—See p. 4.

Plunket, 4th Baron of Louth.
Sir J. Bellew of Willystown, M.P. for Louth in 1637.
Gernon of Killencowle d. in 1613; from his brother, Richard Gernon of Gernonstown, descends
Sir Garret Moore of Mellefont, whose father settled in Ireland.
Sir W. Taaffe, who distinguished himself in fighting against O'Neill.
Peter Taaffe of Pepparstown.

The 13th Baron of Louth.
Lord Bellew of Barmeath, Louth; Sir C. Grattan Bellew, Mount Bellew, Galway.
Gernon of Hammondstown, Louth, and Athcarne Castle, Meath.
The Marquess of Drogheda, Moore Abbey, Kildare.
The 10th Viscount Taaffe of the Castle of Elixhaw, Bohemia.
Taaffe of Smarmor Castle, Louth.

DOWN.—See p. 6.

Russell of Quoniamstown and Ballystrew, m. Miss Fleming of Slane; he d. in 1605.
Patrick Savage, 'Lord of Little Ards,' d. in 1603. From his brother descend
Sir E. Chichester, brother of Sir Arthur, who was Lord Deputy in 1604.
Sir Moses Hill came in 1573; was Governor of Olderfleet Castle.
Captain Needham, a settler.
Pottinger, a settler.
Ward, a settler in 1570.

Count Russell of Killough; Dr. Russell, President of Maynooth.—*Ulster J. of Arch.*
Savage (now named Nugent) of Portaferry; and Savage of Ballymadun.
The Marquess of Donegal; and Lord Templemore.
The Marquess of Downshire; and Viscount Dungannon.
Earl of Kilmorey, Morne Park, Down.
Sir H. Pottinger of Mount Pottinger.
Viscount Bangor, Castle Warde, Down.

ANTRIM.—See p. 13.

Brian Mac Felim O'Neill, Chief of Clannaboy, and Senior of the Kinel-Owen; m. 1° a dau. of Magennis, 2° a dau. of Brian Carrach O'Neill. From his son, Shane Mc Brian of Edenduffcarrick, now Shane's Castle, who d. in 1619, descends

O'Neill of Ballymoney, Co. Down, a farmer, who, since the death of Viscount O'Neill, is head of the Kinel Owen. The present Lord O'Neill of Shane's Castle is of the family of Chichester. — *O'Donovan's Four Masters*, p. 1678.

APPENDIX. 261

Families of 16th century.

Hugh Oge O'Neill of Shanescastle joined Tyrone; his son Brian, Lord of the Feeva, is ancestor of O'Neill of Mullaghgane in the Feevagh.

Sorley Boy McDonnell m. a dau. of O'Neill 1st Earl of Tyrone, and had five sons; his eldest son was Sir James Lord of the Route and Glynnes. His second son was Sir Randal 1st Earl of Antrim.—*O'Donovan's Four Masters,* p. 1896.

Grogan or Geoghegan of Antrim. His son settled in Wexford.

Cahal O'Hara of the Route, owner of Loghgiele, Legan-lic and Crebilly.

Shane Dhu McNaughtone came to Ireland in 1580 as Secretary to McDonnell.

Dalwaye, who came in 1573, and was Mayor of Carrigfergus in 1592. His nephew is ancestor of

J. Dobbs came to Ireland with Sir H. Docura in 1596.

Captain Upton came in 1598.

Representatives in the 19th century.

C. H. O'Neill (Clannaboy) Blessington Street, Barrister-at-law.

J. F. O'Neill Lentaigne, of Tallaght, Co. Dublin, maternally.

From Sir James descended Sir Randal McDonnell, Colonel of the Irish Brigade, who d. in 1740, when the property fell to his brother John. From the 1st Earl of Antrim descend (maternally) the Earl of Antrim, and Armstrong-McDonnell of New Hall, Clare, and the Marquess of Londonderry.

Grogan Morgan of Johnstown Castle, Wexford, represented by Lord Muskerry, and the daughters of the Earl of Granard.

O'Hara of Cleggan.

Sir E. Macnachten, Bart., Dunderrane, Antrim.

Dalway of Bella Hill, Carrigfergus.

Dobbs of Castle Dobbs.

Viscount Templeton, Castle Upton, Antrim.

ARMAGH.—See p. 19.

Donnell Mac Canna, Chief of Clanbrassil.

O'Neill of the Fews.

Sir W. Caulfield, brother of the famous Sir Toby Caulfield, a settler.

Dawson, a settler *temp.* Eliz.

Vesey came *temp.* Eliz.; his son became Archdeacon of Armagh.

The late Major Mac Cann of Louth was his representative.—*O'Donovan's Notes to Tribes of Ireland.*

The Right Hon. R. More O'Ferrall of Balyna, Kildare (maternally).—*MS. Pedigree of O'Moore, by the last O'Moore.*

Earl of Charlemont, Castle Caulfield, Armagh.

Lord Cremorne of Dartrey, Monaghan.

Viscount De Vesci, Abbeyleix, Queen's Co.

MONAGHAN.—See p. 23.

Families of 16th century.
Colonel Sir E. Blayney came in 1598.

Representatives in the 19th century.
Lord Blayney, Blaney Castle, Monaghan.

FERMANAGH.—See p. 24.

Hugh Maguire, the famous general of O'Neill's cavalry, and Chief of Fermanagh, got two bullets in his breast in 1599 from Sir Warham St. Leger, 'whom he strake into the brain.' Hugh's brother, Cuconnacht, d. in 1608, leaving a son Brian, who was restored to a part of his property called Tempodessel, now Tempo.

Hugh Maguire, who mortgaged Tempo; his eldest son, Constantine, was murdered in 1834, leaving a son. His second son, Brian, a brave officer and famous fire-eater, left several sons, who are sailors in coal vessels sailing between Dublin and Wales.—*O'Donovan's Annals*, p. 2366.

Archdall, a settler *temp*. Eliz.

Archdall of Castle Archdall, Fermanagh.

Sir Basil Brooke, Elizabethan officer.

Sir V. A. Brooke of Cole-Brook, Bart., Fermanagh.

Barton came with Essex.

Barton of Clonelly, Co. Fermanagh; B. of Grove, and B. of Rochestown, Tipperary; B. of Straffan, Kildare.

TYRONE.—See p. 25.
None.

COLERAINE OR DERRY.—See p. 28.

O'Kane of Dungiven.

O'Kane, gardener to Mr. Bruce of Donnhiel, Londonderry.—*O'Donovan's Annals*, p. 1829.

Donal O'Cahan, Chieftain in 1598.
O'Carolan of Culkeragh Castle.

Kyan of Ballymurtagh, Co. Wicklow.
Carolan of Dublin.—*Cronelly*.

DONEGAL.—See p. 29.

Nial Garbh O'Donnell Baron of Lifford, who was proclaimed O'Donnell *circ.* 1602; imprisoned in the Tower from 1608 to 1628, where he died.

O'Donnell of Ross, in Mayo, 'The O'Donnell,' an officer in the 88th Regiment; and Sir R. O'Donnell, Bart., Newport.

Hugh Buidhe, next brother of Nial Garbh; one of his descendants was a Field Marshal of Austria, who commanded at the battle of Torgau.

O'Donnell of Larkfield, Co. Leitrim.

APPENDIX. 263

Families of 16th century.

Con Oge O'Donnell, another and younger brother of Nial Garbh, was slain in 1601 by Hugh Roe O'Donnell's soldiers, who were besieging the castle of Donegal, which was defended by Niall Garbh.

John, brother of Sir Cahir O'Docherty, Chief of Inishowen.

Captain Paul Gore, a settler.

McClintock, a settler *temp.* Eliz.

Wray of Carnegilla, a settler *temp.* Eliz. (?).

Representatives in the 19th century.

O'Donnell of Castlebar. The Duke of Tetuan, in Spain. Graf O'Donell von Tyrconell.—*O'Donovan's Appendix to Four Masters*, pp. 2378 to 2420.

Lieutenant-General Sir R. Doherty, son of Doherty of Coolmoyne, Tipperary.

Sir St. George Gore, Bart., of Manor Gore, Donegal.

McClintock of Drumcar, Louth.

Wray of Oak Park, Donegal.

DUBLIN.—See p. 37.

The 21st Baron of Howth d. in 1606.
Archbold of Dublin or Naas.
Bellew of Weston. Compare note ᵉ at p. 39.
Blacknie of Rickenhore.

Luttrell, of Luttrelstown, whose male line ended in the 3rd Earl of Carhampton.
Alderman Alexander Palles of Dublin, whose descendants in Dublin and Cavan were attainted in 1641. He d. in 1603.

Sir Christopher Plunket of Dunsoghly.

Sarsfield of Lucan.
Walter Segrave of Cabra, Lord Mayor in 1588; d. in 1621. His son John was m. to a dau. of Alderman Fagan about the year 1598.
Sir R. Talbot of Malahide.
J. Talbot of Templeoge.

J. Ussher, Mayor of Dublin in 1561; d. in 1600, leaving a son, Sir William of Donnybrook.

The Earl of Howth (the 30th Baron).
Archbold of Davidstown, Kildare.
Stronge-Hussey of Westown, Dublin (maternally).
Blackney of Philipstown, late of Ballyellen.
Luttrell Saunderson of Northbrook House, Hants; and Sir S. H. Stuart of Hartley Mauduit, Hants.
Palles of Mount Palles, Co. Cavan, father of Chief Baron Palles.

Dunne of Brittas and Dunsoghly (maternally).
Colthurst Vesey of Lucan (maternally).
O'Neill Segrave of Cabra, Dublin, and Kiltimon, Wicklow.

Lord Talbot de Malahide.
Talbot of Mount Talbot, Roscommon. and Talbot-Crosbie of Ardfert, Kerry.
Ussher of Eastwell House, Galway.

264   STATE OF IRELAND ANNO 1598.

Families of 16th century.	*Representatives in the 19th century.*
Dr. Loftus, Protestant Archbishop of Dublin, came to Ireland *circ.* 1562, and d. in 1605. He had 20 children.	Loftus of Ballycummin, Co. Dublin, descends from the Primate's son, Sir Thomas; and the Marquess of Ely (maternally) from his son, Sir Dudley of Rathfarnham.
Daniel Molyneux, Ulster-King-of-Arms in 1586, whose father came to Ireland in 1576; he m. a dau. of Sir Wm. Ussher.	Sir Capel Molyneux, Bart., Castle Dillon, Armagh.—*Burke's Peerage.*
Simon Purdon of Tallaght.	Purdon of Tinerana, Clare; Purdon of Lisnabin, Westmeath.
J. Rider, Dean of St. Patrick's, and afterwards Protestant Bishop of Killaloe.	De Rythre of Williamstown, Kildare.

WICKLOW.—See p. 40.

Byrne of Ballintlea m. a dau. of Byrne of Ballycurbeg.	Lord de Tabley; Miss Byrne of Cabinteely; Mr. O'Byrne, author of *The Naval Biography.*
A son or grandson of J. Byrne of Ballinacor settled at Killany, in Louth, *circ.* 1600.	Byrne of Lisnawilly, Louth; Byrne of Allardstown.
O'Toole.	O'Toole of Buxton, Co. Wexford.
J. Rochford of Aghery, father of Colonel Prime-Iron Rochford, who was executed in 1652.	Rochford of Cloughgrenane, Carlow.
Sir E. Brabazon, M.P. for Wicklow in 1585; became Baron Brabazon in 1616; d. in 1625.	The Earl of Meath, Kilruddery, Wicklow; Brabazon of Mornington; Brabazon of Rath House.
Sir E. Wingfield, a distinguished Elizabethan officer.	Viscount Powerscourt, of Powerscourt, Wicklow.

KILDARE.—See p. 44.

Thomas FitzGerald, brother of the 14th Earl of Kildare, whose monument is in the church of Walton-upon-Thames.—*Archdall.*	The 4th Duke of Leinster, of Carton, Kildare (who is 23rd Earl of Kildare); Lord de Ros of Strangford, County Down.
Aylmer of Lyons.	Aylmer of Derry House, Tipperary; Aylmer of Painstown, Kildare.
Sir Gerald Aylmer of Donadea, son of George A. of Cloncurrie, and grandson of Richard A. of Lyons, was a Baronet in 1621.	Sir G. Aylmer, Bart., of Donadea Castle, Kildare; Aylmer of Walworth Castle, near Darlington; and (perhaps) Aylmer of Courtown, Kildare.

APPENDIX. 265

Families of 16th century.
Sir H. Cowley of Castle Carberry, grandson of Walter Cowley, Solicitor-General of Ireland in 1537.
W^m· Eustace, brother of the 3rd Viscount Baltinglass, who rebelled in 1583; m. Miss Ashe of Great Fornaughts, Kildare.
Lattin of Morristown-Lattin.

Whyte of Leixlip d. in 1599, leaving a son aged 16.
Wolfe of Forenaghts.
Burrowes m. a dau. of Sir A. Savage of Rheban, and 2^{ly}, in 1585, a Miss Eustace of Gilltown.
Dr. Meredith, Protestant Bishop of Kildare in 1589.

R. Weldon, came *temp.* Eliz.; his son Walter was of St. John's Bower, Kildare.

Representatives in the 19th century.
The Earl of Mornington, of Dangan Castle, Meath; the Duke of Wellington; Lord Cowley.
Eustace of Robertstown, Kildare, who claims the title; Eustace of Corbally, Queen's Co.

Mansfield of Morristown-Lattin; Lattin Thunder of The Lodge, Westmeath, both maternally.
Whyte of Loughbrickland, Down, Captain of H.M.S. the Warrior.
Wolfe of Bishop's Land, Kildare.
Sir E. Burrowes, Bart., of Gilltown, Kildare.

Sir E. Meredith, Bart., Madaleen, Kilkenny; Sir H. Meredith, Bart., of Carlandstown, Meath.
Sir A. Weldon, Bart., Rahenderry, Kildare.

CARLOW.—See p. 50.

Butler of Cloughgrenan, who became a Baronet in 1628.
Doyle of Clonmoney (?).
Morgan Kavanagh of Borris, who d. in 1636.
Kavanagh of Ballyleigh.

Drought of Co. Carlow, *circ.* 1600; they seem to have been in Ireland since the 13th century.

Sir E. Butler, Bart., of Garryhundon, Carlow.
Sir F. H. Doyle, Bart.
McMorough Kavanagh of Borris House, Carlow.
Kavanagh of Bauck, near St. Mallins, Carlow.—*O'Donovan's Four Masters*, 1839, note.
Drought of Lettybrook, King's Co.

WEXFORD.—See p. 57.

Cheevers of Ballyhaly.
Devereux of Ballybarna in 1598, descended from Devereux of Balmagir.
Sir L. Esmonde of Johnstown commanded in 1601 a troop of 150 horse and foot; he became Lord Limerick in 1622.

Cheevers of Killyan, Galway.
Devereux of Ballyrankin House, Wexford.
Sir J. Esmonde, Bart., of Ballynastra, Wexford.—*Sir B. Burke;* but see above, *circ.* p. 255.

2 L

STATE OF IRELAND ANNO 1598.

Families of 16th century.	Representatives in the 19th century.
N. Forde of Coolgreany d. in 1605.	Forde of Seaforde, Down.
Hore of Pole Hore.	Hore of Pole Hore.
Hore of Harperstown m. in 1607 a dau. of Keating of Kilcoan.	Hore of Harperstown, Wexford.
Kenny of Kenny's Hall, Royal Commissioner, Escheator and Feodary General in 1596; he died in 1621.	Kenny of Kilclogher, and Kenny of Correndoo, in Galway; Kenny of Ballyforan, Roscommon.
Lambert of Ballyhire, who d. in 1631.	Lambert of Caruagh, Wexford.
A. Peppard of Glascarrig, grandson of Patrick Peppard of Louth.	Peppard of Cappagh House, Limerick.
Rossiter and Devereux, 'ancient houses, whose heiress, Letitia Little,' m. the ancestor of	Sir W. Sarsfield-Rositer-Cockburn, Bart., of Cockburn, Berwickshire.
Stephen Synnot, son of Synnot of Ballytramon.	Synnot of Ballymoyer, Armagh.
Talbot, Clerk of the Crown for Wexford, m. a dau. of Bolane of Talbotstown, Wexford; and his son m. a dau. of Sir W. Synnot of Ballyfarnage.	Talbot of Castle Talbot, Co. Wexford.
Bryan Tenche of Mullinderry.	Tenche of Ballyhaly House, Wexford.
Captain Paul Gore settled *temp.* Eliz.	The Earl of Arran, Saunderscourt, Wexford; Sir G. Gore-Booth, Bart., of Lissadill, Sligo; Gore of Woodford, Leitrim.
Rev. T. Ram came in 1599; he was Bishop of Ferns in 1605.	Ram of Ramsfort, Wexford.
Swan came with Essex in 1599.	Swan of Baldwinstown, Wexford.

KILKENNY.—See p. 67.

The 2d Viscount Mountgarret.	The 14th Viscount Mountgarret.
Richard Baron, *alias* FitzGerald, the Baron of Burnchurch.	Sir Henry P. T. Baron, Bart., Baron Court; Baron of Carrig Baron.
Bryan of Bawnmore.	Bryan of Jenkinstown, Kilkenny.
E. Butler, 1st Lord Galmoy, son of Butler of Duiske Abbey.	Garret Butler of Garrendenny, Queen's Co., who claims the title.
Gerald Grace (*Marcach* or the Horseman) d. in 1618; his son Oliver (*Sciavach* or the Handsome) d. in 1626; his grandson lost 17,000 acres of land under Cromwell.	Sir W. Grace, Bart., of Grace Castle, Kilkenny; Grace of Mantua, Roscommon.

APPENDIX.

Families of 16th century.	*Representatives in the 19th century.*
Purcell of Rathetam.	Purcell of the Little Island, Waterford, who bears the name of Purcell-FitzGerald, and is seated at Boulge Hall, Suffolk.
Sir R. Shee of Upper Court and Cloran d. in 1608.	From his son Lucas descends Shee of Cloran; from his son Marcus comes Power O'Shee of Sheestown, Kilkenny, and Gardenmorris, Waterford; Colonel Count O'Shee in France.
Elias Shee of Clanmore, brother of Sir Richard.	Sir G. Shee, Bart., Dunmore, Galway.
Sir G. Flower, a distinguished Elizabethan officer, appears to have settled in Kilkenny.	Viscount Ashbrook, Castle Durrow, Kilkenny.

QUEEN'S COUNTY.—See p. 73.

FitzPatrick, 3rd Lord of Upper Ossory, m. a dau. of O'More.	FitzPatrick of Grantstown Manor, Queen's Co.; Baron de Robeck of Gowran Grange, Kildare (maternally).
Barnaby O'Dunne of Brittas, Chief of Iregan, d. in 1614.	Dunne of Brittas, Queen's Co.; Doyne of Wells, Wexford, is said to be of the same stock.
O'Lalor of Desert, brother of the Chief of that name. His son or grandson, the Confederate Major, Jeremiah Lawlor, settled in Tipperary *circ.* 1666; he d. in 1709, aged 83.	Lalor of Cregg, and (maternally) Power Lalor of Long Orchard, in Tipperary.
Calbhach O'More, uncle of the Chief, Owney McRory O'More, petitioned Elizabeth for his country of Leix; he was transplanted to Balyna, the property of the Delahoyds of Kildare. In 1600 he m. a dau. of Scurlog of the Frayne, Co. Meath.	Right Hon. R. More-O'Ferrall of Balyna, Kildare, great grandson of James, the last O'More, who d. in 1779.— *MS. History of the O'Mores,* written in 1775 by the last O'More, whose only child m. Richard O'Ferrall, Esq., of Ballinree, Longford.
Pigott, who got a grant of Dysart in 1562, had a son, Sir A. Pigott of Dysart.	Sir C. Pigott, Bart., Knapton, Queen's Co.
Cosby of Stradbally Abbey, whose father and brother were slain at the battle of Stradbally Bridge, fighting against the O'Mores.	Cosby of Stradbally Hall, Queen's Co.
Brereton got in 1594 grants of Shanamullen, etc.	Brereton of Carrigslany, Carlow.

Families of 16th century.	Representatives in the 19th century.
Sir C. Coote of Castle Cuffe served against O'Neill.	Sir C. Coote, Bart., of Ballyfin, Queen's Co.; Sir C. Coote, Bart., Dublin.

KING'S COUNTY.—See p. 81.

Brassil Fox of Kilcoursey, Chief of his name, m. a dau. of Mac Geoghegan of Castletown; he died in 1639; he was nephew of Hubert 'The Fox,' who d. in 1600.	Fox of Kilcoursey, King's Co.
Mac Cochlain.	The last chief died 40 years ago, and his estates passed to the Dalys and Armstrongs.—*O'Donovan's Notes to the Annals*, under the year 1585. Mr. Coghlan, near Castlebar, Mayo, is head of one of the most respectable branches.—*Notes to Tribes of Ireland*.
O'Carroll.	The late Marchioness of Wellesley, whose grandfather in America was the undoubted head of that name.—*Notes to Annals*, an. 1585.
'Cahir, Maurice and John O'Connor were the last who obtained the chieftainship in 1600.' One of these, says Sir B. Burke, was ancestor of	O'Connor of Mount Pleasant, who d. in 1818. His daughters m. the Earl of Desart, Tuite of Sonna, and Rev. B. Morris, whose descendant is now O'Connor Morris of Gortnamona or Mountpleasant.
O'Molloy of Fircale.	O'Molloy of Clonbela, King's Co.—*Notes to Annals* an. 1585, *and Tribes of Ireland*.
Briscoe m. Eleanor Kearney of Scraghe, near Tullamore; from an inscription over the door of the now ruined castle of Scraghe, it seems he built that castle in 1588.	Briscoe of Riversdale, Westmeath.
Sir J. Moore of Croghan Castle, whose father settled at Croghan.	Earl of Charleville (maternally).
L. Parsons, brother of Sir William the Lord Justice.	The Earl of Rosse, Parsonstown, King's Co.

MEATH.—See p. 92.

Preston, 4th Viscount Gormanston.	13th Viscount Gormanston, Meath.
Plunkett, 9th Lord Killeen.	The Earl of Fingal, Killeen Castle, Meath, 19th Lord Killeen.

APPENDIX. 269

Families of 16th century.	*Representatives in the 19th century.*
Plunkett, 8th Lord Dunsany.	The 16th Baron Dunsany, Dunsany Castle, Meath.
Barnwall, 6th Baron of Trimlestown, d. in 1598, and was succeeded by his son Robert.	The 16th Baron of Trimlestown, Turvey, Dublin.
Aylmer of Balrath. I think he was a son of 'Elmer of Dullardstown,' Meath.	Lord Aylmer, Baron of Balrath.
Sir Patrick Barnwall of Crickstown.	Sir Reginald Barnwall, Bart., of Crickstown; seat, Grenanstown, Meath.
Bath of Knightstown.	Sir H. De Bathe of Knightstown, Meath.
Cheevers of Macetown—perhaps *recte* Moreton.	Cheevers of Killyan, Galway.
Cromp of Muchalstown.	Crumpe of Co. Kerry.—See *Miss Hickson's Records of Kerry.*
R. Cusack, 14th Lord of Gerrardstown, d. in 1632; his tomb is in Killeen Church.	Cusack of Gerardstown; seat, Abbeville House, Dublin. Barker of Dunboyne, Meath (maternally).
D'Arcy of Dunmow m. a dau. of Brandon of Dundalk.	D'Arcy of High Park, Westmeath; and (maternally) D'Arcy Irvine of Castle Irvine, Fermanagh.
Dease of Kilrue.	O'Reilly Dease, Charleville, Louth.
Dillon of Lismullen.	Sir J. Dillon, Bart., Lismullen, Meath.
Drake of Drakerath.	Drake (late) of Roristown, Co. Meath.
Patrick Everard of Randalstown d. in 1611.	Everard of Randalstown.
John Netterville of Dowth, M.P. for Meath in 1585, d. in 1601, leaving a son, who became Viscount Netterville.	Viscount Netterville.
Plunket of Rathmore, born in 1563, m. a dau. of Dillon of Moymet.	Lentaigne of Tallaght, Dublin (maternally).
Honourable Martin Preston m. in 1584 Alison Herbert.	Preston of Ballinter, Meath.
Richard Read of Meath, who d. in 1631.	Read of Wood Parks, Scariff.
Dr. Jones, Protestant Bishop of Meath from 1584 to 1605.	Viscount Ranelagh.
Teeling of Mullagha.	Captain Teeling, Leitrim Rifles, late of the Pontifical Zouaves.

WESTMEATH.—See p. 102.

Families of 16th century.	Representatives in the 19th century.
The 14th Baron of Delvin d. in 1602; his son became Earl of Westmeath in 1621.	The Earl of Westmeath, who is 23rd Baron of Delvin; seat, Pallas, Co. Galway. Also Count Nugent of Killasonna, and Prince Nugent of Austria; maternally the children of Lord Greville of Clonyn.
Dease of Turbotstown.	Dease of Turbotstown.
Sir Patrick Fox of Moyvore, of the elder branch of the O'Caharnys or Foxes, d. in 1618.	Fox of Fox Hall, Longford.
Magawly of Calry.	Count Magawly-Cerati.
Mageoghegan, Chief of Kinaleaghe.	O'Neill of Bunowen Castle, Co. Galway, whose real name is Mageoghegan; maternally, the late Sir R. Nagle of Jamestown.
Nugent of Carlandstown d. in 1599.	Maternally, the Duke of Buckingham.
Nugent of Clonlost d. in 1613.	Nugent of Clonlost.
Nugent of Coolamber.	Maternally, J. Conmee, Esq., Kingsland, Co. Roscommon.
Nugent of Donore m. in 1580, a dau. of Barnwall of Crickstown; he d. in 1616.	Sir Walter Nugent of Donore, maternally. The name of his family was FitzGerald.
Nugent of Dysart succeeded his brother in 1620; his wife was dau. of O'Ferrall of Mornin.	Count Nugent of Ballynacorr, Westmeath (maternally); Nugent of Portaferry, and Sir C. Nugent, Bart., of Ballinlough.
Tuite of Sonagh, born circ. 1588, made Baronet in 1622.	Sir M. Tuite, Bart., of Kilruane, Tipperary; Tuite of Sonagh, Westmeath.
Sir E. Packenham came with Sydney in 1576; his grandson had the lands of Tullynally, Westmeath.	The Earl of Longford, Packenham Hall, Westmeath.
Captain Piers came to Ireland in 1566; got 1000 marks in 1569 for bringing the head of Shane O'Neill; got the Abbey of Tristernagh.	Sir E. F. Piers of Tristernagh Abbey, Westmeath, 8th Baronet.
Captain Pollard of Essex's army came in 1598 or 1599.	Pollard Urquhart of Castle Pollard, Westmeath.

LONGFORD.—See p. 113.

O'Ferrall of Ballinree, &c.	Right Hon. R. More O'Ferrall, Balyna House, Kildare, and Ballinree, Longford.

APPENDIX. 271

Families of 16th century.	*Representatives in the 19th century.*
O'Farrel of Mornin.	Maternally, O'Farrell of Dalystown, Galway; and Nugent of Ballinacorr, Westmeath.
Sir Francis Shaen (O'Farrell).	Maternally, Kirwan of Castlehacket, Galway.
The Edgworths settled *circ.* 1583. The brother of Edgworth, Bishop of Down and Connor, was ancestor of	The Edgeworths of Edgeworthstown and Kilshrewly, Longford.

CAVAN.—See p. 117.

Edmund O'Reilly of Kilnacrott, a Chieftain, who d. in 1601.	O'Reillys of Heath House, Queen's Co.; of Knock Abbey, Louth; Count O'Reilly of Cuba; O'Reilly, Attorney-General in Jamaica; O'Reillys of Baltrasna and Scarvagh.—*O'Donovan's Notes to Annals*, year 1601.
O'Reilly, whose descendant was Hugh O'Reilly of Ballinlough, Westmeath.	Sir Charles Nugent, Bart., of Ballinlough, Westmeath.
Nugent of Enagh, Cavan, son of Nugent of Rathwire, Meath.	Nugent of Bobsgrove, Cavan.
Sir Oliver Lambert came with Essex, became Baron of Cavan in 1617.	The Earl of Cavan; Lambart of Beau Park.
Hamilton of Coronary.	Hamilton of Abbotstown, Dublin.

CLARE.—See p. 124.

O'Brien, 5th Baron of Inchiquin.	The Duke of Leinster (maternally).
Brady of Tomgrany.	Brady of Myshall Lodge, Co. Carlow.
James Butler of Shanagollen.	Butler of Ballyline, Co. Clare.
Comyn of Kilcorney.	Comyn of Woodstock, Galway.
FitzGerald of Rynana.	Sir A. FitzGerald, Newmarket-on-Fergus, Clare.
Hickie, near Killaloe.	Hickie of Killelton, Kerry.
MacMahon, Chief of Corcabhascin.	Coppinger of Barryscourt, Cork (maternally).—*Tribes of Ireland*, notes. McMahon, Marshal, President of the French Republic, is of this race.
Finin Mac Namara of Rosroe d. in 1601. His son Shioda was ancestor of	Mac Namara of Ayle, Clare.
His son Convea Reagh of Clonmoynagh and Ardclony, who d. in 1625, was ancestor of	Major McNamara Bouchier (maternally).

272   STATE OF IRELAND ANNO 1598.

Families of 16th century.	*Representatives in the 19th century.*
Mac Namara, of a junior branch of the 'Eastern McNamaras.'	Mac Namara of Ennistymon.—*O'Donovan's Notes to Annals*, year 1585.
O'Brien of Carraduff, whose son Donal lost his lands in 1652.	O'Brien of Ballynalacken.
O'Brien of Duagh.	(Maternally) Marshal MacMahon, President of the French Republic.—*Cronelly's Irish Families*.
O'Briens of Leaghmenagh and Dromoland.	Lord Inchiquin of Dromoland; Stafford O'Brien of Blatherwicke, Northamptonshire.
O'Brien, son of Sir Tirlough O'Brien.	O'Brien of Glencolumkille, Clare.—*O'Donovan's Notes* to year 1585 of the *Annals*.
O'Hogan of Cross.	O'Brien of Ballynalacken, Clare (maternally).
O'Loghlin.	O'Loghlin of Newtown; Sir Colman O'Loghlen is a junior branch.—*O'Donovan's Notes to Annals*, an. 1585.
O'Molony of Kiltannon, whose grandson was Bishop of Limerick in 1687.	The Molonys of Kiltannon and Granahan, Clare.
Cuffe, merchant of Ennis, and nephew of Hugh Cuffe, who got 6000 acres of the Desmond lands.	
Lewin settled in Ireland in 1586.	Ross-Lewin of Ross Hill, Clare.

GALWAY.—See p. 131.

Ulick, 3rd Earl of Clanrickarde, d. in 1601.	The Marquess (15th Earl) of Clanrickarde, Portumna, Galway.
Edmund Burke of Kilcornan, son of the 3rd Earl of Clanrickarde.	(Maternally) Redington of Kilcornan.
The 13th Lord Athenry d. in 1614.	Bermingham of Dalgan, Galway; and (maternally) Lords Howth and Clonbrock.
Athy of Galway.	Athy of Renville, Galway.
Robert Blake of Ardfry, father of the Speaker of the Supreme Council.	Lord Wallscourt, Ardfry, Galway.
Andrew Blake of Cummer and Ballyglunin.	Blake of Balglunin, Galway; and Sir — Blake, Bart., of Langham, Suffolk.
V. Blake FitzWalter FitzThomas, Mayor of Galway in 1611; a Bart. in 1622.	Sir V. Blake, Bart., of Menlo, Galway.
Blake, Mayor of Galway in 1564, m. a dau. of Valentine French.	Blake of Renvyle, Galway.

APPENDIX. 273

Families of 16th century.	*Representatives in the 19th century.*
Blake, son of Marcus Blake of Galway, bought lands in Mayo from David O'Kelly of Dunamona; he d. in 1633.	Blake of Ballynafad, Mayo.
FitzRichard Blake of Kiltullagh Castle, Mayor of Galway in 1578.	Blake of Kiltullagh, and Blake of Cregg.
Bodkin, Sheriff of Galway in 1570, was father of John Bodkin.	Bodkin of Annagh, Galway.
Browne of Barna m. a dau. of Sir Morogh O'Flaherty; he d. in 1596. His son Oliver is ancestor of	Browne of Kilskeagh, Galway.
His son Geoffrey ancestor of	Lord Oranmore and Browne; Browne of Browne Hall, Mayo.
His son Thomas.	The Brownes of Newtown, Ardskea, and Cooloo.
His son James.	Browne of Tuam.
His son Andrew.	Browne of Moyne.
Ulicke Burke of Castlehacket, son of John Burke, and Miss O'Kelly of Mullaghmore.	Burke of Ower.
Burke of Glinsk, Lord of Clanconow.	Sir J. L. Burke of Glinsk, 11th Baronet; also Burke of Knocknagur.
Burke of Gortenacuppoge.	Sir T. J. Burke of Marble Hill (*alias* Gortenacuppoge), 3rd Baronet.
Burke of Meelick.	Burke of Elm Hall, Tipperary; Burkes of Slatefield and St. Cleran's, Galway.
Theobald Butler of Cregg.	Butler of Cregg.
D'Arcy *Riavagh* (the swarthy) Vice-President of Connaught, d. in 1603. His monument is in the Franciscan Abbey, Galway.	D'Arcy of Newforest, D'Arcy of Wellfort, and D'Arcy of Kiltulla, all in Galway.
Thomas Dillon of Clonbrock in Galway, and Curraboy in Roscommon, Chief Justice of Connaught, d. in 1606.	Lord Clonbrock of Clonbrock, Galway. —See *Archdall's Lodge*, vol. iv., p. 138.
William Dolphin of Turoe.	Dolphin of Turoe, and Dolphin of Danesfort, Galway.
Redmond Dolphin of Brackloonmore.	Dolphin of Corr, Galway.
Fonte, Mayor of Galway.	Geoffrey Fonte d. in 1814, aged 104, the last of the race.—*Hardiman*.
Ffrench of Castle Ffrench.	Lord Ffrench of Castle French, Galway.
French of Monivea Castle d. in 1618.	French of Monivea Castle, Galway.
French of Mulpit.	St. George of Tyrone House, Galway.
Patrick Kirwan of Cregg.	Kirwan of Bawnmore.

2 M

Families of 16th century.	Representatives in the 19th century.
Edmund *Airgid* Kirwan (2nd son of Patrick Kirwan of Cregg) d. in 1608.	Maitland-Kirwan of Dalgin, Mayo, and Gelston Castle, N.B.
Martin O'Quirivane of *Tobercaoch* (Blind Well).	Kirwan of Blindwell, and perhaps Kirwan of Moyne.
Lawrence of Ballymore, whose father settled in that place, m. in 1603 a dau. of Garret Moore of Breeze, Mayo.	Lawrence of Lisreaghan.
Martin of Ross; his son Jasper d. in 1630.	Martin of Ross House, Galway.
Martin of Tullyra.	Martin of Tullyra Castle, Galway.
In 1578 O'Daly of Killymore got a grant of the manor of Larha; his sons were Teig and Donough.	Daly, Lord Dunsandle, of Dunsandle, Galway.
O'Donelan, Protestant Archbishop of Tuam, 'though never in Holy Orders.'	The Donelans of Ballydonelan, of Hillswood, of Sylane and Peter's Well, and of Killagh, all in Galway.
Murrough na d'Tuagh O'Flaherty, 'Chief of all the O'Flaherties' in 1598.	O'Fflahertie of Lemonfield, Galway.—*O'Donovan's Notes* to year 1585 of *Annals*.
O'Halloran of Barna.	Lynch of Barna, Galway, (maternally).
O'Kelly of Aughrim Castle.	Kelly of Newtown.—*Hy-Many*.
Hugh *Caoch* O'Kelly of Mullaghmore, Chief in 1598.	Kelly of Castle Kelly, and Count O'Kelly of Montauban.—*Hy-Many*.
Conor *na Gearbhach* O'Kelly of Gallagh, sub-chief of Hy-Many, d. in 1612.	Count Conor O'Kelly of Ticooly, formerly of Gallagh, Co. Galway.—*O'Donovan's Hy-Many*.
Donall O'Madden.	Madden of Streamstown.—*Notes to Annals*, an. 1585. (Maternally) More-O'Ferrall of Ballyna.—*MS. Account of the O'Mores, by James, the last of the O'Mores.*
Gilladubh O'Shaughnessy.	Mr. Bartholomew O'Shaughnessy of Galway.—*O'Donovan.*
Sir Dermot O'Shaughnessy, who d. in 1606.	The late Catholic Bishop of Killaloe; Sir W. O'Shaughnessy of Calcutta; the late James O'Shaughnessy of Clongowes, Kildare; R^d O'Shaughnessy, Esq., M.P. for Limerick.—See *O'Donovan's Annals.*
Skerret.	Skerret of Finvara, Clare; Skerret of Athgoe Park, Co. Dublin.
Blakeney, who settled *temp.* Elizabeth.	Blakeney of Abbert, Castle Blakeney, Galway.

APPENDIX. 275

MAYO.—See p. 140.

Families of 16th century.

Bingham of Castlebar, whose father, the Governor of Sligo, was killed in 1596.

Bourke of Moneycrower.

Richard *Ruadh* Bourke of Rathroe Castle, Inniscoe, and Carrowkeel, m. a dau. of McWilliam.

Browne of the Neale, High Sheriff of Mayo, whose grandson was made a Baronet in 1622.

Sir C. Dillon of Bealalahin, son of the 1st Viscount Dillon.

Shane McCostelloe of Castlemore, Chief, m. in 1586 a dau. of O'Kelly of Screggs, Roscommon.

Edmund McJordan, Chief in 1586.

O'Higgins of Moyna.

O'Malley (son of Brian) of Morska Castle.

O'Malley (Edmund), nephew of Granauille O'Malley, b. 1579, d. 1651.

Captain Atkinson, Elizabethan officer.

Representatives in the 19th century.

The Earl of Lucan, Castlebar, Mayo; Lord Clanmorris, Newport, Mayo.

The Earl of Mayo, Co. Kildare.

Bourke of Carrowkiel; Bourke of Curraghleagh.

Lord Kilmaine of the Neale; Marquess of Sligo, Westport, Mayo; Browne of Breafy, now Sir C. M. de Beauvoir, Johnstown, Dublin; Browne of Manulla; Browne of Raheens, Mayo.

Viscount Dillon, Loughglynn, Roscommon.

Costelloe of Edmundstown, Mayo.

Jordan of Rosslevin Castle, Mayo

Higgins of Westport.

Sir W. O'Malley, Bart., Rose Hill, Mayo.

O'Malley of The Lodge, Co. Mayo.

Atkinson of Rehins, Co. Mayo.

SLIGO.—See p. 144.

Donal O'Conor-Sligo.

O'Crean of Annagh.

Dathi O'Dowda, son of Dathi (slain in 1594) and nephew of O'Dowda, elected by O'Donnell in 1595.

The last Chief, General O'Conor-Sligo, d. in 1756; the last Lady of the House of Hapsburg erected a monument to him in the Church of St. Gudule, Brussels. The present senior of the race is a farmer. The descendants, maternally, are McDermot of Coolavin, and O'Connor-Donellan of Sylane.

Crean-Lynch of Clogher House, Mayo (maternally).

O'Dowda of Bunnyconnelan, 43rd in descent from Eochaidh, Monarch of Ireland in 358.—*Hy-Fiachra, pedigree by O'Donovan.*

STATE OF IRELAND ANNO 1598.

Families of 16th century.

Cormac O'Hara of Coolany m. a dau. O'Gallagher; he d. in 1612; his son Teig was High Sheriff in 1608.

Sir Tibbot Dillon of Costello Gallen, Sligo.

French of Gortrassy, and Sessueman Castle, Co. Sligo, m. a dau. of O'Conor-Sligo; he d. in 1624.

Patrick French obtained an estate from Donagh O'Conor-Sligo.

George Bingham, Governor of Sligo in 1596.

Dodwell settled at Tanrago *circ.* 1590.

Representatives in the 19th century.

O'Hara of Annaghmore, Co. Sligo (maternally).

Viscount Dillon of Loughglynn, Roscommon.

Lord de Freyne, Co. Roscommon.

French of Cloonyquin, Co. Roscommon.

Lord Clanmorris, Newbrook, Mayo.

Dodwell of Glenmore.

LEITRIM.—See p. 147.

Magrannell of Magh-Rein, Chief of his name.

O'Rourk.

O'Rourke of Dromehaire.

The last head was Squire Reynolds, who was murdered at Sheemore, Co. Leitrim. His dau. is Mrs. M'Namara of Lough Scur House.—*Tribes of Ireland*, p. 35.

Prince O'Rork of Russia.

O'Rourke of Ballybollen, Co. Antrim.

ROSCOMMON.

Brian M'Dermot of *Carraig Locha Cé* (now Rockingham).

O'Beirn, Chief of Tir-bruin na Sinna.

Sir Hugh O'Conor Don of Ballintubber, b. in 1541, submitted in 1581, d. in 1632. He mar. a d. of Sir Brian O'Rourke.

O'Conor Roe.

Rory O'Kelly of Aughrane, Lord of the Manor of Screen, and High Sheriff of the Co. of Roscommon in 1590, m. a dau. of O'Kelly of Belanamore, or of M'Edmond of Gaillé, and had two sons—Wm. Reagh and Captain Colla. Wm. Reagh's sons entered into Holy Orders. Colla d. in 1615; his descendants are

M'Dermot, 'Prince of Coolavin.'

O'Beirn of Dangan-I-Beirn in the same territory.—*O'Donovan*.

O'Conor Don; O'C. of Mount Druid, of Dundermott, and of Milton.—*Cf. Memoir of the O'Connors*, by R. O'Connor, Esq., also *The Annals*.

O'Conor Roe of Tomona; O'Conor Roe of Lanesborough.

Kelly of Castle Kelly; Count Conor O'Kelly, officer of Grenadiers in France, 43rd in descent from Maine Mór; Thomas L. Kelly, Esq., of Gardiner Street, Dublin.—See *Tribes and Customs of Hy-Many* for an account of the Roscommon families.

APPENDIX. 277

Families of 16th century.	Representatives in the 19th century.
O'Kelly of Athleague.	Kelly of Glencarra, Co. Westmeath.
Conor Na Garvach O'Kelly of Gallagh.	Conor O'Kelly of Ticooly, 42nd in descent from Maine Mór.
Captain Anthony O'Mulloy, called the 'Green Mulloy,' got land in Roscommon early in Elizabeth's reign; had a son, 'the Great Mulloy of Uchterthera,' Governor of Roscommon.	Mulloy of Hughstown, Co. Roscommon.
Moylin O'Mulconry of Tullon, 'The O'Mulconry,' m. a dau. of Teig O'Flanagan, Caencloin.	Sir J. Conroy, Bart., of Bettifield, Roscommon, and Pennant Hall, Montgomeryshire.
O'Nachtan, Chief of the Fews in the barony of Athlone.	Naughton of Thomastown Park.—*Hy-Many*, p. 71.
J. Crofton of Ballymurray, Auditor-General.	Baron Crofton of Mote Park, Roscommon; Sir M. Crofton, Bart., of Mohill House, Leitrim; Sir Malby Crofton, Bart., of Longford House, Sligo.
Sir J. King of the Abbey of Boyle.	Viscount Lorton; Earl of Kingston.
Lyster of Milltown Pass.	Lyster of Lysterfield.

WATERFORD.

Lord Power.	The Marquess of Waterford (maternally).
The Lord FitzGerald of Decies.	Lord Stuart de Decies (maternally); Mansfield of Morristown-Lattin, Co. Kildare (maternally).
Aylward of Fathlegg.	Aylward of Shankhill Castle, Co. Kilkenny.
Edward FitzGerald of the Little Island.	Purcell FitzGerald of the Little Island (maternally).
FitzGerald of Gurteens.	FitzGerald of Turlough Park, Mayo.
Grant of Ballygrant.	Grant of Kilmurry, Co. Cork.
Walter Mansfield (perhaps originally Mandeville) m. a dau. of the Lord of Dromana.	Mansfield of Morristown-Lattin, Co. Kildare.
Richard Nugent of Cloncoscraine, descended from the 2nd Baron of Delvin.	Sir J. Nugent Humble, Bart., of Cloncoscoran (maternally).—See *Lodge*, vol. i., p. 221.
Power of Ballyhane.	Power of Belleville Park.
Power of Clashmore.	Earl of Huntingdon of Clashmore (maternally).
Wise of of the Manor of St. John.	Wise of the Manor of St. John; General Henry Wise of America.

278   STATE OF IRELAND ANNO 1598.

Families of 16th century.	Representatives in the 19th century.
Captain Drew of Kilwinny, settled circ. 1598.	Drew of Drewscourt, Co. Limerick.
Osborne of Ballintaylor.	Sir W. Osborne, Bart., of Beechwood, Tipperary.

CORK.

Lord Barrymore.	Smith-Barry of Foaty.
Lord Courcy, 18th Baron of Kinsale.	29th Baron of Kinsale.
Earl of Desmond.	A descendant of an Earl of Desmond put to death in Elizabeth's reign, is said now to be a brogue-maker in Kerry.—*Dynely's Tour, circ.* 1689. Maternally, the Duke de Choiseul-Praslin, and the Right Hon. J. Fitzgerald, who d. in 1835, aged 93, were descended from the 16th Earl of Desmond.
Wm. Barry of Lislee (son of Viscount Buttevant, who d. in 1582), mar. Selah ny vy Carty; he d. in 1594; had a son James.	James Redmond Barry, who claims to be Viscount Buttevant.—See his *Case in House of Lords*, 1825.
Garret Barry of Leamlary m. Miss McCarthy of Tuadrommeen; his son John *Laidir* (the Stout) m. Miss Nagle of Moneanimie.	Barry of Leamlara.
Barry of Lisnegar and Rathcormack, styled 'Mac Adam Barry.'	Barry of Ballyclough, who claims to be senior to the Barrymore family.
Burke of Clogher, near Castletown-Roche.	The famous Edmund Burke, and his descendant Haviland Burke.
S. Coppinger of Ballyvolane d. in 1620.	Coppinger of Ballyvolane and Barry's Court; C. of Middleton.
T. Coppinger, Alderman of Cork in 1610.	Coppinger of Leemount.
Creagh of Cork m. in 1557 a grand-dau. of Waters, who aided Perkin Warbeck; he d. *circ.* 1601; his son m. a dau. of G. Archdeken; he d. in 1614, leaving a son who m. Miss Roche of Poolnalong Castle.	Creagh of Hermitage, and (maternally) Brazier-Creagh of Creagh Castle.
Duggan of Mount Infant, barony of Duhallow.	Cronin-Coltsman of Glenflesk Castle (paternally).
FitzGerald of Corkbeg and Lisquinlan.	(Maternally) Uniacke Penrose Fitz-Gerald of Corkbegg and Lisquinlan.

APPENDIX. 279

Families of 16th century.	*Representatives in the 19th century.*
French of Cork, who d. 1651, leaving a bequest to the poor of St. Finn Barr's Church, which is still paid from property belonging to the family.	French of Cuskinny, Queenstown.
Galwey of Lota, descended from Galwey of Dundannion Castle.	Galwey of Lota.
Gould of Cork.	Sir H. V. Gould, Bart., of Oldcourt; Goold of Rosbrien, Limerick.
Lysaght of Mountnorth, of the Race of O'Brien.	Lord Lyle of Mountnorth.
Mac Awliffe of Castle Mac Awliffe, near Newmarket.	Mac Awliffe, though born to a handsome estate, was weigh-master in Kenmare in 1840; he was head of this clan.—*Tribes of Ireland*, p. 66.
McCarthy of Carbry.	Count McCarthy of Toulouse.
McCarthy of Drishane Castle m. Honora McSweeny.	The late Alexander McCarthy, M.P. for Cork; McCarthy O'Leary of Coomlegane.
Cormac McCarthy of Blarney Castle, Lord of Muskerry, d. in 1616.	McCarthy of Carrignavar.
Teig-anFhorsa McCarthy, L^d of Glean an Chroim.	McCarthy Duna of Cork; McCarthy Glas of Dunmanway.—*Cronelly.*
Wm. MacCotter m. Miss Hodnett.	Sir J. L. Cotter, Bart., of Rockforest.
Meade of Ballintobber, M.P. for Cork in 1585; his son, Sir John, m. a dau. of Sarsfield, 1st Viscount Kilmallock.	The Earl of Clanwilliam; Meade of Ballintobber; and Meade of Ballymartle.
Conogher O'Callaghan of Clonmeen, Chief in 1598, m. a dau. of Tirlagh McSwiny; his son's only child Ellen m. O'Callaghan of Drumaneen. The last head of this race, O'Callaghan of Kilgorey, who d. in 1791, was grandfather of—	Father O'Reilly, S.J.; the Earl of Kenmare; Mr. Dease, M.P., and Major Dease. The eldest dau.(Mrs.O'Reilly) is erroneously said, in Burke's account of the Dease family, to have d. unmar. See a description of her husband's tomb, p. 544 of *Lenihan's Hist. of Limerick.* Lord Lismore and O'Callaghan of Cadogan represent junior branches.
Donal I I O'Donovan, 40th Chief of Clancathal in 1584, lived in the castle of Rahine, rebuilt Castle Donovan in 1628, as appears by an inscription there. He lived to the year 1639; his 1st wife was Helena Barry of Lislee. By his 2^d wife, a dau. of McCarthy Reagh, he had 7 sons; some say he had 11 sons.	J. O'Donovan, the great Irish scholar, descended from the eldest son, Donal; O'Donovan of Montpellier from his son Teig; O'D. of Cooldurragha, in the parish of Myross, from his son Donogh; Lieutenant O'D. of Cork City, from Captain Richard; O'D. of Lisheens House, and O'D. of Ardahill, from Keudagh.—*O'Donovan's Notes to the Annals.*

Families of 16th century.

Diamaid an-Eich (of the steed) O'Donovan of Gortineeher, parish of Dromaleague.

Donal Oge Na Carton O'Donovan of Cloghatrabally Castle, 41st Chief of Clanlochlain in 1580, surrendered and received a regrant of his possessions in 1616; d. in 1629.

O'Driscoll Mór, Chief of Collymore.

O'Mahony of Fonn Iartarach, in the South-West of Carbery.

Kean O'Mahony, Chief of Kinalmeaky, with his 7 sons removed to Kerry.

O'Sullevan Mór.

Murtagh O'Sullevan Mór.

Rory O'Sullevan Mór of Drominage Castle, m. Julian M'Carthy of Drishane.

O'Sullevan of Cappanacus, from whose house the O'Sullevan Mór was elected in case of failure of the elder branch.

John Purcell of Pullen, 'of the Croagh line of the Purcells of Loughmoe.'

Roche of Castletown.

Roch of Tourin and Cregg, m. in 1566 Miss Fitzgerald of Kerrycurrihy; he d. in 1635; he had 5 sons, George, Maurice, David, John, and Ulick.

Representatives in the 19th century.

O'Donovan of O'Donovan's Cove, in West Carbery.

— Donovan, Esq., of Wood Street, Dublin, Solicitor; Donovan of Ballynore and Clonmore, Co. of Wexford.—*Appendix to Annals*, pp. 2430 to 2483.

W$^{m.}$ O'Driscoll (son of Denis, son of Florence), who d. in 1581, 'was of noble countenance, and in pitch of body like a giant.' A. O'Driscoll, J.P., of Skibbereen, of 'boundless hospitality,' d. in 1849, 'while in gaol for debt to a wine merchant.' The last known Chief was Conor O'Driscoll, called 'the Admiral.'—*O'Donovan*.

O'Mahony of Dunloe Castle.

O'Mahony of Dromore Castle, and Castle Quin.

O'Sullevan of Tomies, near Killarney, in the last century.

Sir E. Sullevan, Bart., of St. Leonards House, Berks.

Sullivan of Curraghmore, Limerick; Sullivan of Wilmington, Isle of Wight.

O'Sullevan of Prospect, near Kenmare, who is probably head of the race of O'Sullevan.

John Mathew Purcell, Esq., of Burton, Co. Cork, 8th in descent.—*MS. Pedigree* by General Creagh.

Roche of Cranagh Castle, Co. Kilkenny; Wm. Roche, Esq., Solicitor, Dublin; and (maternally) Grehan of Clonmeen, Co. Cork.

Roch of Woodbine Hill, Waterford.

APPENDIX.

Families of 16th century.	Representatives in the 19th century.
Sarsfield of Sarsfield Court.	Sarsfield or Doughcloyne.
Sir R. Smith of Rathcogan.	Smith of Headborough, Waterford, and (maternally) Moore of Ballinatray, Waterford.
Supple of Aghadoe.	Sir W. De Capell-Broke, Bart., of Oakley, Co. Northampton, and Aghadoe, Cork (paternally).
J. Uniacke, of the Geraldine family, d. in 1623; was succeeded by his cousin, Uniacke of Ballyhubbert, from whom	Uniacke of Mount Uniacke; Uniacke of Curragheen.
Thomas Uniacke of Youghal, m. Miss Fitzgerald of Lisquinlan.	Uniacke of Woodhouse, Waterford, and Sir J. C. Judkin Fitzgerald of Lisheen, Tipperary.
Wallis of Curryglas, who d. in 1630.	Wallis of Drishane Castle.

SETTLERS.

Aldworth of Short Castle, near Mallow, father of Aldworth, Vice-President of Munster.	Aldworth of Newmarket.
Beecher.	Sir H. Wrixon Beecher of Ballygiblin (maternally).
Francis Bernard.	The Earl of Bandon.
R. Boyle, who became 'the Great Earl of Cork;' he d. in 1643.	The Earl of Cork; the Earl of Shannon.
Cook settled before the reign of Elizabeth, and Edward Cook was a resident in Cork long before 1641.	Cook of Castle Cook, Cork; Cook of Cordangan; and Cook of Kiltinon Castle, Tipperary.
M. Cox settled at Kilworth.	Sir F. H. Cox, Bart., of Dunmanway, Co. Cork.
Captain Crofts came to Ireland in 1596; settled at Bandon; his wife 'placed a cross to his memory in the church of Kilbrogan, which is still in a good state of preservation.'	Crofts of Velvetstown; Crofts of Churchtown.
Daunt of Gortgrenane and Tracton Abbey in 1595.	The Daunts of Gortgrenane, Fahalea, Tracton Abbey, and Kilcaskan.
Dunscombe settled in Cork *circ.* 1566.	Dunscombe of Mount Desert.
Captain Fermor.	Farmar of Dunsinane.
Heard of Bandon came with Sir Walter Raleigh.	Heard of Pallestown, Kinsale.
Arthur Hyde, first settler, had a son, Sir A. Hyde of Carrigonede.	Hyde of Creg, late of Castle Hyde.

STATE OF IRELAND ANNO 1598.

Families of 16th century.	*Representatives in the 19th century.*
Elizabeth, dau. of Sir Thomas Norreys, Lord President of Munster.	Sir C. Jephson-Norreys, Bart., Mallow.
Sir H. Power, general in 1598, was son of Sir H. Power, Master of the Horse in Ireland. From his brother descends	Power of Hill Court, Hereford.
St. Leger, President of Munster.	Viscount Doneraile.
J. Ware settled in Cork in 1588.	Ware of Woodfort.

KERRY.

Conor Mac Gillicuddy, 'Lord of the Reeks.'	Mac Gillicuddy of the Reeks.
Jeffry O'Connell, Lord of Ballycarbery, was High Sheriff of Kerry; he d. in 1635.	O'Connell of Darrynane.
John, son of Conor O'Conor-Kerry, of Carrigafoyle Castle.	Daniel O'Connell O'Connor-Kerry, Commandant of Lodi in 1848.—*Tribes of Ireland.*
Jeffery O'Donoghue of Killagher and Glenflesk, attainted in 1603.	The O'Donoghue; O'Donoghue of Prover, Cheshire.
Trant of Cahir Trante, Dingle.	Trant of Dovea, Tipperary.
Patricin Mac Maurice, 17th Lord of Kerry, b. in 1541, d. in 1600.	Marquess of Lansdowne, 25th Lord of Kerry; also the Earl of Orkney.
Fitzgerald of Rathannan, 'Knight of Kerry,' whose wife was a dau. of O'Sullevan Mór.	'The Knight of Kerry,' Valentia.
FitzMaurice of Cosfeale or Duaghnafealla.	FitzMaurice of Duagh House.
Hussey of Dingle Castle or Daingeanni-Hushy, Castle Gregory, and Castle Minard.	Hussey of Dingle.
Rice of the Dingle.	Count Rice of the H.R. Empire.
Captain Annesley, Munster undertaker.	Viscount Valentia.
Sir T. Blennerhassett.	Sir R. Blennerhasset, Bart.; and Blennerhasset of Ballyseedy.
Sir N. Browne of Rosse, son of first settler, m. a dau. of O'Sullevan Beare.	The Earl of Kenmare.
Chapman, cousin of Sir W. Raleigh, got lands in Kerry.	Sir Montague Chapman, Bart., of Killua Castle, Westmeath.
Crosbie, Protestant Bishop of Ardfert, mar. a dau. of O'Lalor; the Earl of Ormond wrote to Cecil that his name was Mac Crossan.	Sir E. W. Crosbie, Bart., of Maryborough—seat, Bray, Co. Wicklow; Crosbie of Ballyheige Castle; and (maternally) Talbot Crosbie of Ardfert.

APPENDIX. 283

Families of 16th century.

Sir E. Denny, undertaker, of Tralee.
Colonel Gun settled early in Elizabeth's reign.
Hickson, Rector of Killiney.
Orpen, whose sisters mar. O'Donoghue of Ross and M'Carthy Mór.
Raymond.

Representatives in the 19th century.

Sir E. Denny, Bart., of Tralee Castle.
Gun of Rattoo; Gun of Ballybunnion.
Hickson of Fermoyle House.
Orpen of Killowen.—*Vide Miss Hickson's Kerry Records.*
Raymond of Killmurry.

LIMERICK.

Arthur of Limerick.
Edmond Bagot of Bagotstown Castle, m. a dau. of Burke of Brittas in 1545; he d. in 1630.
Burke of Ballinagard, near Limerick.
Burke of Ballyvomeen or Ballynaguard.

Burke of Castle Connell and Drumsallagh.
Burke of Drumkeen.

Piers Creagh of Adare, M.P. for the city of Limerick in 1639.
Edmund Fitzgerald, 'The Knight of Glin,' m. a dau. of M'Carthy Reagh.
Thomas Fitzgerald, Lord of Clenglish, m. a dau. of Cormac M'Dermot M'Carthy of Muskerry; he d. in 1635.
Maurice Hurley of Knocklong Castle m. Gursell Hogan, and was father of Sir Thomas Hurley.
J. Kearney of the Co. of Limerick settled at Garretstown, Cork, early in the 17th century.
Mahony Mac Keogh of Clooncliève had a son John of Castle Troy.
Naish of Ballycullen.
Donogh O'Grady of Kilballyowen, m. a dau. of Browne of Camas; in 1612 he settled his estates on his sons, Darby, Morogh, and Brien.
Donogh O'Quin of Kilmallock, whose son mar. the heiress of O'Riordan.

Arthur of Glanomera, Co. Clare.
Bagot of Ballymoe, Galway; Bagot of Kilcoursey, King's County.

Burke of Prospect Villa, Cork.
Haviland Burke (maternally).

Sir R. De Burgo, Bart.; and Burke of Thornfield.
Hussey de Burg of Dromkeen and Donore; Lady Clonmel, and Lady Seaton.
Creagh of Dangan, Co. Clare.

FitzGerald, Knight of Glin, Glin Castle, Co. Limerick.
Sir G. FitzGerald, Bart., of Castle Ishen, Cork.

Conway Hurly of Tralee, Kerry.

Cuthbert-Kearney of Garretstown, Cork (maternally).

Keogh of Kilbride, Carlow.

Naish of Ballycullen.
The O'Grady of Kilballyowen; Viscount Guillamore; O'Grady of the Grange.

The Earl of Dunraven.

STATE OF IRELAND ANNO 1598.

Families of 16th century.	*Representatives in the 19th century.*
Stephen Sexten of Limerick.	The Earl of Limerick (maternally).
J. Evans, a settler in Limerick.	Baron Carbery of Cork.
E. Seymour, whose son was Mayor of Limerick in 1659.	Seymour of Castletown, Queen's Co.
Stokes, an officer, whose son John of Dummoylan was living in 1622.	Stokes of Mount Hawk, Kerry.

TIPPERARY.

The 2^d Lord Dunboyne m. a dau. of the Earl of Thomond, and had a son, Edward of Clare, Co. Tipperary.	The 15th Baron of Dunboyne, Ballyvannon, Co. Clare.
Piers Putler, 3rd son of the 3rd Baron of Cahir.	Family of the late Earl of Glengall.
Sir W. Butler of Kilcashe, who became 11th Earl of Ormond.	Marquess of Ormonde, who is 21st Earl of Ormonde.
Sir James Butler of Lismallon, whose son was made Viscount Ikerrin in 1629.	Earl of Carrick, Mount Juliet, Kilkenny.
D'Alton of Grenanstown.	Count D'Alton of Grenanstown.
Hely of Gertrough?	Earl of Donoughmore.
Morres of Knockagh, whose son John was made a Baronet in 1632.	Viscount Mountmorres of Castle Morres, Kilkenny; and Viscount Frankfort de Montmorency.
Donal Connachtach Mac-I-Brien-Arra.	O'Brien of Kincora Lodge, Killaloe.— *O'Donovan.*
Donogh O'Carroll of Buolebrack, m. a dau. of O'Kennedy of Ormond.	Father J. O'Carroll, S.J., of Clongowes Wood.—*MS. Pedigree of O'Carroll of Ardagh.*
Donogh O'Fogarty of Inchy O'Fogarty, Fishmoyne and Ballyfogarty.	Lenigan of Castlefogarty (maternally).
Bryan O'Kearney of Knockanglass, b. 1534, d. 1623; his wife was a dau. of Wm. Butler of Ballynadlea; his son Patrick, b. 1561, m. a dau. of Teig Currane of Mohearnain.	Kearney of Blanchville, Kilkenny; Kearney of Ballinvilla, Mayo.
O'Mulrian, Chief of Owncy.	O'Ryan of Bansha House; and Ryan of Inch are chief representatives.
Ryan of Ballymackeogh.	Ryan of Ballymackeogh.
Power of Barretstown.	Sir R. Power, of Kilfane, Bart.
Prendergast of Newcastle-Prendergast.	Viscount Gort (maternally).
John Stapleton of Thurlesbeg, m. Sarah McEgan.	Sir F. Stapleton, Bart., Grey's Court, Oxfordshire.
Cromwell Lee d. in Ireland in 1601.	Lee of Barna, Tipperary (?)
Osborne settled in 1558.	Osborne of Newtown-Anner.

THE CATHOLIC BISHOPS.

See p. 233.

ARMAGH.—Edmund Magauran (*Mag Shamhraidhin*) was Primate from 1587 to 1593, when he was slain by the English while hearing the confessions of wounded soldiers. He was succeeded (1601 to 1625) by Dr. Peter Lombard, who in 1598 was sent to Rome as the representative of the Universities of Louvain and Douay. Lombard was a man of great genius and piety.—See a memoir of him, and a list of his works, by *Dr. Moran*, Bp. of Ossory. Dr. Lombard was succeeded by the celebrated Franciscan, Dr. McCawel.

CLOGHER.—Dr. McBardill was Bp. in 1592, and Dr. Mathews or McMahon in 1509.

DOWN AND CONNOR.—Connor O'Devany (*O'Duibheanaigh*) Bp. from 1582 to 1612, when he and his chaplain, Fr. O'Lughairen, were hanged, drawn, and quartered in Dublin. O'Sullevan says he was 'omnium virtutum ornamento fulgens doctrinam eruditus, ingenio comis . . .' The *Four Masters* call him a 'chaste, wise divine, a perfect and truly meek man;' and they add that no prisoner of Irish blood could be got by the promise of his life to act as executioner. The Bishop's friend, Fr. Hollywood, S.J., says that this 'sanctus Antistes, non multo ante caperetur, nomina ad nos, diemque obitus transmisit eorum Episcoporum, et sacerdotum omnium, quos, a morte Primatis Creagh, in hoc regno novit a Protestantibus peremptos, eum in finem ipsorum uti res gestas investigaremus . . .'—*Fr. Hollywood's Letter to Fr. Acquaviva.*

KILMORE.—Richard Brady, Bp. from 1580 to 1607, 'vir sanctus,' arrested thrice, once cruelly beaten and flung as dead into a brake of briars.

DROMORE.—Patrick Maccual, Bp. from 1576 to—

RAPHOE.—Nial O'Boyle (*O'Buidhil*) Bp. in 1591; imprisoned in 1598, d. in 1611, says Dr. Brady; but the *Annals* give the 6th Feb. 1612.

DERRY.—Redmund O'Gallagher (*O'Galchobhair*) Bp. from 1569 to 1601, when he was slain by the English in O'Kane's country.

ARDAGH.—Rev. J. Gafney was V.G. in 1597.

DUBLIN.—In 1587 there was an Archbishop, name unknown; in 1600 Dr. de Oviedo was Archbp., succeeding 'Donald of happy memory.' Dr. Mathews or McMahon, 'vir virtute et religione insignis,' was Abp. from 1611 to 1623. R. Lalor was Vic. Gen. of Dublin, Kildare, and Ferns from 1594 to 1606.

OSSORY.—Dr. Strong Bp. from 1582 to 1602. He remained in disguise in Ireland; but at length had to retire, and he d. at Compostella. His successor was the celebrated David Rothe (1618-1650.)

KILDARE.—Dr. Ribera of Toledo, Bp. from 1587 to 1605; but, it seems, he never came to Ireland. The Rev. J. Latin had extraordinary powers from Dr. Lombard in 1611.

CASHEL—Vacant in 1598; Dr. O'Kearney was Abp. from circ. 1604 to 1624. He was a man of great zeal, and he lived for years in disguise, and often had to hide in the woods, as appears from his letters and those of his brother, Bryan O'Kearney, S.J. He d. Aug. 14th, 1624, in an Irish Monastery near Bordeaux.—*Letter of his nephew, W. Wale, S.J.*

CORK AND CLOYNE.—Dermod Mac Craghe, Bp. from 1580 to circ. 1602. O'Sullevan calls him 'Mac Carrhus, vir integerrimus et clarissimus; . . . disertus atque sapiens.' He professed Theology some years at Louvain, and was remarkable for a prodigious memory. He wrote an Irish catechism. Fr. Purcel, O.S.F., calls him, 'Graius vir valde prudens et in rebus agendis versatus.' The *Pacata Hibernia* tells us that in Nov. 1600 'the Earle of Desmond and Dermond Mac Craghe were surprised in a poor ragged cabbin in Drumfinnim woods;' but escaped. Carew wrote to Cecil on the 18th of June 1601—'I am promised for £100 to gett Bishoppe Craghe.' On the 24th April 1604 Fr. Holywood, S.J., writes to Fr. Gen. Acquaviva—'Hactenus visum fuit *nostris cum consilio Episcopi Corcagiensis piae memoriae* . . .' This shows that Dr. Mac Craghe was dead before this date.

ROSS.—Owen Mac Egan, integerrimae et innocentissimae vitae sacerdos, Doctor S$^{æ.}$ Theol$^{æ.}$ Bp. elect of Ross, was slain in battle in 1602.—See *O'Sullevan.*

KILLALOE.—Conor O'Mulrian, Bp. before 1579, and after 1615.

LIMERICK.—Conor O'Neill, Bp. in 1591; he was then in Spain.

TUAM.—Marianus O'Higgin was Abp. circ. 1597. His successor was the celebrated Dr. Conry, O.S.F. (1608-1629), whose epitaph at Louvain says he was 'pietate, prudentia, doctrina maximus.' He wrote some works on Theology, and an Irish book called *The Mirror of Christian Life*. His friendship for Jansenius carried him too far.

ACHONRY.—Owen O'Hairt, O.S.D., Bp. from 1562 to 1603, when he d. aged 100 years; he had been among the Fathers of the Council of Trent in 1563.

CLONFERT.—Teig O'Ferral, O.S.D., Bp. from 1587 to 1602, when he d. of old age at Kinsale, after many years spent in preserving the Faith.—See *Rothe's Processus Martyrialis.*

KILMACDUAGH.—Malachy O'Molony, Bp. from 1570 to 1610. I presume he is the 'Bishop Muldowny' in Connaught, to whom Langton of Kilkenny went in 1588 to get a dispensation to marry his cousin, Lettice Daniel.—See *Langton Documents in Kilk. Journal of Arch.*

These details have been taken from the works of Dr. O'Renehan, Dr. Brady, Dr. Moran, Dr. Kelly's ed. of *O'Sullevan,* De Burgo, and the Rev. J. C. Meehan; also from *Calendar of S. Papers,* and a few contemporary letters.

1592, 28 July.—A memorial of sundry things commanded by her Majesty to be well considered by the Lord Deputy, &c. '. . . Through the whole Realm, yea and in the English Pale, there are Jesuits and seminarie Priests, all labouring to . . . in many places openly maintained and followed, and in some places— namely, the English Pale—secretly maintained in the houses of some noble persons, and in many gentlemen's houses partly disguised in apparel of servingmen . . .'

1st. In Ulster is one Redmundus O'Galligher, Buisshopp of Dayrie, *alias* Daren, legate to the Pope and Custos Armaghnensis, being one of the three Irish Buishoppes that were in the Councill of Trent. This Buishopp used all manner of spiritual jurisdiction throughout all Ulster, consecrating churches, ordaining priests, confirming children, and geving all manner of dispensations, ryding with pomp and company from place to place, as it was accustomed in Queen Mary's days. And for all the rest of the clergy there, they use all manner of service there now, as in that time; and not only that, but they have changed the time according to the Pope's new invention.

The said B. O'Galligher hath been with divers Governors of that land upon protection, and yet he is suffered to enjoy the Buishoprick and all the aforesaid aucthorities these 26 years past and more.

Likewise one Cornelius McBardill, Buishop of Clogher these 22 years past, ys not yet reformed, nor compelled to yield any obedience to her Ma^{ty's} lawes, though he hath been divers times before diverse governors.

There was one Rapotensis Bishop who died three years since, used the like authority there sithens he came from the Council of Trent, being with divers Governors, and never brought to acknowledge his duty to her Ma^{ty.}

In O'Reilly his country, being thirty miles or thereabout from Dublin, is Richard Braday, Buishopp of Kilmore, and although there is a kind of custodium granted to a priest there in her Majesty's name, yet he is in the possession, using all manner of jurisdiction therein, although the country is governed by English laws and officers.

In the same Ulster ar at the least at this day, more than 16 monasteries wherein are divers sorts of fryers and munks . . . ; using their habit and service as in Rome itself is used.

In Munster are—1° Doctor Creagh, B. of Cloyne and Cork, who came into Ireland in the time of the late Rebellion of the E. of Desmond, being in action of rebellion with him. He is kept in the country these 11 or 12 years past without pardon or protection, and altho he appeare not in any publicque assembly where Englishmen be present, yet he useth all manner of spiritual jurisdiccions within the whole province, being the Pope's Legate, consecrating churches, making priests, confirming children. . . . It is well known that this Creagh is one of the most dangerous fellowes that ever came to this land, continued there longest of any of his sort, and hath done more harm already there within these two years than Dr. Saunders did in his time . . . he draweth the whole country to disloyalty, his credit is such.

There is one James Karney, supposed Bp. of Imley, that came over from Rome last year.

There is one Sir Teig O'Swyllivan, an ernest Precher of Popery, still preaching from house to house in Waterford, Clonmel, and Fethard, and in the country about these townes.

There is one Dr. Thomas Rachtor, born in Fethard, and lately come from Roome.

There is a seminary born at Cashel, named W^m O'Gorhye, who came with the said Buishop and Doctor the last yere.

There is one J. O'Clearie, a seminarie, who came with the foresaid company the last yeare, and brought a dispensation for the town of Galway for the killing of the holy Spaniarde.

J. Buenagh of Fethard, lately come from Rome, a seminarie, dwelling at Fethard and thereabouts.

Sir W^m O'Cherohy, a seminarie, lately come from Rome, and now dwelling at Clonmel, Cashel, and Fithard.

Sir Conly McNi Marie an ernest precher, semynarie.

Morice Keating, seminarie, chapleyn to the said Dr. Creagh, one of his ordinarie messengers to great men when occasion requireth.

Sir Donogh Oge O'Nahane, one of said Dr. Creagh's chapleins.

Piers Kelly, ordained by Dr. Creagh.

Rory McCragh, very familiar with Dr. Creagh.

J. Morrice, priest reconciled to Papystry.

R. Gyanan, priest, took upon him the ministry once, now reconciled to papistry by Dr. Creagh.

Morice Ohillane, priest, one of the chieftest mayntainers Dr. C. hath in the whole Knight's country.

At Clonmel, Garret Reken and Sir Walter. At Cahir, Darby Calavan.

At Cashel, Patrick Yonge, dwelling always with Nicholas Haly.

At Boyton Rath, Sir Dyonis, priest. At Kilternan, Philip Stackbolde.

In Waterford, Rich. Eneas. At Loghonoy, Mat. O'Dellany.

At Kilkenny, G. Power, also Patrick Oholen, dwelling with R. Rothe.

Sir Donogh O'Casshey, Chancellor of Limerick, according to Romish institucions.

Other priests are— Rory O'Fahy, Thomas Coherey, Morice O'Hownim, Richard Bowdrave.

Certein rich merchaunts and good gent. within the citye of Waterford do specially relieve and mainteyne seminaries and massing priests :—

1° J. Sherlock, who hath been Mayor the last yere, doth retain in his howse one Dr. Teig O'Swillivan, a Jesuyt seminary, which priest hath divers times preached publicly in the house of one Wm Lyncolle and other places in the citye and country, and also in Clonmell.

P. Graunt FitzJames of Waterford, merchaunt, and Rich. FitzNicholas of the same, merchaunt, do retain by them both one Sir David, priest of Kilmallock.

J. Leay FitzNicholas, P. White, R. Comerford, and J. Browne fitzHenry of Waterford, merchaunts, do by them retain one Sir Morren, priest.

Belle Butler, wife unto T. Comerford of Waterford, merchaunt, who is himself in Spain these 12 months, and one J. Myller, and J. Whyte FitzWilliam, merchaunts, do retain one Sir John White, priest.

T. Porter and J. Miller of Waterford, merchants, do retain in their house Teig O'Cane, priest.

Richard Agnes, priest, reteyned by the whole city in general, who doth dwell in the new building of Alexander Brewers of Waterford, merchaunt, who sometimes professed religion, and now revolted.

Thomas Wadding, counsellor att lawe, doth reteine in his howse one Kealinge, a priest.

Richard Power, gent., is very willing and able to inform on such matters.

Abridged from *State Paper in Kilk. Jour. of Arch*, year 1856, p. 81 ; see other Lists of Catholic Clergymen in *Cal. of S. Papers, Ireland* (1606-1608); and in the *Kilkenny Journal*, Aug. 22, 1874.

CATALOGUS IBERNORUM IN SOCIETATE, 1609.

(Ex Archiv. Soc. Jesu, Romae.)

	Provincia.	Aetas.	In Socte.	Gradus.
In Ibernia.				
P. Christophorus Holivodius	Dublinen.	50	25	4 vot.
P. Thomas Sheyn	Clonmell.	46	25	3 ,,
P. Barnabas Carnaeus	Cassilien.	42	20	4 ,,
P. Nicolaus Leynich	Clonmell.	48	23	3 ,,
P. Andreas Mulron	Clonmell.	46	29	4 ,,
P. Patricius Lenanus	Medensis	48	13	
P. Walterus Waleus	Cassilien.	35	13	
P. Mauritius Wisaeus	Waterforden.	44	15	
P. Jacobus Everardus	Fetharden.	34	12	
P. Robertus Nugentius	Meden.	28	8	
P. David Galvaeus	Corcagen.	30	5	
P. Joannes Gerottus	Dublinen.	56	30	4 ,,
P. Jacobus Saulus	Cassil.	30	2	
P. Thomas Kiranus	Conacen.	34	2	
P. Thomas Briones	Kilken.	27	5	
P. Joannes Barnevallus	Meden.	33	10	
P. Henricus Cusacus	Dublinen.	26	4	
P. Robertus Bathaeus	Meden.	27	5	
In Lusitania.				
P. Cornelius Rocha	Toumen.	40	10	
P. Petrus Nash	Fetherden.		1	
Andreas Nolanus	Galven.	24	9	
Joannes Morus	Meden.	27	9	
Robertus Queitrotus	} Dublin.	20	4	
Robertus Coutinus		23	5	
Robertus Birnus			4	
Gulielmus Crevaeus	Cassilien.		4	

APPENDIX. 291

	Provincia.	Aetas.	In Socte.	Gradus.
LUSITANIA—*Continued.*				
Joan. Bap.ta Dugin	Ostrien.	25	5	
Michael Barick	Rossen.	24	3	
Michael Cantuel	Tipperar.		4	
Gualterus Lincaeus	Galven.			
Edoardus Clarus	Waterforden.	29	5	
IN BELGIO.				
P. Thomas Halaeus	Kilmaloc.	30	4	
P. Joannes Birmingamus	Galven.	36	2	
P. Isacus Briverus	Waterforden.	34	1	
P. Petrus Wadingus	Waterforden.	26	8	
P. Henricus de Simone	Dublinen.	42	18	4 vot.
Michael Geraldinus	Dublinen.	20	3	
IN ITALIA.				
Joannes Lombardus	} Waterfor.	25	5	
Thomas Comefortius		26	5	
Odoardus Barnewallus	Dublin.	23	5	
Georgius Geraldinus	Meden.	25	5	
Robertus Netervillus	Meden.	27	5	
Joannes Shaeus	Kilken.	28	5	
Gulielmus Malonus	Dublin.	23	3	
Jacobus Morganus	} Meden.	24	1	
Nicolaus Nugentius		22	1	
Bartholomeus Hamlinus	Meden.	20	1	
Georgius Galtromus	Dublin.	19	1	
Stephanus Gouldaeus	Corcagien.	26	1	
IN HISPANIA.				
P. Jacobus Archerus	Kilken.	64	36	4 vot.
P. Richardus Conuaeus	Rossen.	37	17	
P. Thomas Vitus	Clonmell.	52	15	Coad. Spirit.ls
P. Stephanus Vitus	Clonmell.	34	13	
P. Richardus Valesius	Waterfor.	27	11	
P. Gulielmus Bathaeus	Dublin.	44	12	
P. Stephanus Mortyns (qu. Mortius?)	Waterfor.	25	8	

STATE OF IRELAND ANNO 1598.

	Provincia.	Aetas.	In Socte.	Gradus.
HISPANIA—*Continued.*				
P. Gulielmus Morganus	} Waterfor.	26	8	
P. Jacobus Valaeus		27	9	
P. Jacobus Comefortius		26	9	
Patricius Sherlocus		25		
Gulielmus Vitus		26	8	
Michael Wadingus		22	5	
Joannes Laeus	Kilken.	26	11	
Jacobus Butlerus	Rossen.	30	10	
Richardus Carricus	Dublin.	28	5	
Jacobus Gripeus, or Griphus	Dublin.	24	5	Coadiutor
IN SUPERIORE GERMANIA.				
Ambrosius Wadingus	} Waterf.	26	5	
Laurentius Laeus		25	5	
IN AUSTRIA.				
P. Florentius Morus	Ultanus	57		Coad. Spirit[is]
IN GALLIA.				
P. Richardus Datonus	Kilken.	30	7	4
P. Richardus Comefortius	Waterf.	30	5	4
IN PARAGUARIA.				
P. Thomas Fildeus	Limbricenjis	62	38	

'Ego, Talbotus Gualterus n. Dublinii 1562, patre Gulielmo Talboto viro nobili (adhuc superstite)? matre Maria Bermingham (in D[no.] defuncta).'—10 Maii 1595.

'Batheus Gul. Dublinii n. 1564 a Joanne, Judice, et Eleonora Preston.'

'Barnwall Joan. n. 1576 in Comitatu Medensi, a Roberto nobili Domino de Stacallan et ab Alsona Brendon.'

APPENDIX. 293

'Wadingus[a] Petrus, Waterfordiensis n. 1581 a Thoma, et Maria Valesia, nobilibus.

' De Burgo Thomas, Limericensis n. 1588 a Thoma, et Joanna Arthur.

'FitzSimon[b] Henricus, Dublinen. n. 1566 a Nicolao, Armigero seu primogenito Equitis Aurati, et senatore Dublinensi, et Anna Edgrave ' (qu. Segrave ?).
—*Extracts from the Album of the Novitiate S.J. of Tournay*, by Father Morris, S.J.

' Carolus Leae n. 1545 in oppido Cluenensi Dioecesis Corcag.; pater erat Mauricius Leae Doctor Medicinae, mater Maria Chihi.

' Nicholaus Sedgrave n. 1538, Dublinii a Jacobo Sedgrave qui exercebat mercaturam, et Margarita Bath.

'Thomas Phildius[c] n. 1549 Limerici, Pater ejus Gulielmus Medicinae callebat, Mater Geneth Creah, ambo nunc (1574) mortui.

[a] A Jesuit, author of several literary and theological works; called in *Sotwell's Bibliotheca*, and in *Smidl's Historia Provinciæ Bohemiæ*, ' Vir in omni scientiarum genere praestans ; ' professor of poetry, rhetoric, and metaphysics at Louvain ; professor of theology at Louvain, Antwerp, Prague, and Gratz ; and for thirteen years Chancellor of two universities at Prague. His brother, Michael Wading, S.J., wrote, besides other works, a little book, on which a distinguished professor of the Roman College published a commentary in two large folio volumes. M. Wading was professor of *belles-lettres* and divinity, and also Rector in four colleges of Mexico. Sketches of his career are given by *De la Reguera*, and by the Mexican *Diccionario Universal*, under the name of 'Godines o Wadingo.' A third brother, Luke Wading, S.J., filled the first chairs of divinity in Salamanca, Valladolid, and Madrid ; he is called in the *Literæ Annuæ of Toledo*, ' Vir ingenio literis eximie culto, . . . quemque summis aequiparare possis ; quicquid doceret scientia et auctoritate implebat, multifarie eruditus.' He edited a posthumous work of his cousin, Paul Sherlock, S.J., and had some works ready for the press when he died. Their first cousin, Ambrose Wading, S.J., was elder brother of the famous Franciscan ; he was professor of theology at Dilingen University, and superior of a seminary attached to it, where he governed 150 chosen young religious sent from 40 monasteries of various orders in Germany. Of him the *Historia Provinciæ Germaniæ Superioris* says, ' Cum juxta divinis humanisque scientiis omnibus excelleret, longe tamen virtutibus magis enituit.'

[b] Fr. FitzSimon is called in *Wood's Athenæ*, ' A pillar of the Catholic Church, being esteemed a great ornament among them, and the greatest defender of their religion of his time.' See *Olliver's Collectanea*, and a memoir of Fr. FitzSimon by E. Hogan, S.J., in the *Irish Ecclesiastical Record*.

[c] Fr. Field spent fourteen years on the Brazillian Mission, and about forty on the Paraguay Mission, of which he may be considered the father and founder.—See *Cordara's Historia S.J.*, an. 1626; and *Del Techo's Historia Paraquariæ*.

Of the other Jesuits named in the catalogue, Holiwood, Carney, Roche, Malone, N. Nugent, R. Conway, Stephen White, and W. Bathe wrote some works ; the life of Stephen White

'Jacobus Barry n. 1552 in Civitate (Comitatu?) Corcagiensi, Pater, Joannes Barry, et mater Joanna Sanaghan vivebant de suis redditibus . . . propria manu.'—*Extracted from the Album of the Novitiate of St. Andrea, Rome*, by the Editor of this Book.

WRITERS WHO LIVED IN THE YEAR 1598.

Laymen.—Walter Stanihurst, Michael FitzSimon, W. Quin, J. Talbot, R. Stafford, H., Burnel, and Sir J. Ware, all of Dublin. R. Barnwall of Meath; Connel M'Geoghegan of Westmeath; R. Rothe of Kilkenny; Ludowick Barry, Captaine Garret Barry, Philip O'Sullevan Beare, and Fineen M'Carthy Mòr of Cork (see *supra*, p. 176). Dermot O'Meara of Tipperary, and T. Russel of Munster (?) R. Bellew of Louth; Dr. Neil O'Glacan and Cucogry O'Clerigh of Donegal; O'Mulconry of Roscommon; O'Duigenan of Leitrim; Darcy of Galway, and Thadeus Dun.

Protestant Clergymen.—Drs. Donelan and Daniel, Archbishops of Tuam; J. Usher, Abp. of Armagh, and his brother, Ambrose, of Trinity College; J. Kerney, Treasurer of St. Patrick's, and Thady Dowling of Kildare (was he a Protestant?).

Catholic Clergymen.—Dr. Lombard, Abp. of Armagh (see p. 285); Dr. O'Devany, Bp. of Down; Dr. Rothe of Ossory, and Dr. Tyrry of Cork; J. Coppinger of Cork; Dr. Keating and T. Carve of Tipperary; J. Wadding of Wexford; Dr. Piers of Westmeath; T. Messingham of Leinster; R. Stanihurst of Dublin, who after his wife's death became a priest, and whose son was author of many works.

Religious of various Orders.—H. Ryan and Daniel O'Daly (of Kerry), called 'Polyhister' on account of his great learning, has been sketched by Dr. Reeves and the Bollandist, V. de Buck. Hollywood is mentioned with honour in the history of the University of Padua; he was professor of theology in some Continental colleges, and after four years in the Tower of London he became superior of his brethren in Ireland for twenty-three years. W. Bathe wrote a book on 'The Arte of Music,' and other works. R. Nugent, a great mathematician, made some improvement in the Irish harp. Thomas White founded the Irish college of Salamanca. James Archer was a very remarkable man. R. Netterville was beaten to death by Cromwell's soldiers in 1649; and Dominick O'Collin, ex-colonel of heavy cavalry in the Wars of the League, ex-captain of the Port of Corunna, who became a Jesuit lay brother in 1598, was hanged in Cork in the year 1602.

Dominicans. O'Daly, says Baronius, became the admiration of Louvain, Madrid, France, and almost all Europe. Wm. Furlong of Wexford, and Sebastian Shortal of Kilkenny, Cistercians; D. Malone of the order of St. Jerome, and Pursell, a monk.

Order of St. Francis.—Dr. McCaghwell of Down, Abp. of Armagh; B. O'Hosey, H. Chamberlain, H. Ward, and Michael O'Clery (the chief of the Four Masters), all of Ulster; D. Mooney of Meath; Miles of Drogheda; R. Rochford of Leinster; Dr. Conry, Archbp. of Tuam; F. Mathews of Cork; T. Strange and the famous Luke Wading of Waterford; J. Ferral of Munster; T. Geraldine, F. Gray, M. Walsh, A. Hickey, and P. O'Connor.

Society of Jesus.—Wm. Bathe, Christopher Holywood, H. FitzSimon, and Wm. Malone of Dublin; R. Conway of New Ross; Wm. St. Leger of Kilkenny; N. Nugent of Meath; N. Comerford; P. Sherlock, Peter Wading, M. Wading, and Luke Wading, all of Waterford; S. White of Clonmel; B. O'Kearney of Cashel; J. Young of Cashel; M. Cantwell (?) of Tipperary; and Conor O'Mahony of Co. of Cork; R. Fleming, R. Rochford, J. Houling, J. Clare.—See *Ware's Writers, Hibernia Dominicana,* and *Bibliothèque des Ecrivains de la Compagnie de Jésus.*

IRISH COLLEGES ANNO 1598.

1. The College of Salamanca, founded by Father Thomas White, S.J., in 1582; opened in 1592 by Fathers White, Archer, and Conway, S.J.
2. Trinity College, Dublin, opened in 1593.
3. Lisbon, founded by Fr. Houling, S.J., an. 1593.—*Historia Soc. Jesu.*
4. Douai, founded in 1594 by Dr. Cusack, a Meath clergyman.—See *Ware's Antiquities,* ed. by Dr. Harris; *Anderson's Native Irish,* p. 79; and *History of the Irish Colleges on the Continent,* published in the *Irish Ecclesiastical Record.*

'From about the yeare 1555, as is well known, these late heresies oppressed religion in our countrie, banished teachers, extinguished learning, exiled to foreign countries all instruction, and enforced our youth either at home to be ignorant, or abroad in povertie rather to glean eares of learning, than with leisure to reap any great abundance thereof. Yet such as travelled to foreign countries, notwithstanding all difficulties, often attained to singular perfection and reputation of learning in sundrie sciences, to principal titles of universities, to high prelacies, of whom some are yet living, some departed in peace.'—*H. FitzSimon, S.J.,* preface to his work, *On the Masse.*

ADDITIONAL NOTES ON ULSTER.

Louth (see p. 3) stretches beyond Meath and the mouth of the Boyne, with a very winding shore to the north; has a soil fit for pasture, and so rich as readily to answer the expense of cultivation. *Drogheda*, called by the English Tredagh, a handsome populous town — *Camden*. *Killingcoole Castle* (see p. 4) has had many outworks and vaults running into one another, and is said to communicate with Castle Derner, six furlongs off; Glass Pistol Castle remains still. Castle Roche (see p. 5) is a noble ruin.—*Gough*.

Down (see p. 7) is an extensive and fertile country. Lecale, a rich country, and its extreme point is called by sailors at present St. John's Foreland. *Ardes* (p. 11) is a peninsula, resembling a bended arm, being joined to the rest of the island by a very narrow isthmus, as the arm to the shoulder. The soil is everywhere very kindly, except where in the middle, for near twelve miles in length, extends a wet and morassy level. The shore is thick set with small villages. *Strangford* (p. 12) is a safe harbour, where the river Coyn rushes with a great fall of water into the sea.—*Camden*. *Dundrum Castle* (p. 12) is strong and boldly seated on a rock, its ruins are of an irregular multangular figure, with a fine round tower about 35 feet diameter within. Ardglass (p. 12) exhibits at present a striking spectacle of its ancient strength and importance, being composed of a number of castles and a ruined church. But what is most worthy of attention is a long range of building in the castle style, 250 feet in length, in breadth only 24 feet; the thickness of the walls 3 feet. It was probably built before 1381, if it be not more ancient.—*Gough*.

Antrim (p. 17), within two miles of Ballycastle, is a castle, and next it an ancient building, called the Abbey, in which is the inscription—'In Dei deiparaeque Virginis honorem illustrissimus ac noblissimus dominus Randolphus McDonnell (p. 17), comes de Antrim hoc sacellum fieri curavit An. Dom. 1612.' Dunluce castle belonged to the McGuillans, who were dispossessed of it by the McDonnells in 1580.—*Gough*.

Armagh (p. 19) is, as I have been told by the Earl of Devonshire, Lord Deputy, the most fruitful and luxuriant soil of all Ireland; so that if any manure be laid on it to improve it, it becomes barren as it were in resentment.

Monaghan (p. 23) is very mountainous and covered with woods.—*Camden*.

Fermanagh (p. 25).—In its centre is the largest and most famous lake in Ireland, Lough Erne, 40 miles in extent, covered with thick woods, and full of inhabited islands, some of them containing 100, 200, and 300 acres. This lake stretches not east and west, as described in the maps, but from south to north, 14 miles in length, and 4 miles in breadth; it afterwards contracts itself like a regular river for 6 miles; on this part of it is *Inis-Killin*, the principal fortress in these parts. Thence it turns and spreads itself to the west, 20 miles in length, and 10 miles in breadth, as far as *Belek*, near which is a cataract and a most noble salmon-leap.

Tir-Oen (p. 25) is rough, fruitful, and 60 miles long and 30 broad, divided by the mountains called Slieve-Gallen into Upper and Lower. In it are *Dungannon*, the principal residence of the Earls, a handsomer house than is common in this country, but has often been fired by its owners to prevent its being burned by the enemy; also *Ublogahell*, where O'Neil, the haughty tyrant of Ulster, used to be crowned in the manner of his country. *Logh Eaugh* (p. 25) is a fine lake, well stocked with fish; the varied aspect of its banks, shady woods, meadows covered with perpetual verdure, fields if well cultivated extremely fertile, sloping hills, and the many brooks that run into it—all conspire to render it most pleasant and profitable. In Upper Tir-Oen is the castle of *Straban*, a famous castle, inhabited in our time by Tirlogh Leinich O'Neil, and some other castles of minor importance—which, as in other parts of this Kingdom, are only high towers with narrow loopholes rather than windows, to which adjoin apartments of turf covered with straw, having large courts surrounded with ditches and bushes to defend their cattle from robbers. All the glory or reputation of this county is derived from its lords, who exercise a kind of tyrannical sovereignty, of whom two were Earls of Tir-Oen, viz., Con O'Neale and Hugh, his son's son.—*Camden.*

Colrane (p. 28).—'O'Cahan had in early life protected the troops of Elizabeth against O'Donnell, had revolted from O'Neill in the height of his rebellion, and made peace with the English, had appeared against Tyrone in a suit of law; and by the grossest injustice he and all dependent on him were deprived of every inch of land they held.' 'The County of Colrane is O'Cahan's fruitful country. We had a jury of Clerke or scholars for the jurors, 15 in number, of whom 13 spake good *Latin*, and that very readily.' They were—2 O'Cahans, 3 O'Mullens, 2 McAtagarts, 2 McCawells, McEvally, O'Heney, McRedy, McGillegan, McCloskie, and O'Heny.—*Ulster Jour. of Arch.*, No. 15, and *Sir J. Davis' Letter*, in No. 16.

ADDITIONAL NOTES ON LEINSTER, &c.

Dublin (p. 35) is a good corn country, abounding in all sorts of game, but so bare of wood in many parts that they are forced to burn turf or English pit-coal; it is well stocked with towns and inhabitants, surpassing the rest of Ireland in improvements, and in a peculiar neatness. Where the little river Bray falls into the sea, a little higher up one sees *Ould Court*, an estate of the Walshes of Carrickmain, of ancient nobility and numerous in these parts. *Dublin* City is defended with strong walls, adorned with beautiful buildings and well peopled with inhabitants. From the quays run very strong walls of hewn stone, defended also on the south with ramparts, having six gates, which open into suburbs extending a great way beyond them. On the west side are two gates—Ormond gate and Newgate (which last is the public prison)—leading to a very long suburb called St. Thomas's.—*Camden.*

A True Description both of the Citty and Citizens of Dublin, by Barnaby Riche, Gent., in the Year 1610.

He that had no other knowledge of the City of *Dublin*, but as it is described by *M. Stanihurst*, in his Chronicle of *Ireland*, woulde thinke it to be far exceeding in Statelinesse of building and in many other Commodities more then it is at this houre, and yet I am sure that within these forty yeares that I have knowne *Dublin*, it hath bin replenished with a thousand chimnies, and beautified with as many glasse-windowes, and yet it maketh no such sumptuous shew. But (saith *M. Stanihurst*), *It dooth exceed in gorgeous buildings, in Martial Chivalrie, in obedience and loyaltie, in largenesse of hospitalitie and in manners and civility.* First, for the gorgeous buildings in *Dublin*, there be Som other Townes in Ireland that do farre exceed it. And to speake truly, the buildings of *Dublin* are neither outwardly faire, nor inwardly handsome: a ruynous kind of building, neither convenient nor well cast: neither do I thinke, that either the Masons, nor yet their Carpenters, are of skill to contrive any better.

For their *Martial Chivalrie*, I will not disavowe them, no doubt they have able men among them, both of body & mind, but I beleeve there are better Souldiers in Ireland, then any be in *Dublin*.

To speake the truth of *Dubline* as it *deserveth*. First, for the Towne it selfe, it is convenient enough, pleasantly seated, as wel for the serenity of the ayre as for the pleasing walks that are round about the Citty.

The Cittizens themselves are wonderfully reformed in manners, in civility, in curtesy: themselves and their wives modest and decent in their apparell (I speake of the better Sort), and they are tractable enough to any thing, Religion only excepted.

For *their largenesse of Hospitalitie*, I will not deprive them of their right: They are bountifull enough of their meat and drinke, according to their abilities. Now lastly, for *their manners and civility*, I confesse, *Dublin* is very well reformed, since *M. Stanihurst* writ his Chronicle. And now hee cometh againe to speake of the pleasantnesse of the scituation, and by seeming, he would make it a town impregnable. But I thinke *M. Stanihurst* had little skil in the Art of Fortification. Then he describeth it with so many Churches, with so many Chapels, with so many streets, with so many lanes, with so many Gates, and with so many Bridges, as I protest, I having knowne *Dublin* these forty yeares, yet know not where to finde the one halfe of them he hath named; and a great many of those that are to be seen, when they are found, make but a sory shew in respect of the Commendation he hath given.

To speake the truth, there are seuerall Citizens of Dubline that are very wealthy & men of good ability, that haue there shoppes well replenished with all sortes of wares, as wel Mercery as Grocery, & Drapery, both linnen & woollen, & their is neither silk-man nor milliner in London, that can shew better wares (for the quantitie) then some of those do that bee called Merchantes of Dubline. But I am now to speake of a certaine kind of commodity that outstretcheth all that I have hitherto spoken of, & that is the selling of Ale in Dubline a Quotidian commodity that hath vent in euery house in the Towne euery day in the weeke, at euery houre in the day, & in euery minute in the houre. There is no Merchandise so vendible, it is the very marrow of the common wealth in Dubline: the whole profit of the Towne stands upon Alehouses, & selling of Ale.—*Barnaby Riche's Description of Ireland.*

Carlow (p. 51) 'is rich and tolerably wooded. In these parts live great numbers of Cavanaghs, good soldiers, famous horsemen, and still breathing the spirit of their ancient nobility in their abject poverty. But as they cherish the utmost inveteracy against each other, for I know not what murders committed on both sides many years ago, they are continually destroying one another with mutual violence and assassination.'—*Camden.*

Wexford (p. 56) is a town of no great size; the county abounds with English, still retaining the old English dress and idiom, though with a mixture of Irish.

Near Ferns, on the other side of the Slaney, live the Cavenaghs, Donells, Montaghs, O'Moors, Irish families of turbulent dispositions, and among them the Sinnots, Roches and Peppards, English families. . . . On this side the Slaney the bulk of the common people are of English extraction.—*Camden.*

Cavan (p. 117).—The O'Reillys were, not long since, particularly distinguished for their cavalry.—*Camden.*

Galway (p. 131) is at least the third city in Ireland, being handsomely built of hewn stone in a form nearly circular, and beautified with towers, frequented by merchants, who with great ease and advantage supply it with the various riches of land and sea.—*Camden.*

Maio (p. 140) is a fruitful and pleasant country, rich in cattle, deer, hawks, and honey.—*Camden.* The castles in this county are very numerous, and all square, says *Gough*, who gives the names of forty-five and the dimensions of six of them.

Leitrim (p. 147) consists entirely of mountains covered with luxuriant herbage; it feeds so many cattle that within its narrow compass it counted at one time above 120,000 head. Here rises the Shannon, that prince of Irish rivers, which sometimes narrow, sometimes broad, by its various windings, washes many counties. The principal families are O'Rorck, O'Murrey, Mac Lochleim, Mac Glanchie, and Mac Granell, all downright Irish.—*Camden.*

O'Rorke's castle, near Dromahare castle, from what remains, appears to have been strong and spacious, the windows still in being are high, narrow and dark. The castles of Longfield, Cloncorrisk, and Castlebar, all of the O'Rorkes, are still to be seen. Dungarbery castle seems to have been of some extent; it was built by Lady Elizabeth Clancy in the reign of Elizabeth.—*Gough.*

Limerick (p. 196) consists of two parts—that called the Upper one, in which are the cathedral and castle, has two gates with handsome stone bridges with battlements and drawbridges, one leading westward, the other leading eastward, to which last adjoins a town walled round with its castle and outworks.—*Camden.*

EVENTS OF THE YEAR 1598.

I.—' *The Cessation.*'

ON the 29th of October 1597, the Earl of Ormond, by virtue of her Majesty's letters, was made Lord Lieutenant-General of the army, and represented the Queen's 'own person.'[a] On the 22[d] of December he went to Dundalk, received O'Neill's conditional submission, and his 'humble' petition. The Petition asks, 'That all the inhabitants of Ireland may have free liberty of conscience, or, at leastways, the benefit of her Majesty's law without being cumbered with the law of reason.' 'For that the abuses of her bad officers hath been the beginning of all this trouble, and that the Irishry cannot away with the rigour of law upon every small occasion, their bringing up being but barbarous,' that Tyrone may be made a county palatine. That her Majesty withdraw her garrison from Tyrone 'and all other parts of the Irishry.' As there had passed an oath between O'Neill and all the Irishry that took part with him, that he would take no agreement for himself unless every of them had pardon and his predecessors' lands—he craves that the same may be granted, and that the Mores and Connors (dispossessed in Q. Mary's time) may have a reasonable portion of their predecessors' lands.[b] This was not a very humble petition made 'upon the knees of his heart.' Mr. Brewer, in his Introduction to Vol. III. of the *Carew Calendar*,[c] writes, 'To Tyrone's honour be it said, on one point he remained unshaken. It was required of him that he should not receive into his country any disloyal person, but, upon notice being given, send them to the Governor.' To that 'he agreeth, save only that he will not apprehend any spiritual man, that cometh into the country for his conscience sake.' 'In all his conferences with the

---

[a] *Car. Cal.*, pp. 296, 277.   [b] *Car. Cal.*, 274.   [c] p. xlv.

English authorities, and in his correspondence with his countrymen, liberty of conscience, and regard for the Catholic faith were put foremost by Tyrone.' Hence, when a Dublin Jesuit, Father FitzSimon, (a Palesman and no friend of O'Neill), was imprisoned in time of cessation, O'Neill wrote, 'I do feel myself more grieved, that any should be for his religion restrained in time of cessation than if there were 1000 preys taken from me. Wherefore, as ever you think that I shall enter to conclude peace or cessation with the State, let him be presently enlarged.'[d]

Ormond on his side proposed—1° 'abstinence from war' eight weeks from the date hereof; Tyrone 'agreeth, provided the like be observed by her Majesty's subjects towards himself and all in action with him.' He agrees to call out of Leinster as many as were sent thither by his direction; saving only, if any do stay contrary to his commandment, that they be used no otherwise than as they be with whom they tarry. He is contented that her Majesty's subjects shall buy necessaries in Ulster, so as his men and dependants may have like liberty among her Highnesses subjects, and he agrees that 'the Ulster men shall not come in troops or great companies around, whereby to take meat and drink of her Majesty's subjects by violence.' Restitution to be made of any prey or *bodragge* taken out of the Pale to the Fues, Ferney or any other part of the North, 'the same being trackted thither'—the like course to be held for any spoils taken from the Earl of Tyrone or his dependants by any of the army of the Pale—he agreeth.[e]

These articles and O'Neill's petition seem to have been taken to England by the Earl of Thomond. The *Annals* say, that 'shortly before Christmas the Earls of Ormond and Thomond went into Ulster, when they and O'Neill and O'Donnell passed three nights together at one place ... and a peace was made between the English and Irish on the oath of these Earls until May following. The proposals ... were dispatched to the Queen by the Earl of Thomond. This Earl went to England in the beginning of January.'[f]

' After the concluding of peace from Christmas to May 1598, between the Irish of Leathchuinn and the Earl of Ormond, the Irish of the North issued orders to all the insurgents of Leinster and Meath, namely, the Cavanaghs, O'Conors, O'Mores, the Gavel-Rannal (O'Byrnes), the O'Tooles, Tirrels, and Nugents, to desist for a short time from their acts of plunder and rebellion—and they did so at the bidding of their Chiefs. The Earl of Ormond permitted them

---

[d] Mr. Brewer's Introduction to Vol. III. of *Carew Calendar*, p. lvii.

[e] *Car. Cal.*, pp. 275, 276.

[f] *Annala*.

to frequent Leinster, Meath, and the East of Munster, and to eat and drink with the inhabitants) until news should come from England, in May, respecting peace or war. By this instruction they continued traversing and frequenting every country from Cill Maintain (the town of Wicklow) to the Suir, and from Loch Gorman (Wexford) to the Shannon. It was not easy for the inhabitants of these territories to bear their inordinate demands during this period.'[g]

In January the Lords Justices write, 'that they find cause of great distrust in Tyrone, and that he receiveth letters from the King of Scots;' in the same month Brounker speaks of 'the lamentable state of this accursed country—the enemy is grown insolent and intolerable; in discipline and weapons he is little inferior to us; the men of most spirit follow the rebels, and leave the rascals to the Queen's service.'[h]

'The 18th of Februarie, Brian Oge Orwarke (commonly called Ororke), Lord of Letrym, submitted himself in a great assembly on his knees to her Majestie, before Sir C. Clifford, Governor of Connaught' (whom O'Ruarc defeated the year after in the battle of the Curliews, in which Clifford was slain.—*Editor*). 'He and his followers promised in all humblenesse to perform all duties to her Majestie.... This goodly submission had all the same issue as followeth in that of the famous Faith-breaker, Tyrone.'[i] The *Carew Calendar* gives 'O'Rourke's fifteen Demands' made on the 8th February, among which are— 'that he may have his country, both spiritual and temporal, passed to him and his heirs by patent; that a gaol be built at Leitrim, and a ward of O'Rourke's choice be maintained by the Queen to defend it; that he may have warrant to confer with gentlemen in rebellion, and that what he promises in behalf of her Majesty be performed. All this was granted.'

The Irish *Annals* tell us that, 'O'Rourke (Brian Oge, the son of Brian, son of Brian Ballagh, son of Owen) was angry with O'Donnell (Hugh Roe, the son of Hugh, son of Manus) because of his having plundered O'Conor Roe against his wish, as we have written before; and moreover he was not at all on terms of peace with his own brother, *i.e.*, Teige O'Rourke, the son of Brian, son of Brian Ballagh (in consequence of a disagreement) about the partition of their territory and land. Wherefore O'Rourke confederated and formed a league of friendship with the Governor, Sir Conyers Clifford. O'Donnell was not pleased at hearing this news, for the O'Rourkes had, from a remote period, been the friends of his

[g] *Annala*, pp. 2045 and 2051.
[h] *Life of M'Carthy Mór*, pp. 165 and 473.
[i] *Moryson*.
[j] *Car. Cal.*, p. 279.

tribe, and he (the present O'Rourke) was his own kinsman, and he did not wish to make an incursion against him or plunder his territory, as he would treat all others in Connaught; but he felt certain that he must needs plunder him unless he should return to the confederacy of the Irish, for he (O'Donnell) was not at peace with any one who was under the tutelage of the English. For a certain time he privately solicited him to return, and at another time he menaced and threatened to plunder his territory unless he should come back. O'Rourke continued to listen to those messages from the beginning of Spring to the May following, at which time he went to Athlone and delivered up his hostages to the Governor; and they made (mutual) vows and promises to be faithful to each other; but though the engagement was sincere (at the time), it was not long kept.'[k]

'On the 15th of March, at a meeting in Dundalk, the Lord Lieutenant-General Ormond signified to Tyrone that her Majesty had been induced by his humble submission to give pardon to him and all the Inhabitants of Tyrone upon conditions following:—1, that he renew his submission in some publike place; 2, that he promise due obedience of a subject, and not to intermeddle with the Irish, but now leaving them to themselves, that they may become humble suitors for their own pardons, in which case it is promised to them also; 3, that he disperce his forces, upon receit of his pardon, and dismiss all strangers, Irish, Scots, or others; 4, that he renounce the name and title of *Oneale;* 5, not to intermeddle with her Maiestie's wriaghtes (so the Irish call the bordering lords, whom the Ulster Tyrants have long claimed to be their vassals); 6, that he build up again, at his owne charges, the Fort and Bridge of Blackwater, and furnish the soldiers with victuals as he formerly did; 7, that he deliver to the L. Lieutenant the sonnes of Shane Oneale, who were her Maiestie's Prisoners till breaking out they fell into his hands, and were imprisoned by him; 8, to declare all intelligence with Spaine, and leave it; 9, that he receive a Sheriff for Tyrone, as all other countries doe; 10, that he put in his eldest sonne for pledge, and at all time come to the State, being called; 11, that he pay a fine in part of satisfaction for his offence, according to her Maiestie's pleasure; 12, that he aid no Rebell, nor meddle with the Inhabitants on the east side of the Ban, yet so as he may enjoy any lands he hath there; 13, that he receive not any disloyal person, but send such to the chiefe governour.'

'To the 5th O'Neill says—he desireth nothing of the wriaghts, but such duties

[k] *Annala*, p. 2053.

as they yielded since his grandfather's time. He refuseth the 7th, because he had not those prisoners from the State. The 10th he refuseth, for the pledges (in particular). For the 11th he agreeth to a fine of 500 cowes, yet praying the L. Lieutenant to be a means to her Maiesty for the remittal thereof. To the last he agreeth, provided that he would deliver no man to the State, who came to him for cause of conscience. . . . Hereupon at the instance of the L. Lieutenant the Lords Justices caused Tyrone's pardon to be drawne, and sealed with the great seale of Ireland bearing date the 11th of April 1598.'

'Tyrone received his generall pardon; but, continuing still his disloyal courses, never pleaded the same, so as upon his indictment in Sept. 1595, you shall find him after outlawed in the year 1600.'¹

The truce, which lasted till the 7th of June, was violated only once, that is, when 'James (the brother of the Earl of Ormond), the son of Edward, son of James, son of Pierce Roe Butler, and the son of Mac Pierce, sheriff of the county of Tipperary, and many other gentlemen, proceeded precisely at Easter on an incursion against Brian Reagh O'More, a gentleman of the Irish party, who was passing Easter in Ikerrin; but disaster and misfortune befell the assailants, for many of their gentlemen, of their followers, and of their soldiers, were slain, and James, the son of Edward Butler, was taken prisoner; but Brian Reagh delivered him up in a week afterwards to the Earl of Ormond on account of the peace we have mentioned, and after it had been ascertained that it was not by the permission of the Earl this attack was made.'ᵐ

2.—*The War in Ulster.*

'An answer arrived from England to the letters of O'Neill, O'Donnell, and the other Irish chiefs in alliance with them. The Queen and the Council did not consent to grant them the conditions they demanded; and therefore the Irish exchanged their peace for war, their quietness for turmoil, and their tranquillity for dissension; so that they rekindled the ancient flame of hatred in the summer of this year.'ᵐ

So the *Four Masters* have written, but *Moryson* says that O'Neill's terms were accepted, yet that he 'wanted not pretences to frustrate this late treaty.' 'The Irish Kerne were at the first rude soldiers, so as two or three of them were employed to discharge one Peece, and hitherto they have subsisted especially by treacherous tenders of submission; but now they were growne

---

¹ *Moryson*, p. 23; *Confer Car. Cal.*, p. 278.   ᵐ *Annala*, p. 2053.
ᵐ *Annala*, p. 2053.

ready in managing their Peeces, and bold to skirmish in bogges and wooddy passages; yea, this yeare and the next following became so disasterous to the English, and successfull in action to the Irish, as they shaked the English Government in this Kingdome till it tottered, and wanted little of fatal ruine. Tyrone wanted not pretences to frustrate this late treaty, and to return to his former disloyalty, and the defection of all other submitties depending on him followed his revolt. First he sent aid to Phelim Mac Feogh, chief of the O'Byrnes, the sonne of Sir Feogh Mac Hugh (killed in Sir W. Russel's time), to the end he might make the warre in Leinster against the English.'º

3.—*Siege of the Fort of Blackwater.*

'Because the English Fort of Blackwater was a great eyesore to him, lying on the cheefe passage into his Countrey, Tyrone assembled all his forces and assaulted the same. But Captaine Williams with his company under him so valiantly repelled the great multitude of assaylants with slaughter of many and the most hardy, attempting to scale the fort (which was only a deep trench or wall of earth to lodge some one hundred Souldiers) as they, utterly discouraged from assayling it, resolved to besiege it afarre off, and knowing they wanted victuals presumed to get it.'ᵖ *Moryson* speaks disparagingly of this fort, which is said by *O'Clery*, in his life of O'Donnell, to have been 'a strong earthen fort, with fighting towers, windows, and loopholes, and a garrison of 300 men.'

The assault mentioned by *Moryson* must have taken place in the year 1597, as we know from Francis Cosbie that the day after it a 'Lord Deputy drewe towards the forte and made an oration to the constable and soldiers.' That 'many assaltes' were made 'to surprize' the fort in 1598 is certain from the letter of the L. Justices, of July 22^d, and from O'Sullevan's account, which I will here insert. 'While O'Neill was besieging Portmore, O'Donnell, who had come to help him, persuaded him to storm the place. Ladders high enough for the wall, and able to hold five men abreast, were, in spite of the fire from the fort, placed against the wall, but as the English, foreseeing the escalade, had deepened the trench; most of the ladders were found too short, and the few men who gained the top of the rampart were killed before they could be supported. One hundred and twenty of the assailants were slain, and among them Morogh Cavanagh, a Leinster gentleman, who had proved himself a stout soldier in the battle fields of Belgium.'ᑫ

º *Moryson*, p. 24.   ᵖ *Moryson*.   ᑫ *O'Sullevan's Hist. Cath.* p. 188.

APPENDIX. 307

This can scarcely regard the assault of 1597 mentioned by the *Four Masters*, in which 30 were slain, or that described by Cosbie, in which over 34 were killed. Cosby says that there were in the Fort 'Cap^n Will^{ms}, with some ccc soldiers . . . the valiantest men of Tiroane's forces undertooke to wynne the same . . . gave a most wonderfull and bould assault, continuing the same very long with great resolution, as well in their fighte as continuallye supplyinge of fresh men in the places of the slayne, hurte, and wyckened; and with great lykelehoode they had wonne the same at that instant, if they had met with a cravynne as they buckled wth a man of worthe . . . Cap^n Williams comforted his soldiers . . . and therefore, said he, pull up your hearts; for this hand of myne, havinge a linstock therein, shall give fyer to this traigne, and both blowe youe and myself up to the skyes rather than that these miscreants shall enjoy this chardge of mine.' Upon which every man that was able to stand and hould a weapon . . . cried out, 'We will die with honor to the last man.' The enemy being advanced to the top of the wall and covetinge by all means to enter . . . the ditches were filled with their dead corpses; yet stood they to it right manfully . . . the two field peeces charged with muscet shot paid them their hyre both comynge, stayinge, and retournynge; and glad they were (although it is a custome among them to carry away as many dead corpses and maimed men as they may), yet for all their cunninge they left xxxiiii behind them in the ditches, wth all their ladders, and some furniture for a witness they had come there; but I ensuer you that there was a nomber slaigne and hurte, that were conveyed away, and very few of the warde either slaigne or hurte.'*

I thought it right to insert this description for the honour of the besieged and the besiegers, though it relates to an assault immediately preceding the attempts 'to surprize' in 1598.

Sir G. Fenton writes on the 11th of June—'The last truce expired the 7th of this month, and within 2 days after Tyrone made this devesion of his forces; one parte he sent before the Blackwater, which he now holdeth invironed, swearing by his barbarous hand that he will not departe till he carry the forte; another parte he thrust into the Brenny, and at this present assaulteth the castle of the Cavan there, promising not to leave the place so long as he can gett a cow out of the English Pale to feed his companies.' The *Lords Justices* write, June 17—'The forte is blocked, the garrison consisteth upon 4 companies of foot.' *Ormond* writes to Cecil, June the 18th—'I confess hit is no small hartgrefe unto me to hold the place I do, and to want the meanes whereby I shold be inhabled to

---

* Abridged from Cosbie's Book on the *State of Ireland*, Aug. 20, 1598.

perform what I most desier. I protest to God the state of the scurvie fort of blackwater, which cannot be longe held, doth more toche my harte then all the spoyles that ever were made by traytors on mine owne landes. This forte was always falling and never victualed, but ons (by myself), without an armye.'

A spy gives this intelligence to Fenton—'The 13th day I made an excuse to goe into the forte, and the Capten tould me all his casse; wch was that he wold keepe the forte yet this moneth; wch he may well doe; for that he hath gott of late into the forte 17 or 18 of therles mares, wch will serve him and his company a good tyme. He prayith yo' Hon^r to haste away the Queene's armye to succor him, or else that he may know from you w^thin 20 daies whether he shall make his composicion with therle or not.

'Therle hath made great plashes betweene Armagh and the blackwater; and there he says he will fight wth the m^rsshall yf he come to vittell the forte. He lyeth there stronge with as great an armye as ev^r I saw in the north, and yet he hath of late geven leave to O'Donnell, M^cW^m, Maguire, and James McSorley to go hoame into their countreys, and to be readie to come agayne when he shall send for them.'

The *LLs. Justices* state, July 22—'The Forte is yet helde by that valyant Gent^m, Capten Williams, who commanded it; althoughe Tyrone have lately lent his whole forces to surprize it, and have lost many men still about yt, who have blocked them in on all sydes of that fort; yet . . . that Captain hath lately issued forth, and, besides killing 2 or 3 principal men, he hath gotten divers horses and garrans of Tyrone's into the forte, which stande him and the garrison in good steade of foode. Tyrone hath lyen before it above a month, plashing of passes, and digging deepe hoales in the Rivers the more to distress the armye that should come to releeve it, and has used many assaltes to gett it.'^s

'Cap^{n.} Williams lying longe in that unhappye forte without any reliefe but suche garrons and horses as he by pollicy could attayne unto for the suffycinge of himself and hungry ward, acquainted the State with this their woeful misery; who, having regarde of their distresses, and the safety of that great bulwarke, sent for the Lo. Lieutenant-Genl to Dublin; where, after debating what course was to be held, in the end concluded that Sir H. Bagnall should have the commande of this expedicion.'^t

The *LL. Justices* write—' On the 2^d of Aug., upon conferment held in coun-

---

^s See these letters in full in *Kilk. Jour. of Arch.*, an. 1857; and in *M‘Carthy Mór*.   ^t Francis Cosbie—See *M‘Carthy Mór*, p. 474.

sell touching the revitlinge of Blackwater, the Marshal being present, sent for expressly by the L. Lieutenant, som of us were of opinion that the hazard were too great. . . . But when we saw his Lo. and the Marshal stande so much upon the honor of the service . . . we wished the L. Lieutenant to undertake the matter in person, as his presence might drawe many of the nobilitye with their followers, and might move Tyrone either from feare or from som other respects to give way to him. We and the Lo. Lieutenant had written to the Captain of the Blackwater to consider how he might make his composition in tyme to the most honour he could for her Ma^{ty} and best safety for himself; but the Marshal stayed these letters.

'His Lo. and the Marshall agreeing afterwards, his Lo. took upon him the matters of Leinster, and left to the Marshal the accion of Blackwater.'[u]

The LL. Justices wrote a private letter, stating that 'it is well knowen to all this table, how much against our advise the same (jorney to the Blackwater) was undertaken. When we could not drawe his Lordship and the Marshall from their purpose . . . we urged muche that his Lp. would himselfe undertake that service. . . . Yet his Lordship, being unable or unwilling to indure that troblesome jorney, answered us, that he himself could not be spared from the service in Leinster.'[v] These Justices must have been bearing false witness against Ormond; for that straightforward and fearless man wrote to Cecil—'Sir, for that I understand that the LL. Justices wrote over to you, after this disaster, that it was not there act to send the Marshal, but that it was a plott sett down between him and me, I have thoght goode for proofe of the contrary to send you the inclosed notes, which I pray you to make known to Her Majestye.'[w] Her Majesty, however, condemned Ormond, saying—'In the arrival of Sir R. Bingham, we knowe that you our coussin of Ormond, our Lieutenant, will find great ease. It being neither fitt nor possible that you shold spend your bodye in all services at all times; and yet we must pleynely tell you that we did much dislike that you did not attend the late accion; for yt were strange to us, when almost the whole force of our kingdom were drawn to a hedd, and a mayne blow like to be stroken for our honor against the cappytall rebell, that youe, whose person wold have better daunted the traytor, and would have carried with it another manner of reputation, and strengthe of the nobilitie of the Kingdome, shold employ yourself in an accion of less importance, and leave this to so meane a commander.'[x]

[u] LL. Justices, 16th Aug.
[v] Loftus and Gardener, Aug. 17.
[w] Ormond, Sep. 17—See *M'Carthy Mór*.
[x] Queen to LL. Justices, in *Car. Cal.*

4.—'The Jorney to the Blackwater.'

On the 2ᵈ of August, the *LL. Justices* write—'It may please yʳ LL's. to understand that uppon consideracion had of the forte of Blackwater, wᶜʰ yet holdeth out, as we are informed, thoughe with great extremetie, and comparinge likewise the state of Leinster endaungered in evʳʸ parte by the rebells of the same province, and aided by forces from Tyrone ... Sir H. Bagnall, the Marshall, is now to drawe into Ulster with parte of the armye, consisting upon 3500 foote by the polle, and about 300 horse to revittle the Blackwater; and with another parte of the armye, I, the L. Lieutenant-Genˡ, wᵗʰ such few companies as remayne, am to attend the prosecution in Leinster. The day appointed for the Rendevoues for the Ulster armye is the 16th of this month, when all the companies are to assemble at Ardye, and from thence to marche to the Newrie, and so to the Blackwater; the successe and accydents of wᶜʰ Jorney shall be advertised to yoʳ lls. as they shall fall out, wᶜʰ we pray God to prosper to Her Mᵗⁱᵉˢ Honor and the saffetie of the armye, onely we understand that Tyrone hath plashed the waies and digged deepe holes with other trenches and fortifications to ympeache the armye between Armaghe and the Blackwater.'ʸ

The troops marched through Drogheda, Ardee, and Dundalk;ᶻ and on the 12th of August they cam from the Newrie,ᵃ and reached Armagh on the 13th without any loss other than the taking of Capᵗⁿ Ratcliff prisoner, and some 4 or 5 others cutt off in the straight between Dundalk and the Newrie, and who straggled after the armye and did not march under the seffety thereof.ᵇ

5.—*Number and Quality of the English Army.*

The Armye numbered 4000 foote and upwards, and 320 horse by pole,ᶜ the most choice companies of foote and horse troops of the English Army,ᵈ and the most loyal and best tried in war;ᵉ but according to the Irish account the numbers were 4500 foot and 500 horse.ᶠ A state paper of the time says that—'In the end of April Her Majesty's army in Ireland was certified to be in heads'—

	Foote.	Horse.
Of English	2319	100
Of Palemen	1785	292
Meere Irishe	2478	129
English sent in July	2000	
Total	8582	521ᵍ

ʸ Lords Justices' Letter in *McCarthy Mór*, p. 477. ᶻ *Annala.* ᵃ Ill Newse out of Ireland. ᵇ LL. Justices. ᶜ Ormond. ᵈ Moryson and Camden. ᵉ *Annala.* ᶠ O'Sullevan. ᵍ S. P. given in *McCarthy Mór*, p. 173.

APPENDIX.   311

The best of these soldiers were sent to the north, and, to use the words of Queen Elizabeth, 'almost the whole forces of Her Majesty's Kingdome were drawen to a head, and a mayne blowe like to be stroken for her honor against the cappytal rebell.'[h]

'Bagnall was skilled in the art of war, as prudent as he was brave, cautious in success, undaunted in disaster, less contumelious to the conquered than most Englishmen, who are never sparing of their insults—he had few equals and fewer superiors among the generals of his country. His army consisted of 4500 foot under 40 standards and as many captains, lieutenants, ensigns, and sergeants (tesserarii), and of 500 horse under 8 standards led by Montague. The English were all veterans, who had served under General Sir John Norris in France, or had come from the Belgian fortresses, or had learned the soldier's trade in the Irish wars. The Irish of Bagnal's army were somewhat more numerous, and had often distinguished themselves in the service of the Queen. There were with him also some young Irishmen of distinction, such as Melmorra O'Reilly (called the Handsome on account of the rare beauty of his form and face), and Christopher St. Lawrence, son of Lord Howth. All these soldiers were well armed; foot and horse were furnished with breastplates, the shot had heavy or light guns, and swords, daggers, and helmets; and the whole host shone gaily in their plumes, sashes or sword-belts, and other military trappings. The brass cannons were on wheels and drawn by horses. There was an abundant supply of the munitions of war; and horses and oxen carried plenty of bread, salt meat, cheese, butter, and beer for the army and the fort of Portmore—while a great number of drivers, sutlers, and foragers accompanied the baggage.'[i]

6.—*The Irish Army—O'Neill's Address.*

'When O'Neill had received intelligence that this great army was approaching him, he sent his messengers to O'Donnell requesting him to come to his assistance against this overwhelming force of foreigners. O'Donnell proceeded immediately with all his warriors, both infantry and cavalry, and a strong body of forces from Connaught to the assistance of his ally. The Irish of all the province of Ulster joined the same army, so that they were all prepared to meet the English before they arrived at Armagh. They then dug deep trenches in the common road by which they thought the English would come.'[j]

Leaving some men to keep the garrison in check, O'Neill, on hearing of

[h] Words of Elizabeth given in a S. P. published in the *Kilk. Arch. Journal*.
[i] *O'Sullevan*, p. 19.
[j] *Annals*, p. 2061.

Bagnall's approach, marched to meet him, and took up his position a mile from Portmore, and two miles from Armagh. As O'Donnell had brought 1000 Connaught men under M‘William, and 1000 of his clansmen of Tirconnell, the northern army rose to the number of 4500 foot and 600 horse; but it was far inferior to the English host in equipment, as it consisted of light armed horse and infantry, with the exception of some heavy shot or musketeers.[k]

According to O'Clery's *Life of Hugh O'Donnell*, very few of the Irish were armed as the English were, in comparison with whom they were 'naked;' but they had enough of 'spears and broad lances with strong handles of ash, of straight, keen-edged swords and thin polished battle-axes, but devoid of the flesca and ecclanna which distinguished the English battle-axes—they also had javelins, bows and arrows, and guns with matchlocks.'[l]

'When the chiefs of the North observed the very great danger that now threatened them, they began to harangue their people to acts of valour, saying that unless the victory was theirs on that day, no prospect remained for them after it but that of being some slaughtered without mercy, and others cast into prisons and wrapped in chains, as the Irish had been often before; and that such as should escape from that battle would be expelled and banished into distant foreign countries; and they told them moreover, it was easier for them to defend their patrimony against this foreign people (now) than to take the patrimony of others by force, after having been expelled from their own native country. This exciting exhortation of the chiefs made (the desired) impression upon their people; and the soldiers declared that they were ready to suffer death sooner than submit to what they feared would happen to them.'[m]

The address given in Irish by O'Clery is thus translated by O'Donovan— 'Brave people, be not dismayed or frightened at the English on account of the foreign appearance of their array and the strangeness of their armour and arms, the sound of their trumpets and tabours and warlike instruments, or their great numbers—for it is absolutely certain that they shall be defeated in the battle of this day. Of this we are indeed convinced, for you are on the side of truth, and they are on the lie, fettering you in prisons, and beheading you in order to rob you of your patrimonies. We have indeed a very high hope that this very day will distinguish between truth, as Morann, the son of Maen, said in the celebrated proverb: *ni fuigbitear breiteam bus firiu cairae—there has not been found, there shall not be found a truer judge than the battle-field*, as we have heard from our poets, who have instructed us from a remote period.

[k] *O'Sullevan*, p. 191.   *Supra*, p. 34.   [l] See *Annala*, p. 2068, *note*.   [m] *Annala*.

"Moreover it is easier to defend your own patrimony against a race of strangers than to seek another's partrimony after being expulsed from your own native country, which has been in your possession from the year of the world 3500 to this very day."

'The gentlemen and chieftains said that what the princes had uttered was true . . . the minds of the heroes, and the courage of the common soldiers were raised, and the *Cinèl-Connell*, *Cinel-Owen*, *Airghialla*, and *Ui-Eathach-Uladh* were filled with fury, vigour and a desire of plying their arms, by the harangues of their princes and true leaders; and they promised to them that they would not yield a foot, and that they would suffer death in that field sooner than be defeated.

'There was another cause for the exaltation of the minds of the youthful soldiers. It was told to them that St. Bearchan, the prophet of God, had prophesied that a battle would be fought at that place against the Galls of Dublin by a Hugh O'Neill and by the province in general, for he had promised that the inhabitants of Ulster would come to his relief, and the Cinel-Connell in particular. The heroes believed that the prophet of God would not tell a lie. The person who first exhibited this prophecy was a certain famous poet of the faithful people of O'Donnell, who accompanied O'Donnell on this expedition, to excite and encourage him. His name was Fearfasa O'Clery. He asked what was the name of that place, and, being told it, he said that St. Bearchan had predicted a defeat of foreigners by a Hugh O'Neill, and that he had for a long time a recollection of the prophecy, which the true saint had delivered; and he proceeded to harangue the heroes, as was proper for one like him, and he said, reciting the words of St. Bearchan :

> A ccath an Atha-buidhe
> As lais tuitfe na danair
> Iar ndithughadh allmuireach
> Bidh faoilidh fir o Thòraigh.

> In the fight of Yellow-Ford
> By him shall be slain the Danair (barbarians);
> After the cutting off of the foreigners,
> Shall rejoice the men from Tory.'ᵃ

7.—*Marshal Bagnall's Address to his Soldiers.*

Bagnal delivered an address to his soldiers before setting out from Armagh. I give the substance of it from O'Sullevan—'Soldiers! I have selected you for this enterprise, leaving the raw recruits to the my Lord of Ormond. We shall

ᵃ *Annala*, p. 2068, *note*.

this day avenge the disasters of General Norris and Lord Borough ; the naked rebels will run away the moment they will see our armed and veteran warriors, and we shall secure all Ulster and a vast amount of spoils. Remember the valour you displayed, under my leadership, in relieving Armagh and driving O'Neill from his camp at Mullach-Ban. Whoever shall bring me this evening the head of O'Neill or O'Donnell shall receive one thousand pounds, and you all according to your services shall receive thanks and rewards from your General and your Queen. Let us march on to victory."[o]

8.—*The March from Armagh.*

On Mondaie the 14th of August, the Armie marched from Ardmagh, leving there all the victualls and some munition[p], the drink, women, and young persons, horses, baggage, servants, and rabble[q]. They started before sunrise[r]. It was concluded by the Counsell the day before, that the syxe regiments shoulde marche in single bodies, till such time as they sawe each other engaged, and then joyne in three bodies for eache others' releife if they found the grounde answerable[s], and turn out their wings, should they see cause[t]. Captains Lee and Turner were commanded with a partie of men to lead the forelorne hope[u]. Colonel Percye having the Vanguard, the Marshal his second, should both join and make one vanguard. Colonel Cosbie having the vanguard of the battle, Sir Thomas Maria Wingfield his second, were appointed the like. Colonel Cunie, then Sergeant Mayor having the vanguard of the rear, Colonel Billings his second, were appointed the like. The Marshal, in respect that his regiment had the vanguard, would go there, notwithstanding that he was advised by Wingfield to come into the battle and leave the vanguard to him ; the like did Cunic, but neither could persuade him. The battle was commanded by Wingfield, the rear by Cunie. The horse were divided into three bodies ; the vanguard led by Sir Callisthines Brooke, General of the horse ; the point by Capt. Montague, Lieutenant General ; the rear by Capt Fleming, marching betwixt the two rear regiments[v]. They marched severally, sum six or 700 paces between each regiment[w], so far asonder as one of them could not second nor help thother[x] ; for when the vanguard was charged they were within sight of our battel, and yet not rescued till they were overthrown[y]. Suer the devill bewiched them that none of them did prevent this gross error, whereof Ormond had warned the Marshal to take especiall care[z].

[o] *O'Sullevan*, p. 192.   [p] Montague.   [q] *Annala*.   [r] *O'Sullevan*.   [s] Colonel Byllinges.
[t] Order given to the Armye as well for their marching as in fighting.—*Car Cal.*   [u] Colonel Byllinges.   [v] *Car. Cal.*   [w] Montague.   [x] Ormond.   [y] Taaffe.   [z] Ormond.

APPENDIX. 315

9.—*The 'Skirmishe.'*

The day was bright and serene, the sun was glancing on the corselets and spears of the glittering cavalry, their banners waved proudly, and their bugles rang clear in the morning air, when suddenly, about seven o'clock, from the thickets on both sides of their path a volley of musketry swept through their foremost ranks[a]. The waye being harde and hillie ground within calliver shotte of wood and bogge on both sides, which was whollie possessed by [500 beardless kerne* of] thennemy continuelly playing upon us, the army was fought withal within half a mile of Armagh[b], in the pace and thick woods beyond it on the eastside[c], and on the right hand side of the common highway in wich my Lo. Borough passed to the Blackwater[d]; and the skirmishe was maintained on all sides up to the trenches, being two miles from Ardmargh[e]. Bagnall, on account of the thickets, was unable to return the fire of these skirmishers or to charge them with cavalry; and he, with difficulty, brought his troops through into a large plain, that stretched up to the Irish entrenchments. Here his horsemen pursued the sharpshooters; but were rolled over by the holes, which O'Neill had got made, and concealed with brambles and grass, while those who came to their assistance had to contend with the Irish light troops. Having got to safer ground, he sent out skirmishers and heavy shot, who were encountered by fresh troops of his enemy. His heavy cavalry armed with breastplates, and bearing lances six cubits long, which rested on their right thigh, were again and again charged by the Irish light horse, who threw at them darts three cubits long, and carried lances more than six cubits in length, which they used only when sure of their blow, and, when using, held poised by the middle over their right shoulders. Bagnal's progress was often arrested by these light troops; yet at eleven o'clock he reached a spot not far from the Irish camp, where his way was flanked by bogs and stopped by a ditch four feet high[f].

10.—*The Vanguard attacks the Trench.*

After a myles marching thus ('played on' by the Irish) we approached thennemys trentch,[g] being a ditche caste in fronte of our passage, a myle longe, som five footte deepe, and four footte over with a thorney hedge on the toppe; in the middell of a bog som forty paces over our vanguard passed the trentch[h], having crossed over the ford at the first bog, where the saker was left without stay, and

---

[a] *O'Sullevan.*   [b] *Car. Cal.* p. 280, and Kingsmill.   [c] *Moryson.*   [d] Taaffe.   [e] The two Kingsmills.   [f] *O'Sullevan.*   [g] Now a drain crossing *Anaha*, at the foot of a hill on which there is a 'sconce.' See p. 316, and note n.   [h] Montague.

so forward¹. The forelorne hope, led by Captains Lee and Turnor 'the great,' and the vanguard possesst the trenche, and passed forward to a skons made upon the top of the hill beyond the same; where they remayned a pretty while, and skirmish being hotlie entertained upon our reare, thennemy on horse and foote chardg our companies and bett them back to the trench again, where they were for the most parte all slaine, and their severall collors taken by thennemyeʲ. The vanguard was so distressed as they fell to runne, and were all in effect putt to the sworde without resistanceᵏ. To this question, what was the reason the vanguard was not seconded, beeing possessed of the trenches? Capt. George Kinsmell, who was in the poynte saieth, that the Marshal's regiment, who was to second the poynte (Percy's regiment), was in distance so far of, and hotly fought withal, that they cold by no means com up to second them, whereby the whole regiment was defeated, and all the captains slayne, Colonel Piercy and Capt. George Kingsmell only excepted, who by a stand made by the horsse recovered their second. What did the broken regiment, when you came to the second? Capt. Ceorge Kingsmell saieth, they joined with the marshal's regiment their seconds, and put themselves in order, and charged agayne to the trenches, which they won the second time and, for want of seconding by the Battayle, was defeated as the first. This onset of the Irish is thus described by O'Clery and the four masters. The English advanced vigorously until they sailled across the first broad, deep trench, and some of them were killed in crossing it. The Irish army then poured upon them vehemently and boldly, furiously and impetuously, shouting in the rear and in the van, and on either side of them. The van was obliged to avoid the onset, bide the brunt of the conflict, and withstand the firing, so that their close lines were thinned, their gentlemen gapped, and their heroes subduedᵐ. As the English shots reached farther than the Irish, the Irish adopted this plan; they scattered themselves around the English on all sides, closed in on them, and fought at close quarters with the Barbarians, drove in their shot and skirmishers from the flanks to the centre, and forced the battalions in armour to move to the flanks, and thus by their fire, and by the firm and compact order in which they were arrayed by their leaders, they retarded the English advance, and finally rolled back their vanguard when it reached the broad deep ditches in the plain of Belanahabuyⁿ.

ⁱ *Car. Cal.*—The saker was a large cannon.
 "The cannon, blunderbuss, and *saker*,
 He was th' inventor of, and maker."—*Hudibras.*

ʲ Lieut.-Taaffe. ᵏ Montagu. ˡ Declaration of Captains Ferdinando Kingsmyl and George Kingsmill. ᵐ *Annala.* ⁿ *O'Cleary's* Life of O'Donnell, M.S. R. I. Academy. The Ordnance Survey officers have mistaken the site of this battlefield.

11.—*The Fighting of the Battayle, or 2nd Brigade.*

What was the reason the Battayle came not up? They say that the saker being bogged, staied the Battayle so longe and thennemies gathered soe about them in such multitudes as they cold not boothe second the vangard and save the ordinance. Yet Cosbie, having the vauntgard of the Battayle, passed the bog and left the saker°. Wingfield coming thither made there a stand as well to carry off the saker [which stuck fast in a forde*], as to attend the coming up of the rear regiments, whom he doubted to be greatly engaged, for that he heard them in great fights, and had no sight of them a long time before, by reason of a hill betwixt them. Of this he went to acquaint the Marshal, thinking to find the vanguard but a little before him, which could not then be seen by reason of the hill, purposing to have it to make good that place, and that himself would go with the battle to fetch off the rear; but it was so far off as the Marshal sent to them to make good their retreat to that hill where he stood, and returned with Wingfield to the saker, which he then brought off by force of men, and went again with the Marshal, thinking that the vanguard had been come up, which was still advancing forward, and in all this time there was no sight of the rear^q. The Marshal coming from the rear of the armye,* when the van was beaten back, charged down with the battle,** and our horses which were in the vantguard; and in going down [having raised his visor***] he was slayne with a shott through his forrhead; after whose death, we that were on horseback found no goinge where the rebells stood, by reason of a mayne bogge' Tyrone, pricked forward with rage and envy of settled rancour against the Marshal, assayled the English first line, and turning his full force against the Marshal's person, had the success to kill him, valiantly fighting among the thickest of the rebels.* And as an army deprived of its leader does not generally maintain the battlefield, the General's people were finally routed by dint of conflict and fighting across the earthen pits and broad, deep trenches, over which they had previously passed—they were slaughtered, mangled, mutilated, and cut to pieces.*

At which time the Marshal was slain, the vanguard, either having received a message to make a retreat, or overlaid with the multitude of the enemy, wheeled about disorderly, which advantage the enemy took and brake them. Captain Evans was shot. Much of our powther took fire, wherewith many of our men were slain or hurt, and the rear of the battle disranked and routed"; these two or three barrels or fyrckens of powther spoiled many men and disordered others,

^o The Kingsmills.   ^p Montague.   ^q *Car. Cal.*, p. 280. Wingfield's account probably.
^a recte from the Battayl, E. H.   ** Qu. the poynte or his own regiment?   *** *O'Sullevan.*
^r Taaffe.   ^s *Moryson,*   ^t *Annala.*   ^u *Car. Cal.* and Montague.

and withall our great peece did us much hurte, staying our marche at every 12 score ende'. After this explosion, the ground was enveloped in a dense, black, gloomy mass of smoke for a considerable part of the day". The Rere of the Battayle mayntained fight for the saker, which cold not be recovered by reason yt was bogged, and the oxen killed that drew it[a], and the wheele broken[y]; upon which accident and the former defeatment the Sergeant Major and Montague came to Wingfield, chief commander, the Marshal being dedd, and they determined to retreat to Armagh; Cosby however, without orders, made an attack on the enemy, and he was fetched off broken like the rest[z]. He advanced with his Regiment for the saffegard of those that were broken, with whom he joining, and the Rere of the Battayle remaining with the saker, for want of seconding his regiment was lost with the rest of the vauntguard, and Cosby himself taken prisoner[a].

Cosby's charge is perhaps that referred to thus by Taaffe, Montague and O'Sullivan in the following terms—After the Marshal's death, we that were on horssback found no going where the rebells stood, by reason of a main bogg, and nevertheless our battel of foote went thither, where they lost the most part of their shott, and four captains, and came by force of the enemy agayne[b]. Notwithstanding the general's death 2 other regiments[c] passed over the trentch; the Battayle coming upp, two barills of powther took fire amongst them by which they disranked, in the whieh whyle those 2 former regiments, being passed the trentch, were for the most part putt to the sworde; then by the helpe of our horse, the enemies municion being well spente, we brought the rest into the plain and so recovered Armaghe[d]. At the time of Cosby's attack O'Neill seems to have been in some danger. He had to cope with the regiments of Percy, Bagnal, Cosby and Wingfield, and the horse of Brooke and Montague, while O'Donnell, M[c]Guire and M[c]Farley grappled with the foote of Cuiny and Billings, and Fleming's horse. He was on horseback beside his troops, with a guard of forty horse and forty shot. He ordered his shot to fire on the approaching English, and, having thus created some confusion in their ranks, he charged with his forty troopers, while his pikemen advanced with a loud cheer, and drove the English back in disorder about one o'clock in the day. O'Donnell's opponents, seeing their comrades routed, broke and ran[e]. O'Donnell's opponents were the rear guard, commanded by Cuiney and Billings, and supported by Fleming's cavalry. Here is an account of their fighting.

[v] *Ormond, Taaffe, and the Billinges.*   [w] *Annala, and O'Sullevan,*   [z] *Billings.*
[y] *Taaffe.*   [z] *Car. Cal. and Billings.*   [a] *Billinges.*   [b] *Taaffe.*
[c] *i. e.* Bagnal's and Cosbys.   [d] *Montague.*   [e] *O'Sullevan.*

12.—*The Rear 'in Great Fight.'*

Wingfield, being come to his own regiment (from beside the Marshal), saw the rear coming up, for whom he made a stand at the boggy ford, and went to tell the Marshal of their coming, at which time he was slain[f]. The vann of the Reare, Cuyny, being Sarjint Major, had; and the rear of all had Byllinge's. So the other regiments marching, the Sarjint Major's regiment and the Reare marched in one bodye to the forde, and at the forde the Sarjent Major's regiment took the vann of the Reare, being his place. The rear noe sooner recovered the hill beyond the forde towards the Blackwater, but the enemy charged us with horse and foote to the nomber of 2000 foote and 400 horse.[*] Having long entertained skyrmishe, and by reason of the great number of the enemy's shott and horse coming so near and faste upon us, we were forced four or fyve severall tymes to charge with our coullors in the heade of the fight, by reason our shott was so beaten and our new men bringing the rest into confusion[g]. Capt. Ferdinando Kingsmell, who was in Cuyny's Regiment in the vantguard of the Rere, saieth that they were so hotely fought withal by the force of O'Donnell, Magwyre, and James M'Sorley theire horse and foote, that in an houre and a halfe they could not marche a quarter of a myle forward, by which means they never understood in the rere of the Killinge of the Marshal nor of the defeating of the former Regiments, until they came upp to fetch off the Battayle, with whom they joined[h]. Being thus in fight, our Regiment could not gain a butt's length in three quarters of an hourr The which the horsemen of the Rere and the Sarjent Major's Regiment canne witnesse, who came to second us which the enemy seeing quitted us[i]. Here was likewise fired in the Rere 2 barrels of poulder to the great hurte and dismay of the Enemy, as appeared by their cry at the sight thereof[j]. When the enemy quytted us, both regiments made tow[ds] the Bogge, where being near upon the entrance of the Boogge the Sarjent Maior's Regiment drue of the right hand, and the Reare directly over the Boogge[k].

13.—*The Retreat.*

Being no soner come over but the Sargent Maior gave Byllinges dyrection to retreate, and make good the forde. And in our Retreate we garded the dead bodye of the Marshal, and Sir Calystynes Brookes being hurte, and most of the hurte men, besides the three peeces of ordynance, and the remainder of the munycion. So being come near the forde we saw the enemye, both horse and

[f] *Car. Cal.* [*] An exaggeration, clearly. [g] The Captains of Kingsmill's Regiment.
[h] Cap. F. Kingsmill. [i] Captains of Billing's Regiment. [j] The Kingsmills. Billings.

foote, with the collours flying, which were taken from the Vanguard of all, mynding to make good the Forde before us. Then we first having attayned the forde made it goode. Then Smythe, one of the corporalls of the feilde, came to Billinges, in the hearing of Cap^n Hawes, with direction to make good a hill betwixt Armagh and the forde tyll such tyme as the rest came upp. The which was performed; and in our retreate tow^{ds} the hill, the enemy's horse coming to cutt betwixt us and Armagh, we shott off the biggest of the three peeces of ordynance, which made thenemy to stande. So leving these our knowledgments for that dayes' service under our handes, to which we will be sworne, and pawne our lyves; commending the same to yor Lordship's judgments to sensure according to our desartes[l]. This statement of Byllings, Hawes and Feteplace can scarcely be reconciled with that of Montague, Lieutenant General of the horse, that the "Rere stood, which, being hard·sett to, retired foully to Armagh^m." The new men sent over for supplies, never offered to fight, but, as their leaders say, ranne away most cowardlie, casting from them their armour and weapon as soon as they were charged; few or none of them brought backe their armes^n. By the reporte of all the officers, there ran away to the Irish no less than 300 of the meere Irish, being Ulster and Connaught men, and two Englishmen of the new supplies, who the next morning called to their fellows, and told them the Erle would give them 20^s a peece for ymprest, if they would serve him; and for all the rest of the new supplies we think the better half of them is lost, for many of them were slayne without making any resistance^o. Those soldiers that survived shamefully laid all the blame, not on their own cowardice, but, as was usual in such cases, on the unskilfulness of their officers^p. However Mr Moylmoora Reylie in presens of many tryed his loyalty and valure; and so, God save me, did the rest of the captains, as much as might be donn in so ill grounde, being wood and bogge on either side of the marche unto the trenche^q. This O'Reilly, surnamed "The Handsome," by word and example strove to rally the fugitives, and gathered some soldiers around him, chiefly men of his own blood; but they, being unsupported, were soon cut down, and O'Reilly, left alone, fell, fighting to the last^r. In one spot specially the carnage was terrible, and the country people yet point out the lane where that hideous rout passed by, and call it to this day *The Bloody Loaning*^{s}.

The Colonel and Captains of Bylling's Regiment; *i.e.*, Byllings, Hawes, and Feteplace.
^{m} Montague. ^{n} Ormond. ^{o} The Kingsmills. ^{p} *Camden*.
^{q} Taaffe. ^{r} *O'Sullevan*. ^{s} *Mitchel*.

14.—*Killed and Wounded.*

The Irish obtained a great victory; I term it great, says Moryson, since the English, from their first arrival in that kingdom, never had received such an overthrou as this, commonly called *the Defeat of Blackwater;* thirteen valiant Captaines, and 1500 common souldiers, (whereof many were of the old companies, which had served in Brittany under General Norreys) were slaine in the field[t]. As the estimates of the English losses vary, I submit a tabular view of them.

English Losses.—(*Compiled from the State Papers, etc.*)

Captains slain—20 or 23.	Lieutenants slain —9.	Ensigne Colours Lost—12.	Voluntarie Gentlemen slayne—4.	Captains slain.
Marshal Bagnai	Bagnal's	Bagnal's	M. Brooke	24—O'Sullivan
Banke			Constable	23—O'Duigenan
Bethel[u]			Harrington	21—Lombard
Bourke[u]		Sir G. Bourchier's	Poule	19—Annala
Brooks	Lord Delvin's			16—English Writers
Elsden		Elsden's		
Evans		Evans'		Soldiers slain.
Fortescu[v]		Eustace's	2700—Lombard	
Foskew[v]		Foskew's	2500—O'Sullivan and Annala	
Harvey			2000—Montague, and "Ill	
Hawes[w]			News," and The King-	
Henserve[x]			Mills	
Henshawe[x]			not less than 1800—Montague	
Hushie	F. Kingsmill's		1700—O'Duigenan	
Langhton	Sir H. Norrey's	Langhton's	1500—Moryson &	
Leigh	Leigh's	Leigh's	Camden	
Morgan	Lieu[t] Massey	Morgan's	over 1000—Taafe	
O'Reilly	Col. Percy's	Colonel Percy's	855 slayne (363 Hurte)—S. Paper	
Pettitt	Parker's	Pettitt's	Other Losses.	
Radcliffe			1200 gold crowns—Lombard	
Romney			All the baggage, all the drums,	
Streete	Street's		34 colours, the Cannon, a	
Turnor		Turnor's	quantity of arms—O'Sullivan	

The first account of the battle runs thus :—

'1598, Aus 14. The Ill Newse out of Ireland: the 12th of August they cam from the Newry to Armaghe; the 14th of August theye sete forwardes towardes the Blackewater with 4000 footemen and 350 horses. Capt. Percy and Cap. Cosbey led the firste regiment of foote being 2000; Cap. Percy was hurte, Cosbey

---

[t] *Moryson* and *Camden*, same name. [u] Prisoners, says Taaffe. [w] *Anthony* Hawes escaped. [v] Perhaps different spelling of the [x] Perhaps the same person.

2 S

slaine, and almoste all the regimente slayne. Sir H. Bagnall ledd the second regiment being of 1000, he was shott in the hedd, slayne, and most of the regimente. Sir Calistianes Brooke led the horses, being 350, was shott into the belly, and thought to be slayne. About 2000 footemen slayne, and Cap. Cosbey, Cap. Evans, Cap. Morgan, Cap. Turner, Cap. Leighe, Cap. Streete, Cap Elsden, Cap. Banke, Cap. Petty, Cap. Henserve, Cap. Bethel, Cap. Fortescue, Cap. Harvey, Cap. Molmarey Orrely, Cap. Bourke. Wm Bule Commesarey a voluntarey slayne, James Harrington soone to Sir H. Harrington, Maximilean Brooke taken or slayne, Mr Connstable a Vollintarey gentleman slayne[7]."

Lieutenant Taafe, who with Montague and the cavalry escaped from Armagh, writes, two days after the battle—

'We lost 18 captains, and seeing there are soe many lost I thought fitt to pray you to be a mean to my L. Lieutenant that I may have one of their chardges, asshuring myself that very few will be sutors for the lyke. The greatest in numbers of their soldiers that escaped is not 12 men to any one company.[z]

The victory cost the Ulstermen less than 200 men killed and more than 600 wounded[a]; according to the English account the Irish lost 120[b] or 300[c] or 700[d] men, and among them 2 sons of Art McBaron, 2 sons of O'Cahan, 2 leaders, Maguire's son, the son of McKennagh of the Trough, and the son of Donell McSorley's son.[e]

15.—*The Siege of Armagh.*

By the help of our horse, thenemies municion being well spente, we brought off the armye into the plaine and soe recovered Armaghe, where the capteins resolved to refreshe their men with victualls and municion, and soe to marche dyrectlie to the Newrie. In the meane tyme thenemies approached and fell round on all all sides of us with their whole force. The capteins seeing thinsufficiencie both in mind and means of ther men, and finding themselves noe way able to returne, resolved that I [Cap. Montague] wold adventure with all the horse in the night to break through them, and soe if I cold to passe to the Newrie, then they had shuch a preportion of vittualls as wold kepe them viii dayes. In which tyme they hope yor Lo (i.e. Ormond) will make some speedy expedition to fetch them off, or ells O'Donnell and McGuoire being also in want of victualls wold returne hoame, and then they would see, if they could pass away in one night to the Newrie ; or ells thenemie seeinge the horse gone might be persuaded that they having a monethe or 2 victualls, which indeed was there

[7] *Kilk. J. of Arch.*   [z] *Taaffe.*   [a] *O'Sullevan.*   [b] *Whitechurch.*
[c] *Taaffe.*   [d] *Montague.*   [e] *Whitechurch and Taaffe.*

but dispossed upon their first resolution, soe as they made account they had not now left meatt for above ten daies at the uttermoste, that thenemy cold not kepe together, hearinge by a prisoner that was taken that O'Donnell and McGwier was then reddy to departe, I thought my lyfe well adventured to save so many, attempted it, and cam away with sum vii score horse with som very little loss, though they continually followed me, and at my passing out of the campe gave me a great volley of shott. They have veray small store of municion, and ther Irish run continually to the rebells. I much feare they will betray them; for I was no sooner gone, but I might here them in very hot skirmishe in the quarters, There remains of ours about 2500 in the church of Armaghe[f].

Montague did not escape so easily, it appears, for O'Sullivan says, that Tirlogh O'Hanlon with part of O'Neill's horse pursued him, killed three of his officers, and captured 200 horses; he adds that Captain Romley was slain the next day while smoking a pipe by the road side.[g] The besieged and besiegers continued to fire at each other for three days and three nights, and then the English ceased, and sent messengers to say that they would surrender the fort [at the Blackwater], if the warders were suffered to come to them, without wounding or danger, to Armagh; and that on their arrival they would leave Armagh itself, if they were granted quarter and protection and escorted in safety into a secure territory. The Irish held a council, and some of them said the English should not be permitted to come out of their straitened position until they should all be killed or starved together[h]. The LL. Justices on the 16th Aug., wrote to O'Neill in 'favour of those distressed companies who remayne in the church there awayting for soch comfort as men in so great calamity may expect.' They say—'We thought good upon this occasion to send to you in their behalfe, thoughe wee think that in your owne consideration you will let them departe without doing them any further hurte. We are to putt you in minde how farr you may incense her Ma[ties] indignation towarde you, if you shall do any further distresse to those companies, beinge as you know in cold bludd . . . Besides your anncient adversarye, the Marshall, being now taken away, we hope you will cease all further revenge towards the rest. . . .'

These Justices, who heard the news only at 9 o'clock on the 16th, wrote to the Privy Council 'that the Irish know as well as ourselves that we are not hable without presente succor out of England, to fetch off these companies cooped up in the church of Armagh.'

Therle offered composition uppon these condicions—First, that we shold quit

[f] *Montague's Reporte, and his Letter to Ormonde*, [g] *O'Sullevan*.
[h] Sic. Annala, translated by O'Donova

the Blackwater, leving there the collors, drumms and municion, the Cap^{ns} having left them onely their Rapiers and hacknies; and, that beeing delivered, the whole army with those men of the Blackwater shold marche away from Armagh with all their carriage and hurte men to the Newrie or Dondalk, for performance whereof pledges were putt in on both sides. For the Army the 2 cap^{ns} Ferdinand and George Kingsmell, and on Tirone's parte two of the Hagans the men of most estimacion in this country, which of each part was accordingly performed. Being pledges for the performance of the conditions Thearle gave [us] for the reason that he offered the composition, that he was at £500 charge by the daye in keping his forces together to attend our Army; and that he supposed we had a moneth or six weeks victuall, in which tyme he knew, as he said, that forces would lande in Loghfoyle, and therefore he thought it better to save that charge, to gayne the forte of the Blackwater, and to bend himself to hinder the landing of our forces in Loghfoyle, then by lyinge by us, with soe great charge to hazard so many inconveniences as he feared he might otherwise fall into—Ferdinando Kingsmill, George Kingsmill.[l] The Annala tells us that one of the conditions was, 'that the English should not carry out of the fort meat or drink, armour, arms or ordnance, powder or lead, or anything except only the captain's trunk and arms, which he was at liberty to take with him. They consented on both sides to abide by those conditions; and they sent some of their gentlemen of both sides to the fort [of Blackwater] to converse with the warders.[k] The yielding of the fort followed, when the assaulted guard saw no Hope of Relief, but especially upon messages sent to Captain Williams from our broken forces retired to Armagh, professing that all their safety depended upon his yielding the fort into the hands of Tyrone, without which danger Williams professed that no Want or Misery should have induced him thereto,[l] so he and his men had to depart in doublet and hose only.[m]

On the 23rd of Aug. the LL. Justices report that the Kingsmeales, being both actors in the same, returned this day, assuring us that all the companies were safely returned to the Newry with bagg and baggage and their collors displayed. At the departing of the companies from Armagh it was agreed that they shold march directly to Dondalk; but they, for som respects knowen to themselves, breaking that agreement took their way immediately to the Newry, from whence it will be veray hazardous to come by Dondalk by land, having to pass by the Moyerye straite, which we heare Tirone hath manned to impeach their passage, taking occasion, as it seemethe, in that they went to the Newry and not to Dondalk according to agreement. We are now in consideracion how to fetch them

---

[j] The Kingsmills. [k] *Annala.* [l] *Moryson,* [m] Chamberlain to Carleton.—*Domestic S. Papers.*

by sea from Carlingford, which though it may be thought not fully honourable, for that heretofore yt hath not bein usuall; yet for that the companies are pestered with sundry hurte men; and that they have much baggage, which otherwise they cannot carry being utterly destitute of garrans and all portage overland, we dowte that this necessity will dryve us to fetch them off by sea.ⁿ After the departure of the English from Tyrone, O'Neill gave orders to reckon and bury the gentlemen and common people slain, and they were found to be 2500 slain, among whom was the General, with 18 Captains, and a great number of gentlemen whose names are not given.º

On the 23rd of Aug. Ormond says: We have heard that the companies are come saffely to Dondalk over the Moyery without any impediment of thenemies and I, the L. Lieftenant General, am now preparing to draw to the borders for disposing of themᵖ. He about the same time announced that the Castle of Alderfleete 'standing upon the north seas towards Scotland,' had been taken, and that he could not procure the liberation of Captⁿ Constable from M'Sorleyᑫ. This M'Sorley was a Barbarian of handsome figure and dignified bearing. On Friday, the 4th of Nov. 1597, he was asked to a parley by Sir J. Chichester, Governor of Carrigfergus, and was treacherously attacked by him and his officers; but he killed 280, and wounded 30 or 40 of the English, slew Chichester and his lieutenant and both his serjeants, Captⁿ Mansell and his lieutenant and both his serjeants, Lieutenant Price with his serjeants and drum. Captⁿˢ Merriman, Hill and Warte were wounded and Captⁿˢ Constable and Banks were made prisoners; the heads of Chichester and Mansell were sent to O'Neill, and their bodies to Capt. Egerton for burial ᵣ.

16.—*The War in Leinster.*

After (Clifford) the Governor of Connaught and O'Rourke had parted from each other in peace, in May, at the town of Athlone, and when O'Rourke saw that the English were not at this time more powerful than the Irish, he was afraid that O'Donnell would plunder his territory; and therefore he came at the first summons of O'Donnell, and did whatever was requested of him. This he did by the advice of his people. Having confirmed his friendship with O'Donnell, he proceeded with his forces, at the instance of O'Ferrall Bán, (i. e. Ross, son of William, son of Donell) into Meath; and they plundered Mullingar, and the

ⁿ *Lords Justices and Ormond.* º *Annala.* ᵖ *Kilk. Jour. of Arch.*
ᑫ *Ulster Journ. of Arch.*, No. 19. ʳ *Balcarres Papers.*

country from Mullingar to Ballymore-Lough-Sewdy[a]. About the 7th of June O'Neill sent aid to Phelim Mac Feogh, chief of the O'Brians, to the end they might make war in Leinster[b]. Six hundred soldiers arrived from England. On reaching Dungarvan they marched to join Lord Ormond, and, as they passed along the borders of Leinster, they were fought with by a party of the Irish of that district, and lost 410 of their number[c]. Owney O'More went to Ulster to obtain help from O'Neill. In his absence Brian O'More had several successful combats with the English and their allies, the Anglo-Irish of Wexford, and took from them 7 colours and 14 drums.[d]

To check Brian O'More a hosting was made by Ormond in the month of June to proceed into Leix. His forces amounted to 24 companies of foot and 200 horse[e], [or 3000[f] men altogether or perhaps only 2000 foot and some horse[g]]. In the evening he encamped on a hill on the borders of the territory. He was informed that night that there were only a few to guard that territory; and in the morning following he ordered his brother's son, (i. e. James, son of Edward, son of James Butler) to go, with 6 or 7 companies [or perhaps 1000 Irish and English foot[h]] through the passes into the nearest head of the territory, to see whether he could perform any exploit. Although James was loth to go on that expedition, early on Sunday morning[i] he set out at the command of the Earl. He found his path cut, deeply furrowed and barred by Brian Reagh O'More, who had come with 150 [or 300 foot[j]] soldiers to defend it on the same day. Fierce and terriffic was the salute, which Brian and his forces gave James and his soldiers[k]. As he was attacked in two columns, he was forced to leave his vantage-ground, and with darts and shot he attacked, in open ground, the column in which Butler was. He was shot himself; but his wound only made him fight more fiercely.* The Anglo-Irish were attacked in front and in the rear, hemmed in and surrounded, speared and shot; in a short time bodies were left mangled and pierced along the pass. A lamentable death occurred here—James, the son of Edward, son of Pierce, son of James[l], son of Pierce—a man of whom greater expectations had been formed than of any other of his age of the Butlers living at that time [and who was a Catholic, was killed by two guhshot wounds**]. And such of his men, as had not been cut off, returned as broken-shielded fugitives to the Earl.[m] The second column, coming to the support of the first, was broken

[a] *Annala*, p. 2055.   [b] *Moryson*.   [c] *Annala*.   [d] *O'Sullevan*. Perhaps the combat mentioned by the *Annala* was one of these.   [e] *Annala*.   [f] *Lombard*.   [g] *O'Sullevan*.   [h] *O'Sullevan*.   [i] 11th 18th or 25th of June.   [j] *O'Sullevan*.   [k] *Annala*.   * *O'Sullevan*. *Annala*. "Pierce," in O'Donovan's Version, is a mistake.   ** *O'Sullevan*.   [m] *Annala*.

also.ᵃ Brian pursued the fugitives, slew many of them, and would have slain more, if Ormond had not come up to fetch them off.ᵒ *Lombard* says that the O'Mores slew 1500 of their enemies.ᵖ Brian Reagh died of his wound within four days, and his death would perhaps have been a crushing blow to Leinster were it not for the opportune arrival of Owny O'More, immediately after the battle.ᵠ

17.—*Owny O'More and Tyrrell come to Leinster.*

On that very day, after the fight, Owny, the son of Rory Oge O'More; Redmond Burke, son of John of the Shamrocks; Dermond O'Connor, and Captain Tyrrell came and pitched their camp opposite the Earl's camp; but he, before noon of the next day, Monday, returned to Kilkenny, and sent his soldiers to their garrisons.ʳ Owney had brought 1500 veteransˢ from O'Neill, and three stout captains, Tyrrell, Burke and O'Connor. Redmond Burke was Baron of Leitrim, son of Shan of the Shamrocks, son of Richard Saxonach, son of Ulick of the Heads. With a party of his young kinsmen, all of the first distinction, he went to O'Neill to complain of the answer he received from his father's brother, the Earl of Clanrickard: 'that if Redmond would be satisfied with one mantle's breadth of his inheritance, he would not give him so much, as a reward for war or peace.' O'Neill promised to assist him and gave him command of some hundreds of soldiers, with permission to plunder and devastate any part of Ireland, which had any connexion or alliance with the English. When he and his kinsmen left O'Neill, they went into the confederation of the Irish of Leinster and remained with them during the summer.ᵗ

As, on the 2ᵈ of August, the state of Leinster was endangered in evʳʸ parte by the rebells of the province, aided by forces from Tyrone, who had sent forces to several parts to assist the traitors there, and sturr up rebellion in Mounster, it was concluded, says Ormond, that [the Marshall should draw to the North and] I, the Lord Lieuten-Genˡ with another parte of the armye should prosecute the traitors of Leinster; in whiche prosecution seven of the chefe traitors were, with divers of there followers, putt to the sworde; others also entering into rebellion in Mounster were stayed by me.ᵘ

18.—*Ormond relieves Maryborough.*

A great hosting was made by Ormond to place provisions in Portleix (Maryborough). His army was met by Owny, son of Rory Oge, son of Rory Caoch O'More; by Redmond Burke and by Captain Richard Tyrrell, son of Thomas Oge Tyrrell. Ormond lost more than the value of the provisions in

---

ᵃ *O'Sullevan.* ᵒ *Lombard*, p. 167. ᵖ *O'Sullevan.* ᵠ *Annala.* ʳ *Lombard* and *Cox.* ˢ *Annala.*
ᵘ Ormond, Aug. 2ᵈ and 18ᵗʰ.

men, horses and arms; he was wounded and escaped with great difficulty.'
O'Sullevan describes an attempt made by Ormond to provision Port Leix, as it
may be the one recorded by the *Annala*, I translate it here.—'As Owny O'More
besieged Portleix, Ormond went, with over 4000 horse and foot, to relieve and
re-victual it; he was attacked at the Black Ford by Owney at the head of 1400
men, and lost 600 soldiers, whose bodies he burned, lest his loss should be
known—the English being accustomed to hide their own dead and to expose in
public places the bodies of their foes. There were 60 Catholics killed and 80
wounded. Ormond, however, by sheer numbers passed on and provisioned the
fort."

19.—*Successes of the Insurgents.*

The LL. Justices report, on the 17th of Aug., that, in spite of Ormond's
authority, the Leinster rebels are exceedingly increased, and daily burning,
preying and spoiling the contrye, having already possessed themselves of all the
Queenes County, called Leix, some 3 or 4 castles at the most excepted, which
cannot long hold out. There they possess the lands so dearly bought by her
Majesty and her predecessors, and doe even in a peaceable manner enjoye the
goodes and cutt downe and gather the cornes of thauncient English gent[n] of that
country. The lyke sturr have they already begon in Offaley, and the lyke ende,
in all lykelihood will they make there . . they do what they list without con-
trolm'. A great parte of the County of Kildare they have already spoyled and
burned, and daylie advertisem[ts] we have of there entraunce into the County of
Dublin, and of there purpose, even this day, as we understand, to make heade
even towards this citie; to which God knoweth they may make an easie
approach; yett have wee sett out this present morning the nomber of six or seaven
hundred of cittizens and others to ympeache their approache. This and worse
than we have said is the state of Leinster.' Ormond was ready to make a roade
against one of these insurgents, Donill Spanaghe, [or Donal called the
Spaniard] when he heard of the M'shal's ill successe.[y] Donal had ravaged with
fire and sword a great part of Meath, because the people of that region would not
fight for the Faith.[a]

20.—*The Queen sends re-inforcements.*

On the 12th of Sep. Elizabeth writes—'We make choice of Sir Richard
Bingham, whom we have appointed to be Marshal of that realm, to repair
thither. Hear him lovingly in all things concerning our service, wherein we
know that you, our cousin of Ormond, our Lieutenant, will find great ease in

---

Annala. " *O'Sullevan.* ᵗ LL. Justices, Aug. 17. ʸ Ormond to the Queen, Aug. 18.
ᵃ *O'Sullev:n.*

every way, it being neither fitt nor possible, that you shold spend your bodye in all services at all tymes. . . It doth not a little trouble us to find such hard effects of all things from thence, considering the notable supplies of men, treasure and victuals more plentifully sent than ever heretofore.[a] For other thinges past we have well observed, that all y[r] Jyorneyes and attemptes upon the Northe have had these successes, that not only our armyes have come backe with losse and doinge nothing, but in their absence other parts of our Kingedome have been left to be spoyled and wasted; and though the unyversalytie of the Rebellion may be used as a reason for the mischiefe, yet it is almost a miracle that, with the charges of an armye of eight or nine thousand men the provincial rebells of Leinster and Wexforde and other places should not be mastered.[a]

Bingham, sent over as Marshal, with re-inforcements [including 50 horse[b]], landed at Wexford, and on his march to Dublin was attacked by the O'Mores and O'Connors, and lost most of his men; he lost the remainder and his own life, and a number of other soldiers in a fight with O'Donnell and O'Rorke in Connaught.[c] This statement of Lombard, who, perhaps, confounds Sir C. Clifford with Bingham, is not borne out by any other writer; on the other hand, Camden tells us, that Bingham died as soon as he reached Dublin.[d] Sir Samuel Bagnal [about the end of August] came over with 2000 foot and 100 horse, to strengthen the Queen's Forces in the heart of the Kingdome; the old companies numbering 1050, drawne out of the Low Countries, were commanded by Bagnall, Jephson, Bodley, Sidney, Foulke Conway, Pynner, Blaney, Tobey Caulfield, Heath and Owen Tewder; the new men were under Roe, Egerton, Bingley and some new Captaines.[e] This did not protect the heart of the Kingdom; for we find that O'Rourke made a hosting in the first month of autumn (*i.e.* from Sep. 23 to Oct. 23), and he did not halt until he arrived at Tyrrell's Pass, and the Pass of Kilbride in Fertullagh [in the south of Westmeath]. He seized a prey, and slew some persons at Tyrrell's Pass, and then returned home to his country without wound or danger.[f]

21.—*O'More Marches towards Munster.*

In the first month of autumn, [towards the end of September], O'Neill sent letters to Leinster, requesting Burke, O'More and Tyrrell to intrust the guarding of Leinster to some of their allies; and to proceed, themselves, to make conquests, and to bring some of the adverse territories over to their cause, and particularly to go into Munster, at the invitation of Thomas *Ruadh*, son of

---

[a] *Car Cal.* [a] The Queen to LL. Justices, Sep. 12, in *Kilk. J. of Arch.*
[b] S. P. in M[c]Carthy Mor., p. 173. [c] *Lombard.* [d] Yet Elizabeth speaks of him as alive on the 1st Dec. *Car. Cul.*, p. 285. [e] *Moryson.* [f] *Anna'a.*

James, son of John, son of the Earl of Desmond. They were persuaded and encouraged to go by Sir Piers Lacy, a brave and eloquent gentleman of Munster;[g] and O'More, leaving the care of Leix to his brother Edmund, led 800 foote and about 200 horse under Redmond Burke (Baron of Leitrim), and his brother William, Dermot O'Conchur and his two brothers (Cairbre and Con), and Captain Tyrrell.[*] When they marched into Ossory, the people came spontaneously to join them, except Mac Gillapatrick (i.e. Finin, the son of Brian, son of Finin). They afterwards went to the northern extremity of Slieve Bloom, in order to induce the Irish of East Munster and Westmeath to join them, namely O'Molloy, and Connell, the son of Cahir O'Mulloy, McCoghlan (John Oge, the son of John, son of Art, son of Cormae), and O'Carroll (Calvach, son of William Odhar, son of Ferganainm, son of Mulrony). Although these chieftains had for some time stood by their Sovereign, they were glad to obtain terms of peace from these strange warriors, who were traversing their country. After agreeing upon terms of peace with them the Leinster men turned their faces towards the two Ormonds in Munster.[h]

22.—*The War in Munster.*

The Irish perceiving that the English had sustained many disasters in the North, Connaught and Leinster, following the current of the present time, began to dismaske themselves; and, being united in strict Combination, did verily persuade themselves, that it would be very feasible to make themselves masters of all Ireland, if the chiefe Lords of Mounster, with their friends and followers would join with them. They did account that Province to bee the Key of the Kingdome, both by reason of the cities and walled townes, (which are more than in all the Island besides), the fruitfulnesse of the Country, being reputed the garden of Ireland, and the commodious harbors lying open both to France and Spain.[a] Early in October the O'Mores burst into Upper and Lower Ormond, and from them they sought neither peace nor friendship, but proceeded to plunder them at once, on account of their enmity towards the Earl of Ormond. They took five of the castles of Ormond, one of which, Druim-Aidhneach, on the margin of the Shannon, Burke kept to himself, for waging war on Clanrickard out of it. They remained for two or three weeks encamped in that country; and the spoils of the region bordering on the Suir were brought to their camp; and their Irish neighbours came to join in the same confederation with them. Among those who joined were, O'Dwyer of Kilnamanagh i.e Dermot, the son of

---

[g] *Annala* and *O'Sullevan*.   [*] *O'Sullevan*.   [h] *Annala*.   [a] *Pacata Hibernia*, p. 2.

Owny, son of Philip; the sons of Mac Brian O'gCuanach, namely, the sons of Murtough, son of Turlough, son of Murtough; the Ryans about Conor-na-Mainge, the son of William Caech, son of Dermot O'Mulryan; and the race of Brian Oge of Duharra. After these Irish (septs) had formed a confederacy with O'Neill's people, and after having induced (the people of) every territory into which they came to join them, they marched with the rising-out of these districts, at the instance of the sons of Thomas Roe, son of the Earl (of Desmond) into the country of the Geraldines. They first went to the county of Limerick. The President, Sir Thomas Norris, was at that time at Kilmallock, and when he perceived that he was not able to contend with the Irish, he went to Cork, to avoid them. They then proceeded westwards, across the River Maigue into Connello and to the borders of Sliabh-Luachra and Gleann-Corbraighe. James, the son of Thomas Roe (Fitzgerald), came to join them in Connello on this occasion; and John,[b] the second son of Thomas Roe, was already along with them, upon these expeditions, for he had come to draw them into the country. At this time they offered and sold at their camp a stripper, or a cow in calf, for sixpence, a brood mare for threepence and the best hog for a penny; and these bargains were offered aud proclaimed in every camp in which they were.[c]

Chief Justice Saxey 'in lamentable wise advertiseth th[r] Hon[ra] Los: (the Council) that about the 5th of October 3000 rebells came (into Mounster) by Arlough, and so into the com. of Limerick under the leading of John Fitz Thomas, second sonne of Sir Thom[s] of Desmond, and of one Tirrell. Presentlie the said John was proclaimed Earle of Desmond, who, as is said, took it upon him, if his elder brother James would not ioyne with them, and assent to be proclaimed Earle himself. They spoyled most of the country townes and villages within that county. On Saturday morning, the 7th, James Fitz Thomas came with 16 horse and 20 foot; and the purpose of the traitors was to create him Earl of Desmond at the hill of Ballioghly.[d] On the 8th in the evening there came to Ballingarrie, out of Rannallaghe, Cahir M[c]Hugh, brother of the late Feagh M[c]Hugh, Thomas Butler, and others with 160 men, the rebells being then uniting betwixt Rathkeale and Ballingarrie.[e] About which time the Vice-President had assembled the forces of the Province, with full purpose to encounter with the traitors, finding the said forces to be in shewe able to equall the strength of the enemy; but albeit divers of the noblemen and chiefe gentlemen of the provincewere then and there ready, as it seemed, to accompany the Governor in this conflict; yet at the very instant the most parte of the followers of the noblemen and gent[n] went to the enemy.[e] Though O'More had sent him a letter

[b] 'James' is a mistake of O'Donovan's translation.
[c] *Annala*. [d] Saxey, in *McCarthy Mor*. [e] Weever to Cecil. [e] Saxey.

to challenge him to fight,[f] Norreys withdrew upon necessarie occasion,[g] and his troops dispersed without so much as seeing the enemy[h]; however, it seems he did not retire unmolested, as the Irish kerne had some skirmishing with his rear guard.[i]

When Ormond heard of the progress of these warlike troops, he set out with all his cavalry and infantry for the County of Limerick, to meet them, and sent a message to Cork, requesting the President to come to meet him at Kilmallock.[*] He wrote also to the Earl of Desmond as follows—From the Campe at Cowlin, Oct. 8. 1598, "James Fitz Thomas, Hit seemed to us most strange, when wee herd you were combined and joined with theis Leinster Traytors lately repayred into Munster, considering how your father, Sir Thomas, always contenued a dutifull subject, and did manie good offices to further Her Mat's service; from which course if you should digresse, and now ioyn with these unnatural traytors, we may think you very unwise, and that you bring upon yourself your own confusion, w[ch] is thende of all traytors, as by daylie experience you have seene. Wherefore we will that you do presentlie make your repair unto us, wheresoever you shall heare of our being, to lay down your greefes and complaints, if you have anie; and, if you stand in any doubt of yourself, theis our letters shall be for you and such as shall accompany you in your coming and returning, your safetyes; and further, on your drawing nere the place, where we shall be, we will send you safe conduct for you, Thomas Ormond and Ossery.'

'Given at the Camp of Cowlin 8 Oct. 1598.

'We need not put you in mind of the late overthrowe of th' Erle your uncle, who was plaged with his partakers by fire, sword and famine; and be assured, if you proceed in any traiterous actions, you will have the like end. What her Mat's forces have done against the King of Spaine, and is hable to do against ani other enemie, the world hath sene, to her immortal fame; by which you may judge what she is hable to do against you, or anie others, that shall become traytors.'

Superscribed 'To James Fitz Geralde geve theis in hast."

Desmond answered thus—

"James: Desmonde to Ormond

R[t] Hon: I received your Lo[s] lettres, wherein your Lo. doth specify, that you think it verie straunge, that I should join in action with these gentlemen of Leinster. It is so that I have ever at all times behaved myself dutifully, and as a true subject to her Ma'tie as ever laie in me; and as it is well known to your Lo. I have showed my willingness in service against my uncle and his adherents,

---

[f] *O'Sullevan.*   [g] *Moryson.*   [h] *Camden.*   [i] *O'Sullevan.*   [*] *Annala.*

whereby I have been partlie a mean of his destruction. Before my uncle's decease, it may be remembered by your Lo, I have been in England from my Father, claiming title to his inheritance of the house of Desmonde, which is manifestlie known to be his righte; whereupon her Ma'ty promised to do me justice upon the decease of my uncle, who then was in action, and have allowed me a mark sterling per diem towards my maintenance untill her Matt's further pleasure were known; of which I never received but one year's paie; and ever since my uncle's decease I could get no hearing concerning my inheritance of the Earldome of Desmonde, but have bestowed the same upon divers undertakers to disinherit me for ever. Having all this while stayed myself, in hope to be gratiouslie dealt withall by her Ma'tie, seeing no other remedie, and that I could get no indifferencie, I will follow, by all the means I can, to maintaine my right trusting in the Almighty to further the same.

My verie good Lo: I have seene so many bad examples in seeking of diverse manie gentlemen bluddely false and sinister accusations cut off and executed to deathe, that the noblemen and chief gentlemen of this Province cannot think themselves assured of their lives, if they were contented to lose their lands and living. As for example, Redmond Fitz Geralde, upon the false accusation of a scurvey boy for safeguard of his life, was put to death, being a gentleman of good calling, being three score years of age, and innocent of the crime charged withall. Donagh Mc Craghe also was executed upon the false information of a villainous Kerne, who within a sevennight was putt to death within yor Lop's Libertie of Clonmell, who took upon his salvacion, all that he said against the said Donagh was untrue, that he was suborned by others. Of late a poore cosen of ours, James Fitz Morrys of Mochollopa is so abominably dealt withall, upon the false accusation of an Englishman accusing him of murder, who never drew sworde in anger all the days of his life, and is manifestely knowen that he never gave cause to be suspected of the like. Piers Lacy who was an earnest servitor, and had the kiling of Rory Mc Morrogho, and the apprehension of Morrogho Oge till he left him in the gaol of Limerick; and after all his services was driven for the sauegarde of his leife to be a fugitive. To be brief with yo: Lo: Englishmen were not contented to have our lands and living, but unmercifullie to seeke our leives by false and sinister means under cullor of Lawe; and, as for my parte, I will prevent it the best I maie.

'Committing yo: Lo: to God, I am yor Lo.'s loving Cosen,

'Ja: Desmonde.

From the Camp at Carrigrone 12 Oct 1598."[1]

[1] *Kilk. Jour. of Arch.* Unpublished Geraldine Documents.

The day Desmond sent this letter from his camp, within four miles of Cork, Ormond wrote to the Queen—' At my coming to Munster I found that all the undertakers, three or four excepted, had most shamefully forsaken all their Castelles and dwelling plases before anie rebell came within sight of them and left their castells with their munitions, stuff and cattell to the traytors and no manner of resistance made."[k]

When the Irish army, who were encamped in the west of Connello, heard that Ormond and Norreys were to meet at Kilmallock, they marched eastwards towards Kilmallock and showed themselves to these lords; the Earl and the President agreed to avoid meeting them and turned towards Magh-Ealla [Mallow]. The Irish pursued them to the gate of Magh-Ealla and proceeded to provoke them (to battle), saying, that they could never wreak their vengeance upon them better than now, when they were all (together) in one place. Notwithstanding this, it was determined that the President should repair to Cork and that the Earl should return to the territory of the Butlers. As the country was left in the power of the Irish on this occasion, they conferred the title of Earl of Desmond, by the authority of O'Neill, upon James, the son of Thomas Roe, son of James, son of John, son of the Earl; and in the course of seventeen days, they left not within the country of the Geraldines (extending) from Dunqueen to the Suir, which the Saxons had well cultivated and filled with habitations and various wealth, a single son [*] of a Saxon, whom they did not either kill or expel. Nor did they leave within this time, a single head residence, castle, or one sod of Geraldine territory which they did not put into the possession of the Earl of Desmond, excepting only Castlemaine in the co. of Kerry, Askeaton in Hy-Connell-Gaura, and Magh-Ealla (Mallow), in the co. of Cork. When these agents of O'Neill had, in a short time, accomplished this great labour, they took their leave of this Earl whom they themselves had appointed. O'More and such part of the forces who adhered to him, set out for Leix; Burke and that part of the same hosting, over which he had command, proceeded to Ormond; and the Ulster troops who were along with these gentlemen proceeded to their homes, not without wealth or booty acquired on this expedition. Tyrrell remained with the Earl, who continued spending and subjugating Munster, and gaining more and more people over to his side, during the remaining two months of this year.[1]

---

[k] *McCarthy Mor*. [*] Moryson says they did not spare the daughters; but his authority needs support. The Earl of Desmond wrote to Carew in 1601, "I defye any English that can charge me with hindering of them in bodye or goods." [1] *Annala*.

23.—*Result of the Inroad of the Leinster Men.*

The Munster confederacy was joined by McMoris, Baron of Lixnaw, Fitz Gerald (the Knight of Kerry), Fitz Gerald (the Knight of Glynn), Fitz Gibbon (the White Knight), by Dermot and Donogh McCarthy of Duhallow, Donal son of McCarthy Mor, Condon, O'Donoghu of Onacht, and O'Donoghu of the Glen ; by Lords Fermoy, Mountgarret, and Caher,[m] and Purcell, Baron of Lochmoe, with many young Butlers.[n] The rebellion brake out like lightning,[o] disobedience had spread from the rural districts to the walled cities and post towns : 200 of Ormond's soldiers had deserted to the enemy, who were an insufferable, disdainful, insolent people ;[p] there was no county in Munster but was impassable for any subject, especially for all who wore hose or breeches after the English manner.[q] Unless Her Majesty shall royally undertake the prosecution, the Kingdom will be lost—there is nothing now left but Dublin and the Port of Wexford[r] ; and the Queen takes it much to heart that with 10,000 men she is in no part able to defend herself.[s] On the 4th of November Cecil writes— 'The disease is general ; the religion bad ; the nobility discontented ; the soldiers beaten ; the discipline corrupted ; her Irishman an after game, except we see a blot and enter and bind. Ulster a country so strong and so wild as never conquered nor quiet ; wholly in rebellion except some scores (?) ; the climate unwholesome ; the passages so difficult as my Lord Burgh—The General Norreys never could look over the water ; good soldiers, well armed, and in blood..'[t] On December the 1st Elizabeth writes to the Council—' We have sent over great supplies, to our excessive charge; yet we receive naught else but news of fresh losses and calamities. Although you have the great number of 9000 men, we do not only see the northern traitor untouched at home, and range where else he pleased, but the provincial rebels in every province, by such as he can spare, enabled to give law to our provincial governors; besides that the Pale is not only wasted, but the walls of Dublin, (where our State is seated), esteemed unsafe, and (as we hear) the suburbs thought a dangerous lodging for some of our principal counsellors...we will send a sufficient force of horse and foot out of England, strengthened with old soldiers of the Low Countries.' On the 3rd of Decr she writes to the L. President of Munster—'We have understood how strange a revolt has happened in Munster. When the first traitor grew to head, with a ragged number of rogues and boys, you might better have resisted than you did, especially considering the many defensible

---

[m] *O'Sullevan.*   [n] *Annala.*   [o] *Moryson.*   [p] Sir T. Norreys.   [q] Sir N. Walsh.
[r] Wallop—an exaggeration.   [s] Cecil. See *McCarthy Mor.*, p. 181.   [t] Cecil, in *Car. Cal.*, p. 523.

houses and castles possessed by the Undertakers, who, for aught we can hear, were no way comforted nor supported by you, but either from lack of comfort from you or out of mere cowardice, fled away from the rebels on the first alarm." We have sent over 2000 foot for your aid, and given orders to increase your 30 horse to 50, in sterling pay, and to send over another 100 horses. There are some out or suspected, who might be used, on their claims for land being granted, as good instruments against the capital rebels. Of such are the White Knight, Condon, and Donogh McCormacke of the Dually.^v

24.—*Fighting in Thomond.*

There was strife among some of the gentlemen of Thomond concerning the division and joint-tenure of their territory lands. Among them was Teig, the son of Conor, son of Donogh O'Brien, by whom the bridge of Portcroisi was taken; and although he was not the first who had attempted to take it (by force) from Margaret Cusack, it was to him it finally fell. He also took the castle of Cluain in Hy-Caisin, and the castle of Sgairbh, in the east of Hy-Bloid, from the attorney of the Bishop of Meath's son. Among these was also Conor, son of Donnell, son of Mahon, son of Brian O'Brien, who took Baile-an-chaislein, in Upper Clann-Cuilein, from Mac Namara Finn (John, the son of Teige, son of Cumeadha). Among them was Turlough, son of Mahon, from Coill O'Flannchadha, who took from George Cusack Derryowen, at first the patrimony of the sons of Auliffe, the son of Cian O'Shaughnessy. Mahon, the son of Turlough Boy, obtained Coill O'Flannchadha. Among the same gentlemen was Turlough, the son of Murrough, son of Conor O'Brien, from Cathair-Mionain, and his kinsman, Dermot Roe, who joined in the war of the Irish. Among them, moreover, was Teig Caech, the son of Turlough, son of Brian, son of Donough Mac Mahon, who, about Christmas in this year, captured an English ship, that had been going astray for a long time before. It happened to put in at a harbour in Western Corca-Bhaiscinn, in the neighbourhood of Carraig-an-Chobhlaigh. Teig took away this ship from the crew, and all the valuable things it contained. It was not long after till Teig found the profit very trivial, and the punishment severe. The same Teig took Dunbeg, one of his own castles, from a Limerick merchant, who had it in his possession, in lieu of debt.^w

25.—*The War in Connaught.*

Ballymote, which had been in the possession of the English, for the space of

---

^u Lombard says 1800 of them and their followers sailed from Waterford in 18 vessels. The poet Spenser was one of these exiles.   ^v Elizabeth's Letters, in *Car. Cal.*   ^w *Annala.*

thirteen years before this time, was taken this summer by its rightful inheritors, the Clann-Donnough of Corran, namely, Tomaltagh and Cathal Duv. Governor Clifford, and O'Donnell (Hugh Roe) were auctioning the castle against each other, in offering to purchase it from the Clann-Donnough. The close of the bargain was, that the Clann-Donnough gave up the castle to O'Donnell for a purchase and contract in the middle month of the autumn. Four hundred pounds (in money) and three hundred cows, was the price which O'Donnell gave. In Autumn O'Donnell sent a body of forces from Tirconnell with Mac William (Theobald, the son of Walter Kittagh, son of John, son of Oliver) into Mac William's territory. He sent with him on this occasion O'Doherty (John Oge, the son of John, son of Felim, son of Conor Carragh) with a great force. They were scarcely noticed in any country through which they passed, until they arrived in the Owles; and it was in these (territories) the greater part of the herds and flocks of all Mac William's country then were. They collected all the cattle that were on the main land, outside the small islands; and though great was the collection of preys they made, they encountered no danger or difficulty, save only the trouble of driving them off. And they returned safe to their territories, *i.e.* Mac William to Tirawly, and O'Dogherty to Irishowen. When O'Donnell had obtained possession of Ballymote in the middle of Autumn, the Kinel-Connel sent their creaghts into the county of Sligo; and O'Donnell himself resided at Ballymote from the time it was given up to him until after Christmas. O'Donnell (at this time) caused his forces to be mustered in every place where they were: first, the Kinel-Connell, with all their forces, came to him; and next Mac William Burke (Theobald, the son of Walter Kittagh), with all those who were under his jurisdiction; and when these had come together to O'Donnell, to Ballymote, (which was) precisely in the end of December, he resolved to proceed into Clanrickard, although the inhabitants of that territory were on the alert and on their guard; such was their fear and dread of him. He marched silently, and arrived unobserved at the gate of Kilcolgan by break of day; he then sent marauding parties in every direction through the level part of Clanrickard; one party went to the borders of Oireacht-Redmond, and another to Dun-Guaire, in Coill-Ua-bhFiachrach. This party who went to Coill-Ua-bh Fiachrach committed lamentable deeds; they slew the two sons of Ross, the son of Owny, son of Melaghlin O'Loughlin, *i.e.*, Turlough Boy and Brian. But a gentleman of the Clann-Donnell Galloglagh, who was along with Mac William on that expedition, namely, Hugh Boy Oge, the son of Hugh Boy, son of Mulmurry Mac Donnell, had been slain on this occasion by Turlough Boy, the son, before he himself fell. By another party of O'Donnell's people were slain the two sons of William, son of John (Burke) of Rinn-Mhil, and the son of Theobald, son of Dabuck, from Doire-Ui-Dhomhnaill, with his brother's son, Mac Hubert of Disert-Cealaigh, namely, William, the son of Ulick Roe, son of Ulick Oge, was taken prisoner by O'Donnell's brother, Manus, son of Hugh, son of Manus. Although the Earl had great numbers of hired soldiers quartered in Clanrickard, O'Donnell carried off the immense spoils, heavy herds, and other booty and property, which had been collected for him, without battle or conflict, until he arrived safe at Ballymote.¹

26.—*Minor Events.*

In March, Murtagh Cam, son of Conor, son of Mahon, son of Thomas Mac Mahon of Cnoc-an-lacna [Co. Clare] died in the territory of East Corca-Baiscin; in Spring died Ogan son of John son of Melaghlin O'h-Ogain of Ard-Croine. [A considerable portion of his castle is still to be seen at Ard-Crony.] O'Cahan (Ruari son of Manus son of Donchadh son of John son of Aibhne) died on the 14th of April, and his son Donall Ballach was installed in his place. Baothghalach, son of Hugh son of Baothghalach, son of Mortach Mac Clanchy, of Cnoc-fionn in Clare, died in April. He was fluent in the Latin, Irish and English tongues. Dermot, the son of Edmund, son of Rury O'Dea of Tully O'Dea was killed in the month of July by the insurgents of Clare. Rickard, the son of John, son of Thomas, son of Rickard Oge Burke of Doire-mic-Lachtna, died in August. Mac Donough of Tirerrill (Maurice Caech, the son of Teig-an Triubhis) was slain in Briefny-O'Rorke, as he was carrying off a prey; upon which Conor Oge, son of Melachlin from Baile-an-duin was appointed the Mac Donough. The Blind Abbot, (*i.e.*, William, the son of David, son of Edmond, son of Ullick Burke) who had styled himself MᶜWilliam after the death of the last lord, namely, Richard, the son of Oliver, son of John, did not happily enjoy his title of lord, for he was expelled from his patrimony by Sir Richard Bingham; after which he went about wandering as an exile from territory to territory until he died in Clan Cuilcin (in Thomond) in the month of September; and he was buried in the abbey of Quin in the burial place of the Sil-Aedha The MᶜWilliam, who was lord at that time, was Theobald (the son of Walter Kittagh, son of John, son of Oliver) whom O'Donnell had nominated MᶜWilliam. Joan Cam, the daughter of the Earl of Desmond, namely of James, the son of John, son of Thomas of Drogheda, died in winter, having spent many years in widowhood after the destruction of her tribe, and the worthy men to whom she had been successively espoused.⁷

¹ *Annala.*   ⁷ Arranged and condensed from the *Annala.*

APPENDIX.

SOME ORIGINAL LETTERS WRITTEN IN 1598.

1. *Articuli quidam cum Supplicatione S. Sanct^{ti} nomine Ibernorum Exulum proponendi.*[a]

Cum pro ea, Sanctissime Pater, quam Ecclesiarum omnium ex officio geris solicitudine, non possit non esse gratum quicquid per quoscumque suggeritur opportunum ad Religionem Catholicam ubivis locorum vel conservandam vel instaurandam ; tanto gratius sit oportet quod ad hunc proponitur finem, quanto magis et ii qui proponunt id officii debent pietati in patriam, et Sanc^{tem} T. decet id quod proponitur peculiari quadam cura habere commendatum. Quoniam igitur impleri nunc advertimus quod ante annos centum supra mille D. Patricio Aplo nostro legimus revelatum Iberniam quam tunc quidem ille in spiritu vidit totam inflammatam christianæ fidei et charitatis ardore, postea paulatim caligine et tenebris usque adeo obducendam, ut exiguae tantum lucernae et rari tandem superessent carbones vivi, iique cineribus involuti. Idcirco tum pietate in patriam moti, tum spe ducti, quod (prout sequuta habet revelatio eidem Apostolo nostro facta) ad splendorem et ardorem pristinum Ibernia postliminio reversura sit, Nos ad oscula pedum Sanc^{tis} T. humiliter prostrati articulos quosdam sive puncta duximus proponenda, quorum consideratione Sanc^{tas} T. et excitari possit ad ea propius et pressius cogitanda quae ad salutem patriae nostrae pertinent, et inclinari merito ad id concedendum, quod ad istum finem nos hic suppliciter petimus.

Primus est, quod Maiores nostri, veteres Iberniae Proceres, tam insigni pietate ac singulari in Sedem Apostolicam observantia fuisse commemorentur, ut postquam christianam religionem amplexi semel, Pontifici Romano, Christi Dni in terris supremo Vicario, non solum tanquam Pastori totius Ecclesiae Christianae sese submiserint, sed etiam Regionis suae dominium et imperium cesserint.

Secundus, cum circa annum Dni 1170 vicini Britanni et Angli Iberniam invasissent eamque armis imperio suo subjicere molirentur, Iberni Proceres non antea illis voluerunt se submittere quam Domini sui Romani Pontificis interveniente auctoritate, misso ad id in Iberniam Legato Vivesio quodam, Rex Angliae inauguraretur Iberniae Dominus.

Tertius, quamvis illo quidem tempore expedire videbatur ob multas causas ut Regi Angliae concederetur dominium quoddam protectionis in Iberniam, tamen, ex quo praesertim tempore Henricus VIII, Ecclesiae tandem rebellis factus, usurpavit sibi titulum Regis Iberniae, tam noxium est Ibernis Anglicani dominii effectum iugum, ut huic soli accepto sit ferendum, quod Ibernia ab Ecclesiae gremio per schisma sit avulsa.

[a] From the reference to Trinity College and to the Irish Jesuits, this appears to have been written between 1595 and 1598.

Quartus, quod licet per Anglicanae istius tyrannidis vim et coactionem materialia passim templa in Ibernia haereticus occupet cultus et religio, tamen Ibernorum animos, viva sua templa, possideat Deus, ut nulla sit in orbe Natio (modo nota illi aut nominata sit unquam haeresis) quae pauciores habeat aut infectos haeresi aut ad eam affectos. Et multi quidem, non obstante illius tyrannidis terrore ac minis, Catholicam adhuc Religionem constanter profitentur; caeteri vero plerique constantiam istam probant ad eamque propendent, et quicquid hic delinquitur ex sufficientis instructionis defectu proficiscitur.

Quintus, cum qui ex aliis nationibus pro fide Catholica exules in Catholicis passim regionibus, assignata sibi habeant ex Sedis Apostolicae pia liberalitate seminaria et scholas, in quibus aluntur, et qui inter illos juniores erudiuntur, sola Ibernia, proprium Apostolicae Sedis patrimonium, beneficii huius non est particeps. Quod tamen si hactenus percepisset et hunc imprimis fructum retulisset, quod submitti possent in Iberniam (ubi et liberius agerent quam in aliis quoquo modo infectis haeresi et schismate regionibus) qui instructiores confirmando et consolando, rudiores instruendo, lapsos revocando plurimum profuissent. Deinde et alterum minus forte observatum sed non parvi aestimandum attulisset fructum, nempe, ut qui Iberni Romam petunt, quippiam solicitaturi, non admitterentur nisi habito ab eiusmodi Seminario Nationis vitae suae et conversationis testimonio ac commendatione.

Sextus, cum Ibernia olim fuerit et religionis et disciplinarum schola eiusmodi, ut et eruditionem in istis accipiendam soliti sint eo ex vicinis regionibus plurimi confluere, et ex ipsa prodire multi ad religionem et eruditionem in exteris propagandas nationibus — hac gloria paulatim decidente sive per externorum frequentes et feroces in Iberniam irruptiones, et grassationes, sive per domesticorum Principum civilia et intestina bella, sive per alias simul concurrentes occasiones et causas—certe Angli, Iberniae effecti Domini, utcunque in principio correxerunt quaedam a christianae religionis instituto illic devia, postmodum, quasi data opera, satagerunt ut Ibernos in ignorantiae et ruditatis barbara quadam retinerent caligine, opportunum id ducentes ad illos tanquam sibi servos et mancipia in subiectione continendos. Unde evenit ut Iberni, religioni Catholicae affectu pio alioqui deditissimi, non satis fuerint instructi ad detegendam et repellendam illam in religione corruptelam, quam aliquot iam lustris Angli qua poterant vi et fraude conati sunt in Iberniam invehere.

Septimus, cum etiam vigente ad huc in utroque Angliae et Iberniae Regno Catholica religione, videbatur hactenus caligo ista ignorantiae et ruditatis opportuna ad Ibernos retinendos Angliae subiectos, ab uno iam vel altero anno alia inita est ratio et consilium, quo Anglia, quae se devovit haeresi, in eamdem secum nassam Iberniam quoque trahat, atque ita illam arctius sibi reddat devinctam, nempe collegii cuiusdam ampli et magnifici extructione iuxta Dublinium, primariam Iberniae urbem, in quo a praeceptoribus Anglis haereticis Juventus Ibernica in haeresi instituatur. Ex hoc collegio et institutione magnum imprimis periculum Ibernis imminet, quia licet hactenus affectum eiusmodi per Dei gratiam, et merita Sanctorum suae gentis, praesertim Apostoli nostri S. Patricii, erga Religionem Catholicam et Apostolicam Sedem insitum sibi ostenderint semper, ut is videri possit in nativam transiisse dispositionem, tamen, quia flexilis valde eorum indoles, timendum merito, ne, deficientibus qui de Catholica religione instruant, haeretica doctrina serio seduloque inculcata affectum istum immutet, et flexilem indolem ad se rapiat. Deinde ex periculi huius consideratione tristitia magna et continuus dolor cum nobis tum cordatioribus in Ibernia Catholicis, eo quod illic desint idonei et sufficientes homines, qui in Catholica religione instruant, ac simul desiderium, velut parturientium, quo optamus eiusmodi homines illuc submitti.

Quare Sanctississime Pater, Clementissime Domine noster, haec nostra et populi nostri, imo vero tui iure optimo, voluntate paratissima offerentes tibi vota, ad oscula beatissimorum tuorum pedum prostrati, imprimis optamus, et Deum Opt. Max. rogamus, ut in diebus tuis, et in universo adimpleatur mundo quod praedixit Isaias: "Venient et adorabunt vestigia pedum tuorum qui detrahebant tibi;" et peculiariter contingat genti nostrae, ut quam Henricus VIII. Ecclesiae rebellis factus ab obedientia Clementis Septimi violenter avulsit, Pastor bonus Clemens Octavus Ecclesiae compagi Iberniam postliminio restituat. Deinde rogamus Clementissimam T. Pietatem, ut digneris Articulos et rationes iam allatas attente considerare, ut quae vel ex iis vel ex aliis quibuscumque pro salute Iberniae tuae Deus bonus cordi tuo inspiraverit, ea pro T. Pietate, prudentia et officio executioni mandari satagas. Denique quia, Clementissimo Deo conservante nobis semen, sunt nostrates quidam e Societate Jesu sacerdotes idonei, qui in patria fructum faciant maximum, obsecramus humiliter, ut sicut ad provincias alias ab haeresi reducendas, aut retinendas in Catholica religione aliorum hactenus factae sunt missiones, sic ex istis sacerdotibus ordinentur aliqui in Iberniam, albam ad messem regionem, auspiciis tuis mittendi operarii.

Sanctitatis T. humill^{mi} Clientes Iberni pro Catholica Religione Exules hinc inde dispersi.

Endorsed—Articuli nōie Hybernorum S. S^{ti} proponendi.

2.—*Dell' Illmo Sig^{re} Cardinale Mattei a N. R. P. G^{n}rale da Ferrara a 21 di Maggio* 1598.

Molto R̄. come fratello. Diedi conto giermatina alla s^{ta} di N. S. della missione che la P^{te} V^{a} era risoluto di fare, quando cosi fusse piaciuto a S. B^{ne}, d'alcuni PP. in Ibernia accio potessero ivi fare, quel frutto spirituale che dalle loro mani si puo fermamente sperare. E si come la S. Sta gradi multo cotesta buona voluntà della P. V., cosi si contenta di concedere come fa a quei PP. che da lei saranno inviati in quel Regno, che possino in esso essercitare tutte le facultà che da Sua B. sono state concesse o confermate ai PP. della Comp^a che sono andati in Inghilter e vuole Sua Sta che questa mia lettera basti per essecutione della presente concessione.

3.—*Christopher Holiwood*,[b] *S. J. to F. Aquaviva.*

Admodum R^de P^r. Pax Chri.

Gratias habeo quantas maximas P. V^ae quod tantam de me curam dignatus est habere. Patavium petam, Deo bene propitio, proxima hebdomada, ibi facturus quod iubebit Provincialis donec aliter Paternitas V^ra disposuerit. Scriptum est ad me nullum esse in Hibernia qui habeat facultatem dispensandi cum Nobilibus Catholicis, ad hoc ut possint, salva conscientia, retinere bona Ecclesiastica, quae iam possident, donec Deus restituat pacem Ecclesiae. Videat P. V.^a an expediat talem facultatem nostros, qui mittentur, habere. Certe expedit Ecclesiae sua hoc tempore a Catholicis possideri; nam illi erunt semper parati ea restituere, et interim aliquid quotannis pendere in pios usus insumendum: quod si omnia Ecclesiae bona ab haereticis possiderentur, id redderet ipsorum conversionem multo difficiliorem et impedirit pacem Ecclesiae, nec quicquam interim subsidii inde pauperes acciperent. Quod superest, oro D. opt. max. ut P. V. incolumem et nostri memorem servet. Mediolani 10 Junii 98.

P. V. servus in X. minimus

CHRISTOPHORUS HOLIVODIUS.

Al m° R^do in Chr° P. il Padre Claudio
Aquaviva Gnale della Comp^a di Giesu a Roma.

4.—*Letter of J. Archer*,[c] *S. J. Aug.* 10, 1598.

R^do in X° P. Claudio Aquaviva, Praeposito G^li Societatis Jesu, Romae, Admodum R^de in X° Pater, Pax Christi, etc.

Quas t. p. ad me dedit 14 Martii, has ego non ante Calendas Augusti accepi, etsi ad patrem Henricum Fitz Symons tribus ante mensibus pervenerint, unde facile perspicere potest occasionem tanti silentii. A tempore quo huc perveni in tantis angustiis versatus sum, ut nihil de ratione mittendi per Angliam didicerim, quam p. Fitz Simons, quem ad horulam tantum vidi, me docuerit. Per Hispaniam plures misi cum pecuniis ad studiosos, et nullum omnino responsum accepi. Unde hoc provenerit non aliter conjicere possum, quam quod mercatores nostri literas ad me vel ex me transferre vereantur, eo quod status hic maximo me prosequatur odio, et frequenti indagine, magno proposito pretio, me

[b] Of Artane Castle, Dublin.   [c] Of Kilkenny.

perquirat, ita ut in sylvis et latebris ut plurimum agam, et regredi ad meos non liceat eo quod mercatores in suas me recipere naves non audeant, quod certo sciant quosdam in quolibet portu a statu designatos qui me opperiantur.

Attamen Societatis munia, prout possum, exercere non desisto; bis mille confessiones...excepi; incultos et barbaros in fide instruxi; quosdam, abiurata haeresi, Ecclesiae reconciliavi, et personam unam nobilem, quae, ablegata coniuge, scortum introduxerat, unde maxima dissensio inter principes viros oriebatur, cum illa in gratiam redire feci; sacramenta in Castris ministravi quandoquidem cum subditis in Civitatibus versari non sit permissum. Mirum est quantus erat concursus ex vicinis locis ut Sacrum audirent et peccatis expiarentur; hinc facile conjicere potest t. p. quanta sit spes uberrimi fructus si plures e Societate mittantur.

De Missione cum nobilibus, praesertim aquilonaribus, egi, qui eam valde expetunt, et maxime opus habent, homines inculti, barbari et plane rudes; religiosos tamen plurimum respiciunt. Illi omnem operam et solicitudinem et praedia quaedam illis designare pollicentur. Ex hac parte, valde inculta, excursiones ad reliquas cum maiore securitate et fructu fieri poterunt. Alii in parte australi missionem quidem exoptant, patrocinium patrum assumere publice non audent, sed fovere, et procurare ut nihil illis desit non renuunt. Maior modo spes est uberioris fructus quam hactenus ob frequentes Catholicorum victorias, unde fit ut haeretici ex multis locis migrare cogantur.

De reformatione Cleri tota difficultas erit ob eorum audaciam et inscitiam ...*Quapropter opus erit ut qui mittantur amplam habeant Jurisdictionem*, quam solam illi respiciunt et reverentur, ad coërcendam eorum insolentiam. Ex eorum restauratione tota res pendet, quod ego compertum habeo, ex eo quod quidam Cornelius Stanle Vic. Apos^{cus} obnixe me rogavit, cum huc venirem ut illi assisterem in executione sui muneris in spiritualibus; cui eo lubentius assensum praebui, quod sperabam inde maiorem Dei gloriam et ingens animarum lucrum, ut res ipsa testatur; brevi namque tempore decem sacerdotes, ablegatis concubinis et schismate abiurato, ad meliorem frugem redegi; quod sane efficere non possem nisi fultus auctoritate et iurisdictione illius. Praeterea ad securitatem conscientiarum illius nomine dispensavi cum quibusdam Catholicis pro fructibus Ecclesiasticis, ab Haereticis perceptis, componendo cum illis pro quota aliqua solvenda *in subsidium Seminarii Hybernorum* Salmanticae, quorum gratia huc missus sum. In qua re non existimo me quicquam fecisse adversus Societatis institutum, et quod non sit gratum Deo, et t. p. acceptum, cui in omnibus, ut semper, meum subjicio judicium. Quod si liceret mihi accedere ad Superiores, nec illud ipsum sine ipsorum iussu acceptarem; enixe rogo t. p. ut nihil mali de me suspicetur in hac nec alia re ex relatu aliorum, qui parum de me aut meis actionibus compertum habent. Dicere non possem quantum rei Christianae proficerem, si liceret mihi inter homines publice versari, quod spero aliis fore permissum eo quod cum adversariis nunquam sint versati, ut ego in Flandria et alibi, nec eorum nomina statim sint cognita. Iter in Hispaniam cogito prima occasione ex septentrionali parte, quo antea pervenire non potui, omnibus viis interclusis. Haec sunt, R^{de} Pater, quae de me et de missione scribere pro ratione temporis potui; t. p. inveniet me semper fidelem, humilem et obedientem Societatis filium. Raptim ex Castris 10 Augusti 98.

t. P. servus in X° minimus,

JACOBUS ARCHERUS.

5.—*Nicholas Lenich[d] S. J. to Fr. Duras, Sep. 25, 1598.*

Ihūs

Pax. X. Quoniam intelligo R. V^{ram} cupidam esse aliquid andiendi ex multis, quae Deus Opt. et Max., opera et industria nostrorum patrum, in Hybernia operatur, ideo non immerito existimavi ad R. V. mittere eo quae accepi ex literis Patricii Hamlii, sacerdotis et olim alumni huius Seminarii, scriptis ex Hybernia 12 Calendas Julii huius praesentis anni, ex Anglico idiomate quantum ego potui Latino donatis.

Haud facile dictu est, quantus in his locis fructus constiterit ex opera Patris Jacobi Archeri, uberior procul dubio futurus, nisi unum illud obstaret quod exploratores a Prorege constituti iam inde a primo Patris in Hyberniam ingressu, in eum diligenter inquirebant: usque adeo ut ab hominum oculis, in quibus versabatur, in latebras sibi confugiendum putaret: in quibus moratus tantum temporis, quantum satis esset ad sui memoriam abolendam, rursus intermissa studia instauravit, hodieque Societatis munia ita exequitur, ut ad fidem Catholicam magnus haereticorum fiat accessus. Hic est alius ex eadem Societate sacerdos e Flandria appulsus, cui nomen est Henrico Simonio,* qui non minori cum fructu animarum saluti operatur, Deo illius conatus favente; nam singulis quibusque festis ac Dominicis diebus frequentem ad populum concionatur, tanto cum animi ardore ut suimet ac suarum rerum oblitus videatur. Multi ab haeresum coeno ad Christianae religionis splendorem convertuntur: utque alios praetermittam verae fidei communionem ingressos, Dublinii, in urbe totius Regni metropoli, ubi Prorex sedem tenet, centum omnino sunt, qui praeterito anno circa festum Paschatis resurrectionis pravo haereticorum more, rituque perverso communicarunt: iidem tandem christianae doctrinae rudimentis probe instructi,

---

[d] Of Clonmel.   * H. Fitz Simon, of Dublin.

apud Patrem anteactae vitae maculas confessione eluerunt; vitæque coelestis Sacramento refecti, tantum pietatis specimen, fluentibus abundanter lacrimis, praebuerunt, ut omnes in admirationem darentur. Ne tamen propter insolentem multitudinem turbae fierent, non omnes uno die sacrum X^i Corpus exceperunt; sed in duos bipartiti, priori sexageni posteriori vero quadrageni: qua in re videre erat pium illorum certamen contendentium, utri prius divinum illud convivium degustarent. Huius rei novitas fuit omnibus tam iucunda, ut multos dies nullus nisi de illa sermo haberetur, singulis immortales gratias Deo agentibus, quod ab errorum tenebris in lucem veritatis traducti essent: unde praecipuus in Deum honor et in Catholicorum coetus utilitas redundabat. Cum vero Catholicorum numerus in dies augeretur, Patri visum fuit nobili in domo** aram collocare, quo Catholici confluentes divinis rebus interessent. Quare, ut maiorem in omnium animis ad pietatem affectum excitaret, aulam peristromatis excoluit, tapetibus instravit, et in medio aram posuit rebus omnibus ad sacrificandum tam eleganter instructam, ut nulli cederet earum quae in istis locis instructissimae visuntur. Curavit insuper, ut res divina cum omni vocum nervorumque concentu celebraretur; itaque, organa si excipias nullum ferme ex musicis instrumentis requisieris: nablia, cytharae, testudines, et siqua reliqua sunt, iucundissimam commiscebant harmoniam. Prius tamen quam Sacrum solemni fieret apparatu ter celebratum est planiori ritu, et quidem sine ullo cantu vocum, non tamen affectionum, quae, in omnium animis adversus Deum mirabiliter incensae, Dei coelitumque aures pertingebant; quippe in singulis Sacrificiis Catholici bene multi coelesti pane pasti et incredibili divinae consolationis dulcedine perfusi, ita ut pro votis nunquam satis Deo gratias decantarent. Stato Missae tempore de rebus divinis Pater sermonem instituit tanta cum utilitate audientium quanta maxima esse poterat. Argumento [est] quod demisso sacro plurimos in sodalitatem B. Mariae coöptaverit, quae ab eodem patre instituta tam ibi quam apud alias primi ordinis familias magna cum Sodalium frequentia efflorescit. Hinc facile erit intelligere quanta laetitia omnium mentes eo die compleverit, siquidem quadraginta abhinc annis hoc primum Sacrum solemni ritu peractum audierunt: quae omnia conjicienda potius relinquo ac meditanda, esset enim opus immensum singula literis complecti quae de horum Catholicorum pietate ac perseverantia scriptu digna videbantur.

Pater, ut omnium saluti consulat, varios quoquoversum excursus efficit, adeo quidem prompto animo et expedito, ut sibimet omnem quiescendi facultatem adimat, tanto flagrat desiderio suos adiuvandi concives. Quacumque iter

** Probably Thomas Fagan's. See Fitz Simon's Letter, *infra*.

vel moram facit, statim de Deo sermones serit, patresfamilias de rebus docet, quae ad reliquum vitae spatium in Dei amore ac timore transigendum requiruntur. Illi praeceptis illius obediunt, mandataque cum sedulitate exequuntur, ut merito eos dicas ad Christianam pietatem ex animo proclives atque propensos esse. Praeterea duodecim pueros bene morigeratos, spectataeque indolis et ingenii collegit in Flandriam mittendos, una cum aliquot virginibus, quae se Deo perpetua virginitate devoverunt, ut suum nomen consecrent alicui familiae Deo sacrae: nunc idoneam navigandi tempestatem Dublinii praestolantur, quam fortunatissimam praecamur.

Igitur, Pater amantissime, si viginti habuerimus e Societate brevi temporis spatio [ab] eis tota Hybernia ad veram fidem compelletur: cui nihilo magis quam viæ duce opus est. Quapropter cures diligenter oportet ut quotquot e Societate nostra Hibernico aut Anglico sermone utentur huc mittantur, suam hisce populis operam daturi, qui indies salutis suae avidiores existunt. Interim unum illud admonitum te volo eos omnes in Regno impune, libereque vagaturos, nemine eorum labores, exercitationesque perturbante. Denique ut scribendi finem faciam perstringo breviter quod nuper cum haereticorum ministris Patri contigit. Prorex certior factus de iis quae a patribus, tum praesertim a p. Henrico agebantur, publicam fidem pactus eum ad certamen cum suis ministris de rebus divinis palam ineundum invitavit. Strenuus Christi miles non recusavit congressum, ad pugnam descendit. Illi, patrem ut agnoscunt, obstupescere; periculum vereri, negare insuper cum Jesuitis Seminariorumque alumnis (quos nihilo differre putant) veluti cum impostoribus rem gerendam: imo affirmare nefas esse quovis praesidio illorum studia fovere. Itaque fugere ante pugnam quam post illam victi discedere maluerunt: hinc eo maiorem ignominiae notam subierunt, quo insolentius antea iactitabant, neminem esse in toto orbe, nedum in Hybernia, qui posset suos inter disputandum impetus sustinere.

Catholici rem divinam audituri armis se muniunt, quibus se ac sacerdotes tueantur. Antea enim haereticorum ministri quamplures exploraverunt domos, siqua ornamenta vestiendis altaribus et sacerdotibus accommodata invenirent, inventa abstulerunt; nunc vero in idem periculum se inferre non audent, metuentes ne ubi velint quaestum facere sumptum faciant. Et haec breviter ex literis Patricii Hamlii.

Quid ergo praestolamur, pater amantissime, et cur stamus tota die otiosi, siquidem Deus nos conducat in vineam suam, vineam iam maturam ad messem; age igitur, pater mi, age inquam, ut quam cito plures amandentur operarii, ut semen hoc in horreum Domini reponatur antequam pereat, devasteturque, et summis a V. R. precibus contendo, ut me indignum et inutilem servum dignetur inter caeteros huius sanctae et felicis missionis nominare, nam tanto temporis intervallo tum a N. R. P. tum a praedecessore R. V. illam expos tulavi. Valeat R. V. in X. Jesu, et me [tuis] piis sacrificiis devotisque precibus me committo. Ex Collegio D. Antonii Ollyssipone 25 Septembris 1598.

R. V^{ae} fr. et servus in X°. NICOLAUS LENICH.

R^{do} in Christo Patri, Patri Georgio Duras Assistenti Societatis Jesu hae dentur.

Endorsed—Fiat extractum et exhibeatur Illmo Protectori.

6.—*H. Fitz Simon to F. General Aquaviva, Nov. 25.*

Admodum R. P. Pax X^i. Nihil mihi in votis prius est quam ut quaecumque circa nos gerantur intelligatis; sed mora est a tabellariis, omnia enim commercia hac rerum perturbatione cessarunt ut literas mittere aut recipere non sit facile. Adversarii congressum refugiunt non sine eorum confusione et gaudio Catholicorum. Multas insidias instruxerunt, quas divina providentia evasi, comprehensis cum ego evaderem aliis. Dublinia est primaria civitas, in qua tribunal regium et proregis sedes, et haereticorum sentina, altera plane Londinia. Hanc a sacerdotibus prodendam Senatui inculcant Angli Justiciarii et iureiurando confirmant, fecerunt fidem adeo ut fratrem frater proderet duos producendo sacerdotes, utque senatus multctam gravissimam proponeret quibuscumque sacerdotes foventibus, evolant omnes deserentes catholicissimam civitatem. Hic exitus fuit, ut insontes probati sint sacerdotes et audaciores facti Catholici ad terrores hujusmodi perferendos. Ego autem ab iis praemonitus fui quorum intererat perscrutari aedes, quamvis vix satis mature, cum non prius efferrem pedes quam adessent inquisitores. Tota aestate varias obivi regni partes non sine operae praetio, sex revocatis haereticis, plurimisque schismaticis, et auditis confessionibus ingenti numero. Singulis festis concionem habeo, ad quam confluunt a vigesimo milliari non pauci non sine optato in aliquot fructu. Jam autem excurrere non licet absque manifesto vitae periculo, ita digrassantur hostes, qui quamvis catholicos se [ia^e] ctitent, non tamen aliud praeter nomen habent, nec ferunt qui a nequitia coerceant, aut qui inscitiam corrigant; sic enim rapinis incumbunt, ut timeam praecipuam eas insurrectioni dedisse ansam, et non aliud militibus manere stipendium. *Arcerius noster tandem ad vos dat literas*, utinam perquas se purget. Implicuit enim se officio Vicarii Generalis, ejus fultus auctoritate qui dubiam habebat potestatem quam etiam alteri contulerat. Inde magna confusio, tantaque utqui ejus usi sunt opera in dispensationibus aliisque id [generis]* incerti sint omnium. Ego sane nec augeo nec

^e Corroded. * d is eaten, i and g are clear; possibly the word was "negotiis."

minuo eius auctoritatem cum nihil de V. R. voluntate habeam compertum. Id enixe supplico V. P., ut collectionum, quas ex tota corrasit Ibernia, aequa pars Duacensibus Ibernis statuatur, qui flos studiosorum nostratium, et quorum intuitu potiorem partem obtinuit. Ideo hoc requiro, quod privatis suis, Salmanticae, nimium studere passim judicetur.

Cum opinione omnium, et ipsorum expectatione haereticorum, diversa totius reipublicae futura facies et conditio sit, consulere divino honori, aliqua Ecclesiastica beneficia praeoccupando, debemus. Tria autem nostris usibus accommodatissima animadverti. Primum Thomae Courtum in ipsa Dublinia, quod aliquando Canonicorum Regularium fuit: secundum Abbatia S^{tae}Mariae quod Bernardinorum: tertium Kilmainam quod equitum Melitensium. Haec etiam posteriora duo in ambitu Dublinensi continentur. Si impetremus primum, partem fructuum etiamnum ad nostros usus consequemur. Quod sane opus est, cum recepto more nihil sacerdotibus erogetur praeter oblationes tempore Sacrificii, et victum. Quare, salvo meliore iudicio, soli illi in principio huc mittendi sunt quibus vel patrimonium vel affinitas ampla. Quantum ad externa nova, tota haec patria licet non subiaceat proceribus qui insurrexerunt eorum tamen incursionibus prostituitur; pervolant enim impune, non minus bonorum quam malorum bona diripientes. Ex iuvenibus qui Duaci studuerunt cum unus in eos improvide incidisset, quod se Henricum Fitz Simon diceret, habitus est benigne, dein dimissus. Venerantur externo cultu omnia veneranda, sed opera eorum longe a Deo. Cum [ed*]ictum vetaret omnes, non exciperent sacerdotes, mihi quamplurima diversoria patuerunt. *Magna et periculosa lis inter* tres primates falsis rumoribus exoriebatur, quae omnes ad sanguinem mutuo effundendum protrahebat, iamque facinus patrandum erat cum nocturno itinere veredariis equis ad auctorem percurrendo, eumque ad palinodiam recinendum inducendo malum diuino beneficio averterim. Feci, in aliis Societatis functionibus, quidquid potui: minutiora per se concipiantur. De facultatibus verbum nullum, deque erecta a me sub ratihabitione sodalitate. Omni animi demissione vestras efflagito sive consolatorias in aestu laborum, sive mandatorias in finibus terrae ut sim semper obedientiae filius. Denique pari conatu contendo, ut insignis benefactor noster, *Dominus Thomas Faganus precibus* totius Societatis extraordinariis commendetur, et significatione gratae acceptionis a V. R^{tla} honoretur. Meipsum eisdem, ut unico fulcro tanto instantius committo, quanto longius absum ab influentiis caeterorum membrorum, quantoque pluribus obnoxius periculis. Ex Ibernia 25 Novembris 1598.

V. R^{tlae} tam promtus in X° servus quam humilis filius—

HENRICUS FITZ SIMON.

* Corroded.

APPENDIX. 349

PARLIAMENTARY LISTS OF THE YEARS 1560,[a] 1585,[b] AND 1613.

Lords.	1560.	1585.	Lords.	1560.	1585.
Earl of Kildare	2d	1st	Lord of Delvin	13th	14th
Earl of Ormond and Ossory	1st	2d	of Killeen	15th	15th
Earl of Desmond	3rd	—	Howth	16th	16th
Earl of Tyreone		3rd	Dunsany	19th	17th
Earl of Clanricard	5th	4th	Trimleteston	17th	18th
Earl of Tomond	4th	5th	Lixnaw or Kerry	18th	—
Earl of Clancare		6th	Dunboyne	20th	18th
Viscount Buttyvant	6th	7th	Upper Ossory	23rd	20th
of Ffermoy	7th	8th	Louth	21st	21st
Gormanston	10th	9th	Curraghmore	22d	22d
Baltinglass	11th	—	Donganyne	—	23rd
Mountgarrett	12th	16th	Inchecoyne	—	24th
Lord Bermingham of Athenry	8th	11th	Burk of Connell	—	25th
Coursy	9th	12th	Cahir	—	26th
of Slane	14th	13th			

Shires—1560.	1585.	1613.
Dublin—Fitz Williams de Holmpatrick	R. Netterville	Sir C. Plunket
Finglas de Waspellistown	Burnell	Lutteral of Lutterelstown
Meath—Sir Christopher Chever	R. Barnwall	Hussey, Baron Galtrim
P. Barnwall de Stackallan	J. Netterville	R. Barnwall
Kildare—Eustace de Cradokeston	W. Sutton	Talbot of Carton
Flattesburie de Johnstown	F. Fitz Morric	Sutton of Tipper
Westmeath—Sir G. Stanley	Nugent de Disert	C. Nugent
Sir T. Nugent	Nugent de Morton	E. Nugent
Wexford—Hore de Harperstown	Fitz Henry	Furlong of Horetown
R^d Synnot de Ballybrenan	Codd	Wadding
Louth—Taf de Ballebragane	Gerlone	
Dowdal de Glasspistell	More	
South Louth		Verdon of Clonmore
		Gernon of Strabane
Carlow—Sir W. Fitz Williams	Sir H. Wallop	Bagnal
Edmund Butler	G. Ffenton	M. Cavenagh
Kilkenny—White, Gall	Blanchville	Grace
	Rothe	Shee
Tipperary—Sherlock, Grace	Butler	Butler of Kilcash
	Everard	Sir J. Everard

[a] Compiled from Hardiman's Statute of Kilkenny, p. 135, 140. [b] Arranged from Rev. P. J. Meehan's Fate and Fortunes of O'Neill. p. 522.

Shires—1560.	1585.	1613.
Cross of Tipperary ...	Archbold	Butler of Cloghcully
	Prindergast	Laffan of Greystown
Waterford—Power of Comshen	R. Ailward	Sir J. Gough
P. Aylward of Faithlick	Sherlock	Power of Campier
Cork	J. Norries, L. President	McCarthy of Logher
	Cogan Fitz Edmond	Barrett
Kerry ...	Fitz Gerald	O'Sullevan of Donolough
	Springe	Rice of Ballinruddall
Limerick	T. Norris	Sir F. Barkley
	Rd Bourk	Sir T. Brown
Clare .,	Sir Tir. O'Brene	D. O'Brien
	Boetius Clanchy	Berty Clancye
Down ...	Sir H. Bagnell	Sir J. Hamilton
	Sir Hugh Magennis	Sir H. Montgomery
Antrim	Berkly	
	Sha. McBrien	
Armagh		Sir T. Caulfield
		Sir J. Bourchier
King's Co.	Sir G. Bourchier	Sir F. Ruish
	A. Waringe	Sir A. Loftus
Queen's Co. ...	Warham St Leger	Sir H. Power
	Harpoll	Sir R. Piggott
Connacie		
Longford	Ffaghny O'Fferrall	Connell O'Ferrall
	Wm O'Fferrall	John O'Ferrall
Galway	Le Straunge	Sir W. Bourke
	Fr Shane	J. More
Mayo ...	Williams	Sir Theo. Burke
	Brown	Sir Tho. Burke
Roscommon ...	Sir R. Bingham	Sir O. St John
	Dillon	Sir J King
Sligo ...	Sir V. Brown,	O'Hara
	Crofton, and	McDonogh
	Marbury	
Ferns ...	Masterson	
	Synnot	
Wicklow	Brabazon	Byrne of Tynepark
	Sir H. Harrington	Phelim Mc Pheagh Byrne
Cavan ...	Philip O'Reilly	Sir O. Lambert
	Ed. O'Reilly	Fish
Coleraine	... ...	Baker
		Rowley

APPENDIX.

SHIRES—1560.	1585.	1613.
Donegal	... ...	Vaughan
		Steward
Fermanagh	... ...	Sir H. Folliot
		Sir J. Davis
Leitrim...	... ...	Nugent
		Reynolds
Monaghan	... ...	Sir E. Blakeny
		Sir B. McMahon
Tyrone...	... ...	Sir T. Ridgway
		Sir F. Roe

CITIES—	1560.		
Dublin ...	... Stanihurst...	... Taylor	Bolton
	Golding ...	... Ball	Barry
Waterford	... Wise ...	... Sir P. Walsh	Sherlock
	Strong ...	... N. Walsh	Wadding
Cork ...	... J. Miagh ...	... J. Miagh	E. Tirry
	Coppinger	... Sarsfield	D. Tirry
Limerick	... Fanning ...	... T. Arthur	Galwey
	E. Arthur	... White	N. Arthur

BOROUGH TOWNS.

Drogheda	... Weston ...	... Barnwall	Blackney
	Burnell ...	... Nugent	Beeling
Galway...	... Jonoke Lynch	... Pe. Lynch	Sir W. Blake
	Pe. Lynch ...	... Jo. Lynch	G. Lynch
Knockfergus	... Wingfield...	...	Hibbots
	Waren ...	...	Johnson
Youghill	... Walsh ...	... T. Coppinger	E. Coppinger
	Portyngall	... Collen	Forrest
Kilkenny	... Bethe ...	... Roche	Archer
	Archer ...	... Shee	Langton
Wexford	... Hassane ...	... Pa. Furlong	Turner
	R^d Talbot	... Pa. Talbot	R^t Talbot
Ross ...	... Heron ...	... Duff	Fitz Henry
	Dormer...	... Bennett	Shee
Down ...	...	...	
Armagh	...	... ...	Ussher
			Conway
Kinsale	... Sir J. Alen	... Galwey	J. Roche
	Agarde ...	... Roche	D. Roche
Dundalk	... C. More ...	... Bellew	Cashel
	Stanley	... Bath	Ellis
		J. More	

STATE OF IRELAND ANNO 1598.

Borough Towns—1560.		1585.	1613.
Trim	...Sir J. Parker	Hamon	Ashe
	P. Martell	Gwire	Jones
Cashel	... ...	Conway	Hale
		Pa. Kerney	Sale
Fethard	...Hacket ...	Nash	Everard
	T. Nasshe	Wale	Hackett
Clonmel	...Stridche ..	G. White	N. White
	H. White ...	Bray	Bray
Kilmallock	... ...	Verdon	Verdon
		Hurley	Kearney
Thomastown	...Cosby ...	Sherlock	Robook
	Cowlye ...	Porte	Porter
Le Naas ...	...Draicot ...	Ja. Sherlock	Latten
	Jo. Sherlock	Lewes	C. Sherlock
Ennestyock	... ...	Power	Wm Murphy
		Archdeacon	Crichen Murphy
Kildare	...Abelles ...	Wesly	Fitz Gerald
	More ...	Shirgold	Farbeck
Mullingar	...N. Casy ...	Pettit	N. Casy
	Relyng ...	R. Casy	Hamon
Athenry	...A. Brown...	Brown	S. Brown
	Sir T. Cusack	Lynch	Bodkin
Carlingford	...Radclief ...	Ap Hugh	Whitechurch
	Jo. Neile	R. Neil	Hope
Navan	...R. Waring	Wakely	Begg
	Jo. [Wakel]y	Waringe	Warren
Athboy ..	...More ...	Brown	More
	Blake ...	Terrell	Browne
Kelles	...Shiele ...	Fleming	Plunkett
	Ledwiche...	Dax	Balfe
Ardee ...	...W. Dowdall	Barnwall	Mathewe
	Babe ...	J. Dowdall	P. Dowdall
Dengenchoishe	... ...	T. Trant	Trant
		J. Trant	Hussey
Dungarvan	...Gifford ...	obliterated	Roe
	Chellyner...		Fitzharris
Callan ...	... ...	Quemerford	Rothe
		Branan	Haydon
Philipstown	...	Frehan	Leycester
		Williams	Phillips
Maryborough	...	obliterated	Sir A. Loftus
			Barrington
Swords ...	...	obliterated	Blackney
			Fitz Simons
Athy	...Mothill ...	...	Sir R. Digby
	Cussyn ...	...	Weldon

APPENDIX. 353

BOROUGH TOWNS—1613.

Charlemont	... More. Fortescue.	Newton in Le	
Antrim...	... Conway. Hill.	Ardes	... Sir G. Coningham, Cartcart.
Belfast ...	... Sir J. Blennerhasset.		
Coleraine	... Trevelyan. O'Brien. Wilkinson	Enniskillen	... Atkinson. Fernham.
		Tuam	... Sir T. Rotheram. Pecke.
Derry ...	... Carey. Crewe.	Tralee	... Blennerhasset. Dethicke.
Carlow...	... Bere. Jacob.	Gowran	... Staunton. Swayne.
Cavan ...	... Culme. Sexton. (W. and T. Brady elected in their stead).	Carrickdrumrusk	... Griffith. Bellott.
		Castlebar	... Sir J. Bingham. Peyton.
Belturbet	... Wirrall. Grimesdich.	Monaghan	... Reeves. Cowley,
Ennis ...	... Thornton. Bloode.	Ballinakill	... Sir R. Ridgway. Brereton.
Limavaddy	... Sibthorpe. Downton.	Roscommon	... Marwood. Smith.
Mallow	... Molyneux. Ware.	Boyle	... Cusacke. Meredith.
Baltimore	... Crook. Piers.	Sligo...	... Andrews. Southworth.
Bandon Bridge	... Sir R. Morison. Crowe.	Clogher	... Watkins. Ferrar.
Cloghnakilty	... Harris. Gosnold.	Dungannan	... More. Pollard.
University of Dublin	... Temple. Sir C. Doyne.	Strabane	... Molyneux. Montgomery.
New Castle, near Lyons	... Parsons. Rolles.	Agher	... Birkinshaw. Scorye.
		Tallaght	... Lowther. Parsons.
Donegal	... Crofton. White.	Lismore	... Boyle. Annesley.
Lifford	... Blundel. Disney.	Athlone	... St John. Nugent.
Ballyshannon	... Gore. Cherry.	Kilbeggan	... Sir R. Newcomon. B. Newcomon.
Downpatrick	... Sir R. Wingfield. West.		
Newry...	... Bassett. Leighe.	Fethard (Wexford)	... Loftus. Pemberton.
Bangor	... Sir E. Brabazon. Dalway.		
		Enniscorthy	... Fisher. Perkins.
Killileagh	... Trevor. Hamilton.	Wicklow	... Usher. Esmonde.

ADDENDA.

Epitaphs in the Franciscan Church of Montorio, Rome.

The Earl of Tyrone died in Rome, July 20, 1616, in the seventy-sixth year of his age; and was buried in the Franciscan Church of Montorio: his tomb bears the simple epitaph—

D. O. M.
Hic. Quiescunt.
Ugonis. Principis. O'Neill.
Ossa.

Epitaph of his son, the Baron of Dungannon.

D. O. M.

Hugoni Baroni de Donganan Hugonis Magni O'Neill Principis et Comitis Tironiae Primogenito, Patrem et Rodericum Comitem Tirconalliae Avunculum, pro Fide Catholica quam multos annos contra haereticos in Hibernia fortiter defenderant, relictis statibus suis, sponte exulantes ad communem Catholicorum asylum, Urbem Romam, pro sua singulari in Deum et Parentes pietate, secuto, cujus immatura Mors spem de eo restaurandae aliquando in illis partibus Catholicae Religionis, ob ejus insignes animi et corporis dotes ab omnibus, conceptam abstulit, ac dicto Roderico avunculo fato simili absumpto conjunxit Occidit tam suis quam totae curiae flebilis Nono Kal. Oct MDCIX Aetatis suae XXIV.

Epitaph of the O'Donnells.

D. O. M.

RODERICO PRINCIPI O'DONNELLIO, Comiti Tirconalliae in Hibernia, qui pro Religione Catholica Gravissimis defunctus periculis in sago pariter et in toga constantissimus cultor et Defensor Apostolicae Romanae Fidei, pro qua tuenda et conservanda e patria profugus, lustratis in Italia, Gallia, Belgio praecipuis sanctorum monumentis ; atque ibidem Principum Christianorum singulari amore et honore Sanctiss. etiam P. ac D. Pauli PP. V. paterno affectu susceptus, in maximis Catholicorum votis de felici ejus reditu, summum doloremsuis, et moerorem omnibus in hac Urbe ordinibus immatura morte quam obiit III. Kalendas Sextiles anno salutis MDCVIII, aetatis suae XXXIII. Quem mox secutus eodem tramite, ut eadem cum eo beatitute frueretur CALFURNIUS, FRATER, periculorum et exilii socius, in summa spe et expectatione bonorum de ejus nobilitate animi quam virtus et optima indoles exornavit, sui reliquit desiderium, et moestitiam coexulibus XVIII Kal. Oct. proxime sequentis Anno Aetatis XXV. Utrumque antecessit aetate et fati ordine frater primogenitus HUGO PRINCEPS, quem pie et Catholice pro Fide et Patria cogitantem Phillippus III. Hispaniarum Rex et vivum benevole amplexus, et in viridi aetate mortuum honorifice funerandum curavit Vallisoleti in Hispania IIII Idus Septembris A. S. MDCII.

APPENDIX. 355

The widow of this Calfurnius or Caffar O'Donnell was buried in the Franciscan Convent of Louvain with this epitaph—

D. O. M.
Excellentissima. Domina. Rosa. O'Dogharty.
Dynastarum. Inisoniae. Filia. et. Soror.
Alti Sanguinis. Decus.
Morum. Temperantia. et Splendidis Conjugiis. Auxit.
Primum. nupta. Inclyto. Heroi.
D. Cafarro. O'Donnello.
Tirconnalliae. Principis. Germano.
Dein. Excellentissimo. Domino. Eugenio. O'Neillo.
Catholici. In. Ultonia. Exercitus.
Archistratego.
Utramque Fortunam. Experta. Et. Miseriam.Rata.
Coelum Studuit. Benefactis. Mereri.
Septuaginta. Major. Denata.
Bruxellis. 1. Novembris. Anno MDCLX.
Suo. Cum. Primogenito. Hugone. O'Donnello.
Praestolatur. Hic. Carnis. Resurrectionem.

In St. Mary's Church, Clonmel.

No. 1 :—Hic jacet Terrentius O'Donel qui obiit 4 Martii 1583 et eius uxor Elena White quæ obiit 24 Aprili 1591 Eorum filii qui hunc tumulum fieri fecerunt A D 1592 : quibus sit propitius Omnipotens. Amen.

No. 2 :—Hic jacet Galfridus Barron qui obiit · 22 Martii A. Dni 1601, et Belina White uxor eius quæ hunc tumulum fieri fecerit A. Dni. 1605 et obiit A. Dni. 1610 quorum aiabus propitietur Deus.

No. 3 :—Johannes gelido jacet hoc sub marmore Vitus ;
Charaque Johannæ conjugis ossa piæ.
Bis Major, Wentworth primum prorege, secundum,
Catholici subiens fœdera martis obit.
26 Augusti 1643.

At St. Patrick's Well, Clonmel.

No. 4 :—Hic jacet D. Nicholaus White Armiger vir pietate constantia mansuetudine et integritate morum conspicuus et amabilis, obiit 30 die Augusti 1622 ; eius corpus ex antecessorum capella quæ borealemsacelli hujus partem respicit in

---

** See these epitaphs in the Rev. C. P. Meehan's Fate and Fortunes of Tyrone and Tyrconnell, pp. 446, 477, 476, 474.

hoc monumentum 22 die Decembris 1623 translatum est, cuius animæ propitieur Deus. Sacellum hoc S N.,i Jesu eius que genetrici B Mariæ Virgin' dicatum construxerunt in perpetuam dicti Nicolai memoriam Barbara White uxor eius vidua et Henricus White filius eius et hæres.

No 5 :—A small tablet, bearing three roses (the device of the White family,) underneath which is this inscription :—

        Et trias est Numero et Natura est una colorem
        En ubi præsidium Vitus et arma locat.

At the R. C. Church, Irishtown.

No. 6 :—A massive tablet, which, perhaps, was set in some conspicuous part of the old chapel of the Whites. It bears in full relief the arms of the family, and around the margin, and at the foot, this legend :—

"Insignia Joanis White armigeri quondam comit. Palatini Tipperariæ Seneschal, comitati Waterfordiæ vice-comiti. Clonmel primi majoris sic transit mundi gloria Benedictus Vitus hæres dicti Joani et Alsona hæc fieri fecerunt 1615."*

In the Franciscan Church is a chalice with the inscription: Orate pro animabus Edmundi Everard, et Joannae Naish uxoris ejus 1645. In the C. Church of Cappoquin there is a chalice with the inscription : Ora pro animabus D. Ricardi Everard et Catharinae Tobyn.

See 120 epitaphs wayside crosses or other souvenirs of the families of the 16th century, in this book, pp. 24, 45, 60, 62, 63, 64, 68, 69, 70, 71, 72, 80, 97, 98, 99, 100, 105, 110, 111, 133, 134, 139, 160, 161, 162, 163, 164, 167, 170, 171, 179, 180, 183, 184, 190, 192, 194, 197, 198, 201, 203, 204. 205, 209, 210, 211, 212, 214, 225, 234, 236.

Corrigenda.

p. 211, notes ' and ᵏ. The Rev. J. Everard, C.C., Clonmel, to whom I owe the two last inscriptions, represents the Everards of Burntcourt. There are still direct male descendants of the Everards of Fethard—the "Little Girl," who is said, at p. 210, to be the sole representative, had six brothers and five sisters older than herself, and her father's brother had a large family.

Clonmel Chronicle.

p. 296.—Camden's description of Armagh was accidentally omitted. He

---

* Inscriptions copied and published by Mr. Kearney, C.E., of Clonmel, and to be republished in Mr. Clark's forthcoming History of Clonmel.

say:—"Armagh church and City burnt by Shane O'Neill lost its ancient splendour; at present it consists of a very few huts covered with twigs, and the ruined walls of the monastery, priory and Archbishop's palace."

Reference letters have dropped out in the notes, before ⁿ Angus, p. 16 ; ¹ In the Fews, p. 21 ;¹ O'Donnell dwelt, p. 31 ;¹ Quaere, p. 32 ;ᵇ Belonging to, p. 51; ᵖ Lords to whom, p. 87 ; ᵍ In 1601 Emann, p. 119; ¹ In 1585 lived Teig, p. 154; James Wyse, p. 161 ; ˢ Supple of Kilmocua, p. 203 ; ᵗ Christopher, 9th Baron, p. 227. At p. 64 line 6 supply in the brackets, [Cavanagh, slain] ; at p. 266, for ' Carvagh ' read Carnagh.

Two ancient maps, specially lithographed for this work, were lost after the death of Mr. Kelly, who was to have been the publisher of the book.

LIST OF THE ROUND TOWERS OF IRELAND.

(Compiled from the works of Ledwich, Gough, Wilkinson, Petrie, Keane, Stokes, O'Neill, and others.)

In Co. Dublin . . . 8.—Clondalkin, Lusk, Swords, Rathmichael ; St. Michael'sᶠ (Ship Street), Christ Church,ᶜ Inismacnessan,ᶠ Finglas.ᶠ
„ *Meath* . . . . . 8.—Donaghmore, Kells, Ardbraccan,ᶠ Clonard,ᶜ Duleek,ᶠ Slane,ᶠ Trim,ᶠ Tullaghard.ᶠ
„ *Kildare* . . . . . 6.—Kildare, Kilcullen, Killossy, Oughterard, Teghadoe, Castledermot.
„ *Kilkenny* . . . . 6.—Aghaviller, Fertagh, Kilkenny, Kilree, Tullaherin, Tullamain.
„ *King's Co.* . . . 6.—Clonmacnoise, (2) Ferbane, Ferbane,ᵈ Seir-Kieran, Durrow.ᵈ
„ *Queen's Co.* . . 5.—Dysert, Killeskin, Teampul na Cailleach-dubh, Timahoe, Rosenallis.ᶠ
„ *Louth* . . . . . 4.—Dromiskin, Monasterboice, Drogheda,ᶠ Louth.ᶠ
„ *Wicklow* . . . . 4.—Glendalough (2) Glendalough,ᶠ Aghowle,ᵈ
„ *Carlow* . . . . . 3.—Kellystown, Killeshin,ᶠ Lorum.ᶠ
„ *Wexford* . . . . 2.—Ferns, Ferry Carrig.ᵈ
„ *Longford* . . . . 2.—Inchcloran,ᶠ Granard.ᶠ
„ *Cork* . . . . . . 9.—Cloyne, Kinneagh, Ballybeg,ˢ Nohoval Daly,ˢ Ballyvourney,ˢ Ballywerk, Brigoon,ᶠ Cork,ᶠ Rosscarbery.ᵈ

N.B.—ᶠ *means foundations ;* ˢ *stump ;* ᵈ *destroyed.*

LIST OF THE ROUND TOWERS OF IRELAND.

In Co. Clare . . . . 9.—Iniscattery, Inisceltra, Drumcleeve, Dysert O'Dea, Kilnaboy,[a] Rath,[a] Killaloe, Clare, Tomgraney.[d]
„ *Limerick* . . . . 6.—Dysert, Carrigeen, Kilmallock, Ardpatrick,[a] Limerick,[f] Dunaman.[f]
„ *Kerry* . . . . . 4.—Rattoo, Aghadoe,[a] Currane,[a] Ardfert.[f]
„ *Tipperary* . . . 4.—Cashel, Roscrea, Roscrea,[f] Emly.[d]
„ *Waterford* . . . 2.—Ardmore, Dungarvan.[d]
„ *Down* . . . . . 7.—Drumbo, Maghera, Cloch-Teach, Mahee Island,[a] Dundrum, Down-Patrick,[f] Castlereagh.
„ *Antrim* . . . . . 4—Antrim, Trummery, Ram Island, Armoy.
„ *Derry* . . . . . . 4—Derry,[f] Drumachose,[f] Dungiven,[d] Tamlacht.[f]
„ *Armagh* . . . . . 3—Armagh,[d] Armagh,[f] Killeevy.
„ *Donegal* . . . . . 3—Tory Island, Braade, Raphoe.[d]
„ *Monaghan* . . . . 3—Clones, Clones,[a] Iniskeen.
„ *Cavan* . . . . . 1—Drumlane.
„ *Fermanagh* . . . 1—Devenish.
„ *Tyrone* . . . . . 1—Erigel.[d]
„ *Galway* . . . . 10—Kilmacduagh, Kilbannon, Ruscam, Ardrahen,[a] Aranmore,[a] Killcoona,[a] Ballygaddy, Annadown,[f] Fertamore,[d] Meelick.[d]
„ *Mayo* . . . . . 8—Killala, Turlough, Meelick, Aghagower, Ballagh, Baal, Newcastle, Moat.[f]
„ *Sligo* . . . . . . 4—Ballymote, Drumcliff, Sligo (2.)
„ *Roscommon* . . . 4—Boyle,[a] Oran,[a] Assylin,[f] Roscommon.

FINIS.

INDEX.

A.

Abbey Leix, 75, 78.
Abbotstown, 271.
Abelles, 352.
Achar, 95.
Achonry, 237.
Acquaviva, 286.
Adams, 111, 171, 236.
Adamstown, 57, 95
Adare, 197, 283.
Adrain, 99.
Agarde, 351.
Aghadoe, 281.
Agher, 95, 100.
Aghery, 264.
Aghviller, 235.
Aha, 253.
Aldworth, 281.
Alene, 256.
Alford, 102.
Allardstown, 264.
Allen, 5, 37, 44, 46, 48, 57, 95, 235, 252, 351.
Allen, Bog of, 75.
Allenstown, 94, 95, 100.
Amerson, 31.
Amalies (recte O'Reillies), 117, 118, 119, 120.
Anaghes, 255.
Andrews, 353.
Annagh, 273.
Annaghmore, 276
Annesley, 282, 353.
Annogh Castle, 249.
Antislon, 96.
Antrim, 13, 31, 240, 260, 261, 296.
Antwerp, 162.
Arbracan, 92, 93.
Archbolds, 37, 38, 263, 350.
Archdeacon, 66, 70, 167, 278, 352.
Archer, 66, 67, 70, 72, 210, 291, 342, 344, 347, 351.
Archertone, 106.
Arclo, 41, 52, 208, 239.
Ardagh, 168, 234, 285.
„ Bishop of, 234.
Ardahill, 279.
Ardchille, 49.
Ardclony, 271.
Ardcrony, 215, 348.
Ardee, 3, 5.
Ardenoch, 239.
Ardes, 6, 10, 11, 232, 260.
Ardfert, 189, 190.
„ Bishop of, 191, 236, 263. 282.
Ardfry, 272.
Ardglass, 12, 238, 239.
Ardloman, 95, 96.
Ardmolchan, 93.
Ardmollan, 92.
Ardmore, 165.
Ardmothe, 95, 96.
Ardre, 252.
Ardremakow, 239.
Ardriston, 254.
Ardroute, 239.
Arland, 67.
Armagh, 3, 5, 10, 19, 20, 23, 24, 25, 95, 233, 235, 237, 247, 250, 251, 260, 285, 296, 306, 322.
Armie, English, 3.
Armoy, 167.
Armstrong, 83.
Arnold, 71.
Arny, 198.
Arolstone, 95.
Aronston, 97.
Arran, Isle of, 138, 238.
„ Earl of, 238, 266.
Arspoll, 254.
Artlanan, 239.
Arthur, 204, 210, 283, 351.
Arward, 100.
Ashbrook, 270.
Ashe, 50, 91, 94, 239, 265, 352.
Asheroe, 31.
Ashpoole, 37.
Askton, or Askeaton, 198, 233.
Asoalye, 256.
Asscy, 92.
Assye, 96.
Athboy, 91, 92, 96, 101, 102.
Athcarne, 93, 98, 99, 260.
Athcourie, 237.
Athenrie, 131.
„ Baron of, 226.
Athleag, 151, 277.
Athlone, 102, 104, 152, 224, 264, 277.
Atronan, 95.
Athlumney, 92, 106.
Athshe, 95.
Athy, 44, 272.
Atkinson, 102, 353.
Audley, 9, 101.
Aughrim, 274.
Austria, 64.
Ayle, 271.
Aylemers, 37, 43, 46, 48, 93, 94, 96, 99, 107, 260.
Aylewards, 161, 163, 255, 350.
Aylewardstown, 71, 255.

B.

Babbarne, 259.
Babe, 4, 352.
Baggad, 72.
Bagnal, 2, 4, 6, 8, 12, 51, 52, 53, 253, 349, 350.
Bagot, 281.
Bagotstown, 281.
Baigre, 256.
Baker, 350.
Balaghene, 8.
Balaia, 239.
Balandsox, 253.
Balankey, 99.
Balduff, 253.
Baldwinstown, 266.
Balebeg, 256.
Baleclockan, 78.
Balecowanne, 256.
Baledungan, 92.
Baleguffindowe, 258.
Balehartin, 256.
Balehorron, 256.
Balemakeyan, 256.
Balenfane, 256.
Balenosky, 258.
Balera, 258.

Balerotherie, 36, 37, 90.
Baletrasnie, 258.
Balevolo, 258.
Balf, 91, 95, 96, 99, 352.
Balgan, 257.
Balgard, 37.
Balgath, 94.
Balglunin, 272.
Balgriffin, 37, 38.
Baliburtane, 151.
Baliesko, 101.
Balinesloe, 134, 151.
Ball, 93, 351.
Ballaghan, 31.
Ballaghtobin, 71.
Ballaigh, 259.
Ballaighene, 257.
Ballakit, 32.
Ballashannon, 32.
Ballawlie, 38.
Ballebockrane, 259.
Ballebragane, 5, 349.
Ballebrennan, 256, 349.
Balleconchin, 166.
Balleconnor, 256.
Ballegerce, 256.
Ballegrand, 258.
Ballegray, 96.
Ballegresaigh, 258.
Ballemony, 258.
Ballenacaidde, 96.
Ballencurre, 258.
Ballendel, 95.
Ballenemone, 103.
Balleneskeagh, 96.
Ballenirton, 107.
Ballenrana, 258.
Ballensar, 257.
Balleouddane, 256.
Balleoulouagh, 258.
Baller, 145.
Balleragat, 66, 67.
Balleteg, 256.
Ballevalle, 258.
Ballevodick, 258.
Ballewallken, 258.
Ballgath, 94.
Ballibrayen, 5.
Balliburlie, 82, 91.
Ballibyan Mountains, 144.
Hallicallie, 254.
Ballicappock, 62.
Balliconiel, 106.
Balliconnicke, 61.
Balliconnor, 61, 63.
Ballicotlan, 48.
Ballicranigambege, 254.
Ballidufle, 254.

Balliellen, 253, 263.
Ballifenync, 253.
Ballihack, 57.
Ballihemoge, 254.
Halliloughreagh, 57.
Ballilowe, 254.
Ballimolchan, 93.
Ballimore, 102, 106.
Ballinabay, 315.
Ballinagard, 283.
Ballinagir, 256.
Ballincapoch, 48.
Ballincor, 40, 41.
Ballinecorly, 110.
Ballinedramey, 96, 101.
Ballinekelly, 56.
Ballinelock, 110, 258.
Ballinerah, 56.
Ballineskelligy, 239.
Ballingarry, 200, 331.
Ballingtoughe, 67.
Ballinhawnemore, 58.
Ballinlough, 105, 106, 270, 271.
Ballinmore, 37.
Ballinree, 266, 270.
Ballintabler, 152, 256.
Ballinter, 269.
Ballintlea, 264, 279.
Ballintubber, 152, 256.
Ballinvacky, 58.
Ballinvilla, 284.
Balliot, 96.
Balliroe, 58.
Ballishanon, 249.
Ballitample, 254.
Balliterney, 254.
Hallivaghan, 126.
Ballneagh, 106.
Ballnekill, 95.
Ballohell, 256.
Ballough, 254.
Ballown, 39.
Ballrodan, 95.
Ballstown, 95.
Balltrasency, 96.
Ballunalheu, 97.
Ballvomen, 110.
Ballyndams, 78.
Ballyaghbregan, 255.
Ballyancaislean, 336.
Ballyandun, 348.
Ballyashhin, 62.
Ballyharna, 265.
Ballybege, 254.
Ballybirr, 255.
Ballybollen, 275.
Ballybort, 77, 81.
Ballyboy, 83.

Ballybracke, 253.
Ballybranagh, 105.
Ballybrennan, 58, 349.
Ballybrett, 233.
Ballybrit, 81, 77.
Ballybrittan, 82.
Ballybrittas, 79, 84.
Ballybunnion, 283.
Ballybur, 70.
Ballyburlie, 82, 91.
Ballyburtane, 82.
Ballycallen, 50.
Ballycashen, 166.
Ballycavoge, 166.
Ballyclough, 166.
Ballycogly, 60.
Ballycomask, 209.
Ballyconin, 104.
Ballyconnor, 63.
Ballycorky, 104.
Ballycorry, 100.
Ballycowan, 83, 85.
Ballycre, 255.
Ballycromgan, 253.
Ballycullen, 283.
Ballycurrin, 209.
Ballydarmyne, 254.
Ballydonclan, 274.
Ballyeane, 39.
Ballyen, 68.
Ballyfarnage, 266.
Ballyfarnocke, 58.
Ballyfennon, 71.
Ballyfoell, 255.
Ballyforan, 266.
Ballyfoyle, 68, 255.
Ballygeary, 58, 61.
Ballygrant, 277.
Ballyhaire, 277.
Ballyhaly, 60, 265.
Ballyharth, 62.
Ballyheige, 282.
Ballyhency, 166.
Ballyhinch, 60.
Ballyhire, 60, 265.
Ballyhomyn, 255.
Ballyhubhert, 281.
Ballyhymickny, 209.
Ballykeogh, 61.
Ballykey, 38.
Ballyknockan, 79.
Ballyleagh, 53.
Ballyleigh, 265.
Ballyline, 271.
Ballylorcan, 71.
Ballylorka, 255.
Ballymacarne, 61.
Ballymack, 70.

INDEX.

Ballymackeogh, 284.
Ballymager, 62, 265.
Ballymaka, 72.
Ballymartin, 68.
Bally McCloghny, 255.
Bally McCrony, 255.
Ballymoe, 283.
Ballymoge, 253.
Ballymore, 58, 60, 89, 103. 274, 326.
Ballymorough, 255.
Ballymote, 145, 336, 247.
Ballymount, 106.
Ballymoyer, 266.
Ballymurray, 277.
Ballynacor, 270.
Ballynasad, 273.
Ballynalacken, 272.
Ballynatine.
Ballyneale, 72.
Ballynebally.
Ballynerowly, 255.
Ballynitie, 199.
Ballynonetie, 209.
Ballyraddy, 255.
Ballyrankin, 265.
Ballyreddy, 72.
Ballyrian, 253.
Ballyroghy, 256.
Ballysax, 252.
Ballyshannon, 31, 32.
Ballysonan, 48.
Ballsop, 61.
Ballystrew, 260.
Ballyteige, 62, 254.
Ballytramon, 266.
Ballyvannon, 284.
Ballyvorish, 209.
Ballywhyghan, 239.
Bally William Roe, 254.
Balmadon, 37.
Balmadroght, 39.
Balmagere, 59, 62.
Balmakeyrie, 256.
Balnegin, 95.
Baloebrack, 107.
Balrath, 95, 106, 269.
Balreske, 95.
Baltimore, 168, 239.
Baltinglass, 45, 48, 49, 226, 230, 284, 349.
Baltrasna, 271.
Balsound, 101.
Balyna, 80, 261, 267, 270, 274.
Banagh, 248.
Banelagh, 36.
Bangor, 259.
Baniekard, 258.

Bann, 15, 17, 20, 28, 234, 258.
Bannockburn, 16.
Bannow, 64, 256.
Bantrie, 62, 168, 256, 257.
Barclay, 198, 206.
Barge, 56.
Bargie, 256.
Bargy, 60.
Barick, 291.
Barker, 269.
Barna, 273, 274.
Barnet, 46.
Barne Veddon, 255.
Barnwall, 4, 5, 38, 39, 96, 97, 228, 269, 270, 290, 291, 292, 349, 351, 352.
Barret, 182, 350.
Barretstown, 284.
Barriestown, 257.
Barrington, 79, 352.
Barringston, 48.
Barron, 68, 253, 355.
Barrowe River, 50, 56, 64, 73, 75, 78, 81.
Barry, 54, 61, 167, 169, 171, 182, 198, 224, 254, 257, 278, 351.
Barrymore, 168, 278.
Barry Oge, 172.
Barryscourt, 271, 278.
Barton, 262.
Basset, 353.
Bathes, 5, 37, 38, 39, 93, 94, 98, 99, 252, 269, 290, 291, 292, 351.
Bauk, 265.
Bawnmore, 266, 273.
Bealalahun, 275.
Bealan, 253.
Bealing, 35, 38, 48.
Bealingston, 38.
Bearchin, 168.
Beare, 372.
Bearra, 168.
Beccanston, 39.
Bective, 92.
Beckell, 23.
Bedge, 97.
Bedlow (or Bellew), 4. 38, 39, 45, 94, 100.
Bedlowston, 92.
Beecher, 281.
Beechwood, 277.
Beerford, 100.
Beg, 38, 92, 94, 96, 352.
Belaclare, 239.
Belalem, 239.
Belanamore, 276.
Belatha Lagain, 5.
Beleareele, 58.

Beleeke, 31, 143, 297.
Belfield, 78.
Belgard, 37.
Bellaborow, 256.
Bellabow, 256.
Bellame, 93.
Bellander, 92.
Belfast, 18.
Belletston, 106.
Bellot, 353.
Belling, 38, 48, 252, 351.
Belleushen, 256.
Bellews (see Bedlow), 4, 38. 39, 45, 94, 100, 260, 263, 351.
Bellewstown (see Bedlowstown), 92, 94, 100.
Bellowe, 252.
Belturbet, 247.
Benburbe, 27.
Benford, 46.
Bengley, 5.
Bennecerry, 254.
Bennet, 351.
Benson, 9.
Bere, '353.
Berkeley, 233, 350.
Berks, 280.
Berlagh, 256.
Berminghams, 45, 46, 48, 50, 91, 93, 101, 105, 235, 272, 349, 281.
Bertiers, 13.
Beste, 92.
Bethe, 351.
Betagh, 95, 99.
Bettifield, 277.
Bewlie, 5.
Bierweisour, 239.
Billingesley, 206.
Bingerstown, 94.
Bingham, 33, 275, 276, 350, 353.
Birford, 93.
Birkenshaw, 353.
Birne (see Byrne), 253, 254.
Birr, 83.
Birrell, 5.
Birt, 32, 94.
Birton, 253.
Bishops, 233, 285.
Bishopscourt, 72, 252.
Bishopstown, 104, 110.
Bisset, 5, 16.
Black, 101.
Blackcastle, 72, 94".
Blackfort, 78.
Blackhall, 98, 252, 253, 257.
Blackhill, 46, 93.
Blackine, 94, 263.

2 Z

Blacklowne, 82.
Blackney, 38, 351, 352.
Blackrath, 47.
Blackwater, 20, 25, 46, 90, 304, 306, 315.
Blackwood, 252.
Blake, 96, 133, 272, 273, 351, 352
Blakeney, 274.
Blanchfield, 71, 255, 284, 349.
Blanchveldstoune, 255.
Blaney, 12.
Blarney, 279.
Blatherwick, 272.
Blayne, 97.
Blayney, 233, 261.
Bleachfield, 254.
Blindwell, 274.
Blood, 353.
Bloomfeld, 67.
Blount, 128, 233.
Blundel, 353.
Boanstown, 93.
Bobsgrove, 271.
Bodkin, 132, 133, 273, 352.
Bodlen, 12.
Bolan, 266.
Boles, 94.
Bolgan, 61.
Bolger, 72.
Bollintollin, 254.
Bolton, 95, 351.
Bonecarry, 61.
Bonneltstown, 69, 70.
Bonnoght, 7.
Boreduffe, 253, 254.
Boresheis, 255.
Borranstown, 38, 39.
Borris, 265.
Bosher (Busher or Bouchier), 61, 82, 86, 87, 205.
Bostock, 167.
Botford, 94.
Bothnan, 5.
Bouchier, 271, 350.
Bourk, 163, 350.
Bouth, 164.
Bowdrave, 289.
Bowen, 78, 79, 80.
Boylan, 50.
Boyle, 353.
Boyne, 23, 35, 90.
Boyle, 150, 277, 281.
Boys, 95, 258.
Boyton, 210.
Boyton-Rath, 210, 289.
Brabazon, 134, 154, 242, 246, 353

Brack, 163.
Bracklon, 106.
Brackloonmore, 273.
Brady, 271, 352, 353.
Branan, 352.
Brandon, 4, 5, 269.
Branganston, 48.
Brangastowne, 253.
Brasell, 66, 258.
Brasilagh, 12, 23, 30.
Bray, 35, 37, 38, 282, 352.
Breafy, 275.
Brecaston, 48.
Breeze, 274.
Brefney, 90, 348.
Brenan, 50, 72.
Brereton, 267, 353.
Bresilagh, 251.
Brett, 5.
Breton, 48.
Brewers, 164, 289.
Breynd, 208, 350.
Breyne, 2.
Brianstown, 256.
Bridges, 99, 100, 133.
Bridgetown, 59.
Brighargye, 256.
Brierton, 78.
Briscoe, 268.
Briver, 164, 291.
Bromestone, 57.
Bromoyle, 32.
Bruncard, 242.
Brooke, 42, 262.
Brosenaghe, 104.
Browalstown, 254.
Brown, 3, 13, 16, 21, 33, 38, 47, 59, 61, 91, 134, 163, 254, 256, 257, 273, 275, 283, 289, 350, 352.
Brownesborne, 255.
Brownsford, 68, 72.
Brownstown, 39, 47. 253.
Broy, 258.
Broymore, 38.
Bruce, 16.
Brune, 57.
Brussel, 275.
Bryan, 62, 214, 293, 331, 350.
Brian Carroghe's County, 13, 14.
Bryanston, 62.
Drymingham (see Bearmingham) 135, 252, 253.
Budge, 97.
Buckingham, 270.

Buggon, 48.
Bunburbe, 34.
Buncrana Castle, 32.
Bundroose Castle, 31.
Bunes. 254.
Bunnyconnelan, 275.
Bunowen, 270.
Bunratty, 126.
Buolebrack, 284.
Burdensgrange, 209.
Burg, 35.
Burgate, 167.
Burgo, 73, 293.
Burkes, 113, 139, 141, 199, 205, 209, 220, 229, 255, 272, 273, 277, 321, 327, 347, 348.
Burleigh, 7, 59.
Burnchurche, 58, 66, 68, 255, 266.
Burnell, 38, 96, 349, 351.
Burrowes, 22, 31, 80, 265.
Burris Leigh, 209.
Burske, 239.
Burtall, 194.
Burweisnowe, 239.
Burwis Oare, 239.
Buss, 236.
Butler, 5, 51, 52, 62, 65, 67, 68, 69, 70, 71, 76, 80, 163, 164, 171, 209, 211, 212, 217, 226, 228, 231, 271, 254, 255, 256, 257, 265, 266, 271, 273, 284, 289, 292, 305, 326, 331, 335, 349, 350.
Butlerstown, 256.
Butlerswood, 68.
Buttevant, 174, 224, 278, 349.
Buxton, 265.
Byrne, 35, 39, 41, 54, 62, 253, 264, 266, 290, 350.
Bysse, 102.
Bwy, 258.

C

Cabboyhe, 135.
Cabinteely, 264.
Cabra, 263.
Cabry, 270.
Caddell, 38, 39, 93, 94, 97.
Cahir, 284, 289, 335, 349.
Cahirminane, 336.
Cahir Trant, 282.
Caire, 30.
Caire MacEwlyn, 32.
Caisleannua, 31.
Calais, 83.
Calavan, 289.

INDEX.

Calboy, 30.
Calcestown, 94.
Calcutta, 274.
Caldanglie, 32.
Calebegge, 33, 238, 239.
Calf, 48.
Calfer, 57.
Calmore, 30, 32.
Callan, 66, 67, 70, 207.
Callonok, 258.
Calry, 104.
Camas, 283.
Cambridge, 234.
Campier, 350.
Campion, 23.
Canerston, 110.
Cantaule, 20.
Canton, 58.
Cantwell, 70, 88, 209, 212, 291.
Cantwellstown, 70, 88.
Cantyre, 15, 16.
Cappagh, 266.
Cappahun, 165.
Cappanacus, 280.
Car, Lord, 5, 211, 288.
Car, 215.
Carberie, 45, 48, 167, 233, 253, 279, 280, 284.
Cardiff, 38, 101.
Carduff, 38.
Caregeschurche, 257.
Carew, 51, 53, 286.
Cargan, 31.
Cargmannan, 257.
Carhampton, 263.
Carie, 15, 353.
Carig, 266.
Carlands, 270.
Carlandstown, 265, 270.
Carlingford, 3, 5, 12, 18, 238, 244.
Carlow, 18, 35, 36, 41, 44, 50, 51, 56, 63, 64, 226, 233, 241, 242, 253, 254, 265, 267, 271, 283, 298.
Carne, 60, 106, 357.
Carnegilla, 263.
Carney, 226, 291.
Carolan, 262.
Carraduff, 272.
Carraghmore, 165.
Carraig Locha Ce, 276.
Carran, 211.
Carrick, 34, 67, 94, 199, 211, 215, 292.
Carrick, Earl of, 284.
Carrickbeg, 164.
Carrick, 211.

Carrickfergus, 18, 238.
Carrickmayne, 38.
Carrickstowne, 253.
Carricknestayne, 254.
Carrig-an-chobhlaigh, 336.
Carrig Teage, 34.
Carrigbraghey, 32.
Carrigfoyle, 189, 196, 282.
Carrigogonnell, 198.
Carrigmenan,
Carrignavar, 279.
Carrignegany, 255.
Carrignory, 255.
Carrigslany, 267.
Carroll, 50.
Carron, 254.
Carrigonede, 281.
Carroughmore, 160, 165, 231.
Carrowkeel, 275.
Carrymar, 108.
Carton, 264, 349.
Carty, 278.
Cary, 353.
Casie, 111, 352.
Caslan-Stoke, 32.
Cashell, 125, 209, 211, 233, 235, 236, 237, 286, 288.
Cashell, 4, 5, 351.
Cashiel, 94.
Cassane, 239.
Castles, passim.
Castle Archdall, 262.
Castlebar, 83, 263, 268, 275.
Castle Blakeney, 274.
Castle Carbery, 97, 265.
Castle Connell, 199, 283, 229, 349.
C. Cook, 281.
C. Cosby, 80.
C. Cuffe, 268.
Castledermott, 44, 252.
C. Dirrhy, 78.
C. Dobbs, 261.
C. Donovan, 279.
Castle Durrow, 267.
Castle Fene, 31.
C. Ffrench, 273.
C. Fleming, 231.
C. Fogarty, 284.
Castle Gregory, 282.
Castlehacket, 271, 273.
C. Hely, 70.
Castlehaven, 168.
Castlehaystown, 60.
C. Howel, 70.
C. Irvin, 269.
C. Ishin, 48, 283.
C. Island, 109.

C. Jordan, 82, 92.
C. Kelly, 274, 276.
C. Kevin, 43, 96.
C. Knock, 37, 38.
C. Lamerby, 92.
C. Lyf, 71.
C. MacAwliffe, 279.
C. Martin, 18, 45, 46, 60, 252.
C. Mayne, 244.
C. Minard, 282.
C. More, 275.
C. Morres, 284.
O. Pigot, 75.
C. Pollard, 270.
C. Quin, 280.
C. Richard, 96.
C. Reagh, 11, 12, 166.
C. Ring, 4.
C. Roe, 28.
C. Talbot, 266.
Castleton Kildrought, 98, 252.
C. Town, 48, 60, 92, 93, 94, 99, 104, 108, 199, 231, 256.
Castletown Roche, 225, 278.
Castletown Lord, 79, 268, 280, 284.
C. Troy, 283.
Castle Upton, 261.
Castle Warde, 260.
Cathaoir Mor, 81.
Catherine St., 98.
Caufelston, 97.
Caufield, 12, 261, 350.
Cavan, 24, 89, 90, 102, 107, 117, 121, 148, 241, 246, 247, 263, 271, 300.
Cavanaugh, 35, 40, 50, 51, 52, 53, 54, 56, 57, 58, 59, 62, 63, 64, 120, 226, 302, 328, 349.
Cavin, 66.
Celcarne, 92.
Chamberlaine, 5, 39, 102.
Chaple, 257.
Chapman, 282.
Charbs, 84.
Charden, 235.
Charlemont, 261.
Charleville, 268.
Chatterton, 19.
Cheevers, 48, 60, 62, 93, 94, 99, 256, 265, 269, 349.
Chellyner, 352.
Chester, 237.
Cheshire, 282.
Chichester, 15, 18, 25, 244, 246, 248.
Chuiseul, 278.
Churchtown, 94, 281.

Ciannacta, 28.
Clagh, 71.
Clancasters, 16.
Clanalasters, 16.
Clanant, 19.
Clanbrasels, 2, 11.
Clanbrassel, 19, 20, 261.
Clancanane, 20.
Clancan, 2, 20.
Clancar, 167, 349.
Clancark, 167.
Clancarties, 168.
Clancarvell, 24.
Clancathal, 279.
Clanchy, 350.
Clanconcane, 21.
Clancurry, 48.
Clandeboye, 2, 6, 8, 11, 13, 14, 17, 34, 260, 261.
Clandonnels, 14, 16, 26.
Clane, 47, 252.
Clankonkeyne, 28.
Clanlochlain, 280.
Clanmore, 267.
Clanmorris, 275, 276.
Clanrickard, 134, 135, 139, 220, 244, 272, 347.
Claragh, 255.
Claranclaris, 257.
Clare 123, 124, 126, 240, 261, 264, 271, 272, 274, 283, 284, 348.
Clare, 291.
Clashmore, 277.
Clastnoe, 255.
Clavagh, 71.
Clayland, 58.
Cleere, 238, 254.
Cleggan, 261.
Cleggs, 99.
Clelande, 56.
Clement, the 8th, 349.
Clenghish, 283.
Clergy, 233, 285.
Clery, 66.
Clifford, 33, 85, 303.
Clinch, 100.
Clinshe, 39.
Clinton, 4, 5.
Cloane, 257, 258.
Cloesse, 256.
Cloghatrabally, 280.
Cloghcully, 350.
Clogher, 234, 235, 250, 278, 285, 287.
Cloghla, 254.
Cloghlack, 166.
Clohn, 25.

Cloine McKnosha, 104.
Clomeen, 168.
Clomen, 256.
Clomesse, 100.
Clomochain, 97.
Clomore, 254.
Clonard, 96, 97.
Clonardran, 93.
Clonbela, 83, 268.
Clonbrassel, 20, 69.
Clonbreve, 96.
Clonbrock, 273.
Cloncare, 169, 222.
Cloncoscoran, 277.
Cloncurry, 252, 264.
Clondae, 257.
Clondalkin, 37.
Clondaly, 96.
Clondonnells, 250, 251.
Clone, 68, 180.
Clone Bishoprick, 170, 172, 263.
Clonebrassel McBoolechan, 9.
Clonecollain, 107.
Clonegawny, 84.
Clonekevan, 96.
Clonelly, 262.
Clonemcknois, 234.
Clones, 24.
Clonfert, 131, 134, 237, 286.
Clongell, 94, 97.
Clongoweswood, 47, 245, 274, 284.
Clonin, 103.
Clonkeraigh, 257.
Clonkyraghe, 62.
Clonlisk, 87.
Clonlonnon, 104.
Clonlost, 105, 270.
Clonmacnoise, 83.
Clonmaghan, 96.
Clonmeen, 279, 280.
Clonmel, 159, 210, 213, 229, 283, 288, 289, 355.
Clonmeny, 31.
Clonmillier, 81, 84.
Clonmoney, 265.
Clonmore, 349.
Clonmoynagh, 271.
Clonmore, 4, 5, 52, 92, 280.
Clon na Ross, 236.
Clonnor, 5.
Clonolyn, 53, 54.
Clonranye, 258.
Clonresse, 93.
Clontarf, 38.
Clonyardom, 259.
Clonygagh, 253.

Clonyn, 270.
Clough, 254.
Clougharde, 34.
Cloughchricke, 253.
Cloughgrenan, 51, 52, 264, 265.
Cloughouter, 247.
Clovey, 165.
Clowater, 253.
Clownebolche, 83.
Clowrann, 258.
Cloyduff, 83.
Cloyne, 286, 288.
Cluain (see Clone), 336.
Cnock-fionn, 348.
Cnoc-lacha, 348.
Coaleshill, 258.
Cockburn, 266.
Cocle, 57.
Codd, 60, 256, 349.
Coe Lough, 22.
Coffee, 50.
Cogan, 167, 350.
Coghlan, 83.
Cohery, 289.
Coill-uí-Fiachrach, 347.
Colambre, 105.
Cole, 256.
Cole, 96.
Cole Brook, 262.
Colclough, 233, 253.
Coleraine, 2, 25, 28, 249, 261, 262, 297.
Coleman, 170.
Collan, 9, 20, 64.
Collanhroe, 110.
Collanstowne, 48.
Collaton, 254.
Collbaneghar, 78.
Collbinstown, 253.
Collen, 351.
Colleges, 295.
Colley, 48, 82, 97, 233.
Colleybeg, 168.
Collymore, 280.
Collmanstown, 39.
Collmoolestone, 96, 99.
Collmollen, 95.
Collum, 236.
Coltsman, 278.
Comerford, 67, 70, 72, 166, 211, 255, 289, 291, 292, 352.
Compostella, 286.
Comsey, 71.
Comshen, 351.
Comyn, 271.
Conagh, 271.
Condon, 163, 178, 179, 182, 225, 335, 336.

INDEX. 365

Confy, 39, 47.
Conmee, 270.
Connaghe, 201.
Connagher, 227.
Connaght, 35.
Connally Barony, 253.
Connaught, 1, 2, 35, 54, 112, 122, 237, 239, 273, 241, 287, 303, 304, 336.
Connor, 2, 83, 235, 271, 285.
Conogarhen, 32.
Conran, 37, 38.
Conry, 286.
Conshelaghe, 208.
Contaule, 20.
Conway, 72, 101, 193, 291, 351, etc.
Coodurragha, 279.
Cooke, 5, 245, 254, 281.
Cookstown, 4, 93, 95, 101.
Coolambre, 106, 270.
Coolavin, 275, 276.
Cooledoyne, 58.
Cooley, 85.
Cooleybeg, 168.
Cooleymore, 168.
Coolgreany, 266.
Coolie, 45.
Coolmoyne, 263.
Coolnamuck, 164.
Cooloo, 273.
Cooly, 87.
Coomlegane, 279.
Coote, 268.
Coppinger, 170, 171, 271, 278, 351.
Coran, 37, 38.
Corballies, 37, 93, 94, 98.
Corbally, 101, 255, 265.
Corbetstown, 83, 106.
Corcabhascin, 271.
Cordangan, 281.
Cork, County, 156, 158, 167, 170, 188, 196, 216, 279, 280, 281, 282.
Cork, Bishop of, 172, 236, 286, 288.
Cork, City, 167, 239, 240, 241, 271, 278, 283, 284.
Corkbeg, 278.
Corlod, 255.
Cormicke, 72.
Corolanstown, 103, 105, 106.
Coronary, 271.
Corr, 273.
Corraghmore, 231, 232.
Corran, 18, 347.
Corranvreddy, 258.
Corratobbann, 258.
Correndestown, 39.

Correndoo, 266.
Correstone, 5.
Corrikeris, 48.
Coruagh, 266.
Cosby, 78, 79, 80, 267, 352.
Cosfeale, 282.
Cosheshany, 208.
Coskayll, 257.
Cosse, 256.
Costelloe, 275, 276.
Costilaghe,
Cotos Lough, 22.
Cotter, 279.
Coubrey, 168.
Council, The, 244.
Courcey, Lord, 9, 171, 229, 278, 349.
Courte, The, 257.
Courtney, 205.
Courtown, 46, 264.
Courtstown, 70.
Coutin, 290.
Cowbrodd, 258.
Cowik, 67.
Cowland, 126.
Cowledoynge, 257.
Cowle Ishell, 255.
Cowlneallven, 94.
Cowley, 18, 82, 252, 265, 352.
Cowlniagh, 79.
Cox, 281.
Coyne Lough, 10, 12.
Crackanston, 97.
Cradockstown, 47, 349.
Craghes, 163.
Craigfergus, 13, 14, 18, 33.
Creal, 48.
Creagh, 205, 278, 283, 288, 289, 290.
Creagh Ballraen, 258.
Crean, Lynch, 275.
Crebilly, 261.
Creegh, 258.
Creen, 30.
Creey-Toune, 67.
Cremorne, 261.
Cregg, 267, 273, 274, 280, 281.
Crew, 353.
Crickstown, 91, 93, 96, 105, 269, 270.
Crint, 256.
Crinton, 92.
Croagh, 280.
Croambeg, 255.
Crobey, 96.
Croft, 73, 281.
Crofton, 277, 350.
Crofty, 106.

Croghan, 82, 85, 233, 239, 268.
Croaghe Patrick, 1.
Croghfenaly.
Croke, 67.
Crome, 198.
Cromelin, 39.
Cromok, 259.
Crommer, 255.
Cromp, 101, 269.
Cromwell, 9, 45, 70, 89, 266.
Crooke, 71, 353.
Crook Haven, 239.
Crookestown, 253.
Crosbie, 236, 282.
Cross, 272.
Crosses, Wayside, 68, 69, 70, 72, 97, 98, 231, 239.
Crosshaven, 167.
Crowe, 353.
Crunchan, 81.
Cruise, 38.
Crumpe, 95, 269.
Cuba, 271.
Cuff, 185, 272.
Culkieragh, 262.
Cullen, 61, 64, 166.
Cullendragh, 95.
Cullenston, 61.
Cullentraigh, 258.
Culliebege, 254.
Cul Mac Tryne, 31.
Culme, 353.
Culmore, 30, 249.
Cumnier, 272.
Cumshaiagh, 225.
Curliews, 144, 303.
Curluddy, 72.
Curmollen, 95.
Curraboy, 273.
Curragh, 37, 38.
Curraghleagh, 275.
Curraghmore (see Corraghniore and Carraghmore), 280, 347.
Curran, 34, 284.
Curry glas, 281.
Cusacke, 5, 27, 91, 93, 94, 95, 96, 97, 105, 129, 269, 296, 336, 353.
Cushingstone, 94, 97.
Cuskenny, 279.
Cussyn, 352.
Cutmollen, 92.

D

Daideston, 99.
Daingean ni-Hushy, 282.
Dale, 256.
Dalgan, 272.

INDEX.

Dalgin, 274.
Daljoy, 239.
Dalkey, 36, 238, 239.
Dallway, 252, 261, 353.
Dalton, 71, 103, 110, 163.
Dalystown, 271.
Danesfort, 273.
Daneston, 93, 99.
Dangan, 70, 85, 125, 265, 283.
Dangan, I. Beirn, 276.
Danganmore, 70, 72.
Danganstown, 71.
Danyell, 252.
Darcy, 64, 92, 93, 94, 96, 100, 103, 106, 107, 133, 273.
Dardesse, 96, 106.
Dardestowne, 93, 94, 103.
Darinlar, 165.
Darlington, 264.
Darrynane, 282.
Dartry, 23, 24, 264.
Daton, 67, 266, 255, 292.
Darent, 281.
Davanargh, 257.
Davels, 72, 79, 253.
Davers, 43.
Davidstown, 57, 263.
Daviestown, 257.
Dawmans, 13.
Dawson, 261.
Daxe, 91, 352.
Dayrane, 257.
Dealbhna Eathra, 83.
Deanes, 68, 70, 254.
Dease, 269, 270, 279.
De Bathe, 269.
De Beauvoir, 275.
De Burgo, 283, 287.
Decies, 158, 160, 161, 165, 225, 226, 277.
De Freyne, 276.
Degert, 216.
Delahoyde, 39, 49, 92, 93, 95, 96, 99, 267.
Delamaire, 10, 110.
Delvin, Lord, 103, 105, 106, 227, 228, 270, 349.
Dempsy, 84.
Den, 39, 68, 232, 254.
Dengan, 95, 96, 98.
Denny, 190, 283.
„ Barony of, 255.
De Oviedo, 285.
Derite, 50.
Dermebeer, 165.
De Robeck, 267.
De Ros, 97, 264.
Derpatrick, 95, 96, 100.

Derran, 85, 100.
Derry, 28, 31, 80, 234, 239, 249, 262, 285, 287, 297.
Derrymollin, 83.
Derrymore, 336.
Derver, 4.
Desart, 268.
De Rythre, 264.
Deseret, 232.
Desert, 267.
Desmond, 45, 52, 67, 76, 156, 166, 168, 170, 181, 195, 199, 206, 219, 231, 278, 286, 331, 333, 338, 349.
Devereux, 57, 59, 62, 164, 256, 257, 265, 266.
Devonshire, 9, 235.
De Vesci, 261.
Dexter, 92, 97.
Digby, 252, 352.
Dillon, 38, 39, 86, 93, 94, 95, 96, 98, 99, 103, 104, 107, 110, 113, 137, 154, 269, 273, 276, 350.
Dingan, 82.
Dingle, 157, 189, 239, 282.
Dipper, 256.
Dirr, 257.
Disert, 78, 349.
Disert Cealaigh, 338.
Dobbin, 67, 71, 163.
Dobbs, 261.
Docwra, 102, 261.
Documents, Original, 124, 290, 339, 348.
Dod, 252, 256.
Dodwell, 276.
Doe, 248, 249.
Doinfert, 45, 48, 50.
Doire-Mac-Lachtna, 338.
Doire-ni-Donnell, 348.
Doherty, 262.
Dollardstown, 93.
Dolphin, 136, 273.
Domano, 165.
Domaston, 38.
Domville, 234.
Don, 276.
Donadea, 46, 48, 107, 264.
Donfort, 253.
Dongan, 48, 98.
Donagh, 36.
Donakernie, 93.
Donamore, 37.
Doncannon, 57.
Dondonnell, 103.
Dondrome, 244, 257.
Doneames, 106.

Donegal, 2, 29, 31, 248, 260, 262.
Donell, 300.
Donelan, 139, 234.
Donemore, 100.
Doneraile, 282.
Donewer, 104, 105.
Dongalpe, 257.
Dongarvan, 164.
Donibroke Castle, 37.
Don Owen, 32.
Donmoghan, 4.
Donmore, 94.
Donnelaghs, 33.
Donnell, 79.
Donnhiel, 262.
Dounybrook, 38, 236.
Donore, 103, 104, 105, 270, 283.
Donoughmore, 284.
Donovan (see O'Donovan),
Doramestown, 95.
Dormers, 70, 351.
Dormondus, 66.
Dorrown, 82.
Douay, 285.
Dougan, 253.
Doughcloyne, 281.
Dour, 46.
Dovea, 282.
Dowalla, 225.
Dowdall, 5, 96, 98, 99, 231, 232, 252, 349, 352.
Dowdingleston, 48.
Dowdontonne, 5.
Dowell, 53.
Dowleck, 91.
Dowley, 72.
Dowlin, 252.
Down, 2, 6, 12, 235, 240, 245, 260, 265, 266, 271, 285, 296.
Downelong, 239.
Downemore, 239.
Downeshead, 239.
Downings, The, 50, 252.
Downshire, 260.
Downton, 252, 353.
Dow O'Loyaghe, 88.
Dowrig, 239.
Dowstown, 93, 97.
Dowth, 91, 94, 98, 269.
Doyle, 265.
Doyne, 50, 252, 267, 353.
Dracot, 93, 102, 106, 352.
Drake, 5, 95, 98, 269.
Drakerath, 95, 98, 269.
Drakestown, 5, 94.
Draper, 91, 234.
Drew, 278.

INDEX. 367

Drewscout, 278.
Drinagh, 62.
Drishane, 279, 281.
Drogheda, 3, 46, 90, 239, 240, 243
Dromahare, 276, 300.
Dromaleague, 280.
Dromane, 126, 160, 226.
Drombar, 96.
Dromconragh, 99.
Dromconran, 37.
Dromehaire, 276.
Dromes, The, 36.
Dromgold, 5.
Dromgoldstoune, 5.
Dromkeen, 283.
Dromnagle, 37.
Dromoland, 272.
Dromore, 235.
Dromore, Bishop of, 285.
Dromore Castle, 280.
Dromsaurie, 96.
Drought, 265.
Drum-tidhneach, 330.
Drumcar, 263.
Drumcashell, 4.
Drumneen, 168.
Drumsallagh, 283.
Drumfinnin, 286.
Drylin, 71, 255.
Dryneham, 38.
Duagh nasealla, 282.
Duagh, 272.
Dublin, 26, 48, 36, 59, 98, 112, 232, 262, 263, 264, 287, 298, 344, 345.
Dublin, County, 35, 36, 39, 40, 42, 44, 64, 89, 90, 113, 269, 280, 298, 299.
Dublin, Archbishop, 37, 103, 285.
Dudley, 264.
Duff, 63, 198, 227, 256, 258, 351
Duffree, 56, 61.
Duffrin, 6, 9, 11, 36.
Duggan, 279.
Dugin, 291.
Duhallow, 278, 335, 336.
Duharra, 331.
Duiske, 69, 266.
Duleek, 93, 94, 98, 100.
Dullagan, 6.
Dullardstown, 269.
Duna, 279.
Dunamore, 24, 93, 99.
Dunamase, 75.
Dunamond, 273.
Dunan-Oir, 168.
Dunas, 78.
Dunavall, 34.

Dunbeg, 336.
Dunboy, 31, 83.
Dunboyne, 31, 36, 92, 93, 211, 231, 269, 284, 349.
Dunbroc, 38.
Dunbrodie, 57.
Dunburie, 239.
Duncanon, 244.
Duncormack, 61.
Duncowig, 167.
Dundalke, Town, 6, 236, 269.
Dundanell, 110.
Dundannion, 279.
Dundeedy, 167.
Dundermott, 276.
Dunderrane, 261.
Dundrum, 12.
Duneen, 167.
Dunfirth, 45, 48, 50.
Dungan, 111.
Dunganmore, 70, 72.
Dungannon, 27, 223, 224, 250, 260, 297, 349.
Dungarberry, 300.
Dungarestown, 257.
Dungarvan, 159, 164, 239, 244.
Dungiven, 249, 262.
Dungorly, 167.
Dun-Guaire, 337.
Dunkellyn, 23, 220.
Dnnkerron, 168.
Dunkit, 91.
Dunlaghlen, 134.
Dunlockney, 254.
Dunloe, 280, 350.
Dunluce, 17.
Dunmanway, 279, 281.
Dunmore, 69, 92, 96, 267.
Dunmow, 100, 106, 107, 269.
Dunmoylan, 236, 284.
Dunnangall, 168.
Dunnas, 126.
Dunne, 79, 80, 263, 267.
Dunnocks, 48.
Dunore, (See Donore and Donewer) 47, 167.
Dunowen, 167.
Dunraven, 283.
Dunsandle, 274.
Dunsany, 92, 93, 101, 231, 269, 349.
Dunscombe, 281.
Dunshaghlin, 37, 93.
Dunsinane, 281.
Dunsink, 38.
Dunsoghly, 38, 90, 99, 263.
Dunworley, 167.
Duriforth, 48.

Durhamstown, 234.
Durrough, 84.
Durnam, 13.
Dyngell, 239.
Dysart, 79, 85, 105, 267, 270.
Dyrr, 252.

E

Eaghe Lough, 11, 12, 13, 18, 25.
Earlstown, 255.
Earne, 29, 122, 144, 148.
Eastmeath, 120.
Edenderrie, 82, 233.
Edenduchar, 18.
Edenduffcarrick, 18, 82, 260.
Edgeworth, 271.
Edgeworthstown, 271.
Egerton, 5.
Eichter, 232.
Elfin, 150, 257.
Elie, 87, 89, 264.
Eliot, 61, 95, 101, 256.
Ellis-Flynn, 34.
Elloghe, 32.
Emly, 207, 211, 236.
Enagh, 271.
Ench, 32.
Eneas, 50, 289.
Enfield, 45.
Englysh, 213.
Ennis, 210.
Enos, 50, 289.
Eniscorthy, 57, 63, 64.
Ennistymon, 272.
Erne, 24, 292.
Erwarde, 95.
Esherowean, 95.
Eske, 31.
Esker, 256.
Echingham, 62.
Esmond, 50, 61, 265, 353.
Essex, 11, 14, 22, 23, 24, 25, 59, 63, 77, 85, 86, 262, 271, 97.
Etherunton, 253.
Eustace, 39, 45, 46, 47, 48, 49, 50, 61, 63, 94, 95, 100, 252, 253, 265, 349.
Evaghe, (Neagh) 6, 7, 12.
Evallo, 257.
Evans, 284.
Everard, 66, 95, 163, 210, 269, 290, 349, 352, 356.
Evers, 43, 93, 94, 97.
Everson, 254.
Evrell, 108.

INDEX.

F

Fagan, 38, 254, 263, 348.
Fahalea, 281.
Failghe, 81.
Fainge, 255.
Fair, 255.
Faly O'Connors, 85.
Fanagh, 248.
Fanne Castle, 30, 31.
Fanning, 67, 255, 351.
Farinhamon, 56.
Farmar, 281.
Farrell, 231.
Fasagh, 255.
Fask, 37.
Fathrath, 96.
Fatlock, 161, 350.
Fawlestoune, 257.
Fattra Kattra, 239.
Feara Ceall, 83.
Feddens, 166.
Feiva, 261.
Felten, 96.
Feltrim, 38, 39.
Fencs, 54.
Fenton, 92, 245, 349.
Fercal, 81, 83, 84, 85, 89, 241, 268.
Fercuolen, 43.
Ferderrogh, 36.
Fermanagh, 2, 24, 210, 220, 233, 247, 261, 262, 297.
Fermoy, 169, 171, 225, 335, 349.
Fermor, 281.
Fernes, 35, 56, 57, 59, 61, 63, 235, 236, 244, 253, 256, 266, 300.
Ferney, 14, 23, 24, 302.
Ferrell, 91.
Ferriter, 192.
Ferto, 11.
Fertullaghe, 107.
Fethard, 99, 210, 235, 256, 288.
Fewes, 3, 19, 21, 23, 36.
Feydorffe, 93.
Ffrench, 273.
Field, 38, 99, 292, 293.
Fieldstowne, 37.
Fingall, 46, 268.
Finglass, 37, 38, 39, 349.
Finne, 258.
Finvara, 274.
Fishmoyne, 284.
Fitton, 199, 205.
Fitz Archer, 70.
Fitz Brian, 253.
Fitz Bryan, 252.

Fitz Edmond, 179, 180, 181, 191, 217, 253.
Fitz Edward, 70.
Fitz Garret, 38, 94, 163.
Fitz Gerald, 40, 45, 46, 47, 48, 50, 68, 83, 87, 96, 101, 104, 108, 202, 220, 226, 230, 232, 252, 253, 254, 255, 266, 270, 271, 277, 278, 281, 282, 283, 335, 338, 350, 352.
Fitz Gibbon, 197, 335, 336.
Fitz Harvie, 256.
Fitz Henrie, 58, 59, 349, 351, 352
Fitz James, 46, 50, 257.
Fitz John, 62, 67, 94.
Fitz Laurence, 70.
Fitz Maurice, 103, 191, 225, 282, 349.
Fitz Neal, 62.
Fitz Nicholl, 62, 256.
Fitz Nicholas, 289.
Fitz Patrick, 67, 79, 80, 267, 349
Fitzphillips, 49.
Fitzpiers, 78.
Fitz Piers, 49, 74.
Fitz Redmond, 50.
Fitzsimon, 9, 38, 39, 106, 291, 293, 302, 342, 348, 352.
Fitz Theobald, 163.
Fitz Thomas, 272.
Fitz Urse, 23.
Fitz Williams, 39, 93, 349.
Flain, 11.
Flattesburie, 46, 50, 349.
Fleming, 4, 5, 48, 94, 95, 96, 100, 167, 182, 227, 260, 314.
Flemingston, 94, 97, 101.
Fleshillstone, 94.
Flood, 50.
Foaty, 278.
Follyot, 73, 74, 351.
Flower, 267.
Fount, 39, 47, 273.
Founteston, 47, 48.
Fonn Iartarach, 280.
Foord, 101.
Foordston, 101.
Forde, 95.
Fordston, 95.
Fore, 90, 102, 103, 111.
Forstall, 67, 69, 71, 255.
Forstallstown, 255.
Forster, 69.
Fortanolan, 51, 52.
Forth, 55, 56, 60, 253, 256.
Foster, 38, 101.
Fotherde, 256.
Foulkes, 43.

Foulksrath, 68, 255.
Fowleing, 93.
Fox, 45, 81, 84, 111, 205, 268, 270.
Foxville, 84.
Frame, 96.
France, 105.
Frankfort, 284.
Franstone, 95, 100.
Frayne, 72, 100, 267.
Freckleton, 12.
Freerstown, 254.
Frefans, 96.
Freghanes, 209.
French, 61, 133, 272, 273, 276, 279.
Frencheston, 97.
Freyne, 72, 352.
Freny, 255.
Frinss, 256.
Fues, 21, 302.
Fullerton, 245.
Furlong, 256, 257, 349, 351.
Furnaghts, 252.
Fursetime, 256.
Fyan, 252.
Fynn, 25, 29, 30, 33, 254.
Fynne, 29, 30, 33.

G

Gafney, 285.
Gaille, 276.
Gainstown, 94.
Gall, 72, 255, 349.
Galleystone, 257.
Gallagh, 274, 277.
Gall von Bourckh, 73.
Gallgath, 95.
Gallin, 36.
Gallocar, 32.
Galloways, 183.
Gallstown, 72, 255.
Galmoweston, 96.
Galmoy, 69, 255, 266.
Galtrim, 91, 92, 95, 96, 232, 349.
Galtrom, 291.
Galway, County, 69, 123, 125, 130, 141, 150, 183, 226, 238, 240, 241, 267, 270, 272, 273, 274, 300.
Galway Town, 125, 131, 138, 139, 279.
Galwey, 290, 351.
Gardenmorris, 69, 267.
Gareston, 39.
Garesinotte, 259.
Garisker, 252, 253.
Garland, 4, 5, 95.

INDEX. 369

Garlondstonne, 5.
Garnegall, 32.
Garrard, 66.
Garreden, 257.
Garrendenny, 266.
Garrenusky, 258.
Garretstown, 283.
Garrevadden, 257.
Garrycastle, 81, 83.
Garryhill, 51, 53, 54.
Garryhundon, 265.
Garrymusky, 58.
Garve, 31.
Garvey, 95, 167.
Gavin, 206.
Gavel Rannal, 302.
Geashill, 75.
Geere, 254, 258.
Gellouse, 93.
Gelloustone, 93.
Gelston, 274.
Gentestowne, 257.
Geoghegan, 261.
Geradstown, 93.
Geraldines, 45, 49, 71, 101, 104, 160, 162, 171, 197, 205, 291.
Gerardstown, 269.
Gerlone, 5, 349.
Gerlonstown, 97.
Gernon, 4, 98, 260, 349.
Gernonstown, 4, 94, 260.
Gerrot, 9, 166, 290.
Geer, 258.
Gertrough, 284.
Gibbonston, 106.
Gibston, 95, 96.
Gifford, 49.
Gilagh, 95.
Gilliglas, 50.
Gillrauston, 92.
Gillston, 95.
Gilltown, 265.
Glanarme, 15, 16, 18.
Glanarought, 168.
Glancarvell, 24.
Glancomkeyne, 250.
Glandeboy, 9.
Glandelagh, 235.
Glandilore, 36.
Glandore, 168, 236.
Glanemagh, 239.
Glanfyne, 248.
Glanomera, 283.
Glaskarge, 258.
Glasscarrig, 56, 62.
Glasse, 86.
Glassepistell, 4, 5.
Glean-an-Chroim, 279.

Gleann, 168, 335.
Glencarra, 277.
Glencolumkille, 272.
Glencorbraighe, 331.
Glenflesk, 278, 282.
Glengall, 165, 284.
Glenmalure, 40, 45.
Glenmore, 276.
Glevecklaan, 96.
Glin, 53, 59, 283.
Glinsk, 273.
Glomemore, 7.
Glynnes, The, 13, 15, 17, 18, 42, 250, 261.
Godolphin, 245.
Golding, 38, 48, 95, 106.
Golmoorstown, 48.
Goodall, 96.
Goodman, 39, 151.
Goorte, 134.
Gorchins, 61.
Gore, 263, 266.
Gorey, 63.
Gormagan, 254.
Gormanstone, 92, 93, 94, 225, 226, 268, 349.
Gortenacuppoge, 273.
Gorst, 253.
Gort, Viscount, 284.
Gortgrenane, 281.
Gortineeher, 280.
Gortnamona, 268.
Gortrassy, 276.
Gorvey, 94.
Gough, 164, 350.
Gould, 167, 182, 183, 279, 291.
Goulding, 253.
Gowlding, 94.
Gowran, 66, 67, 71, 254.
„ Grange, 267.
Grace, 67, 70, 226, 254, 255, 266, 349.
Gragene, 256.
Gragrobben, 257.
Granahan, 272.
Granard, 114, 261.
Grange, The, 5, 38, 39, 48, 253, 283.
Grange Castle, 72.
Grangowin, 255.
Grant, 72, 162, 164, 167, 255, 277, 289.
Grantstown, 267.
Gratkerock, 58.
Gratz, 162.
Graves, 73.
Graye, 62.
Greame, 48, 49, 252.

Great Fornaughts, 265.
Great Ardes, 11, 12.
Green-Castle, 12, 31, 32.
Greenfields, 185.
Greenore, 60.
Grehan, 72, 280.
Grenan, 68.
Grenanstown, 269, 284.
Greville, 270.
Grey, 194.
Griphy, 292.
Grogan, 261.
Growe, 254.
Growgane, 256.
Gruanfort, 254.
Guatemala, 162.
Guillamore, 283.
Gun, 283.
Gurteen, 254, 255, 277.
Guyre, 91, 352.
Gwery, 258.
Gyanan, 289.
Gybbes, 66.

H

Hacket, 38, 352.
Hacketstown, 164.
Hacklee, 111.
Hadsor, 5.
Hagans, 21, 24, 26.
Hah. (Howth?) 238.
Hacket. 66.
Hall, the, 256.
Halvestown, 252.
Haly, 197, 284, 289, 290.
Hambige, 94.
Hamill, 344.
Hamilton, 10, 11, 271, 350.
Hamlin, 38, 94, 101, 290, 291.
Hammondstown. 260.
Hamon, 91, 94, 111, 352.
Hane, 256.
Harberston, 48, 99, 252.
Hardwell, 48.
Harman, 253.
Hare, 256, 257.
Harestown, 256.
Harperstown, 62, 266.
Harpole, 53, 350.
Harpoole, 78, 79, 253.
Harrington, 37, 43, 45, 48, 76, 245, 350.
Hartpoole, 253.
Hartley Mauduit, 263.
Harvey. 93, 102.
Haskinston, 111.
Hasquin, 252.
Hasson, 62.

3 A

INDEX

Hatton, 94, 185.
Hauberston, 253.
Havens, 238.
Howlet, 48.
Hay, 59.
Hea, 256.
Headborough, 281.
Heath,
Hegan, 208.
Herbert, 43, 48, 82, 269.
Herbertstown, 93.
Herford, 67.
Hetherington, 79.
Hewitt, 39.
Hickie, 271.
Hickson, 283.
Hide, 93.
Higgins, 275.
Higgs, 252.
Hi-Kinselagh, 63.
Hill, 94, 95, 100, 266.
Hill's Court, 282.
Hillswood, 274.
Hinch The, 39.
Hoar, 256, 257.
Hodnell, 269.
Hogan, 208, 283.
Holde, 94.
Holdhall, 257.
Holicrosse, 211.
Holywood, 28, 93, 285, 286, 290
Holme-Patrick, 37.
Holmpatrick, 38, 239.
Holstein, 73.
Hoodgrove, 71.
Hooke, 59, 61, 164.
Hoorton, 59.
Hops, 104.
Hore, 62, 164, 266.
Horsfall, 235.
Hovendon, 79.
 „ Captain, 22.
Howel, 67.
Howling, 67, 255.
Howth, 1, 37, 92, 97, 227, 263, 272, 349.
Hughstown, 277.
Hullen, 91.
Humble, 277.
Huntingdon, 277.
Huntstown, 38.
Hurlestone, 5.
Hurley, 201, 283, 352.
Hussey, 95, 96, 99, 232, 282, 352
Huysceethy, 54.
Hyde, 281.
Hyde Park, 107.

Hy-Many, 274.

I

Ibaun, 224.
Iberton, 255.
Ibrackan, 221.
Ichers, 93.
Ida, 255.
Idrone, 51, 64, 253.
Idough, 54, 71, 255.
Igroin, 255.
Ikethy, 252.
Ila, 30.
Iland Castle, 109.
Iland Magie, 13, 14.
Ildefonse, 162.
Illanstrassock, 258.
Imokillie, 179.
Inch, 284.
Inchequin, 126, 127, 228, 272, 349.
Inchy O'Fogarty, 284.
Ingland, 148, 152.
Inisbafin, 238.
Inishannon, 167.
Inishowen, 32, 263, 337.
Iniskillen, 25, 227, 248.
Inistioge, 66, 67, 68.
Inniscoe, 275.
Inniskae, 239.
Inver, 238.
Ionoclestowne, 256.
Iregan, 79.
Ireland's Eye, 36.
Iriell, 23.
Irish Exiles, 341.
Irishtown, 95, 96.
Itchinghane, 256.
Isham, 62.
Isle of Wight, 280.
Iveragh, 168.
Ivers, 94, 95, 97.

J

Jacob, 252.
Jacobus, St., 99.
Jamestown, 270.
Jansenius, 286.
Jenkinstown, 266.
Jephson, 43.
Jesucellin, 92.
Jesuits, 290, 295, 340, 348.
Jobston, 38.
Johnston, 46, 50, 61, 100, 351.
Johnstown, 265, 275.
Jones, 91, 97, 103, 233, 234, 244, 269, 352.
Jordan, 9, 38, 205. 275.

Jordanstown, 93, 96.
Jura, 30.

K

Kalbally, 239.
Karne The, 104.
Karron, 67.
Kavanagh, (see Cavanagh) 41, 62, 67, 76, 253, 254, 256, 265.
Kealy, 66.
Kearney, 268, 283, 284, 352.
Keating, 50, 52, 60, 96, 256, 257, 266, 288.
Keelan-a-long, 88.
Keenan, 236.
Kell, 67.
Kellis, 13, 14.
Kells, 90, 91, 101, 255.
Kelly, 223, 252, 274, 276, 277, 287, 288.
Kenmare, 279, 280, 282.
Kenna, 252.
Kennadies, 212.
Kenny, 235, 266.
Kent, 60, 93, 94, 99.
Keogh, 283.
Keppoch, 5, 39.
Keranston, 96.
Kerlis, 255.
Kerovan, 237.
Kerry, 156, 167, 170, 187, 195, 240, 263, 271, 278, 280, 282, 284.
Kerrycurrihy, 167, 280.
Keudagh, 279.
Kidderminster, 233.
Kieran, St., 99.
Kieran, 390.
Kierie, 239.
Kilamonine, 254.
Kilary, 255.
Kilayne, 254.
Kilballyowen, 283.
Kilbeggan, 38, 104.
Kilberagha, 255.
Kilboy, 94.
Kilbracan, 253.
Kilbreede, 254.
Kilbrew, 93, 94, 99.
Kilbride, 94, 95, 97, 107, 258, 283.
Kilbrogan, 281.
Kilcarne, 93, 99.
Kilcaskan, 281.
Kilcashe, 284.
Kilclogher, 57, 239, 266.
Kilcoan, 266.
Kilconelin, 56.

Kilconnell, 135.
Kilconyney, 253.
Kilcorney, 271.
Kilcoursey, 84, 268, 282.
Kilcowan, 60.
Kilcullen, 44, 226, 230.
Kildalkey, 96.
Kildare, 35, 36, 41, 44, 45, 49, 51, 61, 81, 82, 90, 106, 112, 231, 240, 252.
Kildare, Town, 44, 65, 66, 70, 72, 73, 241, 252, 260, 261, 264, 265, 328.
Kildare, Earl, 217, 252, 264, 349.
Kildare, Bishop of 81, 235, 265, 286.
Kildergan, 74.
Kildowdy, 258.
Kildrought, 252.
Kilfeacle, 215.
Kilfeneraghe, 125.
Kilferagh, 69, 255.
Kilgholm, 239.
Kilgorey, 279.
Kilgrage, 101.
Kilgreany, 253.
Kilheele, 48, 252.
Kilhobock, 56.
Kilhussey, 48.
Kilkallatin, 254.
Kilkea, 245.
Kilkele, 239.
Kilkenny, Co. 56, 207, 208, 240, 254, 266, 267, 277, 284.
Kilkenny City, 67, 70, 98, 254, 289.
Kilkenny, West, 99, 102, 104.
Kilkevan, 256.
Kilkerell, 255.
Kilkregan, 254, 255.
Kilkullin, 253.
Killagh, 274.
Killagher, 282.
Killala, 237.
Killaloe, Bishop of 115, 236, 237, 271, 274, 284, 286.
Killalon, 111.
Killany, 5, 264.
Killare, 104.
Killarie, 94.
Killasonna, 270.
Killa, 280.
Killaughe, 106.
Killconkey, 256.
Killcowlen, 259.
Killeen, 105, 268, 269, 349.
Killeglan, 38, 93.
Killegagre, 38.

Killeigh, 75.
Killelongart, 254.
Killelton, 271.
Killen, 252.
Killenan, 103, 107.
Killencowle, 260.
Killenfaghney, 104.
Killenkillie, 239.
Killensu, 257.
Killeon, 103.
Killerghe, 38.
Killester, 38.
Killglass, 144.
Killian, 256.
Killineighnan, 95.
Killinessan, 95.
Killiney, 283.
Killmanahan, 257.
Killmehell, 258.
Killmurry, 283.
Killnehell, 258.
Killollegha, 255.
Killoncowle, 5.
Killough, 260.
Killoutry, 2.
Killovany, 257.
Killowen, 283.
Killpatrick, 258.
Killred, 255.
Killrowe, 93.
Killta, 253.
Killtymen, 258.
Killua, 282.
Killuber, 104.
Killulto, 2, 7, 8, 11, 28.
Killyan, 62, 233, 265.
Killyen, 93.
Killymore, 274.
Kilm, 165.
Kilmacduagh, 131, 237, 287.
Kilmacoole, 98.
Kilmadin, 165, 166.
Kilmaine, 275.
Kilmainham, 348.
Kilmaledie, 85.
Kilmallock, 107, 229, 279, 283, 332.
Kilmanahim Castle, 165.
Kilmannaigh, 257.
Kilmarocke, 37.
Kilmarton, 100.
Kilmerrish, 31.
Kilmlapock, 253.
Kilmodalin, 226.
Kilmodally, 255.
Kilmore, 38, 63, 121, 235, 285, 287.
Kilmorey 260.

Kilmac Thomas, 165.
Kilmurry, 277.
Kilnacrott, 271.
Kil O'Donnel, 31.
Kilree, 253, 255.
Kilrmdony, 255.
Kilruane, 270.
Kilruddery, 264.
Kilrue, 269.
Kilshany, 168.
Kilshaughlin, 37.
Kilsheshane, 215.
Kilshrewly, 271.
Kilskeagh, 273.
Kilsoghlie, 39.
Kiltannon, 272.
Kilternan, 289.
Kiltimon, 263, 281.
Kiltober, 107.
Kiltulla, 273.
Kiltullagh, 273.
Kilulto, 6, 7, 11.
Kilune, 48.
Kilvashlan, 62.
Kilwarlin, 2, 6, 8.
Kilwarten, 8.
Kilwinny, 278.
Kilworth. 281.
Kinalea, 85.
Kinaleaghe, 270.
Kinalewarten, 6, 8.
Kinalmeaky, 278.
Kincleartie, 8.
Kinel-Connel, 34.
Kinel-Owen, 260.
Kindellane, 95.
King, 38, 96, 277, 350.
King's County, 35, 44, 76, 77, 78, 81, 83, 84, 86, 87, 88, 90, 92, 102, 240, 241, 268.
Kingsland, 37, 270.
Kingston, 277.
Kingstown, 83, 98.
Kinnafad, 92.
Kinnalmeaky, 168.
Kinnals, 167.
Kinsale, 1, 171, 229, 233, 238, 278, 281, 349.
Kinsellagh, 56, 57, 61.
Kinvarre, 239.
Kirwan, 271, 273, 274.
Kissak, 38.
Kirvarlin, 6.
Knapton, 267.
Knaresborough, 66, 72.
Knight, 233.
Knightstown, 269.
Knock Abbey, 271.

Knockconor, 99.
Knockcosger, 104.
Knocke, 95, 101.
Knocklough,
Knockfergus Bay, 6, 11, 38, 244.
Knock la Glynche, 34.
Knocklig, 201.
Knocklofty, 165.
Knockmarke, 95.
Knockmoan, 166.
Knockmoella, 255.
Knocknagur, 273.
Knockscur, 253.
Knocktopher, 67, 69, 255.
Knockyngen, 38.
Kowlungiste, 259.
Kyan, 262.
Kylbrowe, 100.
Kyledonoghoue Killy, 72.
Kyllyne, 92.
Kylmorry, 252.

L

Laccagh, 252.
Lacie, 67, 200, 205, 257, 330.
Lade, 15.
Ladle Rath, 94.
Laffan, 61, 350.
Laffer, 25.
Lalor, 80, 267, 286.
Lambay, 36, 239.
Lambert, 57, 60, 73, 74, 245, 266, 271, 350.
Lanan, 31.
Lanesborough, 276.
Landsdowne, 282.
Langton, 66, 71, 72, 287, 321, 351
Laragh, 47, 50, 104, 107.
Larha, 274.
Larne, 15, 18.
Laspelston, 39.
Latin, 286, 252.
Laughanston, 39.
Lawless, 66, 72.
Lawrence, 274.
Lea, 42, 43, 49, 50, 163.
Leamlara, 278.
Leap, The 168.
Leas or Lees, 163, 289, 292, 293.
Lease, 78.
Leath, 163.
Leaugh, 253.
Lecagh Castle, 45, 47.
Leck, 39.
Lechaell, 8, 9.
Ledwich, 72, 95, 105, 110, 352.
Lee, 45, 46, 93, 100, 284.

Lefallyan, 254.
Leganlic, 261.
Leigh, 12.
Leighlin, 51, 52, 53, 234, 244, 253, 256.
Leinerocke, 53, 122.
Leinich, 290, 344.
Leins, 96.
Leinster, 3, 46, 135, 235, 236, 264, 271, 298, 302, 304, 325, 327.
Leipsig, 73.
Leitrim, 2, 24, 113, 120, 123, 134, 147, 266, 276, 277, 300, 303.
Leix, 74, 75, 76, 78, 79, 80, 86, 231, 267, 328.
Lemavadie, 249.
Lemonfield, 274.
Leixlip, 44, 48, 49, 252, 265.
Lenough, 34.
Lenan, 290.
Lenigan, 281.
Lentaigne, 161, 169.
Le Poer, 72.
Lescartan, 94, 95, 100.
Lesmollen, 91, 93, 97, 99.
Lettybrook, 265.
Leverough, 36.
Leweston, 62.
Lewin, 272.
Lewis, 62.
Lexnaw, 190, 191, 230.
Ley, 66, 244, 246, 257.
Leyn, 254.
Licianstown, 93.
Lickdowne, 201.
Liegan, 226.
Liffer, 25, 30, 31, 32, 249, 250, 262.
Lighe, 79.
Limerick, Co., 125, 156, 158, 169, 188, 196, 216, 229, 234, 241, 244, 274, 278, 283, 286.
Limerick Cittie, 196, 283, 284, 289, 300.
Limevadie, 28, 89.
Linch, 39, 95, 96, 101, 132, 235, 274, 275, 291.
Lincol, 289.
Lingstown, 58.
Lington, 18.
Liscarrol, 225.
Liscarton, 92.
Lisheens, 279, 281.
Lislee, 278, 279.
Lismain, 68.
Lismallon, 284.
Lismore, 158, 159, 166, 233.

Lismoyne, 104.
Lismoyny, 83.
Lisnabin, 264.
Lisnawilly, 264.
Lisnegan. 278.
Lisquinlan, 278, 281.
Lisregghan, 274.
Lissadill, 266.
Lissinuskie, 85.
Lister.
Listrange, 152.
Lisurgh, 257.
Little, 266.
Little Cappoth, 252.
Little Freian, 95.
Little Island, 267, 277.
Little Rath, 252.
Lixnaw, 190, 191, 349.
Lobenstone, 94.
Lock, 39.
Loch Gorman, 303.
Lodi, 282.
Loftus, 37, 43, 50, 57, 79, 256, 264
Logh, 58.
Loghbracon, 94.
Loghgiel, 261.
Loghmoe, 212, 289.
Loghtie, 23.
Loghuen, 239.
Lombard, 164, 166, 285, 291.
Londonderry, 262.
Long, 46, 167, 252.
Longfield, 300.
Longford, 89, 90, 102, 113, 116, 148, 149, 231, 240, 267, 270, 271.
Lords passing, 217, 349.
Lorknan, 67.
Lota, 279.
Lougharlachnought, 108.
Loughbrickland, 265.
Lougherey, 96.
Lough Earne, 297.
Lougherne, 24.
Loughfoyle, 230, 238.
Loughmey, (see Loghmoe) 216.
Loughglynne, 275, 276.
Loughgoure, 93.
Lough Hyne, 168.
Loughrowe, 24.
Loughshearnes, 213.
Loughswilly, 239.
Louth, 2, 3, 5, 24, 33, 88, 90, 94, 98, 100, 231, 232, 240, 260, 271, 296, 349.
Loughton, 39.
Loughty, 23.
Louvain, 162, 286,

INDEX. 373

Lovell, 72.
Lowgrange, 69.
Lowyston, 68.
Loynes, 97.
Lucan, 37, 50, 100, 262, 275.
Luffane, 257.
Lamaigh, 258.
Lurgan Rac, 233.
Luske, 36.
Lusmagh, 83.
Luston, 93.
Luttrell, 39, 95, 97, 98, 105, 263.
Luttrelstone, 37, 39, 105, 263, 349.
Lye, 66, 252.
Lyle, 279.
Lynam, 95, 96.
Lyons, 46, 48, 107, 234, 236.
Lyrath, 254.
Lysaght, 279.
Lystmayne, 256.
Lyster, 71.
Lysterfield, 277.

M

McAdam, (Barry) 183, 278.
McAdin, 277.
McAlexander, 80.
McAndrew, 194.
McAronlhy, 16.
McArte, 7, 8, 19, 24, 34, 250, 257.
McArtmore, 259.
McAtagart, 279.
McAuly 100, 102, 104, 108, 110, 128 167, 169, 176, 270.
McAwliffe, 169, 176, 177, 279.
McAwnly, 16.
McBardill, 285, 287.
McBaron, 23, 34, 251, 322.
McBrady, 118, 120.
McBrane, 257, 258, 259.
McBrasil, 136.
McBrenan, 151.
McBrene, 257, 258, 259.
McBrian, 11, 13, 34, 88, 145, 157, 194, 201, 212, 253, 331.
McCabe, 247.
McCahir, 32, 53, 63, 258, 259.
McCann, 20, 251. 261.
McCanna, 261.
McCanny, 205.
McCarnock, 16.
McCarr, 258.
McCartan, 8.
McCarthy, 8, 157, 158, 160, 168, 178, 183, 185, 187, 194, 195, 201, 205, 219, 221, 222, 225, 229, 230, 239, 278, 279, 280, 283, 335, 350.

McCawell, 102, 253, 297.
McCawer, 53.
McClanchy, 125, 126, 127, 129, 130, 149, 199, 205, 206, 300, 338.
McCleyne, 27.
McClintock, 263.
McClosky, 249.
McCnavin, 139.
McCochlan, 35, 81, 82, 83, 111, 112, 132, 213, 268.
McCogh, 152.
McConmea, 124.
McConnell, 15, 16, 31, 32.
McConnor, 124, 127.
McConsidine, 127.
McCoolechan, 6, 139.
McCooly, 24.
McCorcran, 87.
McCorman, 193.
McCormac, 177, 178, 182, 186, 194, 258.
McCostilagh, 140, 141, 232, 275.
McCotter, 279.
McCragh, 127, 163, 206, 208, 215, 233, 234, 286, 288.
McCreen, 258.
McCrohan, 168, 194.
McCrossan, 193, 282.
McCrylly, 283.
McCual, 285.
McCullenan, 231.
McDa, 206.
McDamore, 56, 63.
McDarig, 258.
McDavy, 135, 153, 155.
McDermond, 155, 157, 174.
McDermot, 56, 123, 144, 150, 151, 153, 254, 257, 258, 276.
McDongonry, 31.
McDonnell, 15, 16, 17, 26, 34, 43, 79, 80, 85, 115, 124, 138, 170, 183, 194, 254, 257, 258, 259, 261, 337.
McDonogh, 139, 144, 145, 157, 167, 168, 169, 174, 178, 209, 223, 225, 254, 256, 258, 337, 338, 350.
McDonoghoe, 72.
McDonologe, 32.
McDowny, 136.
McDuff, 32.
McDuilechan, 6.
McDurlaigh, 258.
McEae, 206.
McEdmond, 36, 70, 115, 135, 136, 151, 154, 183, 191, 257, 258, 259.
McEdward, 43.
McEf, 258, 259.
McEgan, 28, 208, 214, 215, 284.
McElligott, 190, 191, 193, 236.
McEnaw, 147.
McEnery, 125.
McEnn, 257.
McEnroe, 118.
McErydry, 143.
McEvally, 29.
McEvilly, 138, 143.
McEvoy, 80, 96.
McFeagh, 40, 63, 64, 78.
McFirbis, 147.
McFollan, 132.
McFun, 190.
McFynyn, 125, 177, 187, 188, 190, 192, 194.
McGagh, 157, 193.
McGarrett, 154, 166, 206, 253, 254, 258, 259.
McGauran, 121, 285.
McGenis, 6, 7, 8, 13, 19, 33, 34, 80, 257, 258, 259, 260.
McGeoghagan, 83, 104, 107, 108, 109, 112, 270.
McGibbon, 144.
McGie, 13.
McGilfoyle, 87, 215.
McGillapatrick, 35, 74, 76, 79, 330.
McGillegan, 249, 297.
McGillicuddy, 168, 187, 190, 193, 236, 282.
McGillo-Newlan, 177.
McGlane, 148.
McGranel, 147, 149, 276, 300.
McGray, 190.
McGuire, 23, 24, 25, 33, 121. 148, 247, 262, 319, 322, 323.
McGuyvelin, 31.
McGyleragh, 127.
McHenrick, 163.
McHenry, 21, 23, 34, 135, 191, 251.
McHubberd, 54, 136.
McHubert, 338.
McHugh, 8, 17, 18, 36, 39, 42, 115, 137, 155, 254.
McHugh Duff, 31, 33.
McI-Brian-Arra, 88, 207, 208, 214, 284.
McJordan, 140, 141, 143, 275.
McKay, 16.
McKeen, 258.
McKenee, 258.

374 INDEX.

McKenna, 322.
McKeon, 16.
McKeough, 205.
McKerra, (Castle) 143.
McKilkelly, 136.
McKowge, 136.
McKowlse, 259.
McLaffan, 61.
McLisagh, 258.
McLoghlin, 32, 124, 125, 147, 300.
McMahon, 3, 20, 23, 24, 33, 34, 87, 121, 124, 125, 126, 128, 206, 231, 257, 271, 272, 285, 336, 338, 351.
McMajoke, 163.
McMalachlin, 259.
McManus, 31, 151.
McMaurice, (McMorris) 50, 57, 140, 193, 225, 230, 253, 282, 335, 349.
McMawen, 257.
McMiertagh, 257, 258.
McMoigh, 257.
KcMorghe, 206.
McMoriartagh, 157, 190, 191, 194, 257.
McMoragh, 45, 52, 53, 54, 62, 65, 127, 128, 254, 257, 258.
McMorris, 140, 143.
McMortogh, 42, 253.
McMoussoge, 258.
McMoyler, 135.
McMulmurry, 206.
McMurry, 147.
McNachton, 261.
McNamara, 124, 130, 222, 271, 272, 288, 336.
McNeill, 7, 8, 11, 18, 21.
McNygel, 16.
McOdo, 167.
McO'Nulles, 13.
McOwen, 182, 194.
McOyn, 257, 258.
McPhadden, 140.
McPhelim, 11, 13, 258.
McPherson, 259.
McPhilip, 206.
McPhilpin, 144.
McQuillin, 13, 17, 31.
McRedmond, 135, 136.
McRicard, 206.
McRichard, 253.
McRory, 8, 74, 124, 256.
McRoss, 258.
McShane, 34, 135, 167, 190, 191, 254, 258.
McShanery, 125.

McSheehy, 183, 191, 194, 199, 204, 206.
McShemes, 259.
McShemon, 258.
McSheron, 254.
McShida, 125.
McSimon, 254.
McSleyne, 27, 148.
McSureton, 232.
McSurley, 15, 17, 34.
McSwiny, 29, 32, 33, 34, 127, 135, 136, 144, 145, 148, 151, 155, 157, 158, 173, 175, 177, 178, 186, 248, 279.
McTeg, 125, 145, 157, 167, 168, 173, 174, 175, 178, 185, 193, 253, 257.
McTelligh, 121.
McTerlagh, 34, 121, 144, 190, 251.
McTernan, 147.
McThomas, 137, 138, 206, 258.
McThomyne, 135, 144.
McTibbot, 137.
McTighe, 206.
McTowaltagh, 151.
McUlick, 190, 191.
McVadin, 146.
McVadock, 56, 63.
McWalter, 88, 135.
McWilliam, 29, 34, 123, 132, 140, 141, 275, 308, 338.
Me y Gilles, 16.
McYllrem, 258.
McYnnes, 13, 258, 259.
Macetown, 93.
Machill, 66.
Macroom, 185.
Madden, 72, 161, 163, 274.
Magheraleny, 145.
Magheramorne, 58.
Magh Rein, 276.
Maglass, 256.
Magner, 179.
Magonitry, 187.
Malahide, 37, 38, 106, 238, 263.
Malbie, 113, 115, 150, 154, 173.
Mallefort, 182, 183.
Mallow, 171, 183, 186, 281, 282, 334.
Malone, 111, 291.
Mandeville, 10, 162, 163, 277.
Mang, 187.
Mangen, 39.
Manglisse, 259.
Mannering, 254.
Mansfield, 265, 277.
Mantua, 266.

Manulla, 275.
Mape, 95, 101.
Mape-Rath, 95, 101.
Mapston, 101.
Marble Hill, 273.
Marchell, 66.
Margue, 167.
Marinel, 210.
Mariner, 208.
Markham, 85, 102.
Marranston, 102.
Marshall, 66.
Marshalstown, 95, 209, 259.
Martel, 182, 352.
Martelston, 182.
Martin, 133, 137, 274.
Marwarde, 232.
Mary's Abbey, 348.
Maryborough, 75, 78, 244, 327.
Mason, 39.
Mastersone, 50, 56, 57, 64, 228, 253, 256, 350.
Mastoston, 94.
Matthews, 285, 352.
Mattei, 34.
Mayler, (see Meyler) 61.
Mayne, 110, 187, 188, 259.
Maynooth, 44, 260.
Mayo, 123, 140, 144, 150, 237, 240, 273, 274, 275, 277, 300.
Meade, 167, 279.
Meaghe, 171, 182, 183, 197.
Meagher, 209.
Measton, 93.
Meath, 1, 2, 35, 36, 44, 46, 89, 92, 93, 94, 95, 102, 104, 106, 234, 237, 240, 241, 244, 268, 303, 328.
Meehan, 287.
Meelick, 274.
Melaghe, 53.
Melans, 250.
Meleck, 104.
Meleeke, 134.
Mellefont, 260.
Menlo, 133, 272.
Menrice, 32.
Meredith, 265.
Merlinstown, 4.
Merrifield, 163.
Merriman, 5.
Merrion, 37, 38.
Meskill, 182.
Mey, 94.
Meylaughe, 92.
Meyler, (and Mayler) 58, 61, 164, 165, 227, 257.
Meynlagh, 145.

INDEX. 375

Meyres, 252.
Michmore, 95.
Middlethird, 20.
Middleton, 194.
Milborne, 42.
Milltown, 135, 277.
Milton, 103, 109, 110, 255, 276.
Misset, 16, 48, 95, 96, 100.
Mitchellstown, 94.
Moat Farrell, 114.
Mocollop, 165.
Mockler, 208, 209, 215.
Mocklerstown, 215.
Moetullen, 130.
Mogangolic, 58.
Moghenees, 126.
Moglass, 215.
Mohearnain, 284.
Mohill, 277.
Moghoony, 127.
Molahae, 99.
Mollenlyeth, 109.
Mollinmighan, 103, 110.
Molyneux, 264.
Molony, 272.
Monaghan, 2, 3, 23, 24, 120, 241, 261, 262, 296.
Monalstrum, 257.
Monasterevan, 36, 45, 75.
Monaster Orys, 82.
Moncell, 215.
Moncktown, 37.
Monclough, 257.
Moneanimie, 278.
Moneycrower, 275.
Monganagh, 248.
Monganestone, 259.
Mongaroe, 258.
Monilea, 107.
Monivea, 133, 273.
Monkstown, 167.
Monroe Lististy, 215.
Montaghs, 300.
Montauban, 274.
Montgomerie, 11, 234, 350.
Montpellier, 279.
Munyvilleog, 58.
Moone, 253.
Mooney, 50.
Moore, 4, 5, 82, 85, 91, 94, 95, 96, 101, 111, 194, 233, 245, 260, 274, 281, 283.
Moore Abbey, 260.
Mooreston, 100.
Mor, 258, 259.
Moran, 287.
More, 85, 168, 292, 301, 390, 350
Morenstown, 95, 101.

Moreton, 38, 48, 99, 105, 106, 269.
Moretown, 208, 252.
Morett, 75, 79.
Morgan, 50, 152, 163, 164, 261, 291, 292.
Moriarty. 188.
Morlow, 96.
Morne Park, 260.
Mornigane, 190.
Mornin, 105, 114, 115, 270, 271.
Mornington, 228, 264, 265.
Morphue, 254.
Morres, 68.
Morrice, 133, 194, 288.
Morris, 268.
Morristown Lattin, 265, 277.
Morrough, 254.
Morska, 275.
Morty, 291.
Moryson, 102, 245.
Mostyne, 129.
Moteing, 67.
Mothell, 255.
Mothinsey, 43.
Moumecloigh, 258.
Mouncktown, 93.
Mounsell, 67.
Mount Bellew, 260.
Mountgarret, 56, 61, 62, 64, 67, 69, 72, 73, 212, 226, 254, 266, 335, 349.
Mount Hawk, 284.
Mountjoy, 75, 77, 249.
Mount Leinster, 60.
Mountmorris, 284.
Mountnorth, 207.
Mount Palles, 263.
Mount Pleasant, 268.
Mount Talbot, 263.
Mourney, 6.
Moville, 32.
Mowberry, 15.
Moy, 145.
Moyagher, 96.
Moyaliffe, 212.
Moyartagh, 129.
Moycarkey, 209.
Moyashal, 108.
Moycashiel, 83, 104, 107, 109.
Moycullen, 137.
Moygare, 92.
Moygarry, 145.
Moyglare, 49, 95, 96, 228.
Moygare, 92.
Moyhill, 253, 254.
Moylagh, 96, 97, 99.

Moylaghoo, 96.
Moyle, 24.
Moybury, 153.
Moylehussey, 95, 111.
Moymmer, 258.
Moymet, 92, 94, 99.
Moyna, 275.
Moynally, 50.
Moyne, 144, 147, 238, 273, 274.
Moynealty, 95, 99.
Moynengeanagh, 124.
Moynish, 147.
Moyntertagan, 81.
Moynterrolis, 148.
Moyobracan, 127.
Moyoise, 104.
Moyrath, 100, 105.
Moyrit, 79.
Moyvally, 92.
Moyvore, 111, 270.
Muchardroms, 95.
Muchalton, 101.
Muchwodd, 257.
Muchalstown, 269.
Muckland, 50.
Mucklane, 257.
Mucknoe, 19.
Muckross, 194.
Muctionoe, 20.
Muinter-Vary, 186.
Mullahassse, 47.
Mouldowny, 287.
Mull, 110.
Mullagha, 94.
Mullaghenonie, 209.
Mullaghgane, 261.
Mullaghmore, 274.
Mullagrash, 252.
Mullinderry, 266.
Mullingar, 107, 111, 115, 325.
Mulloy, 83, 277.
Mulpit, 273.
Mulrancan, 59, 225, 256.
Mulrian, 200.
Mulron, 390.
Munckton, 37.
Munster, 1, 2, 156, 181, 186, 195, 237, 241, 247, 281, 303, 330, 343.
Murphy, 352.
Muscry, 208, 308.
Muscry-Wherk, 208.
Mushanaglass, 186.
Muskerry, 157, 167, 168, 261, 283.
Muyno, 124.
Myagh, 157, 197.

Myller, 289.
Mynloch, 135.
Myross, 279.
Myshall, 271.
Myssell, 254.
Mysett, 252.

N

Naale, 38.
Naas, 35, 44, 47, 48, 49, 50, 90, 233, 252, 263.
Nagle, 83, 171, 192, 278.
Naish, 66, 206, 283, 290, 352, 356
Nall, 94, 97.
Nangle, 92, 96, 103, 104, 110, 113, 232, 252.
Narraghe, 232.
Naughton, 277.
Naul, 92, 103.
Navan, 91, 92, 94, 95, 98, 99, 101, 232.
Nazeby, 47.
Neagh, (see Evagh and Eagh) 20.
Neal McBryan, 11.
Neale The, 275.
Neece, 15.
Needham, 260.
Nelson, 102.
Netterville, 37, 39, 91, 94, 98, 101, 269, 291, 349, 350.
Neur, 56, 66, 68.
Nevill, 62, 257.
Nevinstown.
Newbrook, 276.
Newcastle, 27, 30, 37, 39, 45, 69, 92, 95, 103, 104, 106, 164, 199, 256.
Newcastle Prendergast, 284.
Newforest, 273.
Newhall, 47, 258.
Newlande, 47, 231.
Newmarket, 281.
Newport, 275.
Newrie, 6, 12, 33.
New Ross, 50, 58, 72, 226.
Newton, 5, 47, 99.
Newton O'Clane, 252.
Newton O'More, 252.
Newtown, 71, 250, 272, 273, 274, 275.
Newtown-Anner, 284.
Neylan, 233.
Neyles, 27.
Nimestowne, 256.
Niemann, 64.
Nogha, 255.
Nolan, 254. 290.

Noraghe, 47, 50, 253.
Normanton, 93.
Norris, 5, 51, 33, 84, 186, 230, 282, 350.
Norton, 18.
Northampton, 281.
Northerborne, 239.
Nottingham, 46.
Nuehowse, 4.
Nugents, 5, 12, 34, 38, 85, 93, 99, 100, 101, 102, 103, 105, 106, 154, 162, 163, 166, 227, 260, 270, 271, 290, 302, 349

O

Oakley, 281.
Oak Park, 263.
O'Banan, 87.
O'Beirne, 104, 151, 152, 153, 203, 276.
O'Bolger, 258.
O'Boyle, 31, 32, 33, 34, 248, 285
O'Breen, 111, 196.
O'Brena, 255, 256.
O'Brennan, 54, 72, 111, 190.
O'Bric, 158.
O'Brien, 59, 111, 124, to 130. 138, 163, 171, 172, 198, 201, 202, 203, 214, 221, 222, 228, 236, 271, 272, 284, 336, 350.
O'Burney, 104.
O'Byrne, 36, 40, 41, 42, 45, 50, 53, 54, 104, 111, 264, 302, 326, 331.
O'Cahan, 28, 33, 34, 249, 262, 289, 297, 322, 338.
O'Callaghan, 157, 158, 167, 168, 175, 176, 177, 183, 194, 279. 297
O'Carolan, 262.
O'Carran, 215.
O'Carroll, 82, 87, 88, 89, 207, 215, 241, 268, 284, 330.
O'Casy, 289.
O'Cherony, 288.
O'Clanchy, 129.
O'Clery, 215, 288, 294, 295, 313.
O'Coffy, 50, 139.
O'Concannon, 135.
O'Connell, 190, 282.
O'Connery, 163.
O'Connor, 32, 35, 78, 81, 83, 85, 86, 91, 105, 126, 138, 141, 145, 146, 152, 153, 155, 189, 194, 219, 226, 230, 237, 268, 295, 302, 327.
O'Conor Dun, 143, 150, 151, 152, 276.

O'Conor Faly, 85, 86, 109.
O'Connor Kerry, 157, 189, 190, 191, 192, 194.
O'Conor Roe, 123, 150, 151, 276.
O'Connor Sligo, 123, 144, 145, 275, 276.
O'Corres, 250.
O'Crean, 145, 275.
O'Cowig, 167.
O'Crowley, 158, 177, 186, 229.
O'Cullen, 177, 194, 201.
O'Daly, 83, 88, 129, 134, 142, 169, 177, 186, 194, 274, 294.
O'Dea, 127, 129.
O'Dempsy, 35, 49, 79, 80, 81, 84.
O'Der, 93.
O'Devany, 285, 294.
O'Devlin, 250.
O'Devoy, 80.
O'Docherty, 29, 30, 31, 32, 34, 39, 250, 263, 337.
O'Doghe, 255.
O'Doiran, 257.
O'Donelan, 139, 274.
O'Donichan, 193.
O'Donin, 186.
O'Donnell, 24, 29, 30, 31, 33, 34, 50, 51, 115, 122, 123, 142, 145, 147, 149, 223, 238, 248, 251, 262, 263, 302, 303, 304, 308, 319, 337, 338, 355.
O'Donnely, 22, 27.
O'Donnoles, 250.
O'Donoghue, 177, 187, 282, 335, 282.
O'Donoghue Glann, 187, 188, 282.
O'Donoghue Mor, 187, 188.
O'Donovan, 72, 177, 180, 186, 187, 195, 279, 280.
O'Dooly, 87.
O'Doonelles, 26, 27.
O'Doran, 80, 257.
O'Dorne, 254.
O'Dowda, 144, to 147, 275.
O'Dowling, 80.
O'Downy, 207.
O'Driscol, 168, 172, 173, 176, 177, 186, 191, 239, 280.
O'Drycan, 256.
O'Duigenan, 294.
O'Dunn, 35, 73, 79, 80, 267.
O'Dwyer, 177, 208, 209, 210, 212, 213, 331.
O'Fahy, 138, 289.
O'Faly, 81.

O'Fallon, 151, 154.
O'Fane, 32.
O'Fanet, 32.
O'Felan, 158.
O'Feolan, 163.
O'Ferrall, 80, 89, 105, 109, 113, 114, 115, 116, 226, 231, 267, 270, 271, 286, 323, 350.
O'Ffalie, 75, 81, 85, 87, 217.
O'Fiernagh, 134.
O'Flaherties, 137, 138, 141, 273, 274.
O'Flanagan, 87, 151, 153, 277.
O'Flinn, 151, 167.
O'Foda, 132.
O'Fogarty, 215, 284.
O'Fox, 82, 84, 86, 111, 112.
O'Furrie, 17.
O'Gallagher, 29, 30, 31, 32, 248, 276, 285, 287.
O'Gallogan, 175.
O'Gara, 145.
O'Gardie, 129.
O'Gilmore, 11.
O'Glacan, 294.
O'Goonagh, 196.
O'Gormagan, 254.
O'Gorman, 68.
O'Gorhye, 288.
O'Gormoghan, 54.
O'Grady, 124, 125, 130, 283.
O'Griffie, 127.
O'Griffin, 187.
O'Guin, 17, 34.
O'Hagan, 21, 26, 34, 84, 208, 250, 251.
O'Halagan, 29, 50.
O'Halloran, 137, 139, 274.
O'Hanlie, 151, 152, 153.
O'Hanlon, 3, 19, 23, 34, 50, 250, 323.
O'Hara, 17, 144, 145, 261, 276.
O'Harrie, 17, 350.
O'Hart, 144, 145, 286.
O'Healy, 186.
O'Hegan, 186, 208.
O'Heher, 193.
O'Heine, 136, 139, 206.
O'Heny, 297.
O'Herlihy, 182, 186.
O'Hery, 137.
O'Hetheriscol, 239.
O'Hicky, 46.
O'Hiffernan, 209, 215.
O'Higgins, 135, 275, 286.
O'Hillane, 289.
O'Hogan, 128, 129, 201, 208, 215, 272, 238.

O'Holen, 289.
O'Hologhan, 137.
O'Horan, 129, 138.
O'Hosy, 295.
O'Hurly, 62, 177, 201, 227, 229.
O'Hynowran, 206.
Oireacht-Redmond, 337.
O'Kearney, 84, 210, 270, 284, 285, 295.
O'Keefe, 158, 167, 168, 169, 175, 176, 177.
O'Kelly, 50, 80, 132, 134, 136, 151, 153, 154, 163, 273 to 277.
O'Kennedy, 208, 212, 213, 216, 284.
O'Lally, 138.
O'Lalor, 8, 80, 236, 267, 280, 282.
Old Abbey, 69.
Old Aboy, 255.
Oldcastle, 96.
Oldcourt, 61, 257.
Oldcross, 57.
Olderfleet, 14, 15, 18, 238, 239, 260.
Oldtown, 253.
O'Lery, 186, 187, 195, 279.
O'Levy, 186.
O'Loghlin, 126, 127, 129, 130, 272, 337.
O'Long, 186.
Olortleighe, 257.
O'Lughairen, 285.
O'Lyne, 138.
O'Madden, 112, 136, 139, 205, 274.
Omaghe, 27.
O'Maghe, 140.
O'Magher, 88, 163, 202, 208, 209, 210, 214, 215, 216.
O'Mahon, 168, 186.
O'Mahon Carbry, 158, 167, 168, 177, 186.
O'Mahon Fionn, 158, 177, 186.
O'Mahony, 177, 182, 280, 295.
O'Mally, 140 to 144, 238, 275.
O'Mallon, 34.
O'Mannin, 134.
O'Many, 132.
O'Mare, 208.
O'Meara, 234, 294.
O'Melaghlins, 78, 102, 104, 112.
O'Melies, 2, 24.
O'Mey, 250.
O'Molhane, 132.
O'Molony, 272, 286.
O'Moloy, 81, 83, 86, 88, 268, 277, 330.
O'More, 35, 41, 51, 65, 73, 76

to 80, 83, 86, 107, 231, 267, 300, 302, 305, 326, 327, 331 334.
O'Moroghoe, 54, 56, 57, 58, 352.
O'Mulhonery, 125.
O'Mulconry, 277, 294.
O'Mullanes, 249, 297.
O'Mulreny, 16.
O'Mulrian, 88, 200, 203, 206, 207, 208, 214, 216, 253, 255, 284, 331.
O'Murribie, 186.
O'Murry, 151, 154, 300.
Onacht, 187, 208, 335.
O'Nachton, 151, 154, 277.
O'Nahan, 288.
O'Neill, 3, 6, 7, 8, 10, 11, 14, 17, 21, to 34, 76, 87, 97, 100, 103, 108, 223, 224, 226, 230, 247, 250, 251, 253, 260, 261, 267, 270, 286, 301, 302, 304, 352.
Oneyland, 21, 129.
Oneylan, 19, 128, 129, 235.
Ongestown, 94.
O'Nolan, 16, 52, 54, 253, 254.
Onulchalons, 13.
Onye, 34.
Ophaly, 253.
O'Quin, 17, 21, 26, 250, 251, 283.
O'Quirivane, 274.
Oranmore, 273.
O'Reilly, 2, 9, 24, 89, 105, 117 to 122, 134, 231, 246, 247, 271, 279, 287, 300, 311, 321, 350.
O'Reilly, 9, 89.
Ordriscall, 169.
O'Regan, 177.
Orey, 30.
Orgial, 90.
O'Rhawley, 50.
O'Rian, 88, 200, 203, 206, 208, 214, 253, 255, 284, 331.
Oriel, 23.
O'Riodially, 26.
O'Riordan, 205, 283.
Orme, 102.
Ormond, 50, 51, 52, 53, 59, 64, 67, 69, 70, 71, 72, 73, 74, 76, 77, 79, 84, 87, 88, 143, 207, 208, 209, 211, 215, 217, 225, 226, 254, 301, 302, 304, 330, 332, 349.
Ornaugh, 19.
O'Roddy, 149.
Orpen, 283.
O'Renehan, 286.
O'Rourk, 34, 141, 147, 148, 149,

3 B

152, 255, 276, 300, 303, 304, 325, 329.
Osbertstown, 45, 46, 252.
Osborne, 163, 278, 284.
O'Scott, 50.
O'Shagnessy, 131, 136, 137, 227, 274.
O'Shee, 69, 267.
Ossory, 61, 65, 67, 71, 73, 76, 79, 80, 217, 230, 231, 235, 254, 266, 285, 349.
Ossory, Upper, 73, 76, 216, 230, 349.
O'Sughrue, 168.
O'Sullevan, 128, 157, 167, 168, 172, 173. 180 to 195, 280, 288, 289, 350.
O'Sullevan Beare, 136, 168, 225, 282.
O'Sullevan Mor, 168, 230, 282.
O'Toole, 36, 38, 41, 42, 43, 54, 62, 264, 302.
Ouran, 134.
Outrich, 206.
Overke, 255.
Owen, 254.
Ower, 137, 273.
Owgan, 47.
Owlert, 58.
Owles, 142, 337.
Owlortvicke, 58.
Owney, 203, 206, 284.
Ownhy, 135.
Ownilechabees, 13.
Owr, 258, 259.

P

Pace, 92, 103, 107.
Packenham, 270.
Painstown, 46, 94, 264.
Pale, The, 4.
Pallace, 78.
Palles, 97, 263.
Pallestown, 281.
Palmerston, 37.
Parke, 15, 58.
Parliament (Members of), 349.
Parres, 107.
Parsons, 268.
Parsonstown, 93, 268.
Passage, 161, 164, 165, 239.
Payen, 255.
Paynestown, 94, 99.
Pembroke, 60.
Pennant, 277.
Pentenie, 93, 99.
Peppard, 5, 47, 62, 252, 258, 266, 300.

Peppardstown, 260.
Perce, 122.
Percy, 18.
Perrot, 13, 16, 19, 26, 104, 107, 119.
Peter's Well, 274.
Pettetstowne, 256.
Petits, 104, 107, 352.
Phersone, 259.
Phelin, 258.
Phillipstown, 76, 81, 82, 85, 87, 244, 263.
Philpotstown, 94.
Phippes, 92, 100, 352.
Phoores, 253.
Phypo, 38.
Piercy, 102.
Piers, 39, 103, 104, 270.
Pierstone, 94.
Pigotts, 78, 79, 267, 350.
Pilsworth, 235.
Piltown, 165.
Pincher's Grange, 253.
Pinner, 73.
Platten, 92, 93, 94, 101, 106, 107.
Plunket, 4, 5, 38, 39, 91, 93, 94, 95, 96, 97, 98, 227, 231, 232, 260, 263, 268, 259, 352.
Poble, 53.
Poer, 162, 225, 231, 350.
Pole Hore, 62, 257, 266.
Pollard, 270.
Polomonty, 226.
Polrancton, 256.
Polrankan, 62.
Pope, 86.
Pormanston, 232.
Portaferry, 105, 106, 260.
Portarlington, 80.
Portcroisi, 336.
Porter, 93, 98, 111, 289, 352.
Porterstown, 106, 111.
Portmuck, 18.
Portnahinch, 73, 81.
Portnehill, 255.
Portrane, 97.
Portriff, 93, 94, 95, 96.
Portumna, 134, 272.
Possicktown, 94, 96.
Pottinger, 260.
Poulescastle, 225.
Prover, 282.
Powers (see Poers and Poors), 67, 78, 161, 165, 166, 205, 231, 245, 255, 277, 282, 284, 289.
Powerscourt, 43, 264.
Powerstoune, 38, 39.

Powers Wood, 72, 255.
Prague, 64, 106, 162.
Prenderfoote, 102.
Prendergast, 61, 162, 163, 257, 284, 350.
Preston, 37, 93, 95, 225, 268, 269.
Priests, 287, 294, 295.
Priesthaggard, 61.
Prim, 73.
Prisugard, 257.
Prospect, 280.
Protfords, 39, 97.
Protfortstone, 94.
Proudestown, 99.
Proudfootstown Cas., 92.
Prountford, 95, 101.
Pullen, 280.
Purcell, 66, 67, 68, 203, 210, 212, 254, 255, 256, 267, 280, 335.
Purcellstiers, 255.
Purdon, 264.
Pygot, 78.

Q

Queitrot, 290.
Queen's Co., 34, 36, 44, 51, 73, 74, 75, 81, 82, 84, 86, 89, 261, 267, 327.
Queen's Fort, 78.
Queenstown, 279.
Quin, 21, 26.
Quin Abbey, 125, 128, 338.
Quoniamstown, 279.
Quylan, 91.

R

Raaour, 66.
Raban, 239.
Rachtor, 66, 288.
Radboy, 15.
Rafeig, 98.
Raferghe, 5.
Raffin, 94, 98.
Raffniall, 98.
Rafoe, 31, 235.
Ragget, 66, 255.
Raghlins, 15.
Rahedin, 253.
Rahellin, 253.
Rahen, 256, 275.
Rahencastle, 265.
Rainduf, 257.
Rahine, 258, 279.
Rahenderg, 257.
Rakeall, 197, 331.
Raleigh, 185, 532.
Ram, 235, 266.

INDEX.

Ramshead Island.
Ramalton Castle, 31, 32.
Ramellon Castle, 32.
Randallston, 95, 269.
Ranelagh, 234, 269.
Randol, 15.
Randolfston, 190.
Ranechadie, 12.
Raphesk, 93.
Raphoe, 32, 234, 285.
Rarrody, 136.
Rarush, 254.
Rath, 101, 253.
Rathaldron, 94, 97.
Rathangan, 45.
Rathalvey, 58.
Ratharding, 254.
Rathannan, 282.
Rathbride, 48, 252.
Rathcally, 72, 255.
Rathclare, 4.
Rathcoffy, 45, 47, 252.
Rathcon, 94.
Rathconnyl, 91.
Rathcormack, 278.
Rathcredon, 38.
Rathdowney, 58, 256.
Rathdrome, 42.
Rathengerge, 54.
Rath Reynolds, 94.
Rathesker, 4.
Rathetam, 267.
Rathfarnham, 264.
Rathfeigh, 94.
Rathfernen, 37.
Rathgarvan, 254.
Rath House, 264.
Rathkeale, 197, 331.
Rathkenny, 94.
Rathlin, 16.
Rathlion, 97.
Rathlonnane, 256.
Rathmagolduld, 84.
Rathmanee, 59, 60.
Rathmokue, 60.
Rathmore, 48, 51, 92, 96, 97, 252, 269.
Rathnegarry, 51.
Rathnetesky, 258.
Rathode, 94, 95.
Rathperise, 258.
Rathpodenboy, 257.
Rathronarie, 257.
Rathroe Cas., 257.
Rathsilben, 239.
Rathshillane, 256.
Rathtain, 94.
Rathvilley, 51, 52.

Rathwire, 103, 271.
Ratoathe, 95, 98.
Ratoryn, 97.
Ratroge, 254.
Ratten, 106.
Rattoo, 283.
Raville, 253, 254.
Rawyre, 102, 103.
Raymond, 283.
Raynolds, 83.
Reade, 93, 269.
Reagh, 257, 258, 259, 271, 276, 279, 283.
Reban, 232, 252.
Reken, 289.
Redbaye, 15, 18.
Redestoune, 256.
Red Haven, 32.
Redington, 272.
Redmond, 61, 256.
Redsherd, 196.
Reeks, The, 282.
Reg, 240.
Rehins, 275, 350.
Reilly, 102.
Remotestoune, 256.
Remremonde, 258.
Renville, 272, 338.
Reough, 253.
Representatives of the Old Families, 260.
Revenue, 240.
Reynel, 73.
Reynolds, 39, 276 351.
Reynoldstown, 39.
Rhahin, 79, 80.
Rheban, 265.
Ribera, 286.
Rice, 4, 163, 192, 205, 282, 350.
Richardstown, 5.
Rider, 252, 264.
Ridgway, 244, 351.
Ricknhore, 38.
Rincalisky, 168.
Risserd, 167.
Riverstown, 92, 93.
Riversdale, 268.
Roan, 92.
Robertstown, 45, 91, 93, 95, 97, 99, 199, 265.
Robinson, 167.
Robinstone, 95, 107.
Roche, 57, 58, 60, 62, 164, 167, 171, 184, 197, 199, 210, 223, 225, 256, 257, 278, 280, 290, 300, 351.
Rochesland, 57, 60.
Rochestown, 5, 69, 262.

Rochford, 47, 50, 57, 61, 72, 94, 95, 96, 97, 163, 252, 256, 264
Rockforest, 269.
Roe, 5, 167, 276, 303, 351.
Rogerstown, 93, 255.
Rome, 288.
Ronayne, 164, 184.
Rooe, 94.
Roold, 167.
Rooth, 70.
Rorie, 226.
Rosbare, 239.
Roristown, 269.
Roscarbery, Bishop, 172.
Rosbrien, 279.
Roscommon, 123, 131, 240, 241, 255, 263, 266, 275, 276, 277.
Roscrea, 215.
Rosegarland, 57, 60, 62, 257.
Rose Hill, 275.
Rosemeane, 99, 111, 141, 144, 150, 151.
Roses, 96.
Rosewood, 48.
Roskain, 239.
Rosmaynock, 258.
Rosroe, 271.
Ross Carbery, 236, 239, 274, 283, 286.
Rosse, 56, 59, 61, 167, 170, 262, 268, 282.
Rosselltoune, 257.
Rossiter, 59, 60, 66, 256, 257.
Ross Hill, 272.
Ross Levin, 275.
Ross Lewin, 272.
Rossmine, 95.
Rossnarowe, 255.
Rothe, 56, 66, 254, 286, 352.
Round Towers, 357.
RouteThe, 13, 15, 17, 18, 34, 261.
Rovan, 100.
Rowe, 48, 93, 258.
Rowen, 93.
Rowestown, 93, 94, 97.
Rowthstown, 94.
Rush, 78, 238, 356.
Russell, 9, 12, 27, 38, 39, 41, 93, 101, 111, 183, 260.
Russellston, 111.
Russellswood, 253.
Ryan, 198, 203, 214, 284.
Rynna, 271.

S

Saintleger, 232.
Sale, 93, 100, 290, 352.
Salamanca, 343.
Salestowne, 93, 100.

Salisbury, 251.
Sall, 215, 290.
Sanders, 8, 28, 252.
Sankey, 82, 161.
Sanshill, 257.
Sarsfield, 37, 48, 50, 60, 99. 100, 167, 170, 252, 279, 281, 351.
Sault, 252.
Saunderscourt, 266.
Saunderson, 263.
Savages, 9, 10, 14, 48, 60, 105, 232, 260, 265.
Scarvagh, 271.
Scarriff, 336.
Scatterig, 12.
Scotland, 234.
Scoyne, 100.
Scraghe, 268.
Scryne, 93, 232, 276.
Scurlogstown Castle, 92. 100.
Seaforde, 266.
Seaton, 38, 283.
Segerson, 252.
Segrave, 5, 38, 39, 93, 263, 293.
Sergeant, 253.
Serment, 254.
Seskinrem, 254.
Sessueman, 276.
Sexton, 284.
Seymour, 284.
Shaen, 134, 135, 271.
Shanagollen, 271.
Shanamullen, 267.
Shandon, 164.
Shane, 28, 88, 89, 103, 104, 106, 114, 116, 350.
Shane's Castle, 260, 261.
Shanganagh, 38.
Shangarry, 254.
Shankhill, 277.
Shannon (see Sheynin), 172, 216, 300, 303.
Shee, 66, 69, 70, 205, 226. 254, 267, 291, 351.
Sheemore, 276.
Sheerhes, 204.
Sheestown, 69, 267.
Sheffield, 73.
Shelmalin, 56.
Shenet Castle, 199.
Sherberre, 56.
Sherkin, 168.
Sherlock, 5, 38, 47, 60, 61, 96, 100, 162, 163, 166, 252, 256, 257, 292, 292, 350.
Sherlockstown, 48, 252.
Shewroyher, 188.

Sheynan, 166, 196.
Sheyne, 290.
Sheynen, 81, 82, 102, 104, 113, 122, 125, 131, 187, 188, 196, 216, 238,
Shebbirne, 256, 257.
Shilelagh, 41.
Shillecker, 255.
Shilmalyre, 257.
Shilogh, 36.
Shirley, 22, 23.
Short Castle, 281.
Shortall, 67, 71, 255.
Shroughbooe, 254.
Shyan, 166.
Shynan Castle, 78, 79.
Sidon, 100.
Sigen, 256.
Siggenston, 253.
Sinot Court, 38.
Skerrets, 133, 274.
Skerries, 238.
Skibbereen, 280.
Skiddies, 164, 183.
Skryne, 93.
Slade, 60, 61.
Sladde, 256, 257.
Slane, 60, 69, 92, 94, 99, 227, 260, 349.
Slaney, 50, 56.
Slaune, The, 258.
Sleggar, 71.
Sleumaghe, 73.
Slevey, 257.
Slevoy, 60.
Slewlogher, 169, 196, 331.
Slewmargie, 30, 74, 232.
Slievebloom, 75, 78, 82, 89.
Slievecomer, 75.
Slieve Gallen, 297.
Sligo, 2, 29, 123, 141, 144, 145, 147, 148, 150, 238, 240, 275, 276,
Slingesby, 175.
Smarmore, 5, 260.
Smith, 10, 67, 71, 80, 97, 252, 281
Smithstown, 38, 72, 94, 101.
Sobieski, 47.
Sonagh, 270.
Sourley Buy, 16.
Southampton, 49.
Sowa Castle, 186.
Sparke, 93.
Spencer, 23.
Spring. 194, 350.
Stackallan, 92.
Stackallen, 94.
Stackpole, 204, 289.

Stackes, 192.
Stafford, 12, 34, 57, 61, 63, 71 244, 256.
Stalorgan, 39.
Stamen, 100.
Stanihurst, 48, 58.
Stanley, 4, 93, 343, 349, 351.
Staples, 94.
Staplestowne, 254.
Stapleton, 284.
Starallen, 94.
Strangford, 238.
Starr, 62.
Starrowalshe, 258, 259.
Staunton, 66.
St. Canice, 68, 70, 71, 72, 226.
Stevenston, 91, 94, 100.
Stephen St., 98.
St. Gudule, 275.
St. James' Castle, 70.
St. John, 61, 62, 151, 244, 350.
St. John's Bower, 265.
St. Kathrens, 39, 45.
St. Laurence, 73, 86, 102, 227.
St. Leger, 52, 71, 78, 185, 244, 255, 262, 282, 350.
St. Mallins, 265.
St. Michell, 46, 232.
St. Mollines, 36, 51, 52, 53, 54, 64, 253, 254.
St. Molyn, 253.
Stokes, 38, 252, 284.
Stookes, 94.
Strabane, 27, 250, 297, 349.
Stradbally, 78, 267.
Straffane, 262.
Straghmor, 259.
Strahard, 80.
Strancally, 166.
Strange, 71, 154, 350.
Strangford, 10, 12, 238, 264.
Streamstown, 274.
Street, 110.
Strong, 70, 71, 164, 286, 351.
Stuart, 263.
Stukeley, 59.
St. Wolstans, 37, 44, 48, 252.
Suck, 131, 150.
Suer, 33, 35, 56, 64, 157, 158, 303.
Suffolk, 152, 267,
Sullevan, 280, 350.
Sunnagh, 104, 107.
Supple, 203, 281,
Surleboy, 16.
Surnings, 252.
Sutton, 38, 45, 46, 47, 61, 252, 256, 257, 349.

INDEX.

Swan, 296.
Swayne, 66, 71.
Swedy Lough, 103.
Sweetman, 67, 71,
Swilly Lough, 30, 33.
Swords, 36, 37, 38.
Sydley, 102.
Sydney, 19, 20, 23, 55, 76, 131, 270.
Sygin, 61.
Syginston, 61.
Sylane, 274.
Syney, 102.
Synot, 38, 56, 57, 58, 61, 64, 256, 257, 258, 266, 300, 350.
Syonan, 104.

T

Taffe, 4, 5, 73, 79, 93, 97. 260.
Taghmon, 59, 62, 105.
Taghunan, 61.
Tagomane, 256.
Tailten, 90.
Tailor, 38, 39, 351.
Talbot, 4, 37, 38, 43, 47, 92, 93, 94, 95, 99, 100, 106, 256, 259, 263, 292, 349, 351.
Talbotstown, 41.
Tallaght, 261, 264, 269.
Tallniall, 106.
Tallon, 93, 94, 101.
Tallow, 37, 166, 171.
Taman, 256.
Tample Wodekann, 257.
Tanconshanee, 59, 60.
Tankard, 93, 99.
Tankardstown, 79, 95.
Tanrago, 276.
Tappock, 39.
Tara, 90, 93, 98.
Tarbert, 109.
Tarturs, 13.
Tartayne, 38.
Tassagard, 39.
Tath-Rath, 95.
Taylor, 38, 39.
Teaquin Castle, 134.
Teara, 43.
Teaghcroghan, 95, 101.
Teeling, 269.
Teenes, 3.
Teffia, 84.
Teighin, 258.
Teling, 94, 95, 100.
Telinstown, 101.
Templemichael, 166.
Templemore, 215.

Templeoge, 37.
Templeton, 262.
Tempo, 262.
Tempodessel, 262.
Tenche, 266.
Tennecarricke, 254.
Tenne-Killeh, 79.
Tennekille, 80.
Tennelick, 231.
Tentober, 257.
Termingraghe, 24.
Termonfecken, 92, 232.
Terry, 192.
Teurelan, 254.
Tew, 163.
Thistle-Keran, 93.
Thomas Court, 348.
Thomond, 124, 127, 130, 216, 221, 231, 302, 336, 349.
Thomnebaghy, 255.
Thomyne, 254.
Thomas St. 99.
Thomaston, 48, 66, 68.
Thomastowne, 96.
Thornburgh, 236.
Thorne, 163.
Thornton, 201, 206.
Thurlesbeg, 284.
Thurles, 215, 218.
Thyvyn, 66.
Tibbotnelong, 142.
Ticooly, 274, 277.
Ticroghan, 92.
Tinerana, 264.
Tinnahinch, 73, 79, 81.
Tinraheene, 58.
Tinterne, 57, 60, 233.
Tintubber, 257.
Tipp, 252.
Tipper, 45, 47, 349.
Tipperary, 65, 68, 71, 74, 88, 156, 158, 196, 207, 211, 225, 226, 234, 252, 262, 263, 264, 267, 270, 273, 278, 281, 284.
Tippersold, 38, 39.
Tippston, 252.
Tiranly, 142, 337.
Tir-Bruin na Sinna, 276.
Tirerrill, 144, 145, 338.
Tirhugh, 32.
Tirke, Mayne, 238.
Tirrell, 34, 100, 103, 107, 112, 302, 327, 352.
Tirriaugh, 19.
Tirriaughelie, 20.
Tiscorre, 259.
Tlachta, 90.
Toam, 234, 237.

Tobberton, 38.
Tobercaoch, 274.
Tobin, 71, 163, 210, 225, 255, 356
Tobragney, 208.
Todd, 66, 235.
Toghrighie, 251.
Tohyrly, 54.
Toledo, 286.
Tolghan, 85.
Tolmalag Haven, 239.
Tomand, 253.
Tombs, 45, 60, 62, 63, 64, 68, 69, 71, 72, 355, 356, et passim.
Tomcoyle, 258.
Tomduff, 258.
Tomgarrough, 253.
Tomger, 257.
Tomhaggard, 60, 61.
Tomies, 280.
Tomlaine, 257.
Tomm Dire, 259.
Tomona, 276.
Tomyne, 253.
Tooles, 35, 40, 41, 42, 43.
Togau, 73, 262.
Towers, Round, 357
Towany, 15.
Tracie, 8.
Tracton Abbey, 281.
Tralee, 239, 283.
Traley, 189.
Traley Castle, 190.
Tramore, 164.
Trant, 282, 352.
Traunts, 192.
Travers, 38,
Trent Council of, 286, 287.
Trevers, 42.
Trevor, 50.
Tribleston, 94.
Trim, 91, 92, 94, 95, 102, 234, 244.
Trimberton, 95.
Trimleston, 92, 93, 94, 269, 349.
Triscornagh, 104.
Tristernagh, 234.
Tristernagh Abbey, 270.
Tristinaughe, 103.
Troddye, 67, 72.
Tromer, 62.
Troneblie, 95.
Trow, 23.
Trough, 322.
Trubly, 92, 97.
Tuadrommeen, 278.
Tuam, 125, 131, 227, 234, 237, 273, 274, 286.
Tubherlomunaugh, 257.

Tuberngan, 253.
Tuite, 90, 96, 103, 104, 107, 154, 268, 270.
Tuitestown, 103, 104, 107.
Tullagh, 253, 254.
Tullaghan, 105.
Tullaghanbroge, 71.
Tullaghagrory, 252.
Tullaghard, 94.
Tullamore, 268.
Tullophelim, 51.
Tullock, 94.
Tullon, 277.
Tullow, 65, 231.
Tully, 48, 51, 79, 252.
Tullynally, 270.
Tully O'Dea, 127, 338.
Tullyra, 274.
Turbotstown, 270.
Turner, 46, 62, 256, 351.
Turning, 48.
Turoe, 273.
Turvey, 37, 38, 97, 99, 101.
Tusher, 257.
Tylin, 99, 101.
Tymogh, 79.
Tymoghe, 252.
Tynan, 34.
Tynehinch, 226.
Tynt, 97.
Tyrconnell, 24, 25, 29, 30, 34.
Tyrconnell, Earl, 31, 47, 223, 248, 251, 263.
Tyrmin-Omungan, 24.
Tyrone, 23, 24, 25, 120, 223, 249, 250, 251, 262.
Tyrone, Earl, 8, 19, 20, 21, 22, 23, 24, 26, 26, 28, 30, 31, 33, 34, 63, 67, 70, 99, 119, 223, 246, 251, 261, 297, 301, 302, 303, 304, 349.
Tywe, 67.

U
Ublogahell, 297.
Uchterthera, 277.
Uisnech, 83, 90.
Ullard, 2, 255.
Ulster, 1, 29, 34, 223, 237, 246, 251, 287, 288, 302, 305, 343.
Ulverston, 59.
Uniacke, 281.
Upper Court, 226.
Upton, 261.
Urquhart, 270.
Uriel, 110.
Usher, 38, 95, 101, 233, 263, 264, 351.
Uskerower, 101.

Uskertye, 256.

V
Valdesoto, Count, 106.
Valentia, 222, 239, 282.
Valley, Knight of the, 202.
Vaughan, 46.
Veldon, 94, 98.
Velvetstown, 281.
Verdon, 4, 5, 107, 203, 352.
Verona, 106.
Vesey, 261, 263.

W
Wadding, 60, 161, 163, 164, 256, 289, 290, 292, 293, 351.
Wafer, 94, 100, 258.
Wakeley, 82, 91, 352.
Wale, 53, 98, 164, 211, 253, 254, 290, 352.
Waleslogh, 255.
Walker, 46.
Wallentimore, 239.
Wallis, 281.
Wallscourt, 272.
Wallop, 56, 57, 63, 64, 235, 349.
Walshe, 38, 42, 43, 48, 50, 62, 66, 67, 70, 110, 126, 129, 160, 161, 164, 170, 198, 203, 214, 244, 252, 253, 254, 255, 256, 258, 291, 292, 298, 351.
Walterstown, 95.
Walton, 264.
Walworth, 264.
Warbeck, 278.
Ward, 260.
Ward Castle, 37.
Ward Hill, 90.
Ware, 282.
Waring, 92, 95, 350.
Warringstone, 93, 95.
Warren, 4, 38, 43, 48, 82, 87, 92, 94, 99, 233, 352.
Warrenstown, 4, 99, 233.
Water Castle, 231.
Waterford, 35, 56, 59, 156, 157, 159, 166, 216, 233, 236, 239, 241, 267, 277, 280, 281, 289.
Waterhous, 126, 129.
Waters, 278.
Waterston, 103, 110.
Waton, 67, 71, 254.
Weafy, 93.
Weil, 95.
Welchetown, 104.
Weldon, 265, 352.
Wellesley, 87, 232, 252, 253, 268.
Wellfort, 273.
Wellington, 48, 265.

Wells, 267.
Wesley, 47, 48, 50, 95, 96, 98, 352
Wespelston, 39, 349.
Westmeath, 82, 83, 89, 90, 100, 102, 105, 106, 107, 112, 113, 120, 149, 234, 240, 264, 268, 269, 270, 271.
Weston, 38, 39, 263.
Westport, 275.
Wexford, 35, 36, 41, 50, 54, 55, 56, 57, 58, 62, 63, 64, 166, 225, 226, 241, 243, 256, 261, 264, 266, 267, 295, 298, 303.
Wharton, 48.
Whitchurch, 235, 352.
White Knight, 231.
Whitfieldstown, 163.
Whyte, 10, 12, 39, 44, 45, 48, 62, 67, 94, 97, 129, 162, 200, 204, 213, 256, 265, 289, 291, 292, 351, 352, 355, 356.
Whytney, 76.
Whytty, 62, 63, 256, 257.
Wicklow, 35, 36, 39, 41, 56, 80, 233, 238, 239, 259, 262, 264, 282, 303.
Wilkenstone, 94, 104, 350.
Williams, 50, 85, 306.
Williamstown, 264.
Wilmington, 280.
Winch, 244.
Windsor, 235.
Wingfield, 42, 244, 252, 264, 351
Wirtemburg, 168.
Wise, 161, 163, 277, 290, 351.
Witchurch, 256.
Wogan, 45, 47, 50, 252, 253.
Woghterard, 252.
Woghtereay, 252.
Woncestowne, 255.
Woodbine Hill, 280.
Woodford, 266.
Woodfort, 282.
Woodgrage, 257.
Woodhouse, 281.
Wood Parks, 269.
Woodstock, 45, 271.
Worrall, 5.
Wotton, 5.
Woulfe, 46, 197, 265.
Wray, 263.
Writers, 294.
Wyartstone, 37, 38.
Wycam, 38.

Y
Youghall, 158, 167, 170, 239, 281.
Young, 39, 47, 289.
Youngstone, 47.